Negro S LOCKED OUT OF PUBLIC SCHOOLS FOR FIVE YEARS

— _September 1959-September 1964_ —

Prince Edward County, Virginia,
ORAL ACCOUNTS

WALLY G. VAUGHN

In Due Season, Inc.

TABLE OF CONTENTS

FOREWORD

This work was birthed at Alfred Street Baptist Church, Alexandria, Virginia. At the time Dr. John Otis Peterson, Sr. was the pastor.

On Sunday, April 8, 2001, after the 7:55 a. m. worship service, the late Ms. Gwen Harrison asked me: "What are you working on now? What project has your interest?" "I am collecting oral accounts in Selma, Alabama; but I am really interested in writing oral accounts in Prince Edward County from people that were locked out of the public schools for five years. I would like to do that for the time I will be in the Washington, D. C. area," was my reply. "Well, there is Ms. Prince Edward County standing at the door on her way out, Gloria Gibson," Ms. Harrison said. "I don't know her." "I will introduce you to her. Come with me." Sister Harrison shared my interest with Sister Gibson.

Sister Gibson said: "Why don't you come to our family reunion in August. You can meet some of my relatives that were locked out of the schools." On Saturday, August 11, 2001, the late Mr. David Patterson, Sr. and his wife the late Mrs. Mildred Womack Patterson, the uncle and aunt of Sister

Gibson, gave me a warm welcome to the Patterson Family Reunion in Darlington Heights, Prince Edward County, Virginia. It was on this occasion that the initial interviews were conducted.

Mr. Carl U. Eggleston, Sr., who was an elementary school pupil at the time of the closing of the public schools in Prince Edward County, designated an office at his establishment, Eggleston Funeral Home in Farmville, for the Editor to sit and conduct interviews the second and third years of the project. Whenever the Editor was in town, Mr. Eggleston would put the word out. One person would come and be interviewed and upon leaving contacted a relative or friend and urged them to stop by my office and share their story. Prince Edward County is more than three hundred square miles. During the initial years of the project, having a central location out of which to work was beneficial until sufficient geographical knowledge allowed me to travel the county independently.

Once the Editor started driving around the county, individuals interviewed upon completing their story directed me to a relative or friend that had been locked out of the public schools. Some of the people to whom the Editor was directed lived in other counties in Virginia. Some interviewees resided in other States.

Interviews were conducted from 2001 until 2013. This work is the largest collection of accounts from individuals that were locked out of the Prince Edward County public schools during the education crisis. The Editor is appreciative to each person that entrusted their story to him for publication. Many who shared their story have been called to their eternal rest. Their voices are silent, still they speak from the pages of the publication they were unable to behold.

Most of the stories from the community of the oppressed regarding the Prince Edward County, Virginia, public school saga, September 1959—September 1964, will never reach the broader public. The stories in this valued collection shared primarily by the oppressed are rich and informative, but only provide a mere glimpse of community and home life during those challenging, regrettable, and horrific years.

Wally G. Vaughn
December 7, 2017
Little Rock, Arkansas

PREFACE

The designation Negro was employed in newspaper and magazine articles, speeches and addresses, court records and litigations, Commission reports and studies during the era of interest. The title of this work *Negro Students Locked Out Of Public Schools For Five Years, September 1959–September 1964: Prince Edward County, Virginia — Oral Accounts* is in harmony with the period during which the Prince Edward County, Virginia, public school crisis occurred. It is the contention of this writer that historical integrity should be maintained to the maximum extent possible.

This writer will produce another work in which he will reconstruct the years leading up to the Prince Edward County school crisis and the five years of the closure of the public schools. The book *Negro Students Locked Out Of Public Schools For Five Years, September 1959–September 1964: Prince Edward Country, Virginia — A Reconstruction Of Events* will employ the sources mentioned above.

Readers will become acquainted in the current volume with an array of authentic accounts from individuals that were locked out of the Prince Edward County public schools, articulating to the best of their ability the twists and turns, and ups and downs, that shaped their lives from that period onward.

Very captivating in this volume are the stories of individuals that were locked out of the Prince Edward County, Virginia, public schools and who in adult life devoted themselves to the teaching profession. Each had a burning desire to be an educator. They were denied an education in their youth but in adult life were unable to deny to themselves the importance of education and that children should have the opportunity to learn, develop, and mature intellectually. Most of the school teachers in this volume taught in schools in Virginia. A small number taught in other States. Several educators earned a terminal degree from prestigious institutions of higher learning.

The most intriguing humble element among the teachers is comprised of individuals that were locked out of the Prince Edward County public schools but enjoyed a rewarding career as teachers in the same public school system that denied them an education for five consecutive years. Upon entering their professional calling, these teachers found it impossible to deny the boys and girls of Prince Edward County access to the rich gifts and talents they possessed that could assist pupils in becoming the person each was created and called to be.

Other careers and vocations of persons impacted by the closure of the schools revealed in this work are of individuals in the field on medicine, pastors, entrepreneurs, public servants, social workers, and an engineer.

There are in this publication the painful and agonizing reflections of persons who shared about never coming close to achieving their childhood dreams and ambitions, which required an education. Many students because of the interruption of their education during the critical foundational formative years were unable to sufficiently recover and master the proficiency required to progress and develop intellectually at a rate that permitted them to pursue lofty goals in life.

Some of the public school teachers who learned around May 1959 for certain that their contract would terminate on the last day of school have heart rending accounts in this work. In September 1959 Negro teachers in Prince Edward County accepted employment in other counties in Virginia and other States. Approximately a dozen teachers remained in Prince Edward County. This was their home and they were settled. By the third year of the school shut down several of the remaining teachers had taken teaching positions in other counties.

When the oppressor shut down the Prince Edward County public schools in September 1959, they had a private school system in place that opened for children of the oppressor group that September. Two stories from individuals that matriculated in that private school system are in this publication.

Many students that were locked out of the Prince Edward County public schools gained access to public schools in surrounding Amelia County, Cumberland County, Lunenburg County, Nottoway County, Buckingham County, and a private church school in Lunenburg County. Individuals that were residents of these counties and remember Prince Edward County pupils coming to schools there provided reflections.

Many teenagers of the same immediate family in Prince Edward County were able to go away and continue their education in parts of Virginia and in other States through the efforts of sponsorship opportunities provided by organizations. In numerous households, mothers and fathers sent children to aunts, uncles, grandparents, older sisters and brothers, cousins, and friends in various locations to attend school. Readers get a glimpse in narratives of the distressing disruption of homes and the resulting dynamics.

Within the community of the oppressed most of the mothers and fathers, grandparents, and aunts and uncles, that reared sons and daughters, grandsons and granddaughters, and nieces and nephews, during the school crisis were deceased when this project commenced. Some living parents were too feeble and void of mental alertness to recount the turns of events in their respective households during the school lock-out. The touching stories of a few guardians are in this collection.

The season is approaching when all the individuals who as children and youths were locked out of the Prince Edward County public schools will no longer walk upon the earth. They and their stories will all be gone. We thank the great I AM for arranging for this collection of stories in this book which will live on.

ACKNOWLEDGEMENTS

The Editor is extremely appreciative to Mr. Carl U. Eggleston, Jr. for providing an office at Eggleston Funeral Home in Farmville. The location was exceptionally beneficial during the initial three years of the collection of stories. Individuals who agreed to share reflections were directed to appear at Eggleston Funeral Home. Mr. Eggleston personally contacted and recruited many of the persons that recounted their stories.

The late Ms. Clara Medlyn Ligon provided food and lodging the early years of my undertaking. My personal funds were used to support the project. Sister Ligon was a God sent.

The Editor is appreciative to each person who after being interviewed communicated with a friend or relative and encouraged that person to do likewise.

Many people upon hearing about this work said: "I am praying for you." There were individuals in various locations on the journey that held my hands and prayed the blessings of Almighty God upon me and the project. Thank you.

In the homes where this traveler was served breakfast, lunch, and or dinner while he was driving from one location to another to secure a story, thank you for your hospitality and kindness.

Gas or money for gasoline was provided to me on several occasions by individuals who wanted to ensure that my traveling was unhindered. The mission is accomplished, and your support proved invaluable.

The Editor met Dr. Kitty Smith the latter part of 2011. A resident of Prince Edward County she immediately dedicated herself to advancing the collection of stories. Dr. Smith arranged several interviews.

Several pastors in Prince Edward County unhesitatingly allowed the collection of stories project to be announced during the Sunday morning worship service. Pastor Bernard S. Hill, Sr., High Rock Baptist Church, Rice; Pastor Darryl McCoy Brown, Calvary Baptist Church, Prospect; Pastor Winston Bland New Witt Baptist Church, Redd Shop; and Pastor James W. Morris, Triumph Baptist Church, Darlington Heights—Thank you. Pastor Darrell Wade, Beulah African Methodist Episcopal Church, Farmville, Virginia, was of immense support to me personally and to the project beginning in April 2011.

INTRODUCTION

The stories in this collection are simple and clear. Several names and events appear often in accounts that will be foreign to readers. Clarification is provided below related to those individuals, events, and places.

The Student Strike of 1951 occurred on April 23, 1951, when Negro students at R. R. Moton High School, Farmville, Virginia, walked out of school. The high school was built in 1939 for one hundred and eighty students. Approximately four hundred and eighty pupils were enrolled in 1951. The school board had shacks erected to accommodate the overflow. The high school students protested. Their protest is known locally as The Strike of 1951.

Training Centers were set up in churches, old buildings, and one home around Prince Edward County by local leaders and concerned parents to facilitate the educational development of Negro children during the school closure years. The sites were called Training Centers because these were not schools. Mothers, grandmothers, aunts, and women who cared and were concerned about the children served as facilitators at the sites. Some of the facilitators were without a high school education. In some accounts the sites are referred to as Centers.

The Academy refers to the private school system established by the oppressor.

Reverend L. Francis Griffin or *Reverend Griffin* was the pastor of First Baptist Church in Farmville and was regarded by the community of the oppressed as their leader.

Vernon Johns was the pastor of Dexter Avenue Baptist Church, Montgomery, Alabama, before the young Martin Luther King, Jr. was called to serve the congregation in 1954. Johns hailed from Prince Edward County, Virginia. He was a dynamic preacher and orator, a respected scholar, and local folk hero. Johns was a mentor to Griffin.

American Friends Service Committee was founded in 1917 and is a Quaker organization that promotes lasting peace with justice, as a practical expression of faith in action. The American Friends Service Committee sent representatives to Prince Edward County, Virginia, to work with local leaders and families to help place older students with host families in other States. The organization coordinated, beginning the second year of the school closure, for Prince Edward County teenage students to go away and live with families in States with concentrated Quaker populations. The American Friends Service Committee also arranged for a small number of students to attend private Quaker high schools.

Jean Fairfax was the principal coordinator sent to Prince Edward County by the American Friends Service Committee to coordinate with Quaker communities, families, and institutions around the United States to secure placement for teenage students, so they could resume their education. She was based out of Prince Edward County, having an office in Farmville, but traveled extensively meeting with and securing support and commitments.

Helen Baker was the second representative of the American Friends Service Committee sent to Prince Edward County. She suspended her studies at the University of Maryland School of Law to go to Prince Edward County. Baker remained stationary in Farmville, while Fairfax traveled, and handled all the coordination at the local level with local leaders, families, and students.

The Free School was mentioned by most of the storytellers that were locked out of the Prince Edward County public schools. In the fifth year of the school crisis, September 1963 – May 1964, a private school system was set-up in Prince Edward County. Donations were sent from around the country and from abroad to support the private endeavor so that students of African descent in particular would not miss another year out of the classroom. The private educational system was called The Prince Edward Free School Association. No student had to pay. School was free. President John F. Kennedy was the motivating personality behind the establishment of The Prince Edward Free School Association.

Chapter One

ACCOUNTS FROM PRINCE EDWARD COUNTY

FARMVILLE

JOE BERRYMAN

I went to Moton High School in Farmville, Virginia, with John and Increase Johns, sons of Reverend Vernon Johns.

The Johns boys were just like any other boys in the community. The school didn't have a gymnasium, but there was an auditorium. The boys would get up a boxing team outside on the grounds. The girls would form a circle and yell for their favorite boxer. John (Johns) was tough. I remember Walter Savage would hit John two or three times and it didn't bother John.

Paige Trent was the king of sandlot boxing in Farmville and everyone wanted to beat him. John beat Paige down brutally one day. In those matches the boys' mouths would be bleeding, but it was all in good sport. When the bout was over, everyone went home happy.

I played on the R. R. Moton High baseball team. Our team traveled in an open flatbed trailer with a light railing on the sides that kept us from falling off. We didn't have a school bus to travel in. The all White school board wouldn't provide a bus for us. We went from one school to another on a flatbed trailer to play our baseball games.

Mr. Harry Royal was the principal. Mr. Royal took us to play the games. He owned a 1939 Buick that had two spare tires, one on each side of the vehicle with a decorative covering. School always got out a little early, about 2:30 p. m., on the days we had a game. Mr. Royal would hitch the trailer to the back of his car and take us to play our games.

Mr. Royal didn't believe in banks. His father lost some money. He kept his money in the garage and in the trunk of the car.

During the week, we rode a bus to school, but it was not provided by the county. Mr. Willie Hendricks owned the bus. I believe Mr. Hendricks purchased a chassis and the school board gave him the yellow body to set on the chassis. It cost $2.00 a month per child to ride. The $2.00 paid for gas and the driver. There were six children in my house. My parents couldn't afford the $12.00 monthly fee. My sister, Majorie, worked for Dr. N. P. Miller, a Black dentist in the town of Farmville and stayed with Mrs. Pettus. My brother Everett drove the bus for Mr. Hendricks and didn't have to pay. So only four children from our family had to pay to ride the bus.

Reverend Johns had a little store in the community. He sold candy, hardware items such as pitch forks and a straw hat or two. He always sold fish.

While serving as pastor of Court Street Baptist Church in Lynchburg, Deacon Ham Johns, who was no relation to Reverend Johns and one of the church officers at Court Street, got on the pastor for selling fish after church. Reverend Johns told the deacon:

"If you Negroes would pay me enough money, I would not have to sell goods."

He never dressed up. Reverend Johns never got dressed up. When he preached, his shirt collar would be turned up or his necktie half-tied. Even as a boy, I remember him holding us spell bound. He kept us on the edge of our seats.

My brother Everett was a preacher. He told me once that Reverend Johns was preaching at a church, stopped in the middle of the sermon and said:

"You Negroes are not listening or comprehending what I am saying."

The people adjusted and got prepared for him to go on in his sermon, but instead of continuing, Dr. Johns sat down.

I never learned whether he got up and finished his sermon.

The White people were afraid of him.

Les Davenport was Reverend Johns' neighbor. Les and Reverend Johns had the Hatfield and McCoy relationship, but it was all in jest.

Reverend Johns said prior to his death: "Bury me facing Les' property so every time he goes by he will have to look at my tombstone."

Les was a Deacon at Triumph Baptist Church, which was and remains the home church of the Johns family. Reverend Johns was buried across the road from where Les lived.

When the schools were closed in Prince Edward County, my brother Everett and his wife, Cula, moved to Appomattox County. There was a White man who owned some land and had a rundown house. It was a sharecropper's house. My brother moved his family into the house, so his children could go to school in Appomattox County at Carver–Price High School. The White man told Everett that he only wanted him to tend the land and do some work on the place in exchange for living in the old shack. The children started school in August or September during one of the years the schools were closed. It wasn't the first year the schools were closed.

One day I stopped by to visit my brother. It was snowing. I knocked on the door and Everett yelled for me to come in. I went upstairs and looked in his bedroom. When he raised up in the bed to talk to me, snow was on the top of his covers, having fallen through the roof. It was the same in the children's room.

In the spring of the year when school was about to close, and the children were doing well, Everett and Cula got a surprise. Someone, a White man in Prince Edward County said that my brother was hitch-hiking in Appomattox County, saying Everett was a resident of Prince Edward County and was living in Appomattox County only so his children could go to school. The children were dismissed from Carver–Price High School just before the school year ended. Though they had gone to school almost the entire year, Everett, Jr., Gloria, Melvin, Sharon, and Connie didn't get any credit for their months of study.

At Virginia State College I was trained to be a teacher, but during the summer I did auto mechanic work. One summer I was working at Sears and fixed the breaks on a vehicle that no one else in the shop could fix. The boss asked me did I have a brother or knew of someone who could do comparable work. I said yes. I went to Appomattox, got Everett, brought him back to Lynchburg and introduced him to the boss. Everett was hired. He moved his family from Appomattox to Lynchburg. He and Cula settled down and the children started school again in the fall of the year.

———

VERA JONES ALLEN

When I was a girl in Charles City, in Charles City County, Virginia, I rode the bus to school. The vehicle didn't look like a school bus but looked more like a truck. It was a flat-bed truck with make shift seats improvised to haul students. The siding was a folding canvas type material, sort of like the covering placed on top of tobacco on a flatbed truck when it was being hauled. It was always dark in the section where the children sat. The canvas, of course, protected us from the elements, cold and rain. In the spring or on warm days the canvas was rolled up and we enjoyed the sunlight and fresh air. The students had to pay $2.00 a month to ride. The bus wasn't owned by the county, but by an individual. We never got new books. When the State said new books were available, they sent the used books to the Negro schools and we had to pay for the used books.

After graduating from high school, I entered Virginia State College in Petersburg, Virginia. While matriculating there, I met and fell in love with a student named Edward Baker Allen. He was from Farmville, Virginia. However, he didn't graduate from high school in his hometown because the White people provided no secondary education for Negro teenagers in that era. Edward finished high school in Cumberland County. I graduated from Virginia State College in 1935 and Edward finished the year prior.

I returned to my home county and taught in a three room school.

After Edward and I were married, we settled in his hometown, Farmville.

The work of Black people to secure a quality and good education for Black children in Prince Edward County was afoot as early as the 1930s. Historians that have written about Prince Edward County schools usually begin their investigation at a much later period. But as I said, the work really began during the latter part of the 1930s.

There was a Black woman in Farmville at that time named Mrs. Martha E. Forrester. The Forrester family name was strong and reputable in Richmond, which was the city from which she hailed. Mrs. Forrester's daughter, Jeanette, married Mr. Stanley Clark, a pleasant business man in Farmville. He owned a service station and restaurant on Main Street in town. Stanley and Jeanette had two children, a boy and a girl. The girl was named Nellie and the boy, I can't remember his name.

Jeanette's mother, Mrs. Forrester, moved from Richmond and relocated to Farmville to live with her daughter, son-in-law, and grandchildren. After settling in Farmville, Mrs. Forrester took a keen interest in securing secondary education for Black children in the county. There was a facility for the Negro children. The building had elementary classes downstairs and high school upstairs. The school was named R. R. Moton High School. However, parents wanted a full secondary education school facility for their children.

Mrs. Forrester was the prime mover in establishing a group of energetic Black women.

The new secondary facility, Moton High School, was from the beginning too small to house the enrollment. The students and not the parents were disappointed mostly with the size. The parents discussed it and the school board made adjustments over the years that prove unacceptable and not conducive for learning. In the spring of 1951 the students took action without our (parents) knowledge.

Much has been written about The Student Strike of April 1951. This is what I recall a little more than fifty years later about the day the students walked out of Moton High School.

That morning I got up and went to work as usual. I was working as Supervisor of Schools in Cumberland County. I came home that evening and my daughter, Edwilda, told me they had walked out. I said:

"You stayed in the house with us last night and did not tell us what was planned."

I did not get upset. My husband didn't fuss about it either.

I heard that the high school students walked out to go downtown to the superintendent's office. The children in the elementary school across the street were looking out the windows and wondered where the high school children were going, since the school day hadn't yet ended. Since The Strike had been planned in secrecy, the elementary students had no clue about what was happening. Most of the teachers at Moton walked out and went home. The students walked to the superintendent's office downtown. A teacher who didn't walk out telephoned the superintendent's office and alerted him that the students were in route to the administration building. The students didn't get in the building because the informant's call gave those in the building time to block the students' entry. The students sat on the steps.

Barbara Johns coordinated The Strike. There were others with her, but she was the master-mind. The students didn't return to school immediately. They stayed out. Shortly afterwards Barbara went to Montgomery, Alabama, to live with her Uncle Vernon because she had been threatened by the White folk in the county. Her uncle was Reverend Vernon Johns who was the pastor of Dexter Avenue Baptist Church. Johns was the fireball pastor prior to Reverend Martin Luther King, Jr. being called to the church.

Regarding the closing of the schools in the September 1959, I heard some people talking about the schools not opening on time. That was how I found out about the closing. When the White school administrators in Cumberland County learned of my position and support for the cause of justice regarding events in Prince Edward County, I was fired immediately.

There was a school in the basement of First Baptist Church and at the Methodist Church (Beulah African Methodist

Episcopal Church). Beulah was across the street from First Baptist and both churches were located on Main Street. Reverend L. Francis Griffin was the pastor at First Baptist and Reverend Alexander Dunlap was the pastor of Beulah. Reverend Goodwin Douglas followed Reverend Dunlap at the church.

I remember some of the teachers that worked with the children during the summer. Mrs. Beatrice Vaughan (called Tootie), she married a man from Farmville last name Vaughan and Mrs. Connie Rawlings, whose husband was a doctor, were teachers that worked at the churches with students during the summer. When the Prince Edward County public school system was shut down, Mrs. Connie Rawlings taught in the public schools in Charlottesville, Virginia. She and other teachers returned to their homes in Prince Edward County during the summer.

Some people came from other counties to work with the children during the summer months. Mr. Maceo Hill taught in Amelia County. During the summer, he would come to the church and work with the children in Farmville. Many of the children went to summer school in Farmville because they missed so much time during the winter.

When the Free School opened only a few White children enrolled. One White child was the son of Dr. Moss from Longwood College. His son, Dicky, was one of the White students. There was a White girl whose parents enrolled her. Her parents weren't professors but sent their daughter nevertheless.

A lot of families moved away. Some families came back home when the schools reopened because they had homes here. Many families never returned to Prince Edward County.

I lost my job in Cumberland County for supporting the

effort in Farmville. I got a job in North Carolina. I had a friend who was retiring, and she got me a job without any references in Wayne County. I worked in Goldsboro, where I stayed during the week and came home on the weekend. I rented with a family. The family was dying out when I went there. When the last family member died in the 1960s, I learned that I had inherited everything. They had two houses. They left the church one and left the other to me. I had to go and pack up everything.

My husband owned and operated a funeral home in Farmville. When Barbara Johns died, my daughter, Edwilda and Paul Wilson, drove to Philadelphia, retrieved Barbara's remains and brought her home.

The story of my people in Prince Edward County is a rich and wonderful story. I have granted many interviews and told my story many times and it is with extreme pleasure and pride that I tell it one more time.

_____

SAMUEL WILLIAMS

I was born in Harlem Hospital in New York and my parents relocated to Farmville when I was young. I attended R. R. Moton.

There was a man named Arthur Jordan in Farmville and his father was a preacher. Mr. Arthur Jordan was an instructor at Moton. One day we had one of our usual assemblies in the auditorium. When the assembly adjourned, the students began returning to their respective classrooms. There were two French doors on each side of the exits leading out of the auditorium. Mr. Jordan yelled across the auditorium and requested that the students be allowed to exit freely. All of the exit doors were not opened, which slowed down the process. A female teacher yelled back across the auditorium to him:

"Mr. McIlwaine said one door must be closed at all times." The name is phonetically pronounced Mack-l-Waine.

Thomas J. McIlwaine was the White superintendent of the Prince Edward County Schools.

Mr. Jordan, a six grade teacher, who also taught physics at R. R. Moton High School, yelled back to the teacher in a rhyme:

"I don't care if Mr. HcIlwaine said it. I said open the other door."

All of the students in the auditorium burst out laughing. I think all of the students were laughing at the second name Mr. Jordan made up. I was the only one who did not laugh, as the episode struck me differently. I thought to myself: 'I did not know a Negro could stand up against a White man like that.' That lady opened the door, but the event opened a new door in my mind.

Every day at school we began the day with a period of devotion. We said a Scripture and sang a patriotic hymn. In Mr. Jordan's classroom were learned all of the old Negro Spirituals — *Go Down Moses*, *Joshua Fought the Battle at Jericho*, and others. He taught Black History every day. He told us about Garvey, Tubman, and many others. We thought he was making up the names and events until we discovered the truth by reading for ourselves.

Several students who were braver than others became fed up with the Moton facility. The facility was too small when it was built. The all White school board built tar-paper shacks as part of an expansion effort to accommodate more students.

Moton had a football team, but there were no lights to practice for night games. If we went to Clifton Forge or Covington to play a night game, Farmville High School, the all White school, would allow us to practice at night on their field to get use to the lights to prepare us for the road game. However, the school board would not put lights at Moton.

We had limited academic facilities. We had a few Brunson burners for the science classes, some microscopes, and a few other science pieces.

Regarding The Student Strike of 1951, this is what I recollect. The students met in the auditorium the morning of The Strike. Someone came and said to me:

"We need you to help lead The Strike..."

I had not been duly informed about it. There had been some meetings and I could tell that extensive planning had taken place. Barbara Johns spoke to the student body that day in the auditorium and so did I. I am not sure whether John Stokes spoke or not. I think he did. Barbara was the chief spokesperson.

The school was closed for two weeks while the students demands were being addressed. We wanted better facilities in general. The bravest and most stalwart defense came from my pastor, Reverend L. F. Griffin, Sr., and the NAACP. Oliver Hill, Spottswood Robinson and Martin A. Martin provided legal counsel.

Mass meetings were held at First Baptist Church, where Reverend Griffin was the pastor. We, the students, were advised to return to school.

I became the senior class president in September 1951. We graduated in May 1952. Following graduation, I joined the U. S. Army. I served my tour of duty, was honorably discharged, and took up residence in New York.

Reverend L. F. Griffin attended Shaw University in North Carolina and so did his father and brother. My pastor made a great impression on me when a youngster and I applied to and was accepted at Shaw University. While there, I became involved in the Student Movement of the early 1960s.

In 1963 I returned to Farmville and was involved in activities. Several of us were arrested in Farmville for trying to enter the Farmville Baptist Church, the all White church. I think about twenty were arrested.

I had a frightening episode while under arrest. One of the officers said to me after I had been finger printed:

"Reverend Griffin wants to see you down stairs."

"Okay," I said.

I went down stairs, but Reverend Griffin was nowhere to be found. They put me and some others who had been arrested in a police car and transported us to the Lunenburg County Jail, where I remained for almost a week.

My wife Lillie Ann Blanton Williams and I were the first to desegregate the eating facility in the local bus station. They were supposed to paint over the *Colored* and *White* signs in the bus station. The White folks only put a thin coat of paint on the signs and you could still see the writing — *Colored* and *White*. The law had been passed. We invited other Black folk in the bus station to come over and eat, but they wouldn't come and join us. Sometime later a heavy coat of paint was painted over the signs and the words *Colored* and *White* were no longer visible.

Words can be painted over and blotted out with heavy coats of paint, but there are some things that cannot be blotted out no matter how much covering and coating are put on.

JAMES P. YOUNG

I was born in Farmville, Virginia, in 1921 to Richard and Josephine Young. My mother was part Indian and Daddy was Black. I started school in Farmville around 1927 at Robert R. Moton High School. I graduated Valedictorian from elementary and Salutatorian from high school. Ms. Hazel Glase was the Salutatorian in grade school and Valedictorian in high school. Students brought their own lunch.

Moton High School had an upstairs and downstairs. The lower grades were downstairs and the higher grades upstairs. It was a brick facility. We assembled each morning in the auditorium. We had a morning devotion which included prayer. The Negro National Anthem was sung and then the Pledge of Allegiance was recited. I enjoyed school life.

We went to the original Robert R. Moton High School in Farmville. We had very good teachers and they were dedicated. Everything was done in the one building. We had activities in the front and back. We had organized football and basketball, and played baseball at recess.

In high school I sang in the Glee Club and remember going to Norfolk, Virginia, to sing. I don't remember the occasion. The Glee Club members went to Norfolk in cars. We had no school buses. When I say we had no school buses, I mean that the all White school board didn't provide school buses for Black students, or Colored or Negro students as we were called in those days. The White children had buses and all the facilities needed to get a good education.

Moton High School received all of the hand me downs from the White school in town. The White school was Farmville High School. I was on the Moton football team. I played end or what is now called wide receiver. I was small but could run fast. The Moton football team sometimes got football shoes with cleats, but they were the shoes discarded by the football team at the White school. Farmville High School football team would get new shoes and send their old worn out cleat shoes to us. Before getting the cleat shoes, at Moton members of the football team played football in whatever shoes they had from home. We played in sneakers or old shoes that someone in the community had thrown away. The White people saw themselves as doing us a favor when sending over these run over worn out shoes.

Moton High School was located in the town of Farmville, but students came from Prospect, Pamplin, and other nearby areas. Some children rode in wagons. Someone, a father, uncle, or grandfather would ride them into town on the wagon and drop them off and came back in the afternoon for the students. Some students hitched a ride in a car. Several students drove their parents' automobiles and picked up others on the way.

Moton High School went to the eleventh grade. I finished in the spring of 1939. The new school opened in August 1939, as a new facility. After graduating, I went to Washington, D. C. I returned to Farmville in 1941 to see who was still around. I saw a friend named Fred Reid. We boarded a bus and went to New York. Overnight I became a New Yorker and Fred remained a country boy. (Mr. Young laughs.)

I enlisted in the Army Air Corps. Benjamin O. Davis, Sr. was my commanding officer. After I enlisted, I went to Fort Dix, New Jersey. Mercer Ellington, Duke Ellington's son, and I went in together. When I enlisted, they had me down as White and never changed it.

I went to Tuskegee and was with the Tuskegee Airmen. I went to the Five and Dime Store in the town of Tuskegee one day to purchase something. I gave the White lady the money and she didn't want to take it. I threw the money to her. She wanted to call someone but didn't know what to do. I stared her down. She didn't want to touch a Black hand, which was why she refused to take the money.

Benjamin Davis, Sr. was moved up to a higher grade. His son was a real soldier. The old man I didn't take to very kindly.

I remember the Tuskegee Airmen training. They had no fear. Bridges were not that high in and around Tuskegee. One day I saw a Tuskegee Airman come out of the sky, fly his plane under a bridge, come up on the other side of the bridge and kept moving. They had no fear. Those guys could fly.

I was attached to the Tuskegee Air Force as a radar support personnel. We left Tuskegee, Alabama, and went to Selfridge Field, Michigan as the 332nd Fighter Squadron. I was still in radar support.

From there I went to Shreveport, Louisiana, because the Buffalo Division was at the time 88% illiterate. I was put in that division because they needed some people who could read and write. I went to Italy. When in Italy, at dusk the Italians would watch to see when the tails of the Black or Negro soldiers come out. White soldiers from the United States had told Europeans that Black soldiers had tails like monkeys and the tails came out at night.

In Naples, I was walking down a street one day and stopped at the corner to cross. A man across the street and I started looking at each other.

"Blink," the voice said. When I was a boy, I used to blink my eyes a lot and my friends called me Blink.

"Griff," I replied. It was my childhood friend and playmate Leslie Francis Griffin from Farmville.

Leslie Francis Griffin and I we close as boys. I never thought he would be a preacher.

When we were children, he was devilish. I don't mean he was violent or anything. I mean Leslie was playfully devilish. We went to the Echo Theater once. Black people sat in the balcony or the buzzard's nest and the White people sat on the ground floor. I was a Nanny to five White kids in Farmville. When I took them to the movie, I sat on the ground floor or lower level with them.

Leslie, some others, and I saw a move called The Invisible Man. The movie was about a person who could make himself disappear. The man had a machine that could make him invisible. Leslie went home and tried to make himself invisible and nearly electrocuted himself. One time he put on a cape and leaped from a tree in an attempt to fly. He never tried that again. (Mr. Young starts laughing.)

From Italy I was sent to the Panama Canal and on to Seoul, Korea. My military career ended in 1946 and I returned to New York.

I stayed in touch with Leslie and Fred. We remained tight friends. Fred returned to Farmville. After I had been back in New York for a while, Fred called and said: "Jim, guess what? Leslie is preaching!"

"No," I said in disbelief, "you're wrong."

But sure enough, Leslie was preaching. I wasn't in Farmville when the schools were closed. Leslie was one of the local leaders in the struggle. We would talk by telephone about twice a year. He would call and say: "Jim, why don't you come back to Farmville." The last time I saw him he said: "Jim, I'm not taking any more operations."

Leslie suffered greatly at times due to his involvement in the struggle for justice in Farmville. Sometimes Mr. Warren

Reid who owned the funeral home (Bland-Reid Funeral Home) had to feed L. Francis and his family. Warren also paid the rent for the Griffin family sometime. The church was not paying Leslie as they should.

I am going to ask Warren to tell his story and he can provide more particulars. I hope the information I have shared will shed some light on telling the full story on events in Farmville.

L. L. HALL

L. L. Hall had given many interviews during the past three decades. Cornell Walker asked me June 2004: "Have you interviewed Mr. Hall?" "No, but I have heard the name many times and several people have said 'you have to talk to L. L. Hall." "His story needs to be included in the book or you don't have a history," Cornell said emphatically. "I'll speak with Mr. Hall and when you come to Prince Edward again I'll take you to see him." "Do you think it can be arranged?" "He's not too keen on giving interviews these days. He always complains that people never write what he tells them. But if I ask Mr. Hall, he will give you an interview."

Mr. Hall agreed to grant an interview. When Walker took me to the home on June 6, 2005, Hall was sitting and after being introduced said to me: "Ask me whatever you like." That was what other researchers had done with him. The Editor said: "This will be your story in a book. Tell the reading public anything you like. I will write what you tell me." "I stopped giving interviews because whatever I told a writer when I saw it in print it was nothing like what I said." The former school teacher and principal quickly noted the difference in approach and yielded readily.

Hall was around ninety years of age when interviewed. The Editor just let him talk and drafted the account as given. The information Hall shared is more important than the order in which he presented events.

I was born and reared in Portsmouth, Virginia, and came to Prince Edward County to work in the school system the latter part of the 1930s.

The Negroes, as they were called in those days, in the county were working aggressively to address certain inequities in the school system. Mrs. Forrester was the founder of an organization comprised of Negro women and was one of the leading women in the group. She had gotten old by this time. Mrs. Kate Wiley was the president of the council. Mrs. Wiley owned a big house and boarded Negro teachers during the school year.

The state law during this time was that a student graduated in eleventh grade. High school consisted of grades eight to eleventh. The Council raised money to pay Negro teachers who taught tenth and eleventh grades so the Negro children in Prince Edward County could complete those grades. Mrs. Wiley and Mrs. Forrester told me this.

When the new Moton High School opened in 1939, the Council purchased the curtains for the facility through the PTA. The school boards gave the school building and that was it in those days.

Mrs. Forrester's daughter was a teacher in the elementary school when I came to Farmville.

One of the young students I remember from my earliest days in the public schools in Farmville was Leslie Francis

Griffin. He was in high school when I arrived in town. I vividly remember him saying on more than one occasion regarding a vocation in adult life:

"I'm not going to be a preacher. My daddy is a preacher. My brother is a preacher. I have an aunt who is married to a preacher and I am not going to be one."

"Don't let me have to say, 'I told you so,'" I said to him.

Leslie went off to the war. His whole unit for the most part was wiped out except for him. After returning to the United States, Leslie went to Shaw University in North Carolina and studied for the Christian ministry. He also met his wife at Shaw, who was from New Jersey. Reverend and Mrs. Francis Griffin came to Farmville to live.

I had charge of the school buses, I mapped out the routes for the drivers. Barbara (Johns) got left one day when it was cold. She came to my office the next day and said: "You told me the driver had to wait for me." The bus driver left her. I said: "I will see to it that he doesn't leave you again."

Regarding The Student Strike, I heard about everything after it was over. They said Barbara talked to me about The Strike. She didn't. Joan (Johns Cobbs), Barbara's sister told me many years later that she (Joan) didn't even know about the planned strike. Joan lived in the same house with Barbara and learned of The Strike the same morning as all the other students.

Joan was able to put some of the pieces together in later years after finding some of Barbara's papers in the family house. Joan told me that after she was grown and married she was in the family house cleaning up and looking for something and found excerpts from the secret meetings Barbara had with her group leading up to The Strike. Carrie Stokes wrote the letter to NAACP. She was in it. There were five or six in the inner circle that planned it.

I knew Vernon Johns. He was from Prince Edward County. Barbara got some of her spark I'm sure from her uncle, Vernon. Johns served as pastor of Dexter Avenue Baptist Church in Montgomery, Alabama. He would come home to Prince Edward County to visit, and when Reverend Johns was in the county he would come by the school and visit with me. He was full of humor, yet serious minded. He was very meticulous in the pronunciation of his words.

Sometime after preaching the famous sermon, he came home for a visit. I remember he came by the school and told me the whole story.

Reverend Johns told me that after he put the title of the sermon on the marquee *Is It Safe To Kill Negroes* the authorities came to the church. He was outside the church and they ask him:

"Do you know Dr. Johns?"

"I've seen him. I've seen the fellow," I told them.

I was struck by this statement, as I could not understand how Vernon Johns could have seen Vernon Johns.

"How had you seen the fellow?" I asked somewhat puzzled.

"I look in the mirror every morning, don't I?"

That made sense to me.

Reverend Johns said the police came back that Saturday, stopping by the parsonage, where he was on the front porch reading the paper and swinging. They asked him, not knowing they were talking to Reverend Johns:

"Is the young man still going to preach the sermon?"

Johns said he told the policemen: "Yes, the young man said he is going to still preach the sermon and you are invited?"

"Reverend Johns, those White folks may kill you down there," I said.

"They are not going to do anything. Those Crackers don't have any guts."

Reverend Johns had a theory that Negroes should go into business, sell to each other, make something, and become independent.

He was very comical and never tied his shoes. Someone said to him once:

"Reverend Johns, why don't you tie your shoelaces?"

"When Negroes start making and selling shoelaces, I will tie them up," he said, enunciating every word with clarity as he always did.

Reverend Johns took great delight in telling how he gained admission to Oberlin Seminary. He told me:

"I went there and the head of the school told me 'you do not have enough points' to enter Oberlin."

I asked him:

"Do you want a man with points or a man with brains? I was admitted and finished at the top of my class."

One day I had to drive Reverend Johns to the post office at Hampden-Sydney College. It was an all White college during this time. He went into the post office and I went to run an errand, while he took care of his business. When I returned to pick him up, Reverend Johns was standing by a plaque of some sort and a small crowd of White Hampden-Sydney students surrounded him. I waited in the car. After a few moments, he left the students, walked to the automobile and got in. He told me that he was reading and interpreting for the White students something written in Latin on the plaque. The students were amazed beyond belief because this Negro who had on farm clothes and untied shoes could read and translate Latin. Reverend Johns made a big joke about it and laughed as we rode along.

After he resigned as pastor of Dexter Avenue Baptist Church, Reverend Johns was in Prince Edward County, came by the school one day and asked:

"Have you heard of Reverend Martin Luther King, Jr.?"

"No, I have not heard of him." This was before Dr. King's fame spread.

"He is a fine young man and has a lot of ambition. I strongly recommended him to the church in Montgomery."

"Are you going to stay down there and help him?"

Johns said: "No, I'm not going to stay. I have to get some Crackers lynched."

"What does integrating the schools means to you?" he asked me one day.

"The only thing I see to come out of it is for southern Whites to see that Negroes are not dumb and that there are as many dumb White people."

Johns said: "Say that again." I restated it and he said: "Can you prove that? I'll put it in my memoir."

In the late 1940s and early 1950s we were the only Negro school on the air. I remember it started before The Strike. We broadcasted on WFLO—Assembly on the Air. It was in the school auditorium. The manager of the station came and did the show. Two or three times the manager couldn't get there and I did the show. Mrs. Johns taught Music. She would have the students to sing. Assembly on the Air was on Friday morning at 11:00 or 11:30. In February we did Negro History Month on the air. If it was Easter season, she did Easter music and at Christmas she did Christmas music. She also had the primary children's group which was a rhythm band.

Denise Tyler followed Mrs. Johns in the school system and worked with the children. Denise wrote the school song.

Maxine Hunt followed Denise. In later years Maxine went to Roanoke to teach and the show went off the air.

Mrs. Johns was the assistant to the head of the music department at Virginia State College, after returning from Alabama State College. She wrote two or three books. A publisher did one, I'm sure.

When Dr. Johns filled in for Gandy, the campus chaplain at Virginia State College, the administration asked Johns: "Do you want us to make chapel mandatory for the students?"

Johns said he told the administration: "If I can't draw them on my preaching, then they ought not come." He packed Virginia Hall every night he was there. I remember Gandy. I lived in room 103 and he lived in 105.

When the 50th year anniversary of The Strike was held, people appeared and participated who were not even in the march in 1951. People were claiming they did things they didn't do. Those posters people said they had, none of it was true. No one had any posters the day of The Strike.

When the man from Parks and Services came to present the plaque, he asked where did I get the school name for Dr. Mary E. Branch. Ms. Branch's father was a shoemaker not a shoe repairman. There is a difference between the two.

All the mail that came for the school came to R. R. Moton. I said to the school board lets name the elementary school to Mary E. Branch. As I understood it, Ms. Branch was the first Negro woman to head a college and it became accredited a few years after she took over. The college was in Texas. The school board accepted the recommendation. I made the recommendation to change the name before the new high school was built.

R. R. Moton lived in Prince Edward County. Ms. Branch was a native of Farmville. I saw Dr. Branch once and that was on the grounds of Virginia State College. I was in the presence of R. R. Moton when I was a student at Saint Paul's College. Dr. A. H. Turner was the business manager at the college for several years. His son Harry and I were friends. Harry taught at Virginia State College. Dr. A. H. Turner and R. R. Moton were very good friends. Turner had cabin in Capahosic in Gloucester County on a lake. Moton came to the cabin during the summer. I was there and talked with him several times. Moton was a smart man. He spoke at Saint Paul's once or twice when I was a student.

I had all of the Negro buses in the county and both schools. I had to chart the routes. The routes were color coded. I had to re-accomplish that each year.

When the schools were closed, many students stood on the side of the road waiting for buses the first day of school in September 1959 and the buses never came. When the schools officially reopened in September 1964, they hired five people to do what I had been doing. Much more money was available. (Mr. Hall laughs.)

In the summer of 1959, I took a job in Snell, located in Spotsylvania County, Virginia, at John W. Wright High School. I was hired to be the principal. Several other teachers from Prince Edward County were also hired in Spotsylvania County. The teachers were Mrs. Herndon, Mrs. Alma Smith and I think there was one more. Mr. Spottswood Robinson and Mr. Lester Banks, President of State NAACP, came to the school one day and when I looked up and saw them I asked:

"What honor has gained me this visit?"

They explained that the NAACP was going to file a suit in September and as a principal I would be involved again. I said to myself: "No way!" I explained to them I was not going through that kind of excitement a second time after Prince

Edward County. I rode with them to the superintendent's office and they told him about the planned law suit to desegregate the schools in Spotsylvania County. After they explained why they were present, I explained to the superintendent that I was resigning, effectively immediately.

"You can't resign," he said to me.

"Well, I am!" I explained to the superintendent that I was not about to go through another law suit for a county to desegregate its schools.

The superintendent looked at Mr. Banks and Mr. Spottswood and said regarding me:

"We picked him from a list of fifteen candidates."

I resigned and returned to Prince Edward County. Dr. Willie Edward Smith, my physician, saw me on the streets in Farmville and asked:

"Will you accept a job in Cumberland?"

"Yes," I said. He went and told Mr. McIlwaine to send me a contract. McIlwaine was superintendent in both counties. Dr. Smith was chairman of the school board in Prince Edward County.

I was hired as a teacher in Cumberland. I taught at Luther P. Jackson High School for two years, September 1959 to May 1961. My oldest child, Veronica, had passed to ninth grade when the Prince Edward County schools were closed. Lelise had passed to the seventh grade. Our young son Crawleigh was to start school in September 1959.

Then I went to Hawkes School for two years, September 1961 to May 1963. Hawkes was a two room school. A law was passed that a Cumberland County school couldn't take a student from Prince Edward County unless Prince Edward County paid. The Brown children went to live with their uncle on River Road and attended school in Cumberland

County. Some Prince Edward County families rented houses in Cumberland County, so their children could go to school. Garfield Smith rented a house on Highway 45 in Cumberland so his four girls and one son could attend school.

Hawkes School was closed the end of the 1962–1963 school year. Mrs. Julia Anderson went to Luther P. Jackson, and I returned. This was my second time at Luther P. Jackson. I stayed there until I retired around 1975.

Crawleigh went all twelve years of school in Cumberland County. He graduated in 1971.

Mr. Luther P. Jackson was head of the History Department at Virginia State College. I took a few courses from Dr. Jackson. He was a medium size man and had written several books on Negro History. He wrote one entitled Free Negro Labor and Property Holding in Virginia.

Mrs. Sarah Green White was the president of Prince Edward County Negro Teachers Association when the schools were closed. Many ladies' loss their hair because of the stress and strain of the closure. People had their financial obligations, children, and other issues that wore on them.

I was with Reverend Griffin one day and a man came to his car and said:

"Reverend, my wife is in the hospital and my baby is sick. Can you loan me five dollars? I'll pay you back."

"I only have ten and you can have that," the preacher said. "It's all I have." He gave the man his last ten dollars.

"That man may go off and buy some wine or beer," I said.

"I rather him buy it than steal it. I rather give him ten dollars than have to get him out of jail." We later learned that the man's wife was in the hospital and the baby sick.

Reverend Griffin drove off and we went to Big Star Grocery Store. I think it was Big Star, or it might have been another grocery store. He said he was going in and get some food for his family.

"How are you going to get food for your family and you're broke?" I asked him.

"The God I serve will not let me starve."

He did not have a cent in his pocket. Reverend Griffin had faith and I mean a lot of faith. He went in and started filling his basket. A church member came in the store and said:

"Reverend, I missed you Sunday."

"The old ticker was acting up," he said, meaning his heart. The lady gave him twenty dollars. He went and got some more food. One of his deacons came into the store. They talked and the deacon gave him twenty dollars. The man's name was Deacon Cary or Kerry. He was the chairman of the Board of Deacons at Tarewallet Baptist Church in Cumberland County, where Reverend Griffin also served as pastor. The church was across from Luther P. Jackson High School. The deacon was the custodian at a school.

When he came back to the car with his groceries, Reverend Griffin said:

"I told you the God I serve will not let me starve." He told me everything that happened in the store.

Johns recommended Griff to Dexter Avenue Baptist in Montgomery. Griff went there to preach, but King was called to be the pastor. Griff told me about several churches that invited him to come and be their pastor.

"Why don't you take one of the larger churches and go?" I asked him one day. "You can name your salary."

"Well, I got the children and the community into this mess and I have to stay and get them out of it."

During the years of the struggle, Reverend Griffin told me once:

"If you see me out on the streets, don't come near me or talk to me. Don't let them (the White folks) see you talking to me. They can fire you, but they can't fire me."

Griff was very concerned about the people's welfare and didn't want to put anyone or their job in jeopardy.

I was downtown one day and heard a White man say:

"Somebody ough'a kill that damn Griffin." The man was talking about me.

The White man standing with him said:

"That's not Reverend Griffin. That man works at the school up on the hill." (Mr. Hall laughed while explaining how relieved he was at the man's correction of the other man.)

It reached a point when the White merchants in town wouldn't sell Reverend Griffin merchandise. "You mean they refused to give him credit?" the Editor asked, seeking clarification. I am not talking about giving him items on credit. They wouldn't sell to him even when he had cash money. That's right, even when he had cash money they wouldn't sell to him. He had to go to Cumberland and shop. He often shopped at Lipscomb's. Mr. John Lipscomb had a family store and it was a good size store. The store had almost any kind of food stuff you needed.

One time they tried to burn a cross in the front yard of the parsonage, but the cross wouldn't burn. It burned a little and the fire went out. You could see where it burned some, but the cross wouldn't catch fire as it was supposed to do.

Griff told me one time: "When I die, there are going to be Black people, White people, rich people and poor people at my funeral."

"As much as you have done for the community, that's how it ought to be. They should honor you."

"That's not why they'll come," he said.

"What do you mean?" I asked. It was unclear to me what he was saying.

"They will come to 'make sure that Nigger is dead.'"

It was Griff and Dr. Miller that got the Quakers here to help place students in homes around the country when the schools were closed.

He was a down to earth person.

When he died, his funeral was broadcasted over WPAK, a local radio station on Plank Road that was Negro owned. Griff was the pastor of First Baptist, but there were so many people at his funeral until they had to open the church across the street, Beulah AME. The people packed both churches. Amplifiers were put in Beulah so the large crowd there could hear the service. Even the two churches could not hold all the people. Many sat in their cars in the parking lot and listened to the service on the radio.

———

THOMAS R. MAYFIELD

I was born in Boydton, Virginia, the county seat of Mecklenburg County, Virginia, on February 9, 1925 to Harriett Grace and Nathaniel Edward Mayfield. I was the seventh of ten children, six boys and four girls. I'm the seventh, meaning I'm the gifted one. (Mr. Mayfield started laughing and so did the Editor.)

I started public school at Boydton Elementary School. The school had four rooms and three teachers and went to the seventh grade. My first grade teacher was Mrs. Viola Moody. She lived to be almost one hundred years old. She was a graduate of Saint Paul's College in Lawrenceville, Virginia.

During this time, the 1920s and 1930s, we went to school seven or eight months. We always went late because of tobacco picking or cotton picking. The crops had to be cleared before we went to school.

There were two high schools for Black students or Negroes as they were called in that era. One was East End High located in South Hill, Virginia. West End High School was in Clarksville. I attended West End High School.

My high school career started in 1939 and I graduated in 1943. There was also one church owned high school in Mecklenburg County, located in Chase City. The church owned school was named Thyne Institute. Thyne Institute was built before West End High School. I'm not familiar enough with the historical background to be able to explain why Thyne Institute was built and then West End High School later.

The all White Mecklenburg County school board didn't provide Black children with school buses even though our parents paid taxes to support public education. In order to get Black children of high school age in my community to West End High School, Black parents purchased a bus and we had to pay for a seat. Mr. Milton Gregory was the owner and driver of the bus. Mr. Gregory put his name on the dotted line for the bus because he had children also. Our parents paid one dollar a month or week, I cannot recall which. I think it was one dollar a month. I was still paying to ride the bus when I graduated from high school in May 1943.

The students who went to East End rode the bus that was also owned by a Black family. I can't recall when the county started providing school buses for Black students; but this much I am sure of — it was after May 1943.

I graduated from high school on May 2, 1943 and was in the United States Army May 3, 1943. I was in the Army until January 1946, when I was honorably discharged. I entered Virginia State College in September 1946 and graduated in the spring of 1950, majoring in Vocational Agriculture.

After graduating in 1950, I was employed in Prince Edward County, Virginia, and started my teaching career on August 30 of that year. My teaching career started in Prince Edward County and the county has never been the same since my arrival. (Mr. Mayfield burst out with a big laugh. The Editor started laughing and so did Mrs. Osa Sue Allen Dowdy who was the Administrator of the Moton Museum at this time where the interview was conducted.)

My course was set in the field of education. I was here in 1951 when the students went on strike. I was teaching in a tar covered shack that day. Yes, my classes were held in one of the tar shacks.

This is the best I can recall events approximately fifty-three years later. From April 1951 to November 2004, the month of this interview is a long time. But as I remember, it was a nice spring day. The teachers and students reported to school as usual and the day started as usual. Classes started as usual and somewhere later in the morning the leaders implemented their plan. I remember later in the morning the school bell sounded. I think the bell was sounded at an off time. It had to be an off time because the students had to get Jones (the principal) out of the building. The student body was instructed to go to the auditorium for an assembly. Someone called the principal's office and said he needed to come downtown immediately and retrieve several Moton High School students who were misbehaving or about to get in trouble. No students were in trouble. The call was designed to get the principal out of the building. So, while Jones was away chasing a ghost the students started the assembly and begin discussing issues. I didn't venture to come to the assembly. I had no idea what had been planned or was being planned.

I will admit that I had one student to mention to me a few days or a week or so before the event that something big was going to happen. I let what he said go off the top of my head. I didn't pay him any attention. There were no signs of anything big about to happen. It was only in later years that I remembered the teenager's statement. It was a male student that told me, and I will take his name to my grave.

The Black PTA had been on the school board for years to build a new school. The school board contended it could never find the money for a new high school. The county would not promise the parents that a new school would be built. So, the students said 'lets try it our way to dramatize we want a school equal to the White high school in town.' That was what led to The Strike in April 1951. The issue was securing equal facilities.

Mr. John Lancaster, a graduate of Hampton Institute, was a county agent. The county agent worked with farmers and rural families and assisted them in improving rural living, their dwelling place, surroundings, social life, and so forth. The agent's salary was paid in part by the State and the other half by the county where he worked. John was also the president of the PTA when the students planned and implemented The Strike. The White power structure thought he was involved in The Strike. The county withheld its half of John's salary. He later left Prince Edward County and went to Maryland.

The NAACP lawyers took on the students cause. When talking to the parents, the lawyers told them that they [NAACP legal team] were no longer interested in separate but equal facilities but was pursuing integration. They talked with the parents and the parents agreed to pursue a legal suit for school integration in Prince Edward County.

It was a strange thing, after the NAACP lawyers revealed they were no longer interested in equal facilities but would pursue integration the Prince Edward County School Board found money and secured land to build a new high school for Black students.

After the students walked out, they were out of school about two weeks. When they returned, school went on as usual. The teachers went on with business as usual.

Between 1951 and 1955 there was talk of the schools being closed. People began to talk about 'suppose the schools were closed by the local all White school board.' That didn't bother me because with my training I knew I could do other things. Livestock, crop production, electric welding and a whole range of vocational skills were included in my training at Virginia State College.

After the schools were closed, I think every Black teacher who wanted to and was willing to relocate found a job. Those who had husbands that could support them were able to stay in Prince Edward County. There were several female teachers who were born and reared in Prince Edward County, went off to college and returned to teach. Their roots were in this community and those who had been teaching for a long time just stayed here rather than move.

I taught at Campbell County High School until September 1963.

When the Free School opened in Prince Edward County, I was a member of the faculty.

While the challenges for the faculty and staff were enormous, there was a good part in all of it. Let me explain.

Children born in 1953, 1954, or 1955 were now ten, nine, and eight years old and in the first grade. They had never been to school. Other students had only attended the Learning Centers around the county. Those who had been to school for several years before the closing, knew what they had missed during the past four years. The good part was — there were no discipline problems. The students were hungering and thirsting for knowledge. You had to have been here to have seen the children getting off those buses. They rushed and ran to the classrooms. I can't describe it, (Mr. Mayfield choked momentarily at this point and had to gather himself. Tears came into his eyes. We briefly suspended the interview.)

Teachers and principals had problems trying to place students. For example, children locked out of school in the sixth grade four years earlier, where do you put them? I can't begin to describe the dynamics.

As a vocational agriculture teacher, the thing I had going for me was I could use a lot of manual dexterity learning activities with the students in the higher grades. This contributed to my success. In a math or English class, the students were engaged for almost an hour with a book and serious intellectual involvement. Unlike math and English, my class was unique. The students learned how to build a chicken coop, baying house for chickens, they could read three or four lines of instructions and then do what was printed. My class offered them an opportunity to read then depart from the book for a little while and engage in some hands-on-activity.

There was the New Farmers of America (this was the Black organization and the White students had the Future Farmers of America organization) that the students could join. The New Farmers of America taught parliamentary procedures, livestock judging, forestry management, crop reduction, etc.

In my class they were not in a book the entire fifty minutes or one hour.

I am frequently invited to the Museum to address audiences. Students from different colleges around the county come to this historic site. When I have an opportunity to address college students, I say: 'We, the United States of America, are trying to export democracy abroad and establish democratic societies in other parts of the world and we do not practice it here at home. Can you conceive of a county that would close its schools for four years and five years officially against a certain element of its population?'

And I now ask readers of this volume: 'Can you conceive of a county that would close its schools for four years and five years officially against a certain element of its population?'

After Mr. Mayfield finished his official presentation, he shared some other personal thoughts. Osa Sue Allen Dowdy and the Editor listened. Mr. Mayfield knew the Editor was taking notes, as he was asked to clarify several statements and repeat names.

There were some strong leaders in the Negro community back then (he used the appellation Negro).

Griffin—We do not have a Reverend Griffin now, someone to be that steady individual who would stay the course.

Vernon Johns—I was a student at Virginia State College and remember anytime the word got out that Johns was preaching on Sunday, ooooohhhh my. Many of the guys who never went to church would come to chapel.

My first knowledge of him in Prince Edward County was that he and some men purchased a lot of land and some Angus bulls. He could not let go, he kept interfering with the man who was to manage the thing. Johns was an idea man. He could not follow through.

We have no Buck Carter who was the president of local NAACP and a main stay. He was from Buckingham but married and lived in the New Hope area of Prince Edward County.

In Prospect there was the Scott, Green, Cobbs and Berryman families. These were old land owners and could not be moved. Ooooohhhh, one couldn't threaten them and say you have to get off my land. The Spencer (Tracy) family in the Darlington Heights area was strong.

These were leaders.

I remember one boy who could really read when the schools reopened, and I asked him: "How did you learn to read so well?" He was about sixteen at the time. He didn't go away to school, but it was apparent he had been working.

He said: "I taught myself."

ERNESTINE WATKINS HERNDON

I was born in Farmville to Ernest and Clara Watkins. I grew up in Race Street Baptist Church.

I graduated from Moton High School in 1943. I was out of school two years. I worked, saved money, and in 1945 went to Bluefield State College in West Virginia. I graduated in 1949 with a Bachelor of Science Degree in Elementary Education.

I started teaching in Prospect, Virginia, in Prince Edward County, in a one room school. It was in the Calvary community and the school was School #20. It was called the Calvary community because nearby was Calvary Baptist Church.

The school had first to fifth grades. I had about fifteen students. The composition was something like two students in the first grade; two or three in the second grade, four children in the third grade and so on. There was a pump on the school yard for water. When it was cold, I had to make a fire.

When the students finished School #20, they went to First Rock School, which was also in Prospect, for sixth and seventh grades. That school was aligned with First Rock Baptist Church. First Rock School was a three room school. Mr. Nealy taught there. I believe Mrs. Alma Smith was there at the time. I can't remember the name of the third teacher. The sixth and seventh grade students were bused to First Rock School. When the students at First Rock School reached eighth grade, they went to Moton High School in town.

I taught at School #20 from 1949-1953. The county started closing schools in rural areas. School #20 was closed in 1953. I was pregnant and didn't work. In September 1954 I returned to work in Farmville at Mary E. Branch No. 1.

I had my second child in August 1956. I stayed out and returned to the classroom at Mary E. Branch in Farmville in January 1957, when a teacher departed after getting a job in Richmond. I worked two years in Farmville and then the schools were closed.

In the fall of 1958 we heard rumors that the schools would be closed. In the new year, 1959, we began to hear there may not be any school the next year. People didn't take the rumor serious because it was hard to believe that there would be a community without schools in the twentieth century. It was almost like returning to slavery when there was no school for Black people. It showed the hate one race had for another. The White people held all the cards and made such a mean decision. The school board was lily White and they did pretty

- 38 -

much what they wanted to do. When school closed in May/ June 1959 our contracts were not renewed. We basically knew that the schools were not going to open in September.

When the schools were closed, I was up for renewal of my teaching certificate and had it renewed. I went to Virginia State College and completed all requirements. I came home once and there was a letter from the superintendent of schools in Spotsylvania County, approximately seventy-five or eighty miles from Prince Edward County. I was hired and started teaching in September 1959 in Spotsylvania County at John J. Wright High School.

Teachers from other areas who had been hired in Prince Edward County in earlier years, departed the area and sought employment elsewhere.

Many of us believed that the higher ups, the Federal Government, would not even let something like that happen. When rumor became reality, we were stunned. The closing was a shock to the entire Black community.

Griffin was our Moses and played a major role in getting the centers set up. There were centers in most of the outer areas.

Moton School was like a family and when the schools were closed many of the people we never saw again.

From the fall of 1959 until the spring of 1963 I taught in Spotsylvania County.

I learned that the Free School was to open in the fall of 1963. My children had been in the school system in Spotsylvania County, but upon learning about the Free School I returned to Spotsylvania County in September, leaving my children in Farmville, worked two weeks and resigned. I came back to Prince Edward County and started working with the Free School. Dr. Sullivan was the superintendent. I don't know how he was appointed. I think he was from California, I'm not sure about that. You'll have to research that.

Free School was ungraded. If you were eight, they assumed you were to be in third grade. Free School lasted one year. The pay for teachers in the Free School was comparable, in fact may have been a little bit more.

In September 1964 the public schools in the county officially resumed. I had another child in September 1964 and stayed out of school until December of that year. When I returned, there was a vacancy at Worsham Elementary. I was hired permanently in January 1965.

———

ETHEL WATKINS WILSON FISHER

I was born to Ernest Watkins and Clara Ghee Watkins. We were poor, but they were lovely parents. They did good for us and reared us to be independent and have integrity. My parents were poor but had the love of God in their hearts. We belonged to Race Street Baptist Church, in Farmville, located on Race Street. Longwood College has Race Street now. Reverend Jacob Randolph was the pastor of Race Street Baptist and lived across the street from the church. There was a Reverend Peter Johnson that served as pastor and then Reverend Hubert Venerable.

I finished high school in 1943. I went to Virginia State College and entered the teachers' college in the summer and extension courses in the winter. I secured a teaching certificate. You didn't need a degree to teach in the county in those days.

I started teaching at Hawkes School in Cumberland County. This was a two room school. I had about twenty-five students. Hawkes went to the seventh grade, but usually there were no seventh graders. Maybe one or two and they were usually combined with the sixth graders. The only thing we had was a broom and a bucket provided by the county. Some papers and crayons were provided, but no instructional material at all was provided by the county. My first check was sixty-five dollars. I spent most of that to buy learning material for the children. That was a lot of money back then. When I went to the Teachers Association they had a lot of material and I enjoyed buying for the children. Hawkes School had no lights. We sold fried chicken, salads, etc. to raise money for electricity. We had an outdoor toilet. I went out one day and a big black snake was on the seat. (Mrs. Wilson started laughing.) We had great parents and children back then. After the sixth or seventh grade, the students from Hawkes School went to Luther P. Jackson High School. He (Luther P. Jackson) was an outstanding educator and historian who taught at Virginia State College. He had a great impact in the State. I remember seeing him at many meetings.

After teaching two years I went to Norfolk State College, then to Hampton Institute, and to New York University to do master's work.

I can talk intelligently about the intense teaching sessions that were held each summer, when certified instructors came to Farmville to work with the boys and girls who were not fortunate enough to go away and live with a family and continue their development.

When the schools were closed, there was a gentleman, Dr. Rupert Picott, who lived in Richmond, Virginia, and was the chairman of the Black teachers' association in Virginia. Dr.

Picott headed a project that was designed to benefit the boys and girls in Prince Edward County who were not fortunate enough to leave home and continue their education. When public school ended in May around Virginia, Black teachers volunteered to come to Prince Edward County for four or six weeks and work with the children who had been taught between August and May by their parents, older brothers and sisters, and adults in the community who were willing to help the children, though these adults were not teachers by profession. Each teacher determined how long he or she would teach during the summer. The summer program ran from something like the latter part of June to the end of July or early August. The Virginia public school calendar dictated the duration of our program. Teachers could not leave their salaried posts before school closed and they had to return in August for the beginning of the new school year.

The teachers who taught in Prince Edward County during the summer came from all around Virginia and a few from as far away as Washington, D. C. These summer instructors were paid room and board and transportation. They received no stipend. All of them were volunteers. Their interest was in the students who were being treated so cruel by the local White establishment. The teachers stayed with families around the county.

Some of the teachers had their own automobiles and others caught the Greyhound Bus from their home town and rode to the bus station in Farmville. Upon arrival, those riding the bus would telephone me and I would go to the bus station, pick them up, and transport each to the home of the family where they would be staying. I did not receive a stipend either. I was reimbursed for gas.

The summer education program was based out of First

Baptist Church, where Reverend L. F. Griffin was the pastor. The teachers held classes in the outlying areas in churches and centers scattered around the county. I think there were about twenty-five teachers that came to town each summer. Mrs. Vera J. Allen, a local resident and educator, supported the project also.

All of the teachers worked hard with the children during the week and departed on Friday afternoon to go home and enjoy the company of their own families. They returned to Prince Edward County late Sunday night or early Monday morning.

I was in Farmville during the summer and was one of the managers of the summer program. I held the purse. The teachers turned in a voucher to me each Friday and would be given a check. They received about $25.00 a week. The $25.00 they received was actually a reimbursement. Each teacher paid out of his or her pocket room and board to the family with whom they were lodging and the check they received on Friday was their reimbursement.

EUNICE RUSSELL McLENDON-WHITEHURST

I graduated from Saint Paul's College in 1947. Saint Paul's was an outstanding school. I worked in the dining hall my first year at school and at the campus store my second year at college. The campus store was a store where students could purchase needed items such as toothpaste, deodorant and personals. I also worked the remaining two years while I was at school.

Every student was required to go to Sunday School and Church. They checked your room on Sunday morning. On Sunday after worship, you left church, which was on the campus, and went straight to the cafeteria and had dinner. This was around 1:00 p. m. You were given a sandwich and a piece of fruit to carry to the dorm to eat later in the evening. After dinner at 1:00 p. m., it was quite time on the grounds for one hour. No radio, no music, nothing. You were supposed to take a nap or something.

I majored in Elementary Education and received the music award at graduation. My parents sent me to piano lessons when I was a girl. My sister, Lena, and I were the only two students at college that could play the piano.

After graduation, I returned home to Cumberland County and taught at Cumberland County Training School, where I had attended public school. My grandfather was one of the three founders of Cumberland County Training School. His name was James Leake Russell. Mrs. Matilda Booker and Mr. Hicks were the other two founders. My grandfather said he wanted to build a school for his grandchildren. He wanted a high school. Seventh grade was the highest grade at the time and he wanted a high school.

I got a job teaching in Prince Edward County around September 1951.

I had been reading about the schools being closed for two or three years. I never took it serious.

Near the end of the 1958-1959 school year I remember one day a White man came to the school and unloaded everything in my file cabinet in my classroom. I was teaching at First Rock School in Prospect. I am sure he went to the other classrooms and did the same thing. All the records of the children were removed. That day I begin to take things serious. I knew the schools were going to close. When I got home that afternoon, I said to my husband, "We better start looking for a job." My husband, James McLendon, taught at R. R. Moton High School.

During the summer, we read in a newspaper that a new school was being built in Warren County, Virginia. The highest grade level for Black children in Warren County was seventh grade and then the students had to go to a school in a neighboring county for eighth through twelfth grades, traveling back and forth daily; or students attended a boarding school in Manassas, Virginia. Many of the children left home at twelve or thirteen years old to go the boarding school in Manassas.

The White children in Warren County didn't have to leave home. The only high school in the county at this time was for White students.

There was an advertisement in the newspaper that applications were being taken for positions at the new high school which was still under construction but would be ready for occupancy by the opening day of school. The new school that was to open in Warren County in September 1959 for Black children was Criser High School. With this school, no Black students would have to travel to another county to attend high school or go away to boarding school.

My husband and I got an appointment with the superintendent of schools Mr. Q. D. Gasque. We stayed at his office all day long. He sent his secretary out to get us lunch. At 5:00 p. m. he said: "I am ready to sign a contract." McLendon, as I called my husband, was hired as the principal for Criser High School.

After he got the principal position, we returned to Prince Edward County and started preparing to move. McLendon said he wanted to take some strong proven teachers with him to Front Royal to be on his staff and open the new school. He recruited four high school teachers from Moton High School. They were: Mrs. Helen Lee, the Librarian; Miss. Royce J. Bland, Business Education teacher; Miss. Mary Malloy, Physical Education teacher; and Mr. James Stanton, a Science instructor. I was an elementary school teacher. Counting McLendon, six former teachers from Prince Edward County went to Front Royal to teach in the fall of 1959.

Front Royal was about two hours or so from Farmville. We came back home every two weeks, and then as time went by we would come to Farmville monthly and even less often.

We came back to Prince Edward County in 1968 to work in the school system.

I have always said that everybody always focused on the students and hardly any attention paid to the teachers. I am glad someone is showing interest in the educators from that era and what we had to do as professionals and family leaders and providers when the schools were closed in Prince Edward County.

———

ARNETTA COLEMAN WINSTON WEST

I was born January 11, 1922 to Ryall and Mary Johnson Coleman in Newport News, Virginia. When I was around three months old, my family moved to Clover in Halifax County, Virginia, where all my father's people were from and were still there. I started school at Clover Elementary in a rural section of the county.

Clover Elementary had three teachers. My mother was the principal. Mother went to Virginia State College. Mrs. Geneva Lewis and Miss. Henrietta Coleman, she was related on my father's side, were teachers. Clover had first to seventh grades.

When I was promoted to the eighth grade, I went to Halifax Training School. I was in the school Glee Club. We would take a bus and go out of town. I remember going to sing and other high school choirs were there, it was a high school choir competition. I graduated eleventh grade, that was as high as school went in the era. I graduated around 1940. The county provided school buses.

I stayed out of school one year and then entered Saint Paul's College. My senior year was the most exciting time because all the men returned from the war. Until this time there were only about a total of six men on the whole campus, I am sure there were not a dozen. When the men came back in January, there was great competition to get a date to the prom. I did get a date. I went with Timothy Rice. He was from down south somewhere.

After graduating from Saint Paul's, I got job teaching in a two room school in Halifax County with Miss Bessie Carr. The school was outside of the town of Clover. I can't remember the name of the school. I taught there for about three years.

I met Charlie Winston when I was teaching at the two room school. His family was well known in the county and strong church workers. I met him at church. We got married and moved to the town of Halifax and rented from Mr. John Bowman. I continued teaching at the two room school.

Our daughter, Roslyn, was born April 11, 1951. In August 1951 we moved to Farmville. Charlie was working at Bland-Reid Funeral Home. He had been working there all along, but we felt it best to just move to Farmville.

I got a job teaching at the elementary school, Mary E. Branch No. 1. L. L. Hall was the principal. I taught at the elementary school for five years and then was transferred to the middle school, Mary E. Branch No. 2. I taught sixth grade there until the schools were closed.

I don't remember who told us or how the word was put out, but I do remember going to school to work one morning in May 1959 and we were told that morning the schools would be closed. It may have been near the end of May, but we were told that when the school year ended there would be no more school. It was a shock to everybody. I mean a shock knowing you would not have a job the next year. Our last check came on May 31 or the June 1st 1959.

I was considering withdrawing some of my retirement out of the account, you could do that in those days. I mentioned to the school superintendent what I was considering. You had to fill out papers to withdraw from your retirement fund and I went to his office to discuss the matter. The superintendent advised me not to withdraw any money saying: 'You'll probably get a job.'

Some teachers did withdraw from their retirement fund. They were so uncertain about the future.

I notified my mother. She was still in the Halifax County School system and she communicated with the superintendent. I knew before the end of June that I would have a job in September.

I had a Ford that didn't give any trouble. Charlie continued to work with the funeral home in Farmville. Roslyn and I went to Halifax and we lived with my mother. This was a good time for Roslyn and her grandmother to bond.

When we relocated in September 1959, I started teaching at Clays Mill Elementary School, a two room school. On the weekends we came to Farmville, so I could be with my husband and Roslyn with her father.

I loved Farmville, my church, First Baptist Church, and I also attended Race Street Baptist. First Baptist was my home church and Reverend Griffin was my pastor.

He was a good person and educated. He expressed himself well.

When the Prince Edward County public schools officially reopened in September 1964, I remained in Halifax County school system.

To this day, August 31, 2011, there are high school classmates with whom I am still in contact. The two girls, Bertha Lanier and Elizabeth Carr, we met in high school and have remained friends.

In later years I married Alexander Shannon West. We were together for thirty years.

———

BARBARA JAMISON ORR

I was born and reared in Charlotte, North Carolina. I graduated from Livingstone College in Salisbury, North Carolina, in the spring of 1956. A friend of mine told me that they were looking for a first grade teacher in Farmville. I applied and was hired.

I met a fine gentleman named Dawes L. Orr and we were married in Charlotte in 1957. Dawes graduated from Saint Paul's College in Lawrenceville, Virginia.

It was the last day of school or near the last day of school when I heard that the schools would not open in September 1959.

Dawes and I were not touched as were many other teachers. It was easy for us to pick up and move. We had not bought a home. Some of the teachers had built houses and made Farmville home.

One day in the summer of 1959, Booker T. Reaves and his wife came to our home. Dawes did carpentry work and was out at the time. Reaves was the principal at Jefferson Elementary School in Charlottesville, Virginia, and he had come to Farmville seeking a first grade teacher. A teacher in town told him about me and he came by the house. This was on a Friday and he asked me could I be in Charlottesville on Monday.

When Dawes came home, I said to him: "A job walked in the house today."

I went for the interview and was hired.

Dawes and I moved to Charlottesville. When the school year started, we were in two different States. Dawes got a job teaching in Maryland. I stayed with a retired school teacher in Charlottesville until we found a house. My husband came home every weekend.

Dawes taught in Maryland for several years. These are my recollections on December 7, 2012; fifty-three years after the Prince Edward County public schools were closed in September 1959.

ADELAIDE PAYNE GRIFFIN

I was born and reared in New Jersey and upon graduating from high school I entered Shaw University in North Carolina.

Shaw University was a small Baptist school and students were chaperoned all the time in those days. If you went to town to get a tube of tooth paste, you had to take an older student along. The older students started asking: 'What's in it for me?' So, you had to have an extra quarter for that person. We started going to town in a group and getting one chaperone. With a group you did not have to contribute as much money.

There were mostly female students at Shaw when I entered in the early 1940s. Most of the males had been drafted and were off to war. They started returning in the mid-1940s. My husband, Leslie Francis Griffin, was one of the veterans who entered Shaw under the GI Bill.

We met on the grounds of the school. I enjoyed playing tennis, but he did not. We were in each other's company during the day primarily. Being a religious institution, you were prohibited from going any place with a young man after dark.

I graduated from Shaw and taught for one year in Pine Hearst, North Carolina. Leslie and I were married November 1946. Expecting our first child, I gave up the teaching job in Pine Hearst and went back to New Jersey to live with my parents. My husband and I thought that would be best, since he had just gotten out of the military and entered school. I stayed with my parents for two and one-half years.

My husband's family lived in Farmville, Virginia. After our first son was able to travel, I took him to Farmville so his grandparents, Reverend and Mrs. Charles Henry Denston Griffin, could see him. Reverend Charles Henry Denston Griffin was the pastor of First Baptist Church in Farmville. Reverend Griffin came to Farmville from Norfolk, Virginia. He was near retirement age and said the church suited him.

When Reverend C. H. D. Griffin passed, the church called Leslie to be the pastor and he accepted.

We moved to Farmville and resided in the parsonage, a two story brick house, located on Ely Street. We had been in the parsonage for about six years when our stay was interrupted. Longwood College began expanding and desired the property. This was during the latter part of the 1950s. Eminent domain was in effect. If you refused to sell, you had to go to court and pay all the fees. The church could not afford it. Many other families also had to vacate their homes. The move and the transaction happened so abruptly until we had to sell our furniture because we had nowhere to store it. My children cried.

The church rented us a place for one year, but it was very dilapidated. Many people who owned property would not rent to us with children. We stayed in the dilapidated house for seven or eight months. I told my husband that we could not stay there. The church built another parsonage, but it was not as magnificent as the first parsonage.

There was no kindergarten in those days and my daughter Cocheyse was ready to enter first grade. She was very excited about starting school. I had been tutoring her at home. Shortly before the public schools were to open in 1959 I was sitting on the porch one day reading the newspaper. I came across an article that shocked me. The article stated that the schools were not going to open.

I told the children and Cocheyse started crying, saying:

"They are doing it because I'm Reverend Griffin's daughter and it's time for me to go to school."

Reading about the closing of the schools was a bomb shell. The White people just did it. They had a meeting among themselves, made the decision, and announced it in the paper. I called my husband at the church and asked:

"Have you seen the paper?"

"Yes," he said. "People have been calling all morning."

The Whites had a meeting one day in a theater that was located near Fourth and Main Streets. White leaders told the White people they were preparing to open a private school system.

The summer ended, and the time arrived when the public schools normally opened. Only the Colored Schools remained closed. The White schools opened on time. The White children never stopped going to school and the buses started picking them up for school as normal. A private school system was opened in September 1959 for White students in Prince Edward County.

Most of the Black teachers took jobs in other counties because they needed their income. Some stayed in Farmville. Meetings were called to organize classes to be held at the churches, so the education of the Black children might continue, though on a small scale. The few teachers left in town volunteered to teach and sometimes the high school students taught the elementary students. Classes were held for about four hours each day. First Baptist Church was centrally located in Farmville and most of the children in the immediate area came there for classes.

Many White people were poor and could not afford to send their children to a private academy, which became a concern. Some Whites were sharecroppers and simply did not have tuition. They made arrangements for poor White people to get loans.

One morning there was a long line of White people at the bank downtown. The line formed around the bank. They had gathered around 7:00 a. m. before the normal banking hours started. Black workers on the way to work saw the lines and thought the bank was about to close or something and White people were withdrawing their money. Some Black folk called

- 53 -

my husband and asked him what was going on at the bank and was it about to close.

Leslie looked into the situation and later found out what happened. The White people had quietly arranged for the poor Whites to come to the bank that morning around 7:00 a. m. before normal banking hours to sign forms and get loans to pay the tuition for their children to go to school in the private school program.

I taught my children at home because I had taught before.

After the schools had been closed for a couple of years, people in other areas started getting interested in the Prince Edward County situation.

Learning about our situation, a library in Massachusetts sent two large truck loads of books, which were donated to the county. All of the books could not fit into First Baptist Church, so arrangements were made to store large quantities in the basement of peoples' homes. Most of the books were given to the children. There were sets of encyclopedias and individual volumes of books.

One year a very refreshing and memorable encounter took place. A group of students from Queens College in New York were moved to take on a project. They paid their own expenses and came to Farmville that summer to teach the Black boys and girls whose education had been disrupted. Black families in Farmville opened their homes and gave food and lodging to the students from Queens College. Their coming was a class project and they were not getting paid.

Their teaching extended beyond the classroom. The Queen College students took the children to a farm one day where many of the boys and girls rode ponies for the first time. On another occasion they took the children to a lake, which was a new experience for many of the youngsters.

A young Black lady organized the Queens College students. She was from New Jersey. I remembered her from my earlier days in New Jersey. I cannot remember her name at present, only her work.

When their summer project ended, and they were preparing to leave Farmville, the students from Queens College asked my husband what was needed in the way of educational materials. He provided them a list. Upon returning to New York, the students sent back tons of pencils, papers, and other useful items.

About two or three years after the schools had been closed there was concern about students having been out of school so long. A program was set up where people around the state of Virginia were asked to take in students from Prince Edward County. There was a form that Black families in Prince Edward County had to fill out granting their children permission to go and live with other families around the State, so they could attend school.

Many of the older Black students went to other communities for one year and some two years.

The Free School opened in September 1963. This was a private undertaking but was open to all students in the county. Some of the former public school buildings, which had been closed and pad-locked for several years, were used by the Free School program. Three or four White children attended the Free School. One of the White students was enrolled in the Free School program because his father was a local college professor and endorsed public education.

The Free School was operated by money donated by the Kennedy family and other rich families in the United States. When the Free School opened, a million dollars had already been donated and was available for expenditures.

There were White and Black teachers working in the Free School. Some were retired teachers who returned to help establish the program.

My husband went on speaking engagements. The children would ask could they go with him. He would say:

"No, it is too dangerous. Stay home with your mother."

Altona Johns, the wife of Vernon Johns, was a gifted musician. She gave concerts. My younger daughter went to Virginia State College. When she mentioned her name on one occasion, Mrs. Johns who was on the faculty at the college asked: "Are you Reverend Griffin's daughter?" Then added: "I taught your father."

PEARL STOKES BROWN

I was born April 1, 1921 on Price Farm. I walked to school about a mile and a half. I walked to R. R. Moton. I worked in the fields as a girl. We had to tote water from the spring. Most times all I took for lunch was a biscuit with some preserve inside. My first grade teacher was Mrs. Mary Griggs.

We had to pick all the tobacco. You had to clear the field before you went to school. We went to school about three months out the year.

I remember asking my mother why couldn't we go to school like the White children and she said 'they don't want to co-operate with us.'

I heard about the schools after they were closed. I couldn't make no arrangements for my children to go away and get an education. There were a lot of parents in the same shape. I was too poor to send any of my children away.

If I could have, I would have sent my children somewhere, but I wasn't able. I worked two jobs — one at the tobacco plant and Cedar Brook Restaurant. Black people couldn't go in Cedar Brook. I was a cook there.

I was with Reverend Griffin and the others when they boycotted the stores in Farmville.

————

RUTH EGGLESTON

My husband Minor Burturance Eggleston and I had six children. Minor, Jr., Carl, Carolyn Ruth, Stanley Dale, Harold Timothy, and Michael Lloyd. Minor was the oldest of the children.

When the schools were closed in 1959, Minor was ten years old. I think Carolyn was about to start school.

The first year the children stayed home. The children were given a lot of books.

Parents had to establish residency in a county in order for their children to go to school in that county. We rented a big house in Cumberland County. The house was just before the Court House. My family didn't just pull up and move to Cumberland County. We still had our home in Farmville but was able to legally claim residency in Cumberland County, so the children could go to school. We didn't have to buy any furniture because the house was already filled with furniture. We would go down there sometimes and spend a night in the house, so we could say we had stayed there.

My husband, Minor, would take the children to the bus stop across the bridge on the Cumberland County side to catch the bus. I would pick them up in the afternoon because he would be at work. He was a cabinet maker. He could do any type of wood-work. He made Communion Tables, pulpit furniture, beds, dressers, and anything else people wanted. He also repaired and restored furniture.

We rented the house until the Free School opened in Prince Edward County.

————

VIRGINIA FAGGINS PATTERSON

When I turned five and it was time for me to go to kindergarten, the schools in Farmville were closed. From about age four or five, I was home schooled. My parents, James and Virginia Faggins, and my older brothers taught me to read and write. My oldest brother, Russell, was twelve years old. My brother Johnny was eleven years old. Both knew how to read and write. Mama and Daddy had them to teach me.

The Black children in Farmville whose parents could afford to send them away to continue their education did so. My parents were too poor to send Russell, James Edward, Carlton and Larry away. All of the children in the Faggins family had to stay in Farmville, while the schools were closed.

My brothers got jobs at the local golf course caddying and did other odd jobs. Mama and Daddy made the boys study a little each day and helped them.

There was a church school in Farmville for the Black children. I don't remember if my brothers attended. I remember them being home mostly during the years the schools were closed.

When the Free School opened in 1963, I went to the second grade.

I remember Robert Kennedy coming to Farmville after the schools opened. He delivered a speech. I was in the audience. State Troopers were present. Mr. Kennedy spoke at Branch #1.

I was very young when the schools were closed, but this is what I remember over forty years later, Saturday afternoon, August 11, 2001.

————

RUSSELL FAGGINS

We heard the news on the radio that Branch No.1, Branch No. 2, and R. R. Moton were closed. Later on while I was out and about, I saw the White children going to school. I saw them on the school buses. I wondered to myself 'why are they going to school and we're not?' I talked to a few of the grown people in the community and they explained to me that the White people didn't want school integration.

A recreation center was set up for us to go to. We got local instructions. The people who taught us at the recreation center were not trained teachers. They were local Black people who could read and write and were concerned about us. They understood the damage being done to the Black boys and girls.

Mama and Daddy tried to explain what was happening to us, but they didn't have a full understanding of things either.

Later we started going to classes at First Baptist Church, where Reverend L. F. Griffin was the pastor. The class sessions were from around 9:00 a. m. to 12:00 noon. The classes were held in the basement of the church. Black school teachers taught us. These were teachers who taught at Branch No. 1 and Branch No. 2 before the schools were closed.

My parents couldn't financially afford to send none of their children away to school. Me and my brother, James Edward, went to Cumberland for one year and stayed with our great grand aunt. Her name was Mrs. Mary Trent. Aunt Mary was my father's aunt by marriage. Cumberland was about twenty miles from Farmville. Me and James Edward attended Luther P. Elementary. We came home on the weekends.

"What year did you and James Edward attend school in Cumberland County?" the Editor asked.

I don't remember which year we went to Aunt Mary's.

The White people in Farmville built Prince Edward Academy for their children.

When the Free School opened, only two White students in the town of Farmville enrolled, I believe. They were two White females, I believe. The rest went to the Academy.

I was placed in the eighth grade when the Free School opened. I was in the sixth grade when the schools were closed four years before. The students who went away and continued their education was on time, that is they was in the right grade. When the teacher had the students to read out loud, the students who had gone away could read well. It was obvious they had been in good schools somewhere. Those of us who didn't leave Farmville or Prince Edward County we were put in classes for slow learners. I was at Branch #1 when the schools closed. I never went to Branch No. 2. When the schools opened again, I went straight to high school. I entered R. R. Moton High School.

I was twenty-one years old when I finished high school

in 1969. I could'a been far more than what I is, (a tear rolled from the left eye of Mr. Faggins and he wiped it away with his index finger), but the closing of the schools harmed me and a lot of other students.

———

ARMSTEAD DOUGLAS 'CHUCKIE' REID

My father's father, Fred D. Reid, spoke his mind. My daddy was a brick mason and my mother worked at Longwood College.

When the schools closed in Farmville, I was eight years old. I had three brothers Lawrence, William, who we called Butch, and Oscar, Jr., nicknamed Tony, and my sister, Loretta. My brothers were older than me and all of them went away. Me and Loretta remained at home. My family was eventually split up. I lived with my mother and maternal grandmother. Loretta lived across town with other family members.

Tony (Oscar, Jr.) and Butch (William) went to Ohio with the Quakers Program and went to school in that State. Lawrence went to New York. Lawrence was in his late teens and went to New York on his own. Lawrence went to New York mainly to work.

My family lived in Farmville proper on Race Street. Race Street was our street, right in downtown Farmville. Longwood College has taken most of Race Street.

When the schools were closed, Black adults in Farmville did what they could to assist us in our education, in spite of the situation. Classes were held in different locations for half a day. They were usually held in the basement of churches.

Some afternoons the neighborhood children got together, and we actually played school to help us learn. One person played the teacher and the rest of us pretended we were students.

I think each section in the county had its own church where the students in that vicinity went for classes. In Farmville we had First Baptist Church, where Reverend L. F. Griffin was the pastor. We also used the Masonic Temple for classes. The Masonic Temple was in the heart of our neighborhood. There were so many students in the half-day program in the town of Farmville until the organizers had to divide us into groups.

Loretta and I went to the program in the basement of First Baptist Church. Our paternal grandmother, Mrs. Lucile Reid, was an instructor. She used to keep children in her home but volunteered to teach. After the schools were closed, some of the Black teachers who had been teachers in the public schools in Farmville taught in the basement of the churches where classes were held.

When the schools closed, being so young, we didn't think they would be closed that long. We, the children, saw the closing as a nice short brake, but then it continued. Even the children, who at first thought the school closing an exciting thing, began to feel and understand the impact. We started to understand what was happening to us.

We went to classes year round for a few hours each day. Parents taught and the teachers who were still in the county taught from August to May.

One summer students from Queens College in New York came and taught us.

Two families in particular I remember being greatly impacted by the school closing. These were the Eanes and Banks families. There were twenty-one children in the Eanes family and the Banks family had eighteen children. The two families lived in the same neighborhood. They lived out by Moton High School.

The Free School opened around 1963. Before the school year started, the students were given a placement test or something like an IQ test. I took the test and was placed in the proper grade. I was placed in the same grade I would have been in had the schools not been closed. I did well each year, after the schools reopened.

When we returned to school in the Free School program, I took an interest in music. I played the bass drum and the bass horn. Mr. Frank Williams was the music teacher. In later years, Mr. Williams formed a group called The Soul Musicians. We traveled around the county and to neighboring counties to play. I remember we played at Saint Paul's College in Lawrenceville, Virginia. I played the keyboard with The Soul Musicians.

During the 1960s, Reverend L. F. Griffin was the local leader in Farmville. He was strong and courageous, but nice. He was a true pastor. He was always worrying about someone else. When I was a teenager, he would let me ride with him to different churches where he delivered speeches to encourage the people in their stand against oppression. I was at the church a lot and would run errands for him and do whatever he asked me to do around the church. All of us called him Doc and he was our hero. The phrase 'being a model to others' was not popular in the 1960s, but that was what Reverend Griffin did for me and many other young men in Farmville and in the county. He was a model and we loved and respected him. There were times the church didn't pay him, but Reverend Griffin kept going.

Reverend Griffin took a strong stand, but he was not violent. He taught us not to be violent. I remember when the students from Queens College came during the summer to teach us, most of them were White students. One night after teaching a class, one of the White students drove us home. After dropping off the last student, he drove back to the place where he was living. As he got out of his vehicle, some White people from the area jumped him. They beat him up real bad. What happened to this student was the kind of thing that made you want to go out and retaliate. It made you angry, but Doc said— 'No! There is no room for getting even.'

During my senior year of high school, the music teacher applied for me to receive a music scholarship from Saint Augustine College in North Carolina. I was still lost and didn't know what I wanted to do and was afraid I couldn't handle it. After graduating from Prince Edward High School in 1970, I joined the United States Air Force.

Barbara Johns came back to Farmville several times. I met her and was very impressed.

After being honorably discharged from the military, I returned to Farmville and got involved in politics. I have been on town council for sixteen years as of 2003. When I first got on the council in the late 1980s, I often wondered were any of the people on the town council directly responsible for the school closing. Many of the White people on the council had the last name of people whose names were popular in the late 1950s and early 1960s when so much harm was inflicted on me and my people in Prince Edward County.

I go to the local schools in the county and speak to the children about the era when the schools were closed. There is a film entitled *The Lost Generation*. It is a short documentary about the school closing. On one occasion I showed it to a group of students. A boy yelled out: "That's my mama!" Some of the kids were surprised to see their mothers and fathers. They had no idea that their parents had been directly involved in the situation in Farmville. The parents had never told their children the story about the closing of the public schools in Prince Edward County.

When I was a junior or senior in high school there was another walk out. T. Robinson, a white English instructor, was fired. We left school and marched to the courthouse. School administrators came out and spoke with us. I think Mr. Robinson finished the school year out. I think it was around April or early May when we walked to the courthouse in support of Mr. Robinson. He was an excellent teacher and cared about the students. Teachers of his kind were not always viewed with favor. I told Barbara Johns about this walk-out on one of her visits back to Farmville and she was very pleased with the report and confessed that she had not heard about it.

Reverend Griffin and his family lived in the parsonage. It hurt me after he died in 1980 the family was asked to leave the parsonage. I felt Mrs. Griffin should have had a life time home in the parsonage, as much as Reverend Griffin did for the town and county, as well as the state of Virginia. I could be wrong, but that's how I felt and still feel. The church did not have a pastor at the time she was asked to leave.

My brother Tony is deceased. Butch worked for the UN for eighteen years and returned to Farmville. Loretta is still in Farmville.

Carl Eggleston told me there was a man in an office at his funeral home who was writing the story of anyone that was locked out of the schools that wanted to tell their story for a book. I am sharing my story on Wednesday, May 21, 2003.

On June 15, 2003 all of the people who were students and were affected by the school closing in Prince Edward County will get a diploma with the name R. R. Moton High School inscribed. Even if a person didn't graduate, and many did not, they will still get a high school diploma from R. R. Moton High School. All a person has to do is submit his or her name in order to be issued a diploma. My high school diploma has Prince Edward County Schools. I applied and want a diploma with my name on it and R. R. Moton High School on it. I will be in the line on June 15, 2003, with my cap and gown on. I submitted my late wife's name, Gladys Gray Reid, for a diploma.

Some of us who were affected by the school closing and are still alive formed a group called The Community Helpers of Prince Edward County. We assist the elderly, troubled youths, etc. This group also established a scholarship fund. We give a female student a book scholarship annually to purchase books while in college. We pay dues and accept donations. Gladys was a prime mover in the organization. We go by the local high school first and get inputs from the guidance counselors. People from the community also recommend students for the scholarships. Our group considers need rather than grade point average. Students with the high grade point average will get what is needed, but the poor child will need some help.

I hope that my story will help people better understand what happened in Prince Edward County.

———

WARREN 'RICKY' LEROY BROWN

I was born in Farmville on South Street, a very poor neighborhood, to Pearl Stokes Brown and Henry Brown. I remember when I was a very young boy playing with my cousin, Lawrence Logan, we made up songs about the school bus. School buses fascinated us because we were near school age and could hardly wait to go to the first grade. Lawrence was one year older than me and went to the first grade in September 1958. He was six at that time and I was five. Lawrence went to school one full year. The next school year, 1959-1960, I was to start school. I was very excited about going to the first grade, but the bus never came for me. I got dressed the first day of school and after the bus didn't come, my mother tried to explain to me what happened. Being six years old, I couldn't really understand what she was telling me.

I can easily tell anybody what happened with me for the next four years—'I played.'

I had a brother, Walter, and a sister, Frances, who were in the lock out. Walter was five years older than me, making him around eleven years old when the schools were closed. Mama sent Walter to Daddy's mother and father in the town of Cumberland in Cumberland County. Cumberland was only a few miles from Farmville. Walter went to Luther P. Jackson High School. I don't remember him coming home often. My grandfather and grandmother raised Walter for several years. One reason Walter was sent to Cumberland was because he was the oldest grandson on my father's side, and my father, Henry, was the favorite child of his parents. So grandma and granddaddy took a special interest in Henry's oldest son.

My sister, Frances, was four when the schools were closed. When she turned six, the schools had been closed two years and Frances stayed home.

For four years many of us in the area just played. My mom was poor, and Daddy didn't live in the house with us. Mama was born on a plantation in Prince Edward County. Her family sharecropped, basically poor and education wasn't on the front burner for them.

While the schools were closed, I did learn to spell and write my name. A boy named James Ghee taught me to write my name. James was about five years older than me and was very smart. Arrangements were made for James to go away and continue his education. I think he went to live with a family in Iowa. When he came home during the summer, James worked with the learning program in the basement of First Baptist Church, where Reverend Griffin was the pastor. He was young, but they let James teach because he was so smart. In fact, they allowed anyone to work with us who could teach anything.

I went to the classes at First Baptist during the summer. As I said earlier, education wasn't a priority with my mother. When she grew up, boys and girls went to the sixth grade and then went to work. She believed that hard work alone was enough. Education played no role. She didn't make me go to the classes at First Baptist held August to May.

Finally, one day the Free School opened. I was ten years old when I went to first grade. The administration was trying to put students as close to their proper grade as possible, but I had never been to school at all. There was some discussion about my grade. The only thing I could do when I went to school was spell my name and write my name, thanks to James Ghee.

When I started school, I had no idea what was going on or what school was about. As a result, I didn't like school. I made excuses not to go. The teachers spent most of their time with the students who were where they were supposed to be. That made me angry. In later years, I looked back on it and

I understood why they had to work with the students who were ready to move on and not give most of their time to three or four students.

When the schools reopened, there were brothers and sisters from the same family two and three years apart but in the same grade.

When the Free School opened, my brother, Walter, returned as a high school student. He did one year and joined the U. S. Army.

I remember Reverend L. F. Griffin. He was very out spoken. He was called 'The Fightin' Preacher.' I used to hang around First Baptist Church with Chuckie (Reid).

As I matured, I became a great athlete in high school. I played basketball, baseball and football. I was a star player in each sport. I can't explain how things happened, but when I was seventeen I was preparing to graduate. My coach said to me one day:

"Ricky, you don't have to graduate. You can go to school longer."

I listened to my high school friends. Surprisingly, I was offered an opportunity to attend college. Mitchell College in North Carolina and Benedict College in Columbia, South Carolina, offered me an athletic scholarship. The coach from Benedict College said he wanted to see what another basketball player name Sam Reid (now deceased) and I could do. Arrangements were made for me and Sam to go to Benedict and play in a pick-up game, so the coach could look at us. Our high school coach, Mr. Levi Wilson, drove us, but we never made it. There was a snow storm and we had an accident in route. Mr. Wilson's vehicle was towed back to Farmville. Me, Sam, and Mr. Wilson rode back home in the tow truck. Arrangements were made later for us to go to Benedict again.

I don't know what happened, but I didn't make the trip. Sam got to go back and tried out. He got a scholarship and became a big man on Benedict's campus. This was in the early 1970s.

I graduated at age seventeen. Following high school, I started working for the State Department of Corrections. It was at that time that it became apparent to me that my educational skills weren't where they should have been or where I wanted them to be. I said to myself: 'I have to teach myself more.' I set out and did just that. Actually, I learned more on my own than I did in school.

I worked seven years for the Department of Corrections. I started playing baseball with the police department in Farmville. The team always wanted to win at all cost. The Chief of Police said to me one day:

"I think I have a position for you."

He brought the application the next day to the ballfield and I signed it.

After working with the Farmville Police Department for a while, I left and went to work for Virginia Power and Electric, where I stayed for ten years. I worked on power lines. We had to take classes and training sessions, and I always felt I was behind everyone else in the class. I was the same age as the instructors and the people in the class were mainly young men who had just graduated from high school.

After working with Virginia Power and Electric, a job came open at the Prince Edward Middle School, in Farmville, for a Resource Officer. I applied and was hired.

As of today, November 3, 2003, I still work at Prince Edward Middle School. The Resource Officer does a little of everything. I'm the link between the local Sheriff's Department and the school. I have to be a mom, a dad, and anything else the children need me to be to make things go smoothly in school.

I'm authorized to make an arrest on the school grounds, if that's required.

People always ask me am I mad with White folks and I say no. What happened to us was real and I'm not making little of it. I feel the impact of the school closing to this day. While I'm not mad with White folks, I do have one major disappointment. My disappointment is with the big part of the government, the Federal Government. They knew what was happening to us was wrong, but they allowed a few White people in this county to make such a decision that was certain to impact many generations to come. Many of the Black students never returned to school after the Free School opened.

Some people were too embarrassed because of their age and others didn't come back for other reasons. Many were married and had families when the schools reopened. When a mother or father has no education, it's a strong possibility that they will not talk to their children about education or stress the positive side of education. Those children probably will not stress education to their children and so on for generations. That is the negative impact and it will be felt for generations.

I stress education to my children and pray they will do the same with their children.

The closing of the schools in Prince Edward County affected many people, and several generations have been and continue to be impacted. I am going to arrange for my brother, Walter, tell his story. I will see if my mother wants to share.

WALTER McKINLEY BROWN

I was born 18 April 1948. I remember going to first grade at Branch No. 1. That was when the trouble started. As a kid, you don't know what's going on. I had a grandfather in another county. A lot of parents tried to send their children off to go to school. Some had no place to send their children. I stayed out of school one full year.

Then I went to my grandfather in Cumberland County. I attended a two room school called Hawkes School. One of the teachers was Mr. L. L. Hall. He taught third, fourth and fifth grades in his room. He had one room and Mrs. Edna Smith had sixth grade in her room. The students who were in first and second grades went to a two room school in the area named R. R. Moton. Mrs. Kate Booker who lived on Hill Street in Farmville used to teach at this two room R. R. Moton school. I was about twelve or so when I first went to Hawkes.

We had an old bus, but it belonged to a private owner and not the State. It would break down two or three times before we got to school.

I stayed at Hawkes for three years. I was able to come home every weekend if I wanted to. I was right across the line about three miles from home in Farmville.

When I was promoted to the seventh grade, I went to Luther P. Jackson High School. Mr. James Lawson was my favorite teacher there. He taught English. The shop teacher was Mr. Scales and was one of the teachers I remember. Mr. Moses Foster taught science. Mrs. Neley (Nealy?) made an impression on me.

Mr. Hall worked in Farmville first. He was the principal at Branch No. 1 and Branch No. 2. When the schools closed, Mr. Hall was hired to teach at Hawkes. His children rode with him each morning. Mr. Hall ended up teaching at Luther P. Jackson.

When the Prince Edward County public schools first closed, about twenty-five children from Farmville would just walk across the bridge into Cumberland County and go to Hawkes School. As the year went on, the numbers increased. Soon there were about seventy-five students walking across the bridge each day to go to Hawkes.

When Cumberland County officials found out that a large number of Prince Edward County children were walking across the bridge to the one and two room schools, the county wanted to start charging a tuition fee. These were all the one and two schools in the outlying areas that the White administrators never checked on. They were only checking now because they had gotten wind about the large number of children coming across the bridge. Once the fee was mentioned the traffic slowed down, but never to a complete stop. The children from Farmville kept walking across the bridge until the Free School opened.

Cumberland was the closest county to Farmville which was why the children from this town walked three miles across the bridge. Students in Prospect, Meherrin and other areas of Prince Edward County were too far away from the Cumberland County line and looked for schools in the county nearest to their community.

There were several one and two room schools in Cumberland County near enough for students from Farmville to walk. Some of the schools were: R. R. Moton, Old Green Creek School near Green Creek Baptist Church, Corner Stone School near Corner Stone Baptist, New Site School near New Site Baptist Church, Sharon School was a two room school next to Sharon Baptist Church. Every little section and community had a one or two room school. Elementary age children in these areas couldn't get to Luther P. Jackson because the White folks wouldn't give buses to Black children.

Mr. Reginald White who owned Master Cleaners rented a house in Cumberland County, so his children could attend school in that county. They didn't live in the house but continued to reside in Farmville.

I remember seeing other children from Farmville. Mr. Hall lived in Farmville, but had his children enrolled in school in Cumberland County. His children also went to Luther P.

We boycotted some stores in Farmville to try and help improve the community. This was in 1963. The leadership said to Black people in the community — 'Why should you all spend your money in a town and community that refuses to educate your children.'

I stayed at Luther P. Jackson until the tenth grade. I came back to Prince Edward County and went to school for two years. I left school and prepared to join the Army. Academics was no problem. You know how it is, you just started feeling mannish. My mother fussed at me, but I enlisted. I go a GED in the Army.

It was only in adult life when you look back that you realized just how drastic this situation was. Just the thought that someone would deny you an education! This is the only county where the schools were closed.

When I went into the Army and shared my story with the men in my company, they disputed me and said I was lying. I was in Company Alpha 1-2. They said: "Nothing like that could happen in the United States. Who'd let something like that happen?"

We had no one to whom we could go and get support. Nothing like this should ever happen again. It was a great tragedy. It is to this day unthinkable and makes you shiver to think that the Federal Government allowed the closing to happen.

———

EDDIE LEE WILEY, JR.

I was born March 15, 1945, to Mr. Eddie Lee Wiley, Sr. and Mrs. Rosa Pannell Wiley, in Amelia County, Virginia. My father was a truck driver and my mother was a housewife.

My public education started in a two room school in Rice, in Amelia County. In 1955, when I was ten years old, I moved to Farmville to live with my grandmother and three aunts. My parents separated. Daddy moved to Philadelphia and Mama moved to New Jersey. I was sent to live with my mother's mother and Mama's oldest sister, Lucy. They lived in the same house at 600 Main Street, next to Mary E. Branch No. 1. My grandmother was named Elizabeth Harris. She and three other daughters, Aunt Gertrude, Aunt Lucy, and Aunt Bernice, all with the last name Harris, lived in the same house.

I enjoyed school and was good at my work. I was in Farmville four years before the schools closed. I was at Moton High School, the new school, when they closed the schools.

I remember that September morning in 1959. I got up, ironed my clothes, and got dressed. Aunt Gertrude and Aunt Bernice said: "There's no school and no school buses runnin'."

I asked: "Why?"

They tried to explain it to me but couldn't make the situation make sense.

I hung around the house for a while and then I started

wondering about my friends and what were they doing. I went out and found _____ _____, _____ _____, and _____ _____. We just walked around town.*

As the weeks and months went by, we spent our time earning money as caddies at Longwood Golf Course and setting up pins at the bowling alley on North Main Street. We started selling soda bottles and digging earth worms to sell as baits. We fished some ourselves in the nearby Appomattox River, across the Cumberland County Bridge.

We used to meet under a light each afternoon and evening. We would give an older fellow money and get him to go to Mrs. McKnight's store and buy us a beer. Three or four of us would share the beer. I was around fourteen. _____ was about two years older than me and _____ was a year older. We would walk to Yank's Pool Room on Second Street and Pee Wee's Pool Room on North Main. Mr. Reid owned it, but Pee Wee ran it. We were too young to get in the pool room, but they used to let us in to help keep us out of trouble.

Late one evening we were standing under a street light across from Branch No. 2. It was me, Nicky Vaughn, and Charlie Will Hatchett. We were playing around with my girlfriend, Ruth Moseley, called Fee Fee and her sister, Mattie, who everybody called Mutt.

Mutt said: "For every window pane y'all break, I'll give you a kiss."

We started throwing rocks. We broke well over twenty window panes. That was the fun for that night. The next morning the police went to every home talking to the parents. I don't know who told. I have always had my suspicion over the years. Our parents had to pay for the damages and each boy was put on one year's probation.

My grandmother called my mother, who had remarried and was living in New Jersey and said:

"Come and get Junny 'cause he is jus' gittin'in trouble." They called me Junny, instead of Junior.

Mama sent for me and I went to Troy, New York. In Troy I worked at a carwash and as a bus boy in a restaurant. Then I moved to New York City. I came back to Farmville. I was still in love with Fee Fee. Aunt Lucy had moved from the house on South Main to 700 Grace Street.

Shortly before September 1961 I was somehow chosen to be among a group of students selected to go away and resume my education. Students were to go and live in what was called *Less Crime* States. The way I understood it was that the students selected to be in the program were to go and live with families in States and areas with low crime rates. I think the organization that sponsored the program was the NAACP, I'm not absolutely sure.

Eighty-four Black youths from around the county were to report to First Baptist Church on Main Street one evening. We were told to bring our bags packed and be ready to leave Farmville that night. I remember there was a spinning basket with the names and addresses of foster parents. Each of the eighty-four students at the church that night got to pick a card from the spinning basket. The card I pulled from the basket had the name Mr. and Mrs. Reverend Lee in Inkster, Michigan.

Pop Ross pulled the name of a family from Inkster. Pop was in the ninth grade with me. The Hunt sisters from Prospect went to Inkster and they were in the tenth grade. Another light skinned girl from Meherrin went to Inkster and was in eleventh grade. All of us got the name of the foster parents out of the spinning basket that night.

My cousin, Shirley Ann Johnson, Aunt Lucy's daughter, went to a family in Langhorne, Pennsylvania.

We left Farmville that night on a Greyhound bus. The co-ordinators of the program must have called the foster parents after the bus left town. When we arrived in Detroit, Michigan, the next morning, families were at the bus station to meet us. The foster parents called out our names and each student answered.

Reverend and Mrs. Lee lived in the suburbs of Detroit. He was the pastor of a church and drove a 1959 Ford. Mrs. Lee was a school teacher. He and Mrs. Lee had a nice home and gave me a nice room. Inkster was a very clean city. You could almost eat off the pavement. I attended Inkster High School. In Inkster I saw the difference in the world being Black people, White people, and Indians. Each school day I used to carry the books of a pretty Indian girl.

When in Inkster, I was cut off from my family back in Farmville. I couldn't even write letters home. Reverend and Mrs. Lee said:

"You are here for one reason—to get an education. No one from home needs to send you money or anything."

After being in Inkster for three or four months, I was told one day I was going back to Farmville. I was never told why I was leaving. The foster family bought me a ticket to the Richmond Airport. My aunts picked me up.

When I got back to Farmville, I saw all of the fellows. They asked when was I going back. I showed them the stub from my plane ticket and told them I was heading back soon.

There was another girl in the program and I can't remember her name, but she said the family she lived with was very mean to her.

I often wondered why I was suddenly sent away from

Inkster and back to Farmville. No one ever told me why. I concluded that the organization that sponsored the students found out about me being on probation and told the foster family, which led to my return. It could have been another reason why I was sent back home, but that was the conclusion I drew.

I'm a barber and live in Richmond. Stop by when you're in town.

———

*When the interview was conducted, the Editor recorded all the names Wiley shared. In later years as the Editor continued to interview people in Prince Edward County, he realized that he had interviewed some of the relatives of the boys named. A lady interviewed was married to one of the individuals named by Wiley. The Editor thought it best to delete the names.

———

EDWARD THORNTON

I was delivered by a mid-wife on February 2, 1951. My parents were Cora Bell Gilliam Thornton and Lee Zille Thornton. I was an only child. I went to first and second grades at Mary E. Branch, No. 1. I had passed to the third grade when the schools were closed. For the next two years I didn't attend school.

At the time my mother was working for Dr. Smith, a White doctor in Farmville. Mama cooked for the Smith family. Dr.

Smith was on the Cumberland County School Board. I guess he heard my mother's cry and became sympathetic to our condition. Dr. Smith arranged it so that I could still live in Farmville and attend school in Cumberland County. If a student didn't live in Cumberland County or proved to be a legal resident, they couldn't attend the public schools in that county.

Some of the Negro parents, as they were called in those days, who could afford it rented a house in Cumberland County just for address purposes. They were able to say they were legal residents of Cumberland County. These parents would drive their children in the mornings to stand in front of the rented house to meet the school bus.

My daddy used to drive me across the Prince Edward County line and I would get on the school bus on the Cumberland County side and ride to school. I started attending a one room school in Cumberland County called Green Creek. I remember there was Green Creek Baptist Church nearby and the school was near the church. Mrs. Hartwell was the teacher and had grades first to fifth in the one room. I can't remember her first name.*

My first day on the bus I saw some other students from Farmville. They were already going to Greek Creek. Once inside that first day the teacher asked me what grade was I in. I told her I was in the fourth grade. She put me in fourth grade.

I had a cousin named Lee Watkins, Jr. who was also out of school for two years. I think Lee had passed to the fifth grade when the schools were closed. Lee's mama and my mama were sisters. Mama told, Aunt Mildred, Lee's mama, to let Lee go to Green Creek also. I don't recall whether Lee walked to the bus stop or whether Daddy picked him up and drove him across the line with me, but he started attending

Green Creek. Lee started a couple of weeks after I had been enrolled. Mama was from Cumberland County, but moved to Farmville when a young lady. She was the youngest child in her family and all of her sisters had moved to Farmville.

Several weeks went by and then there was a unique turn of events. Some of the children in Farmville who lived in an area called The Bottom and the area near Virginia Street found out Lee and I were in school at Green Creek. They also discovered that the school bus stopped across the river, not very far away. One day a large number of boys and girls joined us at the bus stop. When the driver stopped and opened the door, they all climbed on board. The driver pulled off with his bus full to capacity. All of the new riders were children with whom I had gone to first and second grades, and Lee had gone first through fourth. Mrs. Hartwell suddenly had a room full of students. All of the new riders went to Green Creek for about two or three weeks, after which time their educational experience ended. The teacher, bus driver, or someone explained that if they did not live in Cumberland County they could not attend Green Creek. Lee had to quit also, but I continued.

I went to Green Creek in fourth and fifth grades. When I turned twelve years old, the Free School system opened in Prince Edward County and I had just been promoted to the sixth grade.

I remember a notice came out stating if you were twelve years old or in seventh grade you needed to meet at the high school for assignments. I went to the high school and attended an assembly where students were rated to determine in what grade each student would be placed. When it was learned that I had just passed to the sixth grade, I was sent back to Mary E. Branch No. 2. I had gone up to the high school to be assigned to a class because I was twelve, as the notice stated, but because I had just passed to sixth grade I was returned to the middle school.

I was formally introduced to music during my first semester in the Free School.

In January 1964, the beginning of the second semester of my first year in the Free School system, they sent me back to Moton High to the seventh grade.

In June 1964, I was passed to the ninth grade. I was doing far better than the average child and to have kept me in with the slower students would have done me harm.

In ninth grade my love for music increased. I think it was the Lion's Club that sponsored an annual musical competition. Black music students competed against other Black music students. White students competed against other White music students. Black students and White students didn't compete against each other.

One year in the competition I played a song called *The Down Fall of Paris*. I played the snare drum solo. I won the local contest for Prince Edward County. The regional contest was held at Longwood College and I won that also. At the regional competition it was still all the Black students. I went to the State competition and came in second. A trumpet player beat me out. The band teacher at Moton, under whom I studied, used to teach at another school before coming to Prince Edward County. The trumpet player who beat me out had been taught at the other school by Mr. Freddie Hall. It was a win win for Mr. Hall. The judges said a point was deducted from me because I was patting my foot while playing. Otherwise, they said everything was exceptional. I didn't give patting my foot while playing a drum solo a second thought. The panel of judges was a mixed group, Black and White.

I enjoyed my high school years and was very involved. I was captain of the baseball and basketball teams. I was All District Baseball and should have been All District in basketball. I was the leading scorer in my senior year and third in rebounds, but I fouled often. I was very aggressive. I played basketball four years, ninth to twelfth grades and played baseball two years, my junior and senior years. I was an All State Drummer.

From ninth grade on, things went normal for me. I graduated at age nineteen. I was Valedictorian of my class. I had the highest grade point average. I wouldn't say I was the smartest student in school.

From the time the Free School opened until I graduated in 1968, I never missed a day in school. I guess I was afraid I would miss something.

According to my high school coach, the basketball coach from Villanova expressed an interest in me. I never spoke to a recruiter or the coach. Once they learned I was not as tall as they thought interest waned. Hampden Sydney College also expressed an interest in me. It was an all male school at the time and that caused some concern with me.

Virginia State College used to host a Senior Day. High school students traveled to the campus and met with representatives. When I saw the Trojan Band, I was overwhelmed. I knew there was no other school for me. Virginia State College gave me an academic scholarship. We were The Marching 110. We were always lined up ten across and eleven deep. But some years there were nearly 140 band members.

The Virginia State Trojan Band used to do half time shows for the Washington Redskins, New York Giants, (the team was in New York at that time) and the Philadelphia Eagles. We did that as well as played at the college games. I also played baseball in college.

The only academic deficiency brought to my attention at Virginia State College was Geography, which I never took in high school. I had to take a three-hour course at State, but received no credit.

I got a degree in Business Administration from Virginia State College in 1973. After I graduated in 1973, I returned to Farmville and worked for eleven months.

Currently I am the drummer for Five Kings of Harmony, a gospel singing group out of Richmond, Virginia. The group has several recordings to its credit.

It is with great pride that I share my story on this 17th day of May 2004.

---

*While at the home of Ms. Clara Ligon, I met a neighbor named Mrs. Ruth Farley Jones who was born and reared in Cumberland County. The Editor mentioned Green Creek School and the teacher, Mrs. Hartwell, about whom he had heard. "Oh, I remember Mrs. Pearl Hartwell who taught at Green Creek. She taught my children at Luther P. Jackson High School," Mrs. Jones said. Pearl was the first name of the teacher.

SHIRLEY JACKSON BROWN

I was born March 2, 1952, in Charlotte County, Virginia, to James Walter Jackson and Nancy Lee Holcomb Jackson. We moved from Charlotte County to Prince Edward County when I was about four years old. We lived on Main Street in Farmville.

Back then you had to be six years old to enter first grade. There was no kindergarten. You went straight to first grade. I started school at Mary E. Brach No. 1 at age six in September 1958 and went to the close of the 1958-1959 school year.

My mother had six children at home. She worked hard to get our clothes, books, paper, and pencils for school. My mom didn't have much education but was a smart lady.

The summer of 1959 was a good summer. Mr. Cole's store was our favorite spot. No one said anything about school not opening in September. Girls were comparing school clothes and talking about what our mothers and fathers had purchased and how the outfits looked. We sold bottles to buy ice cream and so forth. Nothing unusual was on the horizon, as far as a six or seven year old was concerned.

Mama was a domestic and left home early each morning.

That weekday morning in September 1959 my brother Clem, my sisters Elizabeth, Patricia and I left home and headed to school, laughing, talking, and stopping to play. Each of us had on a new outfit.

When we got near Branch, No. 1, the elementary school, we noticed something was not right. Normally there would be hundreds of students lined up and teachers outside directing the students to classes on the first day of school. There were far fewer students that morning. There were no buses that morning either. The buses normally rolled around in front of the school on the dirt, there was no pavement, to pick up the students going over to Moton High School. We hadn't heard anything but knew something was going on.

We went up to the door and saw this big lock. There were chains, big chains, on the door handles. The chains had been rolled in knots to make sure no one could get the chains unloose. The children started talking among themselves. There were a few teachers there to support us. Those teachers explained to us that the schools weren't going to open.

We went back home crying and talking. I was going to the second grade. We really wanted to go to school. No one could explain the situation to us to help it make sense.

The first year the schools were closed we played around with our friends. There were eleven children in our family. Several of them were now adults and had their own families. Those of us at home would go and visit our sisters in Prospect and Charlotte County.

The second year of the school closing, 1960-1961, we went to school in the basement of First Baptist Church and Beulah African Methodist Episcopal Church on Main Street. We went there for a year and they taught us well. We sat on benches. I remember there were no backs on the benches. I remember Mrs. Fred Reid, Chuckie Reid's grandmother, telling those in charge: "We need something with backs for these children or they will be humped-back when they get grown."

Some of the teachers at the churches were: Mrs. Fred Reid, Mrs. Harriett Allen, Mrs. Vera Jones Allen, Mrs. Mary Madison, Mrs. Alice Brown, and Mrs. Griffin.*

The schools at the churches were opened every day, Monday through Friday, and the students who lived in Farmville could go each day if they wanted to or if their parents sent them. We started around 8:30 a. m. or 9:00 a.m. and stayed until about 1:00 p. m. There were a lot of students in attendance.

I remember the teachers saying to each other: "What are we going to do with all of these children?"

When we were going to church schools, the White children would be on the school buses going to the Academy.

Things started looking hopeless. My sister Mary Frances and her husband Franklin Gee lived in Charlotte Court House. Mary Frances asked Mama did she want her and Franklin to take the three of us — me, Elizabeth, and Patricia — so we could go to school in a formal class setting. Mary Frances and Franklin had three small children not yet in school. Mama was reluctant to send us and gave a lot of thought to accepting the invitation. Mary Frances and Franklin convinced Mama to give it a try and she gave in.

The third year of the school closing me, Elizabeth, and Patricia moved in with Franklin and Mary Frances in Charlotte Court House in Charlotte County. We attended Central Elementary School. The principal and teachers were waiting for us the day we arrived. They knew we hadn't been to school for several years. The teachers had taught our older brothers and sisters before Mama moved to Prince Edward County.

The principal at Central Elementary School, Mr. Douglas Cooley, was waiting for us the first day of school in September 1961, and so were Mrs. Lillie Mae Robinson and Mrs. Jefferson.

"Come on in here, Jacksons. We have a seat for each one of you. Those people ought to be ashamed of themselves for what they are doing in Prince Edward County. But God will take care of them. You all come on in," I remember the principal and teachers saying to us, as we walked in the building.

We were like celebrities.

The teachers used to hold us up as examples saying to the local children:

'These students have been out of school for years and look at how they work.'

We came home about once every two or three weeks. Franklin and Mary Frances had no telephone, so we couldn't call home. They had no television either. They had a radio and used to listen to the news. We always listened to the news hoping to hear that the schools were about to reopen in Prince Edward County.

We stayed with Mary Frances and Franklin one school year, September 1961 to May 1962. We couldn't return to Mary Frances and Franklin the next school year because additional people in their home was too much of a financial strain on them and on our family back in Farmville. We returned to Farmville and stayed out of school another year, September 1962 to May 1963.

I remember some White students from up north started coming to help teach in the summer.

When the Free School opened in September 1963, I went to the fifth grade. Students were placed by age until the faculty could determine their academic skills.

I am going to let my sister Patricia share some of her reflections. Some of what she shares will be similar to mine.

———

*Some of the ladies named taught in the Summer Remedial Program and did not work at the churches August to May. During the regular school year, Mrs. Allen and Mrs. Madison worked in other public school districts.

———

PATRICIA JACKSON LEVERETTE

I was born May 7, 1953. I also remember my mother starting around June buying school clothes. I remember Shirley telling me all that I was going to do at school. We would lay in bed and she would tell me about school and the activities. I became more and more excited.

When the White family Mama worked for brought her home one afternoon, we asked her what was wrong. She said: "I don' think y'all children will be goin t' school this year."

This was a blow for me and our family for more than one reason. Mama and Daddy had recently divorced, and she moved to Prince Edward County to make a new start. As children, we had not gotten over them being divorced and now the closing of the schools.

Shirley has already described the first day of school in September 1959, but I want to give my personal testimony. We got up that morning laughing and talking, and after getting dressed in our new clothes we walked to Branch No. 1. I remember some teachers were outside on the grounds to meet us. In my mind I can still see a Black female teacher on the grounds with a blue dress on with a belt. The belt had one of those big buckles on the front. We walked up to the door. We saw the chains on the doors at Branch No. 1 before we got to the entrance. You know how sometimes you might say to yourself when a door is locked against you: 'I should break it open and go on in.' I felt like breaking the chains on the doors because I wanted to see everything inside the school that Shirley had told me about.

You know how it was when you were children—me and Shirley used to say we wish we were White, so we could go to school. The White people had actually made us think and believe that something was wrong with us, when the truth was the opposite. The opposite was the case. Something was wrong with the White folks that they would treat people the way they treated us.

Those were days when if a Black person was walking down the street and a White person was coming, the White person would cross the street rather than walk pass a Black person.

You would be in a store, the first person in line, but when it all ended up you would be number ten or fifteen because the White folks would get in front of you and you had better not say anything. What was so disturbing was White adults, grown people, doing this to children like me and to other little Black boys and girls. That was sick.

We started attending classes at the church. To the names of some of the teachers at First Baptist and Beulah AME my sister Shirley named, I will add Mrs. Ernestine Herndon and Mrs. Ethel Wilson Fisher.* They taught also.

The White folks were mad because Black adults started teaching us at Beulah and First Baptist. The White people must have thought that our people would just let us sink but got mad when adults in our community and among our race started teaching us. During the school hour, we also got Bible instructions. Reverend Griffin would come in and talk to the children.

When we went to Central Elementary, I didn't like being away from my mother. I liked school and learning, but I didn't like being disconnected physically from my mother. Mrs. Lillie Mae Robinson was my teacher that year at Central Elementary. She always made me feel special. She knew I was detached from my mother, but Mrs. Robinson didn't take any jive either. She would report to Mary Frances at church on our progress. We attended Saint Andrews Baptist Church the year we were away from home. But our home church in Farmville was Race Street Baptist Church where Reverend Williams was the pastor.

When we returned home, we missed another year of school and then the Free School opened. We were placed in classes by age. They had trailers set up outside the school because there were so many students. The building could not hold them all. We were tested in the trailers. After those tests, we were put in classes. But there was still much moving around until they found out where you were supposed to be.

The great thing is to find out where you are supposed to be in life and that is on the side of right and what is just.

---

*Mrs. Herndon taught in the Summer Program. From August to May, she taught in a public school in Spotsylvania County, Virginia. Mrs. Ethel Wilson Fisher worked with the children until she was hired to teach in Lynchburg, Virginia. She started there in September 1960. Mrs. Wilson worked with the summer program for the children.

LILLY JACKSON SCOTT

I had completed tenth grade when the schools were closed. At that point it was a sad time when the schools closed. The pastor at Beulah African Methodist Episcopal Church, in Farmville, Revered Dunlap, wanted me to go to North Carolina and live with his parents and finish my education. I can't recall which part of North Carolina they lived in. Mama (Nancy Lee Jackson) wanted me to go and live with Reverend Dunlap's parents, but I didn't want to go.

That morning, I knew the schools were closed, but I couldn't believe it. I got up, opened the front door and just stood there. I heard no noise. Usually children would be coming through the streets talking and laughing. It was quite that morning.

My brother Clem was home with me. I took care of him and took care of the house when Mama went to work.

When Shirley, Elizabeth Nancy and Patricia went to Charlotte Court House, I stayed in Farmville. When Shirley, Patricia and Elizabeth came back, I took care of them.

When the Free School opened, I was married.

Some of the high school teachers I remember before the schools were closed were: Mr. Stanton, he taught biology; Mr. Lowell White, he taught science; Mrs. Martin taught Art, I think she was there in the 1958-1959 school year and I can't remember her first name. Mrs. Minnie Miller taught Home Economics, I know she was teaching that last year because I remember her talking about the Miller Building and hosting a tour of the building. The Miller Building was supposed to open in 1960. Mrs. Rawlins taught Social Studies and History. Mrs. Vanessa Venerable taught Math.

———

JO ANN RANDALL

I was born August 22, 1952, to Catherine and Johnny Randall at 615 Vernon Street. My parents had eight children: James Edward, Joyce, Jo Ann, Willie Mae, Gary, Diane, Debra and Catherine.

I was sick a lot with asthma during my early years. The

first school I attended was the school held at Beulah AME Church on Main Street, after the public schools were closed.

After the schools didn't open for several years, my father sent me, James Edward, Joyce, Willie Mae, Gary, Diane, and Debra to his mother in Newark, New Jersey. My grandmother's name was Mrs. Willie May Venerable.

My public school education started in Newark, New Jersey. They put me in the third grade. I was ten years old. I remember seeing boys and girls serving as safety patrols. Teachers would be talking in class, but I wouldn't hear a thing they said. I was always thinking about home. My grandmother was old, and it was hard for her to handle all of us. We went to school in Newark for one year, but I don't remember anything from that year.

Daddy came and picked us up that summer. When I got back to Farmville, they said the schools were going to open. This was the Free School. It was still hard for me. I started thinking about New Jersey. All the moving made no sense to me and no one could help it make sense to me. While in the Free School, I begin to wonder what would happen the next year and would I be sent to another school.

The move to New Jersey took a toll on all of the children in my family.

Even in high school I often thought about New Jersey. All of my life I have felt something has been missing. When the lives of children are disrupted, and they have to move back and forth, voids are created in their lives.

Home life is the most comfortable place to be if home is meaningful. I am fifty-one and I still have pain. What I experienced as a girl still troubles me. I can still see the look on my mother's face and in my father's eyes when they had to send us away and didn't know what to say.

CARL U. EGGLESTON, SR.

When the schools were closed, I had been promoted to the third grade. For two years I didn't attend school. I played in the streets and I went to something like a training center in the basement at First Baptist Church. I don't remember the teachers who were there.

I returned to school in September 1961 for the 1961-1962 school year. My parents rented a house in Cumberland County, so their children could go to school. We attended R. R. Moton School. It was a two room school that had a pot belly stove, outdoor toilet, and no running water. It did have electricity. Students made the fire during the winter months. The school went to the sixth or seventh grade. Mrs. Brown was the teacher and principal. She moved between the two rooms and taught the students. First, second, and third grades were in one room. The higher grades were in the next room.

President John F. Kennedy and Attorney General Robert Kennedy took a special interest in the Prince Edward County school situation. They lobbied for money that would be used to open the schools, while the court case was being worked. The Free School opened in Prince Edward County in September 1963. My parents discontinued their rental agreement in Cumberland County.

My father was in the woodworking business. I worked with him one and a half hours before school and reported to him at the end of the school day. My father died in 1966. I graduated in 1969, one year later than I should have. Many students were impacted in a similar way.

After graduating from high school, I went to Galax, Virginia, and attended a Man Power Training Center, a program that came under the Virginia Employment Commission. Students could go there and learn a trade. I enrolled to learn more and sharpen my skills in upholstering, reupholstering, and refinishing furniture. I was there about a year and then my interest in mortuary took over. I went to Richmond, Virginia, and did an internship with Mimms Funeral Home. I enrolled at John Tyler Community College in Richmond and graduated in 1978 with an Associate's Degree in Applied Science and majored in Mortuary Science. Then I took the National Funeral Director Exam and the State Funeral Director and Embalmers Board Exam and was successful with both.

I remained with Mimms for another year or a little more. In 1979, the mortician at Mealy Funeral Home in Goochland, Virginia, died. I ran and operated the establishment until one of his sons became licensed. Later I became part owner of a funeral home in Culpeper, Virginia. The family closed the business. In 1983, I opened my own funeral home in Farmville.

In my first year of operation I had no funerals. My first funeral was in January 1984. My grandfather Mr. George C. Eggleston, Sr. died. His funeral was the only funeral I had that year. Gradually people in the community began to accept my services. The next year I had about ten funerals and the following year seventeen.

I have been very active in the political arena. In 1983 I took an interest in town council elections. I ask the city of Farmville to abandon the At-Large Voting System. Several African-Americans had run unsuccessfully for office. The community was 76% White and 24% African-American. Farmville leaders declined to move away from the At-Large Voting System. I sued the town in Federal Court. Then I came up with and drew a ward plan that allowed the town to be broken down into five wards. Two of the wards are majority Black. In May 1984, I ran for town council and was elected. I am the first person of African descent to ever serve on the town council in Farmville. I ran for mayor in 1986 and received about 31% of votes. In 1998 I ran again and receive 46% percent.

The year 2005 will be twenty years that I have served on the 5th District Democratic Committee. In 1992 I was the first African American elected to serve as Chair of the 5th District Democratic Committee. The congressional district is about 70% White.

I'm the president of the R. R. Moton Museum located in Farmville. I am Chairman of the Trustee Board at First Baptist Church, a position I have held for twenty-five years. The first meeting I attended I was appointed chair and have been it ever since.

CARRIE CLARK BLAND

I was born June 12, 1949, in Prince Edward County to Willie and Mary Clark. I started school at Mary E. Branch No. 1. One of my favorite teachers was my third grade teacher, Mrs. Mary Smith. She was from Farmville. She was an older teacher and she wanted you to learn. She wanted to prepare you for life. Mrs. Smith would discipline you without hesitation. She reminded me of a grandmother more than a teacher.

I had been promoted to the fifth grade when the schools were closed. I didn't attend public schools any more until

September1963. That was when the Free School opened. I missed years of public education.

During the years the schools were closed, my mother home schooled all of the children in the house in math, English, and geography.

My father worked part-time for a White retired school teacher name Mrs. Elizabeth Haskins. She lived in Farmville. Daddy was her chauffer, but also did some cleaning around house and yard. Mrs. Haskins provided him with textbooks for us. She knew we wanted to learn. I had three sisters and a brother—Velma (Robinson) Mattie (Bolden) Willie Clark, Jr., and Hazel (Patterson).

My mother went to the fifth grade and Daddy went to the seventh. Velma was the oldest. Mama did the teaching. At the time she was crippled with rheumatoid arthritis, but she did not let that stop her classroom sessions. Mama made sure we read each day and did arithmetic from the book. All of us could read, write and do math.

When the schools closed, Mattie had been promoted to third grade, Willie to second and Hazel was just starting. Velma was going the ninth grade.

When the Free School opened, I was placed in the seventh grade. I think Mrs. Dorothy Statler was my teacher. Willie and Mattie were placed in the same grade, as I recall. I think both were placed in the sixth grade. Hazel was in fourth, if my memory serves me right. I think she may have been advanced a grade. Velma was eighteen or nineteen when the schools reopened, and she never returned. She got married. Willie and Mattie graduated together in 1969.

After high school, I worked with Stackpole Components Company for one year. Then I moved to Richmond and entered business school. After receiving my certificate, I sought employment and worked for Ceridian Employer Services, which was formerly Service Bureau Cooperation. I held various positions and worked there for thirty-one years. In 2001, I was laid off due to downsizing.

I was blessed to be able to have parents who had a strong interest in education and made sure we continued to learn. I have tried to do the same for my children.

———

MATTIE IRENE CLARK BOLDEN

I was born September 1950 and am the third of five children. We had a very good time when children. My mother could never do that much for us because she was disabled. We had to make sure lunch was made for our father. I remember doing this until the schools were closed. I remember my little sister Hazel was to start school the year the schools were closed.

When the schools didn't open, we were kind of confused. None of us understood; we were all small. My mother tried to explain it to us. My father couldn't afford to send us away and Daddy also needed us at home. We also had my father's mother who lived with us. She was getting up in age and we had to help with her. As children, we were living now almost like adults.

Hazel was six; my brother, Willie, who was next to me was seven; then there was me and I was eight, and an older sister Carrie was nine. Velma who was the oldest in the family was around thirteen. Velma was with my grandparents at this time. These were my mother's parents, Mattie C. Miller

Williams and Frank Williams. They lived in Rice down near High Bridge.

Daddy couldn't afford to send us all away to aunts and uncles. We had aunts and uncles in Pennsylvania, Maryland and Lynchburg, Virginia.

Mama really couldn't get up and do for herself, she couldn't do anything for herself or for us. We had to do whatever was required for her. If we didn't do it, there were consequences. Mama taught us with the books we had and with the books people gave us.

When school teachers came to Prince Edward County in the summer to work with the children, we went to the classes at First Baptist Church. These were the Summer Crash Programs. We did our studies and recreation and then went home. I remember the teachers coming in to work with us, but don't remember any names. I remember Reverend Griffin, his wife, his sons, and children.

Mama continued to work with us during the school year and we only went to the classes at the church during the summer. I got hurt one day during the summer. I left something at home, I didn't want to get a bad grade or upset the teacher. I went back home but fell and busted my knee and had to stay home anyway. I stayed at home about a week and went back.

The first three years the schools were closed we were at home and Mama taught us. We lived in Farmville off of Hill Street.

The year before the Free School, this would have been the fourth year the schools were closed, my parents decided to try and get us in a school. They didn't expect the schools to be closed this long. In the fourth year Mama and Daddy tried to get us in the Cumberland County schools. In order to go to school there you had to live in that county. Daddy couldn't afford to move.

One of Daddy's cousins had a house on Plank Road in Cumberland County. My family moved into the house. My father, mother, grandmother, and all the children all moved in.

Carrie, Willie, Hazel and I started going to a two room school named R. R. Moton. The teacher was Ms. I. N. Brown. I remember being in the third grade. I was now twelve years old. I was placed in the third grade because that was where I had stop at the time of the shut-down.

We didn't take everything out of our house in Farmville. The house we moved into had some furniture, so we only had to take a small amount of things from our Farmville home. Daddy left the heavy furniture. Of course, we took all of our clothes. Daddy would go back to Farmville and check on the house. The house we rented on Plank Road was less than two miles from our home in Farmville. Sometimes we, the children, would walk to Farmville.

We had been taught previously some of what was being taught at the two room school in Cumberland County. The teacher would call on us first to help show the Cumberland children what was to be done. I remember many of the Cumberland County children were not reading at the rate they should have. We were reading at the proper rate because that was all we did at home with Mama. We read and did math. I was twelve and in the third grade.

At the end of the school year we were all promoted, and we graduated. We came home one day and found out that the schools in Prince Edward County would be opened. I can't remember how we found out. We were still in the house in Cumberland County. When Mama told us in Cumberland the schools would open, and she had heard the news, we jumped, we hollered, and we cried. We were just so happy, so happy that we would go back to our own school. In the summer of 1963 we moved back to Farmville into our old house.

When the Free School opened, I remember many faces to this day. There were so many children and teachers. Everybody was just glad to be there. They were packed in like sardines. Getting down the hall was a challenge. There were twelve and thirteen year olds; seventeen and eighteen year old students and some people were in their twenties. Our classes were so large. It surprised me how the teachers could teach. Everybody wanted to learn.

My sister Velma didn't come back to school. Velma came back to school for a little while and stopped. Carrie started in the eighth grade and I started in the seventh grade. Willie was also in the seventh grade. Carrie finished high school in 1968. Willie and I finished in 1969. Hazel finished in the early 1970s.

Willie and I graduated the same year. Hazel was almost where she should have been.

I remember Martin Luther King, Jr. came one summer, I think it was in the summer. My sister Carrie, I believe, got to meet him.

This is as much as I can remember as of today, Saturday, September 15, 2012, about the school closure years.

CHARLOTTE HERNDON WOMACK

I was born March 31, 1954. When I was five years old and my brother was three, we closed up our house in Farmville and lived with our grandmother who was in the same town. My mother, Ernestine Watkins Herndon, was a teacher in the public schools, but when the closure took effect Mom was hired to teach in Spotsylvania County, Virginia. She went there, and my brother and I remained with Grandmother. My brother, Charles, and I were not yet old enough to go to school. Mom came home each weekend.

I did not understand why we closed up our house and moved in with Grandma. I could not get any answers because at five years old you did not ask questions in those days. You just did what you were told.

In 1960, I turned six and was ready for first grade. My mom took me to Spotsylvania County with her and I was enrolled in school there. I didn't think this was abnormal. I didn't know we had schools in Prince Edward County and that the schools were closed. When my brother turned six, Mama brought him to Spotsylvania County also.

We would pack the car on Thursday night and head back to Farmville on Friday afternoon when school ended. We would spend the weekend in Farmville and leave Prince Edward County early Monday morning, heading back to Spotsylvania County.

During Christmas, school was out for about two weeks. We would open up the house in Farmville, that is we would have the electricity and water turned on and the same in the summer. Our home in Farmville was more like a summer home for Mama, Charles and I, since we were in Spotsylvania County most of the year.

I had a very good friend nicknamed Poogie. Her proper name was Barbara Oliver. I only saw her during the summer. Poogie's parents rented a house in Charlotte County and moved their entire family there. The family would come to Farmville in the summer. There were four children in the Oliver family at the time. Their Farmville home became their summer vacation home.

"Poogie's sister, Sylvia Oliver, works as a substitute teacher and you should interview her," Charlotte said to the Editor. "Sylvia has a moving story that you have to write."

When the Free School opened, my mother returned to teach in Prince Edward County. I felt that moving back was a disruption to my education. I still had not made sense of everything and no one had taken time to explain it to me. When I was told school was reopening at home, I had already been in school for three years and being told the schools were reopening at home made no sense.

I was nine when we came back to Farmville. Having missed no time out of school, I was on target. Many of the students were placed in classes by age. There were students in my fourth grade class who had never received any formal education. They had been taught in the basement of churches and in homes. These children made me look like a gifted student. I was not smart as such, but I had been in a formal school setting for several years and that made all the difference.

When I graduated from high school in 1972, there were students in my class who were twenty and twenty-one years old.

Our story in Prince Edward County is a very rich and powerful story and I am glad that many people are sharing their recollections.

———

SYLVIA F. OLIVER

When the Editor arrived at the home of Sister Oliver, her grandson was mowing the lawn and she engaged in yard work. She was expecting me.

"Would you like to go inside?" she asked, as it was hot that afternoon.

"We can stay outside, I'll just sit under this tree," the Editor said, finding something to sit on.

She came, sat by me, and continued to supervise her grandson.

The land on which you are sitting has been in my family since 1872. I was born April 12, 1951. A mid-wife delivered me on this property. I started school at Mary E. Branch No. 1 in September 1957. I had been promoted to the third grade when the schools were closed.

My mother prepared us for school that year. She did not believe the schools would close. At that time, I had two sisters and one brother. Tawanna Jean was born May 9, 1950, Barbara Marie, was born May 30, 1954 and Fred Douglass Oliver, Jr. was born on July 13, 1959. Mom purchased all of our school clothes. She did not believe school would not open. But by September she knew school was not going to open. She found out through the Farmville Herald the local paper.

Mom got prepared to teach us at home. She had been a substitute teacher in a one room school. Mom was born in Henrico County, near Richmond, but was raised in Prince Edward County.

The first year out of school my sisters and I watched the White children go to school. The Academy bus came up Longwood Avenue pass our house and turned on Catlin Street. (She pointed in the direction of Catlin Street).

Let me tell you about the first year under Mom's tutelage. That was a rough year. She had the three of us at the kitchen table, not from sun up to sun down but it was close. (Sylvia chuckles.) She taught and left no academic stone unturned. This was long before home schooling became popular and there were guidelines for the program.

When it became obvious that the schools were not going to open the second year, Daddy packed us up and moved to Charlotte County the second week in September 1960. Daddy was born and reared in Charlotte County. That was how we were able to go to school. He was returning to his home county. We lived in a small section called Eureka. We missed the first week of school. Mom was still amazed that the schools were closed. Two years in a row was unreal. When we moved, it was Mom, Daddy, Great-grand father George Price, and my grandfather, Percy Brown. These were my mother's father and grandfather. Daddy worked at Burlington Industries.

The first year in Charlotte County we were tested. Tawanna tested out in the seventh grade, but in Prince Edward County had passed to the fourth grade. I tested out in the sixth grade but had passed to third grade the last year of school in Prince Edward. Barbara who had never been to school tested out in third grade. Mom had done an excellent job.

All of us attended Central Elementary School. Mr. Douglas Cooley was the principal. My third grade teacher was Mrs. Jeffries. Then I had Mrs. Allen and I don't remember the third teacher. These two, I guess, made an impression on me.

My grandfather was overwhelmed by the closing of the schools. My great-grand-father could have easily passed for White but did not. He would not participate.

We stayed in Charlotte County for three years. Charlotte

County was our permanent address. Rental homes for Black folk in Charlotte County included well water and a path. The path led to the outhouse. In Farmville we had running water and a bathroom.

The family came to Farmville every Friday to buy groceries at A&P. Before leaving, we would stop by to check on the house, walk through, and cry because that was home. It was located at 701 Longwood Avenue.

September 1963 the Free School opened. We packed up and moved back home. We returned without my great-grandfather and grandfather. Both were called to their eternal rest while we were in Charlotte County.

I think I was placed in the sixth grade when we returned. I think we were placed according to age and not grade. They started placing by grade the next year when school officially reopened, and students were tested. I tested out in the eighth grade. During my school career I never sat in a seventh grade class.

I was the smallest one in eighth grade. The other children were fifteen, sixteen and seventeen years old.

After high school, I worked for the State outside of Richmond. I was working at Beaumount Juvenile Correctional Center and a co-worker name Demarco Harris found out I was from Farmville. I remember a man telling me that his high school played Moton and when the Moton football team came on the field they were astounded and asked their coaches — 'Where did these grown men come from?' He said some of the guys had mustaches. He was correct because many of the males impacted by the school closing were graduating at age twenty and twenty-one.

To people who will read this story one hundred years from now I want them to know that the worst thing you can do to children is to deny them an education for any reason. To say, as was said to us, we are closing the schools because you do not fit, you are different is unacceptable.

Children understand getting up in the morning, getting dressed for school, saying their prayers; we had no awareness of Black people and White people. It made sense to adults but to children it made no sense to us.

———

DOUGLAS METTEAU VAUGHAN

I was in born on Appomattox Street on October 15, 1943. Appomattox Street was located across the train tracks. That was a poor neighborhood. It was sort of off limits to Black and White people. The prominent Black people didn't even come to the area. It was a neighborhood that was basically forgotten. We had a sock-ball for a baseball and used a stick for a bat. We never had any modern facilities to do our daily playing unless it was at school.

When I was five, my grandmother was sick with diabetes. My mother was an alcoholic until she died. I had one brother and two sisters. We basically raised each other. It was tough at times. We had electricity and water, but no finances to pay for upkeep. Water was $2.00 a month and it would get cut off. The lights stayed off. We went to the neighbors to listen to the radio and watch TV.

When I started school, I didn't even have a pair of boy shoes. My sister had two pairs of shoes and because I wore a pair of her rusty bucks, they were called, some boys knew and teased me. I had a pair of brogans that the sole flapped on. I learned to walk to keep the sole from flapping. Sometimes I used some wire to mend them.

I went to the store once and asked for some Nabisco Crackers. The White man grabbed me behind the neck and literally threw me out of the store and said:

"You ask for soda biscuits and never ask for crackers again."

My second open encounter with racism was some White boys used to chase us each day and try to whip us up. One day we got tired of it and stood firm and fought them on the corner of Main Street. One of the White boys was the son of a local official. The official got with the principal of the school. A specific route was laid out for us to go and come to school. The principal followed us in the evening, or sometimes the local police.

A teacher who knew my family plight asked me one day:

"How would you like for me to adopt you?"

"What about my brother and my sister?"

"I just want a boy."

"I couldn't live with leaving my family."

Over the years she adopted about five boys. One is a lawyer.

When the schools were closed, I was in the ninth grade. There were two groups, the A and B groups. I was in the B group.

My older sister, Irene Vaughan, had already graduated. Mary ran away. She went to Maryland and about six months later she married. My brother Godfrey was also in ninth grade.

As a boy, all I wanted was to be loved. I saw that in other homes and always wanted it for myself.

When I was about eleven or twelve, my older sister had a baby. I had a job and had to use the money to buy diapers and similac. In the winter we would get between the two mattresses we had with our coats on top and tried to stay warm.

School was a safe haven for me. It was a place where I could go and have friends and feel loved or liked. When the schools were closed, that was the most devastating time of my life. Home wasn't the most pleasant place to be. Most of the people in the town had someone looking out for them. Children moved out of state and to surrounding counties.

I wrote a letter to my uncle, Robert Lockett, in Philadelphia, Pennsylvania, and asked could I come and go to school there. I was working in a veterinarian hospital in Farmville. Uncle Robert said I could come, but I had to pay my own way. I saved my money and went to Philadelphia. When they took me to register, the school board people realized I was from Prince Edward County, Virginia. The only way I could go to school in Philadelphia was pay the tuition of a little over five hundred dollars. I was given thirty days to get out of Philadelphia. I returned to Farmville and got my old job back at the veterinarian hospital.

Later I got a job at Hampden Sydney College. I was trying to learn how to cook. I was working as a third cook. I got about $30.00 every two weeks. The supervisor said I had to take a test to get paid as a third cook. I agreed to take the test. The first question was: What is a root? I had no idea because I had never heard the word. I later learned that it was the flour and grease that made the gravy and then you added seasoning.

Seeing I was being taken advantage of, my brother Godfrey and I decided to leave Farmville. We went to a friend in New York. We had a room and paid ten dollars a week for rent. To keep enough money for the room, we went to a restaurant that served butter beans for twenty-five cents a bowl. We ate there at lunch and dinner for thirty days. Godfrey found a job before I did.

My sister wrote and told me she had a baby and the child died. I returned to Prince Edward County to support my sister. I stayed for a year. I went to New Jersey. I worked in the garment industry. I learned to put children's clothes together. I got married in 1963.

My wife and I went to New Jersey with two children, two girls. I stayed with my sister. In 1968 there were the riots in New Jersey. We had to go through that area each day. The National Guard was present and there was looting. We got an apartment and someone broke in. We moved to another area and had the same experience. This happened six times. It reached the point when we came home from work we would knock on our door, sit outside a few minutes, and give anyone inside time to leave.

I vividly remember the last break-in. The last time it happened my wife was cooking dinner. When it was about time to eat, she said we didn't have anything to drink and said: "Let's go to the store and get some Kool-Aid."

We went to the store and when we returned fifteen minutes later they had taken the pot roast, television, camera, etc. The following Monday we left and returned to Farmville and stayed with my wife's mother. Her mother had no running water, but we had saved some money and got the house fixed up.

I got a construction job, but the man said I was too small. I said I could do the work. If you're not satisfied at the end of the week then let me go. My wife had to rub me down at night. The work was extremely difficult. My wife was willing to return to New Jersey but I said no. She got a job at Stackpole Components in Farmville.

In 1972 I earned my GED.

Bricklaying impressed me. A fellow invited me to try and lay some bricks one day. The foreman gave me a job and the blue prints. I completed the job and was hired as a full-time bricklayer. I had to go to school in the evening to take classes for the proper certifications. I passed. Carpentry impressed me also. In time I was able to build anything I wanted to build.

My wife and I decided to build our own house. We laid the foundation ourselves. My daughters were not quite ten years old, but already knew how to use a skill saw. I would mark the boards and they would cut. Every brick, board and block in this house my wife, daughters and I put in place. (The interview was conducted in the house Vaughan, his wife, and daughters built. He and Mrs. Vaughan were living in the house in August 2004.) When it was time to put the roof on, they were up there laying shingles.

In 1975 I went into the building trade for myself. In 1980 the bottom fell out of the building industry. I left the business and went to the Department of Corrections. I made about a third of what I had been making but could do all the over time I wanted. I worked about sixteen hours a day. The prison was old, and the State closed it. A new prison was built in Nottoway. I applied for a position and got it. I started going to Longwood College and Southside Community College. I went from an Officer to a Major in the Department of Corrections in about six years. Every time something opened I applied. I was a major for nine years. Last month, July 25, 2004, I was named Assistant Warden.

There have been obstacles to be sure, but I have not allowed that to stop me. I have always been a determined person. If I set my goals, I pursue them. I have been married forty-one years to Jo Ann Robinson Vaughan from the Sharon community in Cumberland County, Virginia. Both of our girls went to college.

The oldest, Chevell (Roan) went to Old Dominion and is an account. She works with Price Waterhouse. The youngest went to Longwood College and she, Chanel (Leslie) works for NASA in Alabama.

We have a close-knit family. My girls were fighting once when children and I whipped both. I told them they have to love each other and you can't love fighting.

I sometimes sit and wonder where would I have been and where would I be if I had gotten a good education. Yet God so fixed it that I could face challenges and with God's help overcome them. I always felt God was preparing me to withstand all of the obstacles that would come before me.

I have, with God's help, and the support of my wife made some wonderful accomplishments. I love her to death.

A fellow took an interest in me and showed me patterns and how sew. I was able to sew my children's clothes. I tried to go to school at night for about a year. I took a test to get a diploma and failed. Basically, I could not read. My wife realized that I couldn't read and started making me read to her at night. I would stumble over words and was so embarrassed, but she wouldn't let up on me. After a while the embarrassment went away; and today — here we are as one.

PHYLLISTINE YVONNE WARD-MOSLEY

I am one of five children born to the late Phillip Madison and Doris Thompson Ward. I grew up in the area known as Baptist Hill, located on Main Street, in a house that was formerly a fourth grade classroom. Before moving to Baptist

Hill, we lived on Ely Street, which is now Griffin Boulevard. We lived with my great uncle and great grandfather Phillip Alexander Ward. My uncle Fred Ward owned a store. As I researched my genealogy, I understand now that he looked like a White man. When you went in the store, he would have on his white apron standing behind the counter and a cigar in his mouth. My great grandfather also looked like a White man. All of them remained true to their heritage and never sought to pass for White.

Genealogy established that my great grandfather Phillip, my grandfather Charlie Ward, and my father Phillip were all bakers at Longwood College. All together they totaled about one hundred ten years of service there. Longwood University was Longwood Normal in earlier days.

We couldn't go to the college as students but could go the kitchen/bakery area where Daddy worked. As children, we got to see some of the elaborate creations of cakes and other delights he made.

My mom grew up on a farm in Nottoway County, Virginia. There were twelve in her family. She knew how to string tobacco and did other farm chores. When my parents got married, my mother's sister, Lois Thompson, came to Farmville to live with them to go to school. We went to Nottoway to Grandma and Grandpa's house each Sunday. We would also go to Grandma and Grandpa's in the summer and we would see them and White people exchanging equipment and helping each other on tobacco farms. The White families were the Franks and the Yates.

When we lived in the Baptist Hill section on Main Street, there were many Black businesses: McKnight Service/Gas Station, and she had a room on the side where people drank beer etc. There was Reid's Restaurant, Master Cleaners (Page

Walker owned Master Cleaners first and Reginald White later purchased it) and Burnell Coles Store. Nurse Nellie Matthews Coles was the public health nurse. The reason she was called Nurse Coles was because when she and others went to training the White women in training were called Mrs. and they refused to call Nellie by the title Mrs. but referred to her as Nurse Coles and the name Nurse Cole stuck. Down through the years everyone in the county called her Nurse Coles. The public health nurse worked at the clinic and received a list of families or homes to visit. Her companion was Mrs. Branch.

Dr. Albert Rawlings was a physician and his office was on Main Street. His family lived in the house and the doctor's office was in the basement of the house. Dr. N. P. Miller was a dentist located on Main Street. He was very short and sometimes had to stand on a box to work on patients. Chairs did not recline that much in that era. He worked for almost charity. Most of the Black people were poor. Dr. Miller also gave scholarships for college. Dr. John Baker was a general practitioner. His office was in his house. Bland Funeral Home was the only Black mortuary initially. The name Reid was added in later years when they became partners.

Mom worked at a refinishing furniture factory, did domestic work around town and then she was a nurse's aide at Southside Hospital in Farmville. This was how she improved herself over the years. She realized she liked what she was doing and wanted to become a license practical nurse. She went to Richmond for a year when I was in eighth grade and got her LP license. Dad was a painter, chauffer, and baker and that was how he earned money to provide for the family.

We saw Colored signs and such when children. But when we needed bread or anything, we went to Mr. Coles. There were two theaters in town — Lee and The State. Black people could go to the Lee, but sat in the balcony, in many States referred to as 'The Crow's Nest.' Black folk couldn't go in The State Theater.

When the walk-out occurred, I was in second grade. My mom was close friends with James and Margaret Brown a family on Hill Street. They had three sons: Phillip, Alphonso and Herbert. Phillip was in the walk-out, the other two boys were in the lower grades. I can remember the adults talking about the walk-out.

I remember when at middle school we had May Day and would wrap the May Pole. My parents allowed us to go to football games and such. My brother was old enough to drive, but we could not date.

I went to the new high school in tenth grade. I was involved in Home Economics, Art classes and basketball. I remember in May 1959 Coach Malloy told us to clean our lockers out because no one was sure what would happen in the fall. Under normal circumstance we would practice and play during the summer and would have left our things in the lockers.

At this time the Farmville Reading Room was the only library available to Black children. The Reading Room was located in the basement of Beulah African Methodist Episcopal Church. The books were donated by The Home Demonstration Clubs through the Virginia State College Extension.

During the summer, Reverend Alexander I. Dunlap and Reverend Griffin tried to figure out what would happen with the high school seniors, if indeed the schools didn't open in the fall. They wanted to take care of the seniors and then the juniors. When the schools didn't open in September, they got with Kittrell College, in North Carolina. I was in the motorcade that left Farmville on September 14. My dad drove and in the car were Mom, Ronnie and me. None of the students that went to Kittrell were chosen or handpicked, but you could go. I went as a junior. My brother Ronald was a senior. My cousin Alfred Redd was a junior.

The student population in the high school department at Kittrell was very small. The news reached home that there was space available at the campus. With room available, other students from Prince Edward County came. Aunt Martha (Ward Smith), my father's sister, said she wanted her children to go to Kittrell. Aunt Martha's husband, Uncle Reginald, worked at Hampden Sydney in the dorms. After we were at Kittrell College a while, two or three weeks at the most, my cousin Ralph Smith joined us.

Life at Kittrell was interesting. Here we high school students were on a campus with college students. There was a library, girls' dorm and a boys' dorm. Just before we arrived, the high school department was re-accredited. There were only three other high school students there who were not from Prince Edward County. The college faculty taught us.

We always looked forward to the care-packages that came on Monday or Tuesday from home. Reverend Dunlap was our weekly link to home. He received all the packages from our parents on Sunday evening and brought them to us on Monday or Tuesday. He would drive up to the girls' dorm first or sometimes the boys' dorm first and everyone would gather around to see what our parents had sent us from home by him. We shared with each other. Some people didn't get anything from home sometime. We had no money, all of your treats, candy, toiletries, personal items, etc. was in your care package. Parents would send new clothes by him.

My older brother Gerald was a freshman at Saint Paul's College on a football scholarship, when Ronnie and I were at Kittrell. When the tar-paper shacks were built, my parents refused to let my older brother Gerald Ward be a student and sit in the shacks. They sent him to Washington to live with Aunt Thelma. He became home-sick and returned home. After graduating from Saint Paul's College, Gerald joined the Air Force and retired as a Major.

My sister Betty Jean went to our grandparents in Nottoway County. She attended Foster High School in Nottoway County because granddaddy owned land in that county. I can't tell Betty Jean's story because I was away from home and there is so much that happened at home that I learned about in later adult years.

Ronnie, Alfred and Ralph played football on the Kittrell High School team. We had a normal high school year. We were not separated from the other students on the campus.

Ms. Anna Johnson, who was on the faculty, was the student advisor for the juniors.

We wanted everything to be as close to high school as possible. The Prince Edward County students at Kittrell College had a Junior–Senior Prom. We approached the administration and told them we wanted to have a Junior–Senior Prom because if we were at home would have one. We told our relatives and our parents sent us the dresses or gowns. I don't know where we got the money from to sponsor the prom; that escapes me. We had a Hawaiian theme. We had the pineapples, palm trees, etc. Remember there were many of us, juniors and seniors, and we had made friends with the colleges boys and the high school students who were there when we arrived; so, eighty plus students attended the prom and there were chaperons.

Ms. Anna Johnson helped us set up the Junior–Senior Prom. Ronnie graduated from Kittrell High School in the spring of 1960 and so did Charles Taylor who was the senior class president for the Moton students.

The commencement ceremony was held outside, and all the families came. Yes, all the families of the graduating seniors came down. We made our stay at Kittrell meaningful. We didn't miss anything but missed the setting where under ordinary circumstances the prom and graduation would have been held.

In the summer of 1960 the American Friends Service Committee came to Farmville and students were invited to go away and return to school. Being adventurous I said I wanted to go. My only question to my parents was: "Will you be there for my graduation?" They said yes.

Meetings were held at First Baptist Church and information was shared about the two programs, the Friends program and the Kittrell College program.

Some students went to Kittrell for the first time the fall of 1960. Many who attended the previous year returned for their senior year.

In August 1960 I went to Yellow Springs, Ohio, with David Patterson, Jr., eighth grade; his sister Kathryn, tenth grade; Sam Taylor, (deceased) twelfth grade; Henry Cavares, ninth grade; and Frank Earley. I'm unsure what grade Frank was in. There were six of us the first year at Yellow Springs.

We attended Bryan High School. I think all of the teachers were White except for one, the P E teacher who was Black. The town's people were very nice. The Antioch chapter of the NAACP provided us bicycles to get around town.

I lived with a White Quaker family, Phillip and Frankie Ruopp. They had four children: Julie, Rebecca, Charles and Douglas. Phillip taught at Antioch College and would always have faculty and students at the house.

I graduated from Bryan High the spring 1961. Daddy, Mom, and Betty Jean came to my graduation. Gerald was in the Air Force and Ronnie in the Navy at this time. I entered Bennett College in Greensboro, North Carolina, August 1961. I learned about Bennett when I was at Kittrell. I was accepted at Hampton Institute, and so was my cousin Alfred. But my mind was made up about Bennett College. I majored in Home Economics. During the summers, I worked in New York and in Connecticut one summer.

Ralph went to Bera the fall of 1961 with the first group that entered the high school department there. I think I drove him once to Bera while I was at Bennett. It was an interesting place. The work force was amazing. They made brooms and things for the hearth or fire place. I believe I was on my way to Yellow Springs to visit and dropped him off.

When I finished Bennett College, I went to Clinton in Sampson County, North Carolina, and worked as a Home Economics Extension Agent. I returned to Virginia and continued to work as a Home Agent.

I am married to Samuel Mosley and we have two children, Kim and Sam; four grandchildren: Phillip, Samantha, Kiran, and Nikhil. The children and grandchildren live in Washington, D.C.

I retired in 1996 and as of this day, March 25, 2010, I am a volunteer for various groups working eight hours a day. I give my time to the YWCA, Legacy Museum of African American History, Central Health Foundation Committee to raise funds for free mammograms, Campbell NAACP, and I do HIV awareness through an HIV coalition.

I received a Master's Degree in Adult Education from Virginia Tech in 1976. We received our Moton High School Honorary Degree in 2003.

I will arrange for an interview with Betty Jean. She can tell her story and about the demonstrations in Farmville.

———

BETTY JEAN WARD BERRYMAN

I was born November 15, 1945, in Farmville. I was the fourth child in the family. I started school at Mary E. Branch Elementary School No. 1. I went first to fifth grades there. In the sixth grade I went to Mary E. Branch No. 2. The old Moton High School (which at the time of this interview, April 17, 2010, is the Museum) housed sixth and seventh grades because the new high school was on the outskirts of town with eighth through twelfth grades. My sixth grade teacher was Mrs. Hazel Jackson. We had to say a Bible verse every morning. In seventh grade my homeroom teacher was Mrs. Kelly. We had a homeroom teacher because we changed classes and went to different teachers for different subjects. Mrs. Kelly came from Massachusetts. I can't remember her first name, but we used to call her Wildcat Kelly because she was so strict. Our principal was L. L. Hall. He used to psyche us up telling us 'we were going to heaven.' (Betty Jean laughs.) He would say: "You all better straighten up because you are going to heaven." Mr. Hall meant we were leaving the junior high school in the spring of the year and would enter eighth grade at Moton High School in the fall. He called Moton High heaven and those of us in seventh grade were truly excited about 'going to heaven' the next school year. In September 1959 we didn't go to heaven.

I remember my mother and father talking about the schools not opening, but no one really believed it. We used to play on the play-ground at Branch No. 1 during the summer. We were playing on the grounds at Branch No. 1 one day and a man said 'you all can't play here this is private property.' The chain was already up. This was during the summer.

Reverend Dunlap got with the people at Kittrell and my sister Phyllistine and my brother Ronnie went there. I had an older brother who was at Saint Paul's College. I was the baby and my parents would not let me go away. There were many parents that refused and would not send their children away to school.

Mama was clear that I was going somewhere for school, but not far away. My mother's sisters and brothers would gather at my maternal Grandma and Grandpa's on Sundays and the subject was discussed. Granddaddy said: "I have land in Amelia and Nottoway." He lived at a crossway. He could come out of his house turn one way or the other and step into Prince Edward County, Amelia County or Nottoway County, and he owned land in all three counties.

My parents discussed the matter at home for some time and the decision was made. I was sent to Nottoway to live with my grandparents. These were my mother's parents, Willie and Betty Thompson.

I was in eighth grade and attended Luther H. Foster High School. The first day of school I had to get on the bus. I had never been on a school bus because I always walked from home to school. I didn't know anyone on the bus and had to ride for an hour.

I knew the principal at the school Mr. Joseph Pervall. He knew I was coming and asked the teachers to help me along. His wife was Mrs. LaVerne Pervall, and she was well known and was into some of everything. I met a girl named Barbara Gills. She said: "Oh, you're the new student." She was in ninth grade. Everyone knew a new student was coming. Then I met Clarice Winn and we became best friends.

I looked forward to coming home on the weekends, but most of my Farmville friends were gone. So, when I came to Farmville on the weekend, I just sat at home.

With your brothers and sister gone, it was different. You didn't have your sister and brothers home anymore to fight with.

Families moved away. The Madison family went to Maryland, but Roger was sent to a school for boys in Powhatan, Virginia. I believe he started at Saint Emma Military Academy the fall of 1959.

The Rawlins family moved. Mrs. Connie Rawlins taught in Charlottesville. Dr. and Mrs. Rawlins had one son, Albert. I think Albert was a junior when the schools were closed. The Rawlins had three older daughters. Two of the girls, Ivy and Sylvia, were out of school when the closing took place. Shirley, the next girl went to Saint Francis Private School in Powhatan during the closure. Saint Francis was an all girls' school. I used to play with the Rawlins children. Dr. Rawlins remained in Farmville and carried on his practice.

Irene Hamilton also went to Saint Francis.

Roger Madison went to the academy for one year and then he joined his family in Maryland.

On holidays it was exciting because you got to see many people who came home for Christmas. But once you leave home, when you return it is never the same.

After two years and the public schools remained closed, people just went on away.

In the third year of the closure Gwendolyn Lancaster (Brooks) went to Massachusetts to live with her aunt.

Annette Taylor, her mother and father were separated,

but she and her mother moved to New York with the father, so Annette could finish school. Annette is deceased.

Ernestine Lane (Harris), she stayed out of school one or two years, I know she stayed out one year. She went to Norfolk to live with a family. An organization made the arrangements for her to live with the family.

My baby sister was born, and my mother was working. I was now old enough to get my driver's license. The third year the schools were closed I started living at home again and drove to my grandparents each day and taking Angela. I would drive to my grandparents in Nottoway County and take my baby sister to Grandma and then I would wait an hour for the bus. After school, I rode the bus back to Grandma's and then I drove us back to Farmville.

In 1963 Reverend Goodwin Douglas a young Black man that worked at Beulah AME Church in Farmville made his presence felt in the county. Douglas was a native of the Islands. We used to call him Goody. He came from down South somewhere, I can't remember which state. He was out of college at this time. The Methodist hierarchy sent him to Beulah African Methodist Episcopal Church in Farmville after Reverend Dunlap left. I think Reverend Dunlap went to North Carolina because he had ties to Kittrelll College.

Douglas got some young people together and talked to them about demonstrating. I remember the first meeting we had at Beulah. Reverend Griffin and Reverend Samuel Williams were there. Reverend Douglas said some SNCC workers were coming to town to teach us how to march, what to do and what not to do. We were so excited at this first meeting until we wanted to go out that night and march, but Douglas said we couldn't march because we were not ready. We were so anxious and pleaded so hard that he allowed us to go out that evening. We went to the College Shoppe Restaurant which was for the White college students at Longwood. We could go in to buy something any time but had to leave after making the purchase. We went to the College Shoppe that night. A Black man named Willie used to mop the floors there. I can't remember Mr. Willie's last name, but when he looked up and saw us he dropped his mop and said:

"Wha' y'all doin' in here?" (Betty Jean started laughing, imitating Mr. Willie.)

"We want to be served!" we said.

The manager came and said: "You all better get out'a here. I'm going to call the police if you don't."

"We want to be served," we said. Reverend Griffin was there, and the manager asked him to please take us out. The manager knew Reverend Griffin.

Griffin said: "I can't make them leave."

"Just take them out for tonight," the man said. He called the police, they came and pleaded with Griffin and with us. They said it was getting late and it was, so we left.

The next day we went to Crute's Drugstore on Main Street. They had counter seats also. The man said: "You all can't come in here, if you do we'll call the police."

We went to a store and they had taken up the seats. There was no place for us to sit and request service.

SNCC made it to town. College students came here the summer of 1963. SNCC took us to the property of Barbara Johns' father and trained us in an open area. SNCC taught us how to protect ourselves. We went through drills. If water was sprayed on us, we were taught what to do. If the dogs were put on you, we were taught how to respond.

Chapels was another café on South Main. They saw us coming one day and locked the door.

By this time, we had the town squirming. The buzz of the town was that the Black folk were trying to take over. We wanted to march through town, but they said we needed a permit. Reverend Griffin got a permit.

Some businesses threatened to fire Black workers if they allowed their children to continue demonstrating and take no action. The manager at Taylor Manufacturing Company said: "If you don't get your children off the streets, you are going to lose your job."

Some parents were fired from their jobs, but you don't hear anything about that.

It was decided that one Sunday morning we would integrate the churches. When we left home that Sunday morning, we told our parents: 'If they call you don't come and get us out of jail.' We were divided into groups. The people knew we were coming. Dr. Moss had invited a group to come and sit with him at his church. My group went to Farmville Baptist Church. A man named Mr. Smith who ran a store, he met us and said:

"You all go on back down the street. You have churches."

They called the cops. When the cops came, we just fell and sat down on the ground. The police didn't know what to do when they arrived.

"You all need to move." We did not. They called for backup.

There were so many of us until the police didn't have enough vehicles to transport us from all the White churches in town. They called the fire department and local citizens to transport us in their private automobiles from the different White churches where groups were.

There was a man named Phillip Gay, I rode in his car. I was heavy, I was always on the chubby side, (Betty Jean chuckles) and it took about four of them to put me in his car. Gay owned a junk yard on the edge of town and was the fire chief of the Farmville Volunteer Fire Department for many years. I rode in his station wagon. I was the only person in the station wagon. Some of the people probably were marched or escorted to the courthouse because it was so close to the church.

When the word got out that we had been arrested, many parents came to the jail.

Reverend Williams, Frances Hayes and Grace Poindexter were separated from the rest of us. Frances and Grace had just turned eighteen and were handled as adults. They put all the rest of us in the courtroom at the courthouse, which was nearby. They couldn't lock us up because we were under age. Samuel Williams, Frances and Grace were taken to a jail in Lunenburg County.

My father bought a new 1960 Plymouth or 1962. It was a 1960s early model car and brand new off the lot. I would pick up the students for SNCC training sessions in Darlington Heights. When the protest period ended, the car was leaning to one side. (Betty Jean held her right arm up and tilted her hand to one side and laughed.) The springs had broken. Daddy was a little upset. (She is still laughing.)

When the Free School opened, I didn't want to leave the friends I had made at Luther H. Foster, but I decided to come back home.

Everyone was excited about the Free School opening, but when we got there you didn't have your same friends.

In the third year of the closure Gwendolyn Lancaster (Brooks), who went to Massachusetts to live with her aunt, didn't return when the Free School opened. She stayed in Massachusetts and graduated.

Two males that had been in the military and separated returned home and enrolled in the Free School. They were in the senior class with me. Had the schools not been closed, one of the boys would have actually graduated in the May 1960 with Ronnie, my older brother who graduated from Kittrell High School in the Class of 1960.

Free School was nice. We took field trips. One weekend we went to Georgetown in the Washington, D. C. area and stayed with families. This was the senior class trip and it was really nice.

Robert Kennedy visited the Free School. The Attorney General gave every student in the senior class a gift. Each member of the senior class was given a small replica of the PT boat that his brother John F. Kennedy served on when in the Navy.

Roger Madison and I were the only two seniors in the Free School Class of 1964 that graduated on time. He and I went to public school all the way together. When the Prince Edward County public schools were closed, I went to school at Luther H. Foster for four years and to the Free School in my senior year. Roger went to school out of the county for four years, and when the Free School opened his mother brought the family back to Farmville. Had the schools not been closed, this would still have been our year to graduate.

After graduating, I went to Virginia State College and majored in Elementary Education. I returned to the area and taught in Charlotte Court House for four years and then I went to Cumberland County. I taught in Cumberland County for twenty years.

In later years my husband collected junk and sold to Gay. Once in the early 1980s Gay gave a party for his employees and Oscar attended and took me. I told Oscar I wanted to remind Gay of that day at Farmville Baptist Church, but he said: "You better not."

Around 1998 or 1999 our pastor, Jim Ashton, pastor of First Baptist Church, and the pastor of Farmville Baptist Church had a joint service at the latter church. That was the first time I had been back to the church since the summer of 1963.

We had a discussion in the fall of 2009 at Hampden Sydney and one gentleman said when he went away to live with a family in a sponsorship program his experience was horrible. He was sent to a family by the Quakers, but they had to move him. I never knew that some of the students in that program had miserable experiences. I always thought because my sister Phyllistine had a good experience, so did all the other students.

It has been over fifty years since the schools closed in September 1959, but you always wonder — what if? What if the schools had never been closed? There is always that cloud over you. Everything would have been different — who you married, your chosen vocation for life, some people never would have left the county had not the schools been closed.

Some people never went back to school. I was talking to a man a couple of years ago and he was in his sixties. He said he quit school in second grade and never went back. He told me his wife taught him how read.

Clarice Winn who I met when I first went to Luther H. Foster, she and I remained best friends until she passed last year, 2009.

Notes from the Editor: After Betty Jean finished sharing her reflections, the Editor asked a few questions for his benefit. Feeling certain she did not know Mrs. Martha Forrester, the Editor asked:

"Did you know Mrs. Clark, the daughter of Mrs. Martha Forrester?"

Mrs. Clark was already an old woman when I became acquainted with her. Mrs. Clark's husband owned a business. My great grandma, Margaret Ward, was one of the founding members of the Forrester Council of Women here in Farmville. When I joined the group around 2008 and saw an original photograph of the founding members, I saw a photograph of my great grandmother for the first time. Emily Ward, my father's mother, was also a part of the Council. My father was born in 1921 and his mother, Emily, died when he was eight. His grandmother, Margaret raised him. My grandmother was in the Council several years before her death. Mrs. Clark, Mrs. Forrester's daughter, was a part of the Council.

Mrs. Forrester and her group were responsible for building Branch No. 1. There was a high school upstairs and elementary classes down stairs. Before this school was built, there was some small building for students. Mrs. Kate Wiley, I believe, became the president after Mrs. Forrester.

Preparing to leave the house, somehow Betty Jean and the Editor ended up talking about the late Ethel Watkins Wilson Fisher. The Editor shared with Betty Jean that Mrs. Fisher told him about her role as the treasurer who paid the teachers that came to Prince Edward County and taught students during the summer beginning in 1961. Betty Jean said:

I remember one summer, 1960 or 1961, two male teachers stayed with us. My daddy went to Vermont that summer to work at a White college and that made room for the two male teachers. But I don't remember Mama being paid.

———

ETHEL POINDEXTER FOSTER

I was born in Farmville at 209 Grove Street, to Lucy Anna McDaniel Johnson Poindexter and Edward James Poindexter. I had an older sister and older brother.

I went to school at Mary E. Branch No. 1. Mrs. Ethel Wilson taught me there in the fifth grade. In the sixth grade I was at Mary E. Branch No. 2 and my teacher was Mrs. Winston (in later years she became a West by marriage). When the schools were closed, I had been promoted to the seventh grade.

My sister Grace and I missed school the first year of the closing. Grace has always been busy. At one time she wanted to be a nurse and then she wanted to be a teacher. Grace was about two years ahead of me.

During the first year of the closing of the schools, Grace tutored me. She also tutored a neighborhood girl named Gwendolyn Lancaster (Brooks).

My older sister Mary Johnson (Mariner) was married to a military man. His name was James W. Mariner, from Norfolk, Virginia. He was stationed at Langley Air Force Base in Hampton, Virginia. Grace and I went and lived with them during the 1960-1961 school year. This was the second year the schools were closed in Prince Edward County. We were a military family for a while. (Ethel chuckles.)

Mary and James had four children of their own: Debra Mariner (Allsop), Denise Mariner, Ronald James Mariner (deceased) and Dianne Mariner (Nash). Debbie, Denise and Ronald were in elementary school. Dianne, I believe, was about two or three years old at this time. Grace and I attended James Weldon Johnson High School in York County.

We lived with James and Mary for two years. My brother-in-law got orders to go to Japan and the family prepared to move. James took the family to Japan. Grace and I had to return to Farmville.

We had an aunt, my mother's baby sister, who lived in Appomattox, Virginia. Her name was Vermont McDaniel Patterson. Her husband was Vincent Patterson, Sr. Aunt Ver and Uncle Duke (we called him Uncle Duke) had three boys. Their names were Vincent, Jr., Harold, and George.

My father owned property in Appomattox and that allowed us to enroll in school in that county for the 1962-1963 school year. Grace and I had to actually live in the county two nights a week in order to attend school and not be dismissed. The two nights qualified us to remain in the Appomattox County school system.

Our family didn't move from Farmville to Appomattox. Grace and I rotated nights. The night I stayed with Aunt Ver and Uncle Duke in Appomattox Grace was at home in Farmville, and the night she stayed in Appomattox I was at home in Farmville.

Mrs. Ruth Watkins was a school teacher who lived in Farmville but taught in Appomattox County and we would ride with her. Mrs. Watkins had three girls and a boy. They were younger than Grace and I. All of us rode with her. Whoever night it was to stay in Appomattox, Mrs. Watkins would drop us off at Aunt Ver's house and bring the other person on to Farmville.

We attended Carver-Price High School. We went there the 1962-1963 school year.

When the Free School Association opened, Grace and I enrolled. Grace was a senior and I was a sophomore.

There were 35 graduates in the Class of 1966 when I graduated.

———

GRACE POINDEXTER FORREST

I was born in Farmville, Virginia, right in the town of Farmville, conveniently located to Southside Community Hospital, Longwood College, which now is Longwood University, the Norfolk and Western Railroad station and the Greyhound Bus station.

My parents were Edward and Lucy McDaniel Poindexter. Both of them migrated to Farmville, Mama from Appomattox and Daddy from the town of Forest in Bedford County.

My parents were not educated per-se. My father completed seventh grade and Mama completed the third grade; but they always wanted the best for their children. My family consisted of an older sister named Mary and an older brother named Warren and my baby sister Ethel.

I grew up as any other child in that day and time. We were happy and lived in a predominately White neighborhood. The judge of the county, the chief of police, White doctors, the mayor, and my next door neighbor's husband who was a barber, and all these were White folks, we lived in close proximity. My family lived close to the college which probably accounted for the large number of White professionals in the neighborhood.

I grew up a happy girl with family and friends, the church being the center of our lives. We attended First Baptist Church, where Reverend L. Francis Griffin was the pastor.

I can remember my parents very early discussing the school situation. When I say early, I mean in the early 1950s. I remember my father saying to Mama one day: "Did you know the students walked out of Robert Moton High School?" "Who knew about it?" Mama asked. "Just the students for the most part," Daddy replied. I remember Mom saying something like: "What's going to happen?" "I pray it will be something good and peaceful," Daddy said.

Some of the high school students were housed in tar-paper shacks which contributed to the walk-out. My brother Warren attended classes in the tar-paper shacks but graduated before the walk-out. A new high school was built in 1953.

I remember in 1954 hearing my parents talking about the Supreme Court decision. I heard the conversations but didn't realize the forthcoming impact.

I attended Mary E. Branch No. 1 and No. 2. At Branch No. 1 I attended first to fifth grades, and at Branch No. 2 I attended sixth and seventh grades. (Branch No. 2 today is the Museum.)

I had an excellent principal all the way through, Mr. L. L. Hall. I loved Mr. Hall. His oldest daughter and I were in school together. The teachers were great. In first grade I had Mrs. Ellen Bigger. Mrs. Julian Anderson was my second grade teacher. In the third, fourth and fifth grades I had the best teacher, and I don't want to be prejudice, but she inspired me, she was a second mother, her name was Mrs. Ethel Watkins Wilson. In the sixth grade I had Mrs. Kelly from Massachusetts. Mrs. Reba West was my seventh grade instructor. I completed seventh grade at Branch No. 2 and then I went to the high school and completed eighth grade.

Again, I heard my parents discussing the school situation. If I remember correctly, my father said: "It seems there will be no school in Prince Edward for the 1959 school year." I could tell they were concerned, but it was too late to do anything.

My sister Mary and her husband James 'Jimmy' Mariner had just come from California to Langley Air Force Base, in

Hampton, Virginia. It was too early for Mama to say anything to them or them to say anything to Mama.

My sister Ethel and I did not attend school the first year of the closure. Mom taught Ethel how to embroider and taught me to crochet. She would read to us to make sure we were keeping up with our work as much as possible, despite her limited education. Dad worked with us to keep us occupied and not get into trouble.

In the meantime, I decided I wanted to do something. I would set up a bunch of chairs in the dining room and teach the chairs. My mother looked at me, but she never frowned. I would have to say the inspiration came from God to teach my sister Ethel and my neighbor Gwendolyn Lancaster. I taught them by rote, recalling the teaching methodology I witnessed the years I was in public school. I imitated all I had seen in my former teachers. I had books that my parents had purchased, students had to purchase textbooks in that day; books were not given to the students. I had all of my seventh and eighth grade books at home. I used the seventh grade books with Ethel and the eighth grade books with Gwen.

Gwen had passed to the eighth grade I believe. Gwen's mother was a domestic worker and her father was employed at Buffalo Shook. Gwen was an only child.

Ethel had passed to the seventh grade.

Sometime during the first year of the school closure Reverend Griffin and some of the teachers that did not go away and teach decided to have Training Centers for the students. The sites were not called schools because that would have defeated the Prince Edward County desegregation case already in the courts.

Ethel and I went to the center at First Baptist Church

where Mrs. Ethel Watkins Wilson was the teacher. We were tutored basically in math and reading.

During this time, Mama wanted me to learn to play the piano. I could play a little by ear. Mrs. Ethel Wilson took me in and taught me the fundamentals of music for about six months. Mrs. Wilson was the musician at her church.

At the end of the school year my sister Mary and her husband decided that if the schools remained closed they would take us in, so we could attend school during the 1960-1961 academic year. Mary and Jimmy lived off the military installation. They lived in York County. Mary and Jimmy had four children. The school age children went to the Department of Defense School for military dependents. Since Ethel and I were not legal dependents of Mary and Jimmy, we could not attend the school. We were enrolled at James Weldon Johnson High School in York County.

I am sure Mary and Jimmy explained our situation to the principal, Mr. J. Murray Brooks. The school was very small, and Ethel and I were readily taken in.

In the summer of 1961 an organization offered to send Ethel and me away. I believe they offered to send us to New Jersey, but Mom and Dad were totally against it. Mama said she wanted us with blood relatives.

We returned to Mary and Jimmy and were enrolled at James Weldon Johnson High School for a second year. I believe Mr. Brooks was the principal both years and shielded us. There were no other Prince Edward County students at the school.

In 1962 Jimmy was transferred to Japan. When Mom and Dad found out about the transfer, Mama said: "There is one thing I know we can do. We can send you all to Appomattox." Daddy owned a small piece of property in Appomattox.

Mrs. Mozella Price was the supervisor for Black schools in Appomattox County. Mama and Dad talked to her. Mrs. Price said: "I will take them in, and if I had known they were going to miss the first year I would have taken them then."

My mother's baby sister (Vermont) and her husband Vincent (called Duke) took us into their home for the 1962-1963 school year. Ethel and I were enrolled at Carver–Price High School. Aunt Ver and Uncle Duke had three boys, Vincent, Jr., Harold, and George.

Aunt Ver treated Ethel and I like her children.

Ethel and Aunt Ver's sons were all about the same age. When Ethel and I stayed in Appomattox, Aunt Ver had a special arrangement to accommodate us. Aunt Ver would send her three boys to an older uncle, Uncle Larkin, who lived hardly a quarter of a mile away. Uncle Larkin (Larkin McDaniel) was my grandfather's brother. Vincent, Jr., Harold, and George lived with Uncle Larkin, but they took their meals at home. Aunt Ver washed their clothes and everything else that was needed.

Sometimes we would commute from Farmville to Appomattox to school because I had a driver's license. We had an old car, but my parents didn't trust it. Dad was always putting the car in the shop. Dad purchased a used car, a 1954 Star Chief, Pontiac. I was the driver. Some days we rode with Mrs. Ruth Watkins.

Ruth Watkins was a teacher in Appomattox but lived in Farmville. I would inform her when I had activities after school and would drive on those days. I didn't miss one day of school that year.

I met Lloyd Forrest, Jr. during the school year.

Note from the Editor: Lloyd was sitting at a nearby table during the interview.

Lloyd: "I actually invited her to my prom, since I was a senior. After that school year, I did not see Grace again for two years."

Lloyd's sister told me that her brother liked me. I asked her: 'Who is your brother?' She told me Lloyd Forrest.

Mama and Ethel drove me to Aunt Vermont's and Lloyd came by and picked me up for the prom.

After the prom, I learned that Lloyd and some of his friends were going to Lynchburg to a dance. A well known artist, I think it was James Brown, was appearing, but Lloyd wouldn't take me, saying: "I promised your mother I would have you back at your Aunt Ver's after the prom."

Mama sat with Aunt Ver until the prom was over. When I returned to the house, Mama, Ethel and I drove back to Farmville.

I worked hard in all the schools I attended.

In the eighth grade I was a member of the Honor Society at Moton High School, and in ninth and tenth grades at James Weldon Johnson High School and the eleventh grade at Carver–Price High School. I was in the Dramatics Club at Carver–Price. I didn't play any sports.

Note from the Editor: Grace took a break from sharing her story and prepared lunch. While she was in the kitchen, Lloyd Forrest shared an interesting account.

"When I was in the ninth grade, this was the 1959-1960 school year, at Carver–Price High School and the first year of the closing of the schools in Prince Edward County, about 10:00 o'clock one morning the principal, Mr. Richard E. Patrick, called out the names of Prince Edward County students."

"Did he call their names over the loud speaker?" the Editor asked.

"No, he came to classrooms and called out the names. He

came to my class and called out some names. In the end, he had rounded up twenty or more students to dismiss from school. We had no idea what was going on or why new students were flocking to our school. We were young and knew nothing of the politics. I remember a lot of the girls started crying that morning when the principal was gathering up the Prince Edward County students."

After lunch, Grace resumed her story.

At the end of the 1962-1963 school year Mom and Dad heard that some sort of school might open in Prince Edward County, not the public schools. I was absolutely elated. I was tired traveling back and forth.

There were people outside the county interested in the Prince Edward County situation. We had what was known as public demonstrations. Ethel and I worked very hard with the Civil Rights program along with Reverend Griffin. Under his leadership and guidance, he led the public protests with the support of other young people from other States.

We heard about how protesters in Danville, Virginia, Wilmington, North Carolina, and other locations were being injured in demonstrations. The SNCC workers that came to Farmville taught us how to protect ourselves in a public forum and not suffer injuries.

The protesting led to the hiring of the first Black female as a clerk in a store in Prince Edward County. I am sure it was a grocery store that hired the lady, but I can't recall which one.

We protested or picketed the College Shoppe on Main Street. I was arrested at the College Shoppe. Mom used to prepare the meals or lunches for us to eat when we took a break and came back to the church to rest and refresh ourselves.

Many of us were arrested one Sunday when we tried to enter White churches in Farmville and join in the worship services. The people who were under age or considered juveniles were taken to the courthouse. They could not be put in jail cells. I was put in a jail cell. I always tell people 'You don't want to go to jail, if you can help it. When that cell door slams and you are locked in, that is a helpless feeling.'

Mom was upset when Ethel was arrested and said to the judge at the hearing: "I don't understand, you all are supposed to be Christian and want to arrest these children for wanting to come to church." Mom was very outspoken when she wanted to be. If she liked you, she liked you; if she did not like you, she did not like you.

Prior to the opening of the Free School many of us went to the March on Washington. I had heard a lot about Dr. King and to hear his speech which was full of vitality inspired me tremendously.

After the Free School Association was announced, Mrs. Minnie Miller arranged for Ethel and me to work with the new teachers who arrived in the county prior to opening day. Mrs. Miller was a graduate of Hampton Institute and was a Home Economics teacher for several years. She had worked with Ethel and I on some of the social graces of life, entertaining, setting up tables, serving, which side of the person to serve on and which side not to serve on. She worked very hard with us. The leadership connected with the Free School Association wanted some dependable young helpers from the local area. That was how Ethel and I ended up assisting during the pre-opening phase.

I think we were tested for placement prior to the opening of the Free School Association.

With the opening of the Free School Association, this was a very interesting year. I say interesting because along with our school work, we had people coming to interview us all the time, news journalists, asking—'How did you feel when the schools were closed?' and other similar questions.

I was in a graduating class of 23 (twenty-three) and what was so interesting was that only a few of us were classmates before the closing of the schools. Others were one or two years behind us before the closing of the public schools but tested out at the twelfth grade level when the Free School opened. They caught up with us!

I had a chance to meet Robert Kennedy in May 1964 when he visited the Free School Association. The Attorney General gave me a small book which he autographed. The book was entitled *That Special Grace* by Benjamin Bradlee. It was a book about President John F. Kennedy.

My senior year was a very good year because I could see the light at the end of the tunnel. No, let me rephrase that—I could see God's light at the end of tunnel.

When I graduated in June 1964, I made an academic circle, graduating from the same school where I started in the 1958-1959 school year.

I applied to several colleges: Longwood College, they turned me down flat. I had an application from Virginia State College but did not want to go that far away. Saint Paul's was my choice. It was small, church related, and I felt I needed that after almost having gone around the world in the last four years. I entered Saint Paul's College in August 1964. I majored in Elementary Education and graduated in 1968, Cum Laude, after all the struggles.

When the Virginia Teachers Association (the Black association) and the Virginia Education Association (the White association) merged, I was elected the first Black student to serve as member-at-large of the Virginia Education Association.

When I graduated from Saint Paul's College, I returned

to Prince Edward County. I felt that I had to return, I felt I owed the young people something. I was assigned to the sixth grade teaching Language Arts. I actually had students who were sixteen and seventeen years old in my sixth grade class I taught. I taught at Worsham Elementary School for one year.

Lloyd came to visit me at Saint Paul's in the spring of 1965. We were married on December 21, 1968. Lloyd permitted me to fulfill my commitment in Prince Edward County and at the end of the year I applied to the Appomattox school district and was accepted to teach at Appomattox Elementary School.

The public schools were fully integrated around 1969 or 1970. I was transferred to Appomattox Intermediate School that housed grades five thru nine. I taught fifth, sixth and seventh grades.

Around 1974 the Middle School concept came into being and I was transferred to the middle school where I taught seventh and eighth grades. Later I taught seventh and eighth grade English. I retired on December 21, 2005. Thirty-five years and four months in Appomattox County and one year in the Prince Edward County schools.

In 1972 we were blessed with a daughter, Lloliza LuMar; she is named after my husband's mother and my mother. Lloliza is a graduate of Lynchburg College with a degree in Early Childhood Education and licensed to teach grades NK (Nursery and Kindergarten) to fourth grade.

I taught Sunday School at Promise Baptist Church in Appomattox for thirty years. I have served as the director of VBS (Vacation Bible School) from 1985 to the present, (The date of this interview April 6, 2011).

For years I nor many of the other people affected by the

closing of the public schools in Prince Edward County could talk about it, but now I am sharing more and more. I have been invited and accepted invitations to address several groups in recent years and am glad I decided to put my reflections in writing.

———

JERRY 'MONSTER' SMITH

I am number eight of nine children. We lived in a three room house. Mama and Daddy had the living room. The first child Dorothy was born between 1936 and 1938. There was Dorothy, Eleanor, Gladys, Valarie, Bill, Marie, Carol, myself, and LaVerne. I think LaVerne was born in 1950.

I started school at Branch No. 1 and Mrs. Helen Bigger was my first grade teacher. I had Mrs. Alma Smith as a teacher in elementary school.

I had been promoted to the fifth grade when the schools were closed. I went to Hawkes School in Cumberland for a short time, about a month. All the work they were doing I had already done at Branch No. 1. I told my mother that I was re-peating work and I stopped attending Hawkes. Then I started going to the centers where you would sit down and read. I used to come down here sometimes. (Interview conducted in the basement of Beulah African Methodist Episcopal Church, Farmville, Virginia, Saturday afternoon, May 21, 2011.)

I will never forget Oscar Berryman and his encouraging words to me every day. Mama used to fix breakfast for Daddy every morning and I had to take it to him around 9:00 a. m. at Harris Cook Ford where he worked. Melvin Branch owned a restaurant, Reid's Café, he owned it. Melvin got the Richmond Times Dispatch newspaper each morning. He opened his restaurant at 6:00 a. m. He would read his paper and give it to me on the way back from delivering Daddy's breakfast. I would sit on the side of his café and read the Richmond Times Dispatch. Oscar Berryman came by every morning about the same time and would say to me: "Young man, read as much as you can."

This was how I kept up my reading skills the first year the schools were closed.

Daddy supplemented his income by delivering the New York Times, Philadelphia Inquirer, Washington Post and Richmond Times Dispatch on Sunday only. The papers would come to him on the Greyhound bus and he would pick them up at the Farmville bus station.

Daddy got me a job delivering newspapers. I started delivering the Richmond News Leader newspaper. I delivered the Richmond News Leader daily.

During the years of the closing of the schools, I read so many newspaper papers until I considered myself a little lawyer. In the Richmond News Leader there was a piece entitled A Point Of Law. It discussed various law issues. It gave insight on certain things and I read it every day. I never missed a day of reading it. I could always figure out a lot of little things. Children started asking me things, as I seemed knowledgeable to them. I gave them answers and advice as best I could. (Mr. Smith started laughing while telling about his days as a child lawyer.)

I would cut grass, paint, and do other odd jobs to earn money.

When the Free School opened, I took a test. They put me in the seventh grade. At the end of the year I took another test and was advanced to the ninth grade.

I have to say that I have been blessed, but I have to say that I have a lot of animosity. I cannot understand how the Federal Government allowed five men to do all that was done in this county.

———

ANTHONY A. FARLEY

I was born December 23, 1949, in Farmville to Alberta Farley. I started school at Mary Branch No. 1. I had passed to the fifth grade when the schools were closed. I went to school on what was supposed to be the first normal day of school. I heard that the schools wouldn't open, but I didn't believe it. We got to Branch No. 1 and saw the big chain and lock on the door. It was one of those old time bull-locks. It was the kind of lock that was put on the gate to keep cattle in or keep cattle out. My cousins walked up to the school that morning also: Wilbur Farley, Norman Grisin, Deloris Robinson, and another girl we called Lo Lo walked with us.

Mrs. Herndon was a teacher, she had a daughter and a son. She taught at Branch No. 1. She lived on Longwood Avenue, three houses down from us. At a later time, my brother Winfred and I went to see Mrs. Herndon. We didn't understand why the schools were closed. She tried to explain it to us, but it made no sense to us.

We went to classes in the basement of First Baptist Church and the Elks House. I attended all of the alternative schools.

When I asked my mother and others 'why can't I go to school?', all she would say was—'White people don't want you to go to school' and that was the only answer you got.

Some families left Farmville the second year of the closing, so their children could start school in September 1960.

My mama had two sisters Shirley Farley Parrand and Lillian Farley Robinson. Both lived in Farmville. Both of my aunts left Farmville after the first year of the closure, so their children could go to school.

Aunt Shirley had two sons and a daughter: George, Jackie (daughter) and Antroin (or Antwan). After about a year in Farmville, Aunt Shirley moved the family to Baltimore. Aunt Shirley's husband was in the military.

Aunt Lillian and Uncle Spencer had two girls, Deloris and Thomasina. Uncle Spencer worked in the boiler room at Longwood College. It was his job to put the coals in the boiler. Aunt Lillian took Deloris and Thomasina to Baltimore, so they would not miss a second year of school. Uncle Spencer had a job and couldn't leave Farmville.

When the Free School opened, that was one of the most exciting days of my life. It was like Easter Sunday. Everybody had their best clothes on. Your mama went out and bought the boys converse sneakers. The girls had on pretty white and pink dresses. We were gathered in the auditorium on the opening day. There were several guest speakers that day and everyone was excited.

But the next week things begin to change. We were told that we would be given tests to see what you had learned in the past four years; or if you didn't go to any classes to see what you remembered since school ended four years earlier. After the testing, some students were fourteen and in the third grade. Can you imagine being fourteen years old and in the third grade with your cousin who was eight years old? Many of the students couldn't handle it and they, the older students, started dropping out of school. They started dropping out like flies.

I tested out at the eighth grade level. I credit my testing abilities to the teachers that worked in the centers.

Uncle Spencer drank himself to death. He was never the same after Aunt Lillian took the girls and went to Baltimore. She wouldn't come back to Farmville. Thomasina was the oldest daughter. She had a nervous breakdown and died young. I believe she was around forty or in her forties when she died.

———

PAULINE ELIZABETH HOLMAN RANDOLPH

I was born in Prince Edward County in Farmville to Sherlock Samuel Holman and Bessie Brown Holman. Daddy was from Prince Edward and Mama was from North Carolina. They met on the Board Walk in Atlantic City. Daddy was working there, and Mama was visiting relatives.

I grew up on Race Street and attended Race Street Baptist Church. I joined Race Street Baptist at an early age. I am the oldest of six children, three girls and three boys. The birth order was Kate (Williams), Eddie Lee, George, Jean, and James. We always called Kate by the nickname Candy.

I started school at age six and my first teacher was Mrs. Bigger. I will never forget her. We had a dollhouse in the classroom. If you were a good student, you got to play in the dollhouse. I remember one day Mr. Hall came in the classroom, Mrs. Bigger asked me a question and I answered from inside the dollhouse and it startled Mr. Hall. He didn't know where the voice came from. (Pauline chuckles.)

Those of us who lived in Farmville were called town-kids and we had to walk to school. When the school buses passed us bringing the children from the rural sections, we always wondered why we could not ride the bus.

I went to Mary E. Branch No. 2 also. Then I entered eighth grade at the high school. I joined all the clubs I could join. I especially remember being in the Honor Roll Club. I was a Student Patrol and a student helper. The student helpers went to the office to assist or passed out flyers for students to take home and help with the various classrooms. I also was a Cheerleader.

1958-1959 was just a normal school year. I'm not sure how I found out the schools were not going to open. I know that at my house it was a lot of 'what are we going to do?' Eddie Lee said he was going to work. Daddy worked at a store named 'Crawley's Market' on Main Street. Eddie Lee started working there moving boxes and sweeping up.

That first week there was a lot of uncertainty and tears from me. Mama said let's go and talk to Grandma Esther. Grandma Esther, as we called her, lived just across the bridge in Cumberland County. We used to walk to her house all the time before the closing of the schools. She lived in Amostown. Mr. Amos, a white gentleman, owned all the land. My granddaddy, George Brown, worked for Mr. Amos for a while.

George Brown was Mama's daddy and Grandma Esther was his second wife. Mama and Daddy sent me, Candy and Jean to Grandma. I don't know how it was decided that only the girls would go to Granddaddy and Grandma. James was too young. Eddie Lee went to work. I can't remember exactly what George did. All the boys remained at home.

The first day of school the bus came, and we boarded. We had name tags around our necks with our address. Of course, being in twelfth grade I took my name tag off when I got on the bus, I was a senior. Before we left home, they told us be sure we knew Grandma Esther's address. We had no problems registering and everyone was helpful.

Being in a familiar household, Grandma and Grandpa's house, was beneficial. There were two aunts in the house. They were Mama's sisters named Shirley Brown and Mary Brown. Shirley and I were about the same age. She too was in her senior year. Aunt Mary was a bit older than the two of us.

I think with Cumberland County knowing the situation the administration at Luther P. Jackson didn't press the issue. It was a good school year, considering what had happened in Prince Edward County. I was the only senior at Luther P. Jackson that year from Prince Edward County. If there was a Junior-Senior Prom I didn't get to go.

When we came home on the weekends, we would work with James on his reading.

I remember the children from the Dean family in Farmville were at Luther P. Jackson High School the year I attended. I believe there were three girls and two boys in the family.

Mr. Brown was the custodian at Mary E. Branch. I believe his first name was Turner. Mr. Brown dated Ms. Penn who was a teacher when I was in elementary school. I don't know if she was there at the time the schools were closed. After the school closure, Mr. Brown became a contractor and built houses. I'm not sure if he returned after the schools reopened.

Some of the other students I recall that had also been promoted to the twelfth grade the year the schools were closed were: Roena Venable and I believe Adele Gibson. I'm not sure what happened to Adele. Elizabeth Cordell was a rising senior and she left the first year of the closure. Elizabeth and I started first grade together.

After my senior year at Luther P. Jackson, I returned home

and went to work. In June 1960 I married James Thomas Randolph of Cumberland County. Everyone knew him as J.T.

There is a group in Farmville called HOPE, directed by Reverend Kitty Smith and they do a senior prom. This outreach program was designed to touch people impacted by the school closing when teenagers and who never had a chance to go to a prom. They had one this year, 2011. It was in July, I believe. Today is September 8, so it was recently. The men put on their suits and ties and the ladies got dressed up. They sent limousines for some. Longwood University opened up their facilities and catered food, provided the music, the dance hall and everything.

GEORGE NOTICE HOLMAN

I was born September 12, 1945, in Farmville, in Prince Edward County, Virginia. The name I was given at birth was George Notice Holman. My grandfather was named George Notice Brown. He was my mother's father.

I started school at Mary E. Branch No. 1 when I was six years old. One of my elementary school teachers was Mrs. Helen Bigger and I remember her very well. I had Mrs. Ernestine Herndon and her sister Mrs. Ethel Wilson. Both were my teachers in elementary school and made an impression on me. Mrs. Herndon put me in a lot of plays and gave me exposure to a lot of things.

I left the elementary school and went across the street to the middle school in the sixth grade. When I was twelve years old, the Lord blessed me to win a corresponding art contest.

At that time an art school had an ad inside of a folding match box with an illustrated picture and the caption underneath the picture read—DRAW ME—to enter the contest. I drew it, sent in my drawing and won an entry in the contest. The company sent me some more specifics. The president of the art company I believe was Albert Dawn. One of the prominent artists on the board of Directors of the Art School was Normal Rockwell. I won a correspondence scholarship. They sent me three big books. The books talked about shadows, depth, symmetry and other fine points of art and drawing. The books taught all the finer dimensions of art. I became very enthused about art work. This was about a year or so before the schools were closed.

I don't remember the names of the teachers at the middle school, but I was at Branch No. 2 before the closure.

When school was to open in September 1959, I found out that school wasn't going to open. Then I sort of roamed around town for a while. When I was fourteen, my mother signed for me to get a work permit and I started working full time at that age.

I worked at a soda production company called the Nehi Bottling Company in Farmville. It was located on Third Street close to where the Farmville Post Office is today.

I worked at Nehi Bottling for a couple of years. When I was sixteen, I left home and went to Newark, New Jersey.

The first month in Newark I obtained a job at Remco Toy Factory in Harrison, New Jersey. When I went there, I told them I was eighteen and was hired the same morning. I stayed there two years.

When I actually turned eighteen, I received my draft notice and I returned home.

When I was home I went up to the high school and talked

to the principal. This was when the Free School was open. I took a standardized test and was put in the tenth grade. I didn't feel comfortable because I had not been in a classroom since the 1958-1959 school year. I attended for several months and then I quit.

I was inducted into the Army when I was twenty years old. After basic training and AIT, I went to Vietnam for one year. During that term, I volunteered for a second tour. I was allowed to come home and then I went back for a second tour. After my three year enlistment ended, I separated from the Army. I gained a lot of knowledge in the military. In the military I was given the opportunity to increase my learning.

In 1968 I got married. My wife and I had four children. I joined a Holiness Church in 1972 in Richmond, Virginia. In 1978 I helped a pastor start a church in Farmville. In 1985 I was given the position of Adult Sunday Teacher and I hold that position to this day, September 28, 2011. I have to do a lot of research to prepare my lessons for Sunday morning. Doing this for twenty-six years, that is where my knowledge increased, and my knowledge improved. I have a knowledge of biblical, secular, political, and world history as a result of studying and reading in preparation for Sunday School lessons.

It was during these years of preparing for Sunday School that I learned to read at a high level. My reading skills had to improve considering the amount of research and preparation I undertook to present good lessons.

In later years, around 2007 when it was time for me to get my social security I had to have a birth certificate. When I got my birth certificate and read it, it had a different name. On the birth certificate my name is George Matis Holman, but all my life I signed all documents George Notice Holman. I had never seen my name as George Matis Holman until this time.

OREATHA LOIS WILEY BANKS

I had just completed the first grade in 1959 when school closed. My first grade teacher was Mrs. Bigger. I recall her as a tall lady of light completion with jet black hair; she wore it short, not the cutie girl type, but short as a mature woman would ware her hair. I remember the classroom being a very large room to a six year old and across one of the walls was a green chalkboard with the alphabets on the top. The letters were in white on a green backdrop. The first few days I was very nervous but wouldn't cry because my parents wouldn't put up with that.

We had devotion each morning. We said the Lord's Prayer, the pledge to the flag, and one other thing which I can't remember. It seems there were three particular elements to morning devotion.

I remember one girl in class name Willie Mae, I can't recall her last name. I remember she only had one hand. I don't remember whether it had been amputated or just didn't grow normal. I felt she needed a friend and I talked with her sometimes.

I remember a girl name Mignon Griffin and that she had a little sister at home name Cocheyse, and that her sister liked cookies. Sometimes I sent a cookie home by Mignon to her sister.

I recall one day in particular we were instructed to copy words out of our reading book and I struggled to make the A that was in the book. It was different from the A on the letter chart in the classroom. I tried to make the letter A that was in the book and when the papers were corrected, Mrs. Bigger marked my paper wrong. She wanted it written like the one on the chart. I discovered there were challenges in learning.

I remember a day that my brother Joseph brought a book home. There was a girl's picture on the front of the book. I asked myself 'who is she and how did she write a book.' I had not yet learned to read at the level to pick up the book and read it, but the cover page attracted me.

During the school year, around October, we had the County Fair. I recall going and it was very exciting to me; the lights, all the lights, tents, and the ferris wheel! I was told by Mama, or my sister, Shirley, that I was too small to ride on the ferris wheel. I said to myself—'Next school year I'm going to ride on the ferris wheel.'

The following school year we did not go to the fair. I asked my parents why couldn't we go. Mama said something like 'We're not giving our money to support people who closed the public schools.' That was the gist of her statement, but it made no sense to me. (Oreatha is laughing.) I kept asking and she always gave the same answer.

When the schools didn't open in September 1959, I thought we were sought of on an extended vacation. I don't recall doing anything the first year the schools were closed. People were waiting to see if the schools were going to open back up. As time went on, I realized that the schools weren't going to open back up and I could not understand why. My parents only told me the schools were closed.

The earliest recollections I have of being in any type of learning environment after the closing was the 1960-1961 school year. I started attending classes in the basement at First Baptist Church.

I quickly determined that the classes held in the basement

of First Baptist Church were not like my first grade class. I made an immediate comparison. I remember Mrs. Lucille H. Reid was one of the instructors at First Baptist. I don't recall specific material that was covered there. There were times at home when my mother had been reviewing alphabets and numbers with me to keep me from forgetting the little I had learned, and to prepare for when school would reopen. I remember one time in particular Mrs. Reid had a group of us reading Scriptures. We were reading from Saint John, chapter one. One child read one verse and then the next child read the following verse and so on, until the chapter was completed. Every child had a Bible. There were hymnbooks and Bibles upstairs in the church and I think the teachers brought them downstairs for us to use. The Bible was one of our reading sources.

I remember there was one situation at the center I was in, something like a spelling contest. The word that was called for me was December. I remembered having looked at the word December on a calendar. One of my cousins, Wilbert Wiley, whispered the letters to me. I thought to myself—'can I trust this or not. If it's wrong, I'll just have to sit down graciously.' What he said sounded right—so I said the letters. I spelled it correctly! (Oreatha is laughing.)

I attended the Remedial Crash Program each summer, when school teachers and college students came to Prince Edward County to teach us. I remember one summer a man taught in the program and he said he was from Australia. I distinctly recall walking in the rain one day on my way to the Recreation House on Longwood Avenue, where classes were held, and he picked me up in his car. I also remember the man from Australia talking about abbreviations saying certain letters could stand for certain things, such as DD for

Doctor of Divinity or Dumb Daughters. (Oreatha started laughing.)

My brother Joseph went to Iowa in the Quaker Program. I believe he went away the second year the schools were closed or the third year. I remember Mama saying she was going to wait until they started placing children in Virginia before she and Daddy would consider allowing Shirley and I to go away to school.

In the 1962-1963 school year, after I had been out of the classroom for three years arrangements were made for me to go away to school. *They*, whoever *they* were, told Mama and Daddy after the school year had started that they could place me with a seamstress in Kilmarnock, Virginia, in Lancaster County, by the Rappahannock River. My sister Shirley was going to a family in Richmond. I don't know the preliminaries, but Mama and Mrs. Ophelia Pinn, the woman with who I was to live, discussed the matter. I remember hearing Mrs. Pinn say that she told the sponsoring organization that she would accept a child around the age of ten. I had just turn eleven in October of that year — 1962.

It was after the school year started that my parents were contacted because I went to Kilmarnock in early October.

We arrived at the home of Mrs. Pinn. A rather tall lady of light complexion greeted us. She seemed to be a nice person. I knew I had to always be on my guard to make sure my behavior was correct. My parents would tolerate no less. I remember feeling nervous about Mama and Daddy leaving. I especially remember sensing nervousness on the part of my Dad, but he smiled as he left.

The next day or so Mrs. Pinn drove me to Morgan E. Norris Elementary School in Kilmarnock. I was introduced to the School Supervisor, Mrs. L. Cheatham Taylor. Mrs. Smith was the school principal. Mrs. Churchill was the teacher for the third grade where I was going to be placed.

I heard Mrs. Taylor, Mrs. Smith and Mrs. Churchill talking in the auditorium. Mrs. Taylor was saying that I should be placed in the third grade in Mrs. Churchill's class. Mrs. Churchill and Mrs. Smith were trying to convince her to put me in the fourth grade. Mrs. Cheatham was insistent, saying she didn't feel I was ready for the fourth grade. I was placed in the third grade under Mrs. Churchill.

Deep within myself I believed Mrs. Cheatham was right. Having not had a lot of formal training in math, particularly multiplication, division, and fractions, it would have been overwhelming and I would not have been able to catch up to where the other children were in their studies. I had had a little practice in multiplications and fractions at home with Mama, but I wasn't prepared to keep up with the children in fourth grade.

Mrs. Churchill was a very nice and compassionate teacher. I liked her a lot. I liked her manner. She maintained order without being harsh. I got along well with the other students in the class. My reading proficiency was up to par, but I was still lacking in math.

Mrs. Pinn was a widow who had lost both sons during World War II. She told me about her sons. She wore her hair in a French roll. That was a popular style at that time. It was a good school year and I made many friends. When the school year ended, and I was to return home, I had mixed emotions. I had fallen in love with my friends at school. I loved Mrs. Pinn and wondered if I would be coming back to go to school the following year.

My parents came and picked me up to take me back to Farmville. I recall seeing my friend Gail Crosby's twin brother and sister Bill and Billie Jean outside playing. I remember them waving good-bye to me. I tried to hold back my tears but couldn't. I can't be sure if they were at their home or visiting at Mrs. Pinn's — but they were the last friends I saw.

In September 1963 the Free School opened in Farmville. I went to Mary E. Branch No. 2. I believe my homeroom teacher was Ms. Holman. Peter Scott and Rodman Lee were in the class with me.

I remember each school raised money to contribute to the Kennedy Memorial Library. A student at each school was selected to present the money collected at the respected school to Robert Kennedy on his visit to Prince Edward County. At Mary E. Branch No. 2, the two finalists to present Attorney General Kennedy the money collected were Barlow Branch and me. I was selected.

Attorney General Kennedy came by Branch No. 2. There was an assembly on the front steps of the building because the inside was too small. Many parents came out, there were two buses of reporters, and people from the community attended. My paternal grandfather was there. When I was walking up to Robert Kennedy, I heard Granddaddy say loudly: "Yeeeeaaah, that's my granddaughter." (Oreatha is laughing and imitating her Granddaddy.)

I won't forget that day. I wrote up a private account for my own benefit, recounting my emotions etc. My friend Carolyn Eggleston said: "He shook my hand. I'll never wash my hand again."

The following year we went to the high school. I remember there was the special feeling about going to high school. I felt a sense of accomplishment. I had to catch the bus — but that was part of the "high school" privilege.

I completed first grade at Branch No. 1 in Farmville. I went to third grade at Morgan E. Norris Elementary and during the year of the Free Schools I did junior high level at Branch No. 2. The students that the administration at the Free School Association felt could work at the junior high school level were at Branch No. 2.

I believe Mrs. Zenobia Archer was my homeroom teacher and gym teacher my first year at the high school. This was also the year the Prince Edward County public schools reopened, September 1964. I remember her because she drove one of the original Ford Mustang cars. Her car had a green body and black vinyl roof with bucket seats. That was the car! (Oreatha is laughing.)

My friend Carolyn and I weren't in the same homeroom. Sylvia Oliver was in my homeroom that year.

I mentioned earlier that my brother Joseph brought a book home when I was in first grade that attracted my attention. In later years after I had learned to read I saw the book again and recognized the girl's picture on the front. I said to myself 'this is the book Joseph had when I was very young. I want to read it, find out its contents and I did. The title of the book was *The Diary of Ann Frank*.

In my junior year of high school, a Mr. Robinson taught English. He was from Richmond and was very motivational. He took a group of us to Richmond to his home church, Saint Giles Presbyterian Church. He had us attend a theater play at a neighboring college. He had us to attend a symphony performance at Longwood College. These were class requirements. Cultural exposure for us, students, was a major issue for him. He endeavored to broaden our intellect beyond the confines of community. He came across in the beginning as being very strict and stern. I remember Mr. Robinson saying to the class: "You will learn the conjugation of the verb 'to be' and you will never forget it!" I have not forgotten it either.

While in high school, I was inducted into the National Honor Society. (National Honor Society Certificate among the personal artifacts Oreatha showed the Editor.) I graduated from high school an Honor Student in 1969. President Kennedy established the Peace Corps. I always had a desire to join the Peace Corps, go to other countries and help people. As time went by, that goal of the Peace Corps subsided. I was accepted at Virginia Union University and graduated in 1974.

————

SHIRLEY ANN WILEY BARNES

I was born March 11, 1948, in the morning at 604 Hill Street, Farmville, Virginia, in Prince Edward County. I am the fourth child of five children born to James C. and Minnie B. Wiley.

I started first grade at Mary E. Branch Elementary School. I enjoyed school. However, I had difficulty concentrating and staying focused. By the time I had completed the fifth grade, May 1959, the decision had been made to close the public schools in Prince Edward County. At this age I didn't understand what was taking place in Farmville.

The fall of 1959 my two older brothers were leaving to go to schools elsewhere. At this time, I still wasn't sure what was taking place, only that the public schools weren't going to open because the people didn't want to integrate. I was very confused and couldn't understand why there was a problem with Negroes and Whites going to the same school.

During this time, I was home with my parents and younger sister. My mother tried to make sure that we did some reading and math. It was hard for me to stay focused on reading and math because of a wondering mind. I preferred to be outside riding my bike and climbing trees.

In 1962 my younger sister had an opportunity to attend a school in another county in Virginia. Shortly after she left home, an opportunity came for me to attend school in Richmond, Virginia. I was very nervous and felt so unprepared. By this time, I should have been in the ninth grade.

The family that opened up their home to me to attend school in Richmond was Dr. J. M. Tinsley and Mrs. Ruth Tinsley. Dr. Tinsley was a dentist and Mrs. Tinsley was a homemaker. She was very active in the NAACP and the Civil Rights Movement.

I chose to go to the seventh grade when the principal at the middle school in Richmond asked me what grade I wanted to be in.

I spent most of my time alone in Richmond, walking to Broad Street, to the Greyhound Bus Station and sitting, and sometimes to a neighbor who had befriended me when I first started school. I would clean, vacuum, and wash dishes for Mrs. Tinsley. School was a struggle. It was hard for me to focus and concentrate on my studies. I was so afraid of failing and not learning and understanding the material, since I hadn't completely grasped the fundamentals of studying when I was in elementary school in Farmville.

In September 1963 the Free School started. Many teachers from other cities and States came to Prince Edward County to help prepare students. There were students who didn't return to school, especially those who were juniors and seniors when the schools were closed and didn't have an opportunity to go elsewhere.

I attended the summer school program and that fall I was

placed in the ninth grade, one year behind. I worked after school during my senior year in preparation to attend school in Baltimore, Maryland, where my brother lived. I graduated in June 1967.

I graduated from Cortez W. Peters Business School, 1969. I attended colleges in Maryland (Baltimore City Community, Liberty Heights Community, Coppin State University, Catonsville Community College, Takoma Community College, Montgomery Community College, and Germantown Community College). I attended Kennesaw State University in Kennesaw, Georgia, and finally the University of North Carolina at Charlotte in Charlotte, North Carolina, where I received my B. A. Degree in Psychology in 2006.

I attended different colleges off and on as my life situations dictated. I have grown children and grandchildren. I was determined not to let the years the schools were closed stop me from learning everything I could and getting a degree.

————

JAMES HARDY, JR.

I was named at birth James Hardy, Jr., but everyone called me Bro. My father was James Hardy, Sr. and my mother was named Ellen Marionett Foster Hardy. Mama was called Pretty by everyone in Farmville. She was born in Farmville. My father was born in Pittsburg, Pennsylvania. Daddy had relatives in Smithfield and Surry, Virginia. He met Mama one year when she was working at Piedmont Hospital. She was an RN. They got married and moved to Farmville.

I was the second child. My sister Ellen was the first child. I was born one year later, September 7, 1951.

I was born right behind Branch No. 1, the school I would later attend. When I became school age, I started school at Branch No. 1. In first grade I was in Mrs. Herndon's class.

When the public schools were closed, I was going to the third grade and Ellen was going to the fourth. My younger brother Leon was to start first grade in September 1959.

After second grade, we found out the schools were closing. My family moved across the bridge to Cumberland County on Plank Road next to Kildare Laundry. Today the building is W. A. Price Electrical Supply Company. Many families moved to Cumberland County to get an address for school, but never lived in the house they rented. My family literally packed up everything and moved to a new home.

We attended Green Creek Elementary School and the teacher was Mrs. Hartwell. Leon started first grade at Green Creek Elementary School. I went there from the second grade to the sixth grade. Green Creek was a big one room school and aisles dividing the sections. I don't think Mrs. Hartwell had any assistants and she did a fine job.

It was a long bus ride to Green Creek. The bus driver had to go around many winding roads and back roads to pick up other students.

Sometime around the 1963-1964 school year a new elementary school opened in Cumberland County. It was named Luther P. Jackson Elementary School. The county started closing all of the one and two room schools. Green Creek, Hawkes, and the other one and two room schools were closed.

When the Prince Edward County public schools officially reopened in September 1964, my family didn't return to Prince Edward County. By this time Mama and Daddy had purchased a house further down Plank Road. This was now home for us.

I continued in high school at Luther P. Jackson. I played basketball and enjoyed school. In my senior year they were about to combined Luther P. Jackson's student body with the Cumberland High School student body which was all White. My coach, Coach James G. Johnson, was asked to go to Cumberland High to work. He also taught Health, PE and Driver's Education. He accepted the job and asked me would I consider transferring. I went to Cumberland High School and played my last year of basketball. I had two other friends Richard Johnson and James Brooks that transferred with me. I graduated from Cumberland High School in June 1969.

I had many friends that I missed. I kind'a wanted to come back to Farmville and be with the guys that I grew up and was tight with. I would come to Farmville on the weekend and in the summer. We would play basketball.

———

JACQUELYN NENEE' REID

I was born in Farmville, March 10, 1954, to Warren Alfred Reid and Geral Dean Reid.

My mother was a beautician and my dad was a funeral director. I grew up on Vine Street. During that time, the college hadn't expanded and there were many, many Black children in the neighborhood. One day recently we tried to count up the children that were in our neighborhood and named sixty or seventy. There was Chuckie Reid and his brothers and sister; the Jackson family: Shirley, Patricia and the other children in that home; the Carter family; the Lee family: Dale, Gene, Larry, and another whose name I can't remember. There were the Branch and Walker families, and all these children and families lived on Race Street. Also, straight up Race Street there were two adult brothers last name White and they had families. What is now Griffin Boulevard was Ely Street. The Hughes and Clark families lived in that area. It was a tight community and kids would play in the streets and ride bikes.

My dad had a close relationship with Reverend Griffin. So, I was close to his kids. Reverend Griffin spent a lot of time at our house, almost as much as at his own house. (Jacquelyn laughs.) He often ate dinner with us.

The schools were closed when I was supposed to start first grade. I ended up going to live with my grandparents John and Helen Dean in Buckingham County. John and Helen were my mother's parents.

I basically commuted. My parents would pick me up on Friday evening and drop me off on Sunday evening. I attended S. J. Ellis Elementary School, which is now Ellis Acres Memorial Park.

I attended school at Ellis in first, second and third grades. In the first grade I had Mrs. Edwards. My second grade teacher was Mrs. Barnslater. Mrs. Irene Hamlett taught me in third grade.

The first three grades were in one little building. It was not a one room building. The school had four rooms. Fourth, fifth and sixth grades and the library were in another building. The cafeteria was in the basement of the larger building.

My mother was from a large family. Her parents had thirteen children. Carol, Helen, Thelma, Wilbert, and Earl were my mother's younger brothers and sisters. Carol was eight, Helen thirteen, Thelma was fifteen and Wilbert seventeen or eighteen. They were graduating during the three years I was there.

I made some lasting friends at Ellis Elementary.

When the Free School opened, I was nine years old. I attended Mary E. Branch No. 1. I can't remember who my teacher was at that time. I was only there from September through December. I guess my biggest memory of going to that school was that was the year John Kennedy was assassinated.

The staff at the Free School was very diverse. There were some seasoned teachers and some new teachers.

After Christmas recess, when we returned in January 1964, I started at Mary E. Branch No. 2. I was in a different class.

I remember when Robert Kennedy came. I know it was warm because I remember having on a pretty dress that tied in the back, but I didn't have on a sweater.

I was in the fourth grade the first semester, came back and tested and was placed in the fifth grade the second semester of the Free School. When the school year ended, I was promoted to the sixth grade. I remained at Mary E. Branch No. 2.

When the public schools reopened, a band was started. I was in the band. All the band activities were at the high school. All students in the sixth grade could be in the band. We were transported from Mary E. Branch No. 2 to the high school for band classes. I was also in the modern dance class.

As my high school years went by, things began to settle down. The schools were still basically segregated. There were a lot of old students in classes. I was one of the younger ones because I had been skipped a grade.

Burrell Robinson was a White English teacher and was fabulous. He was terminated, and the students didn't like it. He was a favorite teacher. The kids respected him, and he respected the students.

We got a good education and we were a lot more disciplined. Respect for our elders, respect for authority, and kids just respecting themselves has changed so much.

I consider myself one of the lucky ones. I missed no time out of school. There was no question about what I was going to do after high school. It was understood I was going to college, the only question was where would I attend.

I graduated high school at seventeen and started at Longwood, which was at home. Attending Longwood was an immersion in White culture. I attended Longwood the summer after graduation from high school, one academic year and another summer. Then my parents allowed me to transfer to Winston Salem State, in North Carolina, where I graduated in 1975 with a degree Music Education.

I returned to Prince Edward County and taught music for a year at the two middle schools, Branch 2 and Worsham, and worked with the beginning choir at the high school. I assisted the high school band director with the marching band.

I decided that teaching was not for me. As a young person returning home, it wasn't that I didn't like teaching, during that time teachers were isolated. Many of the teachers that taught me were still in the school system and this was the extent of my social network. A social life didn't exist for young teachers. If you went on a date with a male teacher and went to the movie, you ran into your students. The pay was very disappointing.

I moved to Northern Virginia and worked odd jobs for a while until I got with the Federal Government and worked at the National Naval Medical Center in Bethesda, Maryland, and then at the General Accounting Office in Washington.

I stayed there until 1993 and decided it was time to return to Farmville and work with my dad and carry on the family business, Bland-Reid Funeral Home. In order to become licensed, I attended John Tyler Community College in Chester, Virginia, and received an Associate's Degree in Funeral Services, graduating in 1995. I became fully licensed in 1997.

As of this day, November 22, 2011, I am co-manager for our location in Farmville and the manager of our site in Dillwyn. My mom owns both businesses.

I enjoy working here and enjoy being back home, basically because I get to come in contact with the people I grew up with and renew old acquaintances. I see many old friends at funerals for their family members, love ones, and friends.

My grandparents had fifteen children and thirteen lived to adulthood. My grandparents were farmers and five out of the thirteen children graduated from Virginia State College. Carol graduated from Longwood. Several of the sons were veterans; one went into the Air Force and two went in to the Army and are retired military men.

BRENDA SMITH POTTER

Note from the Editor: On Tuesday afternoon, September 27, 2011, the Editor traveled to the home of Leon Hill in Prospect, Virginia, where his story was drafted in full at his dining room table.

As the Editor was preparing to leave, Leon said: "I wan'a give you something." He left the dining room, went to another room, and returned with some papers. "I found this among the things of my late wife when I was cleaning up. I think she was writing her story. Sort'a like what you're doing." The

Editor took the papers, reviewed the pages and said: "Yes, she was writing her story." "You can have it and do whatever you want with it." "I will retype her information as it is written and include it with the other stories in the book. I cannot change anything because if I do it will no longer be authentic," the Editor explained. "I understand," said Leon.

At the top of the account was the name Brenda Smith Potter. Her unaltered draft, which she probably planned to edit but was called to her eternal rest before accomplishing the task, is below.

Being born in 1947, placed me in the middle of a segregation war. The Whites did not want their children to attend school with Blacks. At the age of 7 years when the war began was of no consequence to me because I was to young to realize what the war would later mean. I also had two friends that were white, they came to visit their grandmother every summer and holidays. We played in my grandfather's garden everyday, swimming in the branch at the edge of the garden and ridding their Great Dane Dog. Despite the fact that this war was going on, Blacks and White continue to live as they had always, everything separate—doctors' office, hospital, movies, drive-in and eateries had a sign – Color Entrance. Even the Court House had a separate entrance.

In 1954, the Supreme Court pass down a ruling that Prince Edward Schools had to be desegregated. For the Whites, this was a disaster. They would not hear of a (nigger) as we were call to attend school with their children nor did they want desegregation in the town period. They closed the schools and open for their children, The Academy, a private school. We discovered later that government monies paid for the education that was given to the White children with Taxpayers' monies-both Black and Whites. The Black children of Farmville attended school in the First Baptist Church Basement. While the older children were being taught by the adults, the younger children were being taught by the older children

Within a couple of years of schools closing, we were told to report the to the First Baptist Church for a meeting. There the parents of the children met with a group called the Friends Committee. They proposed a plan to educate the older children. We first had to be tested for placement to determine what class we would be placed. This was done because some of us were still learning while the schools were closed. After the results of the test were received, we reported to the church for placement. There, representatives from the Friends Committee told us that some of us had been selected to attend schools out of State. We would live with host families, both Black and White. Having to leave home to attend school with White Children and live with White Families is not the greatest gift you can give a child who has been told that Whites do not want you to attend school or mix in any way with their children or them. I remembered thinking — how can we leave home because of whites not wanting to go to school with us and now we will live with them elsewhere. Maybe they are not prejudice in other states as they are here and further down South. We watched the demonstrations on the television as well as listen to the news, community people as well as leaders were being arrested and beaten for trying to have a right to live as others that were not Black. I would later find out my thinking was wrong.

I was among those chosen to go to Massachusetts. My family agreed to my leaving and readied me for the trip.

We left Farmville to meet in Boston, Massachusetts. This was the meeting place for introduction to our host families who lived throughout the State of Massachusetts.

As we traveled, my mind wondered back into my past. I could see everyone chattering, but could not hear. My heart long to see my grandparents, who I always felt that I would never be separated from under any circumstances. Not wanting the group to see the tears, I allowed my heart to cry. I felt my heart had a whole inside that was leaking my tears. I began to remember my life before all of the unhappiness began. In all the years I spent with my grandparents, I never considered myself as the grandchild. They had raised me from a baby with my uncles and aunts as one of their children. We were always treated as sisters and brothers, therefore leaving me to respond to my mother as a sister. I went almost everywhere with my grandfather, to work on his truck selling ice, cleaning the movies and drive-in and going to the college to carry his lunch and sit while he ate. He also collected tickets at the State Theatre, we would go their, but had to sit in the balcony to watch the movie. My grandmother would take me with her to shop and run other errands. I paused in my thoughts to say a prayer, asking God to please watch over my grandparents while I went away to school.

My grandmother was injured while working at the movie cleaning uup. A trash can hit the back of her heel. We did not think anything of this accident at first, but when she got so sick and had to go to the doctor, it was time to worry. She was later diagnosed with Lukemia, a type of blood cancer.

An announcement of a rest stop brought me back to reality. I remember some of the group purchasing keepsakes for themselves, but I purchased post cards to send home.

During our brief rest stop, the committee members explained the itinerary to us. We would meet our host parents in the church parking lot, after which a get acquainted luncheon had been prepared. It would be time to leave after the luncheon, the host parents lived quit a distance. We said our good byes and started off to begin our new life.

At the time school closed, I was in the fourth grade. This fact is very important because after being tested, I placed for seventh grade in a business course.

My first family was a doctor and his wife (white and no children). They lived in West Springfield, Massachusetts, a predominately white neighborhood with a school attendance of three blacks. I was one of the three. You would think in a situation like this, the black children would have been friendly, wrong. The children turned their heads when I passed them in the halls. The white children were my associates, later becoming my friends. Living with the doctor and his wife wasa major adjustment. They treated me with the utmost of kindness, trying so hard it seemed phoney. Little did they realize that it was the prepared food and the fact they there were no blacks. Because of my inability to adjust, I asked for another family.

They moved me to the Uttlerlys, still in West Springfield. My second family was a television cameraman and stay at home mom. They had two daughters and a dog. I still resided in West Springfield because of school. Moving with this family would be my first encounter with prejudice and the worst food ever. This was my introduction to Tuna and Spam Casseroles and Skim Milk. The family were large people as were the children, so they always ate and drink diet products. I, on the other hand weight approximately 100 pounds soak and wet. Being from Virginia and always eating well, I had never heard of or eaten these types of dishes. Our milk was fresh from the cow and delivered each Friday. One night the host mom asked if I would bathe the younger daughter, I agreed and proceeded to give the daughter a bath. While giving the bath, she asked "what color is this" pointing to her hands. I said pink, pink because of the warm water burning her skin pink. She then asked "what color is this" point to my hands, I said brown, "she said no you are a Nigger". I refused to stay with them on my return from the holidays. I never told anyone what happened, but stated that I did not want to return to the family. Not wanting to make a big issue, I did not say why, I just said I was not going back. I told everyone that I wanted to stay at home with my grandmother instead of going back after the Christmas Holidays. This was partly true, because by now my grandmother had gotten worse. I did not want to leave her side nor did I want to experience what I could stay at home and get, prejudice and I could eat well. I believe they knew it had to do with race, so my next placement, which was temporary was Springfield, Massachusetts. The Boyds were originally from Georgia. I loved the Boyds as they did me. They gave me my first surprise birthday party. They were southerns, showing genuine hospitality. I really wanted to stay with them, but as I said it was temporary. They had adopted two boys just before I got there, making it impossible for living arrangements.

The next year I was sent to New Beford with a Portugese family who was of dark skin. My roommate was my girlfriend from home. I will never forget because Mrs. Lopes treated the roommate like a queen and me like a maid or hired help. What she did, I would use them later in life, an explanation as to why she treated me this way. In being kind, she baked some biscuits, but left the flour on t hem. Well because I had seen my grandmother do this, I brushed the flour off with a napkin. She got very upset and left the table. I did'nt know what was wrong until Mr. Lopes told me. I tried to explain and apologize but it was to late — the damage was done. I spent my time with Mr. Lopes, who spent his time trying to make up for all the things she did wrong to me. At the end of the school year, she found out that my roommate really did not like her — this opened her eyes to see me exactly for the true way I was and today I am the same. I don't mistreat people at any time nor do I past judgments. Everybody must live their lives for themelves.She apologized and come to Virginia two or three summers trying to repair the damage, but I could not or would not deal with her, not even for a visit.

Doing the time away from home, the love of my life past, my grandmother torned, I blamed everything on having to leave home to go to school with (now they had become white dumb devils) rather than just white kids. Attending school with them, I found that they were not superior but dumb, bad and spoiled. Mr. Lopes helped me through this rough time.

I remembered all the things that whites had said about black children in Farmville. We were bad, distructive, dumb spoiled riding around in cars getting in trouble, they were really talking about their children.

The children of Prince Edward County whose parents were able to relocate or send them with family members should be very grateful.

The story of the schools closing became worldwide. People came from everywhere to assist us in every way possible. Organizations such NAACP, SNCC, CORE sent representatives. The Black Leaders and these organizations began meetings to demonstrate. Our meetings and training was held in the church basement. We demonstrated with sit ins at eateries, churches, made applications to the colleges, rallied on the Courthouse steps and marched through the town. We continued to do this, even though some of us were arrested. Every time we went to a place, the police would be there waiting. We discovered a snitch, on of our older members was reporting to the police. He was frighten away when his car was rocked and threaten to be pushed in the branch behind the church. This problem prompted the leaders to close the meetings. If you were not a participate, you could not be in the building at the time of the training or the meetings.

I was one of many children who demonstrated to have the same freedom in our town as did whites. Picketting the place where my grandfather worked. Many of us went to jail and when they day in court came, the judge asked each of us if we knew what we were doing. The answer was yes, I want the same freedom that everyone else has in Farmville.

My last year would be at R.R. Moton. When it was time to graduate, they said I had enough credits, but that I had never had Algebra I., for t his reason I had to attend school the next year. That was stupid, since all through school I had business courses. I felt this was an injustice, since that should have been detected long before graduation.

An update—I got married, had four children. I left Virginia and attended Essex County College and Rutgers in New Jersey, J. Sargeant Reynolds in Richmond and Queens College in Jamaica, N.Y. Most of my employment history comes from the Urban Leagues. I worked for the Newark New Jersey Branch, Urban Leagues. I worked for the Newark New Jersey, The National Office in New York under Vernon Jordan and the Washington D.C. National Headquarters under Ronald Brown. The Richmond, Virginia Branch sent me to help create the Multi-purpose Center on Churchhill. When we started the program, it was a proposal. The last I heard, the program is a twenty million dollar center. Working in Baltimore, Maryland with the circuit court, I was instrumental in starting a program called Community Re-Entry. As director of the Greenmount Community Association, I wrote several propoosals that began new programs within the community. I was the third black person to work in the office of United Parcel Services in Secausus, New Jersey. I am a Real Estate Agent for the State of New York.

At present I reside in Newark, New Jersey. Future plans include returning to Virginia to give some of my expertise to my hometown

---

CLARA LOUISE GIBSON JOHNSON

I was born in Farmville, January 10, 1948, to Vernell and Maggie Scott Gibson. I was the sixth of eight children: Thomas Edward Gibson, Rosa Mary Gibson, Vernice Gibson (Miller), Adele Gibson (Smith), Madelean Gibson (Holcomb), myself, then Floyd Robert Gibson and Anita Gibson (Jones).

My sister Adele graduated in 1959 from R. R. Moton High School. I attended the ceremony and remember someone on the dais saying: 'this might be the last graduating class from this school.' Of course, nobody believed it. We went through that summer. When it was time for school to open in the fall, there was no school. At this time my mother had four children of school age. Madelean was going to the eighth grade. I was next and should have gone to the sixth grade. My brother Floyd was going to the third grade. My younger sister Anita was not school age. There was no kindergarten in those days.

My mother had been a worker in the kitchen at Longwood College. Dad was a bricklayer and worked away from home and came home on the weekend.

My sister Rosa Mary graduated from high school in 1955 and went to Virginia Union University. All of her books from college she bought home at the end of each year and put them in a trunk on the back porch. We had a big screened in back porch. I've always loved school and highly excelled in school, so in an effort to keep up I started reading those books from college the first year the schools were closed. That kind of help. I read on my own. I would read all morning and all afternoon sometimes. I didn't understand many times what I was reading, but having books made me feel like I was in school. This was my self-study program.

Adele who graduated in 1959 would help us with math and sit and tell us stories.

The first year went by with us doing that.

The next year there was a hint that the schools would open, but that did not happen.

It was proposed that my Dad take us to Richmond where he did construction work. It was agreed that wouldn't happen because at the construction site all the men lived together, and this wouldn't be a practical living situation for girls.

The second year the schools were closed a family friend named Mrs. Ellen Hardy talked to Mama. Mrs. Hardy lived in Cumberland County and worked at Southside Hospital in Farmville at night. Nurse Hardy was the first Black nurse that could work at Southside Community Hospital here in Farmville.

She told Mom that we could live with her and keep her younger children at night and ride the Cumberland County school bus in the morning with them. This worked until about November. There was such an influx of Prince Edward County students that the Cumberland County School administration sent a letter home saying 'Prince Edward

County children had to pay tuition in order to attend their schools.' Mama was now involved in the real estate business and owned several properties, but she didn't make enough to pay for Madelean and I to go to school in Cumberland County, pay tuition for Rosa at Virginia Union University and Vernice at Hampton Institute. So, school ended for me and Madelean.

We were dismissed from school and this hurt more than the first year of being out of school.

Community Centers had opened. There was one at Beulah and at First Baptist Church. My mother was a proponent of education and she purchased books for us. We also used the Reading Room at Beulah African Methodist Episcopal Church. We could not use the public library. It was for White people only.

By the third year of the school closing, Vernice had left Hampton, married and decided to move north. She and her husband, James Miller, from Rice, Virginia, moved to South Norwalk, Connecticut. She told Mom: "Send the girls. The place is small but send them. We'll make it work." She and James had a one bedroom apartment and Madelean and I went to South Norwalk, Connecticut.

My mother was always an advocate for people who had nothing to eat or women who were being abused or someone needing shelter. There was a lady whose husband was allegedly abusing her. This was years before abuse became a public issue.

When I was a girl, it was common for women from this area to move north to serve as live-in maids for White families. This lady went away to live with a White family and my mom took in the lady's three children while she went away to work. The lady saved her money and years later when

she had enough saved, she came and got her three children–
Beverly Marie, Sarah Virginia, and Lionel Paige from Mom.

Mama believed that if you 'do good good will come back
to you.'

When we went to Connecticut, Mrs. Nettie Paige Johnson
was in Stamford, Connecticut. This was the lady whose three
children Mama kept and raised earlier. Mrs. Johnson convinced
Mama to let me come to Stamford and stay with her. For better
living accommodations it was decided Madelean and I should
be split up. Madelean stayed with Vernice and James and took
care of their children while Vernice worked and went to night
school. I went to live with Mrs. Nettie. She was always so very
good and nice to me. Whatever her children had, she made
sure I had the same.

In Stamford I attended Franklin Elementary School. I went
in as a sixth grader. The school was predominantly White. I
felt out of place and isolated for two reasons. First, all of the
elementary aged children were not nearly as large as I was; and
secondly, I went in with the pre-conceived notion that all White
people did not like me and did not want to go to school with
me. In elementary school there were little tables and benches,
and no one wanted to sit with me. I was a rather large girl.
However, I was still happy that I was in a classroom and that I
was finally back in school!

I was tested, and I think they were under the impression
that being from the South I wouldn't be up to par academically.
I have always been a high achiever. I was excelling in school
and the next semester when we returned after Christmas break
they moved me to Burdick Junior High School and placed me
in the seventh grade. Now I felt better about myself because
there were seventh, eighth, and ninth graders around me. I was
in school with people my size and with the girls I lived with.

The hard part about Connecticut was the extremely cold weather. Also, I missed my mother tremendously. We were very close to my mother. We used to sit on the back porch at night and she would tell us stories about life in general.

My oldest brother Thomas lived in South Norwalk, Connecticut, and had a house cleaning service. We would always want to come home. He cleaned the houses of celebrities. We would say to him: 'We will help you clean, if you will drive us home.' I remember the day we cleaned Mia Farrow's house. I was impressed. People live like this!

We would leave early Saturday morning around 4:00 a. m. and get to Farmville early that afternoon. We would leave late Sunday night to be back Monday morning for school. Some Mondays we did not make it back in time for school, but we had been home to see Mom.

I had a good year, and this was the third year of the school closing.

We came home that summer and things went relatively well. When we got ready to leave Farmville to go back to Connecticut, Mom had decided: 'Floyd can go too.' He didn't say he was going and didn't say he was not going. Floyd had not been to school for three years now. Mama packed his bags. Mama didn't drive. When Mama and our cousin Clara Allen got ready to take us to the Greyhound bus station to catch the bus to go to Connecticut, Floyd had run away. We later found out he didn't really run away but went into the woods and watched the car roll away.

I went back to Mrs. Nettie and back to Burdick Junior High School. Madelean was with Vernice for a second year.

When we came back home the summer of 1963, this was a very interesting summer. A lot of Black youths that had been away were dissatisfied with the situation.

I remember Ivanhoe Donaldson, Charles Sherrod, and Reverend Goodwin at Beulah AME and SNCC workers led us in peaceful demonstrations in an effort to try and change things in this area. All of our parents felt threatened because of our involvement and by repercussions that would come. Many parents worked in White people's homes or in the local lumber factory and were in fear of losing their jobs. My mother wasn't working for anybody, but when she had to deal with businesses in town and it had been made known that Mag Gibson's children were involved there as a difference in the treatment she received.

Back in that day you could order goods over the telephone. You could call the grocery store and put your whole order in and it would be delivered. They would ask your name and if they knew your children were involved in the demonstrations they treated you differently.

Buffalo Shook workers were afraid of repercussions. Many people withdrew their children. My mother told us that if we felt that it is the "right thing to do" that we should continue, and she would back us 100% and pray for us. We went to the College Shoppe and Farmville Baptist Church and met resistance.

Madelean and I were among the bus load of youths and youth sponsors from the Farmville area who went to the March on Washington in August 1963.

The Free School system opened in September 1963 and many of the displaced youths of Prince Edward County returned to attend school. Many didn't return. Some of the kids had to be tested because they had been out of school all four years. Many had never been to school at all.

One day a resource teacher brought Floyd home and said: "Mrs. Gibson, Floyd doesn't want to be in school and I have brought him home." Mama said: "You put him back in the car and take him back to school. I'm not equipped to teach him here at home. He has to go back." The man took Floyd back to school.

That afternoon Mama talked to Floyd and explained to him that when he turned thirty-five he wouldn't want to have to learn then what he had the opportunity to learn at this time in his life. Floyd stayed in school and graduated.

I graduated in 1967. I should have finished in 1966 but lost one year. I should have finished with my friend Shirley Wiley. Arlene Bailey was Number 1 in the Class of 67. Eva Wilson was Number 2 in our class. I was Number 3 in the class of 40 graduates.

I got married to Bruce Johnson, Jr. We have three children—Darryl Sherrod is the oldest, then there is Dawn Michelle, and Cheryl LaNae.

I attended community college and did some course work. Longwood had one Black office personnel prior to me. I was working at Uniroyal in Prince Edward County. The company left town, just up and left. My husband worked there too. A fellow co-worker said to me: "Clara, why don't you try Longwood." I applied there and was told, 'you have to take a test for typing and shorthand.' Because this position was a State job, I went to be tested at the Virginia Employment Commission. I aced the typing test, but in shorthand I fell short. The job opening closed out in two weeks. I thought to myself 'the job might not be there in two weeks.' I went home and had my husband and children to read to me and I wrote in short hand as fast as I could. I practiced intensely and went back four days later and passed the test.

I started out at the ground level and retired from Longwood University in 2010 as Executive Administrative Assistant. I had the opportunity to take a class each semester while working at Longwood and that was wonderful.

All of our children earned their undergraduate degree from Longwood College. It was not a university at that time. As of today, May 31, 2012, our son is a software designer engineer and resides in Raleigh, North Carolina. Dawn teaches fifth grade at Prince Edward Middle School. Cheryl was trained in the area of Human Resources Management and lives in Raleigh, North Carolina. Cheryl is pursuing a doctorate degree.

God has taught me how to release the past hurts. In earlier years it was a strain and very difficult for me, but I have learned and am still learning. I still have to have those "come to Jesus moments" to get past some things sometimes.

It is as the song writer said: 'We Will Understand It Better By and By'.

———

JOHN AREHART

Dad was born in 1908. His sister Pauline was the oldest. He had a brother named Raynard. Uncle Raynard was also a Presbyterian minister. Dad and Uncle Raynard were students at Hampden Sydney College at the same time, but Uncle Raynard was a couple of years ahead of Dad.

Dad was a great athlete. He played football, basketball, baseball and ran track. He lettered in all sports and among the small schools he was nominated as an All American. That was a different era for sports. Dad was not headed in the direction of professional sports and had no such ambition. Back in that era you were a student first. He graduated in 1932 I believe.

My father went on to attend Union Theological Seminary in Richmond, Virginia, on Brook Road. I am unsure when he graduated from seminary.

Dad's name was Carl Lloyd Arehart, but he went by Lloyd. The name is inadvertently reversed on the wall at Farmville Presbyterian Church where the photographs and dates of each respective pastor are displayed.

I think Dad's first position as a clergyman was as an assistant pastor in the area of Huntingdon, West Virginia. My mother was a teacher in the public schools and was the pianist at the church. That was how they met. I am not exactly sure of the years he was at that church. I was born December 9, 1941.

Dad then went to Glenville, West Virginia, to serve as pastor of a congregation. I believe this was his first charge as a pastor and he stayed approximately three years.

My first recollection of living in a place was Dunbar, West Virginia, which was a suburb of Charleston. We were in Charlestown around 1946 and I started first grade in Charleston. Dad was in Charlestown from around 1946 to 1956.

I don't know when Dad did all of this, but he had a master's degree in Psychology from the University of Virginia. I thought he only studied theology. My son went to the University of Virginia, where I had earned a Doctorate in Education. He looked me up and called home one day and said: "I found you and also found Granddaddy's thesis."

To tell you how my family got to Farmville, I will repeat the story I so often heard my mother tell.

She said Dad came to the church and interviewed with the Session. At this time, they did not want Black folk in the church. The balcony in the church was for the slave population back during the era of slavery. So, there had been a presence in the church. Dad was asked: "What would you do if a Negro came to the service on Sunday?" Dad said: "I would shake his hand and welcome him." Some people didn't like his answer.

He told Mother about it when he returned home and said: "Based on my answer and some of the reactions of the people, I don't think they will call me."

Mom was a little reluctant to leave Charlestown because she had many friends there.

We were out working on my grandfather's farm one day and Dad got a long distance telephone call. My grandparents had one of those telephones that you had to turn and ring up. (John turned his right arm a few times, showing how callers rung up in the old days.)

Mother took the call and yelled the news out to Dad that the church in Farmville wanted him to come and be the pastor. Mother said Dad was in the garden and dropped the hoe. He dropped the hoe in surprise.

When all of this was taking place, I was going to the ninth grade. This was the summer and fall of 1956. I had taken Latin in Charles Town, at Charles Town High School. I remember I had started Latin and was worried that I would be behind in school. I was about fifteen.

As a fifteen year old, I was running around in my own world. Dad was delighted to return to the area and I believe he felt he could do some good here. He was aware of the difficulties in the county.

Turning to the year the schools were closed, it had already been decided in the summer of 1959 that the schools would be closed, and Dad was aware of the decision. The whole affair began to take a toll on him.

I don't remember how the news came to me, but I was

part of the gathering at the theater where it was announced to us that we would be in a different school setting. It was comparable to a high school assembly. The theater was near First Baptist where Griffin was the pastor. Dad was at the theater that day and gave a prayer.

When the school year began, I attended high school at Farmville Presbyterian Church. The fellowship hall on Farmville Presbyterian Church today was the library for the high school. I remember two classes explicitly. I had Geometry in the basement with about twenty students. I think I had a Government class on the first floor in the church annex, and a Sunday School class was held in the same room on Sunday. In the private school many of the teachers I knew from my public school days.

Farmville Presbyterian Church provided six high school classrooms. The annex where the high school classes were held, this section was added after Dad came in 1956. So, the facility that housed the classes was new.

In my own family the feeling was that the closing of the schools was not the right thing to do. Both my parents had strong opposition to the closing of the public schools, but they didn't openly challenge the local leadership on it. If you went to a party, the advice was 'don't talk about politics, religion, etc.'

I have the dubious distinction of being in the first graduating class of what was Prince Edward Academy.

I graduated in the spring of 1960 and entered Southwestern at Memphis in the fall. Today the institution is named Rhodes College. A donor named Rhodes made a huge contribution and the school was given his name.

I was in the Peace Corps for a couple of years after graduating from college. I returned to Virginia around January

1968. I studied math in college and taught math in different school systems around Virginia.

They discovered my father had esophageal cancer. Somehow the doctors missed it. Dad did not smoke or anything. I remember initially Dad's condition was not treated as a physical ailment, but more emotional.

He died in the spring of 1960. I suspect that the school crisis contributed to his early death and my mother often alluded to the same.

I found a letter my father's sister gave mother after Dad died. Mother wrote the letter to my father's sister asking her did Dad ever have emotional troubles (my phrase Mr. Arehart said) in early life. I believe Dad had serous internal struggles about what was happening around him. The letter suggested the same.

I spent many delightful years teaching at Longwood University until I retired.

———

SLYVIA SHEPARD MEADOWS

I was born in Farmville at Southside Community Hospital, February 28, 1955. I was the middle of three daughters in a family that was not wealthy. My father worked for the post office and my mother worked for a local department store.

Many of my best childhood memories are from my grandparents' home in Farmville. The fine food, family gatherings, some people weren't related, they were people you called aunt that really wasn't my aunt. I remember the Black couple that cooked for my grandparents. I remember where they lived. I remember going to their home and picking them up. I remember feeling a love and esteem for them. I have no memories of people being treated with disrespect.

A great aunt of mine owned a country store on River Road in Cumberland County. Ruby Trent a young Black woman lived with my great aunt and worked in the store. We went to Ruby's house, we bathed with her, we slept with her. I thought Ruby had the most gorgeous hand writing. My great aunt's house was not a great big house, but the houses where many of the Black people lived were much smaller.

I remember being at the homes of the Black people and hearing music and dancing.

I can remember the picketing in Farmville. I remember my mother pulling up to the grocery store and there was a line of picketers going back and forth down the side walk. When she got out of the car, she said: "Don't look at them or look at their signs." I, of course, looked. "Why buy where we can't eat" was on one sign. I did not understand what that meant. I understood later in life they could shop there but could not eat at the establishment.

My older sister was in the first class that went all the way through Prince Edward Academy. She started in the first grade class in the fall of 1959. We never knew there was any other school possibility. As a child you're not thinking about that. As a child, you accepted what you saw. If you live in a bad household, you think all households are bad. I went twelve years in the private school system never thinking it was odd or that there could be a Black school and White school.

I'm not sure Mama was working then. I remember late at night the phone ringing for my father to come and get tuition cost. It was very frightening to me when the calls came. I remember the calls came late at night after all the house was asleep.

I went to kindergarten in the Episcopal parish house associated with John's Memorial Episcopal Church. I went to first grade at the Farmville United Methodist; classes were held in the educational building. I went to second grade at the old telephone building on Randolph Street. It was vacant at the time. Third, fourth, and fifth grades were at Farmville United Methodist Church. When I started middle school in sixth grade, I went to Prince Edward Academy. I went to the Academy sixth to twelfth grades.

Somewhere along the line the world I lived in taught me there was separation. I don't really know who, what, how, or why. I was never taught to be unkind and I never viewed my family being unkind to others.

I started Longwood College after graduating from Prince Edward Academy in 1973. My second year at Longwood I quit college and went to work at Prince Edward County Elementary School as the first White teacher's aide every hired in Prince Edward County. I got the job because I had been working part time at Baldwin's Department Store and a Black friend called someone at the school board on my behalf. I probably would not have gotten the job except I had a Black friend.

I worked with Mrs. Barbara Toney who was an amazing teacher. Being in a predominantly Black setting was very interesting. After being her aide for a year, I knew I wanted to teach. I returned to Longwood and got a degree in teaching.

The first job offered to me was in Appomattox County where I worked for a few years. Then I started teaching in the Prince Edward County public schools.

My children went to the Prince Edward County public schools. I believe every child is entitled to a good public school education.

The transformation was still taking place; so much so that I felt comfortable sending my children to the public schools.

I got my degree and was a Guidance Counselor in the Prince Edward County public schools.

I am back in Farmville serving as pastor of Farmville United Methodist Church.

Today, August 11, 2011, I am in my fifth year as senior pastor of Farmville United Methodist Church. I serve as president of the Farmville Area Ministerial Association; president of the Heart of Virginia Free Clinic, in the process of beginning the first free medical clinic in the area; and on the board of the Youth Empowerment Center.

I believe that God has called me to ministries of justice, mercy, reconciliation and love. It is such a privilege to have the opportunity to be involved weekly with people of all backgrounds striving to be all that God has created me to be and trying to help others do the same.

FRANKLIN WEST

Reverend Alexander I. Dunlap was assigned to a church in Danville, Virginia, and left Beulah African Methodist Episcopal Church, Farmville, in the spring or summer of 1960.

The Virginia African Methodist Episcopal Conference met in April or May of 1960 and I was assigned to the pastorate of Beulah AME, Farmville, Virginia. I arrived to assume the position of pastor in the summer of that year. My wife Marylene and I came to Farmville with our young daughter Priscilla. Priscilla was not school age when the bishop assigned me to Beulah.

After arriving and setting up our home in the parsonage, which was next to the church, I recall teachers from around Virginia coming to Prince Edward County to work with the students. These teachers taught free of charge. Marylene and I took in two female teachers the following summer. They lived with us in the parsonage.

One of the teachers that stayed with us was named Mrs. Tyler. I can't remember her first name.

Classes were held at Beulah African Methodist Episcopal Church. Classes were held in the pastor's study and in the library located in the downstairs area of the church.

I remember a male teacher that came one summer. I can't recall his name and he lived with another family in town. I remember him because he was also a pastor but taught in the public schools. I don't remember where he was from, but he went home on the weekends to his church. We used to take walks in the evenings and discuss the Prince Edward County situation and just have long talks in general.

The church paid me $30.00 a week. Many people around the county sympathized with me. Some of the pastors and churches would have me preach at afternoon Sunday services around the county and give me a stipend. I got more money on these special outings than I did weekly at the church where I served as pastor.

There was a man who was a member of Beulah named James 'Huck' Gee, Sr. One Sunday it snowed, and no worship service was held. Huck went to all the families in the community, asked everybody for a donation and he brought the money to me at the parsonage. He collected over $100.00. Huck would take a drink, but the people trusted him. That's why they gave him the money. They knew he would give every penny to me as he told them.

Our daughter Priscilla was to start school soon. We heard nothing about the schools opening in September, so I asked the Presiding Bishop to move me to a church where I could serve as pastor and my daughter start school. I was sent to a church in Bell Mill, Virginia. Bell Mill was in Norfolk County.

———

MARYLENE COUNCIL WEST

My husband Franklin was assigned to be the pastor of Beulah African Methodist Episcopal Church, Farmville, Virginia, and we arrived in Farmville in the summer of 1960.

After we were settled in the parsonage, teachers came to Farmville to work with the students for several weeks during the summer. This was in the summer of 1961. Two female teachers lived with us at the parsonage. One was named Mrs. Tyler and she was from the Eastern Shore of Virginia.

I was over the library, which was in the basement of the church. Students could come and check out books. The books were very old. I was given a small stipend for operating the library. Mrs. Maida Vaughan McKnight paid me, and that is all I can say about the stipend. The money probably came from the Forrester Women's Council. There was an old lady from Buckingham County running the library when we came to Farmville and I took over from her. I can't remember her name.

In January 1962, I gave birth to our second child, Franklin, Jr.

Mrs. Tyler came back to teach the children the summer of 1962 and stayed with us again. We also had another female teacher that year that lived with us.

We took in two teachers both summers. Franklin and I didn't charge any rent, we were glad to have them and overjoyed to help. When I cooked, I prepared enough for the teachers that lived with us. When they came in from school in the evenings, I had dinner ready. When we ate, they ate. They were like members of the family.

Many years after leaving Farmville, Franklin was given a pastoral charge at Macedonia African Methodist Episcopal Church in Accomac, Virginia. While at Macedonia, we reunited with Mrs. Tyler.

LEOLA MILES ENTZMINGER

I was born January 20, 1943, in Darlington, South Carolina, to Mr. Leo and Mrs. Ethel Miles. My public education started at Cherry Grove Elementary School. It had grades first to seventh. It was a rural school located near Cherry Grove Baptist Church. The school had seven rooms and then there was an area for preparing lunch. Lunch was cooked at the school and students went into the serving area and got their trays. You took your tray back to the classroom because there was no cafeteria with tables and chairs.

My father was one of the leaders in our community. My sister, Mildred, was ten years older than I and was a student at Mayo High School in Darlington. I remember my father getting together with some other Negro men, as they were called in that day, and they purchased a school bus. My sister had to walk to the bus stop, which was a good distance from the house. The high school was about four or five miles away from where we lived.

We walked to Cherry Grove. I did that for two years or so. My father got together again with some of the other Negro men in the community and got the county to give us a bus. The White children already had school buses and our tax money was being used to purchase the buses for them. Daddy and the men told the county: 'We pay taxes. Give us a bus for our children.'

There was a graduation ceremony of sorts, when we left seventh grade at Cherry Grove and went to the eighth grade at Mayo High School. I didn't encounter any problems in high school and classes were great. We had great teachers. My favorite teacher was Mrs. Wilson. I can't remember her first name. Back in those days you only saw the initials of teachers, and you hardly ever knew the first name.

I think a Mrs. Jordan, who owned Jordan's Funeral Home, in Darlington encouraged me to become an elementary school teacher. After graduating from Mayo High School, I entered Benedict College in Columbia, South Carolina. I finished Benedict in 1965.

In the spring of 1965 students in the field of education received information from the registrar's office at Benedict about school districts in search of teachers for the upcoming academic year. Prince Edward County School District, Farmville, Virginia, was on the list. I sent for applications for teaching positions in various counties and received one from Prince Edward County. I said to myself, as I was filling out the application: 'I know I will not get hired there because that is where they closed the schools.' I had seen some of the story on television about the closing of the schools in Prince Edward County. I filled out the application and returned it. I received a letter from Prince Edward County and later a contract in the mail. Before I signed the contract, I let the principal at Brockington Elementary in Darlington review it. His name was Mr. Bonaparte. Mr. Bonaparte reviewed the contract and said it looked okay. I signed the contract and returned it. I later received a letter stating I had been hired. I received offers from other counties in Virginia that I had communicated with, but decided to honor my contract with Prince Edward County.

The Free Schools operated from September 1963 until the summer of 1964. The Prince Edward County public schools officially reopened in September 1964. I came to Prince Edward County in the fall of 1965, entering the classroom in September.

I had no idea what I was about to encounter but went with the educational training received. I was assigned to teach first grade at Mary E. Branch, No. 1. Mrs. Vera Jones Allen was the principal. We had a lot of over aged students at the elementary school. Some were nine or ten years of age and in the first grade. To have to see a child ten years old trying to learn to read was a very moving experience. However, I can honestly say that I experienced no discipline problems thanks to the parents of the students. Many parents were determined that their children would go to school and learn, regardless of how old they were at the time. The children in the class got along well, despite the fact that ages ranged from six to ten. We encouraged the students and reminded them that they were at school to learn. There was no time for a lot of correcting behavior. We were too busy trying to bring them up to their proper grade level.

I have had a wonderful career in the Prince Edward

County Schools. Just as recently as May 11, 2004, the day after Mother's Day, a first grade student of mine from over thirty years ago brought me a fresh bouquet of flowers. I had not seen her since first grade. It is a humbling moment like this one that makes it all worthwhile. I get a check every month, but a moment such as the one I just mentioned you cannot put a price on. When a student comes by the school, and finds one of their elementary school teachers, and tells the teacher about things he or she said and the difference that teacher made in their life, it is so meaningful. That young lady told me so much that I had done for her.

I have been in the county long enough now to see every school building that has been added. I have witnessed positive growth in the educational system. I have been here long enough to see students who I taught return and join the faculty. People have worked hard to see to it that Prince Edward County students have better facilities, facilities that can assist in their intellectual development and prepare them to live richer and fuller lives and make their unique contribution to society. I have seen how a school system can blossom, if you have people in the system that are serious and committed. Dr. James Anderson, who served as Superintendent of Schools for a while, in particular was one of these.

As of this day, May 19, 2004, we have committed leaders in the Prince Edward County school system and I am delighted to still be an educator in this county working at Prince Edward County Middle School.

PROSPECT

FLOSSIE SCOTT WHITE HUDSON

I was born February 22, 1924, to Otis E. Scott and Susie Lindsey Scott in the Prospect area.

My father was a leader in the county. He and Mr. Reverend James A. Carter from Lynchburg used to go to county meetings to try and get school buses for the Negro children in the county. They worked the issue some three or four years. Reverend Carter came to Sulphur Spring Baptist Church around 1938 and he and Daddy started working the bus issue at that time.

When I was a girl, I attended Five Forks Elementary School located in Prospect near Five Forks Store. It had one room when I started in the late 1920s and another room was added when I was in second grade. The school had first to seventh grades. One teacher taught all seven grades. Her name was Ms. Pearl Carrington Allen. She was my father's sister, making her my aunt.

I started working with the boys and girls in my community in October of 1959, when it was obvious they (the White folks) would not open the schools. All of the children who came to my house were in walking distance.

My son, Harold White, (deceased) was in third grade. He stayed home the first year the schools were closed and joined the other children who came to our home for class. The second year the schools were closed Harold went to Newport News, Virginia, and lived with my sister Ruth Scott Lewis so he could continue his education. After my Harold went to Newport News, I continued working with the children in Prospect.

I had as many as fifty children in my basement the second year the schools were closed, the 1960 to 1961 school year. We had old chairs, old bus seats, and a few chairs from schools that the children sat in. We did English, math, and so forth each day, but we didn't call it school. We didn't want the children to think they were in school because they weren't in a formal learning environment. They went out for physical education each day.

The first or second year, I can't remember which, I had two helpers, D. Althea Jones and Pearl C. Allen (Lyle). They helped me a short while and then they opened another site at Five Forks. We had two learning sites in the area, mine and theirs. There was a building that was used for Sunday School, Long Branch Sunday School. Worship service was held only on the second Sunday of the month. Sunday School was still held even on the Sundays when there was no worship service. Sister Jones and Sister Allen took this building and used it for class.

The children who lived close to where Althea and Pearl were teaching started attending there and the boys and girls that lived close to me stayed in my classes.

We always started class with devotion each morning, a song, a prayer, and sometimes each child said a Bible verse and sometimes we read a passage of Scripture. I did a lot of current events. The students had to read the newspaper and give a report each day.

I had a few high schoolers, but mostly elementary students came to my house for class. Many of the older children were sent away, but the older ones who attended my class assisted with the younger ones. The first one or two years I had about eight or ten older students. Out of that number, there were about two that I depended on greatly to assist me with the other forty or so younger ones.

The children brought their lunch from home each day. They usually brought a peanut butter and jelly sandwich or bologna sandwich.

I was young then and I enjoyed it. After the students left in the afternoon, I opened up my beauty parlor.

We always did the upcoming Sunday School lesson on Friday morning because most of the children would be in Sunday School at their church on Sunday morning. On Friday afternoon we danced. I had a record player in my home. I would bring it down to the basement and play records. The students taught me how to do 'The Pony', but I've forgotten how to do it now. (Ms. Flossie started laughing.) There was a record called Pony Time. The singer sang: "Do the pony with your partner." We had fun-time or down-time on Friday afternoon, since we had the religious part in the morning. I tried to provide a good balance for them.

We received learning materials from other locations. People in other States and around Virginia sent books to Farmville for the children who remained in the county because their parents were too poor to send them away to continue their education. The books were sent to Reverend Griffin at First Baptist Church and he would distribute them. Friends and neighbors would drive me into town and I would pick up some books for my students.

A class day went from 9:00 a. m. to 3:00 p. m. All of the children walked to my house. In order to assist with my expenses, I made homemade ice cream and sold it to them for a nickel. Classes went from September to June and then I recessed.

All my work with the girls and boys was volunteer. I didn't get paid. Several of the churches in the Prospect area held classes for the children. I'm sure Saint James African Methodist Episcopal Church held classes. Sulphur Spring Baptist Church didn't have any classes. I think Reverend Cleophus L. Brown was the pastor.

There was a boycott in the 1960s led by Reverend Griffin. The schools were closed, and we didn't want to spend our money in Farmville. My family shopped in Lynchburg and Appomattox. People shopped in Richmond and in other counties. This was during the period when the schools were closed.

He (L. Francis Griffin) was really a leader. We had confidence in him. He went to high school here in Farmville. He was just like any other teen age boy and in most cases went farther in his actions than most. In the end, we concluded he had too much brains for the lessons being taught in the public schools at the time. When he started preaching people said: "You mean Leslie is preaching!" The question was always asked in surprise because the announcement really shocked us.

Harold returned home when the Free School opened. The Free School opened with the help of Reverend Griffin.

After the schools opened, I started working in the Community Action Program (CAP). I got to see many of the students who gathered at my house for classes. When CAP started, Reverend Griffin recommended me to the program and I was hired.

From September 1959 to the spring of 2003 is a long time, but time has not come between me and the children. I am still very close to all the students who are still in the area.

LIBBY HILL JORDAN

When conducting a second visit with L. L. Hall on June 5, 2006 to go over his story which was mailed to him months earlier, he asked as we were concluding: "Have you spoken to Libby Jordan?" "No, I have never heard that name." "No one has mentioned her name to you?" Hall retorted, his voice elevated, wide eyed and a surprised look on his face. "Honestly," the Editor said and explained that he had been interviewing people in the county for several years now and no one had ever mentioned her. By this time, Mr. Hall was standing at the dining room table with the telephone book in his hand and was flipping pages. "I can't believe no one has mentioned the name Libby Jordan to you!" he said with some disgust, still turning pages. He put on his large brown frame eyeglasses, stopped at a page, ran his index finger up and down the page, found her number, started dialing and mumbled again: 'I just can't believe no one told you about her.' I heard a jubilant voice on the other end. I could tell from the comments of Hall that the two old friends had not talked for some time. "Libby, a young man is here interviewing me, and he is interested in the years the schools were closed. I asked him had he spoken to you and he said he has never heard of you. I told him 'you have to talk to Libby Jordan!' I want you to talk to him. You remember some of what happened. I'm going to put him on the phone. Hold the line," he demanded and asked, all in one in his soft voice.

"Hello, Mrs. Jordan, may I come by your house and speak with you?" the Editor asked. She replied: "I don't have much to tell and you don't need to make a special trip." "Okay," the Editor said, "I am sitting at Mr. Hall's dining room table and I am ready to type. My laptop is on. I just need you to start talking. Tell me a little about your girlhood days and move forward."

When I started to school, I attended First Rock School, a one room school down across the railroad. Mrs. Bethel was one of my teachers and one of the ministers from Saint James African Methodist Episcopal Church was also my teacher. First Rock School went to the seventh grade. When I was in the seventh grade, Mrs. Beatrice Davenport was my last teacher.

Students at First Rock who wanted to go beyond seventh grade had to go to Farmville. The county didn't provide buses for us. Only the White children rode school buses. There was a teacher, Mrs. Snead, whose son went to school in Farmville and my parents paid her and I rode with them.

I graduated from R. R. Moton High School in 1931. It had just been named R. R. Moton.

After the schools had been closed for some time, Reverend Griffin and others started setting up Learning Centers in the various areas of the county. Mrs. Beatrice Davenport was given a class of students and she contacted me directly and asked would I assist her. I said yes.

Mrs. Davenport was in charge of the Learning Center that held classes in the basement of Saint James African Methodist Episcopal Church in Prospect. I don't think there were quite twenty children in the class. Some of the children had never been to public school and most were in elementary school. Several had already completed first, second, third, fourth grades and such.

Class went from around 8:00 a. m. to 12:00 or 1:00 p. m.

I think it was 1:00 p. m. Mrs. Davenport had the children in the higher grades and I worked with the ones who had never been to school. Some of the parents brought the children in cars. I would pick up Mrs. Davenport each morning and then we picked up as many children as we could take. The car would be full.

I don't remember whether the children brought their lunch or not. I know no lunch was served at the church. They ate lunch at home. Reverend John Henry Allen was the pastor of Saint James at this time.

We didn't use regular school books. Mrs. Davenport was an experienced teacher and made up work to meet the needs of the boys and girls. She knew what they would have been doing if they were in school and prepared work at their level. I don't remember how many months out of the year the children came to us, but they didn't go nine months like regular school.

The positions at the Learning Centers were volunteer positions. I got a small donation but can't recall how much. It was nothing like $50.00 a month. The money wasn't given to us on a regular basis. Whenever they had some extra money, they would give us a small amount.

Ms. Helen Baker would have all of the volunteers to come together every now and then to talk to us. She was one of the organizers of the Learning Centers. I believe the meetings were held in Farmville. Ms. Baker also took the volunteers who worked with the children on trips. I remember us taking a trip to the House of Burgesses in Williamsburg. On another occasion we went to Washington, D. C. We always went on a bus and no one was required to attend. All of the trips Ms. Baker arranged were educational outings. She took us to places where we could learn.

I was a house wife when contacted by Mrs. Davenport to work with the children. I hope I did something during that time that made a difference.

———

NANNIE REBECCA HARRIS CARR HILL

I was born September 27, 1921, in Prince Edward County, in Prospect, to Floyd and Ruth Elizabeth Green Harris. The house in which I was born still stands. I started school at First Rock School and Mrs. Alease M. Snead was my first teacher. When we arrived at school, the day started with morning devotion. Each student said a Bible verse on Friday morning, but we said the Lord's Prayer every morning and sang a song. Then the teacher called the roll. In the winter the children went out and got the wood for the fire. They would bring in big pieces of wood and a man named Mr. Ed Hicks would come and cut the wood. The school went from first to seventh grade, but had two seventh grades, which were the high and low. Everyone went through seventh grade for two years.

After the seventh grade, we went to high school in town at R. R. Moton High School. Reverend W. J. Hendricks drove the school bus. He operated the first bus in the county for the Negro children, as we were called then. I think our parents paid $3.00 a month for us to ride the bus. It was that amount or something close to it. I enjoyed high school very much. I remember Mrs. LaVerne Pervall who taught English and Miss. Irene Dabney who taught Home Economics. Mrs. Nelson taught Vocational Guidance. Mr. Gasden was the Math teacher. School went to the eleventh grade in those days, but I had to quit school when in tenth grade to help care for my father. I was the oldest of five children: Floyd Thomas, Jr., Ruth Naomi (Davis), John Herodious, and James Leamon were the names of my brothers and sister. Daddy was ill for fourteen years and went home on Christmas morning 1952.

I was the Secretary of the Sunday School Department at Saint James African Methodist Episcopal Church in Prospect. I also used to organize the children for the Easter Program, Vacation Bible School, annual Children's Day, and Christmas Program. I would write out the poems and speeches and then give them to the children. The boys and girls would rehearse after school. All the boys and girls in the neighborhood would come out and participate, whether their parents came to church or not.

When the schools were closed, I felt the children needed an education, but they had no place to go. I had already worked with most of the boys and girls in my neighborhood over the years with various children programs at church. I took it upon myself to ask for permission to use the basement of Saint James AME so the children could come in and get a little learning. The pastor gave me permission to use the church. I don't remember the exact date I started holding sessions, but I do know I was holding classes around the time of my birthday in 1959, which was September 27.

I walked to the church each morning and walked back home. The walk was not very far. We had a wood heater in the basement. We had devotion each morning just like they did in school. The class started at 8:30 a. m. and ended at 12:00 noon. Lunch was never an issue because the children went home around lunch time. I was the only teacher at first. I had twenty-something children in the class.

After I had opened up the Learning Center and got things

settled in very nicely, Mrs. Davenport was sent to take over. I don't remember exactly when she came, but I know it was winter, probably November or December of 1959. I know it was winter because we had fire in the stove. Reverend Griffin and others were trying to get a more organized structured learning environment for the children. Mrs. Davenport taught in Prospect before the schools were closed and many of the parents and children knew her, which was probably why she was sent to Saint James.

I remember Mr. Oliver Hill and Mr. Spotswood Robinson came to the basement of Saint James Church to visit. Mr. Hill didn't ask too many questions, he was observing mostly.

I think classes were held in the basement of Saint James until the Free School opened in September 1963.

Saint James was built in 1954 and still stands. The facility as it is today is the same basement in which the children were taught.

I just tried to help the children at a critical time in our community and in the lives of the boys and girls.

———

GERTRUDE SCOTT STIFF

I was born January 18, 1923. The first school I attended was Five Forks School and we walked about three miles one way. My first teacher was my aunt, Mrs. Pearl C. Allen. Five Forks was a one room school when I started in the late 1920s. When I was in second or third grade, another room was added. Five Forks School went to seventh grade. Students who wanted to go beyond seventh grade and attend Moton High

School in Farmville had to go into town and rent a room with a family. Most families were so poor until parents couldn't afford to pay rent for teenagers to live in town with a family. Mr. Willie Hendricks got a bus.

After completing seventh grade at Five Forks School, I went to high school at R. R. Moton. I started going into town to school in 1936. I rode the bus that was owned by Mr. Hendricks. His name might have been William, but we called him Mr. Willie. Mr. Hendricks took the children from the Prospect area into town to Moton High School. Students had to pay a fee of $3.00 a month to ride the bus. The $3.00 was to help buy gas and pay for the upkeep of the bus.

The situation was the same in the Hampden Sydney, Darlington Heights, and Worsham areas. Students from these areas who wanted to go to high school after finishing the sixth or seventh grade, had to go to town and rent with a family. The other choice was to ride a bus owned by Mr. Ben Marshall who lived in the Hampden Sydney area. Mr. Marshall went through the Hampden Sydney, Darlington Heights and Worsham areas picking up children. Students in those areas also had to pay a fee to ride the bus, something like $3.00 a month.

The new R. R. Moton High School was opened around my last year of high school, which was around 1939 or 1940. I graduated in 1940 and was still paying $3.00 a month to ride the bus.

Our parents paid taxes, but the White people wouldn't give us school buses. The White people took all the tax money and bought buses for their children. Reverend James A. Carter who was the pastor of Sulphur Spring Baptist in Prospect and lived in Lynchburg, and Mr. Otis Scott, Flossie's father, were the leaders in the Prospect area. These two men started going to meetings in Farmville to address the school bus issue. Finally, school buses were given to us.

Flossie said she finished high school in 1943 and rode the public school bus one year without having to pay. The county must have given the buses during the 1941-1942 school year.

When the schools were closed, my children went to the home of Mrs. Hazel Carter (H. B. Carter) a Black school teacher and was tutored by her. She lived in Prospect. Mrs. Carter taught in Prince Edward County at First Rock School. After the schools were closed, she was hired in Cumberland County and taught at Luther P. Jackson High School. Mrs. Carter worked with my children during the summer. I think they also went to her home in the afternoon throughout the school year, after she got home from school.

———

HELEN RUTH WALKER

I was born in Hampden Sydney to Emma Florence Abram Walker and Morris Lawrence Walker, August 27, 1938. My parents were married in June 1932. They had four children: Morris, Jr., Margaret, Helen, and Freddie.

When a child, I attended Mercy Seat Baptist Church and was baptized at the age of eight. We didn't attend Sunday School or church that much. We didn't live close enough and it was quite a distance to walk.

I started school at Mary E. Branch No. 1. I rode school bus No. 23. Mr. David Patterson, Sr. was the driver. We had to walk about a mile to get to the bus stop and some days the bus left us because we were late getting to the stop. On that day we went back home. That didn't happen but a few times. On real rainy days the bus would get stuck in the middle of the road, the road wasn't paved like it is now, (Sister Helen is laughing) and we had to walk another muddy dirt road to get to that one. The bus broke down a couple of times and they had to send another bus to get us home.

In the fourth grade I was asked to play the part of an Indian girl. That was okay, and I really liked the part that I was to play. Here comes trouble! Then the teacher Mrs. Brewer wanted me to play the part of a white girl. I said no, I don't want to. I told her there was another girl in the class that looked more like a white girl than me. Guess who got to play her part. Me! I was hotter, madder than a wet hen. There was a lesson to learn and I learned it well. When your teachers see potential and the ability to do things, listen, take heed and shut your mouth!

I left school in seventh grade at the age of fourteen. I was at Mary E. Branch No. 1. I had gotten pregnant and didn't even know it. I was never told the facts of life. I never went to the new high school which today is the Museum. Mary E. Branch No. 1 went to the seventh grade.

My parents talked to the man that had gotten me pregnant and insisted that he marry me, and he agreed. His name was Matthew Washington Holliman and he worked for Norfolk Western Railroad. We got married the 25th of December 1952. Everybody said in that day 'get yourself a railroad man.' They thought railroad men was a good catch as a husband.

My oldest son Matthew was born February 19, 1953 at Southside Community Hospital. Five more children came along: James Lee (May 1954), Angeline Gloria (June 1955), Carl Mitchell (April 1956), Peggy Leila (February 1958) and the last one and the spoiled rotten one in the bunch Adrienne Denise, but we called her Chollie, was born in 1963.

The year Matthew was to start school they closed up the schools. We were living in Prospect. I got a teacher to come in and teach the children. Her name was Beatrice Lawson Davenport. She had a brother who was a lawyer in Roanoke, Attorney Bernard Lawson. Mrs. Davenport was my husband's aunt. She married into his family to Lovin Davenport. That's what everybody said his name was and that was all I ever called him. Uncle Lovin's sister, Mattie Davenport Brown, raised Matthew Holliman, my husband. Matthew's mother, Angeline Brown, was married to Reverend Peter Thomas Holliman out of Prospect and became Mrs. Angeline Brown Holliman. Reverend Holliman was from Augusta, Georgia, and was well to do at that time because he was driving a car. Matthew's mother passed and his Aunt Pearly Brown Bland, Angeline's sister, started raising him. She treated him so bad that he ran away to Mattie Brown.

I remember it was chilly when we hired her, Mrs. Davenport. We hired her, but she refused to take any money. She came to my house to teach. Each day she could come I would go and pick her up in my car. I was driving a 1949 red and black Ford. We had no set time. Sometimes she would stay a half day, whatever project she was working on she would stay until it was finished.

When I came to know Mrs. Davenport she was not teaching any place. She was living about a mile down the road from me at that time. Lovin and Beatrice belonged to an Apostolic Church. Lovin was later known as Elder Davenport, along with his brother Elder Isaac Davenport. They started the Church of All Nations in Buckingham County.

They were staunch AMEs at first. They started at Saint

James AME. The pastor was John Henry Allen. He had a club foot and was hard to get along with sometimes. Mrs. Davenport at first was a member of Saint James. Then they had an Elder from another church to bring the message one Sunday evening. He was an apostolic preacher. After that Sunday the Davenports' started All Nations Church in Buckingham. They tell me when they pulled out of Saint James it was never the same. (Mrs. Walker started laughing.) The Davenports was a big family and when they left it left a big hole in the membership.

When Mrs. Davenport started working with the program in the basement of Saint James, Matthew started going there. All my children went to Saint James because I was a helper, and no one could stay home alone.

The Bishop moved Reverend John Henry Allen to another charge. He was sent to Rocky Mount, North Carolina.

I was helping when Reverend Richard Hale and his wife was there (Saint James AME). His wife and I had the younger children. Mrs. Davenport and Mrs. Libby Hill Jordan had the bigger children in the basement. I can't remember Mrs. Hale's first name, but I remember they called her Peach. You know how it is when you call people by their nickname, as the years pass you forget their real name. Reverend Hale's wife and I were upstairs in the sanctuary with the toddlers, teaching them songs, most likely amusing them. (Sister Walker started laughing, while talking.) They were too young for school. The toddlers had to come with their larger brothers and sisters who were in the basement. The toddlers couldn't be left at home, so their older brothers and sisters brought them along.

We were fortunate to get a sixteen year old young fellow from Farmville, Virginia, by the name of James Edward Ghee,

II, who later became Attorney James Edward Ghee. During the summer he taught the children. Someone from town drove him out to Saint James each day.

Mr. Turner came from Lynchburg, I think he was a school teacher there and I think he was at Virginia Seminary. He came to the house and had some literature and shared with me what the children needed to know to start Free School and he also talked to the children.

Neil Sullivan was superintendent of the Free School. I think the Free School started at the regular time, September.

I remember teachers that came after the public schools reopened. A teacher from Wichita, Kansas, Mary Lee Foster, came the year the public schools reopened. She and my oldest son kept in contact with each other until her death.

As for my children, Matthew retired from the U. S. Armed Forces, worked thirteen years for the state of Maryland and now owns his own auto mechanic shop. James also retired from the United States Armed Forces and now lives in Douglasville, Georgia. Angeline retired on disability from B & W in Lynchburg, Virginia. Carl is the only minister in the immediate family. He spent four years in the Armed Forces and fifteen years in the Reserves and now works in Petersburg at Southside Training Center. Peggy lives in Columbia, South Carolina, and works at First National Bank. Adrienne lives in Maryland and works for the Department of Defense.

In spite of all the ups and downs, life has been good. I've been up and I've down, but God has really been good.

Note of the Editor: Following the interview, Sister Walker served me lunch.

———

LEEMAN ALLEN

I was born June 5, 1922, to George B. Allen and Lena Anderson Allen in Prospect. I started school at a one room school called School No. 22. My first teacher was Mrs. Redd. I don't remember her first name. I think she was from Richmond. I think she went to Richmond on the weekends.

When I was a boy, there were many one, two and three room schools in the community. Sulphur Spring Baptist Church had a school; it was about two hundred yards from the church and had two rooms. I remember Mrs. Thelma Bailey taught there. Ruth Bailey was a teacher from Roanoke and Thelma Bailey. Both taught in Prospect at different times, when I was a boy. Hazel Carter taught there for a little while also. Mrs. Beatrice Lawson taught there, she became a Davenport when she got married. First Rock was a two room school. Peaks School was a one room school, when I was a boy. There was a one room school at Calvary Baptist Church near the Hendricks Store and the school was on the grounds of the church. Viola Anderson Pride taught there. There was Five Forks School that was a two room school. Mount Moriah School was near Mount Moriah Baptist Church.

Other sections had their schools. There was a one room school in Hampden Sydney named Mercy Seat School. They had a one room school next to New Hope Baptist Church. Darlington Heights had a two room school and later it was made a three room school and the school was next to Triumph Baptist Church. That's all I can remember in this neighborhood.

Most all the schools went to the seventh grade. School No. 22 went to the seventh grade. When I was at No. 22, there were about twenty boys and girls in the class. We brought lunch from home. I lived close to the school and I went home for lunch. Some of the students brought beans, cornbread, a biscuit or whatever they could get from home, vegetables, hotdogs. Most had a sandwich like tuna fish or chicken or something like that.

Well, a man name Mr. Willie Hendricks had a bus. I think the county paid a portion, but every child that rode the bus had to pay three or four dollars. Whoever drove the bus went free. When I was going to high school the bus driver was an Allen, I can't remember his first name. He rode free or rather he worked for his.

I started going to R. R. Moton High School in Farmville around 1938. I liked agriculture. The Four H Club was headed by Mr. John Langston. Then a Mr. Wood came and taught agriculture. He was from Alexandria. They had two teachers working in the 4 H Club, Langston and Wood.

Mr. Langston and Mr. Wood would get together and take us to Virginia State College to workshops. They weren't called workshops back then. It was more like a demonstration. They never had more than one or two goats and a big dairy. They had about forty or fifty cows and about forty head of hogs. They would take us to see the hogs and cows and other farm animals. Dr. Settle (Unsure of spelling) was head of the animals at Virginia State College. He had a bull that weighed about 2000 pounds. He started acting up one day. The bull had a ring in his nose and Dr. Settle caught the ring, held his head up and the bull calmed down.

Mr. J. P. Pervall was the principal at R. R. Moton when I was in high school. Mrs. Altona Johns taught music. I was in the choir and she was the directress. She used to take us to Virginia State College for the high school choir competition. Choirs from all over Virginia came. We won first place one year. I think I was in ninth grade. This was about the 1940-1941 school year.

In December 1941 or thereabouts, that's when they got after me about joining the Army. I was drafted and had to leave school.

I had to register, and they sent me a letter. Then I had to report. I was gone around January 1942. I was in the Army.

We left and went to Fort Meade, Maryland, stayed there six or eight weeks, and then went to Camp Davis, North Carolina. We stayed there for basic training and then left for Fort Hood, Texas. Then left there and went to California and overseas.

I was honorably discharged in 1946. I came home and started farming.

I was in Virginia when the schools were closed.

I think the first time one of my children went to school was after we moved to Norfolk. I got a job working in Norfolk, but my family, my wife and children were still in Prince Edward County. I was working on the railroad, Norfolk and Western. It was time for Ronald to start first grade and the schools were closed. So, I moved the whole family to Norfolk, my wife, and children, Ronald, Wanda Faye, and Carol. Everybody had been born when we went to Norfolk, but only Ronald was school age. Ronald was born January 21, 1954. Ronald started school in Norfolk.

I was laid off and we decided to go to New York to my wife's sisters, Christine Hendricks and Avis Joner.

There was a building in Prospect on Road 626 called Hill Top Store. Floyd and Minnie Hill owned Hill Top. They sold candy, cookies, sodas, and everything a little country store might have. I think it was closed by the time I moved the family to Norfolk.

Hazel (Carter) started teaching children in the old store. She didn't teach them on the weekends the first year the schools were closed. People thought the schools would re-open the second year, but they didn't. Hazel started teaching the children in the area at the old Hill Top store on the weekends probably around the second year the schools were closed. They put some benches and chairs in the old store for the children and she taught. She taught them on the weekends until the schools reopened.

When the old Hill Top was no longer a store, we used to have Sunday School in there. Floyd and Minnie didn't have no children. The store was his living and after it closed he went to the farm equipment place in Farmville and worked. Minnie was a housewife and did domestic work.

There used to be a Sunday School in School No. 22 on certain Sundays. When the schools closed, they moved the Sunday School from School No. 22 to the old Hill Top Store. The Sunday School was associated with Calvary Baptist Church. Calvary Baptist Church met once a month at that time, on the first Sunday. The church members who lived out this way attended Sunday School on the non-church meeting Sundays at School 22 and later at the Hill Top location. Those who lived near Calvary Baptist had Sunday School at the church.

Many of the churches in the area had worship service one a month at that time. First Sunday was Calvary, second Sunday was Sulphur Spring, third was First Rock and fourth Sunday was Triumph Baptist. If you wanted to, you could go to a worship service every Sunday in the month, but you had to move about.

The old Hill Top Store today is the Prince Edward Community Hunting Club building.

The whole family stayed in Norfolk one year and we

moved to New York. Ronald went to school in New York for a while. Wanda Faye started school in New York. The schools in Prince Edward County were still closed.

When I was called back to Norfolk and Western Railroad in Norfolk, we moved back to Prince Edward County. The schools were open then, the regular public schools. We must have come back to Prince Edward County in the fall of 1964.

GRACE ESTELLE FERGUSON MOTON

I was born in Roanoke, Virginia, December 26, 1926, to Daniel Thomas Ferguson and Helen Estelle Hill Ferguson.

When I was eight, we left Roanoke and came to Prospect. We came because this was my father's home and he decided to move back. We were registered for school and attended School No. 22 where Mrs. Hazel Benton Carter was the teacher. It was a one room school and she taught first through seventh grades; she taught all grades. During that time, when a teacher taught they really taught. They made sure that you got it. They didn't have the attitude that I have mine and you have to get yours. It was at least two and a half miles from home to school; rain, sleet, snow, it didn't matter. We would be wet, and usually by the time we got dry it was time for Mrs. Carter to ring the bell.

She had a hand-bell that she used. She rung it in the morning for us to get in line and start the school day. We had devotion, a prayer and the Pledge of Allegiance. Most times it was the Lord's Prayer. We sang a song—'We are taken in together, Whatever the weather, We will take in together.' At noon we would have lunch. We had a well that we pumped water from. There was a little cabinet in the room where you put your jar that you drank out of. It was an old mayonnaise jar or something you brought from home. You held your hand up and she would acknowledge you and you asked: "May I have a drink of water." "Yes, you may." You got your glass and pumped water. Then we prepared for lunch. Some children had more than others. One day my mother said: "All I have today is a roll and I'm going to put some butter on it and sprinkle a little sugar." The sugar was a substitute for the jelly.

White people use to ask us to pick them some berries or something. They would come back the next day and give you a quarter or a little dress or something.

During the war, we had a garden. We had greens and no meat to eat with them. Some of us children would be playing and a White man working on the road would give us his lunch. One day we told him we had no meat and the next day he brought us a shoulder, (pork shoulder). There was no television, radio etc. When it was time to do your chores, sometimes you walked as much as a half mile to get water.

In eighth grade, I returned to Roanoke and attended Lucy Addison High School. My oldest sister was ill and couldn't attend school. Mrs. Carter used to come to the house and teach her. Daddy was working on the railroad in Roanoke and my older brother, Herman, and my youngest brother went to Roanoke. It was not a family split and we would come together on weekends in Prospect.

Florence Estelle Dozier, my daughter from my previous marriage, was sent to Norfolk to live with her father because there was talk of the schools closing. So being unsure whether the schools in Prince Edward County would open for the

1958-1959 year, I sent her to Norfolk. The next year Florence remained in Norfolk because the schools didn't open in Prince Edward County.

On December 21, 1959, I married Leon Moton. He was in the U.S. Army and in August 1960 we went to Europe, to Hanau, Germany. We took Florence to Germany with us and she graduated in Germany.

In June 1964 we left Germany and returned to Prince Edward County. We had a daughter born in Germany in 1963 and she started public school at Mary E. Branch No. 1 in 1968 or 1969.

ALBERTA STIFF FORD

Note of the Editor: The mother of Moses Ford was unavailable the afternoon he was interviewed in December 2011. The Editor was in Prospect on Thursday, May 24, 2012, and stopped by their home. Mrs. Alberta Stiff Ford was at the house. Moses was young when the schools were closed and unable to recall some details when interviewed. The Editor asked the mother to share how she made arrangements for the children to catch the bus in Pamplin City in the third year of the closure of the schools.

I knew Mrs. Alma Lockett. I went to her house in Peaks one day and I asked could I bring my children to catch the bus. She said it would be alright. I heard people were going over there to catch the bus and I asked could I bring my children.

The year I started driving them to the house to catch the bus I had seven children—Moses, Howard, Rosa, Edward,

Shirley, Edora and Sturt.* Edora and Sturt were not school age at the time.

Later we rented a house in Appomattox County up on a hill. It was a three room house. Me and all seven children lived there during the week. My husband Bennett stayed at the home house in Prospect, he had to work. Me and the children came home to Prospect on Friday evenings.

———

*The Editor asked Mrs. Ford to spell the son's name and she spelled it as printed. The name was spelled for her and asked was it correct. She said: "That's how I spell it."

———

CLARA MEDLYN LIGON

I was born December 20, 1928, to Mable Watkins and Otis Ligon in Farmville. My parents lived in Farrell, Pennsylvania, and returned to Farmville each Christmas. I was born while they were on their Christmas visit. They returned to Farrell, and years later Mother moved to Long Island. In 1935 Mother returned to Virginia. We lived in Prospect about ten miles from Farmville. Being an only child, Mother did not want me to go to school in Prospect. I had an aunt in Bedford and went to live with her. I went to Longwood Village Elementary School in Bedford. I graduated from there in 1943, having completed seventh grade. Then I started high school at Moton in 1943 and finished in 1947.

Students came to school and enjoyed it. Teachers were busy teaching and students were unaware of the educational opportunities being denied them. There was no cafeteria or gymnasium. Students went outside for physical education. I was not permitted to do so because of an injury suffered when I was eleven. I took music from Mrs. Altona Johns and Mrs. Vaughan. I cannot remember Mrs. Vaughan's first name. I was a member of the Moton Choral Group.

I rode a bus to school. The county was providing school buses when I started at Moton. Black students were no longer paying a fee to ride a bus to school. In 1947 I moved to Washington, D. C.

My father's sister, Iva Cobbs, who lived in Prospect raised a boy and a girl, Margaret (Evans) and Arthur Lee Foster. When the schools were closed, Aunt Iva tried to make arrangements for them to continue their education. Arthur Lee went away to Massachusetts, I believe that was the state, and lived with a White family. I remember seeing him during the summer when I returned to visit family. Margaret didn't have the opportunity to go away. Margaret went to the classes that were held in local homes and churches.

In 1993 I returned to Farmville. Moton School is now a Museum and a historical site. I am one of the tour guides at my old high school.

TRAVIS DAWSON HARRIS, JR.

I was born October 29, 1947, to Travis Dawson Harris, Sr. and Celestine Allen Harris, in the Prospect community. I was born at home. A midwife named Mrs. Rosha Randolph delivered me.

My parents went to School No. 22 when they were

children. That was the name of the school. It was a community school and had four rooms. I don't know how it got the name No. 22.

When I started to school, I went to First Rock Elementary School. There were two school buildings. First to the third grades were in one building and the fourth and fifth grades were in another building. The building where the fourth and fifth grades were had a divider to separate the rooms. The divider was pulled opened for more space when we had special programs.

The public schools were closed in 1959, when I had been promoted to the sixth grade.

When it was time to return to school in September 1959, we didn't do anything. Many children from different areas went to live with relatives in other counties so they could continue their education.

I started working in the summer of 1959 to earn money. When the schools didn't open in September 1959, I kept on working. My family had no relatives in other counties. All of our relatives were in Prince Edward County. So, I was not able to go away and attend school. I worked in the fields for local White farmers, who paid $2.00 a day. I earned $10.00 a week and some weeks you were paid $15.00, depending on how the farmer felt. I was hired as a boy but worked like a man. I was large for my age.

While the schools were closed, I went to some of the church classes when I could. Classes were held in various churches in the Prospect community. It was announced in church during the Sunday worship service at the announcement time that classes would be held at such and such a church on such and such days this week.

My family went to First Rock Baptist Church. Some classes

were held at First Rock Baptist Church. The adults who organized the classes arranged them in such a way that the boys and girls throughout the Prospect community could benefit.

For example, classes would be held at First Rock Baptist Church for a month so all the boys and girls in that area could get some learning. Classes dealt primarily with the three Rs. Then the next month the classes would move to another church, maybe Sulphur Spring Baptist Church, also in the Prospect area. Sulphur Spring Baptist was about six or seven miles from First Rock Baptist. When they moved it out there, it gave the boys and girls who lived near Sulphur Spring Baptist Church a chance to attend some classes and learn. Then the classes were moved to Peaks Baptist Church, also in the Prospect area. The classes rotated in Prospect within these churches, insuring that all the children went to classes even if only for a short time.

Many of the older boys worked during the day and couldn't attend classes. So, evening classes were started. Night classes were usually held only one night during the week. The preacher or the Church Clerk would announce at the Sunday worship service: "A class will be held on Tuesday night at such and such a church." Any of the larger boys who wanted to attend knew where to go. The night classes were usually held during the winter months.

I can't remember which church it was, but one of the churches had an old school bus to pick up members on Sunday, but it was also used to pick up students for the night class.

The classes at night always started with reading. That gave the teacher a good idea of where each student was academically. If you could not read, you could not do much else. I think the night classes were held because many of the larger boys worked during the day and the night classes were for them.

I was getting on near thirteen or fourteen and was working every day. Many adults saw that the larger boys were lacking in certain areas and were trying to help them.

Most of the girls went to classes during the day because they did not work. They went half a day and then helped around the house in the afternoon. The girls usually got home in time for lunch.

What happened in Prospect, as I have described, was pretty much the way it was throughout the county during the time the schools were closed.

But the best part of our education in Prospect came during the summer when teachers from other counties came to our county to teach. These teachers had taught nine months in the public schools in various locations and then came to Prince Edward County to work with us during the summer. They knew we needed help and dedicated themselves to enhancing our development. The churches also setup a better schedule during the summer.

The Free School opened. I was eleven when the Prince Edward County Public Schools were closed and sixteen in October the year the Free School opened. I had no formal schooling during the years the schools were closed. They tested us academically to determine whether students had been attending one of the church schools or were in a normal school setting in another county in Virginia or some other State. I was placed in the eighth grade. Even though I was in the eighth grade, I had sixth, seventh and eighth grade books. As I remember, I took mostly eighth grade subjects, but there were some subjects that the teachers felt I needed additional help and improvement. I had one or two books from sixth and seventh grades.

If you were placed in eighth grade, but your math skills

were at the sixth grade level, you did sixth, seventh, and eighth grade math. You didn't have to do all of the sixth and seventh grade work, the teachers picked the areas they felt were needed to strengthen and sharpen your skills.

I had tutors and most of them came from Hampden Sydney College. They came to the school. The tutors taught us during study hall periods and after school for students who needed to stay. An activity bus was running for students who needed to stay after school. I had to stay some days for help.

I felt like quitting initially, but my parents would not let me quit. I felt awkward. I had been in the company of grown men for the past several years, going to the bathroom when I wanted, and moving at my own pace. I was not used to holding my hand up in the air and asking for a hall pass to go to the bathroom.

Even the White people I worked for said: "Stay in school because you do not want to farm all of your life."

One White fellow told me: "Farming is going down." Tobacco was big back then. "A time is coming when you will not be able to make it as a farmer. Farming won't always be big." He was right.

In the eighth and ninth grades, if I could have returned to the farm, I would have gone back. I worked hard, studied, and passed each year. I began to feel more and more at ease in the classroom. By the close of my sophomore year, I was beginning to feel real comfortable. This wasn't the case for many students.

My older brother, Thomas, worked like I did on farms for a while. He went back to school. He was born in 1945, I believe, and he was placed in the eighth grade with me when the Free School opened. When Thomas was old enough, he quit school. Thomas quit school in the tenth grade.

Some students were in the tenth grade when the schools closed. Their parents waited a year to see if the schools would reopen. The schools didn't reopen and many of those older students got married. By the time the schools reopened, these people had families and could not return. Some were already nineteen, twenty, and older. In later years many went back to school and got their GED.

I graduated in 1968. I think there were 150 or 152 students in my class. I was twenty years old when I graduated. I knew others who were older. I knew some who were twenty-two and twenty-one. Twenty or twenty-one was the average age that year for a graduate. There were no White students in my graduating class. There were about two or three White students in the entire R. R. Moton High School.

I graduated in June and was drafted into the United States Army in July. I got married September 11, 1968. I came home on leave and got married. I stayed with my wife for about five days and returned to duty. I did two years active duty and eight years inactive. While on active duty, I was assigned to Fort Benning, Georgia, Fort Sam Houston, Texas, and ended up at Fort Carson, Colorado, where I was honorably discharged.

I returned to Farmville in August 1970. Things were busy, and some struggles were still taking place. The public schools were desegregated.

I went to work for The Carpet House in Farmville, where I remained for a couple of years. Then I went to work for the Capitol Police in Richmond in 1972. I remained with the Capitol Police until December 1975. Then I came to work at the Prince Edward Sheriff Department in 1976. I was a Deputy, a Sergeant, and Chief Deputy. The Chief Deputy carries the rank of Captain. I was the Chief Deputy for six years.

In 1999, I ran for the Office of Sheriff of Prince Edward County and won in the November 2, 1999 election. I was sworn in on January 1, 2000 as Sheriff of Prince Edward County. I am the first person of African heritage to hold this post in the county.

I am glad my parents insisted that I remain in school after the reopening. I am equally glad, on this date, May 22, 2003, to share my story with the reading public.

DORIS ELIZABETH ROBINSON BROWN

I was born March 16, 1944. The first school I attended was First Rock School. First Rock was a three room school. I remember Mrs. McLendon who was the teacher. My family lived in a section called Browntown. Browntown was about a mile and a half or two miles from the school. Sometimes in the winter my mother carried us to school in the car. First Rock went to the fifth grade. After fifth grade, we went to Mary E. Brach No. 2 in Farmville.

When the public schools were closed in Prince Edward County 1959, I had been promoted to the tenth grade. The first year of the closing all the children in my house of school age remained at home.

The second year of the closing of the schools my mother, and two other mothers, Mrs. Emma Paige and Mrs. Pryor, got together and found a house they thought was in Appomattox County. They rented the house so their children that were of school age could attend the Negro high school in that county. From my family there was my sister, Elsie, and I. I don't remember whether my brothers Louis, nicknamed Buster, and James, Jr., went to school with us in Appomattox County. From the Paige family there was Marie [deceased] and Whit Junior, who we called Ned.

If I remember correctly, my mother stayed in the house one week with all of the children, while Mrs. Paige and Mrs. Pryor stayed at home in Prince Edward County with their husband and children. The next week Mama was at home in Browntown and Mrs. Paige was in Appomattox with us. The third week Mrs. Pryor stayed with the children and so on. The three mothers took turns staying with us in the house.

After school had been in session for six or eight weeks or so, the county decided to do a survey of the house and property that Mama, Mrs. Paige, and Mrs. Pryor were renting. The surveyors came out, inspected the property and determined that the bedrooms where the children slept were in Prince Edward County, and the kitchen and other rooms were in Appomattox County or something of the sort. All of the Paige, Pryor and Robinson children were dismissed from the school in Appomattox County. I think someone or some people encouraged the county to survey the property. We started school in September, but I don't think we went up until Christmas. Yes, we were dismissed before Christmas break.

We returned home and worked on the farm.

The Quakers came and talked to many parents about their sons and daughters going away to live with families and continue their education. They talked to Mama and Daddy about me and Elsie going to school in Berea, Kentucky, at Berea College. The college had a high school program on the grounds.

We left Prince Edward County in September 1961 on a Greyhound Bus. It was the weirdest feeling leaving home for the first time. I weighted about two hundred and fifty pounds. I had been spending a lot of time with granddaddy and he spoiled me with good food, sodas, peanuts and such. I remember we used to pour our peanuts in a bottle of soda and drink and eat. I was the first grandchild of the late Jessie Hendricks and he took delight in me.

Someone from the college met us when we arrived at Berea College. The bus stopped on the campus. The students from our area that went to Berea College with Elsie and me were Marie Paige, Doretha Pride, and Frances Hayes. We were taken to the dorm. Elsie and I shared a dorm room. We came home at Christmas and for the summer.

We spent two years at Berea and they were good years. I lost a lot of weight. We had to walk too far to get breakfast, so I seldom got up for the early meal. All the high school students were on one side of the campus and the college students were on the other side of the campus. All the students, college and high school students, interacted at the student-hall, basketball games, and other social events and activities.

There were other children from Prince Edward County who went away to other locations in other programs. I remember Roger Madison was in a program, I believe; but I can't remember what State he went to in order to continue his education.

We were home in the summer of 1963 when the news came out about the Free School. I was nineteen and went to the twelfth grade in September 1963. It was not as structured as the academic program at Berea College, but being home with my family and familiar surroundings, that structure meant more to me than academic structure. I graduated in June 1964.

I went to New York after graduating. My parents gave me a set of luggage as a graduation gift. I stayed in New York until November 1964 and then moved to East Orange, New Jersey, having gotten married. I returned to Prince Edward County in 1997.

The one thing that came out of the school closing for me was the importance of family. I tell my children how important the family is and how a strong family can encourage and support its members.

My sister, Elsie, is younger than I and has a much better memory. She will clarify some things.

ELSIE ROBINSON WALKER

I was born December 22, 1945. I started school at First Rock, as did my sister, Doris. At First Rock School, we had to bring our own individual cup for water. There was a bucket in the room with a ladle and when you wanted a drink of water you dipped the ladle full of water and filled your cup.

I was thirteen years old when the schools in Prince Edward County were closed. I had just finished the seventh grade. During the summer of 1959 parents talked about the schools not opening. My mother and father, as well as many other parents in the county, didn't believe it. They refused to believe that the schools would not open. But when the schools didn't open in September, it was a shock to them and to many other parents. We stayed out of school the first year, from September 1959 to the summer of 1960.

My parents were anxious for us to return to school, as were the mothers and fathers of all the children in the county. The second year of the school closing, my mother and father, along with two other families rented a house in Appomattox so the children from the three families could start school in September 1960. The two other families sharing the rent and property in Appomattox County were the Pryor and Paige families. Yes, there were three families renting the house: the Pryor, Paige and Robinson families. All the children living in the rented house were enrolled at Carver–Price High School.

I need to explain how things went and the procedures for the house. All of the parents did not stay in the house with the children. The three mothers, Mama, Mrs. Paige, and Mrs. Pryor, took turns keeping us, the children. Every third week a mother took her week to stay with us. The mother that stayed did not have to do all the cooking, washing, and so forth for the children. The mother whose week it was to stay kept the children. That was her only duty for the week. The two other mothers came up during the day to do the washing, cooking and cleaning. The three mothers had a well-organized team approach.

One day a surveyor came to the house and said he had to survey the property. After conducting the survey, he told our parents that the bedrooms where the children slept were in Prince Edward County, but the kitchen and other rooms were in Appomattox County. The Robinson, Pryor, and Paige children were removed from the roll at Carver–Price High School. We attended the school for about two months.

The Quakers came to the county to arrange for Black students to go away and continue their education. Jean Fairfax was the organizer and co-coordinator of the American Friends Service Committee in Prince Edward County. My sister, Doris, and I were selected to be in the program. When I left home I was fifteen years old. The first year I was in the program it was only girls. There were no boys that went with us to Berea from Prince Edward County the first year, as I can remember. I was the youngest one to go in our group.

Arrangements were made for several children in our community to attend the high school program at Berea College. As I mentioned earlier, when the schools were closed, I was in the seventh grade. Berea's high school program started at the ninth grade. I was allowed to enroll on a trial basis. I was given a test and passed. I was enrolled and pressed full speed ahead. I was elected president of the dorm one year. The dorm was Talcott Hall. The American Friends Service Committee paid the tuition for each student from Prince Edward County. I worked in the cafeteria. All the students who worked had to put their money in a fund from which they could draw. You had to get permission to withdraw money. I made the Dean's List at Berea.

One year we brought a White girl home to Prince Edward County for Christmas. The White people in the community saw the girl at my family's store. The White folks in the area called the local police. The sheriff came to the store. The girl was named Betsy. They got Betsy to give them her parents' telephone number. These local White people called Betsy's family to make sure they knew that she was staying with a Black family.

While at Berea if there were problems we could write to Ms. Fairfax and express our concerns. If parents could pay anything to help defray the cost, they were encouraged to do so. The second year Doris and I were at Berea Mama wrote a letter and said we may want to bring all of our clothes home at Christmas, because Daddy could not afford to send us back. I wrote to Ms. Fairfax. She wrote back and told me to leave my clothes at Berea because I would be back after Christmas.

I joined Reverend Griffin, Reverend Franklin, Reverend

Williams and others marching downtown Farmville. Many Black people joined them. The White store owners would call us names and demand we get out of their establishments. White people passing by would also call us names. There was a five and dime store in downtown Farmville and the seats were removed so Black people could not sit down.

During the summer of 1963, I participated in the March on Washington. I wanted to go because I had been so active in the marches in Farmville. Mama went to Washington also. She and Daddy drove me to town to catch the bus to go to the March on Washington, but when the coordinators saw her they asked Mama did she want to go. She said yes and boarded a bus.

In the summer of 1963 it was announced that the Free School would open in Prince Edward County. I went to the eleventh grade in September 1963. It was different coming back home. It was good to be back. Leaving home at such a young age was a challenge. You did not have your mother and father or younger sister and brothers to talk to when you wanted to talk to them or share things or thoughts with them. I had to get use to family life and intimacy again. It was nice being in a new environment like Berea College, but you really missed your family. You never knew when someone in the family back home was sick or just what was happening back home.

After graduating from Moton High School in 1965, I went to Washington, D. C. and took Ward Clerk training at Arlington General Hospital. I returned to Prince Edward County and married Cornell Walker. We had two children. He was in the United States Army. I remained in Prince Edward County for a while and then went to Germany. Our family traveled and enjoyed several military assignments. Cornell and I returned to Prince Edward County in 1972. Jobs took us out of the county again in 1976.

Ms. Fairfax was in Prince Edward County about four weeks ago on May 15, 2004 for a portion of the *Brown vs Board* celebration. Many of the children who participated in the Quaker program returned to Prince Edward County from different States as well as counties in Virginia to meet with her. About twenty participants met with Ms. Fairfax. I talked with her a while. I will contact Ms. Fairfax and ask her to share some reflections for this book.

The closing of the Prince Edward County Schools was devastating to many children. While the opportunity was extended to me to go away and continue my education for two years, nothing can satisfy or take the place of not being able to grow up with my family. People have told me how privileged I was to go away and live in a new environment and meet new people. A new environment and meeting new people was no substitute for home.

There is no substitute for family and no substitute for education. I am telling my story hoping to stress these two points, and to help insure that an event such as the closing of the Prince Edward County Schools will never happen again in these United States of America.

MARCELLA ANN ROBINSON

When it was time for me to start school, the schools in Prince Edward County were closed. My mama drove me each day to Charlotte Court House to school. I don't remember the name of the school or any of the teachers. I was born June 8, 1956. Mama drove me for one year to Charlotte Court House and picked me up each afternoon. In September 1963 the Free School opened in Prince Edward County. I don't remember much from this period either. I didn't miss any years in school. I went to Branch No. 1 and then to Branch No. 2. I didn't miss any years in school.

My sisters Doris and Elsie have already told about the house my family rented with two other families, so the children could go to school in Appomattox County. I wasn't school age at that time. Doris and Elsie went away to school, but Mama and Daddy still had to make arrangements to get me started in school.

My parents did the best they could in light of the situation. They were determined and didn't let the evil done against us turn them around.

ALDRENA PRYOR THIRKILL

I was born in 1948 to Flossie Ligon Pryor and Henry Pryor in Prospect. I went to First Rock Elementary School when a girl. My first grade teacher was Mrs. Hazel Carter. I never left First Rock. The school had first through fifth grades. One portion of the school had what was called tar paper shacks.

In June 1959 they decided to close the schools because they didn't want to integrate.

The last day of school in 1959 I can remember coming home on the school bus and the bus was totally quiet. It was like no one had anything to say. The teacher told our class before we left school that day that school would not open in the fall. When we got home, Mama had nothing to say, there was silence at home.

During the summer, I took care of my sister's children. I had two brothers Roy and Charles that worked on the farm for our White neighbors. My grandmother lived with us and she was paralyzed. Mama did domestic work in homes in Farmville. When Mama went to town to work, I had to take care of Grandma. My mom did farm work and maid work in houses in town.

When the schools didn't open in September, I can only imagine what Mama was going through. Mama and other parents thought the schools would be closed for a short time.

My father lived in Baltimore and I remember Mama sending me there and I stayed about a week with him and came back home. Daddy lived with Uncle Floyd (Ligon) and Aunt Inell Ligon. Aunt Inell was from Alabama. Uncle Floyd was Mama's brother.

Then I went to New York and stayed with my sister, Arlean (Cobb Jones) for about a month.

In November 1959 Grandma died and in March 1960 Daddy died in Baltimore. Mom and I were there when he passed. We were visiting. Daddy was ill and was in the hospital. Mama and I returned to Prince Edward. We brought his remains back to Prince Edward County. Daddy was born in Pamplin and his funeral was held at Sulphur Spring Baptist Church.

The second year the schools were closed, 1960-1961, several families from Prospect, the Pryor, Paige and Robinson families, rented a house in Appomattox so the children in those families could attend Carver–Price High School. Elsie and Doris have already told the story in their account and

I will not repeat it. My brothers Roy and Charles went to Appomattox also to live in the house, and my cousin Willie Darnell Epperson.

The only addition I will make to the stories shared by Elsie and Doris is that there were four families in the rented house rather than three, as they said. The fourth family was the Allen family. The mother was named Marie and the father was named McCarthen Allen (Aldrena was unsure of the spelling of the first name). Everyone called the father Buddy. Mrs. Allen didn't stay up in Appomattox in the house but sent her daughter Shirley to live at the house with us.

After the surveyor determined that the house was situated in Prince Edward County, we had to dis-enroll from Carver–Price. This was the first semester of the second year of the closing of the schools. Mama was distraught. I am sure she probably said something like: "What am I going to do now?"

We only went to Carver–Price High School for a very, very short time. Mama decided right after we were dismissed that Roy, Charles and I were going to Baltimore to Uncle Floyd and Aunt Inell and go to school. My mama's sister, Estelle Ligon Epperson, had her grandson Willie living with her. Aunt Estelle and Willie lived right across the road from us. Willie Darnell Epperson was the grandson's name. He was some years younger than we and was I guess in the third or fourth grade, elementary school for sure.

When we went to Baltimore, Aunt Estelle and Willie went also. Aunt Estelle went primarily to take care of the four of us — Willie, Roy, Charles, and I. Aunt Estelle went to take some of the pressure off Aunt Inell. Uncle Floyd wasn't well from time to time, and he and Aunt Inell had a son that had down syndrome. We got to Baltimore early enough in the semester to get in school without any difficulty.

What was traumatic to me was the setting. When you grew up on a farm and all you know are fields, we had a well for water and an outhouse, and went to indoor plumbing, sidewalks and streetlights. Now you have three kids from the same family that had heard no noise at night and such and put them in a new environment.

Mama was left behind in Prospect to run the farm. Roy, Charles and I used to help out with the hogs, chickens and the cow, but now Mama had to do everything by herself. Mama had made a huge sacrifice to see to it that her kids got an education.

Now I am going to try and share of my experience in Baltimore, I say try because this is the portion of my life from which I have no memory. I can remember I was in Baltimore and I remember going out of the door each morning to school, but I don't remember anything at school. I don't remember one teacher or any of the students. I remember one incident when I had to leave school because I had had an accident. I remember a boy and I had grades where we could advance. I was lower in math than he; he was advanced, and I remained.

It was sort of bitter sweet. Mama sent money and food from the farm — ham, greens, chicken and other foods to Uncle Floyd and Aunt Inell. Most times the food was not shared with us from Prince Edward. It was a three level house and we lived on the second level. On the second level were Aunt Estelle and the four children. Most of the good stuff Mom sent from Prince Edward County they took for themselves. My two brothers have the same memory regarding the food. We were given foods such as oatmeal, beans, and hot dogs instead of the fresh farm staples that my Mother struggled and sacrificed to provide for us. My oldest brother would tell Mama, but Mama always said, 'I know it, but I have to send it.'

My brother Roy became homesick and returned to Prospect the first year we were in Baltimore. That left Charles, Willie and I in Baltimore with Aunt Estelle. We came home during the summer and for the holidays. We stayed in Baltimore until the Free School opened.

We often caught a ride with a relative or someone from Baltimore to Prince Edward County to visit. One time when I was courting a guy named Aaron Clark he brought us home. While in Prince Edward County, we went to a drive-in movie. Someone one in our car wanted some popcorn or something and when the person got out of the car and the people around us saw us, they reported us for being parked in the wrong area. There was a Colored parking section and a White parking section. We had to move to the Colored parking section, which had pot-holes and everything else.

When we came home in the summer of 1963, we joined the demonstrations. SNCC leaders came to the worship service at churches in the community and asked the parents to let their sons and daughters be a part of The Movement. The leaders came to Sulphur Spring Baptist Church during a weekday evening and word of mouth carried the news around the neighborhood.

We would catch a ride into town. Our parents wouldn't go into the stores that we picketed. They would honor the decisions of the leaders.

We attended workshops to learn how to be non-violent. The seasoned people would tell us if you get arrested 'just fall down and don't fight'. We got all the information at First Baptist. Charles was arrested. On that day Charles and Roy told me: "You're not going today." They must have known something was going to happen. Charles said Mama told him as he was leaving the house: "Charles don't get arrested."

We carried signs by the movie theater. We would try to purchase a ticket for a movie, but they wouldn't sell you one. You would ask, and they would just go away from the window.

Everyone was so happy that the Free School would open. We did not have to go back to Baltimore. Hearing the news was like having a birthday party.

I was placed in the eighth grade or ninth grade. I only recall one White student being in the high school and that was Dickey Moss.

I remember when Robert Kennedy and his wife visited Moton High School. They came down an aisle and I was sitting nearby.

After I returned home, events from that period and onward are clear to me. I graduated from high school in June 1967.

I left home in September 1967 to attend Cortez Peters Business College in Washington, D. C. The gentleman who taught me his father was the world's fastest typist on the old manual typewriter. Technology in my opinion slows one down in speed and accuracy. On the manual typewriter you had to be perfect. On the computer you can delete and go back.

When I was in business school, I went into the workplace after the first year. Mama had taken out loans for me to go to school. I took a job in the law office of Dovey J. Roundtree. She was a Black attorney. I started with her part-time as a clerk typist.

In December 1968 I started working for the Federal Government as a clerk typist, rated as a GS-2. I started working during the day and attended classes at night. I graduated from business school in June 1969.

I got married in 1971. In March 1973 I gave birth to a girl we named Erika Francine. I stayed with the Federal Government until 1973. My husband was in the Navy and we got transferred to London, England, and when we were there I returned to the Federal Government. I gave birth to my second girl named Robyn Arlean in Middlesex, England. I retired in January 2005.

I returned to Prospect in September 2006. It has been difficult over the years to talk about the closing of the schools and the impact on my life. It was in the fortieth year after the closing of the schools that I began to open up and talk about that time period. I owe the opening up to my granddaughter, Mykhayla Thirkill. Mykhayla used to ask me about events from the 1960s and I shared my school experience with her.

I was at a gathering recently with some other people who were students when the schools were closed. The people that brought us together gave each of us an index card, a 3 x 5 index card, and asked us to write our story. How can you tell such a story on an index card? I didn't write anything. The people that hosted the event did say we could write the story on our own and send it to them.

I am delighted to share my story on this day, Sunday, January 8, 2012, in this manner. I say in this manner because I am able to share my whole story.

———

CHARLES PRYOR

At the age of ten the talk about the closing of the schools was just a rumor. During this time, older people didn't talk to children about the issue. We heard it from other kids who overheard their parents talking. The rumor was out the previous year.

As it got close to time for school to reopen, my mom and

other parents in the neighborhood came to the realization that the public schools in Prince County would not be opening. Then there was a mad rush to get us in school. Once armed with the information, parents learned that in order for their kids to attend schools in the adjoining counties, they had to live in those counties.

Just growing up, my household always had plenty of love and enough to eat. The clothing wasn't always fashionable, but it was clean, and I was too young to know the difference. But the cash flow was not plentiful, not only for my household but for the households surrounding us as well. So, my mom and some other parents in the neighborhood knew they would have difficulties maintaining their homes and renting an additional property to allow their children to go to school.

The first year the schools were closed I went to Mrs. Carter's house for a few weeks or months. I remember us walking to her home.

The second year the schools were closed several parents in the community along with my mom decided to pool their resources together and rent one house with three bedrooms in Appomattox County, so their children could attend the Carter-Price School. In the house there were four girls, five boys and an overseer. The school year began. Each day we caught the bus to school until about one month later when an announcement over the school P. A. system requesting that all the students whose names were called were to report to the school main office. We were told that we could no longer attend the school because we did not live in Appomattox County.

Later we found out that due to the overcrowding conditions in the neighboring schools a survey had been conducted and the home which we had moved into was not within the boundaries of Appomattox County. In fact it was only a few feet from the Appomattox County line but still in Prince Edward County.*

My mother then had to find another way of getting us into school. She considered sending us to New York to live with my oldest sister. At that time her house wasn't big enough to house three additional kids. So meanwhile we would go to Mrs. Jackie Allen's house to avoid losing too much of our schooling. But as it stood we still missed the remainder of that year of being enrolled in a public school.

Somewhere along the line they decided that Uncle Floyd in Baltimore had a big enough house.

In Baltimore, we lived at 1826 Saratoga Street. I now went to Abraham Lincoln Elementary School. It was tough being a kid from the country now in the big city. We got into fights. We were teased about how we talked and how we dressed coming from the country.

We had fights going to school, in school, and after school. After the first year and people got to know us, it got better.

We lost one year out of school. I wasn't an Einstein. Some kids can catch up, but I remained a year behind. I struggled through elementary and junior high school in Baltimore.

While we were in Baltimore, Mama was home alone. My aunt moved to Baltimore with us. My aunt had to shut her house down. Mama had to oversee two houses.

When the Free School opened, we came back home. That was when I realized how segregated it was in Prince Edward County. When I left, I didn't know I could not eat in Roses Five and Dime. Mama protected us from all of that. We never went to the movie. Four years or so later I returned to the county as a teenager. I learned how bad things really were. The Movement started, and it was like a rebirth for me. I learned about all the things that I could not do in the county I was from.

I always thought Mama was afraid, but she wasn't. She knew how to survive. Dad passed the same year the schools closed.

The Civil Rights Movement started. The leaders of The Movement gave training to the young under aged (teenagers) volunteers at First Baptist Church anticipating that they would be arrested. The teens were used because the leaders believed that the older adults, if arrested could be charged with a misdemeanor and the fees to get them out of jail was too costly. They taught you not to say anything or offer any resistance when approached by the police when demonstrating without authorization, just sit down. Finally, the Friday came when we were going out to actually demonstrate. They asked for volunteers of the people who had actually been trained. I had missed the trainings, but I wanted to be a part of this Movement, so I raised my hand. After all — 'How hard could it be?' The police had blockaded the street nearest the church anticipating that this would be the Friday that we would start our demonstration. The leaders decided to drive ten of us around town so that we could enter Main Street from the other side. That day we were arrested. Afterwards the sit-ins and demonstrations to boycott the stores were continued on Fridays and Saturdays. Typically, the Black folks did their main shopping in Farmville on those days. The idea was since we couldn't eat here why should we spend our money here? The arrests continued.

Going away to school helped me in a lot of ways. It made me adventurous. Had I not gone through all the things that the closing of the schools caused, I don't know if I would have been as courageous.

I graduated from high school in 1969. I went into the

United States Army for two years. I remember we left from Fort Benning, Georgia, to go to Fort Polk, Louisiana. We stopped in uniform to get something to eat from a restaurant. The sergeant or lieutenant went inside to arrange for us to eat. The White fellow told him: "The White fellows can come in and eat, but not the Niggeras." This is when I realized that it did not matter what your status was as a Black man you were still less than a human being to some if not most Whites. Still I was not discouraged. Life has taught me that there was still a place for me in this world that I should always continue to move forward. But in my mind at that time I must say it did paint a ceiling as to how high I could go in life.

I have never been out of a job and never drew unemployment in my life. I moved to New York in 1972, and got a job changing tires, and then I moved sheetrock for a while, and also drove chartered buses. In 1980 I joined the United States Postal Service as a truck driver, Level 5, where I studied and trained for advancement, becoming a Supervisor of Dispatch Level 14, then onward, upward to a Supervisor of Distribution Operations Level 17. Then finally I decided that I wanted to break that imaginary ceiling that I had painted for myself and seek an even higher position in management. Knowing that this journey would not be an easy one, I prepared myself for disappointment and rejection. I had to compete with college grads and me with only a high school education I had to rely on perseverance and my knowledge of the job. I was always driven by the fact that my mother probably only went as high as the fourth grade in school but was able to manage a household, care for a farm, raise five kids and stay financial. In 2010 I retired from the United States Postal Service as the Manager of an 88,000 square foot facility with over 100 employees and seven supervisors under my supervision.

The thing that has been most beneficial to me in life is that I have always known when to fight, when to step back, and when to move forward. Life is only good when you pursue it.

This is my story shared with the public on March 8, 2012, almost fifty-three years after we were locked out of the Prince Edward County public schools.

---

*The story of Charles Pryor regarding the surveyor and outcome is different from the accounts rendered by the Robinson sisters. The common strand in the accounts is that the geographical position of the house had something to do with the students being dismissed from Carver–Price High School.

ARTHUR LEE FOSTER

I was born May 30, 1944, in Newport News, Virginia. I don't know all of the details because I was very young, but I ended up in Prospect, Virginia, with a family last name Cobbs. They were not related to the Cobbs in the area. Iva and Hunter Cobbs was the couple that took me in when I was a child. They had six children of their own but took in other children. They took me in and Margaret. There was another girl named Frances Davis that they took in. Frances' parents came and got her on an Easter Sunday, they had bunnies and so forth. I remember it well. We were near school age and about ready to start. This would have been around 1949 or 1950.

I started first grade at Prospect Elementary School, a one

room school. A highway now runs through the area where the school was located. The school was near Saint James African Methodist Episcopal cemetery. I started in what was called Pre-Primer. If you did good in the Pre-Primer, they would move you to the first grade the same year. I was moved to first grade. Prospect Elementary had grades first to fourth or fifth. Our teacher was Mrs. Morton. She was unbeliev-able. She taught all the grades. We were divided according to grade level. Mrs. Morton was also the cook. Her desk was in front of us and the kitchen was behind her. We sat facing the kitchen, but Mrs. Morton was always facing us. There was a big square stove in the kitchen to cook on. Then there was the potbelly stove in the class to keep us warm in the winter. Many of the bigger boys had to go out and chop wood to start a fire. I was young, and the bigger boys made the little boys carry the wood they chopped. I went to Prospect Elementary School for one year and the school was closed. Mrs. Morton had two years of college. In those days a person could go to school for two years and teach. The school board was trying to get teachers with four year degrees in the schools.

In the second grade I went to First Rock School and Mrs. Alma Smith was my teacher. In the third and fourth grades, Mrs. Lottie Jackson taught me. I repeated the fourth grade. I passed to the fifth grade and had Mrs. Fisher (not Ethel Wilson Fisher). Mrs. Fisher and I had a terrible personality conflict. We did not get along. She did not pass me that year. The next year I was in fifth grade and a Mr. Reynolds came to teach. After a short while, he said to me one day: "Arthur, come and see me after class before going to recess." I went to see him, and he asked: "Why are you in fifth grade?" I told him the story and he said: "I see." He went to the school board and explained my situation. The school board said it would not reverse a teacher's decision, so I had to repeat the fifth grade.

I passed to the sixth grade and went to Mary E. Branch No. 2 in Farmville. Mrs. Winston was my teacher. I don't recall her first name because you didn't know teachers by their first name in those days.

This year school ended as normal and it was during the summer that we found out the schools wouldn't open in September. They chain-locked and pad-locked the schools.

Leading up to 1959 White people would be on the local radio station saying their children wouldn't go to school with Black children. A school system was arranged for the White children to go to school.

I went to the center at Saint James AME Church the first and second years of the school closure. Mrs. Elizabeth Hill Watkins taught me at the seventh grade level. She felt that I wasn't taking it serious. She called me aside one day during the second year of the closure and said: "You need to take this serious because I know you can do this work. I want you to go to the ninth grade when school opens."

A group started arranging for students to go away and work during the summer, but you had to have been promoted to the eighth grade the year of the closure. In the summer of the second year of the closure, my aunt Marie Otey, in Bedford, Virginia, arranged for me to go away and work. (Her husband ended up being the first Black mayor of Bedford. His name was Russell Otey.)

Aunt Marie knew someone in Bedford that had a list and she got my name on the list. I don't know the name of the organization. Aunt Marie got everything in order. After everything was arranged, one day I left Prospect and went to Bedford which was about sixty miles away and spent the night. The next day we got on a bus, myself and a bunch of other boys from the Bedford area and the town itself. We went to Bloomfield, Connecticut.

When we arrived, the tobacco was already planted. Our first job was to sit on our buttock and bring dirt up to the young plants. After that when the plants were larger, a tractor came through and pushed more dirt on the plants. As the plants grew, they would bend. Then we had to tie them up. There was a wire on a pole that ran from one end of the tobacco row to a pole on the other end of the row. These were long rows. We had to tie the plants up until they were strong enough to stand on their own. Some tobacco fields were as much as six hundred acres. This tobacco was grown for one purpose, to wrap cigars. At that time one tobacco leaf was worth five cents. They didn't want you losing any leaves. (Arthur let out a roaring laugh.) Once the plants were fully grown we had to go back and pick one leaf at a time.

I was teamed up with a boy from Bedford. You had a picker and a dragger. The picker would pick the leaves and lay one leaf on top of another. A dragger would come and get the pads. You picked two rows at a time. You started at the bottom of a plant and picked three leaves at a time. When you had a stack of six leaves, the leaves were placed in something like a wagon without wheels, more like a sled. I think my partner was named Wendell. He was rather slow. I would get far ahead of him, so I decided to let him pick and I be the dragger. We did piece work, you got paid based on how much work was accomplished.

Many of the students working in the tobacco fields were talking about their senior year in high school, going to college, or joining the military. Some of them asked me what about my plans. I didn't answer.

I had gone to the sixth grade and was now seventeen years old. Suddenly I felt ashamed. The end of the summer I returned to Bedford and then went home to Prospect.

I went to Farmville to the home of Mrs. Vera Allen and talked to her about going to school. She said: "We have sent and made final arrangements for everyone who is going to school this year. You're too late." I was walking down the steps and before I got to the last step, she said: "Arthur, I have a boy in Meherrin who is ten years old, but his mother is having problems with the idea. He will be going to a White family in Bethesda, Maryland, but his mother is not for it. If he can't go, will you be willing to go?"

"I'm still packed from my Connecticut trip," I told her, "and can go."

I went home and ran an errand for my mother. When I returned, she said Mrs. Allen had telephoned and asked me to call her. I called her, and she asked could I leave the following morning.

I left Farmville the next morning on a Greyhound or Trailways bus, I can't remember which carrier. I arrived in Washington, D. C. and Mrs. Esther Delaplane of the Quakers picked up me, Irene Mitchell and Frances Mitchell. I think there were five of us she picked up and dropped us off at the families we would live with in Bethesda.

I lived with Lloyd and Gladys Swift and their four sons. I think they were expecting a boy about ten or twelve years old. The Swift family was Quakers. The public schools had already opened when we arrived in Bethesda. Mr. Swift took me to Leland Junior High School. I was seventeen and had passed to the seventh grade. They called the school board and they came to the school. After a short time the school board representatives said — "We have a real dilemma. You were promoted to the seventh grade, but we are unsure if you can do seventh grade work." They tested me all day at school. At the end of the day, they said: "We are not going to put you in the seventh or eighth grade. You will be placed in the ninth grade with a condition," which was explained to me. I didn't do well on the English part of the test. It was decided I needed a tutor for that subject. Everything was explained to Mr. and Mrs. Swift when they came to pick me up the end of the school day.

Mr. and Mrs. Swift couldn't afford a tutor for me. Mrs. Swift was talking to a Mrs. Watson one day. Mrs. Watson was a legal secretary on Capitol Hill. Hearing the story, Mrs. Watson said she would tutor me and did so two days a week at her home. She lived one street over. We lived on Highland Street and she lived on Chelsea Lane near the Naval Hospital.

Attending the Quaker church with the Swift family was different. There was no pastor or a choir. Nevertheless, they were serving Jesus Christ and praising God. They were right where we were spiritually. I had a lot of questions. The Swift family started looking for a church for me where I could worship in a tradition with which I was more accustomed. They found an African Methodist Episcopal Church in Washington, D. C. I can't remember the name of the church. They took me there each Sunday, dropped me off, and then went on to the Quaker meeting house. After the Quaker worship service ended, the Swift family came back by the AME church and picked me up, and we went home. The church I was attending emphasized Episcopal, the church didn't meet my spiritual needs. Then Mr. and Mrs. Swift found a Presbyterian church for me in D. C., but for all practical purposes the people were Baptist.

We did not eat out much. Each of the children, including me, had chores. All of us took turns doing chores: washing dishes, mowing the lawn, or whatever else needed to be done around the house.

Mr. and Mrs. Swift told me they could only keep me for one year. When school closed in May 1962, I didn't return to Prince Edward County, but went to my foster sister, Juanita Cobbs (Barnes) in East Orange, New Jersey and worked. She got me a job at East Orange Hospital as an orderly. When they took me around and showed me what I would be doing, I said no. I found a job at a restaurant and worked until the end of the summer.

I returned to Prospect and the Watson's sent me a letter and some money. The Watson's had asked Mrs. Delaplane where was I being placed and she told them I was not placed for the coming school year. Mrs. Watson asked in the letter was I in school. I told her I was not in the placement program and had not been placed for the upcoming school year. Mr. Watson was building small computers before computers were fashionable. He was an engineer. I think I called them, a number being in the letter. Mr. and Mrs. Watson decided to take me in themselves. I was invited to come and live with them for a few weeks, because Mr. Watson traveled a lot. With his travels, that would have left me and Mrs. Watson in the home. I was enrolled at Chevy Chase High School in tenth grade. I was not in the Quaker sponsorship program this year. Don and Kay Watson took me in out of the kindness of their hearts, so I could go to school. Several weeks passed and I remained with them.

When I received my report card at Chevy Chase High School, I noticed the letters NCP. Students compared grades and I didn't see the three letters on anyone else's report card.

I asked some of the students what did NCP mean, and they did not know. I asked the guidance counselor and it was explained that the letters were the designation for Non-College Preparatory.

The Watson family took me to First Baptist Church in Bethesda. Unlike Mr. and Mrs. Swift who took most of their meals at home with their children, the Watson's were more dinning out people, so I was exposed to many restaurants. I stayed with Mr. and Mrs. Watson the entire school year.

I passed to the eleventh grade. I returned home and entered the Free School system in September 1963 as an eleventh grader.

In my senior year the Watson's called and asked had I applied to any colleges. I said no. They asked what was I going to do. I said go into the military or something. They said apply to some colleges and see what happens. They said they would pay my tuition.

I graduated in 1965. There were 27 graduates in the Class of 1965.

Mr. and Mrs. Watson paid the tuition for my first year and for the first semester of my second year at Virginia State College. They had to reduce their support. The college administration gave me funds for the second semester, allowing me to complete my second year.

In July 1967 I ended up back in Bethesda, Maryland. Mrs. Watson knew someone and wrote a note on my behalf. I was hired to drive a bus picking up handicapped people. I had to have a physical examination and they found a spot on my lung. It was determined I had tuberculosis. I went to a facility near Roanoke, Virginia, and it was projected I would be there a year in the hospital, but I was cleared in six months.

Note of the Editor: Mrs. Foster was preparing lunch. The Editor had stayed longer than planned. As we were talking informally, Arthur said:

Many of the White people were opposed to the closing of the schools, but you don't hear much about that. I remember once when I was coming home on break from Maryland I had to change buses in Richmond. When I got on the bus that was going to Farmville, nearly all the seats were taken. There was an empty seat where a White girl was sitting and I asked — "Is this seat taken?" She said: "No." While riding we began to talk and discovered the both of us were from Prince Edward County. She told me that she was returning home on break also. She said her parents were opposed to the closing of the schools and had sent her away to attend school.

Arthur showed the Editor his high school yearbook, which was perused from cover to cover. He told of the accomplishments of some classmates.

"Willie Richardson is a dentist and I believe he lives and has his practice in Baltimore."

"Do you have his contact information?" the Editor asked.

"I sure don't."

"A boy locked out of the schools who became a dentist, that story needs to be told. I will see if I can locate him. May I use your name?"

"Sure, anything I can do to help," said Arthur and added, "We are so glad you're doing this work."

The Editor enjoyed the afternoon meal prepared by Mrs. Foster and departed.

———

MARY FRANCES MITCHELL JONES

Ms. Clara Medlyn Ligon arranged with Mrs. Flossie Scott White Hudson to identify some people from Prospect for me to interview on Wednesday, August 11, 2004. When the Editor arrived at the interview site where senior citizens gathered but referred to as Ms. Flossie's Center, four sisters from the Mitchell household were present.

Ms. Flossie said to the Editor: "I have some of the students that came to class at my house when the schools were closed. I sent for them to come and talk to you."

The Editor explained that each person would be interviewed separately. Mary Frances was first and said she was ready to answer any questions. The Editor said: "I have no questions." A strange look crept over her face. "I don't ask questions and print the answers as other researchers do. This is your story, your contribution to history. What is it that you want to say to the world about the period of the school closing in Prince Edward County? We cannot allow your story to be minimized by having you answer a few questions. Tell your *story*. Am I making any sense?" the Editor inquired, after his explanation. "Yes," Mary Frances said smiling and began to recount events.

I was born October 31, 1944 and am the oldest of eight children born to Alonzo and Othea Wright Mitchell. The first school I attended was Five Forks School. My first grade teacher was Mrs. Baker. In the higher class was Mrs. Flossie Wormack.

Several of the children in my family were impacted by the closing of the schools in Prince Edward County. I was going to the sixth grade. Irene was going to the fourth grade. Naomni was going to the third, I believe. Alberta was going maybe to first grade. My two brothers, Alonzo and Roy, and my baby sister, Beulah weren't school age when the schools were closed, as I remember.

When I heard the schools weren't going to open, I thought we would just have a few additional weeks out of school and then return. But after several weeks, school didn't open, I got concerned even though I was young.

I went to Cousin Flossie's house, where she was the teacher. We had prayer each morning and talked about current news. We always had to bring a newspaper clipping. Most of the people in our community were poor. But one student would get a newspaper somehow and the others of us would cut out an article.

I went to classes at Cousin Flossie's for two years. Then the Quakers came and began to select children to go away to school. My sister, Irene, and I were chosen to go to Bethesda, Maryland. We left home in August or September 1961.

We lived in separate homes in Bethesda. I lived with Ed and Sandy Rovner. Both were government workers and had two young children. This was a White family and they lived in the Bannockburn community in Bethesda.

Irene and I were the only Black people in the community and there were only a few at school. Irene lived with Ms. Vogeli. Ms. Vogeli was single and belonged to the upper class. Irene had all of the privileges and received a large allowance. (Mary Frances laughs.) Irene was more or less able to go and come as she pleased. I had more restrictions. At the Rovner's house I was treated like the children, Mark and Julie. When it was time for bed, all went to bed. Mark and Julie were younger than I. They were about eight and nine.

We attended Western Junior High School. At this school

I remember the children would get up and get a drink of water and return to their seat without asking. That was so strange to me. In Prince Edward County we had to raise our hand and wait to get permission from the teacher to get a drink of water or go to the restroom. There were only a few Black children at the school. I began to think things out at a more serious level. The schools were closed in Prince Edward County because they (White people) didn't want us to go to school with White children and now I was flung in the thick of White children. I had always heard there was a difference and believed it. But once I went to Western Junior High and started working and learning I determined or reasoned in the end there really was no difference.

We came home for the summer of 1962. In August we left home again to go off to school. The second year away from home, August 1962 to May 1963, I lived with Ms. Eloise Twitty in the District of Columbia. She was originally from Peaks, Virginia. Peaks is in Prince Edward County, between Pamplin and Farmville, and about six miles from Prospect. Ms. Twitty was single, but her father lived with her. I can't remember his name. Ms. Twitty took her role seriously, like a mom. I had less freedom with her than at the Rovners'.

It was announced in the summer of 1963 that the Free School was going to open in September. When I entered the Free School, I think I was placed in the tenth grade. I was born in 1944 and was now almost nineteen years old. I went to school for two years and quit. I took the test for a GED in 1965 and passed. I was twenty years old and wanted to work. I felt more mature than the other children at school. That was the main reason for leaving. Furthermore, I wanted to start getting settled in life like an adult.

As of the date of this interview, August 11, 2004, Ms.

Twitty is still alive. I still communicate with her. I usually see her at the revival at Peaks Baptist Church each year.

Looking back, I wonder how did this great country of ours allow this (the closing of the schools) to happen to us and no one say anything. I cannot to this day figure that one out and nobody has any answers.

NAOMI MITCHELL CAREY

Naomi came to the table next. Mary Frances stayed and listened. Again, the Editor explained no questions would be asked and said to Naomi: "Just tell your story."

I was born August 26, 1948 and started school at Five Forks School. Mrs. Helen Baker and Mrs. Flossie Wormack were the teachers. I had passed to the third grade when the schools were closed. I remember that because I never entered the third grade at Five Forks.

When the schools didn't open, the children in my family of school age started going to classes at Cousin Flossie's house. We had been going there for almost two years when I noticed that White people started coming by the house and talking to Cousin Flossie. These White people caught my attention because they just started showing up. I thought they were from the Prince Edward County school board and were checking to see how things were going. I later learned that these White strangers weren't from the local school board but were Quakers.

The Quaker representatives were visiting the various Learning Centers in the county and talking with the teachers.

The teachers, such as Cousin Flossie, talked to our parents. I knew things were brewing and plans being made for children to go away to school. I got excited. I began to see myself sitting in a classroom again and reading and writing and learning. The Quakers talked with Mama and Daddy about children in our house going away to live with families and attend school.

I was so happy. I'm going back to school I thought to myself. Mama and Daddy sat me down and explained the rules of the program that would find homes for students to stay during the school year. Mama and Daddy explained to me that a limit of two children would be taken from each home that was selected and there was an order as to who would be selected. The two oldest children in the family had priority. I was number three in the birth order. I just missed the cut off. That meant Mary and Irene would be going off to school. I was crushed and started crying. I really wanted to go to school. I was very sad. There were no families or schools that would take me. That made me feel real bad and it stayed on my mind.

When Mary and Irene left home it did something to the house. It was never the same. After they were gone, all during the year every time I thought about it, how our house was different, I cried. Whenever I thought about Mary and Irene I cried. We had never been separated. When Mary and Irene left home that was their first time leaving. We had never been out of each other's company. There had never been a day in any of our lives when we had not seen each other. Our family had never been separated.

I remember the first march in Farmville. It was down Main Street to Walker's Dinner. We were taught when we sat down in these restaurants that if a White customer put a lit cigarette in our hair we were not to touch it but was to let the person sitting next to us take it out or put it out. If the person whose hair the cigarette was put in had taken it out, that person may have gotten excited and become violent. That did happen to some students. I actually saw White people put lit cigarettes with flaming red ends in the hair of Black people.

Then I remember Jessie Jackson and Martin Luther King, Jr. coming to Farmville. They held a meeting at Reverend Griffin's church on Main Street. I was small, but I attended. People would come around and pick folk up to attend meetings and so forth in those days. The meeting where Martin Luther King and Jessie Jackson were present was held in the evening, it was not quite dark when we were in the church. I remember Reverend King talking about the closing of the schools and how we had to have non-violent marches in Farmville. I don't know how long he was in the county, but I recall seeing him on more than one occasion in Farmville.

A lot of times when we met we would sit at tables and talk and sing. One of the favorite songs was We Shall Over Come.

The next thing I remember was the buses going to the March On Washington in 1963. This was the first time I left Prince Edward County. It was so many people in Washington. You had to push your way to make even one step. As far as you could see, there were people. People were falling out because they were so tired and exhausted. I remember a boy from Farmville got too hot and fell out. I will not give his name.

After this, the meetings in Farmville stopped.

When the Free School opened in September 1963, I was fifteen years old and was put in the fourth grade. This first year was, I don't know, the feeling is hard to explain. (Naomi struggled to find words to express her feelings.) It was as if I was lost. In my mind I was wondering could I do it, could I make it because I had been out of school for so long.

I remember Robert Kenney came to the school.

When I went to the eighth grade in the 1967-1968 school year, I quit school because I was almost twenty years old. I was more mature than the other students. I was almost as old as some of the young teachers coming out of college.

The closing still has an impact on me. I made sure all of my children went to school. My grandchildren have to go to school. A few of my grandchildren live with me. They have to get up in the mornings for school. That's the rule.

———

IRENE MITCHELL LEGIN

Mary Frances and Naomi remained at the table while Irene told her story.

I started school at Five Forks School. Mrs. Baker and Mrs. Womack were the teachers and they sort of controlled the community. Back then teachers had great influence. I left Five Forks and went to First Rock School for one year in the sixth grade. I was to go to Mary E. Branch No. 2 in the seventh grade in town the next year, but I never got to enter Mary E. Branch No. 2.

When the schools didn't open, we attended the various centers in the area. Mary and I went to Cousin Flossie's Center. She taught reading and arithmetic in the basement of her home. We just did basic elementary school work.

The Quakers came around and started talking to the teachers at the Learning Centers. I think there were male and female representatives that talked to teachers such as Cousin Flossie. When I first saw these White people at the center, I thought they were just people from the local county school board or something checking in on the centers and were in charge of things. Later it was explained to me who the Quakers were and their mission in Prince Edward County.

I think Cousin Flossie was the one who told me about the Quaker program. She explained that they were going to start placing the older students who were most likely to succeed. The restrictions were two students from a household could participate in the program and the two most likely to succeed. Usually they took the two oldest children, but if one of the oldest gave evidence that they wouldn't likely succeed the next child in the family was selected.

Mary and I were selected to participate in the program and went to live with families in Maryland. I stayed with Ms. Vogeli. She was single. She lived in Bethesda. She had two little children, Mark and a girl. I can't remember the girl's name. Mark was about eight and the girl about six. I attended Western Junior High School. Mary and I saw each other at school every day and were permitted to visit in the afternoon. We lived only a few blocks from each other.

Ms. Vogeli was rich. I had my own section of the house. I had my own private section of the house, private bath, room, and study. I also had a maid. My maid was named Marion. Marion was Black. She would take me to the beauty parlor on her side of town on the weekends to get my hair fixed.

Mary and I came home on holidays. I earned money for receiving good grades. Ms. Vogeli gave me an allowance. She also gave me so much money for each A earned in school. I would save my money. When there was a long weekend, I rode the Greyhound bus home to Farmville and Mama and Daddy would meet me in town.

The next year Mary and I lived with families in Washington, D. C. I lived with Mr. and Mrs. Henry Brock. Mr. Brock was affiliated with the national body of the AFL-CIO. I think Mrs. Brock was a teacher.

This home was a little different from the one I stayed in the previous year, but I still had my own private area. All I had to do was go to school and study.

I was a member of the National Honor Society at one of the schools. I remember carrying a white pillow case, a box of cornflakes, a real fork, a plastic knife, and wearing one loafer shoe. Whatever they told you to bring or wear you did. That was part of the initiation. Students already in the society would tell you what to do.

When the Free School opened, I returned home. Though I had privileges, these were not enough to make me forget my home and family.

When the Free School opened, I was placed in one of the high school grades. I remember I was at Moton High School which had eighth through twelfth grades. I think the last grade I completed in Washington just before returning to Prince Edward County was the eighth grade. So, I was placed in the ninth grade when I entered the Free School. The year the Free School was in session was very challenging for me. The challenge was not academics. I had done well in Maryland and Washington, D. C. schools. The challenge revolved around age. I was so much older than the other students in my class. Academically I was fine. It was the age difference. I was a little more mature than they.

I went to school for about a year. As I said earlier, I was

much more mature than the other students in my class, and I was ready to get on with my life. Under ordinary circumstance I would have already graduated from high school. I earned a GED the same time as my sister, Mary, did.

I started working at Stackpole Components in 1966. While working there, I did a home study course for four years and earned an Associate's Degree in Industrial Engineering.

———

ALBERTA MITCHELL LIGON

The three older Mitchell sisters remained at the table and listened to Alberta give her account.

I started school at Five Forks School. We carried our lunch. Some days Mrs. Baker, who taught the lower grades, would put a pot of beans on the old potbelly stove. She would teach and watch the pot all at the same time. When the pot came to a boil or ran over, she would stop teaching the lesson, go to the stove and stir the pot. There were cups and bowls and odd pieces in the room for the boys and girls to eat out of. Some cups didn't even have a handle. Mrs. Baker cooked because the children from the real poor families didn't have any lunch to bring. She cooked basically for them because she knew students couldn't learn if they were hungry. (The sisters remembered the soup, talked briefly about the experience and then allowed Alberta to resume.)

I was nine years old when the schools were closed. I didn't understand or know what was going on. Back then a child didn't ask a lot of questions. I didn't understand why I was not in school. I was at Five Forks and was in the second grade. I was one year under Naomi, who was around third grade.

I started going to Cousin Flossie's center. I remember it was fun. To me it was like being back in school. I had never seen anything different, so as far as I was concerned I was back in school at Cousin Flossie's. At Cousin Flossie's we received free lunch. We were served peanut butter and jelly sandwiches, crackers, and bologna sandwiches. We never received lunch at Five Forks. So, getting it at Cousin Flossie's was an advantage. We had to carry lunch at Five Forks. As I said earlier, some days Mrs. Baker would cook a pot of soup on the potbelly stove.

I remember when Mary and Irene went away to school. I remember them packing. I didn't want them to go but was happy they could go off to school. (Alberta is crying and telling her story. Naomi became teary-eyed and left the table where all of us are sitting).

I would hear people talking about the closing and in my mind I always wondered how could people do something like that and cause families to have to split up. They were treating us as though we didn't matter.

The Free School opened, and I was put in a grade higher than the last grade I completed before the closing. When in eleventh grade, I quit school. I think I went following my sister, Naomi, who had moved to Paterson, New Jersey. I worked a year and a half and then went to a community college and earned my GED. I took courses beyond this. I entered college and took computer courses but couldn't work and go to class.

It pains me to this day to think about the closing of the Prince Edward County Schools and the impact it had and continues to have on families and individuals.

FRAN HARRIS

I was born Frances G. Harris, February 25, 1948, in Prospect. I was born in the same house in which Aunt Nannie (Nannie Rebecca Harris Carr Hill) was born. My mom was Ruth Naomi Harris. Mom was the Valedictorian of her R. R. Moton Class of 1945, I believe. (Fran was uncertain of the year.) When I was about two years old, my mom went to New York City where economic employment was greater, and I was left in the care of my grandmother, Ruth Elizabeth Harris and my Aunt Nannie.

One of my earliest memories from girlhood was attending worship services at Saint James African Methodist Episcopal Church. In September 1954, I started school at First Rock School, which was a three room school. Mrs. Hazel Carter was my first teacher. My second grade teacher was Mrs. Eunice McLendon, who was also my third grade teacher. There was a tar paper shack on the side of the school where the second and third grades were held. Mrs. Lottie Jackson was my fourth grade teacher. My fifth grade teacher was Mr. Henry Powell. First Rock School had a wood heater, outdoor toilet, and a hand pump on the school yard.

I remember the Weekly Reader, which was comparable to a newspaper for elementary school students, and it had good information. I was Goldie Locks in the school play when in the second grade. I had yellow crepe paper hair. (Fran started laughing.)

When in the fourth grade, I remember being so excited about the teacher reading Pinocchio. Fifth grade was coming to an end and I was so thrilled about going to Farmville to begin sixth grade. Little did I know that in September 1959 the schools in Prince Edward County would not open.

There was talk all summer that the schools wouldn't open, but with most families the thought of the schools not opening was unbelievable. My family, and no other family could imagine the Federal Government allowing the schools to be closed and children denied an education.

From September 1959 to May 1960 I was without any formal education. During the first year the schools were closed, I attended the Learning Center at Saint James AME Church. I walked each morning with Aunt Nannie until she stepped aside as the primary worker with the boys and girls and Mrs. Davenport assumed the leadership role. Then I started walking to the center with other children from my neighborhood. The center was critical in helping us maintain the three Rs. We did some history and other things, but they kept the basics before us.

Also, I recall students coming to the Learning Center from Michigan State College. They came during the second session of the year, from January or February until the spring and these were all White students. There were three of them and I distinctly remember. I know there were two female students and they stand out in my mind. I cannot recall whether the third was a male or female. I went to the Learning Center at Saint James for one year and I don't know whether any Michigan State College students returned in succeeding years or not because I went away to school.

In September 1960 the schools remained closed. My grandmother arranged for me to go and stay with a distant cousin who was an educator in Appomattox County,

Virginia. Her name was Wilsie Womack Smith. She taught at Carver–Price High School in Appomattox County. I had never seen this cousin before going to live with her. She was not a relative with whom my grandmother was in frequent contact. I don't even know how and when Grandma made contact and negotiated the arrangement for me to go and live with her. Cousin Wilsie had a foster daughter with whom I shared a room and we became close friends.

I lived with Cousin Wilsie from Sunday night until Friday afternoon. Each Friday evening, I returned home. Next door to Cousin Wilsie was a rental house where three families from Prince Edward County lived. Eight children lived in the house and the parents did weekly rotation of parental responsibilities. Whichever family was taking the others back would stop by and pick me up on Sunday evening. There were always two cars going back on Sunday evening because there were usually about ten or twelve people when we went back to Appomattox County.

Living with Cousin Wilsie was a real learning experience for me in many ways. I left a house with no indoor plumbing and went to Cousin Wilsie's where there was indoor plumbing and other niceties and facilities that made life enjoyable. She had a beautiful home. I went from a public school that had an outdoor toilet and a wood heater to a school with everything indoors. I didn't only go from a different learning environment to another, but also from a different living environment to another. It was a happy time.

I came home in the summer of 1961 expecting to hear school would open and I would go to the seventh grade in Farmville, but that didn't happen, nor did I return to Appomattox County to live with Cousin Wilsie and attend school. Instead, my mom and my step-father came to Prospect from Washington D. C. for Labor Day 1961. Everyone knows that schools open the day after Labor Day. I observed a lot of closed door activity at our house that Labor Day weekend. Little did I know all of the conversation was about me going to live with my mother and step-father and attending public school in Washington, D. C. Two days later we left Prospect and I cried all the way to Washington. One day after arriving in Washington, I was standing in line at John Phillip Sousa School registering for class. Ironically John Phillip Sousa School was the D. C. school that was part of the *Brown vs Board* of Education suit, as had the Prince Edward County School District.

I made a relatively quick adjustment, but I missed Prospect. Whenever we returned to Prospect at Christmas, summer and holidays, I would cry when it was time to return to D. C. When I was large enough, my mother and step-father would put me on a Greyhound bus and I would ride to Richmond. My uncle, John Harris, mother's brother, would meet me in Richmond so I wouldn't have to change buses in Richmond and ride on to Farmville. I graduated from Anacostia High School, Washington, D. C., in 1967.

The years have passed, and I have been truly blessed. I have been the recipient of many blessings. Nonetheless, I often wonder what my life would have been like without the chapter of the closing of the schools in Prince Edward County. Had things been different would I have been at the head of my class as my mother was at the head of her class? Even to this day I cannot get my mind around the idea that the schools were not opened in September 1959.

LEON HILL

The name given me at birth by my parents was Hazel Leon Hill, but everyone, family and friends, has called me Leon as far back as I can remember.

I was born September 5, 1945. I started public school at No. 22 School and Mrs. Hazel Carter was my teacher. No. 22 School had first to fifth grades. I went one year and then it was closed. Then I went to First Rock in the second and third grades. We were in the tarpaper buildings, which are not there now. Mrs. Eunice McLendon was my teacher.

When the schools were closed, I had passed to the ninth grade. I missed school the first year of the closure. I worked on the farm and we cleared ground for William Henry Stiff. His sons and I and my brother cleared the low land, so he could make a pasture.

The second year the schools were closed my family and two other families, the Ligon and Stiff families of Prospect, rented a house together in Appomattox County. The house they rented had two rooms and a kitchen. Eight children and two adults stayed at the house Monday through Friday, and we came back to Prospect each Friday evening. The rental house was ten or twelve miles from Prospect and was rented from Wilsie Smith. Wilsie was our cousin and she taught English at Carver–Price High School. The rented house gave us students an Appomattox address for school. All the children were enrolled at Carver-Price High School. We had to stay in Appomattox County during the week, which was why we came back to Prospect on Friday evenings.

In my family there was me and my brother Andrew. Andrew had passed to the sixth or seventh grade when the schools were closed.

I will tell about the Ligon family. The father was named Raymond Ligon and his wife was named Martha Robinson Ligon. Mr. Ligon owned his own construction business. He built houses, worked on churches and so forth. Mrs. Ligon worked at the Appomattox Garment Factory. In the Ligon family there was Elaine; she was in the sixth or seventh grade. LaVerne was one grade ahead of Elaine. Raymond their brother was around fifth grade. Their mother, Mrs. Ligon, stayed every week with us.

The parents in the Stiff family were William Henry Stiff and Mamie Bland Stiff. Mr. Stiff worked on the rail road and farmed. Mrs. Stiff was a housewife. Her father, as I recalled, was Mr. Leonard Bland and his wife was Mrs. Elenora. Elenora was my daddy's sister, but she passed before I was born.

There were three boys in the Stiff family — William, Ray, and Oliver. William was around the sixth grade; he and my brother Andrew were together. Ray was one grade behind William, and Oliver was one grade behind Ray.

While the three families lived in the house in Appomattox, Mrs. Ligon continued working at the garment factory. Mrs. Ligon left the house around 7:30 a. m. I think she had to be at work at 8:00 a. m. She had a car and drove herself.

Mrs. Stiff was a housewife and she was always with us. Probably after we went to school she would go back to Prospect and be back at the two room house when we got home from school. Mrs. Ligon got off work at 4:00 p. m. and was at the house around 4:30 p. m. Mrs. Stiff and Mrs. Ligon did the cooking.

I can't remember the details of the sleeping arrangements. But I know the girls slept in the room with Mrs. Ligon and Mrs. Stiff, and us boys was in the other room. We had cots and small beds all around the two rooms. (Mr. Hill started laughing.)

When we did our homework in the evenings, we sat on the side of our beds because we had no tables. There was one small table in the kitchen. The kitchen was so small that we had to eat in shifts.

The house had indoor plumbing and running water. Everybody knew their bathroom time in the morning and at night.

My mother did not stay at the rented house with the children. She had to remain in Prospect and take care of her mother who was ill.

All of the children in the rented house were related, blood relatives.

Edwin Paige drove his father's car. Everybody called him Ned. I was back in Prospect for the weekends and would ride to ball games and dances or other school events with Ned and Phillip.

I went to the Junior-Senior Prom. Ned took Juanita Lawing from Appomattox to the prom.

I play baseball on the Carver–Price High School team. I played third base. Ned played football and baseball. I think he played second base.

There were thirty-three students in the Carver–Price Class of 1964 and three of us were from Prince Edward County — Edwin Paige, Phillip Walker and Hazel Leon Hill.

Ned lives in Florida and I am going put him and Wally in contact with each other, so Ned can tell his story.

There were other Prince Edward County students at Carver–Price High School, while I was there. I remember Edward Lockett and his sister were at the school.

Mrs. Goode taught at Carver-Price and she took her sister-in-law named Ernestine Goode. All of us, me and Ernestine, were in sixth grade together Mary E. Branch. Ernestine didn't miss a beat. The first year of the closure, she started riding to Carver–Price with her sister-in-law, Mrs. Goode, the school teacher. Ernestine would have graduated in 1963, since she did not miss anytime out of school. If I had not missed one year out of school, I would have graduated in 1963.

Ernestine's brother was named Darius Goode. Mrs. Goode was from Appomattox County, I believe; but after she married Darius, she moved to Prince Edward County. Her homestead address was in Appomattox County.

Prince Edward County students went to schools in other counties nearby.

My aunt, named Libby Hill Jordan, had three girls, but one daughter, Ithro, graduated from Moton High School before the closure. Phyllis and Lillian Jordan graduated from Central High School in Charlotte County. They caught the bus. They caught the bus at the house of Mr. Wilson, who lived on the Charlotte County side. Mr. Wilson was in the pulpwood business and so was the father of Phyllis and Lillian. Their father and Mr. Wilson worked everything out.

After graduating from high school, I enlisted in the United States Army. I did two tours in Vietnam. I received the Bronze Star Medal and the Purple Heart Medal. I was in the military for twenty-seven years.

My father was named Hazel Hill and my mother was named Leola Womack Hill. My father worked on the Norfolk and Western Railroad for forty-two years. My mama was a teacher's aide in the Prince Edward County Public Schools after the schools officially reopened.

GLORIA ALLEN LOCKETT

I was born in Prospect to Donald and Annie Allen, September 12, 1957. I was two when the schools were closed. When I turned five, I didn't go to any center in the area where classes were held. I lived about a half mile from Saint James African Methodist Episcopal Church. I don't know why, but my parents did not send me there when I turned five.

When it was time for me to start school, the schools were still closed. No one in my house ever said anything like 'it's time for you to go to school, but the schools are closed.' Life just went on every day. I had no concept at that young age of what was happening or where I was supposed to be or what school was all about. I had no idea what school was.

I started first grade in September 1964 and that was my introduction to school. We grew up poor and didn't have what other children had.

I never really fully comprehended the school closing and its impact on people until around 2006 when I learned that the State had allocated money for students that had been impacted, but who wanted to continue their education. You could get money to assist in securing basic Adult Education, GED, Associate's Degree, Bachelor's Degree, and Master's Degree. I'm unsure about the Ph. D.

Under ordinary circumstance I would have gone to kindergarten at five years old and first grade at six, but I missed both and started public school at seven. So, I qualified for State funds when it was authorized.

I enrolled in the Saint Paul's College satellite program in Farmville. Classes were held at the Moton Museum. I earned a Bachelor's Degree in Business Administration. I am as of this day, October 19, 2011, enrolled in a master's degree program in Human Services at Liberty University, Lynchburg, Virginia.

Gloria said following her presentation: "You need to speak with Evangelist Lillie Jordan Johnson. She has a powerful story." Gloria also mentioned her sister, Polly Allen Wise, that was a nurse. "You make the contact with them and I will get with Evangelist Johnson and your sister, Polly," the Editor said.

———

LILLIAN GLORIA JORDAN JOHNSON

My twin sister Phyllis and I started public school at First Rock School on Highway 460 and we walked to school. My first grade teacher was Mrs. Alma Smith. I remember an old freight train came around 9:00 a. m. and we always tried to cross the railroad tracks before it came. The train always had what seemed to be hundreds of cars. My older sister Ithro was six years older and she would leave us and walk beside the moving train. Mama would get after Ithro and soon Mama put an end to that.

In the second grade Mrs. Smith taught us too. My sister and I looked exactly alike, we were identical twins. In second grade the photographer came to take student pictures. When he developed the pictures, he thought he took a picture of the same student twice and he destroyed the other set. When they sent the one set of pictures home, we figured out as closely as possible that it was Phyllis. It was not a positive identification. Phyllis had a mark on her left upper cheek and that was the primary way people knew one of us from the other. The way the girl was sitting in the picture you could not see the left check; nevertheless, the family settled on Phyllis. (Lillian started laughing.)

In the third grade we went to a tar paper building in the back of school. Only the third grade was there and Mrs. Eunice McLendon was the teacher.

In fourth and fifth grades we went back to the main building. Our fourth grade teacher was Mrs. Lottie Jackson and we had Mrs. Fisher in the fifth grade. I can't remember Mrs. Fisher's first name.

In the sixth grade we started at Mary E. Branch No. 1 in Farmville and Mrs. Kelly was the teacher. She was ambidextrous. Before she met us, she had been in a terrible accident and the scars were still visible. She had learned to use the other hand. She could write on the board with both hands.

I think my seventh grade teacher was Mrs. West. I remember she was very beautiful. I say I think it was Mrs. West because I'm not absolutely certain.

The following year I went to eighth grade at the high school. Going into town was an adventure. Our elementary school years had been at a small three room school with boys and girls we knew. We saw the same kids each day and at church on Sundays, and many were our relatives. In town we met students from Rice, Hampden Sydney, Darlington Heights and so forth. Making new friends was adventurous and exciting.

My sister and I were very popular because we were twins and Mama still continued to dress us alike. In eighth grade we changed classes for different subjects. I believe my homeroom teacher was Mrs. Mary Madison. I distinctly remember taking classes from Ms. Malloy who taught P. E., Mr. White who taught science, and Mr. Stanton taught us Math. I remember having Ms. Glaze and Mr. Paul Martin.

In eighth grade, the 1958-1959 school year, my parents had not discussed anything about the possible school closing in our presence. We ended the school year telling our friends 'See you next year.'

Daddy's sister, Aunt Gertrude (Gertrude Load Holt) came to visit the summer of 1959. This was the first time I recalled having seen her. I remember shortly after she left Mama and Daddy started talking about 'them not opening the schools.' As we overheard adult conversations, Phyllis and I began to put some things together. We would hear Mom talking because she was very upset. I can remember her saying – "I will have to send my babies away." Towards the start of school, Aunt Gertrude called and said send us to New York to live with her and Uncle Frank. I remember Mom and Daddy taking us to the train station in Farmville and putting us on the train. I remember Aunt Gertrude meeting us at the train station in New York City. Imagine being in New York City when you had never been outside of Prince Edward County!

New York City was quiet overwhelming. The information about Prince Edward County and the school situation was beginning to appear in the news. Phyllis and I heard it on the news. Aunt Gertrude put us in a school about two and a half blocks from her house called Morris High School. She took very good care of us. Knowing nothing about New York, we were unaware that we lived in a bad neighborhood. Aunt Gertrude took such good care of us until it was unnoticeable what kind of neighborhood we lived in. She used to call us 'her dolls.'

I remember when she enrolled us in the school and the teachers found out where we were from whenever there was a recitation or report for class the teachers wanted Phyllis and I to talk about Prince Edward County and the school situation. The teachers had heard about it in the news and read stories in magazines, but they had two real live human beings in the school that had been impacted by the experience and they wanted to hear our first-hand account and wanted the students to hear about it.

I remember sometimes teachers would say to other teachers regarding Phyllis and I—'they are from Prince Edward County.'

When we came home in the summer things were so different. We did not know the depth of it until we would come home. When we would come, it made us feel kind of bad being around our old friends and many of them having not gone to school anywhere. Guys started working and they were comfortable. They were able to put money in their pockets. In the summer we went to the lake and had fun, but there was no discussion about education. You felt bad that your friends did not have relatives somewhere to whom their parents could send them. My parents really wanted us to get an education.

Phyllis and I went back to Aunt Gertrude and Uncle Frank in August 1960 to go to school a second year. We finished our second year of school in New York.

Aunt Gertrude died. Mama came to New York and stayed with us and Uncle Frank. Within a short time, Uncle Frank decided to get married. The bride to be told him that his nieces could stay in the house, but his sister-in-law (Mama) had to return to Virginia and couldn't stay.

Mama told Daddy about it and he said—"All y'all come home." At the end of the first semester, December 1961, we came back to Prince Edward County. Phyllis and I had about a year and a half left before graduating high school.

When we got back home, somebody had told Daddy there was woman in Charlotte County in the Jeffries family that wanted to take in some children from Prince Edward County. A Mr. Wilson Jeffries and his wife, who the husband called Mae, made it known that they would take in some children from Prince Edward County. They had five children themselves—Jessie was the oldest and there were two other boys and two girls, whose names I can't remember, younger than Jessie.

Phyllis and I stayed with the Jeffries during the week and Daddy would come and get us each Friday evening. This started in January 1962. We stayed with Mr. and Mrs. Jeffries the entire second semester of the 1961-1962 school year.

Some of our friends got involved in The Movement and started going into stores in Farmville to shop. I remember once I saw a policeman with a dog. We came back home and told Daddy about it. He didn't let us go back into town. He said: "If anything happens to you all, I'll go crazy." We knew what that meant. That meant Daddy wouldn't allow any harm having come to us to go unaddressed.

During the summer of 1962, Mrs. Jeffries said her health would not permit her to take us the upcoming school year. So that was when Daddy and Mama had to figure out what to do so we could finish our senior year. I remember in our last year of school Daddy started taking us to catch the school bus at a bus stop in Charlotte County. They said it was against the law to take kids to other counties. It wasn't so much the White folks that was turning in Black children, but Black folks turning in Black students. There was a lot of jealousy. You couldn't talk to anyone about school or where you went to school because people were jealous and would report you.

Daddy started driving us to the Appomattox County line

in the mornings. He drove us to that part of Appomattox County where the Appomattox County line and the Charlotte County line touched. We boarded the bus on the Charlotte County side to ride to Central High School where we had attended the previous semester. Some mornings Mama used to drive us to where the lines converged, and she also carried some of the Hendricks children in the car with us. The bus driver that we rode with was very kind. He would always stop at the store in the afternoon and he would purchase candy or peanuts to give to me and Phyllis. He never gave any of the other children candy.

Where the Appomattox County and Charlotte County lines met a very large number of Prince Edward County students began to congregate. Some students got on an Appomattox County bus that took them to Carver–Price High School in Appomattox, and the others of us got on the bus that went to Charlotte Court House. The bus driver that drove the bus that we rode to Charlotte Court House told Daddy one day that there were so many Prince Edward County students gathering where the two lines converged catching a bus that soon it would attract attention.

Daddy stopped taking us to the bus stop where the two county lines converged and started driving Phyllis and I deeper over into Charlotte County to catch a bus.

There was a man named Mr. Wilson. According to my mama, Daddy and Mr. Wilson met, and Daddy explained everything to Mr. Wilson. Mr. Wilson said: "If you can get your children to my house, they can catch the bus with my children." Mama would get up in the mornings and take us to Mr. Wilson's house. It was about thirty miles one way. Mama drove back and forth each day. Phyllis and I had to travel about sixty miles a day, so we could go to school or three hundred miles a week. Mama drove over one hundred miles a day. She drove us to Mr. Wilson's house, then drove back home to Prospect, drove back to Mr. Wilson's in the afternoon to pick us up, and then we came back to our house.

Phyllis and I were in the Central High School Class of 1963. We were the only two Prince Edward County students in the Class of 1963.

Mr. George H. Binford was the principal at Central High School.

In later life due to circumstances in my life I had to bring my daughters to Prince Edward County for my mother to raise. I remember my daughter Liana being at the high school. I went there once during the school day to just walk the hallways and see, and it was so good to see the young White students and the young Black students talking. One thought came to my mind—Satan, you tried to stop it, but you could not. The children were like oblivious to the past.

That made me feel so good.

———

POLLY ALLEN WISE

I was born on December 24, 1953. When I was to start school, the schools in Prince Edward County were closed. I don't remember all the details about how I ended up at Saint James African Methodist Episcopal Church, but that was where my education began. I went to school in the basement of the church.

Saint James was about two miles from my house. My sister Dorothy and I walked to the church each morning. Dorothy was a year older than I. There were some others that walked with us. There were four or five of us from my area that went to the church for school.

At Saint James we had books that were very old but were readable. We had the Dick and Jane book, and Mid Night Cat. I remember those two books.

I remember some White college students came and worked with us. They were from outside of Virginia. I think they were from Wisconsin or a State in that region of the country. I remember them putting us in their cars and driving us into town to the Elks Lodge for dance lessons. The Elks Lodge was on Ely Street, which today is Griffin Boulevard. I took ballet lessons.

I went to school in the basement of Saint James until the Free School opened. When the Free School opened, we were tested. I tested out at the second or third grade. I believe I started in the third grade. I was reading and working with numbers. We had mastered reading and elementary math at Saint James. We could add and subtract when we went to the Free School.

I was glad to be in a real school and not a basement. You know when you are little, and you want to go to school; I had that kind of excitement. Being in a classroom, a real classroom was a wonderful thing.

I dropped out of high school in 1970 and got married and moved to Maryland. When in Maryland, I studied and earned my GED. I became a Certified Nursing Assistant around 1972. Later in the 1970s I moved back to Prince Edward County. I started nursing school in 1980 and graduated in 1982. I earned my LPN License in 1982. I worked at Southside County Hospital from 1982 to 1996. In 1996 I graduated from Lynchburg General Hospital School of Nursing, Lynchburg, Virginia. I obtained my Registered Nurse (RN) Diploma.

I love my work. In 2005 I got my certification for Ambulatory Surgery, CAPA which is Certified Ambulatory Perianesthesia. This year, 2012, March 23rd to be exact, I got CRNI, which is Certified Registered Nurse Infusion.

I have five children—Dorita, Melissa, Tammy, Crystal, and Joseph. I had all five when I studied for the various nursing courses and degrees. Tammy is thirty-eight years old, as of the date I am sharing my story, which is June 26, 2012. She has been disabled most of her life. Tammy contracted meningitis when she was six weeks old. My other children took care of her when I was in school or took classes. My children always say they don't know how I do it or how I have accomplished so much in life.

It has been a hard journey I will admit. But the race is not given to the swift, but to the one who holds out to the end.

————

CATHERINE ALFREDA 'FREDA' SCOTT

I was born in Harlem and came to Prince Edward County at age two to live with my grandparents, Gladys Berryman Scott and Robert Scott in Prospect. I went to Calvary School in Prospect, a one room school. I grew up in Sulphur Spring Baptist Church and it had a school at one time, but there was no school when I turned school age. I lived closer to Calvary. Calvary School was on the grounds of Calvary Baptist Church. Mrs. Ernestine Herndon was my first grade teacher. I entered first grade in 1952.

There was one teacher and five grades. Calvary, I think, went to fifth grade. You were grouped according to age. The first graders sat at a table near the front of the room. The second graders may have had at table to the side and other grades sat at desks. Ms. Naomi Harris, the mother of Fran Harris, was a substitute teacher. We had an outdoor toilet and I believe had electricity. There was a potbelly stove in the middle of the room. They burned coals in the stove, not wood.

The county started closing the one and two room schools in outlying areas about this time. Calvary School closed in May 1953.

In second grade I started taking the bus to First Rock School. I spent second and third grades in the tar-shacks called the chicken coop. Mrs. McLendon was my teacher. She taught me for two years in the chicken coop. Then I moved over to the main building at First Rock which housed three grades, first, fourth and fifth grades. Mrs. Lottie Jackson was my teacher in fourth grade. In fifth grade I had Mrs. Fisher (not Mrs. Ethel Watkins Wilson Fisher). Everyone brought lunch from home. Ice cream was sold. In elementary school I was in the Glee Club.

When I was promoted to sixth grade, I rode the bus into town to Mary E. Branch No. 2. I had Mrs. Hazel Jackson in sixth grade. In Mrs. Hazel Jackson's class, we had to recite a Bible verse each morning as part of our devotion. We said the Pledge of Allegiance but had a devotion also. In seventh grade I had Mrs. Kelly from Malden, Massachusetts.

My parents did not let me go to the movie because we had to sit in the balcony. Mrs. Kelly, in seventh grade, took us to see The W. C. Handy Story. Our classroom was the only class in the theater, but we still had to sit in the balcony that day. This was a school day and a special trip. We walked down to the theater from the school.

We didn't even believe it was going to happen. I remember

an address I heard Mrs. Ethel Wilson give around 2004, she said the teachers knew the schools were not going to open, but many parents were unsure. I recall Mrs. Wilson telling how many of the teachers started crying when they came to the realization that the schools would be closed, and they not be rehired. Many of the teachers had just purchased new cars and had other financial obligations.

Some of the teachers I remember affected by the closing were: Mrs. Eunice McLendon and Mr. McLendon, he taught high school, they went to Front Royal to teach. Mrs. Lottie Jackson left the area after the schools closed. I think she was close enough to drive. I think Mrs. Hazel Jackson went to Charlottesville. Mrs. Mary Madison, the mother of Roger, Dorothy, Victor and Wilfred went to Chestertown, Maryland.

My grandma Alice Gilliam Carrington Scott was a slave girl. I remember her saying: "I don't wan' you goin' to school wid'em any way because I don' wan' White people tellin' my children and grandchildren what to do; and beside they will always think they are better than you."

I stayed home the first year the schools were closed. I went to Cousin Flossie's center. We read and did a little math and paid attention to current events. We kept up with what was going on in the county. I was a newspaper girl for a little while for the Norfolk Journal and Guide Newspaper and I read about updates on the court situation.

Mrs. Hazel Carter lived nearby and tutored my siblings in the evenings when she came home from teaching in Cumberland County. Elzora and Claudette went to Mrs. Carter in the evenings.

The second year the schools were closed I went to New York to live with Wilsie, she was my aunt, my mother's oldest sister. Aunt Wilsie had four children and I was the fifth in a three bedroom apartment in the projects. At that time the projects didn't have the negative connotation it has today. Back then if you ever got kicked out of the projects, you could not move into another project area. You were out for good. The projects afforded people an opportunity to move up. Families stayed in the projects until they could do better. You never expected to stay there all of your life.

I stayed in New York for two years. I did grades eighth and ninth in New York. I missed a year back home, but when they reviewed my report card the administration marveled at my grades. I remember them saying: "And she has missed a year out of school. Look at these grades." I was placed in the eighth grade. They put me in a class where I had to prove myself and then later I was moved to a higher level in the eighth grade.

In the fourth year of the school closure I went to Aunt Alice (Alice Rucker) who lived in Roanoke, Virginia. I attended Lucy Addison High School, a Black High School. Lucy Addison was a large school.

When I came home each summer, I attended all the special classes set up for students. Robert Green had a group here from Michigan State. Ernest Green, one of the Little Rock Nine, was a part of Dr. Green's team.

There was a summer course at Saint James AME in Prospect I attended in the summer of 61 or 62. Some of the college students that taught us were from Michigan State. In 1963 we were in town, so I know it was not that summer.

In the summer of 1963 I came home and was involved in the demonstrations and NAACP Youth Council.

I remember in the summer of 1963 Safeway Supermarket was throwing food away and probably the A&P Store also. People were carpooling to other counties to shop. Safeway was near First Baptist Church and we could see everything. The store is not there today, the college has built up.

I told my aunt, Mattie Johnson Scott, that she should apply for a cashier's position at Safeway. When she went to apply, they gave her the book immediately to study. She studied and passed the test. She was the first Black person hired in a store downtown that previously had employed only White people.

SNCC came to town. Charles Sherrod and Ivanhoe Donaldson came to Farmville.

Also, in the summer of 1963 Queens College students and other college students came to the county and taught elementary age boys and girls primarily. The older teenagers were demonstrating.

Some of us said we were going to J. J. Newberry, a five and ten cents store, (Longwood Art Gallery today). "We can't serve you." Someone said they were going to call the police. We said okay and left. We came back the next day and all the seats had been taken up. Everyone had to stand and eat.

In August 1963 some of us went to the March on Washington.

The Free School opened. I went to the eleventh grade. Public schools opened the next year. My class was the first graduating class after the county was ordered by the courts to appropriate funds for a public school system. We graduated in May 1965.

I went to Berea College in August 1965. The American Friends were here and that is how I learned about Berea College. Nancy Adams was a Quaker representative here. Nancy would talk to me about Berea College. I knew some of the students that had been placed in the high school department at Berea when the schools were closed. I majored in

Spanish. I took Spanish in ninth grade. I also took Spanish in tenth grade in Roanoke. When I returned to Prince Edward County, Spanish was just being offered and I had already been exposed to the material and did not enroll.

I went to graduate school at Boston University and got a master's degree in Spanish. I worked for a State agency for the blind for one year and was invited to teach at Berea College, I accepted.

AUNDRE LINELL CARTER PEARCE

I was born in Norfolk, Virginia. My mother (Hazel Benton Carter) was from Norfolk County and her family was still there. In 1926, Mama came to Prince Edward County to take a teaching position. She had attended Virginia State College for six weeks and received a provisional teaching certificate that allowed her to teach. Shortly after coming to Prince Edward she met and married my daddy, G. Andrew Carter. She later earned a Bachelor of Science Degree from Virginia State College.

Mama was from a family of ten, nine children lived, and one child died when an infant. Mama's father died when several of her siblings were in elementary school. Her mother died when the two youngest sisters, Christine Benton and Jacqueline Benton were in college. At that time Mama became the matriarch of the family. On holidays when Aunt Christine and Aunt Jacqueline were on college break they came to Prospect and lived with their older sister, my mama and Daddy. Aunt Christine met and later married Grover 'Jack' Hendricks of

Prospect. Aunt Jacqueline, the baby in the family, and Leeman Allen of Prospect fell in love and were married.

When I started school in September 1949 at School No. 22 in Prospect, Mama was my teacher. I went to School No. 22 my initial four years of elementary education and Mama was my only teacher. School No. 22 was a two room school and at one time had two teachers, but when I started first grade Mama was the only teacher. After I completed the fourth grade in the 1952-1953 school year, School No. 22 was closed. The county was consolidating the rural schools. In the fifth grade I went to First Rock School. I attended one year and when promoted to the sixth grade I went to Mary E. Branch No. 2 (today it is the Museum). I was a student at Branch No. 2 for two years, sixth and seventh grades. Then I entered R. R. Moton High School in the eighth grade. The high school was relatively new. I was one of the many students that benefited from The Strike of 1951. The new high school resulted from the student strike.

I was enjoying my high school years. You know how a student feels comfortable, in a comfort zone, I was excelling academically and accepted socially. I was an only child.

During the 1958-1959 academic year, I was in the tenth grade. Some of the teachers I remember from high school were: Mrs. Venable (homeroom), Miss. Furr (Math), Mr. Stanton (Science), Mrs. Rawlins (Social Studies), Miss Malloy (Physical Education), Mrs. Miller and Mrs. Madison (Home Economics). When school closed in June, I had been promoted to the eleventh grade. Many people had heard that students would not return to classes in September. Parents with school age children had three months to finalize arrangements for them to continue their education. Parents and students were concerned. Mama was concerned because she was the primary bread winner. Daddy was a small-time farmer and did not have a huge income.

The NAACP was very strong in Prospect and the Scott family was a well-known supporter of the organization. Whenever you heard NAACP, you heard the name Scott.

I remember attending meetings the summer of 1959 at Sulphur Spring Baptist Church. People were brain-storming about what might happen and what adjustments families needed to make. There were also discussions about fund-raising projects. Prince Edward County was a farming community and the NAACP needed funds to assist with litigation in the court case. I was fifteen at this time and am unable to recall fifty-two years later all the details related to events. But I do recall personally writing a letter to nationally known Rhythm and Blues singer LaVern Baker, sharing with her the local situation and asking her to come to Prince Edward County and assist us in raising funds. She recorded *Tweedle Dee, Jim Dandy To The Rescue*, and other popular songs. I found the letter recently that she (LaVern Baker) wrote to me explaining she couldn't come.

Mama made arrangements for me to enter Saint Francis De Sales School for girls in Powhatan, Virginia, in September 1959. I remember my mother talking to Mrs. Connie Rawlins and Mrs. Geneva Hamilton about the school. Mrs. Rawlins had a daughter named Shirley already at the school and Mrs. Hamilton had a daughter enrolled named Irene. Shirley and Irene were students at Saint Francis before the Prince Edward County public schools were closed. After getting information from Mrs. Rawlins and Mrs. Hamilton, Mama went to the school and talked to the administration. She was told that the school did not accept eleventh graders. They accepted freshmen students primarily; a small number of sophomores were permitted to enroll.

The administration agreed to accommodate me. Shirley Rawlins, Irene Hamilton and I were the only Prince Edward County students at the school. As I mentioned, I was the only one there as a result of the closure of the schools. Saint Francis had many students from Louisiana and other locales that had a large Roman Catholic population.

Mama was hired by Thomas J. McIlwaine, who was the superintendent of schools in Prince Edward County and Cumberland County, to teach at Luther P. Jackson Elementary School in Cumberland.

Many Prince Edward County families relocated so their children could enroll in another location and attend school. Uncle Leeman and Aunt Jacqueline now had three children — Ronald, Wanda Faye, and Carol. Uncle Leeman and Aunt Jacqueline moved the family to Norfolk, Virginia.

Saint Francis had a college track and a business track. These were the only two options available. Because of the preparatory classes I had taken at Moton, I followed the college track. I took French at Moton and it was the foreign language at Saint Francis, so I enrolled in French II. I took trigonometry, having completed Algebra at Moton. R. R. Moton High School had an excellent curriculum. Many of the high school students that went away to school during the closure excelled and went on to college. Saint Francis was a Roman Catholic school, all students regardless of their faith background took Catholicism and were encouraged to convert. I did not convert. We were permitted to come home for the Christmas holidays and summers. Families were encouraged to visit the girls during other holidays.

When I graduated in the spring of 1961, I had been accepted at Hampton Institute, Hampton, Virginia, and Xavier University in New Orleans. Although, I attended pre-college at Hampton, I selected Xavier to continue my education. I studied there for one year and transferred to Hampton Institute. Xavier was just too far away from home.

While at Hampton Institute, I participated in demonstrations during the era of The Movement, the 1960s. I remember being part of a group from school sent to Prince Edward County to conduct a survey. I believe students from other colleges were part of the team sent to the field. We had questionnaires and went into the different homes. I went to an area of the county with which I was totally unfamiliar. Prospect was not a well to do community but was not like the area in which I was conducting the survey. I was astonished at the conditions of the homes. I can now, after all these years, clearly see in my mind one home in particular that had card-board windows; yes, card-board served as window panes, and the floor was dirt; not wood, but dirt. This was in 1963 or 1964 when we conducted the survey.

I don't know how long Uncle Leeman and Aunt Jacqueline stayed in Norfolk, but I know they later moved to Brooklyn, New York. Aunt Jacqueline lived in Brooklyn before she and Uncle Leeman were married. She also had two sisters living in Brooklyn when they relocated there with the children.

Ronnie and Wanda Faye continued their education in Brooklyn. Carol, I believe, started pre-school in Brooklyn. I remember it was the summer after I graduated from Saint Francis, the summer of 1961, or the summer after my one year at Xavier, the summer of 1962, I went to Brooklyn to keep the children until their school closed and I accompanied all three back to Prospect to spend the remainder of the summer with my parents. Carol had just started school.

The family moved back to Prince Edward County when the schools reopened.

I graduated from Hampton Institute in 1966 with a degree in Health Physical Science and Biology.

Uncle Leeman still lives in Prospect. I will contact him and ask him to share his story for the book.

———

RAYMOND EVERETT LIGON

My father was named Raymond Daniel Ligon and my mother was named Martha Mae Robinson Ligon. Most people think I am a junior by name, but I'm not named after my father. My name is Raymond Everett Ligon. Everett was my grandfather's name.

I was twelve years old and had passed to the third grade when the schools were closed. I was at First Rock School at the time. I had Mrs. Carter in first grade and I can't remember the name of my second grade teacher.

My parents were thinking school would open late in 1959, but as the year progressed they realized the schools were not going to open up.

The first year the schools were closed my parents made us read and do arithmetic. They thought the schools would open later in the first semester. My big sister LaVerne did the tutoring for the most part.

I had about thirty (30) cousins that lived around us. Mama had five sisters and three brothers and all of them and their families lived in this community. As time went on and the schools didn't open, the older cousins started tutoring the younger cousins. Sometimes they would come to our house and sometimes many of the cousins would all meet at another house and the older cousins would teach us younger ones.

That was how we learned the first year the schools were closed.

I had a cousin named Adell Dungee who was in high school and the first year the schools were closed she went to stay with Mrs. Price in that big house on Highway 460. Adell was the daughter of Christine Robinson Dungee and Alfonso Dungee. Christine was my mother's sister. Adell was in tenth or eleventh grade.

My mother worked at the garment factory in Appomattox and the factory was next to Carver–Price High School. So, at the beginning of the second year the schools were closed we started riding with her to work; my sisters, Elaine and LaVerne, and I. Mama had to be at work at 7:00 a. m. We sat in the car until 8:00 a. m. and then walked over to the school, Carver–Price High School.

We got out of school at 3:00 p. m. and walked back to the car. My mother got off work at 3:30 p. m.

This went on for about two months and then officials realized they had a lot of students who were not at the school before. So, my parents had to rent a house in Appomattox County.

My parents and two other families rented the house.

The three families were: the Hill family, Leon and his brother Andrew.

Then there was the Stiff family. There was Ray, Oliver, William, and Elaine. Oliver and I were in third grade. Elaine was in the sixth grade and Ray was in the fourth grade.

In the Ligon family it was me and my two sisters.

My mother and Mrs. Mamie Stiff were in charge. All of us lived in a three room house. There were so many people we were on top of each other.

All the families came back to Prospect each Friday evening and went back to Appomattox on Monday morning.

Appomattox County school officials came and checked two or three times to make sure we stayed there. After a while they stopped checking. We stayed in the house about four months, and after they stopped checking on us we closed the house down and all the families came back to Prince Edward County.

My sisters and I started back riding to school with our mom. This went on to the end of the second year of the school closing.

Also, during the second year of the school closing, I had some cousins that left Prince Edward County to go to school. My mother's youngest sister, Ethel Robinson Morton, and her husband, Arthur Morton, had four kids. Uncle Arthur had about four or five brothers in New Jersey and a sister in Philadelphia. The mama and daddy and all four children moved. The children were John, Freddie, Mary Etta whose nickname was Honey, and William whose nickname was Tony.

John and Freddie were sent to New Jersey the first year of the school closing. John stayed, and Freddie got home sick and came back.

At the beginning of the third year of the school closing, 1961-1962, my parents realized they would have to rent and they rented a house closer to Appomattox. This year the Hill and Stiff families were not with us.

A new family rented with Mama. It was the Hendricks family. The mother was named Mattie and the father named Herman Hendricks. The children were: Delores, Marlee, Willie, Warren and Howard. Mattie was my mother's sister, so these were my cousins living with us.

Another person also lived with us, Bernice Hendricks. She had already graduated and worked at the garment factory and needed a ride. She didn't have a car. She lived with us and rode to work with Mama.

We stayed at the house until around February of the school year. They checked regular and after they stopped checking we moved back home early in the second semester.

The fourth year the schools were closed we didn't rent a house. They had stopped checking and we stayed in Prince Edward County.

In the summer of 1963 I was in the demonstrations in Farmville. There were people who would take us in to Farmville on the back of a truck or we would catch a ride. Daddy was a farmer but would let us go and picket even though he needed us on the farm to help him. We were trained at First Baptist Church. We were trained in front of the pulpit. They taught us how to fall on to the ground and fold up and protect your head.

We demonstrated in front of the movie theater and at the drugstore. Some people got arrested at the drugstore. Safeway Grocery Store was throwing away so much food because no one was shopping there. Mattie Scott was the first Black person hired as a teller at Safeway in Farmville.

When the Free School opened, all in my family went to the Free School. I had passed to sixth grade in Appomattox. In the Free Schools I was supposedly in the sixth grade. I got to shake the hand of Robert Kennedy when he visited the schools. All the kids who had not missed a day in school up until the day he came got to shake his hand. The next year I was placed in the eighth grade.

I remember my cousin Adell who went to stay with Mrs. Price the first year of the school closing didn't come to the

Free School. When the Free School opened, Adell had already graduated from high school at Carver–Price. She stayed with Mrs. Price in tenth, eleventh and twelfth grades or eleventh and twelfth grades. I believe she stayed three years, but I know she stayed two years. When the Free School opened, Adell had graduated.

Things started getting more back to normal the next year when the public schools reopened in September 1964. I graduated in 1969 and there were sixty-nine (69) students in the Class of 1969.

I worked a little while and then went into the United States Army. I spent three years in the Signal Corps. I got out a Sergeant, came back home, and went into business with my father. He was a contractor. You are sitting in my building right now.*

Note of the Editor: *Interview was conducted in the Fellowship Hall at Calvary Baptist Church, Prospect, Virginia, Sunday afternoon, January 22, 2012.

———

MARY FRANCES HENDRICKS BROWN

I was born here in Prince Edward County to Clara Robinson Hendricks and Cassell Hendricks.

There was a big wreck on the train track off of Highway 460. My grandfather John Robinson was driving the bus. It was pouring down rain, and rather than stop, he opened the door and he looked out and all of a sudden there was the train. Five of my cousins got killed. My oldest sister, Lorraine Hendricks (Sanders) was on the bus. The children were making a lot of noise and my grandfather had just made her come and sit near him. The train struck the back of the bus. A White man brought my sister home. I was looking out of the window and said to my mother: "Lorraine in the car of some man." Mama got excited and ran to the door.

When I was little, I went to school in a little shack near Calvary Baptist Church. It was a one room school. I wasn't school age but went with Lorraine. Mrs. Herndon was the teacher. So, when I got to be school age, I started at First Rock. Mrs. Hazel Carter was my first grade teacher. Mrs. Eunice McLendon was my second grade teacher. When I went to Mary E. Branch No. 1, Mr. Hall was the principal and you walked a straight line with Mr. Hall.

Lorraine graduated in June 1959. When I passed to the fourth grade, the schools were closed.

Three of us were at home the first year the schools were closed — Bernice, Joyce and me. I did not go to school the first year the schools were closed. The next year my father told me I had to go to school. I was born March 16, 1947.

When it was learned that the schools would be closed for a second year, my parents made arrangements for me, Joyce and Bernice to go away to school.

Bernice was sent to Washington, D. C. She had passed to the eleventh grade when the schools were closed. She lived with our uncle named Hubert Hendricks. This was my father's brother. Lorraine and Evelyn had gone to New York to live.

My father and my mother knew Mrs. Helen Dennis who lived in Charlotte Court House, in Charlotte County. She had been a teacher at Moton High School and taught my older sisters, Evelyn and Lorraine. Mrs. Dennis was a Home Economics teacher.

Daddy made arrangements for me and Joyce to go and live with Mrs. Dennis for the 1960-1961 school year. Joyce was in eighth grade at the high school.

The first day of school was unbelievable. We were at the bus stop in Phenix where the bus picked us up. The high schoolers got on the bus, but the driver told me I had to wait for the next bus. All the students on his bus went to Central High School. I was to ride the bus that went to Central Elementary School. There was a high school bus and an elementary school bus.

When the second bus came, the driver stopped, opened the door and I climbed aboard. The bus was full — but it was full of White children going to Randolph Henry Elementary School in Charlotte Court House. This was the White elementary school. (Mary Frances started laughing, while recounting the event. She was laughing so hard until she had to stop telling the story and relax.) The driver looked at me standing at the bus stop and must have assumed I was White. When he stopped and opened the door, I got on. I went to Randolph Henry with the other children and was let off. I cried, and I cried.

I was taken to the administration office and they asked me where I lived. I told them the address of Mrs. Dennis and I told them to call Central High School because that was where she taught. They called, and she came. When Mrs. Dennis got to Randolph Henry Elementary School, all hell broke loose. She said: "Why did they send you to this school." I said: "I don't know. The bus driver told me to wait for the next bus. I did, and the bus came, and I got on." So, Mrs. Dennis straightened out everything and got me on the right bus. This was the opening day of my first year in school in Charlotte County. It was a rough day. I don't think I ever stopped crying that day. (Mary Frances is still laughing.)

Joyce and I would help Mrs. Dennis with her kids. She had

two boys Carlos and Alvin. They were toddlers. Joyce and I had individual chores. Joyce helped Mrs. Dennis in the kitchen and inside the house. I had the outside duties. I took the boys out for fresh air and exercise until dinner was ready. Then I gave them their baths and got them ready for bed.

Mrs. Dennis used to keep an old man and he was over one hundred then. All of us shared the task of feeding him. He used to tell me stories about being sold for a horse or a sack of corn.

Joyce and I came home every weekend. My father came and picked us up. Daddy worked on the railroad. He came home on Friday and had to leave on Sunday at 2:00 p. m. Daddy took us back to Mrs. Dennis before he went to the railroad.

It was a lonely time for Mama. Mama was alone when we went to Charlotte Court House, all the children were out of the house. Daddy worked on the railroad and was gone all week and she did not drive. Mrs. Dennis had us to call home one or two times a week.

Other Prince Edward County students attended school in Charlotte Court House. Phyllis and Lillie Jordan were twins and they caught the bus at Mr. Wilson's house in Charlotte County. His name was Thomas Wilson and his brother was Junior Wilson. Mr. Wilson and the Jordan sisters' father were friends.

I remember some of the children from Charlotte County that I went to school with—Jackie Jeffries, Jessie Jeffries and Cynthia Jeffries and girls from Red House.

Joyce and I stayed with Mrs. Dennis until the end of the 1962-1963 school year.

Bernice graduated at the school she attended in Washington in 1963.

When the Free Schools opened in September 1963, we came back home. Joyce went to the twelfth grade and I went to high school in eighth grade. I would have been in ninth grade had not the schools been closed. I was a good basketball player and made the team that year. I was named team captain and my girlfriend was the co-captain. Her name was Evelyn Hunt. Evelyn left Prospect during the closure and went somewhere to school, but I don't know where she attended. There were only two White students in the high school when the Free School opened, Dickey Moss and Brenda Abernathy. Brenda used to come and stay with me sometimes.

I held the title of captain of the girls' basketball team from eighth grade to the twelfth grade. My girlfriend Evelyn was the co-captain.

————

MOSES FORD

I can remember the first school I attended, that was First Rock School. There was no such thing back then as a principal. You just had all teachers at the school. I was in the third grade when they announced that the schools would close. I was sitting in class, I was in Mrs. McLendon's class. I think she announced it. We got on the bus that day and came home. It was in the morning when the announcement was made.

The first year the schools were closed I don't remember, but I don't think we did anything. We just mostly played the first year. There were three of us in my family. I was in third grade, my brother, Howard, was behind me in the second grade, and my sister, Rosa, was in first grade.

Then when the schools didn't open the second year, we went to Miss. Flossie's in her basement to classes. Some of the other students I remember being at Miss. Flossie's was Vivian Scott (Nunnally), Roland Berryman, Jr., we called him Junny; he had a sister named Gloria. There was another sister named Shea, but I'm not sure whether Shea was old enough to be at Miss. Flossie's. All of us went to Miss. Flossie.

In the third year when the schools were closed we started going to school in Appomattox at Carver–Price High School. Mama drove us each day to Pamplin to meet the bus. I believe Mama had a Pontiac station wagon. We would catch the school bus at a lady's house. Mama would drive me, Howard and Rosa there every morning and pick us up in the afternoon. I can't remember the lady's name, but I remember she had a son and a daughter. The girl was a little older than me and her brother was older than she was. The lady was an older woman, she was about my grandma's age. Mama drove us about seven miles one way each day.

The school didn't ask for an address. I'm pretty sure they knew we were from Prince Edward County. Then the school started getting over crowded.

Sometime during the 1961-1962 school year they sent a letter home I believe telling parents that all children had to live in the county to go to school in Appomattox. I can't remember exactly when, but sometime during the school year my parents rented a house in Appomattox County from Mrs. Price, the lady who the school was named after. The rental house was right across from her house. It was a two room house, it might have been three rooms with the little kitchen. I was in third grade at Carver–Price High School.

Mama stayed up there with us during the week and Daddy stayed in Prospect and worked. Daddy worked at Hicks and Carson in Prospect. It was next to where the post office is today. Hicks and Carson was like a general store. Daddy was the butcher, he cut the beef and other meats. He delivered fertilizer for the store. We had one car and Daddy would take us to the shack in Appomattox on Sunday evening or early Monday morning, and he would come back to get us on the following Friday evening.

We went back to the two room house in Appomattox when the schools were closed for the fourth year. I was in the fourth grade.

I remember Ethel and Grace Poindexter were at Carver–Price; and a girl named Lucy who was from Prince Edward County stayed with Mrs. Price, Lucy was at the school.

I remember we demonstrated up and down Main Street. I was born in 1949, so I was about fourteen during the demonstrations. We found out about the demonstrations through Miss. Flossie. I believe her husband Reverend Hudson was still living. I think he was still living. Miss. Flossie's son Harold demonstrated with us. When we demonstrated, Junny drove the truck and took us into town. His daddy had a truck.

When the Free School opened, we came back to Prince Edward. I can't remember how I heard, but we got the news that the schools would reopen.

I started in the fifth grade. I was two years behind. They gave a test and some scored high and they were moved to a higher grade. Some were asked did they want to move up. If people felt they were smart enough to skip a grade, they could take the test, and some did.

I drove the school bus in high school and graduated in 1968.

When we were old enough, still in high school, we encouraged Daddy to leave the store and go to Lynchburg and work. We would tell Daddy: "You can do better." He got a job at the foundry in Lynchburg.

I started working and then was drafted in the United States Army in 1969. The service didn't agree with me. I had trouble with my nerves. The Vietnam War was going on. I knew I couldn't kill nobody and I think that was part of my problem with my nerves. They told me the name for my condition. I was discharged and came back to Prince Edward County. I started working at Prince Edward High School as the custodian, bus driver and worked in food service all at the same time. I was also a part-time deputy sheriff.

JOYCE STIFF HENDRICKS

I was born March 30, 1952 to Helen Stiff. I was raised by my grandmother Rosa Cunningham Ford. We lived in Prospect.

I started school at First Rock School and I think I went to school one year before the schools were shutdown.

I missed three years out of school. I went to Ms. Flossie's. I walked to her house. There was a bunch of us that walked to her house. Moses Ford, Howard Ford, Rosa Ford, Shirley Ford, and a bunch more walked to Ms. Flossie's.

I think it was the fourth year the schools were closed when my mother and her sister, Alberta Stiff Ford, got together and rented a two or three room house in Appomattox County. My mother and me, and Aunt Alberta and her children lived in the house.

Mama and Aunt Alberta worked at the garment factory in Appomattox. Aunt Alberta worked some while we were in that house. I went to Carver–Price High School.

When the Free School opened, I was enrolled. I don't

remember what grade they put me in. I went on to high school and graduated in 1972.

I got married and moved to East Orange, New Jersey. I stayed there six or seven years and came back to Virginia and raised my family.

I went to work at the Thomasville Furniture Plant in Appomattox and worked there for thirty-two years.

This is what I remember on this day, Thursday, October 4, 2012.

———

JAMES ALLEN

I was born September 14, 1950, to Morton Allen and Emma Ruth Ford Allen.

I went to Five Forks School one year. I had completed the first grade when the schools closed.

Ms. Flossie said 'the children need to do something, if they learn no more than how to write their name, write your address, and count money.' Seemed like Ms. Flossie was the only one who cared. A bunch of students went to her house for the classes she taught. I remember Liana Mitchell, Betty Mitchell, Hattie Dungee, my sister Emma Allen, my sister Fannie Allen, Elizabeth Lyle, Paul Lyle, Alfred Lyle, James Lyle, Wilbur Ford and a whole lot more was in the basement of Ms. Flossie's house.

When the Free School opened, they put me in the fifth grade at Branch 2. I was put in the fifth grade! They gave you a grade. They didn't know where to put us. They put you where they thought you could handle the grade. I was about thirteen.

They put me in the fifth grade, but the gap was so wide. It may not seem like it now, but it was real. What you learned faded in four years. A lot of your knowledge faded, so you basically started from zero. The teachers didn't realize that in those four years you kept growing in body size, but you kept losing knowledge at the same time. How could you catch up with two things against you, body size increasing but your memory of what you knew before decreasing? (The question was emphasized by Mr. Allen.) How was you supposed to go from first grade to the fifth grade and do the work?

They sent some of us from Branch 2 to R. R. Moton High School to the seventh grade. We started working with clocks to learn how to tell time. We started working with clocks at Moton, learning about a. m. and p. m., a. m. for the morning and p. m. for the afternoon. The teacher would call out different times — something like 1:30, 2:45 and so on and we had to set the time on the clocks. We couldn't do it. We never completed the cycle needed to do these things. We couldn't handle the work at Moton.

They sent us back to Branch 2 to the fifth grade. My first year at Branch 2 in the fifth grade they had us on our ABCs. I went to the first grade before the schools closed and we didn't learn all of our alphabets my first year at Five Forks.

Like I said — the gap was so wide. It may not seem like it now, but it was real. What you learned in school faded in the four years you didn't go to school. A lot of your knowledge faded, so when the Free School opened you had to basically start over.

In the meantime, you had great big children in school with little children and it didn't even look normal. Many students just fell out. (Expression for quit school.) I quit, my brother Morton, Jr. quit. I quit in sixth grade and Morton was about two years in front of me. He went one year beyond Free School and quit.

People need to raise their voice and be heard. People have a chance now to let their voice ring out.

To be handicapped, uneducated, things you should know and don't know, you have to remain silent until you learn the ins and outs and then speak.

Have your own faith and belief. I didn't finish high school, but I put all four of my children through school, so you can make it if you try.

The only thing I can't get was why was Black people so silent. No town meetings, no arguing. At the time most of the Black people didn't own land but lived on someone's land. If they said anything, the White people would have put'em off the land.

Note of the Editor: The Editor stopped by the home of Allen on another occasion and asked as we talked: "How many of your relatives do you believe were locked out of the schools?" Several persons had mentioned the number of blood relatives impacted by the school closure and knowing that Allen had numerous cousins in the area inquiry was made of him of an estimate. He started listing households and naming children. They numbered in the dozens.

————

LEWIS FITCH

I started school at School No. 20 in Prospect. It was a one room school next to Calvary Baptist Church, located in the Calvary community. Mrs. Herndon (Ernestine) was the teacher. I was born February 1, 1942 and started school when I was about six years old. I left Calvary School and went to First Rock School. Then I went to Branch No. 2 in Farmville. I had just completed the ninth grade at R. R. Moton High School and promoted to the tenth grade when the schools were closed. During the summer, I heard about the schools possibly not opening.

The first year the schools were closed I don't think I went to school. I worked in the field. We lived on a farm.

The second year the schools were closed, they started sending children north to go to school. I went to Palmyra, New Jersey. I stayed with James and Edna Webb. Mrs. Webb was a school teacher and Mr. Webb was a mail carrier. They had a daughter named LaVerne. She was around thirteen years old.

I started school at Moorestown. Mrs. Webb taught high school in another location and I had to wait for her to come and pick me up. Rather than wait an hour or longer for her, she had me transferred to Palmyra High School, where I only had to wait a short time for her to come and pick me up after school. I had an enjoyable one year.

The next year I moved to Appomattox, Virginia, and lived with my parents. We lived in an area called Gladstone. I did eleventh and twelfth grades in Appomattox at Carver–Price High School. I played baseball on the school team one year. There were a lot of students in the school from Prince Edward County.

I graduated in 1963 from Carver–Price High School. Ruth Dungee graduated in 1963 also from Carver Price. There might have been two or three others in the graduating class from Prince Edward County. I am only sure about two, me and Ruth.

I got drafted into the service, the United States Army. I did

Basic Training at Fort Gordon, Georgia, and Advance Infantry Training (AIT) at Fort Lewis, Washington. Then I did special cold weather training in Norway and Alaska. I also had some desert training. Most of my time was in special training. I was in the military two years, 1964-1966.

I came home and went to work at Lee Smith Foundry in Lynchburg, Virginia. I worked twenty and one-half years there. I quit and moved to New York in 1987 and have been here ever since, until the time of this telephone interview on Monday, August 13, 2012.

———

LEWIS MONROE WATSON

My parents were Walter Watson and Elva Christine Watson.

I attended Peaks School, a two room school. The teachers were Mrs. Hendricks and Mrs. Davenport. Mrs. Hendricks had first, second and third grades. Mrs. Davenport taught fourth and fifth grades. When students at Peaks School finished fifth grade, they went to Branch No. 2 in Farmville or First Rock for sixth grade. Mrs. Sanders did the cooking at Peaks School. She was in a kitchen off to the side. There was a small cafeteria. Mrs. Sanders did full time cooking every day. Some kids brought lunches, but there was enough work for her to cook each day.

We had to walk three miles one way to school. We cut through the woods and walked up to the highway. The teacher rung a bell, something like a cow-bell, to start the school day.

The school day started with morning devotion. Every child had to know a devotional Bible verse. You recited your Bible verse, then we said the Lord's Prayer, and then the Pledge of Allegiance.

During my early years, each teacher had her own assembly with her class. When I was around third grade, we started having the morning devotion in one large group.

My daddy was a sharecropper and raised tobacco, wheat, and corn for Willie Vaughan, who was on the Board of Supervisors in Prince Edward County.

I never will forget it! One day Daddy came home and said to Mama: "Elva, we're moving. I heard ole man Vaughan say to somebody 'before I allow my child to go to school with Niggers, I'll close it down.'"

And they did, they closed the schools down.

We moved from Prospect, Virginia, to Pamplin, Virginia, in 1959. Daddy started sharecropping again.

I started attending James Murray Jeffress School in Charlotte County. The house we moved into was so situated near the Appomattox County and Charlotte County lines that I could walk out of the front door and across the road and be in Charlotte County.

Reverend Howard Flood was a preacher that lived in Charlotte County and his house was near our house. His children always went to school in Charlotte County and the school bus stopped near their house. I would walk to the bus stop and get on the bus.

I was never asked about my address because the bus came from Pamplin and Pamplin was nowhere from Charlotte County.

I rode the bus and went to school in Charlotte County for two years, 1959-1960 and 1960 to 1961.

My brother, Walter, tested and passed to drive bus for the Appomattox County public schools. In September 1961 I started attending Carver–Price High School. I rode the bus Walter drove.

When the Free Schools opened in Prince Edward County, I stayed at Carver–Price High School. I stayed at Carver-Price until I was in the ninth grade. Daddy started getting sick. This was around 1966. I am the baby out of fourteen children. I dropped out of school to take on some of the load at home on the farm.

I came home one day, and Mama said she heard about LBJ starting up the Job Corps program for students who had dropped out of school. Mama said: "You need to go." I signed up and went to Morgan Field, Kentucky, an old Army post that the government fixed up. I studied electronics. The qualification of the program was if you successfully completed it you got a GED. I was seventeen when I completed the program.

You had to be eighteen to get a public job. When I turned eighteen, I got a job. At nineteen I got drafted and went to the United States Navy for two years. After being discharged, I came back home, and was employed at Lynchburg Foundry, (1971) for 21 years. I married Arlene Marshall (Watson) in 1972. We've reared three sons, who are doing well and are married with families also.

In 1977 I started singing Gospel. I sang with the Echoes of Glory. I was a deacon in my church, (Peaks Baptist Church, Prospect, Virginia) for three years, and then was called to preach in 1983. I went to Virginia Seminary and College in Lynchburg, Virginia. I had two sons getting ready for college also. I had to come out of school and support them.

One day I said to my boys: "I believe I'll start school

again." I applied to Liberty in Lynchburg. They said: "You need to get a GED." I said: "I thought I had it." I went to an Adult Learning Center in Lynchburg and earned a GED. Then I went on to earn a bachelor's degree from Virginia University of Lynchburg (formerly Virginia Seminary and College).

I have been the pastor of Mount Zion Baptist Church in Red House, Virginia, for twenty-one years, as of the time I provided my reflections, which is Tuesday, January 24, 2012.

———

BERNETTA STIFF WATKINS

My most vivid memory from when the schools were closed was walking up the dirt road in front of our house on a moon lit snowy night with my sisters Claudette and Elzora, and my brother, Kelvin. We were going to Mrs. Hazel Benton Carter's house which was about a quarter of a mile from our home. My family lived in this same house where we are sitting now. Prior to the 1959 closing, the county school division was divided into districts and each neighborhood had its own elementary school and everyone attended high school in Farmville. Mrs. Carter had been the first grade teacher at First Rock School in Prospect when the schools were closed in 1959. She then began teaching in Cumberland County and allowed us to come to her house at night for instructions. She taught us reading, writing, and arithmetic.

I was born August 6, 1953, in Prospect, Virginia, to Thomas Russell and Gertrude Scott Stiff. I was five years old, turning six when the schools were closed in June 1959. Prior to the closing I had attended school unofficially at First Rock School for several months until I was caught. I was only five years old and back then one began school at age six. (Mrs. Watkins started laughing while sharing this episode.) I don't remember how I got to go, but I wanted to go to school so bad and my mother said go; and I went until they checked birth certificates and caught me. This was in the spring of the 1958-1959 school year. When they caught me, they said something that sounded like — 'Don't come back until you are six years old.'

When they had the end of school year program at First Rock, Mrs. Carter, allowed me to come back to say a poem in the program. I can still remember my part as of today, October 8, 2012.

> The school bell will grow red with rust.
> The corners filled with webs and dust.
> How lonesome will the school room be,
> With Claudette gone, Alisa and me.

This was Claudette's part that I memorized also:

> Goodbye first grade reader.
> Goodbye desk and room.
> I'm going off to sunny land.
> I'm leaving all of your gloom.

I learned to spell words backward and forward just for the fun of it. "kciD" — DICK and "eeffoc" — coffee are two that I remember now. I had also learned to read while attending school those months before they put me out. I was doing school work with Claudette at home.

I was really looking forward to school starting the next year.

Elzora would have been going to sixth grade. Claudette had passed to the second grade. I was all ready for first grade, having had my "unofficial kindergarten." Kelvin was born in May 1955, so he had a couple more years before he could start school.

But to my dismay sometime during the summer of 1959 my parents told us that there would be no school in the fall.

During the first four years that the public schools were closed Elzora, Claudette, Kelvin, and I attended no schools. We all went to Mrs. Carter's house at night and she taught us. I am not sure if we went every night during the week; nor do I remember whether we went every year. I believe Kelvin went along with us from the very beginning although he was too young for school.

During the summer, they had the summer reading programs, but we didn't go to all of them because we had to work in the tobacco fields. Kelvin was the youngest and since the girls were the oldest we did the work. My father farmed to supplement his railroad income and he raised tobacco, corn, wheat, garden, and livestock — pigs, cows and chickens.

We made use of any old books that we could get our hands on at home including the old textbooks Elzora and Claudette had from school. We had other old textbooks. I don't know from where we got them, but we had them, and we did work at home on our own. Mrs. Carter would work with us at night at her house on the material we had worked on at home during the day. She would give us the assignment before we left on the nights we had school with her.

We used to get the Sunday edition of the Richmond Times Dispatch and would read the obituary page to help our reading. (Mrs. Watkins started laughing hard at this point.) We would also read the society pages with the engagement and wedding announcements. We didn't even know the people but reading helped us. We read the Sunday paper from cover to cover, but I especially remember the obituaries.

We had offers from aunts to go to live with them and attend school. Aunt Janice Ola Scott Thomas, this was mama's sister, lived in Richmond. She had no children. We were invited by Aunt Alice in Roanoke and Aunt Wilsie in New York. Daddy would not break up the family, he constantly said—'No, I will not break up my family.'

One of the big things was sitting around daily listening to WFLO radio station waiting to hear the schools would reopen. We had a radio, but we didn't have a television. When the news came on there was dead silence in the house because we had to hear about school reopening. You couldn't talk when the news was on. You knew to sit down and shut up.

After the first year the schools were closed, every year thereafter we were waiting to hear and saying to ourselves, it must be this year. And then when it didn't happen, we would say "It must be next year."

I remember the school Mrs. Carter had at the old Hill Top Store, but we didn't attend. I cannot remember why not, we probably had to work. I don't think the school at Hill Top was operated very long.

When the Free School opened in 1963, I was ten years old. During the year of the Free School, we were placed by age not by grade. The school was ungraded, and I was placed with ten year olds who were with varied levels of academic ability. I don't remember doing ABC or 123 in my first year of organized school. Where I was placed in the Free School wasn't beneath my abilities, nor so high up I could not comprehend. The lessons I did in Free School seemed appropriate for what I could do.

There are two things I vividly remember about the year of the Free School. One was the assassination of John Kennedy, November 22, 1963, and then during the spring of 1964 Robert Kennedy came to visit the Free School and I carried a flag. They had little hand size flags and every student that had perfect attendance up until that time got to stand in the front row with a flag and got to shake his hand. I was at Mary E. Branch No. 2 in Farmville. Today Mary E. Branch No. 2 it is the Moton Museum.

The next year I was placed in the sixth grade which was my appropriate grade. I went on to graduate Number 3 in a class of seventy-eight students in 1971.

There were older students in high school with me who got married and they dropped out. They were adults that had to go on with their lives. Then there were the "*Skippers*". This was the name members of my class gave to certain students. *Skippers* were the older students who were allowed to take extra credits to graduate early because they were older and behind their appropriate grade levels. Some of them were approaching their twenties. If students were one to two grade levels behind, they were allowed to take double English and Government in the twelfth grade or whatever they needed to have in order to graduate earlier. This allowed them to catch up and skip a grade, so we called them "*Skippers*". I can remember at least three students that were with me from seventh grade up until the eleventh and then they skipped the eleventh grade and went to twelfth grade and graduated a year early.

After graduating from Prince Edward High School in June of 1971, I entered Norfolk State College in August 1971. I majored in History and was awarded a Bachelor of Arts Degree four years later. I wanted to be a lawyer, I wanted to go to law school, but after the four years I didn't want to do any more formal education then. I had no backup plan and became a Social Worker. Back then you took a test and went in as a Social Worker Trainee. You were in training for a year and then became a Social Worker, but you had to have a bachelor's degree to become a trainee.

I have been a Social Worker all my adult life. I started at the Nottoway County Department of Social Services in February 1977 and I am still there as of this day, Monday, October 8, 2012. My first year I was a Social Worker Trainee, then I was promoted to Social Worker after the first year and promoted to Senior Social Worker after the fifth year. I have been the Social Work Supervisor for Nottoway County for nearly thirty years.

It was much later in life that I could fully identify some of the impacts on me that missing the first five grades had. I had to teach myself to write cursive. I never learned all the proper strokes on certain alphabets. When the schools reopened, we couldn't go back and get all of the basics. We couldn't go back and get everything missed during the four years we were out. Some gaps couldn't be closed. I didn't truly realize some of the gaps in my own education until I had kids and started helping them with their homework. When my oldest son was in third grade, he brought home a blank outline of the United States and asked me to help him put in the States. I couldn't because I hadn't been to third grade to learn that. I began to see a pattern. When each of my three children was in elementary school and asked me for assistance, I was lacking in certain areas.

Although I have always loved to read and learn new facts, my bachelor's degree is in History and I have done numerous papers and research, I often wonder what could have I done further, better, or on a larger scale had not my education been interrupted.

————

MARY JONES BANNISTER

I was born in Prospect to Alease Matthews Jones and Gassie Jones on November 30, 1939. I was the fourth child in my family. We lived on a farm. Henry and Elizabeth Matthews were my mother's parents. Elizabeth's father was a full blooded American Indian. My grandfather's father was born in slavery. Robin Hill was the name of my great grandfather who was born in slavery.

I started School at Prospect Elementary School. It was located up on Highway 460 in Prospect. I think it had one room and Mrs. Virginia Morton was the teacher. My sister Catherine and my brothers Willie H. Jones and Gassie Thomas Jones took me to school.

I went there a few years and my family moved. I started attending First Rock School and went to the seventh grade. In 1952 I went to R. R. Moton and in 1953 I went to the new high school. I graduated in 1957.

After graduation, I went to Atlantic City, New Jersey. I was a chamber maid at a hotel. It was a resort city and had plenty hotels. I became homesick and after the summer ended I came back to Virginia and stayed to the following June 1958.

I returned to New Jersey and worked as an elevator

operator at Lit Brothers. As time passed, I worked up to sales manager.

Catherine came to Atlantic City in the summer of 1959 to work. I found her an apartment. When she found out that the schools were not going to open, Catherine went back to Prospect and got her husband and their children. The whole family moved to New Jersey that summer. Most of the seven children were in school.

My mother moved to Atlantic City in 1959 and my younger brother Cornelius Conrad Booker. Cornelius was born in 1953. Mama lived with my sister Catherine for a while and then got her own place. Cornelius started school in New Jersey.

The children that moved to New Jersey do to the closing of the schools never missed a year out of school. When the schools reopened in Prince Edward County, all the families and children remained in New Jersey. They never came back to Virginia.

I have three children: Walkeena Branch, Patricia Young and Jennifer Preston; six grandchildren and three great grandchildren. They all live in New Jersey.

———

FIVE FORKS

———

CYNTHIA ALFREDA VAUGHAN

My first school was Five Forks School in the Five Forks community, where I started in September 1958. It was a one room school and the teachers were Mrs. Womack and Mrs. Baker. Five Forks had an outdoor toilet and there was no electricity at the school. The light in the classroom was the sunshine. We took our lunch, usually a peanut butter and jelly sandwich peeping through a greasy bag. We had to walk. No bus was provided. My younger brother Richard went to Five Forks and so did my sister, Sarah. Sarah was two years older than me, and Richard was four years older than me.

I was born February 3, 1952, to Lessie Bell Vaughan and the late Wyatt Vaughan, Sr. I went one year to Five Forks School, first grade only. I went there from September 1958 to June 1959.

In September 1959, when I was to go to the second grade at Five Forks School, the schools in Prince Edward County were closed. The children in my family didn't do anything the first year the schools were closed. Most of the boys in the area started doing odds jobs for White people.

About a year or so went by and Ms. Flossie Hudson started her school in her house.* My mama found out about the school at Ms. Flossie's and started sending us.

My sister Sarah went I'm sure. I don't remember whether Richard went with us to Ms. Flossie's. We didn't do anything for a long time. We started going to Ms. Flossie around 1960. Ms. Flossie lived near the Hendricks Store on the corner of Highway 626 and Highway 657.

We made porcelain trays and plaques and little things to hang on the walls at home. We didn't do a whole lot of reading and math. We did some, but not a lot. I think we went every day. Ms. Flossie, as we called her, prepared lunch for the children. It was fun. We used to walk to her house from Five Forks. It was about a mile or a little more from where we lived. There was nothing in Five Forks for us. No one had taken it upon themselves to start any classes.

In October 1962 my family moved into a house in Prospect near Calvary Baptist Church, the same house we're sitting in now and talking. We stopped going to Ms. Flossie's.

In September 1963 the Free School opened and I went to Branch No. 1. I was placed in the second grade. I was eleven years old when I went to the second grade. Some students in the second grade were even older. Many of the boys wouldn't tell their age. (Ms. Vaughan chuckled.) I liked school. I really loved home economics and math. I never cared for reading. I didn't like history and social studies. I took those classes but didn't care much for them. I graduated in 1970.

I've been in Prince Edward County all of my life. I want to tell all young people coming up now to get an education. Many of us lost out because of what happened in Prince Edward County. But I haven't lost focus. I know children need an education.

———

*Ms. Flossie held sessions in her house the first year of the school crisis, but the Vaughan family was unaware, or circumstances precluded the children from attending.

———

WILLIE SYLVESTER VAUGHAN

I was born July 7, 1946. I started first grade at Five Forks School. Mrs. Baker was my teacher and so was Mrs. Womack. There were two teachers in the one room school. Five Forks went to the fourth grade and the one room class was split down the middle. One teacher had the first and second graders on one side and the other teacher had the third and fourth graders on the other side of the room. Five Forks had an outdoor toilet and a pump outside. We had to walk about four or five miles to the school. There was a big potbelly stove in the middle of the room. Usually the first student to arrive when it was cold made the fire. There was a wood shed out back. We got the wood from the sawmill. I think the county bought the wood from the sawmill. After fourth grade, we went to First Rock School, next to First Rock Baptist Church. First Rock school had three rooms, I believe, and three teachers. I don't remember the teachers because I only went one year.

When the schools were closed, I was around thirteen. After the schools closed, I started helping my father on the farm. You couldn't stay in the house. You had to work. I got no education at all while the schools were closed.

In 1963 the Free School opened, and I went back to Moton. I was around seventeen years old and I was put in the fifth grade, the last grade I completed. I stayed in fifth grade that whole year. I went back to school each year until I reached the tenth grade. I was well into my twenties by that time. I couldn't take it any longer. It wasn't the school work, but the children teased the older ones saying things like: "Look at the old man in this class." "Hey, ole man." (Sylvester was mimicking the children.) I was so old, and the other students were so much younger that it made it difficult for me to concentrate.

I quit school and went to Southside Vocational School in Crewe, located in Nottoway County. I went for eighteen weeks studying in the area of service station auto mechanics. Reverend James Franklin, from Prince Edward County, was the teacher. I started doing mechanic work. In your twenties you want to start living like a young man and have a car. I was ready to move on with my life.

I have been singing gospel music since I was three years old. I sing with a group today called The Gospel Traveliers of Farmville. We sing around the state of Virginia and have sung in Ohio, New York and other locations. Our first recording was called *Move On Up To Heaven*.

The Prince Edward County story is a story people don't believe to this day. When we travel to sing and share this story in other States and even counties in Virginia, people say 'No, that could not have happened. Nothing like that could happen in the United States.'

They gave us a diploma recently, but those of us who received it don't have the education. So, what does the diploma mean? I was blessed to learn to work with my hands. I went eighteen weeks to Southside Vocational School, but really I should've gone for four years of mechanic training, but I had to get some training and start working. The closing of the schools affects me to this day.

———

WYATT VAUGHAN

I started school at Five Forks School. Mrs. Baker and Mrs. Womack were the teachers. Mrs. Baker had first and second grades. Mrs. Womack had third and fourth grades. After fourth grade, you went to First Rock School for fifth grade. Then we went to R. R. Moton in sixth grade. I was going to the seventh grade when the schools were closed.

When the schools were closed, I experienced a double slam. I was denied an education and I got polio that year, in October 1959 I got it. I went from 120 pounds down to seventy-six pounds in a matter of weeks. I stayed in the hospital for three months and twelve days.

The first year the schools were closed we worked on Norman Southall's Farm in Prospect. There were four or five Southall brothers and they all owned farms. When one had no work, you could go to one of the others and find work. I still had some of the effects of polio, but still worked.

I attended some classes at First Baptist Church for a little while. Some of the adults from the Prospect area drove us into town for the classes. I think they had a bunch of cars and the children were loaded up and brought to town. The little ones in the Prospect area went to Ms. Flossie's, but the older students they tried to get us some more stable learning.

When the Free School opened in September 1963, they tried to put me in the eighth grade. I was almost twenty years old. I was born October 18, 1944. Trying to go back to school and readjust was difficult, especially for those of us who were old and had gotten into many things, including debt. I owned a car and had to make payments. The choice was to pay for the car or go to school. It was just hard to make the transition and go back to school at that age and be in junior high school.

In 1969 I went to Richmond with six other fellows coming out of high school to get a physical exam for the Army. I was the only one who passed the physical exam. I entered the Army in 1970 for two years. I began to see things differently.

I went to Southside Community College in 1972, I believe that was the year. I took up auto mechanics.

It is hard to explain how I feel. The closing of the schools put me at a handicap and down a road that I know under ordinary circumstance I would not have traveled. We had nothing to do. The educational handicap sent many of us down the road of drinking. Many got married, but without an education you couldn't do for your family as you wished. Things just happened and happened until you got to the point where you didn't care.

I am the pastor at Mount Lyle Baptist Church, Madison, located between Charlotte County and Prince Edward County.

ERNEST 'BILL' WILLIAMS

I was born July 12, 1948, the youngest child of eight children. There were seven boys and one girl. The area of Prospect where we lived was known as Rattlers Branch. I attended elementary school at Five Forks School in Prospect, Virginia. I started in 1955 and Mrs. Pearl Baker was my first teacher. She also taught me in second grade. My third and fourth grade teacher was Mrs. Flossie Womack. Five Forks School was a frame school building, without running water. It had an outdoor toilet, no paved driveway or anything. We played stick ball at recess. We had a Spalding ball and we got a stick out the woods nearby and used it for a bat and played ball.

When I was promoted to the fifth grade, I left Five Forks School and started at First Rock School. The situation was similar—no running water, no indoor toilet, we still played stickball. I only went there in fifth grade. I was promoted to the sixth grade in June 1959.

Due to the interruption caused by Brown *vs* Board of Education and Prince Edward County not wanting to integrate, the schools were closed.

There were eight children in my family but only four of us were impacted by the closing: John, James, Doris (Berryman) and I. John was promoted to eighth grade and James had been promoted to the eighth grade. Doris was promoted to the seventh grade when the schools were closed.

At first for a year being out of school was all fun, we played stickball all day in the neighborhood. It was fun.

Then some of my friends started to go away. Isaac Dungee, Jr. went I believe to school in Appomattox. I think he and his sisters and brother lived with an uncle in Appomattox County. Harold White, Miss. Flossie's son, went to Hampton to an aunt so he could attend school.

The second year of the school closing, 1960–1961 school year, we started at the Five Forks Sunday School building known as the Long Branch Sunday School Building. No running water and no electricity. There was one outdoor toilet for the boys and the girls. When the girls went to the bathroom at recess, the boys just went on down in the woods. There was no drinking water and no well. I can't remember how we got water to drink during the school day. There was a store nearby, about three hundred yards away called Five Forks Store, but no one had money to buy a soda. Mrs. Pearl Lyle

and Althea Jones were the teachers. We called Mrs. Jones —
Aunt Della.

A typical school day at the Long Branch Sunday School
Building we started in the morning with the Lord's Prayer
and we saluted the flag. There was a flag in the building. We
did reading and arithmetic, these were the basics. They taught
us Freedom songs.

I believe in the second year of the school closing my sister
Doris went to live with Curtis our older brother who was in
New York.

The third year the schools were closed I started classes at
Miss. Flossie's in the basement of her house. We had lights,
and utilities, and so forth. This was a step up for me.

Miss. Flossie had a 4-H Club. It was called the Greenwood
4-H Club. Miss. Mary Moody (Stokes), who was a Saint Paul's
College graduate and Mr. Rudolph Doswell came by to run
the 4-H Club. When the schools were opened, Miss. Moody
was the Home Extension Agent. Miss. Flossie said she thinks
Miss. Moody came to Prince Edward County in 1958. Mr.
Doswell and Miss. Moody worked in the school system as
4-H workers and leaders before the schools were closed. Miss.
Flossie negotiated with them to come by and work with us.
Mr. Doswell taught us farming and raising livestock. I took
on a project under him and ordered a small pig to raise so I
could take it to the Five County Fair for a prize. In the fall of
the year the big fair was held in Farmville, but five surrounding counties shared in it — Cumberland, Charlotte, Prince
Edward, Buckingham and Appomattox.

"What happened to the pig you raised," the Editor asked.

I think my family slaughtered the hog and we ate it. (Mr.
Williams started laughing and so did the Editor.)

Each morning we had devotion and prayed. Each Friday

Miss. Flossie had a social. She put the record player out and we would dance. At recess we played baseball in her front yard. Miss. Flossie said only one of her windows was broken during all the years of the closure. During the year, we had seasonal events such as the Easter Egg Hunt and other events.

In the fourth year of the school closing I went to public school in Charlotte County. I used to ride with Mrs. Nellie Robinson. I was at Hendricks Store hanging around one day. This was around August in 1962. She said: "Why don't you ask your mother can you come with Buster and Junior (Lewis Robinson and James Robinson who were her sons) to school. I asked my mom and she said yes. I had to pay a fee, .25, (twenty-five cents) a day to ride with Mrs. Robinson.

Buster and Junior had two older sisters that had gone away to the high school department in Berea, Kentucky, in the Quaker sponsorship program.

Mrs. Robinson took us on Highway 47 to some friends' house and we caught the bus from there to James Murray Jeffress Elementary School in Charlotte County. I was in sixth grade that year and was promoted at the end of school to the seventh grade.

I was the only one in my home that rode with Mrs. Robinson.

The third and the fourth years of the school closing my sister Doris went to Christiansburg Academy in Blacksburg, Virginia. Doris and a female student from Farmville named Rita Mosley stayed in the same home and attended school.

In September 1963 the Free School opened in Prince Edward County. At that time, I guess because I had attended some school during the closing, I was placed in the eighth grade. I never did sit in seventh grade. In eighth grade I could pick things up right away. I had done multiplications, and was taught world history in the sixth grade, and had a little science in sixth grade, so I could pick things up real good.

John and James went to work when the schools were closed and when the Free School opened they were nearing adulthood and continued working. Doris returned to school.

I went to Connecticut the summer after tenth grade to work at an inn, Ragga Mount Inn in Salisbury, Connecticut. I came back to school in the fall for the eleventh grade and completed that year. I was promoted to twelfth grade and went back to the same place in Connecticut to work that summer, but I left there and went to work at New York State Hudson Valley Psychiatric Center.

I decided to quit school. In 1967 my grandfather died, and I came down to Virginia to the funeral. So, my mother said to me: "Your grandmother (Jenny Coles Scott) wants to talk to you before you go back to New York."

Grandma said to me: "You know your grandfather is gone and we need you to help about around the farm."

I said: "I got a job in New York and I'm not coming back."

Grandma took her glasses off and said to me: "Boy, next Monday you better be on dat school bus, cause I'm gon' be on it." I went back to New York, worked one week and drew my last $48.00 a week check and came back to Prospect.

Mama said: "Son, do me a favor, please finish high school." None of my older brothers of six brothers had finished high school. Mama went on to say: "If you finish, one day you will probably have more than your friends and the people who don't finish high school."

Monday morning, I was on the school bus. This was in October. I went back to school and graduated.

Many kids went back to school when the public schools reopened but dropped out later. Many of them just didn't have clothes to wear and they dropped out. I had older brothers who would send me clothes, so I could dress and be up-beat.

I graduated from high school in 1968. I was eligible for the draft and went to Richmond and registered. I failed the physical examination. I came back home, and Mama said: "Son, you know your Daddy got you a job on the railroad; or do you want to go to New York with your brothers."

I said: "I want to go and talk to Grandma." Grandma said: "We need you round here, but you're a young man now and have to take care of yourself." A girl name Irene Mitchell drove me to the bus station in Farmville to catch the bus.

I took a job in a factory named Eagle Electric in Queens, New York. I worked there eleven days. I said 'this is not for me, I have a high school diploma.' Each day I went outside and sat on a ledge and ate my lunch. I asked a guy one day:

"Where does that train go?" It was the L train.

He said: "It goes to New York."

One Friday I faked sick saying I had to go to the dentist. I boarded the L train and rode to New York and I got off at Broadway and 42nd. I saw a Chase Manhattan Bank and said to myself: 'I want to work there.' I went inside and asked the security guard what did I need to do to get a job there. He directed me to 1 Chase Plaza. I went to personnel and they gave me an aptitude test. I scored a 98 and was hired immediately.

"Can you come Monday morning? We want to start you off in the assistant manager program," they said.

I worked there twenty-eight months making $125.00 a week. In my neighborhood my brothers' friends were always encouraging me to take the city test: fire department, police department, and I took them all. The police department called me, and I called my mama to discuss it. She said: "Please don't take that job."

I got a job with the New York City Transit as an Officer Associate. I stayed there four months and was called off another list to go with the New York Environmental Protection as an Officer Associate. This was in 1970. In 1976 I was promoted to New York City Water Inspector. In 1982 I was promoted to Supervisor of New City Water Department. In 1990 I was promoted to District Supervisor Water and Sewer in the Borough of the Bronx. In 1998 I was promoted to District Superintendent Borough of Manhattan Water and Sewer Distribution.

I am a World Trade Center survivor. I responded to the location and was there eleven minutes after the plane hit the North Tower. I saw everything, bodies, people jumping out of windows, bodies lying in the streets. The only reason why I am alive today, Sunday, January 8, 2012, one of the chief engineers called and said: "I want you to take a pressure reading on a fire hydrant off a twenty-inch water main on the sidewalk in front of the North Tower. The only reason I didn't go and do it was because I didn't have my assigned vehicle with my tools. (Pressure gauge etc.) I said 10/4 and contacted my office asking them to bring me a pressure gauge to my location. While I was waiting for them to bring my tools, the South Tower got hit and that's when holy hell broke loose.

After that everything started coming down. I started running south on West Street, but the crowd was coming from the south on West Street. I turned around. I went to the basement of 1 World Financial Center and we were trapped for two and one-half hours. While we were there people started dying in the basement. A chaplain said: "Let's have a word of prayer." The prayer was never completed. Someone yelled: "We can get out." They had a yellow rope that was passed from one person to the other. It was like a lead rope. They told us to head to the Hudson River and be prepared to jump into the water in case any other buildings were attacked. I got back to my office and we regrouped. At 5:30 p. m. we met with the FBI and CIA and went back in for the rest of the night until 5:30 a. m. the following morning. While working through the night, we could see people, the dead at their desks. The next morning, we had to secure our water main. We went up to the Jarvis Center at 12th Avenue and 34th Street. For the next thirty-one days, we worked around the clock. I was supervising the crews and operations.

In 2002 I retired from the City of New York. I relocated to Chesterfield, Virginia. I was unemployed for about four months and took a job with the Chesterfield County public schools as a facility coordinator at Meadow Brook High School. I worked there for six years and seven months.

Looking back, I see now the encouragement from my mom and grandma about staying in school has paid off. I remember Mama said: "If you stay in school and graduate, one day you will have more than your friends that quit." All the opportunities that were afforded me resulted because I had a high school diploma.

The closing of the schools taught me a lesson, the lesson being — Not to be denied an opportunity due to lack of ability.

PEAKS

ANNIE MAE BEASLEY WASHINGTON

Cornell Walker and Mr. William Junious Miser drove me through the Peaks community on an earlier visit to Prince Edward County. When in the county in June 2006, the Editor decided to return to Peaks on his own. Down the road from Peaks Baptist Church the Editor saw some children in a yard. He parked on the side of the rode in front of a house, went on the porch and greeted an old lady who apparently was the matriarch of the family and possibly of the neighborhood. The Editor introduced himself and explained the nature of the project. The matriarch immediately agreed to share her story. She understood the need for such chronicling and capturing information on paper. It was as though she was sitting on the front porch waiting for the arrival of the Editor and his appearance was no surprise to her. As she was talking, the children played in the yard and walked about on the porch. She was peacefully watching the children, monitoring their movements, and talking to the Editor all at the same time. There were one or two vehicles parked in the front yard. One car with a New Jersey license plate was packed for traveling. A young woman came out of the house, spoke, went to the vehicle and put several more items inside. The Editor reasoned that some of the people seen moving about were visiting and the matriarch was the mother, grandmother, and possibly great grandmother of the individuals moving around. Mrs. Washington began.

I was born in Prospect, May 1, 1913, to Joe and Anna Beasley. My parents was sharecroppers. We lived on the land of a White family and I don't remember the family's last name.

I went to a one room school when I was a girl. I think I went to school whenever I could. When we got to school, we said a Bible verse and sung a song, a church song. The school had a potbelly stove in the middle. The teacher would send the boys out for wood. There was a pump on the yard for water. A bucket of water was kept in a lil' room where you came in the one room school. Mrs. Lucy was the teacher. I can't remember her last name. The school went to the seventh grade. After seventh grade, you went to Farmville to school.

Mr. Hendricks drove a bus, but he picked up the children who went to Number Twenty-two and Five Forks and took them to Moton High in town. No bus came to my area. Most of the boys and girls who lived in my section dey education ended after seventh grade 'cause no bus came to our area. Our parents was sharecroppers and was too poor to pay rent to a family in town for us to live wid' dem. After seventh grade, I stayed home and helped my parents on the farm.

"Do you remember when the public schools were closed?" the Editor asked.

When the schools closed, I had three of my gran'chil'ren livin' wid' me — Barbara Ann Beasley, Alfred Beasley, and Beverly. Dey' was Roxie's chil'ren.

Note of the Editor: Roxie, the Editor concluded, was the daughter of Mrs. Washington.

Peaks School was a two room school. I was real upset when I heard the schools was closed.

Note of the Editor: Peaks Baptist Church was very close

to this house. "Were classes held for the children at Peaks Baptist Church like was held at Saint James or at First Baptist in Farmville?" the Editor asked.

As far as I know, wasn' no classes at Peaks Baptist Church for the chil'ren when the schools closed.

————

BERVELY BEASLEY HATCHER

A younger woman passed Mrs. Washington and the Editor on the front porch several times going in and out of the house. Each time she came out, the lady had several items in her hands that she put in the back of the sports utility vehicle parked in the front yard. It was the vehicle with the New Jersey license tag.

Mrs. Washington stated that the woman had been impacted by the school closure. The Editor could tell from her swift trips in and out of the house that she was ready to leave the area. She heard in passing the dialogue between the matriarch and the Editor. When the Editor asked the lady if she was willing to share her story, nothing much had to be explained.

"I don't have long," she said, while walking. "I'll give you five minutes. What do you want to know?"

"What do you want to tell the world about what happened here when you were a girl and the schools were closed? All the stories gathered will be in a book and the many stories will give a fuller and richer view of what happened," said the Editor. "I can write as fast as you can talk."

The woman started talking but was talking fast while standing on the porch. She was ready to get on the road.

I started school at Peaks School on Peaks Road. Peaks was a two room school and Mrs. Hendricks was my teacher. She taught first, second and third grades and all the students were in the same room. The fourth, fifth and sixth graders were in another room and were taught by another teacher whose name I can't remember.

One day we had to draw a rooster. A girl named Lottie tore a page out of a book with a rooster and we traced it. Mrs. Hendricks beat us with the ruler in the palm of our hands.

Note of the Editor: At this point a calm seemed to have come over the narrator. She was still anxious to get on the road back to New Jersey but was now more than willing to stay for a little longer on the road that took her back to childhood. She continued:

When the schools closed, I was eight years old. I learned that the schools were going to be closed before September 1959. When school closed for the summer, people were already saying there would be no school in the fall.

A boy name Tom Tick Scott told us there wasn't going to be any school in the fall. We were walking home from Peaks School and had gotten our report cards. Tom Tick tore his report card up and we said to him:

"Ooohhh, you're goin' to get in trouble."

"Ain't no school next year," he said.

I remember thinking that can't be. I loved school.

I didn't understand why I wasn't going back to school. My mother came home for summer vacation. When she heard that the schools weren't going to open in September, Mama took me and Barbara back to Connecticut with her, where I started school in the fall.

I was eight years old. Barbara turned six on August 21, 1959 and was ready to start first grade. My little brother,

Alfred, stayed in Prospect with Grandma because he wasn't school age.

Two years later my first cousin, Charlotte, turned six years old. Alfred also turned six. My mother brought Alfred and Charlotte to Connecticut, where both started school.

Charlotte was my mother's sister's child, Aunt Dorothy Washington Jones.

When school reopened in 1963, all of us came back to the Free School. Many of the older students got married.

My aunt named Venessa Jackson got married and my Uncle George Washington got married and never went back to school.

Peaks School was cut in half and today the school is two houses.

Note of the Editor: The Editor thanked Barbara, then turned and thanked Mrs. Beasley who gave every indication that she understood the nature and importance of the project and was appreciative of the undertaking. Her old wrinkled face and piercing eyes were consoling to the Editor. "I'm glad somebody is doin' dis kind'a work," she complimented.

SADIE SCOTT WALKER

After interviewing Helen Ruth Walker on May 20, 2011, the Editor said to her: "I'm going to ride over to Peaks and see what the good Lord will do." Mrs. Walker gave directions that took the Editor directly into the community of Peaks. Two young ladies were seen standing in a front yard. The Editor pulled in the driveway, greeted them, and said: "I have a question, but I need to talk to someone who is around sixty years old." "My Mama is eighty-one," the more vibrant of the two said, "I'll go in and get her."

The mother came to the door. She was dark, had white hair, and was full of energy like a woman in her early sixties. The Editor explained that he was trying to find out the names of the two teachers at Peaks School the year the Prince Edward County public schools were closed. "Mrs. Davenport was one," Mrs. Sadie Scott Walker began. The Editor called out the full name, "Mrs. Beatrice Lawson Davenport." "That's right and the other teacher was Mrs. Hendricks, but I can't remember her first name. Somebody over by the store in Prospect probably can tell you."

Learning that several of her children were impacted by the closing of the schools, the Editor asked the matriarch would she share her story. She consented.

We sat on the front porch. Mrs. Walker composed herself and began her story.

I was born in the Peaks section of Prince Edward County, October 4, 1928, to Alonzo and Louise Harris Scott.

When I first went to school, I went to Peaks School, but I wasn't enrolled as a student. Back then when you cried they just said 'come on' and you went. I went with my Aunt Emily once or twice. Mrs. Hazel Carter taught my aunts when they were girls. I remember Mrs. Carter, but she didn't teach me. Peaks School had one room at the time an'a outdoor toilet.

When I was old enough to go to school, they had built a new school with two rooms and I started there. There was two big rooms and a very small kitchen. Mr. L. L. Hall was my first teacher when I went to Peaks School. Mrs. Brown taught me also, but I can't remember her first name. Then Mrs. Beatrice Davenport taught me. Mrs. Davenport came after Mr. Hall left. I went to the seventh grade at Peaks School.

Mrs. Mae Lou Booker was the cook. She was the first cook I knew at Peaks School. Mrs. Mary Walker was also a cook when I was in school. Then Mrs. Davenport got me to cook. I think she sent one of the childr'n to get me. I cooked there from 1942 to 1943 or 1944. I left and went to Philadelphia, Pennsylvania. Then Mrs. Alma Saunders started cooking at Peaks School.

I came back from Philadelphia in 1949. Mrs. Saunders was the cook then.

My husband was working with Reverend Griffin. There wasn' that many people voting at the time. Back then there were classes to teach you how to write. The classes were held at the churches, most times at First Baptist Church, where Reverend Griffin was the pastor.

They taught you in the classes what to say and how to write it out, so when you went to register to vote you would get everything right. When you went to the courthouse, you had to write out—My name is Sadie Walker. I was born in Prince Edward County, October 4, 1928. My occupation is housewife. Then put your address. If you could write all of that out, you could then go and vote. If you couldn't write it out, you didn't vote. In 1959 we had to write this information out to vote.

When you voted, there was a box on the ballot and you had to check the little box. They taught us how to make the X in the box very neat. (Mrs. Walker, using her hand, and without pencil or paper, demonstrated how the X had to be made.) If you went outside the box, they said during the training, it would not count.

Carolyn, Betty, Oather, Jr., Geraldine and Delores stayed

home the first year. We had one car and my husband drove it to work. They started going to classes in the basement of Saint James Church and would walk. It was between three and three and a half miles from our house to the church.

I started taking the childr'n to First Rock in the third year of the closing of the schools. The classes was in First Rock School.

When the childr'n went to First Rock, I would go all through the community and pick up childr'n. Back then you could ride childr'n on the fender of a car and nobody would say a thing. I had'em everywhere.

Note of the Editor: The Editor said to Mrs. Walker: "I have never heard of a learning site at First Rock School, only at Saint James AME in this area. I have been collecting stories for publication for ten years now and this is the first time I have heard about classes being held in First Rock School. I have been working under the impression that all of the public schools were pad-locked during the closure years."

I'm sure the childr'n went to classes at First Rock School for a year. I drove'em.

"Git the phone and call Carolyn," the mother said to the daughter that greeted the Editor upon arrival. The daughter went in the house, brought the phone out on the front porch, dialed the number and gave the telephone to her mother.

"Carolyn, you remember goin' to First Rock School when the schools were closed? Y'all went to Saint James for a while, y'all had to walk and y'all carried Earnestine on your back." Mrs. Walker looked at the Editor, smiled, and whispered, while continuing to listen to Carolyn — "She remembers goin' to First Rock School." The mother listened another minute or so and hung up. "She said if you have any more questions just call her."

"Thank you," the Editor said.

I knew they went to First Rock School for one year.

"How did they get into the school to have classes if the county had all the schools locked up?" the Editor asked, remaining unclear.

Mrs. Inez Hicks owned the property where the school was. She owned it all and they couldn't tell her what to do.

The fourth year the schools were closed everybody went to Carver–Price in Appomattox. I had cousins, Flossie and William Walker, that lived in Appomattox. This was my husband's relatives. William and my husband was cousins. William came over to the house one day and said to Oather: "The childr'n been out'a school three years. Bring'em over and sign'em up at Carver–Price and use my address."

My husband was born in Appomattox and his roots was in that county.

William and Flossie went with me and Oather to register the childr'n in school. Carolyn, Betty, Oather, Jr., Delores, Geraldine, and Earnestine got registered.

They never stayed a night in Appomattox County. I carried them each morning to meet the bus. I took them to the bus stop where Flossie and William's childr'n caught the bus, not far from Flossie and William's house. Flossie and William had about ten childr'n. They had ten. (Mrs. Walker named the ten children and displayed a finger for each person she named. She doubled back once or twice when enumerating. It appeared she was trying to name them in birth order and missed someone.) I had to drive about five miles, maybe a little more, one way to the bus stop. They normally caught the school bus near Gravel Hill Baptist Church. If they missed the bus, I drove them to the next bus stop, which was next to Mount Pleasant Baptist Church.

Oather bought a second car so I could drive'em back and

forth each day. At first I had a Buick and my husband took it. Then he gave me a station wagon of some sort. I picked'em up in the afternoon. Sometime I didn't get there on time.

I didn't like that second car. It looked like a hearse. He said: "It's your car, now take dem chil'lun to school." (Mrs. Walker chuckled, when imitating her husband.)

I took the Jackson children and my children. I packed them into that station wagon to go to Carver-Price.

Geneva Jackson (Jones) and Juanita Jackson (Vaughan) were twins. Jessie and Juanita Jackson was their parents. Their uncle, George Jackson, brough'em (Geneva and Juanita) to my house each morning. They went to school the whole year at Carver-Price. I don't know how they got registered. All I know is their Uncle George came one morning and said the girls grandma said to ask could they ride wid' me and I said yea.

Sometimes the childr'n would knock on the door in the morning and I would be sound asleep. Some mornings Juanita and Geneva would help comb hair. They were older than my girls. They were maybe ninth or tenth grade. They were two or three years older than Carolyn.

One morning there was a lot of snow on the ground and I slid off the road near the woods and skimmed a tree. I was driving a little fast that morning trying to get to the bus stop on time. (Earnestine, who had made her way to the front porch from her house next door, whispered to the Editor: Mama wasn't drivin' a lil' fas' that morning, she was drivin' real fas'. Earnestine chuckled.)

Junior Paige and Luevenia Paige went to Buckingham County. They lived on 460 going toward First Rock. They stayed in Buckingham County most of the school year. They owned a restaurant on 460. During the week Junior drove back and forth to work in Farmville. Mrs. Paige came from Buckingham each day to run the restaurant. I worked for her sometimes.

They had training classes at Saint James for the youths, training them how to act when they protested. They were taught what to do if somebody put a cigarette on you. Sometimes the White people would put a lit cigarette on you. (Mrs. Walker drew up her arms and shivered as if a cigarette had just been put on her.) I took my children—Carolyn, Betty, Oather, Jr., and Delores.

We picketed downtown, and I marched once or twice. The older people didn't march. Whole lot'a stores just locked up because they didn't want the Black people to come in. On Saturdays we would go into town and stand but wouldn't buy nothing.

Sometimes Reverend Griffin would be here (at the Walker house) before daylight to pick up Oather. He thought Oather was a strong man. Reverend Griffin would pick up Oather and the older Mr. Scott in Prospect and they would go to a meeting.

My children went to the Free School in Prince Edward County when it opened in September 1963.

———

*Note of the Editor: Later Friday evening, May 20, 2011, the Editor returned to the home of Helen Ruth Walker and inquired about the First Rock School learning site. "If all the schools were pad-locked by authorities, I don't understand how children could have attended classes inside First Rock School during the third year of the closure," the Editor reasoned aloud. "I was told Mrs. Inez Hicks owned the land. What about the building? Who owned it?"

"I don't know anything about it," Sister Walker com-menced, "but I know who can tell me, Emma Wade."

Saturday morning May 21, 2011, around 10:00 a. m., Sister Walker telephoned me in Farmville and shared: "I spoke with Libby Jordan who is ninety-nine years old and she said Inez Hicks bought the land from the Brown children, Roy, Bennie, Pearly, and Angeline Brown, after the schools were closed. The land belonged to Inez and Ed Hicks, the husband. I called Emma Wade, she is eighty-one, and she and Libby Jordan said they never remember First Rock School being locked up or a lock being on the door. Whoever owned the land also owned the school. The school was always in the hands of a private family."

EARNESTINE WALKER LEE

I was born March 12, 1956. When I was supposed to start school, the schools were closed. I started attending classes in the basement of Saint James AME. I remember the larger girls, Margaret Smith was one of them, helped Mrs. Davenport with us younger ones.

During the 1962-1963 school year, I went to Carver–Price High School in Appomattox. I had Mrs. Virginia Goode for my first teacher. Mama had a station wagon that looked like a hearse. Children would be in the front seat, back seat, and in the hole in the back of the station wagon. Wherever there was a space somebody sat.

Some days Mama would not get there on time to pick us up after school, somedays she was late. When she was late, we would start walking from Appomattox toward Prince Edward County and she would meet us. We would be playing and walking until we saw her.

Some mornings we would miss the bus. When we got to the bus stop the bus would be gone and we would have to go to another bus stop. We knew the route and could tell Mama which way to go and where to turn and we would get on at another stop. Sometimes we had to run behind the school bus.

I remember the morning Mama ran off the road. It was snowing, and Mama was speeding. She was trying to get us to the bus stop on time. She actually went off the road and then got back on. We got to the bus stop on time.

It was about ten miles from our house to the bus stop in Appomattox. Going to school was exciting. The days were long. We were up early, most times by 5:00 a. m., went to school, back home, did our chores, you still had to do them, then homework, and before you knew it, it was time to go to bed, and before you knew it again it was time to get up.

———

LEROY CARR

I was the baby in my family. There were four of us, but the other three, my brothers Lester and Lander and my sister Grace, graduated before the schools were closed.

I had passed to the eighth grade when the schools were closed. They were saying 'they were going to close the schools,' but I didn't believe it. When the schools didn't open in September 1959, Daddy said: "Son, I can't move, so you have to get a job.' Daddy worked for the railroad.

I was a good basketball player on the playground and was looking forward to trying out for the junior varsity basketball team at Moton High School. I was hurt.

I stayed in Prospect from the time the schools closed until I was twenty-one. Between eighth grade and when I turned twenty-one, I worked for Newton Glenn. He had a farm. I left there and went to Robert Taylor Sawmill in Prospect off Route 460. Then I went to Kyanite Mining in Dillwyn, Virginia. I left there and went to Carter Shoe Factory in Farmville.

I got married in 1962. My oldest daughter Tammy was born February 9, 1963.

Some of my friends and I started a band around 1965 called 'The Imperial'. I was a singer, I was the lead singer. Phillip Walker was the drummer. The organist was Plummer Jones. Our first job was at Pine View Café. Plummer got drafted and I started playing the organ by ear. We played at places all around Virginia. One night we played at the University of Virginia. The night we played James Brown was performing on the other side of the campus. We had about one hundred and fifty to two hundred people. We thought we were doing something because we had that many people, when James Brown was on the other side of the campus. (Leroy was laughing.)

Then I left and went to work on the railroad in New Jersey.

When I was in New Jersey, I went to truck driving school and learned how to drive an eighteen-wheeler. I bought my own truck and became my own operator. I started driving truck at twenty-five.

When I started driving truck, I couldn't even read the map. I went to a White man and said: "Show me Chicago," and he showed me how to find Chicago on the map. He said: "If you're looking for Chicago, on the back of the map it will have E.13. Go up the line and across the line and your finger should be on Chicago."

When I first started driving, I didn't trust the map. For example, if I left New Jersey, I took Interstate 80 because I could read numbers. I looked at the map and saw the next town. Then I started looking for signs for that town. When I saw a sign for the town, I knew I was on the right road. In time I learned that the map didn't lie. If it said the town was there, the town really was there.

I basically learned to read from the road map. I had to regain all that I had lost after the schools were closed. Most of the jobs I had since the school lock-out started didn't require me to read. When I was plowing on a tractor on a farm in Prince Edward County, all I had to do was get on the tractor and drive. There was nothing to read. No reading was required at the saw-mill where I worked for a while.

I left New Jersey and went to Birmingham, Alabama, in 1999 and started my own trucking company. I ran thirteen eighteen wheelers in my company the first year in business. The name of the company was L CARRGO Carrier. My wife Gwen picked out the name. She said L was for Leroy; my last name Carr; and Go was for going or forward movement.

The first year in business my gross earning was 1.1 million dollars. I decided to sell out. I enjoyed the work and the business, but it became overwhelming and everything happened so fast. I had no education. I was unfamiliar with all the tax laws and other laws related to business. It was just me and my wife, Gwendolyn Howard Carr. We were the front office. Gwen was from Augusta, Georgia. I stayed in business until 2001 and sold the business. I kept one truck for myself.

As of today, August 13, 2011, I still have my one truck. I have been driving about forty-two years, starting at twenty-five and I am sixty-seven years old now. I run forty-eight States and I pull chemicals. My average gross per-year now is $230,000.00.

I can add and work with numbers, but I cannot read well. I often think if I could have had a full education and just *one* year of college, how far I could have went is unimaginable!

———

DOROTHY LOCKETT HOLCOMB

I started my public education at Peaks Elementary School and Mrs. Beatrice Davenport and Mrs. Mary Hendricks were the teachers. The last year the schools were opened Mrs. Davenport taught me. Peaks was at this time a three room, two classrooms and a kitchen. There were no indoor facilities, but we had a strong learning environment.

When the school closed at the end of the year, I had no idea it would not reopen in the fall. We said 'good bye' to each other like we normally did at the end of the school year, expecting to see each other in September. Later during the summer Dad informed us that school was not going to open.

I remember the day vividly when he broke the news. I was outside the house sitting on the steps on the back porch. My brothers, Edward and Macy, and I were on the back steps. I don't know why Dad told us at this particular time, but I remember he said: "You all won't be going to school this year." Being ten years old, you asked why. Dad said: "The folks (meaning White folks) don't want to integrate."

Then we entered into a dialogue with Dad, asking: "Where are we going to go to school?"

He said: "Well, don't worry about that right now. I promise you, you will be educated."

We kind of left it like that that day. We were so shocked. So as time went on, Dad said one day: "Okay, next week you all will start going to the Methodist Church (Saint James).

We said: "The Methodist Church, what are we going to do there?

He said: "Mrs. Davenport will be there to teach you."

So, we said: "Okay."

I remember Ed and I talking afterward about how we would get to Saint James. Ed said: "I guess the bus will come and get us." He was getting ready to go to Mary E. Branch in Farmville when the schools were closed, and he would have ridden the bus to town.

When we got ready to go to Saint James, Dad took us the first day on his way to work. He worked for the Norfolk and Western Railroad in Pamplin. But after that day, we had to walk, and we are talking about three miles to the church and three miles back home. There was no bus. (Mrs. Holcomb started laughing.)

Me, Edward, Macy, my nephew (my sister Eloise son) John, my cousin, Louise, (she was my mom's sister's daughter), Leroy Carr, and a bunch of the other neighborhood children walked to school each morning.

We all attended Peaks Baptist Church in the Peaks community, but Peaks Baptist did not have a learning program. That was how we all ended up at Saint James. Saint James was the nearest location to us with a Learning Center. Edward, Macy and I went to Saint James for two years. The schools still did not reopen.

In the third year of the school closing, the 1961-1962, school year, my parents decided to try and get us in school in Appomattox County. The only way to do this was to have a residence in Appomattox County. My parents rented an old dilapidated house and we pretended to live there. The house was uninhabitable. You could see the earth beneath when standing inside the house. There was no furniture in the house. Dad and Mom did not intend to live there at first. This was a stop gap. They were hoping that the schools in Prince Edward County would not be closed for a fourth year and we would only need to rent in Appomattox for this school year. The house was right in Pamplin City, a small community in Appomattox County.

Dad took us to the old house each morning and dropped us off on his way to work. After he let us off, we had to stay behind the house outside. We stayed behind the house and waited for the bus because the house was not livable, so we remained outside. When the bus arrived, we went in the back-door, through the house, then out the front door and boarded the bus. We attended Carver–Price High School.

This was the third year of the closure of the Prince Edward County schools. Macy who had passed to the tenth grade when the schools were closed discontinued his education and never enrolled at Carver–Price. At the house each morning was me, Ed, John and Larry, my nephew, and another nephew and niece Phillip Goode and his sister, Edith. Phillip and Edith were the children of my sister Otelia. All of us rode with Dad each morning. And this was the era before seat-belts. (Mrs. Holcomb chuckled.)

When the school day ended, and the bus driver dropped us off at the house, we went through the front door and out the back and stayed in the backyard until Dad came. We did that on a daily basis. After work, Dad would come and pick us up.

Other children started coming to the house in the morning

to catch the bus. Remember my family lived in Peaks and we attended Peaks Baptist Church and the entire community was close knit. People heard about the house. All each student needed to do was get to the house each morning in order to board the bus. This house provided everyone with an Appomattox County address to register at Carver–Price High School.

When the Prince Edward County public schools did not open for the 1962-1963 school year, Mama and Dad rented the old house in Pamplin City for a second year; only this year Dad did not drop us off each morning. He fixed up the house enough to make it habitable and our family moved in.

The second year Dad rented the house, often as many as twenty-one students boarded the school bus at the house. Other students that started coming to the house the second year we were there were Alfred Carr, Edward Carr who we called Eddie Ray, George Jones, and Mable Carr. These were my cousins.

Many of the students used our address; but not all students that came to catch the bus at our house used our address. Many had another Appomattox County address, but our house was the closest bus stop for their parents to drop them off, coming from the Peaks community in Prince Edward County. Sometimes people missed the bus at their primary bus stop and came to our house to catch the bus.

The next year, the 1963-1964 school year, the Free School opened in Prince Edward County. Of the twenty-one students that often boarded the bus at the house, all returned to the Free School, except me, Edward, Phillip and Edith. Phillip and Edith parents were in Maryland at this time and their grandparents, my mom and dad, were raising them.

The next year, September 1964, the Prince Edward County public schools reopened, but we did not return to the county.

All four of us completed our public education in Appomattox County. Edward graduated from Carver–Price in 1966 and I graduated from the same school in 1968. Edward was Number 2 in the Class of 1966 and I graduated Number 2 in the Class of 1968.

Edward went on to Livingstone College in North Carolina on a football scholarship. I went to Johnson C. Smith in North Carolina on an academic scholarship.

I worked for the Virginia Employment Commission for thirty-two years. I served on the Prince Edward County School Board from 2000-2004. I retired in 2004 and as of today, October 19, 2011, I serve on the Board of the Moton Museum.

This is an abbreviated version of my experience. I have written a book and provided greater details. I hope to have the work published.*

---

*Since this interview, the book by Dorothy Lockett Holcomb, *Educated in spite of...A Promise Kept*, has been published.

MABLE BOOKER

I was born February 14, 1955, to Lander Carr and Louise Stiff Carr. The Prince Edward County public schools were closed when it was time for me to start first grade.

My mother's sister, Alberta Stiff Ford, bought an old run-down shack, an old house, no shingles and little wood on the side; a strong wind would have blown it down. Aunt Alberta's house was not a rental, she bought the house.* Her husband was named Ben Ford. Uncle Ben worked at the Lynchburg Finery, a steel factory in Lynchburg. Aunt Alberta and Uncle Ben's house was in Appomattox County and they bought their house there before the schools were closed.

My mama's other sister, Helen Jones, lived in Prospect, but she went to Appomattox each day. Aunt Helen worked at the Appomattox Garment Factory. Starting in September 1962, Mama arranged for me to ride each morning to Appomattox with Aunt Helen. Aunt Helen would drop me off at Aunt Alberta's house on her way to work. Aunt Alberta had four children older than me. I caught the bus with them. Aunt Alberta could stand on the porch and see us get on the bus.

I started first grade at Carver–Price High School and used Aunt Alberta's address for school.

I know ten, twelve, or thirteen other children from my community that started first grade in Appomattox with me in September 1962. Donnie Walker was in Mrs. Goode's first grade class with me. His brother, Jessie Walker, was in second or third grade at Carver-Price. We all completed the first grade at Carver–Price High School. It was a good school year. I remember we wrapped the May Pole. I loved it!

When the Free School opened in Prince Edward County in September 1963, my parents enrolled me for the second grade. My mom got all my papers together and took them to the school administrators. To her surprise, I was not given credit for my first grade work. None of the other students from my community that started first grade the year before at Carver–Price were given credit. The people that ran the Prince Edward County Free School Association said that we should not have gone across the line.

Mom was devastated and said it made no sense for them not to accept the credit for the one year after riding nearly forty miles round trip each day.

None of the nearly fifteen children that completed first grade at Carver-Price in the 1962-1963 school year received credit for that one year when they started in the Free School.

---

*Alberta Stiff Ford rented in Appomattox County for two years. She her story in this volume.

GEORGE LEE JONES, JR.

When it was time for me to start first grade, the schools in Prince Edward County were closed. I started first grade at Carver-Price High School in Appomattox County in September 1962.

My great grand aunt, Aunt Alma, use to live in Prince Edward County, then later she moved to Appomattox County. Alma Booker Lockett was the sister of Lucille Booker Carr. Lucille was my mother's mother.

My mama, Grace Carr Jones, would drive me to Aunt Alma's house each morning. Mama also picked up several other boys in our neighborhood and they rode with us to Aunt Alma's house. All of the boys Mama picked up were my cousins.

The car started out at my house, I was an only child. Then Mama would pick up Larry and Johnny Boy, they lived within walking distance from us, about one hundred yards. Then we picked up Alfred (Lander Alfred Carr, Jr.).

Mama would drop the four of us off at Aunt Alma's to catch the bus to Carver- Price High School. We used Aunt Alma's address to register in school. All of us were in elementary school.

Aunt Alma had two children Dorothy Ann and Edward, and both were in high school at Carver-Price.

I went to school in Appomattox for one year, first grade only.

When the Free School opened in Prince Edward County, I went to Mary E. Branch No. 1. When I got to Mary E. Branch, I thought I was going to the second grade, but they put me back in the first grade. I had to start over. They said I had crossed another county line and gave me no credit for the year's work I did at Carver-Price.

I went to Branch No. 2 in fourth and fifth grades. There was overcrowding and many of us were sent to Worsham School. We went to Branch No. 2 in the morning, then boarded a bus and was taken to Worsham. We were brought back to Branch No. 2 in the afternoon to catch the bus home.

I went on to high school and went to school every day I could.

LANDER ALFRED CARR, JR.

When it was time for me to start first grade, the schools in Prince Edward County were closed. I started first grade at Carver-Price High School in Appomattox.

My aunt, Grace Carr Jones, this was my father's sister, drove us to Appomattox County each day to catch the school bus. Aunt Alma (Alma Booker Lockett) and her husband Uncle Leonard rented a house in Appomattox County. In the car with Aunt Grace was her son, George; Larry Jordan and I'm not sure what grade Larry was in, but I think he was in elementary school; and John Jordan, Jr., Larry's brother, was in junior high. My sister, Mable rode with us sometimes.

Aunt Grace had a 1955 tan four door Ford. I remember Johnny Boy and Larry used to sing Do-Whop in the car in the mornings. They sang songs by The Temptations and Four Tops each morning. They had beautiful voices. They had voices like The Temptations and could mimic them.

Aunt Grace would drop us off at Aunt Alma's and we caught the bus with her children Dorothy and Edward. Some of Aunt Alma's grand children also caught the bus with us, Phillip and Edith.

There was a house next door to the rental. A White girl named Cathy Bates lived there and she caught the bus that went to the White school.

A highway came through later, but the big tree that was in the front yard is still standing in the median between the two lanes.

I went one year to Carver–Price and then the Free School opened. I remember Robert Kennedy came to Mary E. Branch No. 1, but I had no idea who he was, but I remember seeing him. When I entered the Free School, they put me back in the first grade. I was in the second grade for a short time.

———

PHILLIP WALKER

I was born November 4, 1942, to Bessie Carr Walker and Henry Walker. I was born in Peaks and started school at Peaks School. Mrs. Beatrice Davenport was my teacher. I went to Peaks School from first to sixth grades. Then I was transferred to Mary E. Branch No. 2 for the seventh grade. I went to Moton High School in the eighth and ninth grades. When I passed to the tenth grade, the schools were closed.

The first year the schools were closed, I went to Connecticut and worked at Ragga Mount Inn, Salisbury, Connecticut. Then I came back home and hooked up with my cousin who was teaching school in Appomattox County. Her name was Doris Walker Goode. I used her addressed in Appomattox to enroll in Carver-Price High School, but I lived in Prince Edward County. I never stayed with my Cousin Doris.

I rode to school with Edwin Paige. Ed's father had a car. My family didn't have a car.

I went to school during the day, came back to Farmville and worked at the bowling alley until 11:00 p. m. One of the guys that worked at the bowling alley would take me home at night.

I would contribute weekly to gas. I did that for three years — tenth, eleventh and twelfth grades. From where we lived to Carver-Price High School was about twenty miles one way.

Edwin Paige, Leon Hill and I graduated from Carver-Price High School in June 1964.

GOLDIE SAUNDERS WALKER

I was born to Myrtle Gordon Saunders and Matthew Saunders on October 28, 1946. Daddy worked for Norfolk and Western Railroad and retired after many years. I started at Peaks School when I was six years old. Mrs. Mary Hendricks was my first teacher and Mrs. Beatrice Davenport taught me in fourth, fifth and sixth grades.

I was excited about going to Mary E. Branch No. 2 in the seventh grade. I had a good mind and enjoyed school.

When I passed from Mrs. Davenport's sixth grade class, I was due to go to Mary E. Branch No. 2 to the seventh grade. My brother, Matthew, who no one in the community knows as Matthew, everyone in the neighborhood knew him as Bayo, had passed to the sixth grade. I will call him by the name Bayo throughout my story.

In the summer of 1959 my mother said she had heard others talking that the schools weren't going to open. She was saying 'that was such a shame. How could they not open the schools?' I said 'that is such a shame. I don't think that'll happen.'

After Labor Day, schools didn't open and as children we sat around and did nothing. Other children in the neighborhood couldn't go to school, so we all just sat around in the community and played around. The girls did house work, washed dishes, washed clothes and other domestic duties. We just sat around and talked and did whatever else our parents wanted us to do.

We had an aunt and uncle who lived across the bridge in Buckingham County; Aunt Ethel and Uncle Freddie Gordon, my mother's brother and his wife. After the first year of being out of school I said to my mother: "Why can't we go and stay with Uncle Freddie and Aunt Ethel in Buckingham County?"

Mother said: "I don't want anyone else taking care of my children and I don't want Ethel and Freddie to be burdened with my children."

I said: "Mama, I don't think they would see us as a burden." Uncle Freddie and Aunt Ethel had one son, named James, Jr. and he was grown.

So, at this point Mama was just silent. I thought she was just thinking 'maybe I can send them over there, I don't know.' After talking with Mama, I spoke personally with Aunt Ethel. We used to go and visit Aunt Ethel and Uncle Freddie about every other weekend.

She was cooking, and I said: "Aunt Ethel, I really want to go to school. Can I come over here and live with you and go to school?"

Aunt Ethel said: "Yes, child, you can come and live here during the week and your Mama can come and pick you up on Friday and bring you back on Sunday."

But then Mama heard someone else saying that some of the children that had gone to live with relatives in other counties their parents had to pay a fine for sending their children to surrounding counties because that particular county was not their parents' tax base. That changed my mother's mind completely about me and Bayo going to live with Uncle Freddie and Aunt Ethel.

I was trying to go to Aunt Ethel and Uncle Freddie and start school the second year of the closing. In the end Mama was against it. After Mama denied us the opportunity to go and live with Aunt Ethel and Uncle Freddie, we just stayed home for the whole four years. What a drag and setback for our minds, Bayo and I.

I always had the yearning to continue my education. It worried me. It concerned me that I was just sitting round not studying. I would hear the statement that 'the mind is a terrible thing to waste.' I was already behind and did not want to get further behind my age group.

In September 1960 me and Bayo started attending classes at Saint James African Methodist Episcopal Church, where my former teacher Mrs. Davenport was working.

There was a man named Mr. James Watkins that drove an older car, it was black, but I can't remember what model. He came around every morning and picked up all the children who were still out of school in the Peaks area and drove them out to Saint James Church. His wife Elizabeth Watkins taught with Mrs. Davenport. Mrs. Watkins was a school teacher also. I don't know where she taught.

When Bayo and I started at Saint James the second year the schools were closed, those who taught the older students were Mrs. Davenport and Mrs. Watkins. These were the only two I remember. School went from 9:00 a. m. until 1:00 p. m.

They taught the older students reading and subject verb agreement, English, and math. Of course, they didn't teach us anything like biology and such. I think they taught us hygiene. They kept us focused on the basics. Sometimes we had homework. They wanted us to continually keep what we had learned in our minds, that's why we had homework.

The goal of the teachers was to keep us from forgetting what we had already learned before the closing of the schools. When we returned home each day after class at Saint James, we tended to our chores and talked.

When I heard the schools were going to reopen, I was happy, very very happy. I said to myself: "Finally, we can go back to school!"

Our parents prepared us with new clothes and shoes to go back to school. I was just happy. I was happy on the day we saw the school buses rolling to pick us up and take us into Farmville, where all the schools were.

When I returned to school, everything was so new. In a way, things were chaotic because I had never gone to school in Farmville. When the schools were closed, I had been a student at a two room school in the Peaks area. Now I had to meet new classmates. The classmates I met I did not know. I met *all* new classmates because my classmates from Peaks School many of them didn't return when the Free School opened. After being out for four years, some had little jobs, some had become parents, and others just lost the desire to learn.

I had a problem with biology and algebra. To jump back into these courses after four years out of the classroom was a challenge.

Once we got into our respective classes, we started studying and went to our assigned classrooms and the educational knowledge started rolling again. I continued on until I graduated twelfth grade in 1968, four years later than I should have finished high school. I would have graduated in 1964 had there been no break.

Bayo stayed in school also. At one time he had almost decided that he wouldn't continue. He started in the Free School and was near quitting. There was a friend, in fact more than one friend, that talked to him. A man named Mr. Moore who was the shop teacher, and another man named Cameron Allen, he was the supervisor of the school buses and not a teacher, they talked with my brother and told him that it wasn't a good idea that he quit school, that he needed to continue to come to school and learn because in later years he was going to need that education. Bayo listened to them and decided that he was going to continue, and he graduated twelfth grade.

I was married in 1969 and moved to Philadelphia, Pennsylvania. I attended Philadelphia Community College which enhanced my education.

I am sharing my story on my birthday, October 28, 2011.

EDWARD 'PEANUT' PATTERSON

Leaving the home of Mrs, Annie Mae Beasley Washington, the Editor drove back in the direction of Prospect. The Editor passed a house on the narrow road and driving slow being cautious, saw a man standing beside the side of the house. The house was old, weather-beaten and had been without paint for many years. It was impossible to tell what color it was in earlier times. The Editor pulled over to the side of the rode, got out of the vehicle and started walking toward the man seen standing by the side of the house, trying to determine his age range while moving in his direction. The Editor surmised that he was at least in his fifties and here was another story from the era of the school closing. When close enough, the Editor reached out his hand and the two greeted each other. The former was more excited about our acquaintance than was the latter. The project of the collection of stories was explained. The man said to the Editor regarding the years the schools were closed: "It didn' both'a me, I was'n born yet." The Editor nearly collapsed and had to quickly recompose himself. The man looked like he was approaching sixty. "Go in the house, he prob'ly can tell you sup'um."

The Editor gathered that he was to talk with a man inside. The old weather beaten-house was hardly a foot off the round. Two thin wooden steps took a guest up to the front door. He knocked on the door and heard a voice say 'com' in'. The Editor opened the door and stepped into a nearly dark living room. It was early afternoon, warm and bright outside. The Editor closed the door and quickly assessing the premises while standing in place and remembering what was seen when driving up concluded he was in a three or four room house. No human being was seen but some sort of movement was heard, as a person turning over in a bed. A man was lying on a sofa next to a window. The sofa was to the left of where the Editor entered the house. The project was explained, and the man said, never rising up on the sofa: "I cain't tell'ya nut'in'. I was out'a school den." The television was on and tuned in to a popular afternoon soap-opera. The volume was very low, and we had no need to elevate our voices.

"Well, would you tell me how life was around here when you were in school as a boy, the years before the schools were closed? All information is important, and everybody has a story, everybody can share something. If not for yourself, tell your story for your mother and father's sake. Tell it for future generations."

When the Editor said, 'everybody has a story, and everybody can share something' and tell it for your parents' sake, for future generations, the human figure rose up on the sofa as though he had suddenly been called forth to some strange something that commanded his attention and support. He put both his hands over his sleepy and somewhat painful face and moved them about as though he held a warm wet invisible washcloth. He looked around, as if he expected to see someone or persons other than the Editor. He collected himself, sat up on the sofa and the Editor sat beside him, and he started talking. The room remained semi-dark, but his reflections brought a brightness to the room.

I was born October 16, 1936, in Prospect. I started school at Peaks School and my teacher was Mrs. Beatrice Davenport. I started school around 1942 or 1943. Peaks was a two room school. Mrs. Brown was the other teacher. Mrs. Davenport had the lower grades. I remember that because she was my first teacher. She had fifteen or twen'y childr'n in her class. There was fifteen or twen'y in the other classroom. There was a hand pump on the yard that we had to prime to git water. We only got water when we went out to recess. You could drink all the water you wanted to drink. The toilet was outside and there was one toilet for the boys and another for the girls.

When I started to school, I remember we took our lunch. My mama would fix a biscuit with a piece of meat between it. That was lunch and then I would drink water from the pump after eatin'. That was how most'a the childr'n did for lunch.

When I was in the third or fourth grade, I remember Mrs. Alma Sanders started cooking at the school. A kitchen was set up next to Mrs. Davenport's room. Each student had a desk. The girls would go to the kitchen and Mrs. Sanders would give them the bowls or plates wid' food. Then the girls came back to the classroom and put a bowl or plate on each desk. I don't remember whether we had to pay or not—been so long.

Peaks went to the fifth grade. After the fifth grade, students went to First Rock School. I went to First Rock in the sixth and seventh grade. I don't remember a kitchen at First Rock, but there was'a outdoor toilet. Mr. Joe Miller was the teacher. He was a short light skinned fellow. I never went to school in town. I stopped after First Rock and went to work.

———

*Some think his name might have been Ernest, but he called himself Edward. When the Editor returned to Prince Edward County several years after the interview and rode by the house, it was obvious that no one lived there. The Editor mentioned the name Edward Patterson when in Peaks on May 20, 2011, and the name was not recognized in the small hamlet. He was asked to describe the man. A description of the man was provided and the house he lived in that was very low to the ground on the main road. "You must be talking about Peanut. He died, but he used the name Edward. Just put 'Peanut' in his story and everybody around here will know who you are talking about."

———

DARLINGTON HEIGHTS

———

MILDRED WOMACK PATTERSON

The White people ran everything and made all of the decisions in those days. We heard that the schools were closed and thought they (the White people) would keep them closed for a short time and then reopen. We thought they were just trying to show us they were in control and after a little while would open up the schools.

My husband David and I had five children that were in school: Daisy, David, Jr., Kathryn, Carolyn and George. Our son, Lionel, wasn't old enough to go to school.

Daisy and George went right on to school.* When we realized the schools were not going to reopen right away, we sent Daisy and George away. We had to pick and choose which children we would send to where and to which relatives. We couldn't send them all to relatives, because our relatives had their own families they had to support. There were not many close relatives nearby. Job opportunities had taken most of my family away and my husband didn't have many relatives nearby. But we felt we had to send Daisy to school right away since she was in her senior year. I think Carolyn was in the fourth grade.

Being a senior, Daisy was really upset about the closing of the schools because she wanted to graduate from Moton. We made arrangements for Daisy to go and live with relatives in Appomattox. She stayed with my aunt, Mrs. Mozella Price. Daisy was about twenty-five miles away from us. She came home about every three months.

George went to live with my husband's sister. My sister-in-law and brother-in-law, Adie Patterson Spencer and Louis Spencer, lived in Charlotte Court House in Charlotte County. That is where George went to live and attend school. He was six years old at the time. George was about fifteen miles away from us and came home every weekend and we were always glad to see him. David, Sr. and I were farmers and sent food to Adie and Louis to help out with George. We gave a little money also. They never asked for money, but we wanted to give it.

David, Jr. and Kathyrn stayed at home during the 1959-1960 school year. Both were also very upset about the closing.

Arrangements were made for the boys and girls in the Darlington Heights area to attend classes. There was an old school, School No.14, in Darlington Heights. My husband went to School No. 14 when he was a boy. The building was now used for other events, but not for any educational purpose. It was old and dilapidated. We needed places to hold classes for our children and School No. 14 was converted into a school for children who lived in Darlington Heights and the Hampden district.

I was not a certified teacher, but I taught the children at School No. 14. I had a car load of students each day and picked up children as I went. There was a teaching schedule for the parents. Reverend L. F. Griffin helped us get organized in the Darlington Heights area. The lady who taught with me was Mrs. Dorothy Croner, who is deceased. We were the two primary teachers at School No. 14. Neither one of us was certified to teach, but our presence in the classroom kept the children out of mischief and assisted them in their learning and kept them focused.

Reverend Griffin assigned Dorothy and I to the positions. Reverend Griffin and I were classmates during our public school days at R. R. Moton. He must have remembered my student days and felt I could be of assistance to the students.

Daisy completed her senior year and her father and I attended her graduation in the spring of 1960.

We sent our daughter Carolyn to New York to live with my husband's sister Cornelia Patterson Perry. Carolyn came home at Christmas and during the summer.

Many children stayed in the county the first and second

years the schools were closed, but after Helen Baker and Jean Fairfax took an interest in affairs arrangements were made for a considerable number of the boys and girls to go away and continue their education.

Well, we realized that the White people weren't going to open the schools back up. Negro parents started making preparations to get their children in school elsewhere. We started having meetings in our homes to figure out what we were going to do.

The American Friends, I think was the name, came in. Jean Fairfax and Helen Baker who were connected with the Friends came to the county. We started having meetings in churches and then they, Jean and Helen, started visiting homes and talking with parents. The Friends, Jean and Helen, were of great support to us.

Helen, who was from Baltimore, and Jean began assisting in locating homes in different States where our children could go and live with host families and continue their education. Helen remained in Farmville to help see things through.

In August 1960, the beginning of the 1960-1961 school year, many of the children from Prince Edward County went to Ohio on a Greyhound bus to live with host families that had volunteered to take them in. When the bus left Farmville that evening, it was packed. There were close to fifty students on board. The Friends chartered special buses to carry children to different locations. The Friends took care of everything. They paid the bus fares and no rent was charged in the homes where the students lived during the school year. Students did house work in the homes where they resided in exchange for living there.

We started having meetings in the county about the re-opening of the schools. NAACP officials would be present, and they would take it to a higher level. Reverend Griffin was always present.

In the following year, 1961-1962 school year, there was no Greyhound bus transportation provided by the Friends. Students had to get back on their own to the families hosting them. The case with my family was a little different. Each year David and Kathryn received tickets to ride the Greyhound bus to Ohio. I do not remember who gave the tickets. My children were also given tickets to come home at Christmas and at the end of the school year.

David, Jr. and Kathryn came home at Christmas and the end of the school year. I got a letter from them about every two weeks. I called them often. I went to Ohio about twice a year to visit my children. I went in the fall after they were settled and again in the spring after they returned following Christmas break. I usually went around March.

Many people from all around the country and the state of Virginia helped families in Prince Edward County. Many who helped I have never met and do not know but appreciate their support to this day.

Quite a few children didn't get to go away. President Kennedy's administration reopened the schools in Prince Edward County and the children, many of them, came back home.

The period when the schools were closed was a very difficult time, but God kept us; as God will always keep and protect those who put their trust in Him.

———

*The Editor got the impression on September 7, 2011, while talking with George after the funeral of his mother that he went to relatives in the fall of 1960.

TRACY SPENCER

I was born July 8, 1919, to Mary Carrington Spencer and Charlie Spencer. My father was at first a sharecropper and later bought his own place. I started school at No. 14. It was a little building that had one big room. There was no electricity. It had window panes and that was how the light we had came in. The only teacher I remember was Mrs. Oliver and then another teacher came, I can't remember her name. I remember Mrs. Oliver because she gave me a good beatin' once. Mrs. Mary Wicks was a third teacher and Mrs. Flossie Womack also taught there. All of these taught me at one time or another. The school went to the seventh grade. There was a pump on the yard for water. I lived a short distance from school and I went home for lunch. Back then everywhere a child went we ran. We ran home for lunch and would be back in no time. Those who brought lunch brought a biscuit or piece of meat. If you got a wiener that your parents brought back from town that was a luxury. (Mr. Spencer started laughing.) We played baseball a lot and pitched horse shoes at school. The boy who could make the most ringers was the main kid at school. The girls played baseball with us but played other games. David Patterson's sister Cornelius was a left-handed pitcher I believe, and she was very good. She could pitch!

A man name Mr. Willie Walker furnished a bus for Darlington Heights and it cost us ten cents a day. You went on to school (meaning high school) and rode the bus if your parents could afford it. There were six of us in my family going to school at one time: Jewel, me, Matliene, Henry, Earl, and Armentha. There was Edna Croner my half-sister. Daddy had to pay for seven children each day to ride the bus.

We lost a lot of school days. We would go a day and stay home a day and work the field, so our parents didn't lose all the crops. I think I was fourteen when I reached the seventh grade. My older brothers went to D. C. and I begged my mother to let me go so I could work. I told her I would come back home and finish school. I stayed two or three years and she came and got me and made me come back home. I returned home and completed the ninth grade.

Most of the students from Green Bay who came to high school, I remember they drove their family cars. The children from Green Bay wore a little better clothes and there were other signs of being a little different.

I returned to D. C. and started working at the candy factory where I was working before.

I worked nine years and was drafted for the war in 1942. I went to China, India, and Burma when I was in the Army. I was stationed at MacDill Field in Tampa, Florida. When we went downtown, we rode the bus. When the bus got downtown, there was a rope that divided the street. The Colored soldiers had to go on one side of the street and the White soldiers were on the other side. If a Colored soldier went on the other side of the street, the Tampa Police and the Military Police would come and arrest you.

I stayed in the Army until 1946. I got out and then reenlisted and got married. I would have gone to Korea. The rule was if you was married you could take your wife. I was a staff sergeant and was told there was no space, but I could go alone as a technical sergeant. My family talked me out of it and that was the end of my Army career.

I returned to Prince Edward County and could find no work. Sharecropping or cutting pulpwood were the two options. I started cutting pulpwood when I first returned in 1946 or so to 1960.

I was living in Prince Edward County when the walk out took place, and my niece, Barbara Johns, was the student that led the student strike. Barbara was the daughter of my sister, Viola. Viola wasn't mentioned earlier in my story because she was a little girl when I was in school. Barbara had some of Vernon Johns in her. She would not take no for an answer.

I ran a store until the early 1960s or the year they started the sales tax. You'll have to check and see what year the sales tax started and that will be the year I stopped with the store.

I don't remember how it came about, but during the school closing they had a White fellow that seemed to take a real interest in the welfare of the Black children. Dr. Gordon Moss asked for permission to use the back room of my store to update the Black parents on the school situation. I don't recall how often he gave updates, but the back room of the store was where the people gathered.

I don't remember who asked about using the backroom of the store to teach the children, but I allowed them to use it and the children would gather for class. The room couldn't hold more than thirty children. I think it was mainly during the summer. There was no fee or anything, I let them have it out of the goodness of my heart. My son was not impacted by the school closing.

As a boy, a number of things I couldn't understand. All we saw in our area was broom straw and further up in Darlington Heights, where the White people lived, there was four leaf clover.

There was a White man who had fifty acres and a Black

man who had five hundred acres. The Agriculture Department was furnishing fertilizer. The local White people were taking the shipments and telling Black farmers there wasn't no fertilizer for them.

The local White merchant would sell fertilizer to the White men, but when Dr. Johns went to buy some the man said:

"I don't have any fertilizer for you."

Vernon Johns took up the matter for the Black farmers in the county. They tell me when he went to D. C. to the Agriculture Department he went in overalls, one strap fastened and the other hangin' down.

Johns went to Richmond first and got no results. Then he went to Washington, D. C. and asked to speak to the head. My brother drove Reverend Johns to Washington. They said he could not see the head. Johns maneuvered around them as he was good at doing. He finally saw the head person and the fertilizer started coming in and Black farmers could buy as much as they wanted.

I heard him (Johns) quote from books and he could cite from anything. If he went to preach and had not fed his hogs, it was nothing for Reverend Johns to go and feed his hogs in a suit and then go on to the church and preach.

Edward Lewis, Jr., my nephew, is the founder of Essence Magazine. Edward is my sister Jewel's son.

Hart, Marks, and Shaffer's were the best men's clothes. When the White people wore a suit a long time, they would sell it to my brother. I always said — 'When I grow up, I'm going to wear Hart, Marks and Shaffer's.'

———

MARTHA CARRINGTON MORTON

When the Prince Edward County schools were closed, I had one child that was school age and her name was Belinda. Today she is Belinda Morton Gee.

Belinda was in elementary school. I lived in Darlington Heights, but I was a teacher at James Murray Jeffress Elementary School in Charlotte County. I took Belinda to school with me and enrolled her. Annie B. Moseley was the principal.

I took at least four or five other children from Darlington Heights to school with us. I had a car load every day. I had a 1956 Ford. It was two tone.

When the Free School opened in Prince Edward County in September 1963, Belinda was enrolled.

I was hired as a teacher in the Free School and resigned my position at James Murray Jeffress Elementary School. I stayed in the Prince Edward County school system until I retired in 1989.

I did my college work at Virginia State College and Virginia Union University.

I don't usually talk much about the era of the school closure, but shared this information on Thursday, March 29, 2012.

———

DAISY PATTERSON EDWARDS

I was devastated when the Prince Edward County public schools were closed. I was a rising senior and was looking forward to my last year of school with all my friends. My mother arranged for me to go to Appomattox County and live with her aunt, my great grand aunt, Mozella Price.

The beginning of the school year at Carver–Price High School was difficult. I didn't know anyone. I began to make friends.

I came home to Darlington Heights every holiday and about one weekend a month. I had an aunt, Elizabeth Womack Wade my mama's baby sister, who worked at a factory in Appomattox. She drove to Appomattox each day. On the weekend that I was to come home she would stop by Aunt Mozel, pick me up, and take me home. Aunt Elizabeth lived about seven or eight miles from my parents.

Some of the girls in twelfth grade at Carver–Price High School that befriended me and became my mentors were Diane Tibbs, Valetta McCoy, Rosetta Lipford, Ora Scruggs, and Frances Pennix. These five students, and really all of the seniors at the school, made sure I had a great year.

Even though I was away from home, it was a good school year. I wrote the Class song. I was the author. I may have had a few other girls to help, but I was the primary writer.

I was crowned the May Queen. I don't remember how I won, whether it was through voting or whether we had to write an essay; neither do I remember whether the queen had to be a senior girl. All I remember is that I was crowned.

My goal that year was to finish high school and I did. My parents came to graduation. The ceremony was held in the evening, not at night, in the school auditorium. There were thirty-three seniors, if my memory serves me correct. I was number six in the Class of 1960. I was awarded a $1,500.00 scholarship to Hampton Institute. I didn't pursue it because my parents would have had to pay some money and at the time my father was not employed. He had been a bus driver for the Prince Edward County public school system. But now that the schools were closed, Daddy didn't have an income.

———

GWENDOLYN WESLEY CRAWLEY

I was born and reared in Farmville. Mr. and Mrs. David Patterson, Sr. were my grandparents. They brought me up.

During the 1958-1959 school year, I was in the seventh grade. That was a happy time because I was going to high school the next year. Moton High School had eighth to twelfth grades. My excitement was increased when my seventh grade teacher took us on a field trip one day to see the high school we would be attending the following year.

The academic year ended, and school closed in late May or early June, as normal. During the summer, there was some activity in the community, but I didn't fully understand events. Adults didn't talk around children in those days. It was in late June or sometime in July that I found out I would not be attending R. R. Moton High School. All of the schools in Prince Edward County were closed. I learned that my family was moving to New York. Mother had to uproot us.

The day we left Farmville I cried from the moment we departed until we got to Brooklyn, New York. We arrived in Brooklyn at night. I did not see any of our new surroundings. The next morning, I was introduced to city life.

Relocating to New York was a shock. As a country girl, I was thrown into the heart of the city. I was unprepared. I had lived a sheltered life in Prince Edward County.

We lived in a fourth-floor walk-up. Eight other families were in the building. In Prince Edward County, my cousins were my playmates. Things were different now.

In New York, I attended an integrated school. There were Puerto Rican students and other nationalities. I had never been close enough to a White child to touch one. Brooklyn, New York, was altogether frightening. It was a whole new world. There were boy gangs and girl gangs. My brother and I didn't know where one gang's turf ended, and another started.

After we had been in Brooklyn for a good period of time, my mother and stepfather purchased a house in New York. They would not allow the children to be separated. I never returned to Prince Edward County to live, though I asked Mother to let me go and stay with Grandma and Grandpa.

In New York, I went through a serious grieving process. I lost contact with my closest friends. Lucille Baker was my buddy-buddy. We never saw each other again. Jean Wesley and I were very close. I lost contact with her also.

After all these years, I have not lost contact with my roots. I still remember with fondness my girlhood days in Prince Edward County, Virginia.

———

HOWARD WESLEY

I was a student at Branch No. 2. Branch No. 2 had sixth and seventh grades. Moton had eighth to twelfth grades. I heard that school was going to close the end of May. Rumors had been circulating for several months, but I paid them no attention. In my mind, based on past experience, school always closed around the end of May. I thought—'Okay and it will open in September.' I was going to the seventh grade.

During the summer, Mother told us that we were going to New York. I had three sisters: Gwen, Ardenia and Charla. I remember the day we left Prince Edward County. I recall stopping in Philadelphia to eat. Arrangements were made for a family member to drive us on to New York.

Prince Edward County was home and leaving was a hard blow. I cried all the way to New York. It was night when we arrived in the big city. When I woke up the following morning, I heard a lot of noise. I got up and looked out the window and saw more people in one block than I had seen in all my life.

I got dressed and went outside. I had a southern accent and was new. Three fellows beat me up. Brooklyn was not an easy place to live. I figured out early that many of the people were not intelligent and if you could think beyond them things would be okay. I played basketball. I went from park to park and many people came to know me. They knew I was not part of a gang.

I think all of us, my sisters and I, returned to Prince Edward County each summer. School ended on a Friday and we were on a bus to the Farmville bus station on Saturday.

My family spent three years in Brooklyn, perhaps the three worst years of my life. My mother and step-father purchased a home in Bronx. Moving from Brooklyn to Bronx was like getting out of prison. People in Brooklyn fought for no reason and I could not understand that.

———

SUSIE MANNS REID

I was born September 12, 1949. A mid-wife named Mrs. Mandy Carter delivered me. My great grandmother Carrie Evans and great grandfather Henry Evans raised me and my brothers and sisters, as well as raised some of my cousins, uncles and aunts. We all grew up in the same house. There was a total of fifteen children Great-grandma took care of.

Of the fifteen children in the house: Richard Evans, we called Butch, Nancy Spencer, Larry Hamilton, John Manns, my brother we called Johnny, and I were in school at the time of the closing. All the others in the house had already graduated from R. R. Moton or had quit school.

Mrs. Victoria Brown was my favorite teacher and she used to correct us when needed. When the schools closed, I was ten years old and going to the fifth grade.

We had a routine at home. We had designated times for work and study. We got up early in the morning and went to the fields. We never had to buy anything from the store except cheese and a few other items. We had our own buggy and wagon, horses, and cows.

After all the work was done, we ate dinner and then we had school. School was from maybe 5:00 p. m. to 7:00 p. m. or whenever you finished. If you played around, Great-grandma would take charge and make you get your work.

You had to be in by dark because of the KKK. Negro girls especially had to be inside by dark. White men would take advantage of them when they could, and nothing would be said or done about it. They used to throw rocks at us and spit at us. It was very dangerous.

There was a Sunday School building in Darlington Heights. When church didn't meet, everyone still went to Sunday

School at that building. During the week on certain days, that building was used for a classroom. This was one of the centers that students could go to. We didn't go every day. There were scheduled days to go to the center. I don't remember the days.

When we weren't in school, we were in the fields. We would see the White children ridding the school buses to school, while we worked for their families.

Ma, as we called Great-grandma, had all kinds of books for us. My great uncle worked for the YMCA in Medford, New Jersey. His name was James Henry Evans. This was my mother's uncle. After the YMCA Summer Camp ended, Uncle James packed up the papers, books, pencils, clothes, and shoes the children left at camp and sent it all to us.

There were also people in Farmville who used to bring us books.

After being out of school for two years, arrangements were made for several of us in the house to go away and live with relatives, so we could continue our education. I was sent to Aunt Sadie Hamilton Monroe in Atlantic City, New Jersey.

The others in the house were split up like this: Larry went to Stanford, Connecticut, to live with Uncle Jim. Uncle Jim was my great grandmother's son. Richard lived with Uncle Hamp (Allen Hamilton) or Uncle Jim, one or the other. I don't remember where John went to live and go to school. Nancy remained in Farmville. She was older than me.

My great grandmother used put a tag on my wrist with my destination written on the tag, which was Atlantic City. Then she would take me to the Greyhound bus station in Farmville and send me off. I went to school each year in Atlantic City for two or three years, I'm unsure about which number.*

When the Free School opened, I returned home. I was the only one who returned when the Free School opened.

- 379 -

Mrs. Carter delivered me in 1949 and delivered my daughter in 1969. I'm going and visit Mrs. Carter after this interview. She's ninety-five years old.

———

*Mrs. Reid went to school in Atlantic City, New Jersey, for two years. She remembered being out of school for two years before being sent away to relatives. She returned to Prince Edward County, Virginia, when the Free School Association opened in September 1963.

———

STANLEY LORENSO WESLEY

The first school experience I had was very pleasant. The first time I went to school or was inside a school building was in late May or early June 1959. My sister, Thelma, who was older than I, took me to school with her at Branch No. 2. Branch No. 2 had sixth and seventh grades, so Thelma was in one grade or the other at the time. Students were allowed to bring anyone they wish on the last day of school. Thelma took me. I was to start first grade a few months later, so going that day was a real joy for me. I remember the excitement around the school and how lively the students were.

My excitement about school grew after going that day with Thelma. This was a time when like any other child I was looking forward to going to school. My sisters and brothers were in school and they would talk about school all the time. At home they were always talking about their friends from school, what they did at recess, and their teachers, and these things excited me.

We started hearing about school not opening and it didn't really dawn on me what was really taking place. When it was my time to go to school as a first grader, things changed. The Prince Edward County schools were closed.

I had five brothers and four sisters. They were: Edward, Bernard, Thelma, Jean, George, Lloyd, Zelda, Aliceteen and Leon. When the schools were closed, I remember Jean was along junior high age and Edward, Bernard and Thelma were older than her. Zelda is one year older than I and had gone to school one year. Zelda completed first grade.

I was around six when the schools closed, but as I recall my sisters and brothers were impacted in the following manner. My sister, Jean, went to stay with Deacon Woodrow Wilson and Mrs. Wilson in an area called Cullen in Charlotte County. Deacon and Mrs. Wilson were no kin to us but had an interest in supporting Jean. There were many Negro families, as they were called then, in surrounding counties that took in children from Prince Edward County, so they could go to school. To my understanding Jean was the only one in our family that had the privilege to go away and attend school.

Eddie (Edward) got married and left home. Thelma and Bernard moved to D. C. I don't recall the order they left home. Jean was next in line age wise. Mrs. Wilson took a liking to Jean and allowed her to come and live with them.

George, Lloyd, Zelda, Aliceteen, Leon and I were still at home. We spent our days playing and doing chores.

I knew I had cousins that attended school in Prince Edward County, but who had left the area and State to go to school. I had no one that I could go stay with and start school. I also had friends who went to live with relatives in Charlotte Court House.

It was hard for me when we were seven and eight years old. Our little cousins would come from other counties to visit. When they played games that involved numbers and counting, I was lost because I had never been to school. I would make an excuse about not wanting to play.

Around 1963 people from up North came to teach during the summer. There was an old church building that belonged to Triumph Baptist Church. The congregation had built a new edifice, but the old one they moved out of was still standing. Classes were held in the sanctuary at the old church during the summer. Each class sat on a pew, and four or five pews back another set of students and so on.

While classes were held at the old Triumph Baptist Church, White students also taught classes at Dick Tracy's place. We used to call it Dick Tracy's place, after the cartoon character. The owner was a Black man named Mr. Tracy Spencer. He owned a store that he stopped operating around 1960 or 1961. I remember going there to buy candy as a youngster before he closed it. There was a back part attached to the vacant store area. Mr. Spencer allowed the community to use that vacant section as a classroom. The school was just referred to a Tracy's. At Tracy's some students were in the store part and some were in the back part. Mr. Spencer also had another building a short distance away on his property that he allowed to be used as a classroom. There were at least three White teachers when school was held at Mr. Spencer's during the summer.

When those students came to teach us during the summer, that was our education for the year.

When I first stepped into a real school setting, I was

nine years old and in the first grade. I entered first grade at Worsham when the Free School Association began operating in September 1963. Some of the teachers at Worsham that year were Mrs. Herndon, Mrs. Martha Morton, and Mrs. McClain. I can't remember their first names.

First grade was different. I was nine, and the majority of the children in first grade were above six years old. While six years old is normal for first grade and being older is abnormal, the reverse was the case in Prince Edward County in September 1963. Any student in my first grade class who was six years old was the odd one.

School was enjoyable. I reached junior high school and during the summer there was summer school. I went on my own.

There was another walk-out around 1969 or 1970. There was a White teacher Mr. Robinson who was fired. The school board was all White and something happened. I don't remember all of the particulars. Mr. Robinson was a fine teacher and gentleman. He moved to Richmond.

I think when my high school class graduated in 1973 it was about this time that the Prince Edward County school system began to get back on track. My class was the last class that had graduates over twenty years old.

I graduated the first of June 1973 and got married June 30, 1973. Having been born in 1953, I was twenty years old when I graduated. I worked for several years and answered the call to preach in 1984. About six months after answering the call to preached, I was called to serve as pastor at Bethel Grove Baptist in Rice, Virginia. This congregation met on the first and third Sundays of each month. I also served as pastor of Old Green Creek Baptist in Cumberland County. This congregation met on the second and fourth Sundays. When Bethel Grove was able to meet each Sunday, I resigned from Old Green Creek Baptist. I served at Bethel Grove for seventeen years. Then I resigned and started an outreach ministry in Farmville.

I attended Virginia Seminary in Lynchburg and did correspondence through Liberty College. My daughter, Lakesha, is a store manager. My son, Lorenso Antwon, graduated from ITT in Norfolk and works with computers. My baby, Teresa, is a rising senior at Old Dominion University.

I shared and continue to share with my children the importance of an education. There are so many today who have the opportunity to get an education and refuse to do it. I always say to children — 'Get an education'.

My wife, Gertrude (Walker Wesley) has been a main stay to and for me.

———

LEANA BEATRICE EVANS WORMACK

I was born October 1, 1945, in Prince Edward County to Reginald and Elizabeth Evans. The first school I attended was Mercy Seat School. I started there around 1951. My teacher was Mrs. Victoria Brown. Mercy Seat went to the sixth grade, after which students went to Mary E. Branch No. 2 in Farmville.

When I was old enough to think about what I wanted to do in life, my goal was to become a nurse. I liked helping people and wanted to devote my life to doing that. I was looking forward to developing and going off to college.

But first I was looking forward to going to high school. But in September 1959 the schools didn't open.

The schools were closed and all of us in the community who couldn't go away missed the first full year of the 1959-1960 school year. They started having classes in Darling Heights the second year the schools were closed.

Mount Carmel Sunday School Building was a place where Sunday School for children in the area was held. Any of the children who wanted to go to Sunday School went to this building. All of the children went to Sunday School because parents didn't allow you to stay home on Sunday morning back in those days.

After the schools were closed, the Mount Carmel Sunday School Building was used for a classroom for school. The Sunday School building had electricity, but no indoor plumbing. There was a wood heater, a potbelly stove that was used when it was cold. Mrs. Spencer made the fire. There were usually about twenty-five of us in the building for class. The Sunday School teacher, Mrs. Agnes Spencer, who attended Triumph Baptist Church worked with us. She was a house wife. One or two other ladies assisted her, but I don't remember their names. We went to class each day. It was at least a five mile walk one way. School started around 9:00 a. m. and was out around 2:00 p. m. School started at 9:00 a. m. in order to give Mrs. Spencer and the other workers time to do what they needed to get done at home.

Someone from Farmville contacted my mother about me and my sister, Queen Elizabeth, going away to school. I have never known all of the particulars. But one day Mom started talking to me about leaving home and going away to school. She explained to me that I would be going away to live with another family. She told me that I was going to Inkster, Michigan. I was happy about going back to school, but was not happy about leaving home. Living with strangers didn't appeal to me.

We left Farmville on a Greyhound bus one night in August 1961 and we had a very long ride. I remember we rode all night. The students on the bus that night who I remember leaving the county to go away to live with families were: my sister, Queen Elizabeth Evans (Brown), my cousin, Alma Watkins (Walker) and Howard Smith, his sister, Alfreda Smith (Hicks), Pop Ross, and Eddie Wiley went on the bus to Inkster.

In Inkster I lived with Mr. and Mrs. Payton. The lady's first name was Clementine. This was a Black family. I attended Inkster High School. I was placed in the eighth grade. School was enjoyable. Queen Elizabeth and I came home at Christmas and at the end of the school year. I don't know which group made the arrangements for us to go away,* but Mom and Daddy did have to provide some financial support.

Queen Elizabeth and I returned home after one school year in Inkster. It was hard on Mom and Daddy. They had to send money to support us and our family was very poor.

When we returned home that summer, Queen Elizabeth went to Charlotte County and lived with our cousin, Myrtle Wilson and her husband, Monroe. She finished high school there.

When the Free School opened, I was placed in the ninth grade.

I feel like I have been cheated. No one impacted by the closing of the schools ever was able to reach their full potential in life. The people who closed the schools and hurt us, there is nothing they can do to make it up.

---

*Participants in the American Friends Service Committee

Emergency Placement Program went to Inkster, Michigan, for the 1961-1962 school year.

———

CLARA PATTERSON CLARK TAYLOR

I started elementary school at Triumph Elementary School, it was near Triumph Baptist Church. I think it was a public school at this time. Triumph was a two room school. We had an outdoor toilet. The boys would go and get the wood in the winter for the stove to heat the room. We took our lunch from home.

I don't remember my first grade teacher, I think it was Miss. Stokes. She was not married, she was Miss. I remember Aunt Addie (Addie Patterson Spencer) was my second grade teacher. I was with her only for a little while. The same teacher taught first and second grades and another teacher taught third, fourth, and fifth grades. I remember going to another room when they moved me to the third grade. They felt my skills were strong enough to skip second grade and I was moved to the third grade. My teacher was Mrs. Fields. I can't remember much about fourth grade. I think Triumph went to fifth grade because I remember in the sixth grade we went to Mercy Seat School in Hampden Sydney. My father drove the bus. All the years I went to school my father drove the bus. Miss Young taught me at Mercy Seat. In seventh grade I had Mr. Johnson, we were still at Mercy Seat. I was the Valedictorian of the seventh grade class. Hazel Suckins (now deceased) was the Salutatorian. The both of us were from Triumph School.

Then we went to Moton (today the Museum) for I believe one year. I think we were there for one year. I remember having Social Studies in a tar shack. Mrs. Connie Rawlins was the teacher.

The next year all high schoolers were at the new school. Mr. Woods was my favorite teacher. He would always call me Clara Bell. I believe he was the English teacher. One of the highlights of high school was being a marshal at graduation for the seniors.

I graduated from R. R. Moton in June 1957 and went to Virginia Union University. The high school principal, Mr. Samuel Griffin, assisted me in getting a scholarship. My friend Doris Scott and I went to Union together. We were best friends.

When the schools were closed, my brother David and my sister Kathryn went to Yellow Springs, Ohio. My little brother George went to live with Aunt Addie, my Daddy's sister, so he could attend elementary school. Lionel had not started school. Carolyn was in elementary school and was sent to New York to live with my father's sister, Cornelia Patterson Perry.

It was a sad time in our family. We had a large family and to be split up like that was very sad.

After graduating high school in Ohio, Kathryn went to Chaney State in Pennsylvania.

After graduating from Virginia Union University, I taught in Orange, Virginia, for about five years at Prospect Heights Elementary School.

When I came home on the weekends from Orange County, I just found it so hard to believe that no agency at the State or Federal Government levels intervened. How people allowed this to be was incomprehensible. Families were separated, and many children were not able to continue their education at all.

Several summers I spent in New York working, but my mom told me about the summer program when the schools were closed.

In the summer of 1964 I taught at Worsham Elementary School. The program in the summer of 1964 was part of the Free School Association. I worked with the elementary school children. It was challenging and rewarding. The children were eager to learn. It was obvious they were delayed in their school performance but were eager to learn.

There was also a summer school program at Mary E. Branch No. 1 in town during the summer of 1964. The reason I taught at Worsham was because I got a ride with my mom, who volunteered to help with the summer program.

I came home in the summer of 1965 and worked with the school children.

My mother told me about Helen Baker. She had cancer and my mother said Mrs. Baker washed all of her dirty clothes each night. Mrs. Baker felt that if she expired during the night she would leave her house in order.

WILLIAM JUNIOUS MISER

I was born in Darlington Heights, January 15, 1929, to Rufus and Alma Scott Miser. When I was a boy, I attended Mercy Seat School. Mrs. Addie Marshall and Mr. Charles Johnson were the teachers. The school had two rooms when I started. We carried our lunch which was not much, but we carried what we had back in those days. We had fried egg between a biscuit. This was a sort of ritzy lunch. Some may have had a piece of fatback between a biscuit which was a standard lunch. We drank water from the pump on the church yard.

I rode the bus to school. Mr. Ben Marshall drove an old yellow bus, I mean a very old bus. I don't remember my parents paying for me to ride. Mr. Marshall always did things out of the kindness of his heart.

We used to walk to Vernon Johns store. Reverend Johns lived in the store sometimes. I recall in the early 1950s I use to go to a place and cut cresses (water cress as some people call it or greens). Reverend Johns asked me one day did I know anyone who could do electrical work. I told him yes, I had a friend, last name Wormack, in Hampden Sydney. I took the man to the store and Reverend Johns had a heater in the store. This was a small tin heater that burned wood that he had heating the store. He had a bucket nearby and took the top off and laid it (the top off the bucket) on the heater. Reverend Johns took an egg and cracked it, and let it drop in the top that he took off the bucket and put on the heater. There was no grease in the top and he added no salt or pepper. He took a screw driver out of his back pocket and stirred the egg, using the top as a cooking pan. When the egg was done enough for him, Reverend Johns took a pair of pliers, picked up the top, which was too hot for him to hold with his hand, and put the egg on a piece of bread and ate it.

Johns sold a little of everything. He sold Watkins products. They produced rubbing ointments, cooking flavors such as lemon extract and so forth.

Johns would come to your house with a red sock and white sock on. He didn't care. He would come out of the field and go straight to the bus terminal, get on the bus and go to Petersburg.

Sometimes the store would be opened or unlocked, and he would be Petersburg.

Mercy Seat School went to the eighth grade and there was no Kindergarten, but I left and went to Washington, D. C.

Mr. Marshall was a plumber by trade and many young men worked with him when they returned home from the service.

———

JOY CABARRUS SPEAKES

Where I am sharing my account, this is the house my grandfather built. His name was George Pierce Morton. There is an interview with Granddaddy in the book *They Closed Our Schools*, by Bob Smith, on page 47. Granddaddy was instrumental in the decision to get a better school for us in Prince Edward County. He was active in the NAACP and the local PTA.

I was born in this house that Granddaddy built. I started elementary school at Triumph School. There was a school next to the church, Triumph Baptist Church, and my grandmother, Emma Evans Morton, was my first teacher. I went to school there for a while and then went to New York to live with my mother and father and I went to school in the Bronx. My mother used to send us down in the summer to be with our grandparents. But later she sent us back to live with our grandmother. It was my sister Cornelia and my brother Henry that Mama and Daddy sent back to Grandma.

After we came back to Darlington Heights, I attended Mercy Seat School. I don't remember any of the teachers. From Mercy Seat School I went to R. R. Moton. By going to school in New York, when I started at Mercy Seat I didn't understand why I had to ride so far to school.

I was in the eighth grade the year of The Strike. One of the things I think pushed her (Barbara Johns) to it, there was a bus accident in Prospect that killed five children on the railroad tracks. One of the children that got killed was a good friend of hers.

One day Barbara left her lunch or something home and went back to get it. While she was back at the house, the bus came. When she got back to the bus stop the bus was gone. The bus with the White children passed her. The bus driver couldn't stop and pick her up because they couldn't pick up Black children.

The morning of The Strike we gathered in the auditorium. When the curtains were drawn back we expected to see Mr. Jones the principal, but instead Barbara stepped forward and addressed us.

When we got home that afternoon, my Grandmother was a little upset. She had been a school teacher. Granddaddy felt good about the walk out and felt something good would come out of it.

I remember sitting at the dining room table and Father, I started calling granddaddy Father, talking about with the plaintiff petition you had to have so much land. Many people were afraid because they were sharecroppers. Father said for anyone who wanted to sign the petition and was afraid he would pledge some of his land for them.

When the lawyers came to Farmville, they told us they were taking no more cases for separate but equal schools but was now pursuing integration. The case went to court in Richmond.

After two weeks we went back to school.

The next school year Barbara was sent to Montgomery, Alabama, to her Uncle Vernon. Her parents feared for her life.

The case went to the Supreme Court. One of the justices died and Warren took his place.

Once the decision was handed down by the court we thought everything would be fine. The new R. R. Moton High School was opened to appease us. I remember a cross was burned on the old school ground.

The house of Barbara Johns' parents was burned down one weekend when the family was away. They never found out what really happened. This was before the Brown *vs* Board was handed down.

I graduated in 1955 from the new R. R. Moton High School. I did not experience what my cousins and brother Henry experienced in 1959.

I had, and I am approximating, forty cousins impacted by the closure of the schools. This would be children in the Wesley, Holcomb, Wormack, Patterson, Morton and Reed families.

My Aunt Martha (Martha Carrington Morton) loaded up her car with children and took them to Charlotte County for four years so they could continue their education. Aunt Martha taught at a school in Charlotte County. My brother Henry Cabarrus went to school in Yellow Springs, Ohio, during the years the schools were closed in Prince Edward County.

HAMPDEN SYDNEY

———

FRANCES GOLDMAN SCOTT

I was born August 7, 1932, to Edmonia Goldman. I started school at Mercy Seat Elementary School. My first teacher was Mrs. Addie Marshall. Mercy Seat School went to the seventh grade. The school had four rooms. One of the rooms was used more or less as a kitchen. One of the ladies from the community, my aunt, Mrs. Bertha Goldman Jenkins, was the cook. We would be served lunch and take our food back to the class room. The plates were provided, but students had to bring their own cup to school for drinking. When it was time to wash your hands, you went outside. One student poured water over your hands and you washed. That student poured the water for everyone. It was a privilege to pour the water. The teacher made that job seem very special. After the seventh grade, we went to the town of Farmville to attend R. R. Moton High School. When I entered eighth grade, around 1944 or 1945, Moton had eighth to eleventh grades. Twelfth grade was added later.

I got married in 1950 to Willie LeGrant Scott. He grew up in the Kingsville area, about a mile and a half from Mercy Seat Church. My oldest son, Willie, Jr., was born in October 1950. My oldest daughter, Valarie, was born in January 1953.

I believe Willie, Jr. had completed first, second and third grade at Mercy Seat School. Mercy Seat School in the late 1950s still had an outdoor toilet, there was a pump on the school grounds and they were still making a fire in each classroom.

Each classroom still had a wood stove for heating in the winter. He took his lunch each day. There was still no cafeteria. He had been promoted to the fourth grade when the schools were closed. When the schools were closed in September 1959, Willie, Jr. was one month short of being nine years old.

I worked with Willie at home the first year the schools were closed, as well as during the second year. When Valerie reached school age, I started working with her at home.

There was a building in the community that belonged to the Beneficial Benevolent Society and Loving Sisters of Worship. The Benevolent Society was connected with Mercy Seat Baptist Church. The building was straight across the road from the church. The society gave permission for the building to be used for instructions for the students. Some of the ladies in the society were: Mrs. Sarah Marshall, Mrs. Mammie Brown, Mrs. Emma Crawley, Mrs. Harrietta Brown, Mrs. Emma Harris, and Elsie Mae Harris.

The society's building began to be used around September 1961 for class.* The children in this area had been out of school since September 1959. The primary teacher at the Benevolent Society building was Mrs. Margaret Fowlks Allen. I believe the children went five days a week. They went from 8:00 a. m. to noon or 1:00 p. m. They didn't go a full day. Mrs. Allen taught basic reading and math. It was enough to keep their minds attuned to elementary school material. Willie, Jr. attended the classes taught by Mrs. Allen.

In August 1962, Willie, Jr. went away to live with a family to continue his education. He was selected to participate in one of the programs that arranged for children to go away and continue their education. I don't remember all the particulars or the organization in charge of the program. He was selected to go and live with a family in Ashland, Virginia, located outside of Richmond.

His father and I drove him up to Ashland to start school. When we drove up and the family opened the door, I knew my son was safe. Yes, I was just meeting the family, but spirit always agrees with spirit. The Jacksons' were beautiful people. Reverend Andrew Jackson, I believe was his name, was a Baptist minister. They were a Black couple. Reverend and Mrs. Jackson assured me that Willie would be all right. They gave us a tour of the house and showed us Willie Jr.'s bedroom. I was sad when it was time to leave. I cried a little.

We returned to Prince Edward County. I had to be strong for Willie, Sr. My husband cried for several weeks. It seemed like it just got to Willie, Sr. when he would come home in the afternoons from the gas station where he worked and Willie, Jr. was not here to greet him. When Willie would come home from work and the children heard the car door slam, they would always run outside and meet their father. Now, Willie Jr. wasn't running out of the house to meet his father. Being separated from his son really bothered my husband. He would cry periodically.

I drove to Ashland and picked up Willie, Jr., every other weekend. I got to Ashland around 3:30 p. m. on Friday and was there to pick him up as soon as the school day ended. We would head back to Prince Edward County immediately after school closed. I always wanted to be back home by early evening. My husband was working and couldn't take off easily. It was a good two and a half-hour drive to Ashland. It is about 90 minutes from Farmville to Richmond and another thirty minutes to Ashland.

Willie stayed with Reverend and Mrs. Jackson for one year. In September 1963, the Free School opened in Prince Edward County.

My daughter, Delores, was born in 1955. My son, Gregory, was born in 1956, and Louis was born in 1959. Valarie, Delores and Gregory went to the Free School when it opened. I remember the children were tested to see where they should be placed.

The Free School opened and Willie, Jr. was able to remain at home. I am thankful for the Jackson family and thankful that Willie was so close to us. Many children who went away to continue their education had to go to states far away such as Michigan and Pennsylvania.

It was a trying time, but we made it through with the help of the good Lord. God promised that He would never leave you nor forsake you. My family was not forsaken. Thanks be to God.

As the Editor was preparing to leave her home, Mrs. Scott said: "If you could come to our reunion in August, that would be a good thing. There're going to be a lot of people here and you can get a lot of stories."

"Rosa, who sent me to you, said the said thing. If God opens the door for me, I will be here," the Editor said.

—————

*The building that belonged to the Beneficial Benevolent Society and Loving Sisters of Worship started being used in September 1960. Several journalists that visited Prince Edward County during the second year of the school crisis visited the site.

—————

WALTER WOOD, SR.

After the early worship service at Mercy Seat Baptist Church, Sunday, August 8, 2004, the Editor was walking to his car when the elderly gentleman that had led some of the songs during the worship service said: "Than'ya for comin' out."

We talked informally for a few minutes. The Editor asked:

"What happened with your children when the schools were closed?"

Clifton, and I believe Steve, moved and went to school at Charlotte Court House.

Brother Wendell Brown had a son long wid' my sons. Brother Brown and I was talkin' one day. God touched Broth'a Brown's heart and he said:

"Bro Wood, brin' dem childr'n and let'em ride wid' me."

We was talkin' it over; me, my wife, him and his wife. They said:

"Brin'em over in the mornin'."

That was how I started drivin'em cross the line (across the Charlotte County line) to go to school. I would pic'em up each evening after school at the same spot.

I drove'em from the house to a bus stop where they caught the school bus. I drove'em about eight or ten miles one way to the bus stop.

There was a teacher in that county, her father was one of the greatest preachers ever around. She said: 'The childr'n from other counties can't come to school in this county.' But when one door closes, God opens eight or ten other doors. (The account is recorded as Mr. Wood told it. The Editor concluded as the dialogue continued that the riding arrangement made with Brother Brown for Clifton and Steve was interrupted and the other door God opened was the offer from a family in Charlotte Court House for the Wood boys to come and live with them.)

I was in the Army in World War II. My Daddy married two times; had twenty-four childr'n, twenty-four (Mr. Wood said the second time with emphasis and started laughing), sixteen girls and eight boys; three livin' t'day, I'm the only boy livin'.

"Where did you go to school when you were a boy?" the Editor asked, trying to determine whether Mr. Wood was from Prince Edward County.

I went to Mission School in Meherrin.

"When were you born?" the Editor asked.

I was born in 1923, February 26.

The Editor remembered a middle school teacher interviewed who was impacted by the school closing. Her maiden name was Wood.

"Are you related to Ms. Angeles Wood Christian who teaches at the middle school?" the Editor inquired.

Mr. Wood smiled and responded proudly:

"She's my daught'a."

He paused and reached for my hand. We shook hands and he said:

"Well, come bac' an' see us agin."

AARON JOHNSON

After parting company with Mr. Wood, the Editor was about to unlock his car and leave the church grounds. A gentleman parked opposite of Mr. Wood was about to unlock his car and leave. We spoke to each other. He asked: "You visiting? "Yes," said the Editor and explained the nature of his visit. Mr. Aaron Johnson agreed to share his story. We stood next to his vehicle and the Editor wrote on some paper in his possession.

I was born September 23, 1938, to Aaron and Hattie Evans Johnson. When I started school at Mercy Seat School, Mrs. Brown and Mr. Charles Johnson were the teachers. My father passed when I was ten years old. My mother, my two sisters, Elizabeth and Nannie, my brother, Hezekiah, and me, we was on welfare. Hezekiah was two years younger than me. Nannie graduated the year before the schools closed.

When the schools closed, I had been promoted to the eleventh grade. Our people had a sense of things and knew that the schools might not open.

I had a girlfriend named Rosa Baker. Her mother and father had died. The year before the schools closed, Rosa graduated from Moton High School. I was working the farm and cutting pulpwood. I said to Rosa one day in September 1959:

"Schools ain't gon' open. Let's get married and I'll take you to the city."

I made $100.00 that week cutting pulpwood and working the farm. I paid the preacher with five one-dollar bills and bought two bus tickets to New Jersey for a total of $70.00. Me and Rosa left Prince Edward County on September 20, 1959, just a few days after getting married.

When we got to New Jersey, we got with people I knew in Atlantic City from Prince Edward County; my relatives. They rented us a room for $10.00 a week for two people.

I went out and got a job at a diner as a chef making $33.00 a week and Rosa got a job that paid $38.00 a week.

I met an eighty-year old Black man, named Mr. Wilson,

who was preparing to retire from the hospital as head chef. This fellow told me to come by the hospital, that because I was young I would probably get hired. I went by the hospital. It had ninety beds and Mr. Wilson told them I was a cook. I went to personnel and they asked when could I start. I filled out the application and was told they would call me in few days. I started working at the hospital in 1960. In 1962 Mr. Wilson was leaving. Personnel asked what was my qualifications. I told them I had to quit school in tenth grade. They put me in as head of the breakfast shift and wanted me to get a high school diploma and the proper training certificates.

There was a dining facility upstairs for White doctors, nurses and floor workers. They ate there. There was a small place in the basement for us (Negro workers).

A new hospital was built, and I stayed on. I worked at the hospital for thirty years. I stayed in New Jersey for forty-eight years. Rosa and me are retired and we travel back and forth, living in Prince Edward County several months in the year and in New Jersey several months during the year.

ANGELES WOOD CHRISTIAN

I was born June 6, 1955, to Walter and Lucile Wood. We lived in the Hampden Sydney area. I had three sisters and three brothers. The girls in the family were: Lucia (Braxton), Maida, (Davis), and Darlene Wood. The boys were Clifton, Steven, and Walter, Jr. (deceased). Clifton was the oldest.

I was four years old when the schools were closed. When

it was time for me to start first grade at six years of age in September 1961, the schools were still closed. Mama made arrangements for me and my younger sister, Darlene, to start school in late August 1961. Mama called our aunts in New Jersey and told them about the school situation in Prince Edward County and negotiated for us to go and live with relatives. Arrangements were made for Darlene and me to go to New Jersey. Darlene went to Newark and stayed with Aunt Rosa (Rosa Spraggs Langston). Aunt Rosa was my mother's sister. I went to Jersey City and stayed with my father's sister, Meredith Wood (Johnson). My parents were from Prince Edward County. Mama was from Farmville and Daddy was from Meherrin.

Clifton and Steven went to school in Charlotte County, Virginia. They stayed with one of Mama's friends. Lucia and Maida were too young to go to school.

Mama tried to explain to Darlene and I what was happening, but it was too difficult and complex for her. As she was trying to make arrangements for us to go away and help the school situation in Prince Edward County make sense to us, which she could not do, the situation started taking its toll on her. Nevertheless, Mama got everything worked out.

One night she and Daddy took us to the Greyhound bus station in Farmville. Mama talked to the bus driver to make sure he let us off in Baltimore. Mama put a band around my wrist and one around Darlene's with important information for anyone who would have a need to know. She and Daddy put us on a Greyhound bus and we left Farmville. As the bus pulled off that August night, we wondered where were we going and why were we leaving our mother, as we had never left our family before. We started crying.

We arrived in Baltimore, Maryland, the following morning.

It was daylight. We were met at the bus station by our cousin, John Stokes. Darlene and I cried all the way to Baltimore, we didn't sleep.

Cousin John took us to his home and called some of our other relatives in New Jersey, the ones with whom Darlene and I were to live. They drove down to Baltimore and picked us up. Uncle Pernell drove down to Baltimore, arriving later in the day and we left Baltimore in his big Cadillac. He drove us to Aunt Rose's house in Newark. It was at this point that Darlene and I got another shock. We were told that the two of us would be separated. Having not heard this until now, Darlene and I threw ourselves on each other crying. They let us cry together for a while. They attempted to comfort us by explaining that we would see each other once a week. We were to live in separate households primarily because of financial reasons. I was to live with Aunt Meredith and Uncle Pernell. Aunt Meredith was a beautician and I can't recall what Uncle Pernell did for a living.

Darlene was to live with Aunt Rose and Uncle Johnny in Newark. Aunt Rose was a coordinator of a Day Care Center. I am not sure what Uncle Johnny did.

Aunt Rose and Uncle Johnny left with Darlene and I began trying to learn how to live in the city. Coming from the country it was very hard. People picked on you. I can't remember my first year of school in Jersey City at P S 11. I can't remember anything about it to this day. I don't know how I have managed to block it out. I can't see anybody, teachers or students in my mind. Nothing is there.

The second year's recollections are similar. I don't remember anything or anybody.

I cannot name one student or teacher from the two years I went to school in New Jersey.

Darlene and I came home one time a year and that was at Christmas. We saw our parents twice over that two-year period.

A date for the opening of the Free School was announced in Prince Edward County. Mama called with the news. Uncle Parnell drove us back to Prince Edward County. The trip back was exciting. Darlene and I were happy about going back home. When Uncle Parnell pulled up into the front yard of our house, Darlene and I jumped out of the car and ran up on the porch. Mama was standing there waiting for us. Daddy was at work.

Our sisters and brothers were there and glad to see us as well.

When we enrolled in the Free School, I went on to my regular grade and so did Darlene. Most of the students in my class were older. I was around nine when we returned and there were students in the class who were ten, eleven, twelve, and thirteen years old.

After graduating from high school, I went to Bennett College in Greensboro, North Carolina. I graduated from Saint Paul's College in Lawrenceville, Virginia. I earned a Master's Degree from Longwood College in Farmville, Virginia, and am endorsed in Mathematics from Longwood. I teach in the Prince Edward County public schools. As of the date of this interview, May 18, 2004, I have been teaching twenty-six years and am still enjoying it, in spite of.

With God's love, mercy, and grace, there are a lot of in-spite of situations in life that can be enjoyed.

———

ROSA MARIE JOHNSON BEDFORD

I was born in Hampden Sydney on September 21, 1951, to Rosa Hunter Johnson and Ned Johnson. Mama was from Hampden Sydney and Daddy was from Cumberland County, Virginia. I had two sisters and three brothers. The girls were Catherine Marie and Anna Ann, and the boys were Stanley Junior, Willie Junior, and Richard Junior. All the boys had the same middle name. Mama wanted them to have a middle name and each was named Junior. The way my birthday fell I started school in September 1956 at a small school in Hampden Sydney called Mercy Seat School. I think it had three rooms. Mrs. Victoria Brown was my teacher. My brother, Stanley, and I were in the same room. I was in the first grade and he was in second grade. The third and fourth grades were in another classroom and the fifth and sixth grades in another. Mr. Charlie Johnson was also a teacher at Mercy Seat School and I think he was the principal also. I can't remember the third teacher. Mrs. Victoria Brown used to bring a big bag of lunch for the students who had no lunch. She would bring a biscuit or whatever she could afford to bring. She was also a teacher who worked to advance us. I learned my time tables up to the threes in the first grade. Mrs. Brown was a good teacher. I was promoted to the second grade.

I went to Mercy Seat School for one year and then my family moved to Farmville. From Hampden Sydney to Farmville is about six or seven miles. When it was time to go back to school in September 1959, Mama said:

"Y'all are not going today." We had no idea why we were staying at home and we were not bothered by what Mama said. We thought school was closed for some reason and would open later. Catherine was getting ready to start first grade that year.

When the schools were closed, I had just passed to the second grade. I could only write my name, and that was in big letters, and say the alphabets. That was all I could do. I hadn't learned to write my last name. My mama had limited education and couldn't assist us at home in the manner she wished.

While the schools in Prince Edward County were closed, my learning experience was unique. I didn't attend classes at the churches in town. Mama worked, and I was the oldest. The task of keeping my brothers and sisters fell to me, though I was only around eight years old.

When I was sent to the store to get something for my mother, that was my opportunity to learn. Since I knew my ABCs, in time I came to know and recognize the names or words on products in the store. The words pork-n-beans, oil, bread, lamp oil, we had no electricity in the early 1960s or television, so I had to go to the store frequently to purchase these items. After a while, the words pork-n-beans, oil, bread, lamp oil, soap, soap powder and other common house items became familiar to me.

Catherine, and my brother, Willie, started going to school. There was a school in Dr. Miller's office. Dr. Miller was a Black dentist in Farmville. He had a three-story facility or house. He and his wife, Mrs. Minnie Miller, lived upstairs, the office was in the middle section and there was a basement. The school was held in the basement. I remember walking Catherine and Willie to that school. I would drop them off and return home to care for the others who were too young to attend. They would walk with me to take Catherine and Willie. Some pictures were taken by *Time* or one of the other national magazines of Catherine and Willie walking from the school in Dr. Miller's office.

The reflections shared is all I can recall from the time the schools were closed until the Free School opened in September 1963. I just don't remember anything much from those years.

The stores in Farmville were boycotted in 1963. The boycotters would meet at the home of Reverend Samuel Williams, get their signs or posters, and go into town and boycott the stores that didn't have Black people working. Reverend Williams lived across the street from us and I would stand at our window and watch the people rally up at his house.

In 1963 the Free School opened. I remember all of us returning to school except my youngest brother Richard who was born in 1959. The day I walked into school I was twelve years old. It was very embarrassing sitting in a class with students who were seven and eight years old. They made fun of students like me. The entire year was a struggle. You couldn't concentrate because the other students would continually tease us. It seemed that the teachers spent most of their time with the children who were in the proper grade or at the proper academic level. It wasn't the fault of the teachers. It made sense to spend the bulk of their time with the fourth and fifth graders who were nine and ten years old. These students knew the sounds, vowels and consonants, and could grasp things more readily than the older students. Students like me who had been out of school for four years had lost all we had learned in first grade. In first grade we only learned to write our name and how to count. I was in a class with a mixture of students from eight to thirteen. Some were probably older. The boys would not tell their ages.

I learned to write my name in cursive. I was able to write my name in cursive because I had two friends who had move to Farmville from Bowling Green, Virginia. Their names were

Lena and Gracie. They were sisters. When they learned that I couldn't write in cursive at my age, Lena said to me during the year of the Free School:

"You are too old not to be able to write your name in cursive," and they taught me.

I remember being given a test the second year of school, which was the year the county officially reopened the public schools.

In 1965 I attempted to learn to play the flute. I couldn't grasp the concepts. I was so upset. I pretended I was playing. The teacher discovered it, but the teachers were sensitive to us.

After seventh grade you went to high school. I missed so many days in sixth grade that I had to go to summer school. Mr. White was the teacher. There were two teachers with the last name White. I can't remember the first name of my summer school teacher.

High school was better because there were older students there, but I was still the oldest in my class. I enjoyed all the teachers at Moton High. Mrs. Patsy Cobbs Franklin and Mrs. Alberta Sims in particular I remember.

On March 29, 1968, I dropped out of high school and married Daniel Bedford who was from Charlotte Court House. I gave birth to two boys and I returned to high school around 1970 or 1971.

My husband had attended college and tutored me in algebra. I finished algebra with nearly an A average. I was determined. I won the Crisco Award in Home Economics. Mrs. Mary W. Madison was the Home Economics teacher. I learned to sew almost anything. She played a very important role in my life. When I could not afford material, she gave me material to make my boys clothes.

I graduated from high school with honors. My mother-in-law

babysat our children, which allowed me to concentrate on my studies.

I thank God for my husband because he was able to assist me with my classes. I was offered a scholarship to Virginia State College when I graduated in 1973 but declined the offer because I was married and had a family.

After graduating from high school in 1973, I stared working with Mrs. Pauline Smith learning the trade of upholstery. In 1982, I started working at a shelter workshop in Farmville teaching upholstering, hand-woven canning, and refinishing woodwork. I was also the head of subcontracting for the Shelter Workshop. In 1992, I went back to school and earned my Nursing Assistance License. I worked for ten and a half years at Crossroad Service Board Rehabilitation Facility. Since 1999, I have been employed at Prince Edward Middle School as a Teacher's Assistant or Para Professional, as we are now called.

I am the proud mother of three boys: Daniel, Jr., Randy, and Antonio Tremain. I have four grandchildren, three boys and one girl.

My sons have done wonderful in great part because I was determined to see to it that they went to school and developed an appreciation for education. My oldest son has a master's degree in computer science and works for HUD. Randy is an underwriter for an insurance company and is pursuing his bachelor's degree. Antonio has a bachelor's degree from Hampden Sydney College and a master's degree from Virginia Commonwealth University and is currently pursuing a Ph. D in Psychology. He is also a part-time professor at John Tyler Community College in Richmond.

Dr. Miller died many years ago. Mrs. Miller died in 2004, earlier this year. She was over 100. She was 103 or 104 years old.

Mercy Seat School, where my public education began, is standing today with just minor remodeling. It is now a store for rent.

I am going to call my cousin, Barbara Baker Simons, and ask her to give you an interview. Barbara and some others in her family went away to continue their education. Her oldest sister, Frances, I think was going to the twelfth grade when the schools closed. I think Mrs. Frances Goldman Scott and Mr. William Page have interesting stories to share. These parents had to arrange for their children to go away and continue their education. I will contact both and see if they will agree to be interviewed.

Education is important, and I hope my story and the stories of others in Prince Edward County impacted by the closing of the schools will make a difference. I am sure it will because the truth will always make a difference.

"If you could come to Prince Edward the first weekend in August for the Hampden Sydney Reunion, you'll get to talk to many people. You should really try to come back for the Reunion."

"If the good Lord opens that door, I will be here," said the Editor.

———

CATHERINE MARIE JOHNSON JACKSON

I was born January 15, 1954. I was five years old when the schools were closed. My family had moved to Farmville by this time. The year I was supposed to start to school I was so excited. I asked my Mom:

"Am I going to school?"

"No, the schools are closed," she said.

I was sad and terribly upset.

My education started at the church. I attended classes at Beulah African Methodist Episcopal Church on Main Street in Farmville. During the years the schools were closed, I also attended classes in the basement of Dr. Miller's dental office. The teachers were always very friendly. They taught us the alphabets and how to sound out words, how to count and so forth.

I don't know where they came from or remember the time period but one year a group of college students came to Prince Edward County to teach during the summer and to work with us. They were mostly White students.

One of the reasons I remember them is because I benefited more than educationally from their coming. One of the students got in contact with a group or with the social workers and made arrangements for me to get my first pair of eyeglasses. I really couldn't see very well. I was from a very poor family and eyeglasses weren't very high on the priority list. Food and shelter were primary. My family purchased a lot of used items. There was a place downtown that sold used shoes and my mother bought shoes for us there. The shoes cost something like fifteen cents or a quarter. The shoes were worn but had enough sole to keep your feet off the ground.

When the Free School opened, we were placed by age. I was nine and was placed in the third grade. I was able to do third grade work and keep up.*

------

*Catherine is the younger sister of Rosa Marie Johnson Bedford.

STANLEY J. JOHNSON

The house I spent my early years in had a few boards on the floor and the rest of the house had a dirt floor. We didn't have a bathroom indoors nor lights, no electricity.

I started school at Mercy Seat School and went there for three years and then we moved to Farmville. In Farmville we had a bathroom and electric lights. I was going to the fourth grade in September 1959, but the schools never opened.

The first year the schools were closed I worked. I was around nine years old. My mother lived in Farmville, but I returned to Hampden Sydney and lived with my grandmother. I helped my uncle, Jessie Hunter, on his farm and cut pulpwood. This was all I did basically from the time the schools closed until the reopening in September 1963.

In 1963 when the Free School opened, I was placed in the seventh grade. I dropped out of school a couple of times, but always returned. My grandmother couldn't afford to take care of me and I quit those times to earn money. I graduated in 1970.

After high school, I joined the United States Army and stayed in for two years. I went to Europe for one year and had assignments stateside in Kentucky, Texas, and the state of Washington.

After being honorably discharged, I returned to Prince Edward County.

The closing of the schools killed a lot of futures. Even though I graduated from high school, I came out still somewhat illiterate. To this day, it is hard when you want to write something out or read something and you can't do it with the ease that you would have had if the schools had not been closed. I feel the impact of the closing to this day. You will feel it for the rest of your life.

It is painful when your child is in the fifth grade and ask you:

"Daddy, what is this word?" Or when you are reading your children a book and the child looks at you strange as you read.

I'm sure you have heard about the honorary diplomas they gave out recently. Giving people a diploma, well, what was that! They can't give you the years back.

———

*Stanley J. Johnson is the brother of Rosa Marie Johnson Bedford and Catherine Marie Johnson Jackson.

———

VALARIE AMELIA SCOTT BREWER

The first time I went to school was in May 1959. My brother, LeGrant, was a student at Mercy Seat School. A May Day program was held at school. I don't recall who all went from my house, but I was there at the invitation of LeGrant. I remember the excitement of the children at school. I was to start school that fall and my excitement about school was lifted at the May Day program.

September 1959 came and there was no school. I don't remember how the news of the school closure came to me.

The first year Mama worked with us at home.* She read to us, and worked with me on the alphabets and counting. LeGrant had a foundation because he had already been to school. Mama was really concerned about me. I had no foundation. School at home had its challenges. One reason it was so challenging was because class was held around the coffee table. That was where we sat so Mama could work with us. It was hard to remain focused. LeGrant had already been to school a few years. I was just starting. Deloris was born in 1955 and Mama just had us all in school at the table. Mama did the best she could with us.

There was a one room house nearby where the Branch family lived. Mr. Branch had a new house built for his family just opposite of his old house. The old house, and I mean it was an old house, was torn down. There was no indoor plumbing. The kitchen and bedrooms were demolished. The front room or living room was left. It was the old living room that was used as a classroom when Mrs. Brown taught us. There were so many different ages in that one room. It was amazing. Along the wall was a long bench the students sat on and a few desks were available.

Then we started attending class at The Hall.** This was the third year or thereabouts after the closing of the schools. Mrs. Margaret Hill, whom we called Missy, was the teacher.

Being out of school made many of us more determined to learn and advance and develop. When I entered the Free School in September 1963, I was placed in the third grade. I graduated in 1973. I stress the importance of education to my children. I have always told them "if I can't give you anything else, I will give you a good education." I work for the United States Postal Service in Richmond, Virginia. The May Day Program I attended in May 1959 sticks in my mind to this day, August 7, 2004.

---

*Mrs. Valarie Amelia Scott Brewer is the daughter of Mrs. Frances Goldman Scott.

**The Hall was another name for the Beneficial Benevolent Society and Loving Sisters of Worship.

JOSEPHINE BAKER BOURNE

I started school at Mercy Seat School. When the schools were closed, I was at Mary E. Branch No. 2 and had passed to the eighth grade, if my memory serves me right. I was looking forward to going to high school.

The first year the schools were closed I stayed home. All of my days were free. There were no classes close to where we lived.

Just before the start of the second year of the school closing, September 1960, I called my Uncle Alex, Alexander Hunter, who lived in New York. I asked Uncle Alex would it be all right if I came to live with him and go to school for the year. He said yes. He treated me like one of his own children. Aunt Juanita, his wife, was very kind to me.

I went to school in Hempstead. I was enrolled at Franklin Elementary School. When the school year ended in May 1961, I did not return to Prince Edward County for the summer. I remained in New York and in September 1961 I went to the ninth grade, attending Hempstead High School. I completed my remaining years at Hempstead High School.

I felt it was a shame what had happen in Prince Edward

County. My sister, Frances, never graduated. Barbara, Shirley and Ralph got to go away and attend school.

I missed my mother and father very dearly, while in New York. Even though I was living with relatives, you only have one set of parents. I missed bonding with them and they with me. All of the children in the county who went away had these types of loss issues.

A lot of children were cheated out of the future they deserved. People are discussing the issue now and talking about what they can, should, and need to do for residents of Prince Edward County, but you cannot undo the past. There is no telling what so many Prince Edward County residents could have been and the contributions they could have made to society.

_____

BARBARA BAKER SIMONS

I was born September 28, 1949, to Joseph and Anna Mae Hunter Baker. I had three sisters and a brother. My sisters were: Frances Mae (Streat), Josephine Elizabeth (Bourne), Shirley Ann (Simpson), and my brother was named Ralph William. I started school at Mercy Seat School. Mrs. Victoria Brown was my first teacher. I started school around September 1955. Mercy Seat Baptist Church was hardly a mile from the school.

The schools were closed in September 1959. I missed the next two years of school. We were just at home. Josephine went to live with our Uncle Alex (Alexander Hunter), my mother's brother.

In the 1961-62 school year, I went away to Washington, D.

C. to go to school. My brother, Ralph, and my sister, Shirley, also went to Washington in August 1961 to attend school. Daddy drove us to Washington that day and Mom rode with him.

Ralph and I lived with a host family. It really wasn't a family. The lady Ralph and I lived with was single. Her name was Miss. Butler. She was a Black lady and I believe her first name was Evelyn. I think Miss. Butler did cleaning work. She took us in out of the goodness of her heart. She learned about us through the NAACP I believe. Ralph and I arrived at Miss Butler's just in time to start school. Miss. Butler lived on 8th Street, in Northwest, D. C. We attended Saint Martin's Roman Catholic School in Northwest.

Shirley lived with another family in Washington. I don't remember who was dropped off first with their family, but Shirley lived with a family that had a home in Northeast Washington.

Organizations did as much as possible to keep children from the same family together when they went away to continue their education but keeping all the brothers and sisters together wasn't always possible. Miss. Butler could not afford to take all three of us.

Shirley lived in Northeast, but also attended Saint Martin's. The school was our way of keeping a link with each other and seeing each other daily. Ralph and I seldom saw Shirley on the weekend, but always looked forward to Monday morning when we would see each other again.

Shirley's environment, as far as I could tell, was different. I think the husband and wife with whom she lived had a daughter. So, Shirley wasn't alone and got to do some things. She got to go shopping, go to the movies, and so forth.

Miss. Butler could only afford to feed me and Ralph and

give us a place to stay. The NAACP paid her to board us and sometimes the money didn't always come on time. My parents would also send their share of money for our upkeep.

There was also another girl from Farmville who lived with Miss. Butler. Her name was Shirley Johnson or Jackson. I can't remember her last name. That was forty-three years ago, as of this summer and the time of this interview. I can remember and see a lot of faces in my mind, but I can't remember the names. Yes, there were three Prince Edward County children in Miss. Butler's home. I think Shirley rode with our family when Daddy drove us to Washington.

Ralph, my sister, Shirley, and I came home at Christmas and then for the summer after school closed.

The next school year, September 1962 to May or June 1963, I experienced a change and so did Ralph.

In September 1962 I started attending school in Bumpass, in Louisa County, Virginia. I was now about thirteen or fourteen. I lived with a Black teacher who taught at the same school I attended. Her name was Mrs. Downing or Doughty or Daphney. I'm not sure of the exact pronunciation. We are talking about something that happened years ago. But I think Daphney was her name. She was an elementary school teacher. I think the NAACP found her. Ms. Daphney had no children and lived with her niece and husband. The niece and husband taught school in Orange County, Virginia. They came home on the weekends and during the week it was just me and Mrs. Daphney. Ms. Daphney was old at that time, over sixty I am sure. She was slightly crippled. She did not allow me to watch television or even change the dial on the radio. It was business only. I studied, and I excelled, and she appreciated it. I must admit that I made high grades that year. (Mrs. Simons started laughing.) But it was very lonely. Compared to when I lived in Washington, being at Ms. Daphney's was very lonely. She did not drive. She caught the school bus with me each morning or I caught it with her. We only got to ride out in a car when Ms. Daphney's niece and husband came home. When they went shopping, they shopped for the month. The outings Ms. Daphney took me on were not very frequent, only once or twice a month. We went to church whenever we could get a ride.

While I was at Ms. Daphney's, my brother, Ralph, was in Toledo, Ohio, with the Jones family. This was a Black family. They really loved Ralph. I think they drove to Prince Edward and picked him up, after learning that he would be with them that year. They thought of him more as a son than as a student. Ralph was about fifteen at this time, he was born in 1947.

I think my sister Shirley returned to the same family in Washington, D. C.

When I heard the Free School was going to open, I jumped for joy. The news broke that summer while I was home. I did not have to return to Louisa County.

We were given a test and students were placed where the administration, in view of the test, felt you belonged. I was placed in the seventh grade. It was exciting. The teachers worked hard to bring us on up to speed. Along with the regular math, reading, social studies, history, and science classes, the Free School curriculum had modern dance, band, and field trips. Many of the students went to the World's Fair in New York. Shirley was in the modern dance group that performed at the World's Fair. I didn't attend. Everything was free. Mrs. Jenkins taught gym. She was strict and made you perform, yet she was gentle. It seemed like they wanted to give the kids everything possible to enrich their educational experience.

Today what used to be Mercy Seat School is a business establishment. I want the world to know that we all feel the same pain. The closing of the schools was an experience that I grew from. All people need to learn how to grow closer together and be one. The school closing shaped me and fashioned me, and I am able to move forward.

There are good and bad people in this world. I got to see both. I got to experience the beauty of strangers taking children in so that their entire childhood would not be lost. Miss. Butler, Ms. Daphney, and the Jones families were all blessings to us. And today I am trying to be a blessing to others.

I'm going to call my sister, Frances, to see if she will give an interview. Her story needs to be told.

———

FRANCES BAKER STREAT

Barbara called Frances and told the sister about having her story drafted. After talking for about five minutes, Barbara had convinced Frances to do the same. She hung up, gave directions to the home of Frances and the telephone number in the event the Editor got lost. When the Editor arrived, Frances and her husband, William Lee Streat, served lunch, after which the interview was conducted.

I was born October 9, 1943. When I was thirteen, I got a job at a nursing home to help make money for my family. I was working and going to school. I had passed to the eleventh grade when the schools closed.

My daddy couldn't afford to send me away to school. My

sister, Josephine, went to New York. I was the oldest and Josey was next. I think Josey was a year younger than me. Josey went to my Uncle Alex (Alexander Hunter) and went on to high school.

"My dream was to be an artist. I could draw anything," Mrs. Streat said, pointing to a picture hanging on the wall in her kitchen. The picture was of a bowl of fruit.

"Did you draw that?" the Editor asked, admiring the painting.

"No, I didn't draw that, but I could draw just that good," she said in a deliberate convincing tone.

"She could draw real good," her husband William added, who was sitting at the kitchen table with us.

I wanted to go to art school and become an artist. But after the schools closed, I stayed in Hampden Sydney with my mother and father.

"You wan'a see my certificate they gave us?" Mrs. Streat asked.

"Yes, I would love to see it," the Editor said, having heard about the ceremony in which students impacted by the closing of the schools were given honorary high school diplomas with the name R. R. Moton High School on it, but having not seen the document. Mrs. Streat went to another part of the house and returned to the kitchen with the certificate.

"It don' mean nothin'," she noted, handing it to me, "but I went and got it anyway. I can't use it to get a job."

After the schools closed, I worked with the younger children who came to the Benevolent Society Building. I can't remember who else taught or worked with the children. We had a good time working with the children.

I made sure that all of my children went to school. Janell Lambert, Patricia Marshall, Thomas Marshall, Deborah

Marshall [Smith], Janet Lambert, and Jacquline (Jenette) Lambert all completed high school.

William Lee Streat said as the Editor prepared to leave: "Let'us know when you comin' back and I'll cook a good meal f'you. I do most'a the cookin'.'"

"I will do that. I will let you know ahead of time. I want to get your story on paper. You had a lot say when Frances was sharing her story, but you need to tell your own story," the Editor ended.

TOMMY HUNTER

I was born March 4, 1944 and started school at Mercy Seat. I don't remember the name of my first teacher.

When the schools closed, I had been promoted to the eighth grade. When the schools didn't open in September 1959, I went to work with my brother in the fields. I worked in the fields from September 1959 to the summer of 1960.

In August 1960, I went to Dayton, Ohio, to go to school. I lived with Mrs. Billie Jackson and attended the Dayton Public Schools. I don't know who made the arrangements for me to go away. One of the organizations paid my expenses. My parents didn't have to pay.

When it was time to go back to school the following August, the sponsoring group wouldn't allow me to return to Dayton or be in any program. I was never told why.

I started back working. I went to New York in 1963. I wasn't in Prince Edward County when the Free School opened. Even though I wasn't here, I would have been around nineteen when the Free School opened.

I still live in New York. My wife, Lil Ann Hunter, and I have two sons. We made it a point to share our stories with our sons. We are proud of them. Our son Ryan Patrick Hunter is the Assistant District Attorney in Suffolk County, New York. Our other son, Thomas T. Hunter, is a detective in New York City.

———

JAMES EDWARD CRAWLEY

I started school at Mercy Seat School. When the schools were closed, I had passed to the sixth grade. When the schools were closed, all the kids in the neighborhood came to The Hall for classes. School was held in The Hall for one year.

Some who were children at the time remember attending classes in a part of my uncle's old house. My uncle, Sam Branch, had not yet built his new house for his family in September 1959. I remember this. Classes were started in The Hall and some of the children who were attending Mercy Seat School before the closing were taught there during the first year, from late 1959 to May 1960. I missed the first year of school, September 1959 to May 1960.*

In September 1960, some of us started attending classes in the one room school. My Uncle Sam had finished building his new house. The old house he and the family moved out of was torn down, except for one of the larger rooms. He gave permission for that large room to be used as a classroom.

In September 1961, me and my sister started attending Saint Matthew Lutheran Church School. The school was part of Saint Matthew Lutheran Church in Lunenburg County.

From my house to Saint Matthew Lutheran School was about fifteen or twenty miles. Saint Matthew Lutheran was a private school and the building was connected to the church. Some professors from Hampden Sydney College supported our travel expenses. I don't know the names of any of the people that gave money. My uncle, Mr. Lester Thornton, drove us each day.

He drove his two children, Claire Polly (Johnson) and his son, Marcellus Thornton. From my family there was me and Elizabeth. I'm not sure whether my brother, Ralph, went or not. Uncle Lester took us back and forth to Saint Matthew Lutheran for one school year, September 1961 to May 1962. We went to Saint Matthew Lutheran School for one year and the school closed.** I don't know whether it was closed because Price Edward County children started attending or because of financial reasons.

After Saint Mathew Lutheran School closed, I was fortunate enough to enter school in Appomattox County, attending Carver–Price High School. I had passed to the seventh or eighth grade when I started going to Carver–Price. My sister, Elizabeth, also went to Carver–Price.

The reason me and Elizabeth were able to attend school in Appomattox County was because there was teacher who lived in Prince Edward County, in Hampden Sydney, who got a job teaching in Appomattox County. Me and Elizabeth rode with her each day. Me and Elizabeth told the Appomattox County school administrators that we lived in Pamplin, a community in Appomattox County. The teacher we rode to school with was Mrs. Victoria Brown, who used to teach at Mercy Seat. She was hired in Appomattox County after the closing of the schools in Prince Edward County. Mama and Daddy wanted me and Elizabeth to go with her because we were the oldest and needed to continue our education. My brother, Ralph, was about six at this time and my sister, Margaret Ann, was even younger.

We rode with Mrs. Brown to Carver–Price for one year, September 1962 to May 1963. Then the Free School opened in September 1963. When the Free School opened, I was placed in the eighth or ninth grade. In high school I was on the football team. I played the tackle position on defense and offense all of my high school years. I graduated from high school in 1968. I was born February 10, 1948 and was twenty years old when I finished high school.

---

*The account given by Crawley conflicts with other accounts as to the year The Hall or the Beneficial Benevolent Society and Loving Sisters of Worship became a center where neighborhood children gathered for instructions. There was no Training Center or Learning Center in Hampden Sydney the first year of the school crisis. The Crawley presentation has events reversed.

**Saint Matthew Lutheran School closed after the 1962-1963 school year. Crawley put the closing one year too soon. There is a historical marker near the church that dates the year the school closed. Also, some Prince Edward County pupils were at the school during the 1962-1963 academic year before entering the Prince Edward Free School Association opened in September 1963.

DORIS DAE MILLER JOHNSON

I was born February 19, 1952. I went to Mercy Seat School for one year, September 1958 to May or June 1959. In September 1959 the schools didn't open. I remember being very confused about why I could no longer go to school.

There was an old abandoned one room house across from where I lived in the Hampden Sydney area. The house belonged to Mr. Sam Branch. He gave permission for the students to have class in it. Mr. Branch had built a new house for his family and had already moved out of the old house. Mrs. Victoria Brown taught us in this one room abandoned house. About ten and not more than twenty students came to the class. We went every day and class was held from about 8:00 a. m. to noon. This was from September 1960 to May 1961.

In the summer of 1961 I went to Brooklyn, New York, to live with my mother's sister, Aunt Lucy (Lucy Venerable Homley). I went to P S 133. This was my first time in the big city. I had to learn how to fight to survive. I also learned to use the dictionary. I excelled and did well. I went to school in New York for two years.

When the Free School opened in September 1963, I returned to Prince Edward County. I was placed in the fourth grade. When the Free School opened, if a student had money they paid for their lunch. If a family was very poor, students from those households were given lunch.

I went to Worsham Elementary School during the year of the Free School. I remember Attorney General Bobby Kennedy came to Worsham Elementary one day to visit.

I hope my brief reflection will shed some light on the Prince Edward County story as it relates to the closing of the schools from September 1959 to September 1963, when the Free School opened.

EVA JOHNSON WILSON

I was born December 16, 1946, in Prince Edward County. I am the oldest of six children, one brother having died at two weeks old. My mother was named Julia Jackson Johnson. My education began at Mercy Seat School. I don't remember my first teacher but remember my last teacher at Mercy Seat who was Mr. Smith.

In sixth grade I was in the Honors class. My grandfather, Mr. Charles T. Johnson, was the assistant principal at the school. I had been promoted to the seventh grade when the schools were closed.

The first year the schools were closed I did not attend school anywhere. The second year I worked and about half way through that year the American Friends came to the county. They somehow secured the Honor students list from the junior high school. My name was on that list because I had been an Honor student.

The American Friends workers were visiting homes and asking parents about letting their sons and daughters go away to school. The Friends secured the junior high school Honor Roll list, as I mentioned, and I had been an Honor student and that's how they got my name, as well as the names of many others who were selected to go away. One of the American Friends representatives asked Mama would she consider letting her daughter go away to school. Mom agreed and in August 1961 I left Prince Edward County on a Greyhound bus. Some of the other students on the bus with me selected by the American Friends to go away and attend school were: Bessie, I can't remember her last name, Casey Edwards, Raymond Wiley, and Emanuel Smith. There were other students, but these are the only names I can remember.

I went to West Springfield, Massachusetts. Some of the students went to Connecticut and other New England states.

I lived with the Utley family, a White family. I was enrolled at Springfield Junior High School, where I was placed in the eighth grade. I came home for Christmas 1961 and again when school ended for the summer in 1962.

I returned to Springfield in August 1962 to continue my education but had to make an unexpected adjustment near the middle of the school year. The Utley family, for reasons I cannot recall, moved. I was placed with a Black family in Springfield. I can't remember the family's last name. I remember my room in the house, which was two blocks from the Basketball Hall Of Fame.

My experience with the second family was somewhat of a strain for some reason.

There was a lady who lived nearby named Margaret O. Carson. Margaret was a Social Worker. She knew that I wasn't very happy in this second home and would let me come to her home and spend time and do work. Margaret would give me money and take me to the movies. I was so impressed with her until I decided I wanted to become a Social Worker.

The families I lived with were Quakers.

One of the most memorable things I recall from this period was the short relaxing trips students from Prince Edward County living with families in New England occasionally took. I am unsure who the sponsors were, but whenever there were short school breaks, someone or some people made sure all of the Prince Edward County students in New England got together to fellowship. One year when on break from school, they took all of us mountain climbing in New Hampshire. I have a picture of us on that mountain.

The 1962-1963 school year ended, and I again returned to Prince Edward County.

While I was home during the summer of 1963, it was announced that the Free School would open in September. I did not return to Massachusetts. When the Free School opened, I entered the tenth grade. I got married in the eleventh grade and quit school. The librarian asked me one day:

"Are you coming back in the fall?"

"No," I said.

"Well, I'll see you in two weeks," she replied, as if she didn't hear a word I said.

I went back to school and I graduated in 1967.

I entered Virginia State College in Petersburg, Virginia, and graduated in 1971. I returned to Prince Edward County and was the first professional person to work in the courthouse. I became a Social Worker and stayed in the field for thirty years.

OSA SUE ALLEN DOWDY

I was born July 1, 1947, to Hal Edward Allen and Dora Lee Allen. I started school at Felden School located off Highway 15 in Prince Edward County. Felden School was about half way between Farmville and Keysville off of Highway 15. There were two elementary schools in the community, Felden and Mercy Seat. Leaving Farmville and heading on Highway 15 South a traveler would reach the turn for Mercy Seat first,

Felden School was down the road a little further. The Felden School had three rooms with a potbelly stove. My first and only teacher from grades first to fifth was Mrs. Mary Foster. About thirty children were at Felden School. Felden had an outdoor toilet. There was a pump on the yard. I think the school had electricity.

The grades were something like first and second in one room, third and fourth in another and the fifth graders were in a room. Mrs. Foster went from one room to the other teaching. She worked with one class an hour, then gave us work and went to the next room for an hour and so on.

The thing I remember about Mrs. Foster was when we misbehaved she made you put your hand out and hit you with a ruler. It was one of those thirty-six inch rulers. For the most part the children were good because we were afraid of that ruler. It left a tremendous burning in your hand.

I completed the fifth grade at Felden in 1958. In the fall of 1958 I entered the sixth grade at Mary E. Branch School No. 1, located in Farmville. This was a meaningful time. I thought I was moving up in the world. Sixth grade was exciting for me because I had so many new friends. We changed classes at school during school hours. All the classrooms were large and pretty compared to the three small rooms at Felden. Mr. Johnson was my favorite teacher. I cannot remember his first name. Mrs. Ethel Wilson also made an impression on me. Mr. L. L. Hall was the principal and he too made an impression on me. The 1958-1959 school year ended.

The summer of 1959 was a normal summer. We played and waited for school to open in the fall. I guess my parents told me the schools were not going to open. My parents and other parents in Prince Edward County thought the schools would be closed for a brief period.

The first year the schools were closed we did nothing. I didn't go to any of the Learning Centers. The organized classes were held in town at First Baptist Church. Daddy worked, and he had to drive to work, so that took away our transportation each day. The second year I didn't do anything much to speak of. We lived too far away even from the Benevolent Building near Mercy Seat Baptist Church and couldn't attend classes there. I would have had to walk about five miles to get to the Benevolent Building.

In the summer of 1961 representatives from the American Friends came to speak with my mother and father about my sister, Ada, and I going to stay with a family in New York. I think there were two representatives that came to the house that day. When one of the representatives mentioned New York, my mind began to envision city life, lights, people and all the rest. Ada was sitting there listening too and also got excited. The lady explained to my father that we would be taken care of. Daddy didn't want his young daughters to go to New York and live among strangers and neither did he want his family split up. The schools had already been closed two years and I am sure my father thought the issue was coming to a head. He had no idea, neither did any of the other families have any idea, that the schools would remain closed two more years.

I remember being crushed when Daddy refused the offer made by the representatives from the American Friends. I did not understand Daddy's position and did not want to understand it at that moment. I was deeply disturbed. I cried, and I cried, but he was the head of the house. Ada and I were very close. She cried and cried and when she stopped crying I would start.

During the third year of the closing, September 1961 to May

1962, I fell in love with a young man named Raymond Eugene Dowdy from Lunenburg County. I met Raymond when I was fourteen.

I remember we started picketing downtown Farmville. I don't remember much about the picketing, but I know we had a march on the courthouse. I remember there was a program at First Baptist Church and we were singing Freedom Songs. The event was televised.

Around the third or fourth year of the closing of the schools, Black people were really getting fed up with the whole school issue. Reverend Griffin held us together. He gave us hope that this thing would end soon, and the schools would reopen.

I remember Daddy would always fuss about having to pay taxes while his children were denied an education. Yes, even though the schools were closed Black parents still had to pay taxes.

The Free School opened in September 1963. I was tested and placed in the ninth grade. I was happy to be back in school after four years. I really enjoyed the 1963-1964 school year. Many of my friends who went away never returned. I had to make new friends at the opening of the Free School.

I dated Raymond for three years and then we were married October 1964. I dropped out of school.

I saw the light and returned to school and got a GED in the early 1970s. Then I started attending Southside Community College where I earned a two-year degree in business management. I transferred those credits to Longwood University in Farmville and earned a Bachelor of Science in Business Administration. I continued my education and entered Virginia State University and earned a master's degree in business administration.

Raymond and I have three beautiful children Loretta, Priscilla, and Raymond, Jr.

I am a retired educator. I taught business administration at Randolph Henry High School. I currently work at the Moton Museum as the office manager.

This is only a sketch of a larger personal story I plan to publish in the future.

Note of the Editor: Osa called her sister, Ada, and arranged for her to come to the Moton Museum and give her reflections.

———

ADA DOREENE ALLEN WHITEHEAD

I was born January 22, 1946, to Hal Edward and Dora Bell Lee Allen.

School always started in September, but my birthday was in January. The year my parents enrolled me in school the teacher asked when was my birthday and I told her. She said I could not start school that year. So, I had to wait and was almost a year late starting school. I started school at Felden School. I think my father went to Felden when he was a boy. It was a very old three room school. My teacher was Mrs. Mary Foster and she was a very good teacher. I remember her being very serious and hard. We learned a great deal under her and she was a strict disciplinarian. I remember she would discipline us with a ruler, or what was called a yard stick. If you misbehaved in class, Mrs. Foster would tell your parents and that meant being disciplined again at home. I was spoiled at home and thought I could get away with things at school. But if Mrs. Foster told my parents, I got disciplined at home also.

We moved to another house about five miles down the same rode and my sister Osa and I started riding the bus to Felden. I remember there was a set of twins that rode the bus and I fell in love with one of them, but he would never look at me. (Ada started laughing.)

After leaving Felden School, I attended Branch No. 2. I really loved school. We were from a very poor family and didn't have the nicest house. I reasoned early in life that if I wanted to live in a nice house that I had to get an education. There was no cafeteria at Branch No. 2. If you wanted lunch, you had to go across the street to Branch No. 1, which was the elementary school.

I think my daddy used reversed psychology on us. He would always say to the girls:

"Gal, why you wanna git'a education? All you gon' do is git married and have babies."

I think he wanted us to come to the realization that the reverse was the appropriate choice and the opposite was the choice my sister Osa and I made in life.

I never dreamed the school doors would be closed on us. There was no such thing as schools being closed and students denied an education. Who had ever heard of such a thing? Being our age, we didn't understand what was going on. I didn't have the type of parents who would sit down with you and explain what was happening.

Initially my parents kept saying the schools wouldn't be closed very long. My brother had just passed to the twelfth grade when the schools were closed. The schools didn't open in a timely manner. The education centers were opened in the various communities.

I remember my father being very involved in civil rights events in the county and being involved in the boycotts. The KKK used to meet in an open field down the road from our house. Daddy had a lot of guns and he was determined to protect his family. We slept with the doors opened and unlocked. Daddy used to say:

"Let'em come on in here if they wann'a."

The American Friends came to visit our home one day. I remember being in the front room of our house and the representatives saying something along these lines to Daddy and Mama:

"We are here to help your daughters. We will get them out of the county." A family had already been identified to sponsor me and my sister. Since the American Friends representatives were in our house talking to Mama and Daddy, I thought that their presence was a sure sign that my parents would agree to let Osa and I go away to live with a family and attend school. The more the people talked the more excited I became. But the more they talked the more Daddy said no.

I think Daddy said no because we were teenage girls and the fact that he would have to provide some money which he did not have, as well as a host of other concerns that came to his mind of which I am unaware to this day. I started crying when Daddy gave his final answer. Daddy did everything he could to support us during the time we were out of school.

The American Friends representatives came by our home to talk with Mama and Daddy in the summer of 1961. Shortly after their visit, when Daddy said no, I left home. I had a sister named Eva who lived in Washington, D. C. She was my oldest sister. I went to live with her, stayed a short time and then went to my other sister, Ida, who lived in New York. Ida was a 1958 graduate of Moton High School.

During the time I was in Brooklyn, New York, with Ida, I worked during the day and attended night school. I think the night school I attended was Fulton Night School. It was a regular school during the day and night classes were held in the evening.

The Free School opened in September 1963. I returned home and was placed in the tenth grade. Fulton Night School sent my transcript to the Free School administration office. While the schools in Prince Edward County were closed, many of our friends went away to continue their education, and it was obvious when the Free School opened that they had not suffered as much as we had educationally. In July 1965, I got married. I graduated in 1966.

I went to work at Stackpole Components in Farmville. In the early 1970s I started attending classes at Southside Community College. After I got started, I encouraged my sister, Osa, to enroll. I earned a degree in Business Management. Then I entered Longwood College and earned a bachelor's degree in Business Administration. I entered Virginia State University and earned a master's degree in Business Administration.

I worked at Stackpole Components for eighteen years. After the local Stackpole Components branch closed, the company wanted workers to go to North Carolina, but I did not want to move to North Carolina. I submitted an application to Longwood College and was hired to work in the science department.

When you miss the foundation in elementary school and junior high, you can tell it when you enroll in a college program. In college everyone I matriculated with had twelve years of schooling and I basically had eight. I missed four full years.

As of the time of this interview in November 2004, I teach in Mecklenburg County at Bluestone Senior High School.

My sister and I attended Southside Community College, Longwood College and Virginia State University together at my insistence. As of the date of this interview, we plan to enroll in a Ph. D program together.

Through it all God has been good to me. Everywhere God has placed me God has reminded me that education alone is not enough.

BARBARA ANN BOTTS CHAPMAN

After arriving at the home of Mrs. Barbara Ann Botts Chapman in Richmond, Virginia, on June 26, 2011, she introduced me to her mother. Then we moved to the dining room table. Mrs. Chapman commenced:

It is interesting that you are doing this particular project. It is a story that needs to be told, but it is a story that is very painful for many of us to tell. I am surprised that I have not written anything because I am capable.

"I believe you will write in the future," the Editor encouraged, sensing the seriousness of her comment and having heard so much about her over the years.

Mrs. Chapman resumed.

When the schools were closed, I was probably twelve years old. I started school when I was seven because my birthday was in October. I started school at Felden, a one room school-house and I guess twenty or twenty-five children were there. I attended Felden through the fifth grade. The next year

I went to Mary E. Branch which started at sixth grade. Branch was in the town of Farmville. I finished sixth grade and the next year the schools did not open.

I had done very well in school. Everyone was shocked when the schools were not opened. I don't know the politics of that time and cannot talk intelligently about what transpired.

The first year the schools were closed, 1959–1960, I didn't go to school. I spent a lot of time at the Beulah African Methodist Episcopal Church reading. They had a reading room. It was a small room with a lot of old books. We could check out books and sit there and read. This was the first year of the closing and I must have read nearly every book on the shelves. My mom (Mrs. Geneva Adele Redd) did day's work in town and when she went in to work she would leave me at the reading room. Mom had a car and drove to work. I would read all day. I don't remember anything about lunch. I may have had lunch, but I don't remember.

"Were any of the elementary school age children at Beulah?" the Editor asked, trying to determine whether a Training Center was set up in that church during the first year of the school crisis.

I don't remember the elementary age children being in class at Beulah the first year the schools were closed.

All during the year I kept asking Mama when was school going to open.

At the end of the year we began to hear about students going off to school. I heard about students going to Kittrell. Mama mentioned it to me, but we learned that the older students were attending. We heard about the American Friends coming to town and talking to children about going to school.

Mama heard about the program and said we were going to inquire. We went to a meeting. I think the first gathering we attended was in the basement of First Baptist Church. We listened to the presentation and them talk about sending children away to go to school. I was excited, and Mom was interested. When we told them how old I was, they hesitated because most of the children they were going to send to host families in other States were older. I am not sure what transpired, maybe me begging my Mom; I guess they saw how interested I was in school. I was accepted in the placement program.

Mama borrowed money from her mother, Katherine Redd, to purchase clothes and necessities for me to go away.

That September (1960) Mom and I got on a Greyhound bus and went to Moorestown, New Jersey. There were other Prince Edward County students that went to New Jersey, but they were not on the bus with us. We got to New Jersey and met the Black family I was to live with for the school year. The lady was a teacher, a middle school teacher I believe. I am unsure what the husband did for a living. They had three children, one girl close to my age.

The family was nice to me. I started middle school and that was a total shock. I had been an honor roll student my entire school career. Talk about bullying and being picked on, the kids made fun of my accent, the way I dressed, I had pimples on my face, and I was rather skinny. I withdrew, it was not easy. I went from making all A's and a B to C's and maybe a B.

It is hard for me to remember a lot of what happened that year. Being uprooted was traumatic and I tried to block things out. I do remember going to a Woolworth store with the girl in the family. I remember the manager saying: "What are you Niggers in here trying to steal?" I had never been called a Nigger. We ran out of the store. I am not sure whether the girl with whose family I lived had ever been called a Nigger.

I came home Christmas of 1960. When it was time to go back in January, it was so traumatic and painful.

I remember attending a Methodist church in New Jersey. I was baptized at New Witt Baptist Church on Route 15 near Worsham (Prince Edward County) and was only familiar with the Baptist tradition. In June 1961 I came home for the summer.

The Prince Edward County public schools remained closed and in September 1961 the American Friends sent me to another family in New Jersey. The husband was a military member assigned somewhere unknown to me. He was not in the home. I only knew he was in the military. The couple had two small children. I was basically the babysitter for the children. I had a lot of responsibility, taking care of the children and cleaning the house, and whatever else she told me to do. That was a very lonely year. The first year I went away was challenging, but this year was lonely because after school I went back home and took care the children and cleaned house. I had very little interaction outside the home. I resented being used as a babysitter and a house cleaner.

I don't remember too much about this year either. Nothing in particular stands out in my mind.

In the fourth year of the closing of the schools and the third year Mom allowed me to go away, September 1962–June 1963, I went to Newton, Massachusetts, and lived with a White family. Dr. Kurt M. Hertzfeld was the vice president at a university. His wife was named Nora. They had to my recollection three or four children.

Each year Mama rode with me to the new location where I was to start school. I always came home at Christmas by myself.

The experience in Newton was interesting in many ways.

It started getting cold in October and did not warm up until May. The Hertzfeld family lived in a big white house up on a hill and all the Black people lived in an area sort of like at the bottom of the hill. There was a name for the section at the bottom where the Black people lived, but I can't remember the name. I remember Mrs. Hertzfeld put forth an effort for me to go and socialize with the Black people at the bottom of the hill. I was about fifteen, closer to sixteen now and was interested in boys. I wanted to go to the parties and wanted to be with the Black folk in the area. I did not always keep curfew and sometimes she (Mrs. Hertzfeld) had to come and look for me at the bottom of the hill.

I remember doing reasonably well in school in Newton. I think I was enrolled at Warren Junior High. I had an English teacher who thought I could write real good. He was a White male. I remember doing a paper. I selected the topic and it was on environment verses heredity; regarding intelligence, whether it was from our environment or whether we inherited it or was a combination. I got an A on my note-cards and an A on my paper. That made me so happy. I felt like I was coming back into my own. (Mrs. Chapman had a big smile on her face when telling this part of her story.) I still have the note cards. They are somewhere here in the house.

I remember the Hertzfelds' were very nice to me. I saw them as being intense intellectual people.

I returned home in the summer of 1963 and that was the summer Reverend Francis L. Griffin began youth non-violent demonstrations in the county. This is the story that I feel has not been told. Demonstrations were taking place all over the country. The story of other communities during the summer of 1963 has been told. Our story from Prince Edward County has not been told.

People came to the county to train us. The trainers were SNCC people, mostly young men as I remember. There may have been some women. We would spend all day practicing and learning, learning and practicing non-violent demonstration techniques. Anticipating we would be touched, they taught us how to sit on the ground and hold ourselves, so we would not move and make it difficult for anyone to pick us up. They taught us how to roll up in a ball and tuck our heads, so no one could beat us in the head.

We made picket signs at Beulah AME Church and First Baptist Church. We would practice all day long. We would practice on the sidewalk of the church. We learned the songs of the Civil Rights Era.

At some point we began to put the training into practice. When they deemed we were ready, they took us to the main streets and we began to picket stores and restaurants that would not serve us. Our whole focus was to draw attention to the fact that the schools were still closed, and we could not go to places where other people could go.

One Sunday twenty-three of us went to worship at Farmville Baptist on Main Street. Of course, they would not allow us to enter. The church was near the courthouse and the juveniles were taken there. They called our parents to come and get us. They cautioned our parents to take us out of the demonstrations. My mother came and got me.

The next day we were back downtown picketing. When Mama left home Monday morning, I was in the car with her. She had an old Plymouth. She dropped me off at First Baptist Church and all she said when I got out of the car was: "Be careful."

To let you know how supportive my mother was of me and how brave I saw her as being at this time, I will tell this story.

She was doing day's work for the Paulette family. The man of the house was the post master for Farmville. One of my girl-friends had a car and we went up to my mom's job. The girl was going rather fast and spinning gravel. Mr. Paulette came out yelling: "Who do you all think you are driving up in my yard like that?" My mom came out and said to him: "Who do you think you are yelling at my daughter like that?" It did not dawn on me until years later what she had done, speaking to her sole employer like that.

During this time, there were older Black people who ignored us and went on into the stores to shop. I asked Mama 'why would they continue to go in when what we were doing was to benefit them'. She explained that they came to town when they could and had to shop where possible. Mama understood both sides. She understood their perspective and supported what we, the teenagers, were doing.

People were getting arrested all the time. The authorities always turned the juveniles over to their parents, but the older ones among us were arrested. We demonstrated the whole summer of 1963.

I was so caught up in the demonstrations. It was so exciting and exhilarating. I had not given returning to Massachusetts or going anywhere else to school any thought. We had spent the whole summer demonstrating for the reopening of the schools and it never occurred to me that I was going anywhere for a fourth year of school other than in Prince Edward County.

The Free School opened. I was seventeen and in the tenth grade. There was a lot of excitement. Robert Kennedy came. We had great teachers. They seemed to be the most important people I ever met in the classroom. They seemed to have been so important and had come to teach us.

I graduated in the spring of 1966 at age nineteen. I had a full scholarship to Virginia State College and I said—'No way!' I turned it down. My mother did not know I had turn down the scholarship. They announced at graduation that I had won the scholarship. I had had enough of school. The one year without school, the year I read in the reading room at Beulah, the three years away in the Friends program, all contributed to my decision.

Having declined the scholarship, I went to Philadelphia and lived with relatives. I got a job as a long distance telephone operator with Bell Telephone Company. I did that for about three years and then returned to Farmville. I worked at Stackpole in Quality Control. I decided I could not do that and left Farmville and came to Richmond. I knew no one in Richmond. I had a distant cousin in Farmville, Magnolia Hayes, who knew a lady in Richmond with whom I could live. I got a room with that lady and enrolled in key-punch school. I got a job with C & P Telephone working as a key-punch operator. I did this for about three years and while I was doing this, I asked myself—"Is this what you are going to do with the rest of your life?" I started attending J. Sergeant Reynolds Community College. I was about twenty-seven years old now. I went there for two years and majored in Education. I graduated Summa Cum Laude. I got married to Robert Gillyard and transferred from Reynolds to Virginia Commonwealth University. I majored in English Education. After graduating I started teaching English in the Richmond Public Schools. I taught three years at Parks School. I returned to Virginia Commonwealth University and earned a Master in Guidance Counseling Degree. I was a counselor for about fifteen years in the Richmond Public Schools and was named assistant principal. I returned to school at George Washington

- 444 -

and earned a Doctorate in Education. I was later named principal at a middle school. I did that for five years and then I retired.

————

MARY VIRGINIA PEACE

I was born February 8, 1947, and my parents took me out of Prince Edward County six weeks later. I was in Washington, D. C. when the schools were closed. My grandmother, Mrs. Mammie Smith, never left the county.

When I heard the schools were closed, I was outraged even though I was not living in Prince Edward County at the time. I was outraged because all of my cousins who still lived in the county were impacted.

Polly Thornton (Struthers), Marcellus Thornton, Marshall Thornton, Ava Marshall, Norma Jean Marshall, Angela Neversome, Norm Neversome, and the list goes on of cousins, and friends, who had to leave home and live with strangers or relatives or make other adjustments to get an education.

Some students went away and lived with host families for one year and refused to return the next school year. Some students went away to live with families and only stayed a few weeks. They were so young, and all were home sick. The homesickness and absence of family was too much for many of them to bear. Many had the resolve to go and live among strangers as children and do well in school.

I have a cousin who is fifty-seven years old. I will not give his name. But he was telling us recently all that he endured while separated from his parents and living with a strange family, and how he cried and cried. He could not take it. He was living with a nice family and in a nice community, but blood family cannot be replaced. My cousin quit whatever program he was in that had sent him away and he returned home. People can see the Prince Edward County story on television and read about it in articles and books, but they cannot feel it. Only those who lived it and lived through it can feel it.

In 1963 when the Free School opened, my sister, Gwen (Williams), my brother, William Harris, and I came to Prince Edward County to live with our maternal grandmother, Mrs. Mammie Smith. My mother, Mrs. Nellie Smith Jeffries, remained in Northern Virginia and sent money to help support us. I was placed in the eleventh grade. The students who were eighteen, nineteenth, and twenty-years old and in tenth, eleventh and twelfth grades had a fire in them. They wanted to learn. They knew what had happen to them and refused to take learning lightly.

When my mother returned to the county in the mid or late 1960s, she became known as a one-woman army. She ran a literacy program out of Mercy Seat Baptist Church and addressed any injustice that came before her.

I know the Editor of this work has interviewed many people and allowed each individual to tell their story for publication, but the truth of the matter is — No one can put into words the Prince Edward County story and the impact the closing of the schools had on families, individual lives, and future careers.

———

JAMES ALLEN

I was born April 20, 1934, to Gracie Allen. My public school education began at Mercy Seat School. Mrs. Addie Marshall was my first teacher. She was from Prince Edward County. Mrs. Marshall also taught a Sunday School class at Mercy Seat Baptist Church where my family attended. In those days a teacher may have taught you in school during the week and in Sunday School at church on Sunday.

Mercy Seat School went to the seventh grade, after which time we went into town to Moton High School. When I passed to the eighth grade, I went to R. R. Moton (now the Museum). I went to the eighth grade around 1948. Mrs. Connie Rawlings was my homeroom teacher. I think it was eighth grade that she was my homeroom teacher.

I loved school and my classroom work, but I also developed a love for athletics when in high school. I played football, baseball, basketball and ran track. Mr. Watson was the main coach. I cannot remember his first name. Mr. C. B. Woods was also a coach. He coached football. I was a halfback on the football team or what they now call a running back. Mr. Truman was the basketball coach. On the baseball team I played left field. I was a guard on the basketball team.

The local all White school board never appropriated any funds for the athletic program at Moton High School. We received from Farmville High School, the all White high school, the hand me down football shoes with cleats and other second hand, worn out sports equipment and attire. My parents paid taxes as did other Negro parents, as we were called in that era, but the White people took the tax dollars and spent it for the most part on the development and advancement of their children.

I lived in Hampden Sydney. I had a choice of riding one of two school buses each morning. One bus came from Darlington Heights and another from the New Hope area. If I missed one bus, I could catch the other.

One afternoon in 1951 while riding home on the bus that went to the Darlington Heights area, I happened to sit by Barbara Johns. She lived in Darlington Heights. I was not into school politics and had no idea of any plans that were being laid by Barbara. On this particular day while riding home she sort of filled me in. Barbara told me what was being planned and asked me would I consider being a leader when it was time to go to the shacks (the dilapidated huts outside that were used as classrooms) and tell the students we were walking out. Barbara said she would take my name back to her committee as one of the persons nominated to alert the student body when it was time to walk out. The next day she told me my name had been approved by her committee. Barbara obviously thought by me being an athlete that would win the students and they would follow instructions and walk out when told. After I had been selected and approved by her committee to be a runner, Barbara told me the whole plan. She told me about the telephone call that was to be made and so forth.

I don't know who made up Barbara's inner circle. I know John Stokes and his sister, Carrie, were in her inner circle. I believe Barbara's committee was comprised of several of the student council members.

On the day of The Strike there was an assembly in the auditorium. The assembly ended, and the students went back to their classrooms. Students that had classes in the outdoor shacks returned. When I was alerted, I started making the rounds to the shacks and announced that the students were walking out. The students had already been alerted about The Strike during the assembly. My task was to go to the shacks and tell them the time to walk out had arrived. Someone else or some others alerted the students in the main building that it was time to walk out.

I was raised by my grandmother, Margaret Fowlks Allen. I had an aunt and uncle in high school the same time I was a high school student. Florence Allen, was the aunt, and my uncle was Herman Allen. Florence was a grade ahead of me and Herman was in my class. When we got home the afternoon of The Strike, my grandmother asked us did we believe in what we were doing, and we said, yes. Grandma said she would support us.

A meeting was held at First Baptist Church and I became acquainted with the NAACP and became involved with that group. I remember one of the lawyers saying—"We are going to take care of you children." That impressed me.

Florence, Herman, and I were plaintiffs in the Prince Edward County case of Davis *vs* Prince Edward County.

In most cases, what I have read about The Strike is accurate. One of my concerns is that you only hear one side of the story.

Also, I have engaged in much reflection over the years about The Strike. In retrospect, I recall Barbara always told me things about her uncle (Reverend Vernon Johns) and some of the things he was going through. Writers and local citizens have speculated about who was guiding Barbara Johns, as she planned, organized, and implemented The Strike. Looking back on it all, I believe her uncle, Reverend Johns, was giving her counsel to some degree.

After high school, I moved to New Jersey. I worked a little while and then I enlisted in the United States Army. After being honorably discharged, I enrolled in college at Johnson C. Smith in North Carolina. I married Angelena Elliott of Fayetteville, North Carolina.

When the schools were closed in September 1959, I was living in New Jersey. I had fifteen or twenty young cousins from the Hampden Sydney area who were impacted by the closing.

One of my cousins, Gretna Carpenter, went to Kittrel College in North Carolina, when the schools were closed. Gretna was my Aunt Margaret's daughter.

We have heard very little about the people who closed the schools. They should tell their story and tell the truth. It is only when they tell their story that we can get a fuller understanding of events.

I earned a master's degree in Business Administration from Rutgers University. I worked for the state of New Jersey as a tax auditor. I lost my first wife around 1986. I later married Carol Taylor. I have six children and nine grandchildren.

I was instrumental in getting my classmates together for a reunion forty-seven years after high school. As a result of my work with that effort, I was asked to serve on the Board of the Moton Museum. As people have an opportunity to read this story and the stories of others associated with The Strike or the closing of the public schools in Prince Edward County, I hope readers will also have an opportunity to visit the Moton Museum.

MEHERRIN

BERTHA EARLEY SHEPPERSON

I was in born in Prince Edward County. We lived in Meherrin and New Bethel Baptist was the church we attended. Reverend Williams was the pastor when I was a girl. We went to church on the wagon with the mules pulling. There were nine of us and we were often late by the time Mother got us ready. I was born March 2, 1934. During the week, we waked to school which was about three miles. That was New Bethel School. It was a two room school. Mrs. Eloise Brown was my first teacher. There was also Virso School in Meherrin, it was a two room school. Both schools went to the seventh grade. After seventh grade, we went to R. R. Moton High School. By the time I completed seventh grade, 1946 or 1947, there was a bus to take children from Meherrin to Moton in Farmville. Before this time, students who wanted to go beyond seventh grade had to go to Farmville and board with a family. My aunts and cousins had to do this. They were in the Earley family.

I started eighth grade at Moton. The bus traveled a long route. There was one bus that went to the Zion Hill area, New Witt area, and on to Moton High School. We had no lunch room. We had no gymn. On rainy days we did exercise in the auditorium, the chairs would be taken down. For lunch you had a choice of milk and cinnamon buns which you had the option of buying.

More and more students began to attend the high school.

The White administrators came up with the tarred paper shacks on the lawn. These were one room shacks with an oil heater and the finishing on the outside was the finishing like they used on the rooftops. These shacks had lights and the heater was inadequate. Students had to wear their coats and hats during the winter. In the spring it was unbearably hot. This lasted up until I graduated.

I was in the walk out. We considered Barbara our leader. In the classes sometimes there would be discussions of 'what if questions'. These what if discussions stirred us to serious thought. The students initiated the questions because they felt comfortable talking about such issues with one particular teacher, I can't remember the teacher's name. Barbara got with other students individually. When she got it to the group, it was all arranged. People were appointed for various tasks. Someone was responsible for getting the principal away from the building. Once he was away, that opened the door for the assembly. The principal was M. Boyd Jones. Someone successfully got him away from the school by way of telephone. While Mr. Jones was downtown, everyone was notified to come to an assembly. We waited for Barbara to give directions. Some students went home on buses. The students who lived in town, Farmville, marched on to the superintendent's office, which was located in the courthouse at this time. Somehow Barbara's personality allowed her to rise up and be accepted by the students as the leader for this event. I didn't march to the courthouse.

Barbara had a committee. This group or committee did the talking and this group stayed together. Academically things returned to normal, but Barbara and her group continued to negotiate with the school administration along with the parents.

I graduated in 1952 and I went to Hempstead, Long Island.

I had several brothers and a sister impacted by the school closing: Frank, Deloris, Vincent, Phillip, and Carolyn. Frank went to the Quakers in Ohio. My sister Deloris went to Hampton, Virginia, to an aunt; my father's sister, Sara Branch. Deloris went to public school in Hampton. Phillip, Vincent, and Carolyn stayed at home.

Carolyn was not school age when the schools closed. When the schools reopened she was nine.

My mother's philosophy was each generation was to do better than the last. When the schools opened back up, one child said, 'I don't want to go back to school,' feeling he was too old. Mama said, 'you might feel you're too old, but you'll go to the school and go to the basement and help the janitor put coals in the furnace, and you'll stay in school all day'.

Daddy would raise a garden and share with Reverend Griffin and his family. Daddy had no money but shared from his garden.

Many children today have no interest in education, but perhaps if they knew the story they would have a greater interest in education.

SHIRLEY ELOISE WALTON
WATSON JENNINGS

I was born in 1937 and started my education in a two room in Meherrin called Virso. We had the potbelly stove and students were assigned to make the fire when the weather was cold. There was no running water at Virso School. We took a bag lunch and in my early school years students went to a spring to get water to drink. The boys would bring the water back in a pale. I graduated from Virso and then attended Moton High School in the early 1950s.

There were some ladies in the area that did some teaching while the Prince Edward Schools were closed. The classes were held at New Bethel. I don't remember the ladies who did the teaching, but I believe Mrs. Josephine Henderson was one of them. The ladies who worked with the children weren't certified trained teachers. They were adults from right around here who were concerned about our boys and girls and did what they could to make a difference. I don't remember how many days a week the children went to New Bethel for class. My son, Cecil, went sometimes.

I wept for Cecil because he wasn't able to start school in first grade on time. My heart went out especially for the children who were already in school and couldn't complete their education.

My husband and I couldn't afford to send Cecil away. We were too poor. Our other children weren't school age yet.

SARA DELORIS EARLEY

Emerson and Susie Earley were my parents.

I started my public education at New Bethel School in Meherrin, which went to the fifth grade. When promoted to the sixth grade, New Bethel students went to Branch No. 2 in the town of Farmville. Branch No. 2 went to the seventh grade. When promoted to the eighth grade, students left Branch No. 2 and went to Moton High School eighth through twelfth grades.

When I was in the seventh grade, there was an annual day called The Seventh Graders Day. It was a day of celebration. In the spring of the year the seventh grade students were transported from Branch No. 2 to Moton High School so they could see where they were going to high school the next school year. We enjoyed our visit to the high school that day in the spring of 1959. The day my class went over to see where we would be attending high school we went to the cafeteria and were served fish sticks and a carton of milk, following our tour of the facility. I distinctly remember these two items being served. Eating in a cafeteria was exciting, since we did not have one at Branch No. 2. We got to talk to the high school students that day and they made us feel welcome. We started looking forward to the next school year. As the 1958-1959 school year was coming to a close, we seventh graders, on the way to the eighth grade, were psychologically prepared to go to high school in September 1959. We were in the high school mental state.

Well, we never made it to R. R. Moton High School because the public schools were closed. It was rumored that the schools would be closed. The White leadership pad-locked the doors at the schools. My parents were civil rights workers. When the schools didn't open in September 1959, my parents were somewhat calm and accepted the closing, believing it would only last for one year at the most. Most of the Negro children, as we were called during that time, stayed home during the 1959-1960 school year. Some boys and girls left home.

In my family the children were Frank, Vincent, and Truman who family members called Phillip, myself and our youngest sister Carolyn. We all stayed home for the entire school year. Carolyn was not impacted at the time because she was young and had not started school.

During the 1959-1960 school year, Frank, Vincent, Philip and I were at home. Mom would pull out a book and say read this or that. We would sit by the fire in the winter and read. This was the extent of our home schooling.

In the summer of 1960, June, July, and August, I was engaged in the greatest amount of learning that I had received in almost a year. A White male instructor came to Farmville. He was from Dartmouth College and taught an English course. He was a teacher by vocation. Those three months with him were the most intense days of learning for me during the 1959-1960 school year. I remember coming into town to many of his sessions, but do not remember where the classes were held. It may have been at First Baptist Church where Reverend L. Francis Griffin was the pastor.

During the summer of 1960, there were several organizations in Farmville saying they would take children and arrange for them to continue their education. The Quakers, other organizations, and just every day citizens expressed a willingness to take a child or children and see to it that their educational development was continued. Parents were making arrangements to send their children away to continue their education. Separations took place and numerous friendships ended. I was separated from many of my girlfriends. Some people I never saw again.

There was a family in Pennsylvania that would have taken me, but my mother said no. I didn't know it at the time, but my mother had already spoken to my father's sister, Sara Branch, who lived in Hampton, Virginia. Aunt Sara and Uncle Thomas said they would be glad to keep me. They had a daughter, Sandra, who was near my age. I went to Hampton and Aunt Sara and Uncle Thomas threw their arms around me and life went forward. I didn't feel good about leaving home. There were many tears and it was not easy.

Virginia had passed a law called Pupil Placement. If you went to school in Prince Edward County, your parents paid taxes there and that was the only county where you could go to school. When my aunt learned I was coming, she went to the school board in Hampton and they said I could not attend the public schools in that city because my parents didn't pay taxes there. Aunt Sara registered me in the school system in Newport News, only a short distance from Hampton. Someone there told Aunt Sara what to do to negotiate the system and then she enrolled me at Y. H. Thomas Junior High in Hampton. Sandra was in ninth grade and I was in the eighth, having missed a year of school. I was older than she.

I wrote home almost every day. My parents were farmers and didn't have a telephone, which was the reason why I wrote home so often. Mama and Daddy had a car, but never drove it long distances.

When in Hampton, Aunt Sara and Uncle Thomas made sure that Sandra and I went to Sunday School. On Sunday morning, Sandra and I caught a bus to Sunday School in Newport News. We rode the Baptist bus from Aberdeen Gardens. We rode to the Baptist church, got off and walked on to Saint Paul Methodist, I think it was AME, on Jefferson Avenue. Aunt Sara and Uncle Thomas came to the worship service and we rode back with them. After church sometimes we went to McDonald's where a shake was twenty-five cents and a hamburger was fifteen cents.

My birthday was January 19. Mama told Aunt Sara that

my favorite cake was Pineapple Coconut. Aunt Sara made that for me each year on January 19, while I lived with her. (Tears began to swell in the eyes of Ms. Earley. Soon a stream of water flowed underneath both eyes. She quietly and mysteriously made a handkerchief appear in one of her hands. She wiped the tears and continued her story.)

After Y. H. Thomas Junior High School, I went to Phenix High School. Phenix was more challenging for me than Thomas. There were a lot of students at Phenix. I looked forward to attending football games. It gave me something to do on Friday. I also joined the choir at Phenix High School. Mr. Charles Crump came to me one day and said try the choir. He knew I couldn't sing, but probably knew of my circumstance and allowed me to join. Once in the choir, I developed a love for the choir more so than singing. Life was lonely for me. We traveled a lot. We went to Petersburg, Richmond, and other areas to sing.

I did not sleep well, but I did well in school. Uncle Thomas was very pushy and strict on the grades. I'm not sure that I was allowed to get a D in anything.

When school was in session, I came home once a year and that was at Christmas, when the public schools were in recess until the New Year. My brother came home from Ohio at Christmas. Frank always beat me home by a day even though I was right in Virginia. I had to ride the Greyhound bus. At that time everything southbound connected in Richmond, Virginia. Sometimes I missed several buses and had to remain in Richmond until I made a connection. I was fourteen years old and couldn't push through the crowds at the bus terminal. I saw my first flasher* in Richmond at age fourteen, while sitting in the bus station.

One year I met a fellow who came out of school with my

older brother. He lived in New York. The young man saw me in Richmond and took me under his wings. He got me up to a bus and left. I guess he thought I got on the bus, but I missed that one also.

Going back to Hampton after Christmas break was okay. The bus ride was long and quiet, but leaving my family was always a strain. Leaving home was always the hardest.

When school ended in May or early June, I came home for the summer. I always returned to Hampton one day before school started so I would not have to wait too long before the first day of school and it gave me more time at home.

Within a short time, I was out of school twice and Aunt Sara had to write me an excuse. The excuse was signed Sara Branch. Upon reading the excuse and noticing the last name was different from mine, the principal or assistant principal, I forget which, found me. He had some papers in his hand and asked:

"Who are your parents?"

I told him, and he took the papers and went away. Someone who knew my situation explained to him what was happening in Prince Edward County. He understood and aided me. Many people around Virginia at that time knew nothing about the closing of the Prince Edward County public schools. The science teacher came to the classroom after this encounter and told the class the Prince Edward County story. The administration at Phenix High School became my silent supporters. They were no longer concerned about Virginia law, they wanted justice. They were not willing to uphold the law and cripple a student.

One day all the teachers at Phenix High School got together and discussed the Prince Edwards County school situation and me. All of them became my supporters. The leadership put forth every effort to protect me and make sure my education was not interrupted a second time.

I came back home in 1963, when the Free School opened. I went to R. R. Moton High School. The educational program was called Free School because we didn't have to buy books or lunch. Our parents didn't have to pay for anything. The buses were school buses, but the drivers weren't paid from local tax dollars, neither was gas purchased with local tax dollars, and the salary of teachers came from another source. The Prince Edward County school case was still in court, as the local school board said it was not supporting public education. I was in the eleventh grade at this time. I graduated in 1965. Had the schools not closed I would have graduated at age 19, but I finished at a later age.

I did not go to college and that was by choice. I didn't seek admission to college because I did not want to leave home again. My parents were prepared to assist me in getting a college education. In fact, they wanted me to go to college, but I made a promise to myself never to leave home again. I told Mama and Daddy that I was not leaving home anymore. I'm not sure whether they fully understood, but they accepted my decision. (Sara told this part of her story with power. The Editor sensed and could feel the beauty and commitment in her decision.) I am taking college courses now, May 2003.

I am the first Black female to serve in uniform in the courts and civil process in Prince Edward County.

———

*A flasher was a person who had on no clothes but wore an overcoat. The man would go before a person or group of people and quickly unbutton his long coat and show himself to whomever was watching. The flasher flashed himself and disappeared.

———

VINCENT LOWELL EARLEY

On Saturday, June 5, 2004, the Editor journeyed to Prince Edward County and drove to Meherrin in the afternoon, having never been to this community, but hearing about the New Bethel School. Seeing the church marquee, the Editor turned onto the grounds. A gentleman was driving away in his truck but stopped and inquired whether assistance was needed.

The Editor got out of his vehicle and explained the project and that he had in his possession a list of names of individuals who taught children in local churches and Learning Centers when the schools were closed, the list was discovered in the Archives at James Branch Cabell Library, Virginia Commonwealth University, Richmond, Virginia.

"Do you now Miss Josephine Earley or Mrs. Susie Earley?" the Editor asked showing the gentleman the list. The two of us were standing outside our vehicles that were parked close to each other.

"I know Miss. Josephine," he said scanning the paper. "I knew Mrs. Susie real well," he resounded with a degree of affection, compassion, and certainty the Editor recognized, "she was my mother. I'm Vincent Earley," he revealed, as we shook hands. Looking further over the list, Brother Earley said he recognized several other names and told me who was deceased and who was alive.

He unlocked the church, took me inside and told me his story.

I was born November 26, 1946. I started school at New Bethel School and Mrs. Eva Earley was the teacher. She was married to my uncle, Phillip Earley, and was my aunt by marriage.

I had passed to the sixth grade when the schools were closed and frankly had no idea there would be no school. During the summer we heard rumors that we would not be going back to school. I was twelve years old at the time. In reality, at twelve years of age I thought it was a blessing in disguise. I thought — 'Great, no school!'

I was at New Bethel which went to the fifth grade and was looking forward to going to school in Farmville. In the fall the doors were permanently locked, and no trespassing signs placed on the doors. The New Bethel School was on the grounds of New Bethel Baptist Church. The county took over the school several years earlier which was the reason why the doors were locked and could not be tampered with. The building belonged to the county.

There were nine children in my family and four were impacted by the closing of the public schools: Frank, Deloris, Phillip and me.

My older brother, Frank, went away to Yellow Springs, Ohio, in the Quaker program. Deloris went to Uncle Thomas in the Tidewater area. My brother Phillip Truman and I stayed home. Daddy was a farmer and we raised our own tobacco and sharecropped the White man's tobacco across the road. Daddy chose for me and Phillip to remain on the farm because we were the youngest. Frank and Deloris were the oldest, and parents wanted the older children in the family to continue their education, as they were the ones who would leave home soon to seek work and start a life as adults.

Phillip and I worked the farm the first year the schools were closed.

In the second year a Learning Center opened at New Bethel Baptist Church. My memory is not perfectly clear on the matter, but I think the center functioned primarily in the summer. When the Learning Center opened at New Bethel Baptist Church, I think Cousin Josephine was the leader because she had the most education, which was a high school diploma. Mrs. Florence Ayers was also a high school graduate. Mama was a helper at the Learning Center. My mother only went to the sixth grade, I think. Reverend B. F. Williams was the pastor and he lived in this community.

White students started coming in the summer from different colleges around the country to work with us. I only remember White college students coming to our area. I distinctly remember some students coming from Michigan State College, but I cannot recall any of their names. Classes were normally held in the evening or at night because most of us still had to do farm work during the day. This was the summer of 1962.

The college students came, if my memory serves me right, for two summers and I believe it was the summer of 1962 that they started appearing in our community to work with us. By the third year other programs had come about. I don't know who was financing the programs, but it was done privately. The programs really enriched the lives of the students whose families couldn't afford to send them away or who were not selected to participate in one of the programs that located homes outside of Prince Edward County to host children.

Then in the summer of 1963 we started hearing about the Free School that would open. No one knew if it would really happen. The buzz around was whether many students would go back to school. I wondered whether I would be put in the sixth grade at sixteen years of age. Many students were placed by age. I was placed in the eighth grade when the Free School opened. I didn't feel out of place because most of my peers were with me.

The students who went away and were able to continue their education without any serious interruption and returned to Prince Edward County when the Free School opened were on their proper grade level.

During the four years the schools were closed, there was unrest in the county. There were those who were trying to get the local White people to open the schools. There were marches in downtown Farmville, but they were non-violent marches. We marched to gain access to the theaters and restaurants and so forth. Voter registration was an issue also. The poll tax was still in and you had to take a test and be able to read in order to take the test; and I assume many of the Black adults couldn't read.

I was twenty-one years old when I graduated, and my parents insisted that we graduate. Phillip graduated and went on to college to Virginia State in Petersburg, Virginia.

Following our interview, Vincent said: "I'll take you to see Mrs. Ayers. She doesn't live very far from here. You just follow me. But I have to warn you, your car might get pretty muddy."

We left New Bethel Baptist Church, drove on the main highway a short distance and turned down a narrow dirt road. It had rained recently. We weaved from left to right to avoid huge puddles of water on the wet dirt road that dipped and rose and curved a few times before we reached the house. The journey took fifteen or twenty minutes. Mrs. Ayers was outside doing yard work when we arrived.

FLORENCE WOOD AYERS

"Ms. Ayers, how are you?" Brother Earley asked, as we got out our vehicles and began walking toward Mrs. Florence Wood Ayers who stopped working in the yard to greet us.

"I'm fine. How 'bout y'all?" Brother Earley and the Editor stated they were well.

"This gentleman wants to interview you about the time when the schools were closed, and you worked at the New Bethel Learning Center."

"That was a long time ago," she said, laughing. "I don't know how much I can remember."

"Just tell what you can remember," said the Editor. "Start with when you were born. Tell a little about your childhood and then continue." The Editor sat down on the steps, while Mrs. Ayers stood and talked. Brother Earley left us.

I was born in Prince Edward County, July 7, 1937, to Spencer 'Sonny' Wood and Beatrice Richard Wood. Really I was born on the 5th, but the birth certificate says 7 and for business purposes I have to use what is on the birth certificate.*

When I was a girl, I went to Mission School over in Meherrin. It was a two room school. My first teacher was Mrs. Crawley and then Mrs. Kerney. Mission was about two miles from where I lived, but we could cut through the woods and come out in the back of Mission School.

Then they started transporting us to Levi School in Green Bay. It was a two room school and Mr. James White and Mrs. Mammie Dell Brown were the teachers. There was another school in Green Bay called Mount Leigh, which was four or five miles from Levi School. Levi went to the seventh grade and then we went to R. R. Moton High School. We took our lunch in a little brown paper bag.

My father drove the bus when I went to Mission, Levi, and Moton. I rode with my father all my school years.

I finished Moton High School in 1955 or 1956. I graduated from the new big building. I went to New Jersey and went to school for IBM Key Punch Operator at Edythe Skinner Roger Secretarial School, One Foye Place, Jersey City, New Jersey, and then went to work for Western Electric in Kearny, New Jersey. I got married in 1957 or 1958.

I came back to Prince Edward County and I think I was here the year the schools were closed. Ms. Helen Baker and others had established the centers. The NAACP and the leading people in the community asked people to volunteer to work with the children.

I was contacted through Mrs. Alease Baker and later Mrs. Susie Earley approached and asked me to help teach the children. Mrs. Alease Baker was the first teacher at the New Bethel Baptist Church Learning Center. She worked alone for a while and managed the students. But as more and more parents brought their children, the numbers increased, and she needed help. Mrs. Baker contacted me about assisting her. Mr. Emerson Earley would drive to my home and pick me up each morning. I worked with the children from September to May.

The classes were held in the sanctuary at New Bethel Baptist Church. Mrs. Alease Baker had the higher grades, fourth, fifth, and sixth and even the high school students that came. I had the lower grades, first, second and third. I can't recall exactly, but either Mrs. Baker remarried or something came up that required her to stop working with the students.

Ms. Susie Earley came to work with me at the church. Ms. Susie took the lower grades and I took the higher grades that Mrs. Baker had. Mrs. Baker was a house wife at this time. She used to teach or was a substitute teacher in the school system.

We taught from the literature and books that people sent to Prince Edward County. We went from around 8:00 a. m. to 12:00 or early afternoon. We didn't go all day. The children brought their lunch and drank water from the pump on the yard. New Bethel Baptist had an outdoor toilet at the time and the children had to go outside to the restroom. We had an oil stove in the church for heat.

I don't recall teaching during the summer, I was busy getting my garden planted and working at home.

People all over would donate funds. We were given a very small financial donation for working with the children. One month you might have gotten $50.00 and the next month you may not have gotten anything. If contributions didn't come in to Ms. Helen Baker, we didn't get anything. The money wasn't the issue with us. We would have taught anyway because we cared about our children. People sent books and literature from everywhere. The literature was stored in the basement of Dr. Miller's building.

My husband Herbert and I returned to New Jersey, Jersey City, early in the summer of 1963. I worked with the children about three years. My sisters, Jean and Margaret Wood, and my brother, James Rufus all lived in Jersey City in the same apartment building. Herbert was out of work. He was a truck driver. My sisters and brother invited us to come to Jersey City and find work. My work with the children at New Bethel ended in the summer of 1963 when we left.

I returned to Prince Edward County in 1970. Mission School where I started as a girl was closed when all the one and two room schools were closed. My cousin, Henry Vaughan, bought the building and fixed it up as a house. His wife lives in it now.

When there is a problem, people need help and you should stretch your hand out to help, especially where education is involved. The mind needs to be active at all times in constructive things and I'm glad I was able to help the children in a constructive way.

----

*Many people across the South had dual days. The mother usually knew the birthday of a child. In rural areas sometimes several weeks elapsed before the mid-wife carried the information to the courthouse in town. It was common for the mid-wife who kept no journal or log to get the days mixed up, having delivered multiple babies.

SYLVIA FOWLKES

I was born September 13, 1957, at Southside Community Hospital, but my family's home was in Meherrin. My paternal grandmother and grandfather were raising me. They were farmers. Their names were Alice Fowlkes and Waverly Fowlkes.

When the schools were closed, I was two years old. When it was time for me to start kindergarten, the schools were still closed. I started kindergarten at Beulah AME Church on Main Street in downtown Farmville.

I had to come to Farmville and live with my father and stepmother on Hull Street. I stayed with them Monday to Friday and returned to Meherrin each Friday evening. My father would take me back. There were a lot of children that attended school at Beulah. I would say there was somewhere around fifty students at least. School was not held every day. It may have been something like Monday, Wednesday, and Friday. School was not a full day either.

We would go to Mary Branch No. 1 for recreation. I remember children used to come from Darlington Heights and other locations for recreation.

When the Free School opened, Worsham Elementary was opened. I entered the second grade. I had gotten a good foundation at Beulah. My second grade teacher was Mrs. Pierce. She was a Black teacher. If you got a low grade in math, she would line the students up, and, well, you can imagine what happened.

My sister, Phyllis, who was a few years older than I, went straight to either the fourth or the fifth grade when the Free School opened.

I was at Worsham Elementary from the second to the fifth grades. Worsham went to the fifth.

I graduated in 1975 from Prince Edward County High School, formerly R. R. Moton High School.

———

CECIL WATSON

I was born July 29, 1953. When I turned six years old and was ready to go to school, the schools were closed. I had been looking forward to starting school. I was the oldest child in the family. I think it was my parents who told me that I wouldn't be starting first grade.

I just stayed around home the four years the schools were closed. My parents couldn't afford to send me off to school. My father worked at the saw mill and traveled a lot to other counties to cut lumber. My mother was a house wife. My father and my mother were from Prince Edward County and had no relatives in other places where they could send me, so I could go to school. I never went to the classes in Farmville held at First Baptist Church or Beulah AME. I was just at home all day every day. My mother can probably tell more about the situation in Meherrin and whether there were any classes for children while the schools were closed.

Had the schools not closed I would have started first grade at New Bethel School near New Bethel Church in Meherrin. I think my mama dealt with some of the basics of school with us at home.

The Free School opened. I rode the school bus from Meherrin into Farmville. I was ten years old when I started school at Mary E. Branch No. 1 in September 1963.

I didn't feel any different being ten years old and in the first grade because I wasn't aware of the difference between myself and the other children in the class who were starting school on time; and no one ever told me about the difference. As far as I knew and understood things, I was just starting school and was where I was supposed to be. The other children in the class who were six or seven years old were just starting school also and were in first grade as they were supposed to be.

I enjoyed school and learning. I remember being skipped in the eleventh grade. I also remember having to take two history classes and two English classes at the same time when in twelfth grade. I graduated in June 1972.

I started working in Burkeville, which is not far from Farmville. I currently work in Prince Edward County as a school bus driver and I still live in Meherrin.

ALFRED FRANK WATSON

I was born in Baltimore, Maryland, September 20, 1940, to Frank Watson and Gloria Neal Watson. My father died when I was a boy and my grandmother, who lived in Meherrin, told Mama to send me and my brother, Ashley Neal Watson, to Virginia. Ashley and I went to live with our grandparents Ashley Neal and Mammie Hurt Neal.

I was eight years old when I moved to Meherrin and I started attending Virso School around 1948. It was a two room school that went to the sixth grade. It had no running water and an outdoor toilet. My teacher was Mrs. Lillie Franklin.

My first day in school a boy told me: "I'm goin' t' punch you in the nose."

He was too slow, and I punched him in the nose first. (Mr. Watson started laughing.) He had a real bloody nose. When I got home, Grandma beat me. Somehow, she found out about it.

When I was promoted to the seventh grade, I started going to school in town. I had to walk about a mile to the bus stop.

When the schools were closed, I had been promoted to

the twelfth grade. I got a job working at a lumber yard stacking lumber. I saved my money and a week before Mother's Day in 1960, I left Virginia and went back to Baltimore.

I got a job in Baltimore and also started taking night classes to get my high school diploma. Mama asked me one day:

"How are you going to work and go to school at night?"

"I don't know," I said, "but I have to do this. I need a diploma to get a job."

I received my high school diploma in 1961. I was hired at Bethlehem Steele Shipyard.

I stayed in Baltimore until June 1980. I came back to Prince Edward County that summer.

———

ANNIE MARIE OWENS DUNGEE

I was born in Meherrin in 1945 to Eva Owens. I started at Mission School. Mission School had two rooms and went to sixth or seventh grade. Mrs. Venessa Venerable was my teacher. She was the only teacher there. A parent would come and cook. Her name was Mrs. Lucile Wood. She lived in Meherrin. She did the cooking. They took one of the classrooms and made it like a cafeteria. Mrs. Wood made biscuits and hot rolls and cooked other dishes. We got together at school and made a garden on the grounds. When the vegetables were ripe we went out and she had us pick'em. She showed us how to work the garden. We planted string beans, onions, greens, peas, tomatoes, carrots and other healthy foods. Mission School had an outdoor toilet and a pump on the yard, but the school did have electricity. I think at least forty students attended Mission School because the families in the area were large.

When I left Mission School, I was going to Mount Leigh to the eighth grade. Mount Leigh was in Green Bay. That's where the county sent us. I went one year to Mount Leigh. Mount Leigh had two or three rooms, I think. My teacher at Mount Leigh was Mrs. Sarah White. Mount Leigh had a wood stove to give heat, but nobody cooked there. We took our lunch. Mount Leigh had an outdoor toilet. There was a pump on the school yard for water.

After Mount Leigh, I went to R. R. Moton in 1958 for one year. When school ended in 1959 and recessed for the summer, I went to New York and worked. When I came back home near the end of the summer to get ready for school to open, I found out the schools wouldn't open in September. I was hurt because I was rather smart.

When the schools closed, I was hoping to go somewhere and finish up. My grandmother was too poor to send me away to school. My mother had a large family in Baltimore. I don't think she could'a taken one more. There were eight children already in the house in Baltimore and I would'a made nine children, plus the mother and the father.

I didn't attend any classes the four years the schools were closed.

When the Free School opened in September 1963, I was too old to be in eighth or ninth grade. When the Free School opened, I was eighteen years old. I think I was in the ninth grade when school closed.

I stayed in Prince Edward and worked in Charlotte Court House at the Moses Nursing Home. Then I worked in the peach orchards and tobacco fields. In 1966 I married Edward Dungee. He was from Prince Edward County, born in Prospect. We had two girls and two boys: James, Louise, Evelyn, and Johnny.

The honorary diplomas they gave out in the summer of 2003 really don' do nobody no good. I'm too old now to even get a job. If it hadn't been for Christ being on our side, I don' know where we would be. I'm in church every Sunday giving God the praise.

———

WILLIAM LEE STREAT

I was born in Lunenburg County, March 16, 1949, back behind Saint Matthew Lutheran Church. I was born a mile or two from the Prince Edward County line. When I was two or three years old, my parents Johnny Allen Streat and Ruth Louise Smith Streat moved to Meherrin. I started school at Saint Matthew Lutheran School. It went to the seventh grade. Saint Matthew was a Black Lutheran Church and the teacher at the school was Black. The school was in Lunenburg County and was about a mile from my house. Virso School and the other small schools in the Meherrin area was too far away for me to walk. The Lutheran school was the closest school to my house. So when I started school around 1955 I walked across the line from Prince Edward County to Lunenburg County to Saint Matthew School. Ms. Grayhab or Rahab, I can't remember her first name, Jackson was my first grade teacher. There was no principal, but only the teacher was at Saint Matthew. The school was a wooden school hooked on to the church.

When the Prince Edward County schools closed, I was still at Saint Matthew Lutheran School in Lunenburg County.

A lot of my cousins from Meherrin in Prince Edward County started coming to the Lutheran school. Dora Reed/Reid, (Mr. Streat was unsure of spelling of the last name), Patricia Streat, Rebecca Lee, Patricia Lee, and a whole bunch more. It's been a long time, but I remember that many of the children from Prince Edward County who started coming to the Lutheran school were high school students. The Lutheran school only went to the seventh grade, but there were Moton High School students in the eighth, ninth, tenth, and eleventh grade when the schools shut-down and they came to Saint Matthew. I guess the students and their parents felt it was better they come to the Lutheran school and do seventh grade work than do no school work at all and loose everything.

A lot of parents from Hampden Sydney would drive their children to Lunenburg to Saint Matthew. Parents used to drive a car load of children over to Saint Matthew from Hampden Sydney. A car load was as many children as the driver could fit into the car.

It was fun walking to school. It would be a crowd of us and all looked out for each other.

Many of the students in Farmville walked across the Cumberland County line to go to school in that county, but when it was found out that they lived in Prince Edward County they turned the students out of the schools in Cumberland County. The children from Meherrin and Hampden Sydney that attended the Lutheran school in Lunenburg County wasn' turned out or dismissed because Saint Matthew was a private church school.

After I finished the seventh grade at Saint Matthew, I went to Lunenburg Junior High. I attended there one year. At this time the order was being enforced that you had to go to school in the county where you lived. Since I lived in Prince Edward

County, I had to attend Moton High School. When the schools reopened, I went to Moton High School.

———

REBECCA LEE RANDOLPH

My mother was Mildred Stokes Lee and my daddy was Edward James Lee.

I have lived in Meherrin most of my life. In my younger days when schools were open, I attended Levi School, which had first to seventh grades. Levi School had two rooms. There was a divider that came down from the ceiling that separated the two rooms.

Our teachers were Mr. James White and Mrs. Mammie Dell Brown. I enjoyed that school. Mrs. Brown taught grades 1-4 and Mr. White taught 5-7. We brought our lunch from home. We were warmed by a potbelly stove in the winter.

After the Prince Edward County public schools were closed, I was out of the classroom in the public school for two years. Four of us in my family were impacted by the school closing. Patricia was a year under me, she had just passed to the sixth grade. Herbert, my brother, had passed to the ninth. My sister Joyce had passed to the tenth grade.

We heard other children in the community talking about the Lutheran School and our parents said: "You all go up there too." And we did.

During the first year the schools were closed, everyone in my family went to the Lutheran School. We walked to Saint Matthew in Lunenburg County. Mrs. Jackson was the piano player and led us in devotion and music. Reverend Ford was an old man and he taught where you could understand him. We learned the Lutheran catechism and we learned Lutheran theology.

Note of the Editor: "Do you know where Reverend Ford was from or what college he attended?"

I don't know where he went to school, but I believe he was from North Carolina. Reverend Ford was an old man at this time.

We also went there the second year the schools were closed. It has been so many years and time has erased some memories of specific events.

In the 1961-1962 school year, I was at Lunenburg High School, in Victoria. Victoria is in Lunenburg County. I had a cousin Mary Frances Watkins and her husband, Reverend Hayward Watkins, that lived in Lunenburg County. Mary Frances' mother (Ossie Lee) and my daddy were brother and sister. Mary Frances made the contacts in Lunenburg and got us to the right people. Mary Frances went and talked to Mr. Galvin Jenkins, the principal at Lunenburg High School and he agreed to let us come.

Once the door was opened for me, Joyce, Herbert and Patricia, that made it easier for others in our neighborhood to go to school. Three other families followed us. In the Reed family Shirley and Joe were the oldest two, they were in high school. In the Winkler family: Joyce, Arlean, Carlye, and James were all high school students. Ten students came out of my neighborhood and went to Lunenburg High School and all of us had missed two years out of the public school classroom setting. This was our first year at Lunenburg High School, but the third year of the school closing in Prince Edward County. I was placed in the eighth grade. The ten of us from my neighborhood in Meherrin were Prince Edward County students in Lunenburg High School.

When the bus rolled up to the school in the morning, other students didn't know where you got on or where you lived.

All the Lee, Winkler, and Reed children that went to Lunenburg High School would walk across the Lunenburg County line to catch the school bus each morning. When it rained, Daddy would carry us to the store on the Lunenburg side and the bus would pick us up there. The other families did the same thing. Everybody stuck together.

There were two exciting parts to being at Lunenburg High School. First, it was a joy to be back in school; and second, we came home every afternoon. We were at home in our house every night. Many children had to go away and live with relatives and came home on the weekend or once a month.

The next year, 1962-1963 school year, all ten of us returned to Lunenburg High School for another year. I was in the ninth grade. Joyce Lee and Carlyle Winkler graduated from Lunenburg High School in the May 1963.

Some students from Queens College in New York came and taught at Levi School in the summer of 1963. They taught us as best they could with the books they brought with them. We read a lot and we learned poetry and read poetry. The poem that I learned and that has stuck with me is *Mother to Son* by Langston Hughes:

Well, son, I'll tell you:
Life for me ain't been no crystal stair.
It's had tacks in it,
And splinters,
And boards torn up,
And places with no carpet on the floor —

Bare.
But all the time
I'se been a-climbin' on,
And reachin' landin's,
And turnin' corners,
And sometimes goin' in the dark
Where there ain't been no light.
So, boy, don't you turn back.
Don't you set down on the steps.
'Cause you finds it's kinder hard.
Don't you fall now —
For I'se still goin', honey,
I'se still climbin',
And life for me ain't been no crystal stair.

Stan Shaw was a student at Queens College and was the teacher at Levi School. I think we had four students in the class. I remember Emerson Hunt, Shirley Reed (Ray), Patricia Lee (Adams), and me.

When the Free School opened, I was in the tenth grade. Seeing old friends that you left four years earlier was exciting.

I'm the secretary for the Lunenburg High School Class Reunion of 1966, though I didn't graduate from that school, they still consider me being part of the student body. I graduated from R. R. Moton High School in the spring of 1966.

Some of the Queens College students returned to the county in October 2009 for a reunion.

Fifty years later, I remember the Lutheran catechism taught by Reverend Ford. I remember it to this day. When I visit Saint Matthew Lutheran Church today, I can still recite everything along with the congregation. I am Baptist by background.

Levi School is still standing and used today for a clothing closet to help families that are burned out or in need.

———

MABLE LEE RICHARDSON SMITH

My mother was Theodora Richardson Bettles Watkins and her mother was Ida Staples Richardson.

I went to Levi School when I was a girl. I remember graduating from Levi. My grandma made me a dress. She made the dress out of one of those sacks that the hog feed used to come in. I remember I was itching during the ceremony. Mrs. Mammie Brown was my teacher the year the schools closed.

When the schools didn't open in September 1959, my mother took us to her sister Rosa Richardson in Baltimore. Aunt Rosa lived at 2024 E. Preston Street. Mama took me, my brother George Watkins and my sister Dorothy Watkins. George was four and Dorothy was two at this time. My mother graduated from R. R. Moton High School. The tenth grade was as high as school went when she finished. She was the baby in a family of ten children and was the only one to graduate high school.

The next school year Mama died from a brain tumor. We were still living with Aunt Rosa. Mama was thirty-three when she passed. I remember Kennedy got killed and Mom died just before that. We was in school that day and school closed soon as the news was out about President Kennedy.

Mama's body was brought back to Meherrin. After the funeral, George, Dorothy, and I were separated but not by choice. They stayed in Meherrin with our daddy Gideon Lorenzo Watkins.

When I got back to Baltimore, I was sent to Aunt Bessie (Bessie Richardson Robinson). She lived at 2412 Reisterstown Road. Aunt Rosa was older and couldn't care for children, which was why I went to Aunt Bessie.

While in Baltimore, I attended Booker T. Washington and I went to 137.

In 1967 when I was sixteen I came back to Meherrin to live with my grandmother. I went to high school and then dropped out and went to the Job Corp. I got my GED and nursing certificate in the Job Corp. I came back to Prince Edward County in 1970.

In 1970 I went to Southside Skill Center in Crew, Virginia. I got my CNA (Certified Nurse Assistant). I worked as a nurse's assistant.

As of today, Friday, May 17, 2012, my husband Matthew of Green Bay is deceased. Matthew Warren Smith was his full name. Matthew was in the fourth grade when the schools shut-down. He stayed in Green Bay and didn't go back to school when the Free School opened.

Our daughter Sherre graduated from Prince Edward High School in 1988. I made sure she graduated. I was determined that somebody in my family was coming out of Prince Edward. Sherre Richardson Williams and her husband have blessed me with three grandchildren Sasha, Jasmine, and Justin.

————

WILLIE RICHARDSON

I started school at Levi School. Mrs. Mammie Dell Brown taught first through fourth grades and Mr. James White taught fifth, sixth and seventh grades at Levi School. This was a two room school, with two out houses; one for the girls and one for the boys. There was a pump on the yard. Sometimes we had to prime the pump and sometimes no water came out. When water did come out, we cupped our hands and drank. When you got good, you could take a sheet of paper and make a cup. We would challenge each other to see who could make the best cup. Sometimes red mud came out of the pump and sometimes a string of human hair. Some students thought the hair was from one of the dead people in the nearby cemetery.

Each school morning started with devotion and the Pledge of Allegiance. There was a board that separated the classes and this board was down for devotion and all of the students from Mrs. Brown's class and Mr. White's class shared in the morning activities together. After devotion, the board was put back up and the two teachers went on with their lessons.

There was a wood shed at the school and local people delivered wood and the county paid. There was a stove in each room. During the winter months, if your bus got to school first you had to make the fire. The day before you had to bring wood in and put in the wood box. There was a light, one bulb, dangling down from a cord. The school probably was built before electricity was provided to the area.

During the winter months in school, sometimes the kids got excited when the teacher said: "Tomorrow we will have a hot lunch." Usually students brought a biscuit or light bread or white bread with tuna or bologna on it. When Mrs.

Brown said, 'tomorrow we will have a hot lunch', that meant she was going to do the cooking during class on the stove in the classroom. She would say to the students: "I want you to bring a jar of tomatoes. I want you to bring a jar of peas, you bring some corn,' and so on. We were in the rural and most of the mothers did canning and had the foods named at home in jars. Mrs. Brown would bring the beef. She poured all the vegetable the students brought in the pot. By 12:00 or 1:00 p. m., the stew would be done. You had to bring your own bowl from home. Mr. White's class always got some of the stew.

During the spring, we made homemade ice cream at school. Mrs. Brown had an old-fashioned ice cream maker that you put the ice in and churn. The kids took turns churning, and by lunch the ice cream was ready. You took your turn churning. The top would come off the container. When the ice cream was being made and it was my turn to churn, I would stick my finger around the edges and get ice cream. The boys churned, not the girls. The girls served the ice cream.

We played marbles and got holes in the knees of our pants. Our parents would sew patches over the holes, and sometimes there were patches over patches.

We had a see-saw at school. It was a small log with a big log across it and we tried to knock each other off. We threw horse shoes also.

I had turn thirteen and was ready to go to high school. I was really excited about going to high school. We learned a little of the school closing that summer and that the schools might not open in September.

My uncle, Plenty Franklin Richardson, came to Meherrin to get his three sons who were living with our grandmother and take them back to Chicago to go to school. I sort of tagged along and they allowed me to go to Chicago with them. Uncle Plenty took me back also.

In Chicago I went to William McKinley High School and graduated eighth grade.

The next year, which was the second year of the closure of the schools, I was back in Meherrin with my grandmother. Uncle Plenty was having family problems and his family was breaking up. So, I didn't go to school the second year the schools were closed.

My mother was the baby of ten in her family. The third year the schools were closed a cousin called from Baltimore and told my grandmother: "That boy needs to be in school. Let me see what I can arrange." I went to Baltimore and attended Clifton Park and finished ninth grade. This was the third year of the school closing.

I passed to the tenth grade and remained in Baltimore. When the schools were closed for the fourth year, I attended Baltimore City College. It was actually a high school. In the tenth grade I had a chance to be on the JV wrestling team.

When the Free School opened, Grandma called and said: "All right, boy, you need to come on home, the schools open."

I came home and went to the eleventh grade. I was eighteen or going on eighteen.

I didn't have a big challenge when I returned home for school. Some students had been out of school for four years. There were children in the fourth and fifth grades who were fifteen years old.

Robert Kennedy was instrumental in getting the Free School in Prince Edward County. When teachers came to teach, they were from all over the country. Woodrow Packer was from Alabama. Mr. Cooley was from Lawrenceville, Virginia. We had outstanding teachers.

I graduated from Robert R. Moton High School in 1965.

After graduating from high school, I went to Baltimore to work during the summer. I got a job with Canada Dry Bottling Company. While there, I wanted to go to school and so I applied to Baltimore Community College.

One day someone called me and said he was Mr. Packer, Woodrow Packer. He taught eleventh grade U S History in the Free School. I guess he made telephone calls around Prince Edward County, located my relatives, and found out where I was living.

He said: "You were the only one who seemed interested in learning." Then he asked: "What are you doing?"

I said: "Working and getting ready to go to community college."

"No," he answered, "you are coming to Saint Paul's."

"I didn't apply."

"Don't worry."

"I have no money."

"Don't worry," he said again.

"When do I need to be there?"

"Monday."

This was around Wednesday when we had the conversation. I left Baltimore on Sunday on a Greyhound or Trailways bus for Lawrenceville, Virginia. I missed the last bus out of Richmond to Lawrenceville. I spent the night in Richmond and arrived at the campus on Monday. Mr. Packer was the Assistant Dean of Men and it was easy to find him.

When I found him, he said: "You missed your placement test."

I missed the English test, but another test was being given on Tuesday. I tested for Math and did well. I was just happy to be there. I got a janitorial job cleaning a building the first semester. The second semester I did well in school and worked. I returned to the soda company during the summer after my freshman year.

When I returned to Saint Paul's for my sophomore year, I was a janitor again. It was called Work Study. This was how I got through college. My major was Natural Science with a minor in Chemistry.

In the spring of 1967 I pledged Kappa Alpha Psi Fraternity. I was on line by myself. This experience made me tenacious and made me more independent.

In my junior year I became the waiter in the teachers dining hall.

In my senior year I was President of the Student Government.

I remember we had a sit-it or sit-out protesting the firing of Dean Law. I remember having a write up in the Richmond Times Dispatch Newspaper.

I graduated in May 1969. My grandmother Ida Richardson came to the graduation. My Aunt Bessie, Bessie Robinson who was my grandmother's second child, helped me buy a 1960 Thunderbird. Aunt Bessie supported me tremendously. I drove to Meherrin and picked up Grandma for the graduation.

I got married shortly after graduating.

After graduation, I got a job in the Shock Trauma Lab at the University of Maryland and drove cab. While working in the Shock Trauma Lab, my interest in medicine peaked. I was having lunch one day and a fellow had a bunch of books. He was a dental student. I made a few inquiries and the student told me what to do if I was interested in studying dentistry. I went to the school's administration office and got additional information.

I applied to Howard University and the University of Maryland and was accepted at both schools. Since I was in Baltimore, I decided to attend the University of Maryland. I was out of college one year before I entered Dental School.

I realized what it would take to get through school. I studied more in one year than in four years at college. I made it through. In my third year I was elected Class President. There were nine Black students in the program. The fourth year I did well. I was one of the individuals to finish in three and a half years.

When I graduated, Mr. Packer came to the ceremony. It was like having a father present.

After graduating, I worked at a hospital and then went into private practice.

I opened my practice in 1976. One of the unique privileges I had after opening my practice was to be a doctor to my elementary school teacher Mrs. Mammie Dell Brown. She came to my office to have some dental work done. She was in the area and learned of my practice.

Another rare event occurred with my grandmother. Grandma called me one day and said: "Boy, you'a dentis'."

"Yes, Grandma, I'm a dentist," I said.

"I wan' you t' come and pull my teeth out."

I was not licensed in Virginia and tried to explain to Grandma that I could not just come to Prince Edward County and pull her teeth out. It was hard for her to understand why her grandson who was a certified dentist could not just come to Meherrin and pull her teeth. (Dr. Richardson was laughing while recounting the episode.) I explained the situation and professional arrangements were made for me to go home and do the work. I went home and pulled Grandma's teeth out.

I opened a second location several years later.

I am a general dentist, practicing wholistically. That is to say I look at the whole person and not just one part of the patient.

LEOLA WATKINS BAILEY

I was born April 1, 1953. The schools in Prince Edward County were closed the year I was supposed to start first grade. When I was maybe seven years old, I started first grade at Saint Matthew Lutheran School in Lunenburg County. We lived near the school and some other children from the neighborhood went there too.

I was in Mrs. Jackson's class. I remember Patricia Lee, Rebecca Lee's sister. I remember learning how to count and to say my ABCs at Saint Matthew.

The next year my brother Alvin started at Saint Matthew and was in Mrs. Jackson's class.

When the Free School opened, I was put in the sixth grade and I tested out at the sixth grade.

We had good teachers when I was in high school. I remember Mrs. Griffin, Mrs. Madison, and Mr. Mayfield, they wanted to make sure you succeeded in life.

I graduated in 1972.

This is my story given on May 17, 2012.

RICE

———

HOWARD HICKS

I was born June 29, 1933, in Rice to Charlie Winston and Marie Branch Hicks. I started school in 1939 at Hubbard School. It had two rooms. Both rooms was very large, but one of the rooms had a section which was the kitchen. There was folding doors that separated the kitchen from the classrooms and when she was cooking the doors were closed. My grandmother, Georgiana Hicks, was the cook. They had tables, like picnic tables in the kitchen area and we sat there and ate. My grandmother said the State paid her. I think the State gave us the food. The food came in boxes and cans.

We had a pump on the school yard and outdoor toilet, one for the girls and another for the boys. There were 'bout twenty-five children at the school, but no mor'n thirty. Mr. Anderson Miller had six in the school. Mr. Aubry Jackson had seven in the school. School started at 9:00 a. m. because all the students had to do chores and then walk to school. Mrs. Young was the teacher. Mrs. Baker, Mrs. Vaughan, Mrs. Bertina Foster, and Ms. Rosa Foster, all taught during the seven years I was there. Mrs. Mary W. Foster was my last teacher. Mrs. Bertina was her daughter-in-law and Ms. Rosa was her daughter. Mrs. Baker and Mrs. Vaughan drove from Farmville. The school went to the seventh grade.

"Why were there so many teachers? Why did the teachers leave so soon?" the Editor asked.

I don't know why the teachers didn't stay long at the school.

I would have to go to the spring and get water early in the morning, so my mother would have water in the house. Boys and girls had to milk cows. We had to feed the horses or mules whichever you had. You had to cut wood in the morning if you didn't cut your wood the nigh' befo'. The mothers usually fed the chickens.

White children rode on a green International school bus and Mr. Curtis Hamlin, a White man, was the driver.

My uncle, Wilson Daniel Hicks, was a carpenter and built the kitchen on to High Rock School. He built it in the late 1940s. My Daddy went in the Navy in 1941 and I know Uncle Wilson built the kitchen after Daddy went in the Navy. Then Uncle Wilson went in the Navy. I think he built it after he came out.

After seventh grade I went to R. R. Moton for a year. Daddy took me out of school to help support the family. I worked the farm and help cut and haul pulpwood. In later years I went to Baltimore. I stayed a few years and came back to Prince Edward County.

I was in the United States Army from August 5, 1952 to 1954. I don't remember the date I came out.

"What were the one and two room schools in the area when you were a boy?" the Editor asked, detecting Mr. Hicks had an excellent memory.

There was High Bridge School that had one room. There was a Scuffle School in the Sailor's Creek area; and then there was High Rock School and Hubbard. Only High Rock School was on the church grounds. These schools was in and around Rice.

Green Bay had Levi School next to Levi Church. There was Mount Leigh, and I think No. 8 was in Green Bay. No. 8 had one room and Mrs. Susie Miller taught there. I know she was teaching there in the early 1950s.

As the Editor sat on the front porch of the home of Mr. Hicks, located near High Rock Baptist Church, around 9:00 a. m., the sun was beginning to make its presence felt on this summer morning. It was quiet. One car may have passed the house on the country road the entire time we were talking. Having heard the name Lucy Dove from individuals that attended classes at High Rock Baptist Church when the schools were closed, the Editor asked: "Do you remember Mrs. Lucy Dove? I heard she was one of the ladies that worked with the children at the church when the schools were closed?"

Her husband was a farmer. She was a house wife. Mr. Dove worked the farm.

Mr. Hicks told the Editor about the Dove family and pointed me in the direction of where Mr. and Mrs. Dove lived during the era of interest.

———

DORETHA PALMER DOVE

I was born May 9, 1925. I started school at High Bridge School. It was a one room school and a place for coats in the back. The boys were on one side and the girls' coats on the other. Sister Willie Belle Green was the teacher. Reverend Anthony Green was the pastor of High Bridge Baptist Church. The school was next to the church. Mrs. Green taught the Sunday School lesson on Friday, so we would be prepared for Sunday morning. I can remember her teaching under the tree. High Bridge School went to the seventh grade. I went to the first grade and then the county determined that Epps School on Scuffle Town Road was closer. So I started attending Epps, which was a two room school and had an outdoor toilet. We took our lunch.

I attended high school and graduated from R. R. Moton. When the schools closed, my children were Roger Dove born October 22, 1945, and he was almost fourteen when the schools closed. He would'a been goin' to the ninth grade. Frances, my daughter, was born September 1948, and was about eleven when the schools closed. Helen was born February 2, 1947 and was around 12. David was born October 4, 1950 and was in third or fourth grade. He had to wait a year later than normal to start school because his birthday fell in October and he wasn't six in September the year he was supposed to start school.

I don't know how I found out about the schools not opening.

Our oldest son, Roger, went to Staunton. Mr. Rudolph Doswell was the County Extension Agent. Roger was in the 4-H Club under Mr. Doswell who was impressed with Roger. Mr. Doswell had a relative in Staunton and that was who Roger lived with for one year. Roger was in high school.

Frances, Helena and David remained at home and went to classes at High Rock Baptist Church where my sister-in-law, Virginia Dove, worked with the children. Parents had to pack a lunch for their children.

High Bridge Baptist Church held classes in the sanctuary for the children. I knew Mrs. Josephine Thompson who worked with the children. Mrs. Thompson was a housewife. Ms. Rosa Palmer also taught there. Rosa was my first cousin. She was a teenager, maybe sixteen or seventeen years old. Rosa was sickly and wasn't in school and was hired to work with the children. Lula Mae Palmer is my sister-in-law by marriage to my brother Robert.

In the second year of the closing Roger, Francis, Helen and David went to North Carolina. I made arrangements for them to go to their uncle Reverend Willie and Lidia Lee in Stovall, North Carolina. Reverend Lee was my husband's uncle. Reverend Lee married a lady from North Carolina and relocated. I don't remember what month William and I sent the children to North Carolina, but it was early in the school year.

Where High Bridge Baptist Church is located today on Highway 619 is the second location. When I was a child, the church and the school was on the High Bridge Road. There was a bridge called The High Bridge and the church took its name from the bridge.

WILLIAM ROGER DOVE

I was born October 22, 1945. I started school at Epps School, a little country school in Rice. All of the country schools were spread around. Miss. Hardaway was my teacher, when I started school around 1951. Epps School had two teachers, Miss. Hardaway and Miss. Gee. Epps School went to about the fifth grade. I went to Epps School in first, second and third grades.

Epps School was closed in the early 1950s and the students were transferred to High Rock School in Rice. Miss. Hardaway and Miss. Gee went to High Rock School when Epps School was closed. I went to High Rock School in the fourth and fifth grades.

When I was in the sixth grade, I went to Mary E. Branch No. 1 in Farmville. I had passed to the seventh grade when the schools were closed and was supposed to go to Mary E. Branch No. 2 the next year.

The first year the schools were closed I worked in the fields. Some people had money and could afford to send their children away. My parents couldn't afford to send all of us away.*

The second year the schools were closed my parents sent me and my sister Frances to North Carolina. We stayed with our uncle, Reverend Willie Lee. I'm not sure whether my brother David went with us. We went to Stovall School which was right in the area. Stovall was a little place in the curve of the road, it was at the edge of Oxford. I think Uncle Willie lived in Bullock.

When my sister Frances and I went to Uncle Willie, Frances Miller who was my first cousin also went from Rice. Walter Lee and Donald Lee who were also from Rice went to Uncle Willie. There were children, all relatives, from three homes in Rice that went to Uncle Willie's the second year the schools were closed.

I was in Stovall for one school year. I came home for the summer and then missed the next year out of school. This was the third year the schools were closed.

The fourth year the schools were closed Mr. Doswell got me in school in Staunton. There were a lot of people that wanted to help kids in Prince Edward County. Different people took in students. I stayed with Mrs. Robinson in Craigsville in Augusta County. She was an older lady and didn't work. I can't remember her first name. Mr. Wesley Scott who was the brother-in-law of Mr. Doswell was the principal of the high school in Staunton. Mr. and Mrs. Scott made arrangements for me to live with Mrs. Robinson. I stayed with the Scott family sometimes, but I lived primarily with Mrs. Robinson. Mr.

and Mrs. Scott were from the Prince Edward County area and would bring me home when they came or when my parents couldn't come and get me.

I remember graduating and then the Free School opened. So, I missed the first year out of school, went to Uncle Willie in Stovall, North Carolina, the second year the schools were closed, missed school the third year, went to Mrs. Robinson the fourth year the schools were closed, and in the fifth year I went to the Free School.

I kept up my interest in the 4-H Club and activities. I was in the Future Farmers of America. Mr. Doswell kept me involved in a lot of things. I started off raising chickens, pigs and all sorts of things. I did all this along with my school studies. I was always raising stuff for the 4-H.

I raised Yorkshire pigs and won. I won prizes for sweet potatoes in Petersburg one year. I can't remember the year. They gave us Silver dollars for prizes. I still have some of the Silver dollars they gave us for prize money. I don't have all of them, but I still have some of them that they gave us. I won first place in Prince Edward County in tractor driving and cutting. I won a trip to the World's Fair in Harrisonburg, Pennsylvania, and came in second place. I don't remember the year.

I always wanted to play baseball, but in the spring time I was always working in the field.

In my last year of high school, I took eleventh and twelfth grade courses. I graduated from high school in 1966. I could have gotten an agricultural scholarship, but I decided not to take it because of the time I missed out of school and my age. I decided to go to work.

Representatives from Craddock Terry Shoes came to school and said they needed young Black employees and so I was one of the first Black people in the area hired. Craddock Terry Shoes made Army shoes and other shoes. At one time the company had ten or eleven plants in Central Virginia.

I started working for Craddock Terry Shoes as a lock-stitcher. This was a person that sowed the soles of shoes. The plant manager said to me one day after I had been there for a short while: "People take months to learn this. You keep this up and I'll give you a ten-cent raise." I got the raise and a man told me: "The most I ever got all the time I've been here is a three-cent raise."

I got involved with the Union. I started out with the Textile Workers Union out of Lynchburg, Virginia. I organized several Farmville plants and other plants. I started out as an organizer and ended up as a Vice President of an International Union out of New York, the Textile Workers Union of America, the AFL-CIO.

Around early 1970 we migrated with Amalgamated Clothing and Textile Union of America, Amalgamated was out of New York and was part of the textile garment district. The new organization was known as AFL-CIO, CLC. I worked primarily up and down the East coast, but as an international representative I traveled across the United States.

I came back to Prince Edward County. I have always had an entrepreneurial spirit. After I came back to Prince Edward County, I opened up a restaurant, catered and raised cattle.

Then I started working for Clayton Homes. Clayton Homes bought out Country Squire Homes. I opened several sale centers for Clayton Homes.

Around 1997 or 1998 I opened up DOVE HOMES in Prince Edward County. These were modular and regular homes. The economy got bad around 2008 and I had to close. I was in business for ten years. My health turned bad also.

I answered the call to preach in 2004. I started at Virginia Union University in the fall of 2004 and graduated in 2007 with a Certificate in Ministry; Certificate of Biblical Studies, I believe it states.

This is my story shared on Saturday, June 30, 2012.

———

*The story of William Roger is more detailed and his recollections more precise than the account of his mother. That is to be expected.

———

MARVIN DOVE

I was born October 4, 1952. I remember during the summer White kids came and taught at High Bridge Baptist Church. I came sometime. I came to classes one or two summers at High Bridge. My family lived in Rice, but Mama grew up in the High Bridge area. During the winter, I went to class at High Rock Baptist Church. My grandma Mrs. Lucy Dove was one of the main teachers.

There were seven of us: Roger, Frances, Helen, David, Melvin, me and Kenny. Mama and Daddy sent the bigger children away. Roger, Frances, Helen and David went to Uncle Buck and Aunt Lil in North Carolina. The rest of us stayed home and worked the fields.

I was out of school for four years and was eleven when the Free School opened. I could write my name when I went to school, and I could count.

———

HILTON HOWARD LEE, SR.

I was born June 29, 1947, in Rice, located in Prince Edward County, Virginia, to the late James A. Lee, Jr. and Ruby Saunders Lee. I started school at High Rock. It was a three room frame school in Rice. There was no kindergarten back then. You went straight to first grade at six years old. We had to pump water at High Rock School. There was no running water. The students used the pump at High Rock Baptist Church that was next to the school to wash our hands before lunch. You had to bring your own lunch. Around 1958 the county added a kitchen to High Rock School. One lady was hired to do the cooking and her name was Mrs. Miller. She would cook, and you got your lunch and went back to your seat. Most of what she served was beans or soup. We had coal heaters in the classrooms. The students had to start the fire. We were starting the fire up in 1958 up to 1959. My first grade teacher was Ms. Hankins. She taught first, second, and third. Mrs. Helen Gee (Carter) taught the fourth and fifth grades.

We played baseball at recess when the weather was warm. One day in the spring of the year in 1959, just a few weeks before school closed for the summer, we were playing baseball. Someone hit the ball across the road and I ran across the road to get it. Some White men were working on the road. They were State Department Workers and were putting up a sign. It was lunch time and the men were sitting down eating. One of the White men said to me as I picked up the baseball:

"Y'all little tottlers are out here playing now, but you won't have this ground to play on next year."

I can't remember the exact word he used, but it was something like toddler. I just said: "Yes, sir."

In those days you always said yes, sir, to White men. I didn't pay much attention to what he said because it made no sense to me. I ran back across the road to the school yard.

Mrs. Gee asked: "What did that man say to you?"

I told her as best I could what he said.

I had been promoted to the fifth grade when they closed the schools.

During that first year the schools were closed, I used to hear my mother crying and talking to my father. Mama used to say:

"These children need an education. What will they do without'a education?"

One day my daddy said to me when we were working tobacco: "Son, you're goin' to get in school some kind'a way."

Daddy got killed in 1961. He had already started working to get us enrolled in school in Nottoway County. Daddy's family was from Nottoway County.

My father's mother still lived in Nottoway County. One of my cousins and his mother lived with Grandma. That was how my mother tried to work us in through the family. We used Grandma's address in Nottoway County to get enrolled in school.

After about two years or so, we got enrolled in Ingleside Elementary School in Nottoway County. Mama got us enrolled. After getting in school, each morning we would walk about a mile and a half across the line into Nottoway County and catch the school bus and ride to Ingleside. The system was told we lived in Prince Edward County.

We went a short time to Ingleside, something came up and we had to leave.*

Black people started boycotting stores in Farmville in the early 1960s. One day a White lady came out of Motley Hardware on Main Street and took the sign from a girl and threw it on the ground and then slapped the girl. Reverend Griffin held the girl back and said:

"No violence!" and then he told the girl: "God will take care of it."

When the Free School opened, they put me in the eighth grade. They slowly found out I couldn't keep up with the other eighth graders. The teachers kept testing and reviewing and after some time they determined that I was still on a fourth grade level. That was my last grade in school four years before. They decided to put me back in the fourth grade.

I started thinking to myself after what I was told and felt I couldn't handle the pressure and embarrassment. I got to thinking about the things children do to each other sometimes. I knew the nine and ten year olds in the fourth grade had no intentions of hurting me, neither did they realize how much they would've been hurting me with their teasing. They weren't the ones who closed the schools.

Here I was fifteen or sixteen years old and being put back in the fourth grade. I never spent a day in the fourth grade because I quit school. I could not handle it.

When I was in my early twenties, it all fell before me what an education meant. I had a job and could do the work, but I couldn't hold up when it came to paper work and writing. Once I was offered the position of foreman on a job, but I couldn't read the blue prints in order to hold the job. I could do the work and was so good I showed and trained other people in what needed to be done.

I decided to improve myself. A teacher named Mrs. Baskerville from Keysville worked with me and another fellow for about three years. She taught at a school in Amelia County. There was also a White lady who used to tutor at the Farmville Library. I studied under her for a while.

It would always hurt me as a father when my children would come and ask me something about their homework and I couldn't help them. That was one of the most hurting things.

I have spent so many hours over the years wondering what could I have been in life had things been different. I pray that the people who did this to the children in Prince Edward County between 1959 and 1963 have asked God to forgive them. God does not accept people like them into His kingdom unless they repent. Those people cut us down in life very early. It was like murdering the mind.

What happened to me drove me to make sure that my children Howard Jr., Adriane Denise, and Helen got an education. Helen teaches in the public schools of Prince Edward County. I made sure that my children got an education.

When I was offered the opportunity to walk across the stage that Sunday in June 2003 and receive an honorary high school diploma, I took it as a slap in the face and I did not participate.

---

*See the story of Cathlean Lee Kirby below. She and young brother Raymond continued attending school at Ingleside Elementary School. Hilton was unable to clearly recall all the details.

DOROTHY LEE ALLEN

I was born September 27, 1942, of humble beginnings. We used to get water from a nearby spring and haul it back to the house.

I started school when I was about seven years old. We lived about four miles from school, maybe a little further. We lived way down in the woods on a bumpy road. We lived about two miles from the main road, which was Highway 460. My mother grew up in Prince Edward County in the Rice community. Mom was born around 1913 or so. She attended High Rock School in the 1920s.

My public education also began at High Rock Primary School. Ms. Mary Hankins was my first and second grade teacher. High Rock was a three room school. Mrs. Ethel Wilson was my third or fourth grade teacher. Mrs. Lancaster was the other teacher at the school. We had a wood stove.

High Rock Baptist Church was nearby, where Reverend Braxton was the pastor. He baptized me.

When I started, the school was burning coal. The girls had to start the fire each morning when it was cold. There was a pump at the church where we got water. There was a bucket, aluminum pale, for the water. Two of us would walk to the church and fill the pale up and bring it back to the school. Everyone had to bring a cup from home. You left your cup at school with your name on it. I think it was something like a little tin or aluminum cup. I had one of those cups that could open and close. It resembled an ice cream cone when opened but had a round bottom. Each student had a lunch pale, and some had brown bags. Sometimes you took fried chicken, pear preserve, or peanut butter and jelly on biscuits. There was no cafeteria at the school. When I was about ten, the older girls were allowed to make hot coco on the potbelly stove in the winter. The little ones could come with their cups and get some.

When promoted to the sixth grade, the students from High Rock went to Mary E. Branch. My seventh grade teacher was Mr. Charles Johnson. He was a real nice man. He always encouraged you to come to school. In eighth grade, I went to the new high school R. R. Moton.

I entered the ninth grade and was very excited about school. I was a freshman and was looking forward to tenth eleventh, and twelfth grades. I was already looking to the future. My ambition was to become a registered nurse. I had taken some science courses and was planning to take more. I didn't have a college in mind to attend after graduating from high school, but I knew I wanted to go beyond the twelfth grade.

The next year, September 1959, the schools didn't open. My family knew the schools weren't going to open. I grew up on a farm. Daddy had lots of work for us to do. I stayed at home and worked on the farm and helped Mom around the house.

Teenagers started dating and in 1960 I got married.

My father died in 1961. Daddy was from Nottoway County and his mother, Mrs. Lizzie Flippin Lee, still lived in the county. My mom tried to get my younger brothers and sister in school in Nottoway County under grandma's name and residence. Grandma paid taxes in Nottoway County and Mom sought to get the children in that way. Mom had talked to Grandma and the agreement was made that her grandchildren from Prince Edward County would use her name, Mrs. Lizzie Flippin Lee, and address to enroll in school.

In September 1961, Hilton, Raymond, and Cathlean started

school again, after being out for two years. I had a driver's license. I think we had a 1955 blue body and white trimmed and striped two door Ford. Mom assigned me to drive Hilton and Raymond, Roger and Cathleen to school some days. I drove them to Ingleside Elementary School. I believe the school was in Burkeville. It was a brick facility and fairly nice, as I recall. I would drive them to the door each morning and they would go inside. I would also pick them up in the afternoon. Their education didn't last long. School for them lasted about a month. I know they didn't attend for two months. The teacher sent a note home by Raymond or Hilton one day. Somehow it had been discovered that Hilton, Raymond and Cathleen were not residents of Nottoway County.

In the summer of 1963 it was announced that the Free School would open in September. I had no plans to return to school in the fall of the year. I had one child in the home and was expecting another child. My second child was born June 19, 1963.

Many of the older students didn't return to school because they had families and responsibilities. Things were very sad because with such little education it was difficult to support a family adequately.

Almost twenty-five years went by before I earned my high school diploma. I earned my GED in 1983. I got it, but it wasn't like earning a high school diploma as a teenager, which was what I really looked forward to before the schools were closed and my education discontinued. I earned a Certified Nursing Assistants License around 1986, which is the closest I have come to my teenage dream of being a registered nurse.

I don't talk often about the era of the school closing. I was hesitant, very hesitant to grant this interview, because it makes me cry, it saddens me, even forty-five years later.

When I talk about that period, I think about how much I missed in life. Each time I retell this story all of my girlhood dreams, visions, and hopes, flash before me. It is very painful. (The eyes of Mrs. Allen began to swell with tears. She pressed on with her story.)

That fake diploma they handed out is a joke. This is the reason why it is a joke—there were people who walked across the stage and received an honorary diploma and could not even recognize their name on the paper. That is sad, it is shameful. Some of them can't even read the words on the diploma. This was a new level of degrading people. There are Black people in Farmville today who sign their name with an X. To give them a diploma is a form of deception and phoniness.

Many people my age have to purchase their own medicine and pay for their own insurance. My job doesn't provide insurance. If those who say they are interested in helping are serious, let them provide something meaningful to the older ones such as insurance.

We serve a powerful God and somehow God will bring good from all of this. We may be resting in our graves and not be here to see it unfold, but God will fix it.

Following the interview, Mrs. Allen attempted to arrange an audience with her younger sister Cathleen. Cathlean said she was unavailable and the Editor should let her know the next time he would be in Prince Edward County.

CATHLEAN LEE KIRBY

I was born in Rice on February 19, 1950, to Ruby Saunders

Lee and James Lee. There were ten children in my family, six boys and four girls. Clyde, was the oldest, Franklin, Bertha (Redd), Fleming, John, Dorothy, Helen, Hilton, myself and Raymond was the older of births. Clyde was the oldest and was at least twenty years older than me, meaning he was born not later than 1930. Raymond was the youngest and was born around 1952.

I started school at age six at High Rock School. My first teacher was Ms. Hankins, who was later by marriage Mrs. Anderson. My second grade teacher was Mrs. Dorothy Brown.

That summer we were out of school. The children had no idea the schools weren't going to open in September. The way I found out was at our church's annual Homecoming Day. Homecoming Day at High Rock Baptist Church was always held on the fourth Sunday in August. Mrs. Brown, my teacher, was at church that Sunday. We were on the church grounds having dinner following the worship service. Mrs. Brown was sitting in her car. The door on the passenger side was open. I think she was eating her lunch. Mrs. Brown had long hair and was a beautiful woman and very smart. I was near the passenger side of her car. All the children were outside eating and playing. "Cathlean, what are you going to do this fall?" she asked casually, while eating her food.

"I'm going to school?" I answered, not taking a second thought.

"Cathlean, there isn't going to be any school this year," Mrs. Brown said.

I took off running. I ran across the church yard and found my parents. I don't like talking about this. (Mrs. Kirby suspended the interview and went to another room in the house and got some tissues. She cried, wiped her tears, and slowly collected herself. She continued her story.)

Each family, for the most part, served lunch out of the truck of their car. You could carry things to the picnic table, but most served out of the trunk. I found my family's car. There was no discussion on the subject of school not opening. I was scared. I knew Mrs. Brown always told me the truth and I could not figure out what she was talking about.

In September my parents and others were talking and saying things such as 'they (the White people) are not going to open the schools'.

Later in the year Negroes, as we were called then, started having classes in churches and any place they could hold a class. There were no buses, so children had to walk to one of the churches.

Reverend Braxton was the pastor at High Rock Baptist Church. I think he was the pastor. Wait a minute. Let me call my cousin, Coosie, in Rice. (We are at the residence of Mrs. Kirby in Farmville.) She would remember.

Note of the Editor: Mrs. Kirby called her cousin.

Reverend Braxton was the pastor, according to Coosie.

"What did your cousin do when the schools were closed?" the Editor asked.

"She went to Kittrell College."

"I have not interviewed anyone who went to Kittrel," said the Editor. "Can you call your cousin back and ask her to grant an interview?"

Mrs. Kirby called her cousin a second time and arranged for an interview with Mrs. Virginia Saunders Foster, nickname Coosie, immediately after this interview. She would be the first Kittrell College attendee interviewed by the Editor.

Mrs. Kirby resumed.

There were classes held at High Rock Baptist Church during the week. The classes were held in the sanctuary. They tried to divide us by age or class. For example, first graders were on the first pew, a few rows back were the second graders and so on.

Mrs. Lucy Dove was one of the helpers. Most of the people who taught us were Sunday School teachers from the church, most who were house wives. These ladies didn't get paid.

We had to walk to get to the church. We walked about four or five miles one way through wooded areas to get to the church. We would stop by Aunt Fannie (Saunders). Her husband, Uncle Arthur, was my mother's brother. We would stop at their house and get our cousins, Geraldine and Juitt, and Cornelius Jones, who lived in the same house. Then we would all walk to the church. Some other children would join us as we passed their homes.

After about two years, my aunt got us in school in Nottoway County. My baby brother, Raymond, and I went to Ingleside Elementary School.

My brother, Frank, and his wife, Vivian, had two school age children named Loretta and Roosevelt. Loretta, Roosevelt, my brothers, Hilton and Raymond, and I had to walk through a bottom and across a creek until we reached a mailbox and crossed the Nottoway County line to catch the school bus. The walk was about a mile or a little more to catch the school bus. It seems like there were some more children who walked with us to catch the bus, but I can't remember. It's been so long. Mr. Parker was the bus driver. Sometimes my sister, Dorothy, would drive us to school.

I think it was the beginning of the third year of the schools being closed that we got into the school in Nottoway County. That would have had us entering school there in August or September of 1961. When I went to Ingleside, I was eleven years old and placed in the third grade. I was embarrassed. I was one of the largest children in the class and was definitely the oldest. To make it worse, I didn't know as much as the younger ones in the class. I remember the year 1961 because that was the year my father was killed in a car accident.

My sister, Helen, went to Baltimore and lived with my aunt, Ms. Lovelean Glandy. Helen stayed one year and returned home. I think Helen was around eighth grade when the schools were closed.

When I was in the fourth grade at Ingleside the children put gum under the chairs one day and the teacher said I did it.

"The gum is under your desk and you did it," Mrs. Lois Farrar said. She made me open my hand and she paddled me.

Hilton had to quit school while we were at Ingleside. Raymond and I continued to lie and told the people we lived with Grandma. I don't know if they found out from Hilton that he still lived in Prince Edward County or what that led to his dismissal.

Raymond and I stayed at Ingleside until the Free School opened. I had been promoted to the fifth grade at Ingleside, but when I entered the Free Schools in Prince Edward County I was placed in the eighth grade. I remember the Free School had teachers here from North Carolina, South Carolina and other States.

I was protective of my books and school meant a lot to me. My mother bought me a geography book that I loved. I was showing the book to my cousin Edith Lee one day while we were sitting in the cafeteria waiting for the bus to take us home. A girl name Jo Ann Epps snatched the book from me when I was showing it to Edith. Mama had paid about $5.00 for the book. That was a lot of money back then. Jo Ann said:

"What kind of little book is that? I'm going to rip it up."

She had it in her hands in the ripping position. (Mrs. Kirby held up her hands demonstrating how the girl was holding the book and preparing to rip it.) I snatched it from her and said:

"No, you're not." I was ready to fight her, and the teachers made me stop.

While at Moton High School, I was on the cheerleading squad in the 1966 and the 1967 school years. During the 1967 and 1968 school years, I was in the Library Club.

Note of the Editor: Mrs. Kirby had several high school yearbooks at her house. We suspended the interview and she showed the Editor photographs of herself from each yearbook and identified some of the teachers and students. Then she resumed her story.

In 2003 the school board issued honorary high school diplomas to students impacted by the closing of the schools. When I heard about the diplomas being issued, I was somewhat excited because I thought the diploma would have some value. I asked a friend of mine named Elsie Hubbard:

"Can you get a job with the diploma? Can it help a person in any way?"

I asked Elsie to find out. She got back with me and said:

"No, the diploma won't help you get a job. It's not worth a thing."

My main question is—Why? Why did they close the schools? What was accomplished? I had to go to school among people I did not know. It all hurt and still hurts. The closing was one of the lowest things that could have been done. I could have been a different person and raised my children differently had my education not been interrupted. But in the end, you can't interrupt God's plan.

My oldest daughter had perfect attendance in school. She

has a master's degree. I made sure my daughters went to school. My youngest daughter graduated from Hampton University. I stressed education to my children. They had a mother behind them to push them. I was determined that they would learn and develop.

———

GLORIA ANN REDD LOVELACE

I was born August 1, 1952, in Rice. I started school at High Rock. I don't remember any of the teachers at High Rock. I think I had passed to the third grade when the schools were closed.

My sister, Majorie, and me were the only two school age children in my family. Marjorie was the oldest. She was born September 24, 1951. My mother, Bertha Lee Redd, got with relatives in Amelia County, a great grand aunt, and asked her could we live with her. Me and Marjorie didn't want to go and stay there, but Mom made us go. I think we attended Russell Grove. We came home on the weekend. Mama and Daddy would pick us up on Friday after school and take us back on Sunday afternoon.

We really missed being at home. Mom tried to put us at ease by explaining we needed to get an education. But I still missed home.

The Free School opened in September 1963. I think I was placed in the seventh grade. We were glad to get back home.

Teachers who made an impact on me during my school days in Prince Edward County were: Mrs. Connie Rawlins, Mr. Tillison, and Mrs. Redd, and Mrs. Moseley.

————

VIRGINIA SAUNDERS FOSTER

I was born March 29, 1942, to Fannie and Arthur Saunders.

When I was a girl, I walked to High Rock School which was about two or three miles from our house. High Rock was a small school that sat on a hill. Ms. Hankins was my first grade teacher. I'll never forget her. Mrs. Lancaster was my second grade teacher at High Rock School.

While I was at Moton High School, Mrs. Mary Madison, Mr. Leo White, and Mrs. Connie Rawlins were some of the teachers who made an impression on me.

When the schools were closed, I had been promoted to the tenth grade. It was in the news that the schools wouldn't open. That was how we found out about it.

Reverend Dunlap came around and interviewed some of the teenagers in Rice. I think Reverend Dunlap was from Farmville. He came to our house and talked to my whole family. Then Reverend Dunlap interviewed me privately. As I recall, he asked me who was my favorite person or the person who had made an impact on me. I said Ms. Hankins was the person who had up to that point made the greatest impact on my life. Then he asked did I want to go back to school. I was anxious to go back to school and said:

"Yes, I want to go back to school."

I don't know all of the workings of events that took place, but arrangements were made for many of the teenagers from Rice to enroll at Kittrell College in North Carolina. The NAACP paid part of the tuition, so we could attend.

Most of the children from Rice were taken to Kittrell by their parents. It seemed like a long journey to me. I had never been out of Prince Edward County. We didn't miss a lot of time out of school. I think we went to Kittrell in late September or sometime in October 1959.

Some of the students who went to Kittrell College were: Phyllistine Ward (Mosley), Fannie A. Turner (Hill), Charles Taylor, Phyllis Ghee, Estelle Nash (Hamlin), Marie Walton (Jackson), Elsie Eanes, I can't remember her married name, Elise Booker and Doris Booker my cousins, both deceased. Doris was my roommate at Kittrell College. Some of the students only went for one year. Shirley Miller went to Kittrell also, but I'm not sure whether she stayed all three years.

Kittrell College had a high school department. I worked in the cafeteria to help pay for my room and board. Doris, my cousin, also worked in the cafeteria.

Many of the boys and girls enrolled in the high school department at the college were from northern states such as New York and New Jersey and had been kicked out of public schools. Their parents sent them to the country to study and stay out of trouble. The children from Prince Edward County were basically the only ones at the high school not there because of disciplinary problems. We were there because the school doors in our home county had been closed against us.

The college was near the town of Henderson. I remember we used to go to church sometimes in Henderson.

The college was maybe a two-hour drive from Prince Edward County. I remember Mom and Daddy used to drive down some Sunday afternoons and bring us fried chicken, potato salad, pound cakes and other delights. We would share with the ones whose parents couldn't come and bring them food.

The first time I ate hominy grits was when I went to North Carolina. The first time I saw cotton growing was when I went to Kittrell. There was a big cotton field next to the school. I went out and picked a few balls. (Mrs. Saunders laughed while telling these vignettes).

Every time it rained at school I cried because I wanted to be at home. If you didn't get up to go to breakfast, you went hungry. Flossie Oliver's daddy owned a store. She kept things like tuna fish and other eats in her room. Flossie would share with us. I was going to quit school and return home. I was young, and the college students took me under their wings. They teased me when I cried to come home, especially when it rained.

We came home at Thanksgiving and Christmas, and then at the end of the school year for the summer.

I remember hearing about and reading about the sit-ins in nearby Greensboro. I was frightened. My mother and father were glad for me to have the opportunity to go and continue my education but weren't thrilled about me leaving home at age seventeen.

I wanted to be a teacher when growing up. I graduated from Kittrell College High School Department in May 1962 and returned to Prince Edward County. I gave up my ambitions to go off to college and become a teacher.

Shirley Miller (Jones) is a nurse and lives in Nottoway.

On May 17, 2004, there was a Brown *vs* Board of Education Fiftieth Anniversary Celebration in Prince Edward County. The students who went to Kittrell gathered that evening. There were about seventeen present that night.*

---

*This was the first interview the Editor conducted with a student from Prince Edward County that had gone to the high school department at Kittrell Junior College.

ROBERT 'BOB' HAMLIN

I was born July 29, 1942, in Baltimore, Maryland, at Johns Hopkins Hospital. I am adopted. I was adopted at birth and the decision was made before-hand. I was adopted by the woman who became my mother's sister-in-law. My birth mother was named Lilly Taylor and my adopted mom was Carrie Hamlin. My birth father was Semion Hamlin and my adopted father was his brother, Jasper Leroy Hamlin.

A little bit of that story. My biological mother had had a love affair with Semion and became pregnant. In the meanwhile, she had fallen in love with George Bowen who was my adopted mother's brother. That being said, it was determined that I should be given up for adoption at birth. A few months after my birth, Jasper, or Jack as they called him, left Baltimore and returned to Prince Edward County and the home of my adopted mother and purchased land in Rice. They built a house on the land. Eventually he moved Mom and myself here.

My father's (Jasper) home was in the Green Bay area. He came from a family of fifteen children. My adopted mother was from around the Rice area. During her growing up years, her family lived in different locations in and around the Rice community. She came from a family of eleven.

In Baltimore my dad worked for Bethlehem Steel and when he returned to Prince Edward County he decided to go into business for himself cutting pulpwood. He connected with a White man out of Burkeville named Joe Terry. Joe Terry presented himself as a real estate man of sorts and would buy large tracts of land and would hire my dad to cut the pulpwood. Dad had an old truck and some equipment. After sometime, Dad was able to buy a power chain saw. As time went by, Dad was able to hire more workers, and buy more saws and equipment.

Joe Terry began to branch out and found timber in South Boston and Danville. Dad and his crew would go to those places, stay during the week and cut pulpwood and come home on the weekend.

In the 1950s Dad began to think: 'I can make more money if I could cut for Hammer Mill Paper and Continental Can Company.' His first big contract was with Continental Can Company to cut three thousand acres of timber at Quantico Marine Base in Northern Virginia. That led to other contracts with Continental Can Company and other organizations. Dad remained in Northern Virginia, staying there during the week and coming home on the weekend.

He cut timber all over Manassas, Woodbridge, Reston, and other sections of Northern Virginia. Dad had a camp for his crew to live in during the week, providing meals and a place to sleep. At the height of his success he had thirty-five men working for him and fourteen or fifteen power saws. Dad's trade mark was on the side of each truck— **L. J. HAMLIN** in oval shape **Trader in Pulpwood** on the sides of the trucks.

During the summer time, a bunch of us kids would go up to the camp and work. We did limbing. That was cutting the limbs off the trees after the trees had been cut down by the men. After cutting the limbs, we would go back and mark the trees using the ax helve, and then the pulpwood cutters would come along and cut the wood where we had marked it.

The truck driver always had a helper. Their job was to come in and load the trucks with those sticks of pulpwood and drive them to Woodbridge to the train car siding. That was where you loaded the pulpwood on to the train.

While all this was going on, Dad branched out more. Somehow, he came up with a contract in Red Bank, New Jersey, and he sent a crew there to cut pulpwood. At the same time, he had all this going, he decided to set up a saw-mill in Manassas, (Northern Virginia). The saw-mill didn't do as well, but he operated it for about a year. He cut flatwood like for bed-slats and such.

Dad purchased one hundred eighty acres of land in the Green Bay area. His life-long dream was to establish a dairy farm. On the property on Highway 696 he built a block home to be used by tenants that would work the farm. He also built a barn for tobacco.

All of this made me realize that cutting pulpwood and dairy farming was not in my future.

Pulpwood was the main stay and it provided a pretty decent living for county Black folk in the middle 1950s and early 1960s. The strangest thing was we never had running water in the home. Mom was the homemaker and took care of everything at home. She raised the garden, canned an awful lot and that meant I was often at the well drawing water. I was a happy child all during my growing up years.

My father began to have some latent or what might be called mid-life crisis issues. In 1956 or thereabouts Dad decided to buy a motorcycle. My dad could not ride a bicycle. (Mr. Hamlin begins laughing, while continuing his story.) I remember I let him get on my bike one day and he rode it into the side of the house.

We noticed that he was not coming home on Friday nights, but coming to Prince Edward County on Saturday or late Friday night. We later learned he was stopping in Richmond to practice riding his Harley 750 FLH. It was the biggest thing going at the time. (Mr. Hamlin was laughing harder and the Editor was now laughing.) The bike weighed at least eight hundred pounds. It had lights all over it and was very pretty.

Finally, he decided to drive it home one Saturday morning. We heard this noise one Saturday morning around nine o'clock. (Mr. Hamlin imitated the roaring hard sound of the huge Harley 750 FLH motor cycle.) He came easing down the road.

Dad was in the habit of buying a new car every two or three years. He had a 1953 Chevrolet Bel-air, a 1956 Holiday Oldsmobile 88, in 1957 he bought the 1956 Harley.

We noticed that when we would go into town the police would follow us. Daddy traded the 1956 Harley and purchased a brand new 1958, a Harley Duo Glide. It was equivalent to the 750 FLH. It was jet black and had chrome everywhere.

Dad then traded the Holiday Oldsmobile 88 for the biggest Buick made called the Limited. Prior to that Road Master was the king. The Limited had more bells and whistles. I recalled on the rear fender of the new car were fifteen hashmarks. The Limited was complete with air conditioner, power seats, power-windows, six cigarette lighters and ash-trays. It had air sacks instead of springs. Under the dash board was a little rod. If you were in the country and hit some low spots the driver pulled the rod out and the air sacks raised the car another six inches higher. The car also had a wonder-bar radio. You could pre-set radio stations and hit the bar and it would scan the stations. There was a button on the floor on the left side near the dimmer switch, and if you were too lazy to lift your hand and lean over to change the radio station, you could change the stations with your foot by pressing the button on the floor.

These were the things that I was accustomed to and I came to realize that Daddy was being watched.

And then he had the gall to join the Nation of Islam in the 1950s. We were the only Muslims in the county at the time. Four gentlemen from Philadelphia came to Prince Edward County. Elijah Muhammad was of the opinion that the Black man would have to be more self-sufficient and needed land. The four gentlemen moved on the property Daddy owned in Green Bay. They were all Brother Xs. Their first names were Redell, Lewis, Charles, and Eddie. Brother Eddie was married.

They began to teach my family about Islam and when I was around nine years old my adopted mom and dad, my real mom and dad and their two children became Muslim. The Colored people in Rice began to distance themselves from us. My dad's father was a Baptist minister and started Calvary Baptist Church. Whenever we would have our meeting or service there would be a knock on the door and when the door was opened there stood the police. "We are just stopping by to make sure you all are not starting any trouble." One of the ministers would ask: "Do you go to the other churches and do the same?"

When I stared sixth grade at Mary E. Branch No. 2 in Farmville, the administrator at High Rock School in Rice contracted me to start the fire each morning in the winter before I caught the bus to come to Farmville. Farmville is twelve miles from Rice.

When the schools closed in 1959, I was naturally hurt, but was not necessarily shocked. I had the feeling something was going to shake out to remind Black people who they were in the eyes of White people.

I was promoted to twelfth grade. I was going to be the first person in the family to graduate public high school. Mom and

Dad went as far as they could in public school, Dad to the seventh and Mom to the sixth grade.

Being out in the country as we were, we were on the eastern edge of the county. I was a mile from the Nottoway County Line. What was happening on the western edge of the county, Farmville, we may not have heard the news.

I was in Northern Virginia working with Dad at his pulpwood camp. We came home on the weekend. When I came home one weekend Mom told me that Flossie's family, Mr. John and Mrs. Flossie Oliver, had stopped by and asked why I was not in school. Their daughter, Flossie Levella, was enrolled at Kittrell in the high school department and home visiting her family for the weekend.

My parents and I went to see the Oliver family that Saturday morning and talked about Kittrell. On Sunday morning, the next day, my parents packed me up, loaded the car and to Kittrell College we went, one hundred and twenty-miles from home.

I had never been away from both my parents at the same time. We had begun to talk about options for school before heading off to Kittrell. I didn't care for either option presented to me. We had relatives in Pennsylvania and New Jersey, and I had an older cousin in Paterson, New Jersey, who wanted me to come and live with him. Mom and Dad had given some thought to me going north. I had already expressed my disdain about going north for school.

We got to Kittrell on Sunday afternoon. I had no idea whether I would be accepted. We rolled up on the grounds in that big Buick. We found Flossie, whose parents had driven her back earlier that day. Flossie got us in touch with the school president Dr. Arthur Camper. Camper was president during the 1959-1960 school year. I think we met Dean Roucsh that Sunday afternoon. He was head of the high school department or more officially — he was dean of the high school. We met the business manager Mr. Wilson.

My dad, if I remember correctly, wrote a check for $400.00 to the school that Sunday. They said, 'if you cannot pay any more that is okay'. Everyone one was on some type of work study scholarship. The college dean was Dean Horton.

The college was going to try and gather the transcripts and records of the students from Prince Edward County, but our records were locked-down in Prince Edward County.

I had a car at home. I got the car in high school, but my parents would not allow me to take it Kittrell. In my sophomore year I bought a motor cycle but had to leave it at home also. Looking back that was a good thing. Mom said:

"You are there to focus on school."

I grew up in a household being an only child. I was shy and bashful, people don't believe that today. I was introverted. I found out that I was going to have a roommate and I needed to learn how to interact with the person. Some of the people at Kittrell I had interacted with in Prince Edward County, so we took care of each other emotionally.

The teachers and administration were totally dedicated to seeing that we got the best education. They did not get paid what they deserved. By that I mean, the instructors at the college also taught in the high school department when the Prince Edward County students arrived.

I had a second challenge at Kittrell. I had embraced Islam and in North Carolina they ate a lot of pork. I had to prepare my own food in the dorm room on a hot-plate. I had never heard of the African Methodist Episcopal Church until I got to Kittrell. The songs they sang were not those that I remembered from the days when my parents were in the Baptist Church. Kittrell had one of the best college choirs around.

The choir went to sing in Maryland on one occasion and the bus was in an accident. The teacher, the choir director, and several students were injured. The bus was totaled. Everyone on campus was disturbed.

Some of the college students got together and planned a protest one month after the Greensboro event. This would have been March 1960. The Greensboro event happened in February. About eight guys got the college bus and would go to protests in Henderson. The bishop found out the college bus was being used to transport student protesters to the town of Henderson where the protests were being held. School authorities on one occasion got in a vehicle and ran the bus down. When the driver of the bus stopped, someone climbed on board and told them the Bishop said, 'Bring the bus back'. The students said:

"You can take the bus back, but we're going on to Henderson."

One of the Bishop's representatives drove the bus back to the campus. The students that were on board walked the eight miles to Henderson to join the protest that day.

People claiming to be the KKK started harassing the campus. They would ride through the campus on weekend nights firing weapons. Kittrell was a religious school and no weapons allowed, but sawed-off shot guns and forty-fives started to come out of nowhere. (Mr. Hamlin started laughing.) We had to form and organize our own security.

I graduated in the spring of 1960.

The experience with the Muslims was very educational and enlightening for me. It made me see myself differently. As

I traveled in later life and developed, I learned that the White man was not the devil. I got to see and hear the Honorable Elijah Muhammad on several occasions. I got to see and hear Malcom X on several occasions.

I later joined the United States Air Force and made a career of it.

ROY R. MILLER

I was born on May 5, 1943. My education began at High Rock School. Mrs. Lancaster was one of the teachers at the school and Ms. Hankins was the other. I went to R. R. Moton High School in eighth and ninth grades. I played basketball and loved it. The coach was Coach Truman. I was looking forward to playing basketball all of my high school years and then possibly going on to college and play. I also played baseball in high school, but basketball was my first love.

I had passed to the tenth grade when the schools were closed. My grandfather, Floyd Johnson, owned a farm. My father passed when I was six years old. My mother, my sisters, and my brothers lived in a separate house on the same farm and so did my grandfather and grandmother. My oldest, brother, Edward, was already out of school when the schools were closed. My older sister, Mattie, graduated in May or June of 1959. She just got out of school in time. Me, Shirley, Jerry, and Flossie were still in school at the time of the closing.

When the schools didn't open in September 1959, me and Jerry went to work with Granddaddy on his farm. Granddaddy raised tobacco.

My sisters, Shirley and Flossie, went away in the 1959 school year. A school had to be found that would accept them. School had already open in the other counties. My family had some friends in nearby Amelia County. They were friends of my mother. I know the family's last name was Eanes. I can't remember the husband and wife's first names. Shirley and Flossie went to the Eanes family and were accepted at Russell Grove High School.

Shirley and Flossie came home each weekend. Amelia was not far from Rice. I would drive them to the Eanes house each Sunday evening and pick them up on Friday after school. My oldest brother Edward had a car. I think he had a Ford. I would drive his car to take our sisters back and forth. When I took Shirley and Flossie back to the Eanes each Sunday, my mama would pack up enough groceries for Shirley and Flossie to have for the week. Sending food for Shirley and Flossie took some of the financial strain off the Eanes family. All of the boys had to work so the girls, Shirley and Flossie, could go to school. Shirley went somewhere else it seems, but I can't remember, it's been so long.

When the Free School opened in September 1963, I went back to school. The bus started coming to Rice and taking us into town. I was placed in the tenth grade, the grade I had been promoted to when the schools were closed. But then I had to quit school. As I mentioned earlier, my father died when I was six years old. My mother started receiving a check for the children after Daddy died. When the children reached a certain age, they couldn't be claimed or considered a legal dependent. My mother's check was reduced because of my age. Since I was considered legally grown, I had to start supporting myself.

There were no classes of any sort offered in the Rice

community for the younger boys and girls locked out of the schools. The children in Rice did nothing for four years, except work on the plantations, as I called them. There were acres and acres to work. When the schools were closed in September 1959, the boys and girls in Rice received no educational training until they returned to the Free School in 1963.

My mother moved to Philadelphia and Flossie finished high school there.

I was drafted into the United States Army in 1966. I went to Fort Jackson, South Carolina, for basic training and to Fort Ord, California, for infantry training. Then I went to Fort Sill, Oklahoma, and trained for enemy warfare in Vietnam. I went to Vietnam for one year.

I returned to Prince Edward County after being honorably discharged from the Army and started working at Stackpole Components Company. A young lady started working at Stackpole Components Company the same day as I and on the same shift. Her name was Elnora Ward from Nottoway. Two or three years later we were married and are still happily married as of the date of this interview, Friday, August 6, 2004. Elnora and I have two boys, Michael and Roy, Jr.

The closure of the schools caused me to miss a lot of opportunities in life. I loved sports and looked forward to playing basketball at the college level, but that didn't happen. I have no idea what I might have been or could have been in life had the schools remained open. I just stopped playing baseball a few years ago. I played until I got too old to play.

I hope a situation like the Prince Edward County School episode never happens again as long as there is world.

———

CALVIN NUNNALLY

I was born October 22, 1946, in Rice and began my public education at High Rock School. Ms. Hankins was my teacher. When the schools were closed in September 1959, I was almost thirteen years old.

After the schools were closed, classes were held at High Rock Baptist Church for the students. Mrs. Lucy Dove, one of the regular Sunday School teachers at the church, was the instructor. The classes benefited the younger children, those around eight and under, more than the older students. The larger children had the option to float in and out of class. Some of the older children knew as much academically, and in some instances more, than the teachers in the church schools and learning centers. I do not say this to anyone's shame but am only stating a fact.

The children in my family affected by the school closing were: my brother, Bennie, Jr., who had passed to the eleventh grade. I had passed to the sixth grade. My sister, Brenda, had been promoted to the fifth. My sister, Barbara, (Eggleston) had passed to the fourth grade. My younger brothers, Clarence and Leon, were going to the third grade. These two were less than a year apart. Doreen, our baby sister, was not yet in school.

Bennie, Jr. started working at the sawmill with Daddy in Nottoway County. After working about two years and the schools not having reopened, Bennie volunteered and joined the United States Air Force.

Daddy was a part-time police officer in Burkeville, located in Nottoway County, and worked at the sawmill.

I missed the first four years of school when the schools were closed. In 1963 my family moved from the community of Rice in Prince Edward County to Nottoway County. My baby sister,

Doreen, was approaching school age and my parents felt she needed her foundation. Mama and Daddy decided to move to a community where Doreen could start first grade. Moving also meant that the rest of us still at home could return to school.

The sawmill in Burkeville where Daddy worked was owned by Mr. King. Mr. King knew of the situation in Prince Edward County, as Burkeville was only about thirty minutes away. Mr. King had two houses built in Burkeville. One house was for the Nunnally family and the other was for Mr. Pumpy Nash and his family. The Nash and Nunnally families had children that needed to go to school.

I started school in Nottoway County in September 1963. The Free School opened in Prince Edward County at the same time. When Mama and Daddy moved the family to Nottoway County, they didn't know when the Prince Edward Schools would reopen.

I graduated from Foster High School in 1968 and was #2 in my class. During the years I matriculated at Foster, none of the counselors ever said anything to me about college.

One day I saw Mr. Macio Hill at the post office in Burkeville and he asked:

"What are you going to do now?"

"I'm going to Vietnam like everybody else and get killed," I said. I had many friends who had gone to Vietnam and gotten killed. I was a National Merit Scholarship Winner and more, but none of the counselors ever said anything to me about college.

"No one has ever mentioned college to you?" Mr. Hill asked, somewhat shocked.

"No," I said.

"No!" he exclaimed. Taking charge of the situation, Mr. Hill said: "You're going to Elizabeth City Teachers College."

I thought he meant there was such a college in Elizabeth City, New Jersey. I became very excited and started looking forward to the venture.

Mr. Hill was at my house the next morning honking his horn. My mother came to my bedroom and said:

"Mr. Hill is outside, and he said come on."

I had no idea the trip would be the following morning. I got up, washed, and went to the car. Mr. Hill pulled off and I prepared for the long ride to Elizabeth City, New Jersey. Well, low and behold, we ended up in Elizabeth City, North Carolina. (Mr. Nunnally started laughing and continued to tell his story while laughing and reflecting.)

Mr. Curtis Bryan was the man we talked to at Elizabeth City Teachers College that day. He saw my grades and was astounded.

"I know we can get you a scholarship."

"Yea, Yea, Yea," I said to myself.

We returned home that night and two weeks later I drove my 1960 Chevy back to college. I enjoyed my years at Elizabeth City Teachers College. On the weekend I would drive up to Richmond, Virginia, to visit my brother, Bennie, Jr., who was a student at Virginia Union University.

Bennie earned his GED while in the Air Force. After being honorably discharged from the Air Force, Bennie applied for admission to Virginia Union University. The institution said he did not have a high school diploma and had to take the Graduate Record Exam. Yes, the Graduate Record Exam. I don't think the school had a strong affection for veterans. The whole country to some extent was like that at the time. Bennie took the Graduate Record Exam, which is for students exiting college and not entering, and passed it.

After graduating from Elizabeth City Teachers College, I

was hired as a teacher in Virginia. When I got my first pay check, I purchased a new 1974 Mustang.

I have enjoyed my years in Virginia's education system. I have been a teacher, a principal, and as a principal opened Amelia County's first middle school. I have served as head of WCVE Educational Public Television for Central Virginia. I was responsible for all daytime educational television. This was the programming that went into classrooms at schools.

Of the seven children in my family, and each was impacted by the closing of the schools in Prince Edward County, all have a Master's Degree except two. Bennie, Jr. has a Ph. D in Finance and Business Law from the University of Virginia. He has been invited to return to the University of Virginia and teach but has consistently declined the offer. Bennie also writes textbooks. My sister, Doreen, is pursuing her Ph. D in Education.

Daddy retired from the Burkeville Police Force around 1999 at the rank of Colonel. The jury is still out, but we think Bennie Nunnally, Sr. was the first Black Chief of Police in the State of Virginia. We are trying to substantiate it.

There is one thing, however, that has already been substantiated for me and that is — the day I bumped into Mr. Hill at the post office was a divine event ordained of God.

————

CLARENCE ALONZO NUNNALLY

I was born September 13, 1951 and started school at High Rock School. The school was located next to High Rock Baptist Church. Ms. Hankins was my first grade teacher.

I had passed to the second grade when the schools were

closed. I went to the classes held in the church during the school year. Mrs. Lucy Dove and some other ladies taught us.

The most exciting time for learning for us was during the summer when teachers and college students came to the area to teach us.

I remember the sessions from the summers of 1961 and 1962. My uncle used to bring us in the morning to the church about 8:00 a. m. or 9:00 a. m. and came back for us about 12:00 noon. Uncle Percy brought me, my brother Leon, my sisters Barbara and Brenda; and his three children Rita, Ronald and Gerald.

Reading, writing and arithmetic were the subjects taught.

Uncle Percy died before the Free Schools opened. His children went to the Free School for that year. After that year, Aunt Pearl moved her family to New Jersey, East Orange, I believe.

————

RUFUS DOVE

I was born July 31, 1946, in Rice, Virginia. I started school at High Rock School around 1952. The school was next to High Rock Baptist Church. I completed the 1958-1959 school year at Mary E. Branch No. 2 in Farmville and Mrs. Hazel Jackson was my teacher.

The first year the schools were closed I didn't do much of anything. I stayed with my grandfather in Tuggle. He had a stroke and was in a wheel chair. He was alone. Mama and Daddy sent me to live with Granddaddy. His name was Sherman Goodhope.

The second year the schools were closed, 1960-1961, I

went to Alexandria, Virginia, and stayed with a distant relative named Louise Jennings.

She was from Nottoway County and was a blood relative on my father's side. She didn't make contact with my family the first year the schools were closed, because like so many other people she thought the schools would reopen the second year.

When it was found out that the schools would remain close for a second year, Louise contacted my parents and talked to them about me coming to Arlington and living with her. Louise and the relatives in Nottoway County didn't know my family extremely well before this time, but remembered they had kin folk in Prince Edward County that had school age children.

One day, when I knew anything, Louise was at the house. I had no idea she was coming or that I was leaving home that day with her. I found out everything when all was explained to me on the spot. I had never seen Cousin Louise before this time.

Cousin Louise, as I called her, lived on 18th Street in Arlington, Virginia, and worked for the Federal Government. I was enrolled at Hoffman-Boston High School in Arlington.

When I went to Alexandria, Cousin Louise introduced me to Mr. Hightower. He owned a construction company. She also introduced me to Mr. Strother who was one of the top blacksmiths. He shoed President Kenney's horses. President Kennedy rode horses and had a stable. Mr. Strother was the top blacksmith. He made his own horse shoes.

My first summer I stayed in Alexandria, the summer of 1961, I worked with Mr. Strother. I learned about horses and went to horse stables with him in Maryland, Winchester, Virginia, and other places. We made the shoes on Monday and

Tuesday and on Saturday we did the work. I learned so much about horses from Mr. Strother. He was in Ebony Magazine in the 1960s. They did a story on him.*

When I went back to live with Cousin Louise in the third year of the closure of the schools, 1961-1962, another student from Prince Edward County named Freddie Cobbs came to Arlington. Freddie lived around the corner from us with Mr. and Mrs. Ernest Johnson. Mr. Johnson was a big shot in the county.

During the summer of 1962, I worked with Mr. Hightower and began to get my construction skills. He was a good teacher.

I stayed with Cousin Louise until the Free School opened.

When the Free School opened, I was placed in the tenth grade. Around December 1963, I got my license to drive school bus and was a substitute driver.

I went to school that one year. School became boring that year compared to what I had experienced in Arlington for three years. In retrospect, I will say that had I stayed at Cousin Louise's house I would have remained in school.

When the Prince Edward County public schools opened in September 1964, I didn't go back to school. I went into the logging business. I went into business for myself. I borrowed five hundred dollars from the woman who had been my seventh grade teacher, Mrs. Hazel Jackson. She had confidence in me and agreed to give me the loan. My parents told Mrs. Jackson it was her decision to let me have the money and they were not involved. (Mr. Dove started laughing.) They told Mrs. Jackson this was between me (Rufus) and her.

I bought my own logging truck, chain saws and other equipment.

My first big job came. I was offered the job of cutting the timber in the State Forest in Nottoway County. The man in charge was so impressed with me being so young that he gave me the job. The timber had to be cut because the beavers had gotten into the wood.

I did pretty good and then things got rough. Wood was not selling for a while. I decided to get out of the business and go back to Cousin Louise.

You had to have a Class A Chauffer's License to drive school bus. Since I had a Class A license, I was able to get a job driving for Thompson Trucking in Arlington on Fort Myer Run Drive.

I drove tractor-trailer for about a year for the company until I got drafted into the United States Army. I went into the service April 5, 1966. I went to Vietnam.

When I went to Vietnam, they found out I knew how to pour concrete and do construction. When we first got there, we had no barracks. They put a team together and some of us built our own barracks. Anyone with a skill in construction played a role. The barracks had everything; rooms, showers and so forth. We still had to go out into the jungle.

When I came back, I got out of service. Mr. Johnson, who Freddie Cobbs stayed with, had a job waiting for me. He put me in charge of a couple of recreation centers doing maintenance work. I did maintenance work for two years.

When I was in the military, a man told me his uncle owned a construction company. I called one day, and the uncle hired me as a security guard. After a little while, the uncle said to me:

"I have a better paying job for you. You were in the military and know how to lead. I want you to be the labor foreman."

The construction superintendent was an alcoholic. He used to take me to his house in the evening. He would take out the blue prints and show me what walls needed to be knocked out of buildings and so forth. He didn't realize it, but he was teaching me how to read blueprints.

He was doing a remodeling job and showed me the blueprints on what to take out and what to put back. He would be late in the mornings because of his drinking problem. The owner of the company found out that this gentleman wasn't showing up and he wanted to know who was running the show. The people told him they reported to me. One thing led to another and the owner asked me would I handle the job. I was not happy being in charge as I was. I thought I could be better off as a contractor rather than as an employee. I told the owner that I was leaving. He said:

"Don't leave. I was in the red before you took over."

The owner of the company took me on as a subcontractor. I started my own business DOVE CONSTRUCTION. I did pretty good. This was during the Nixon Administration. Then things fell apart. The people I was doing work for couldn't sell houses. They came to me and said:

"I have to shut down." Within thirty days the total operation was over.

I looked around and landed a job with United States Service Industry. They saw on my resume that I had been in business for myself and thought I would be a good manager. This company took care of 60% of high-rises in the District of Columbia, Crystal City, and in Maryland. I ran the day operations and after a year and a half I became Director of Operations. This company had 3,500 employees. When I became Director, I had to sign a statement that stated, 'if I left the company I could not work within a two hundred mile radius.' I worked for them for seven years and they forgot to renew my contract.

I worked one year with a company out of New York.

I had an idea for a business. I had a friend who wrote a proposal for some people to back me in the business. H. Humbert Anderson, who worked for AXA Equitable Life Assurance Society didn't want to give me the money but wanted to be a partner. The company named GLOBAL SERVICE CORPORATION, based out of Columbia, Maryland, was formed. Anderson and I were the owners. GLOBAL SERVICE CORPORATION was a janitorial service and mostly took care of office buildings.

There was a program that the SDA had. If you classified as a minority and qualified, they let you bid on Federal contracts. I ended up getting the Walter Reed Commissary. I got the Commissary at Aberdeen, Maryland, this was an Army post. I got other Government contracts. I also got a lot of private contracts in the Washington, D. C. and Maryland areas. I got the contract for the Jefferson Building and the Monroe Building in Richmond. I had five or six buildings in Richmond. I have forgotten the name of some of the buildings. I had 300 employees; 60 full-time and the remainder part-time, these made up my night crew.

I was in the business for nineteen years. After 9/11, we started having problems. We had bi-lingual people working for the company and there were employees that had something in their record. Many of our workers couldn't get the clearance needed to work in a Government facility or on a Government installation. GLOBAL SERVICE CORPORATION started getting fined by the Government. One thing led to another and we decided to close the business down.

I took a year or so off and lived on my savings. I started a trucking business, but the economy got bad again.

Today I drive truck for a private company.

My work with Mr. Strother made a great impression on me. In later years I had my own horse farm in Prince Edward

County in Prospect. My family and I would go there and spend time together and ride. I still have my property in Prospect.

I was thinking to myself recently that for a little country boy that came forward and did the things I did I said to my-self—I didn't do too bad.

———

*See the story on Mr. Edward D. Strother and his craft/trade in *Ebony Magazine*, September 1966.

———

JEAN HASKINS

I had passed to the fourth or fifth grade when the schools were closed.

The first year the schools were closed my mother and father arranged for me and my two sisters go away to school.

I was sent to Baltimore, Maryland, to my uncle, Albert Stokes. This was my mother's brother. His wife had died, and Uncle Albert was raising seven children. A lady moved in the house and started taking care of us. The lady was his girlfriend. Uncle Albert tried to get me into Dunbar, that was the name of the school and it was across the street from where we lived.

Mama and Daddy sent my two sisters, Shirley and Ruby, to Nottoway County to go to school. Shirley and Ruby went to Aunt Slovine and Uncle Henry. Uncle Henry, Henry Haskins, was my daddy's brother. The way things happened Shirley and Ruby couldn't get in school in Nottoway County and they went back home to Mama and Daddy.

I was still in Baltimore and Uncle Albert was still trying to get me in school. I stayed in Baltimore for about six months and could not get in school. So, I came back home.

We just played until the Free School opened.

When the Free School opened, I went to R. R. Moton High School.

I remember in high school there was a White girl that befriended me. One time we went to a little shack of a place on Main Street in Farmville that sold hamburgers. We both wanted a burger. No Black people were allowed to go inside. She went in and bought one hamburger for each of us.

I stayed in high school until I graduated. Then I got the heck out of there (Prince Edward County).

I attended Smithfield Massey Business School and completed my studies in Business Administration. I returned to Farmville and worked at the telephone company for one day. I went to lunch and never went back. I returned to Richmond.

These are my reflections shared on Thursday, April 19, 2012.

GREEN BAY

CYNTHIA LEA JOHNSON

I was born in Green Bay and started first grade in 1955 at Mount Leigh Elementary. It was on the corner of what is now

Green Bay Road and Leigh Mountain Road. Mount Leigh was a two room school. First, second, and third grades were in one room, and fourth, fifth, and sixth in the other room. There were two teachers, Mrs. Sarah White and Mrs. Susie Miller. Mrs. Miller had first, second, and third grades.

After I completed the fourth grade in 1959, there was no more school. Mount Leigh Elementary School was locked. There was no chain put on the doors, but the doors were sealed tight. The amazing thing was no one believed school was not going to open in September 1959. The children and parents found the closure hard to believe. Some of the teachers may have known.

My father had moved to Baltimore a few years earlier to find work. The first year we were out of school the children just played. My mother finished R. R. Moton. We did some school work at home. I knew the basics, having gone to the fourth grade. My sister, Frances (Hicks), was in the fifth grade. My brother Eugene was in the sixth. My oldest sister, Vivian, was in seventh grade at Branch No. 2. We played school and worked the farm.

Vivian fell in love and made plans to marry. My mother called my father and said:

"Your oldest daughter is planning to get married."

My father got one of his friends to drive him from Baltimore to Green Bay. The man was named Sonny Boy Fowlkes. He had a big Cadillac with the long arrows on the back. Daddy loaded all of our clothes and us in that car. There were the four children, Daddy, Mama, and Sonny Boy in that car. The three adults rode in the front seat and the four children in the back seat. Everything else was in the trunk.

Daddy was living with a cousin, Evary Johnson, also from Green Bay, in a two-bedroom apartment. When he returned with his wife and four children, all of us were in the two-bed-room apartment. We stayed there until my father was able to rent a house around the corner. He rented a three-story row house.

In the fall of 1960 we all enrolled in school in Baltimore and all of us started out pretty much where we left off. I went to the fifth grade. We lived in East Baltimore at 1003 Rutland Avenue.

Though I attended a two room school with three grades in a class in Green Bay, I was far ahead of my contemporaries when I entered the Baltimore public schools. How did I get such a strong solid foundation in that two room school? Dedicated teachers and a strong family structure made the difference.

It was a big adjustment for me living in the city. The other major adjustment involved attending school. Back in Green Bay I always went to school with my brother and sisters. In Baltimore, it was decided that some of the children at our school would be bused to another school, as our facility was too crowded. I was bused to Harriet Tubman Elementary School at Broadway and Banks Streets. This was the first time I had been to school without having my brother or one of my sisters in my company and on the same grounds. The teachers were great at Harriet Tubman.

Other than the two adjustments mentioned, things went well for me in Baltimore. I think one of the great benefits of my situation was that we departed Prince Edward County as a family.

When I entered Clifton Park Junior High School, I was with my sister Frances again. Then I went on to Paul Lawrence Dunbar High School, my brother was still there. I finished Dunbar in 1968.

I always said that I was going to return to Prince Edward County one day and teach in the same school system that denied me an education.

I went to work in August 1968 for the Baltimore Police Department. I knew I could work there thirty years, retire and still be under fifty and do what I said I wanted to do— returned to Prince Edward County and teach.

I attended the Community College of Baltimore, today Baltimore City Community College, got an AA Degree with honors, and then matriculated at Coppin State and graduated summa cum laude in 1997. In May 1999 I submitted my resume to the Prince Edward County School Board and was hired to teach math.

I always told people as I was growing up that I would return to Prince Edward County and teach in the school system that refused to educate me.

I wish students would at a very early age realize the importance of education. But parents have to help children understand the importance of education. Therefore, I guess my real dream is for parents to come to realize the importance of education and pass it on to their children.

MARY BARKSDALE

I was born in Green Bay. I went to Mount Leigh School. I believe it was a one room, that was about fifty-five years ago. I started there when I was five years old. Mrs. Susie Miller was my teacher. I was born October 30, 1943, to Edward and Rebecca Spradley Barksdale.

When the schools were closed in September 1959, my family was still living in Green Bay. My older sisters, Daisy Barksdale (Granger) and Bernice Barksdale (Byrd) were in New York. Bernice was a Moton High graduate. They lived in Manhattan. Daisy and Bernice were living with Homie Barksdale our cousin in New York. My mother and father talked with Bernice and Daisy and Homie about me coming to New York to live with them.

I left Prince Edward County on a Greyhound bus in October or November. I didn't enter school when I got to New York. I went to work. I stayed in New York until 1997, when I returned to Prince Edward County.

I filled out the papers and sent them in to get the honorary high school diploma. It was put in the mail to me as I wished. I couldn't bring myself to walk across the stage and be handed the honorary diploma. There was something not real about it all.

———

ERNESTINE HUGHES SMITH

Rosa Johnson Bedford came to me at the August 7, 2004, reunion in Hampden Sydney and said: "There is a lady I want you to talk to, but she said she is not going to give you an interview. I explained to her why she needs to tell her story, but she keeps saying no." With some frustration, Rosa said: "We'll talk to her together," and added with emphasis, "but you need to get her story." It was now mid-afternoon and the reunion events for the Mercy Seat Baptist Church and Hampden Sydney community very lively. The Editor secured his laptop computer and awaited instructions. Holding my hand and pulling me forward, Rosa guided, and we stopped under a big tree.

Sitting at a table under the tree was the lady. Rosa introduced us and shared the importance of the project. The woman shook her head, while crying. Her facial expression said to Rosa—'I told you no.' "I don't like to talk about it," the lady said in a mild trembling voice. "You have to tell your story," the Editor said. "You have to tell it for yourself, for your mother, for your father, and for a host of other people. If you don't tell your story, who is going to tell it? We cannot entrust it to others. You have to tell your own story, and nobody can tell your story like you can. Nobody can tell what happened to you better than you. I need you to try and tell it." She kept crying. The Editor remained seated in front of her in a folding chair. Rosa stood beside her. After several minutes of solitude, the lady wiped her eyes, blew her nose, and nodded in the affirmative. "Just say what you would want to see in a book," the Editor said softly. "I will only type what you say."

My parents were George Edward Hughes and Mary Ghee Hughes. I was born in Charlotte Court House, March 6, 1950. Then my parents moved to Prince Edward County, when I was a baby and settled in Green Bay. The first school I attended was Mount Leigh.

From my elementary school days, I wanted to be an LPN. I always wanted to care for people and take care of people.

I had passed to the fourth grade when the schools were closed. My mother told us the day school was to start that we wouldn't be going. I enjoyed school and was deeply hurt.

I helped my mother raise the children. There were eight children and only three of us were school age. My brother Earl was the oldest. I was next and then my sister, Beatrice.

The five children younger than us we had to help take care of. I didn't understand why Daddy wouldn't move to another town or county, so we could go to school.

Some people contacted my parents inquiring about me, Beatrice and Earl going away to school. Daddy was not for it, but my mom was agreeable to the idea. We ended up staying home.

When the Free School opened in September 1963, I was placed in sixth or seventh grade. It was a good school year. There were students of all ages in classes. The next year when regular school opened I went to the eighth grade.

I have taken nurses' aide courses. I'm a Certified Nurses' Aide. This is the closest I've come to my childhood dream of becoming a nurse.

It is very hard to put into words how I feel about what happened to me and others in Prince Edward County when the schools were closed. I have shared this little bit under great strain. I didn't want to give this interview, but Rosa Bedford insisted, and I yielded.

Note of the Editor: Mrs. Smith cried during the entire interview and the world rejoices because she summoned the strength to share her painful account. Mrs. Smith, on behalf of readers you will never meet, and the many people who will read this book generations from now, THANK YOU.

JOHN HURT

I was born April 7, 1951, to Irene Trent Hurt and Elmore Hurt. My parents were from Prince Edward County and they both grew up in Green Bay.

There were twelve children in my family: Daisy, Shirley, James, Elmore, Jr., Estelle, Rosa Lee, Earl, myself, Ernest, Josephine, George and Christine.

Daisy and Shirley were not affected by the closing. Shirley finished a year or two before the schools closed. James, Elmore, Estelle, Rosa Lee, Earl, and me were locked out of the schools. Ernest, I believe, was starting the year the schools were closed.

I had passed to the second grade when the schools were closed. I was at Branch No. 1. Mrs. Bigger was must first teacher. My sisters and brothers went to Mount Leigh, but by the time I started to school it had closed.

I think me, Earl, and Ernest were impacted the most. James, Elmore, Estelle, and Rosa Lee were already in the higher grades.

We were told over and over that the schools would open. Mama and Daddy didn't believe they would do this to us. Each night we went to bed thinking the next day school would open. Especially after the weekend we always thought on Monday we were going to school. But after so long, well....

My father died around 1960 or 1961 at a young age. Looking back, I think stress contributed to it.

When the Free School opened, I was twelve or thirteen years old. I was put in the sixth grade. Can you imagine being put in sixth grade and had never completed the second grade. When the schools were closed, I was reading 'See Jane run." In fact, I was looking more so than reading. This was the book I ended with. I was expected to do the same work and keep up with the children who had gone away to continue their education. I had been out of the second grade for four years and had forgotten everything I had learned in first grade. I was bigger than any of the children in my class. It was so embarrassing. I just could not keep up. It was impossible.

As I was growing up, I never really understood the impact of the closing. We came up in a situation where many, many people couldn't read and write, and you almost thought it was natural. But it was when we would visit other counties and be around people our age that we realized how damaged we were. We spent all of our time in Prince Edward County around many others who couldn't read and write so we had no comparison.

We lived on a White man's farm and had to work. That was why going to school was not such a big thing. Renting a house in another county or moving wasn't an option for my parents. We were too poor. We worked the farm those four years. We were brain washed. We worked on a farm and the White owner always told us:

"Y'all don' need no schooling. Y'all will always have a place to work and live. You can always live on my place."

Most of the people I hung out with they couldn't read and write, so I didn't feel out of place.

I was about twenty-five years old when I was able to fill out a raffle ticket or if I was at the grocery store and they gave us something to fill out to win a prize. I could not fill it out until I was about twenty-five.

I heard an advertisement on the radio one day that said something like:

"If you are in a company of people and you can't read, you will feel like a misfit." Then she would say over the radio: "Perhaps you are a misfit but let me help."

I called the telephone number they gave. The lady's name was Mrs. Virginia Booker. She would come to my home. She came twice a week. I was about twenty-five or maybe a little older when I started with her.

I got my wife in the program, my brother, Earl and my

brother Ernest. Ernest is still in the literacy program in Farmville to this day, November 6, 2004.

What did I learn in this program other than reading? I learned that if you are in your twenties when you begin to learn to read and write it will not happen — *just like that.* Many of the grown folk in the program with her quit because they thought the information would be gotten instantly. But the truth of the matter is — It was a struggle!

When I got saved, when the Lord saved me, something came over me and I wanted to read the Bible. The 1st Psalm, Psalm 117. (Brother Hurt movingly recited some of the Psalms to the Editor.) I joined the Holiness Church and had to lead the Testimony Service. To be able to stand there and be able to testify and read the Scriptures to the people was a great feeling.

The Bible says that every deed done in this body you will give an account for. How could a people be so evil as to do something like close the schools? They did not only deny me, they denied my children.

I went to Richmond to the State Capitol to help get the scholarship bill passed. The state of Virginia is working to appropriate several million dollars for people impacted by the closing of the schools, so they can return to school and further their education. I think the bill should even include the children and grandchildren.

The number one priority for the Hurt family is education.

I know the basics you get in first to about fifth grade. If you miss that, it will be difficult from that point on.

I want to say that there is no shame in not knowing how to read and write. The shame is in and with those who closed the schools. The other shame is when people refuse to brace up and go on and learn how to read and write.

I always tell our people don't be afraid or ashamed to tell your story; but tell it without hating.

———

PAMPLIN

———

ALMA BROWN ROBERTSON

I was born April 14, 1930, to Alfred and Lizzie Carter Brown. I went to Old Brown School in Pamplin. It was a one room school. Mrs. Wilsie Smith was the teacher. The school went to the fifth grade. There was only the White school in Pamplin at that time. Pamplin is on the border of Prince Edward County and Appomattox County. I could walk across my yard and be in Appomattox County. Children in my area went to Appomattox. I used to cross the line and catch the bus and go to Carver–Price High School. I graduated from Carver–Price High School. Prince Edward County didn't provide buses to the Pamplin area for students that wanted to go beyond elementary school.

There was a family in Pamplin who sent their daughter to Carver–Price when the Prince Edward County schools were closed. She could do as I did as a girl. She could walk across her yard and literally cross the county line and be in Appomattox. She was an only child. I won't give the family's last name. The girl did this the whole time the schools were closed. She would come out of her house, walk across the yard, and be in Appomattox County. She would stand there and wait for the bus with the Appomattox children. She caught the bus near the old Saint John's Service Station. The old Saint John's Service Station was on the line.

She stayed in the Appomattox school system even after the Free School opened and the regular school started back.

————

SARAH DOROTHY COUCH

I was born August 25, 1949, in Pamplin to Leroy and Sally Ann Paige Couch. I started school at Mercy Seat School. Mrs. Victoria Brown was my teacher and I loved her to death. I lived in Pamplin but had to walk several miles to catch the bus that brought us to Mercy Seat. All the Negro children in Pamplin had to go to Mercy Seat. There was a school in Darlington Heights at a church. We lived too far on the other end of Pamplin to walk to the school in Darlington Heights. We were closer to Mercy Seat in Hampden Sydney than to the school in Darlington Heights.

I was in fourth grade when the schools were closed. The children in my house locked out of the schools were one brother, Isaac Leroy, and six girls: Shirley Ann, myself, Mildred, Edith, Gladys, and Florence.

While the schools were closed, Mama taught us reading and spelling and math at home. We lived on a White man's farm in Pamplin. My daddy worked for the man. Mama gave us three hours a day for school. You could only get up to go to the bathroom. On top of that she cooked and washed clothes.

As far as I recall, there was absolutely nothing in Pamplin

for the children, no classes and such. Everyone was schooled at home or nothing. Then they worked in the tobacco fields.

When the Free School opened in September 1963, I was placed in the seventh grade, though I was in fourth when the schools were closed. Mama had done a good enough job at home and I could work at the seventh grade level. They gave me the Free School test and I passed at the seventh grade level.

I graduated in 1970 from R. R. Moton High School.

―――――

SAMUEL A. COBBS

I was born to Lacy and Minnie Cobbs in Prince Edward County, May 9, 1942. I was one of ten children. I was born and raised on a farm, as were most Black children in Prince Edward County during this time. We planted and gathered crops.

I was affected when schools closed on June 5, 1959. When it was announced that the public schools were closed, I could not believe it. I had been promoted to the eleventh grade.

My brother Freddie and I were out of school for a year. During that year, we helped farmers gather their crops. We were also able to earn money shucking corn, harvesting tobacco and tying bags when farmers combined their wheat.

After we had been out of school a year, the American Friends Service Committee came to Prince Edward County. I remember Dr. Martin Luther King, Jr. came to Prince Edward County also.

We must have heard about the American Friends Emergency Placement Program at church, Sulphur Spring Baptist Church where my family attended. Consequently, Freddie and I went to First Baptist Church, in Farmville, where a meeting was held. The American Friends representative Helen Baker interviewed many of us. Somehow, I was chosen to go to Moorestown, New Jersey, with six other students, where we would live with foster parents and attend school. Freddie was not selected and did not leave home the second year of the school closing.

Students were also selected to attend schools in Iowa, Pennsylvania, Massachusetts, and Ohio.

My father didn't want me to go away to school. He was opposed to my going away. Daddy wanted us to stay home and work with him on the farm, but my mother was of a different mind.

Those of us selected to go to Moorestown, New Jersey, left Farmville the same night on a bus bound for Philadelphia, Pennsylvania. Students in the Emergency Placement Program that were going to other locations and points north were on the bus that night. I believe Cornell Walker, who went to Media, Pennsylvania, was on the bus.

When the Moorestown group arrived in Philadelphia the following morning, American Friends Service Committee representatives were there to meet us. The representatives that picked us up were Juniata Morrissey and Charlotte Meacham.

I was placed with a Black couple, Mr. Clarence and Mrs. Ruth Jenkins Baylor. They had no children. It was a mutual adjustment for Mr. and Mrs. Baylor and for me. Mrs. Baylor was a middle school math teacher at Moorestown Junior High and her husband was a butcher for a local company.

I was chosen to attend an all White private preparatory school, Moorestown Friends School. I recall that Moses Scott attended Moorestown High School, the public high school. Moses was from Prince Edward County and selected to be in the American Friends Emergency Placement Program.

In September 1960 I was the first Black student to attend Moorestown Friends School in its one hundred seventy-five year existence. It was a big adjustment for me to go to the all White high school having attended all Black schools in Prince Edward County. The teachers at Moorestown Friends School were kind and so were the students. I had some difficulty in math, namely geometry. I was given a tutor for history, but really needed a tutor for geometry in which I was unsuccessful. I enrolled in chemistry, but dropped and enrolled in French III.

The Baylor family was very good to me. They took me on trips to Atlantic City, New York City, and Philadelphia. They bought me clothing for school and gave me a small weekly allowance. I was very active in Second Baptist Church in Moorestown. I was in the junior choir and active in Sunday School.

Mr. and Mrs. Baylor exposed me to different foods that I had never eaten, stuffed peppers, crème dried beef, which I detested, cow tongue, which I hated and corn-beef. Mrs. Baylor was an excellent cook. She often served beets and I liked beets. I learned to eat and appreciate many foods.

Mrs. Baylor's sister lived down the street and I would go there sometimes and eat. This sister was a special education teacher in Philadelphia. Her name was Anne Jenkins Anderson. Mrs. Baylor also had a sister in Trenton who was very, very nice to me. This sister was the Assistant Superintendent of Schools in Charge of Curriculum and Staff Development. Her name was Mrs. Ada Bernice Jenkins Munce.

Mr. and Mrs. Baylor really tried to make me feel like a high school student. They arranged for me to be in a Debutante Ball. I had to take a bus from Moorestown to Camden weekly for about six weeks to rehearse. The big ball was held at the Latin

Casino in Cherry Hill. I didn't want to be in the Debutante Ball and didn't wish to be a part of it. Otherwise, Mr. and Mrs. Baylor were very good to me.

When I returned to New Jersey in September 1961 for my senior year at Moorestown Friends School, I went back to the Baylor home.

The beginning of the second year the behavior of Mr. and Mrs. Baylor toward me changed and I had no idea what was happening. At the end of the first semester of my second year, I learned that Mr. and Mrs. Baylor were experiencing difficulty paying their mortgage and had the house up for sale. That contributed toward the change I concluded. The Moorestown Emergency Placement Committee, which secured our foster parents each year, made arrangements for me to move.

During the second semester, January to the end of the school year in the spring of 1962, I stayed with four different families, living with each family for approximately one month. I lived with two Quaker families, one French Canadian family and a Black family. All the families treated me nice.

The first of the four families I lived with was the Wildman family. This was Edward and Hannah Wildman, and they had three children, a daughter and two sons. They had a huge house. Mr. Wildman was a physician and Mrs. Wildman a housewife.

The second family was the Hull family. The husband was named James, and the wife was named Alta Mary. I know one of the boys was named Regan. This boy was in my class.

The French-Canadian family's last name was Phillips. The husband was named Henry and the wife named Phyllis, I believe. They had a son named Bill who was one year behind me in school. One day the Phillips family took me on a boat trip out on the mighty Delaware River outside of Philadelphia. I was very frightened. I thought I wanted to go on the outing until I got in the boat. We stayed on the river a very short time and they came back in on my behalf.

The fourth family was Lloyd and Mary Stark. I believe Lloyd was a major in the United States Army. They had two sons in middle school Craig and Eric. Mrs. Stark, believe it or not, was raised by Mrs. Ruth Jenkins Baylor's mother.

As Moorestown Friends School was a Quaker institution, we had to attend Meeting every Thursday at around 10:45 a. m. You sat there for forty-five minutes and remained quiet. If the Spirit moved you, you would get up and shake or shake in your seat. Most people shook in their seat if they felt something had moved them. Sometimes those who felt the Spirit would say something, but for the most part these were older people. The students remained quiet throughout the service. I never heard a student say anything.

While at Moorestown Friends School, I was in the French Club, the Cupola (the Cupola was the school year book, so I was on the Year Book staff), Nominating Committee, and a member in the Senior Play. In the senior play I had the role a deaf mute.

The first year at Moorestown I spent adjusting. The second year I was busy moving from family to family, so I never got involved in sports.

I was from a poor farming community, as I mentioned earlier, and couldn't afford all of the extra memorables associated with a senior year in high school. The senior class at the school had a car wash and raised enough money to buy my high school ring.

Being the first Black student at Moorestown Friends School, I was also the first Black student to graduate from the school.

During my senior year, I was encouraged by the guidance department to apply at Earlham College, a Quaker School in Indiana. I also applied to Southern Illinois and was accepted, applied to Howard University, West Virginia State College and Hampton Institute.

I chose Hampton Institute. The reason I selected Hampton was because Mrs. Munce, Mrs. Baylor's sister, took Moses Scott and I to Williamsburg, Virginia, to speak to the LINKS organization about our experience coming from Prince Edward County. On the way back to Trenton, Mrs. Munce took us to Hampton Institute and I fell in love with the campus instantly. Hampton was also the only school that offered me financial assistance, $250.00, which was a considerable sum in that era.

My first year of college I needed eyeglasses and Anne Anderson, Mrs. Baylor's sister, sent me the money to purchase the glasses. I saw her that summer and she said, 'if you need anything let me know,' which I thought was very nice.

The Moorestown Friends School paid all of my expenses for four years at Hampton Institute. The cost my first year, the 1962-1963 academic year, was $725.00. My last year 1965-1966 tuition was $1,175.00.

I majored in Elementary Education. After graduating in 1966, I joined the National Teachers Corps and trained at Indiana State on techniques in teaching disadvantaged under privileged children. I interned two years in the Gary, Indiana, school system and accepted a position in the Gary school system, where I taught for two years. So, I worked in the Gary, Indiana, system for four years.

While in Indiana, I began working toward my master's degree. I received the degree after two years of interning in the Gary school system.

In the spring of 1970, I was offered a job by Dr. Martha Dawson at Hampton Institute to work in a non-graded federally funded early Childhood Education program called Follow Through. My job was that of demonstration teacher and we had federal sites in Little Rock, Arkansas, Atlantic City, New Jersey, the Archdiocese of New York City, and Bradley County, Tennessee. I traveled extensively for four years conducting demonstrations and working with teachers who would work with disadvantaged students in those areas.

I joined the Hampton public school system in 1974 and worked in that system for twenty-seven long years, teaching self-contained elementary students for thirteen years and moving to middle school when the system converted and moved sixth graders to middle school in 1987. I taught Social Studies and Language Arts in middle school for fourteen years. During this time, I earned a second master's equivalence degree attending Hampton, the College of William and Mary, Norfolk State University, the University of Virginia, Lynchburg College, Christopher Newport University, Old Dominion, and Appalachian State. Some courses were taken on the grounds of institutions and other courses taken through extension classes. I retired from the Hampton public school system in 2001.

My wife Sadie and I have been traveling since retiring. A Miami-Key West, Florida, trip was most memorable. I have had time to spend with my family, visiting my brother Leon who teaches German at Wayne State University, in Detroit. Leon has a Ph. D and was also affected by the closing of the schools. Sadie and I have also gone to visit family in Charles Town, West Virginia and Atlantic City, New Jersey.

Of the ten children in my family, eight of us went to college.

FREDDIE COBBS

I was born on September 14, 1945, in Pamplin, Virginia, and attended Five Forks School. Mrs. Pearl H. Baker and Mrs. Flossie Womack were my teachers. In the fifth grade I went to First Rock School, where Mrs. Helen Fisher was my teacher. Then in sixth grade I attended Mary E. Branch No. 2. in Farmville. I don't remember my sixth grade teacher's name. I was also at Mary E. Branch No. 2 in the seventh grade. I went to R. R. Moton High School in the eighth grade. I completed the eighth grade school year and was promoted to the ninth grade before the schools were closed.

In the fall of 1959, the schools didn't open. My father was a farmer and I stayed at home for two years helping Daddy on the farm. During these two years, there were schools in some of the churches. So, I went to one in Prospect at Saint James African Methodist Episcopal Church.

In the summer of 1961, one of the teachers that came to Prince Edward County to work with students was Neal Haygood. He was from Arlington, Virginia, and taught at Hoffman–Boston Junior Senior High School in Arlington. Mr. Haygood taught at Saint James in the summer of 1961. There was also a female teacher from Arlington that came to the county to teach that summer, but I can't remember her name.

Mr. Haygood said that he knew a couple in Arlington who wanted to take in a young girl so that she could attend school. He saw that I was eager to learn, and he said that he would tell them about me when he returned to Arlington.

He told the couple about me and my parents decided to let me go and stay with the family. Mr. Haygood was a coach at Hoffman-Boston, so he had to leave Saint James before it was time for school to open in Arlington. He had a female teacher from Arlington take me to Arlington to meet the family that I would be staying with. All arrangements were made directly with my parents. There was no sponsoring organization involved.

The female teacher took me to the home of Mr. and Mrs. Johnson. The man's name was Ernest and he was the Supervisor of Recreation for Arlington County. His wife was named Mignon Johnson. She was a Counselor in the Washington, D. C. Public School System. I stayed with them for two years and completed the ninth and tenth grades. I attended Hoffman-Boston Junior Senior High School.

Pop Johnson was the way I addressed Mr. Johnson. He loved football and he used to take me to all the high school football games in the area. When the Hoffman-Boston team went to other counties, he followed the team and would take me along.

I called his wife Mom Johnson. I vacuumed and waxed the floors every week for her. I also had a paper route in the community. I got up about 5:00 a. m. and it took about thirty to forty-five minutes to deliver the papers to my customers. I delivered the Washington Post Newspaper.

My parents received a letter from the Johnson family in the summer of 1963 saying they could not take me for a third year. But then we learned that the Free School was going to open in Prince Edward County. I was glad that I was going to be back home with my parents.

I enjoyed the Free School very much. They had excellent teachers from all over the country.

I completed the eleventh grade in the Free School System. The next year the public schools reopened, and I completed my senior year graduating in 1965.

After graduating from high school, I entered Virginia State College. I majored in Electronics Technology. In my junior year I participated in the Cooperative Education Program. I worked for IBM Company in Endicott, New York, for two years and two semesters. I met a young lady who worked for IBM named Gertrude 'Pattie' Van Dunk. She was the Secretary in the Education Center for IBM. Pattie caught and held my attention. We were married on August 28th, 1971.

I graduated from Virginia State in 1971 and got a job with General Electric Company in Lynchburg, Virginia. I was hired as a Planning & Methods Specialist. I wrote procedures for placing components on printed circuit boards and applied pre-determined time standards. I was one of the first Black Engineers to be hired in that department. After several years in that position, I was promoted to be a Cost Estimator. After working a few years in that position, I became a Cost Analyst.

We lived in Lynchburg for fourteen years. I worked for General Electric for ten years and then I was laid off. I was hired by Stackpole Components Company in Farmville, Virginia, as their first Black Manufacturing Engineer. The plant there manufactured switches. I worked at Stackpole in Farmville from 1981 to 1985. In January 1985 I was transferred to the headquarters in Raleigh, North Carolina. Shortly after moving to Raleigh, Stackpole started producing keyboards for home computers. I was chosen to go to Stackpole's plant in Taiwan to train the operators how to assemble and test keyboards. I spent approximately one month there. At the same time, we were assembling keyboards for Atari Home Computers in Hong Kong. We had a problem with a lot of keyboards that we had shipped there, so I was chosen to go to Hong Kong for two weeks to train operators how to repair and retest the keyboards. Stackpole also had a plant in Haiti.

I was chosen to go to Haiti for a month to train operators how to assemble and test keyboards. Then Stackpole opened a plant in Juarez, Mexico. I was sent there several times over the years to train operators how to assemble and test keyboards and switches.

In 1986, Ark-Les Corporation from Watertown, Massachusetts, purchased Stackpole Components Company. This was a good acquisition because Stackpole produced switches up to 15 amps, and Ark-Les produced switches from 15 to 30 amps. Ark-Les produced appliance and automotive switches and I became a Quality Engineer. Around the year 2000, Ark-Les built a plant in Dongguan, China. This plant was located about a two-hour boat ride from Hong Kong. I was sent there for a few weeks to train the operators in inspection and testing of the switches using statistical process control. I worked for Ark-Les until February 28, 2003 when the plant was closed in Raleigh and moved to Juarez, Mexico. I had some excellent work and travel experiences with Stackpole and Ark-Les.

I always had a desire to learn. I was the youngest child in my family. When schools were closed, I had two brothers and two sisters that were either in college or had graduated from college. I thought that I had to do the same. I also had a few goals of my own. I never knew exactly what occupation I wanted to pursue growing up, but I knew I wanted to be in a field that paid a good salary. I grew up poor as a farm boy. Even though I wanted to enter a vocation that paid a good salary, I also knew I had to study to achieve and enjoy any reasonable level of success.

As of today, April 23, 2011, I am semi-retired. For the past six and a half years, I have been driving the school bus for the Wake County Public School System. I also drove school bus during my junior and senior years of high school. I never thought that I would be driving a school bus forty years later.

On August 28th, 2011, Pattie and I will have been married for forty years. We have enjoyed a wonderful life together.

———

ALFRED LEON COBBS

Born on September 12, 1943, I was the ninth of the ten children that my parents, W. Lacy and Minnie (Booker) Cobbs raised on a tobacco farm in Prince Edward County, Virginia. Our family like most Black families at the time was large. The extra hands made a difference on the farm when it came to planting, tending, and harvesting the crops. Despite the manual labor needs on a tobacco farm, my parents did not keep us out of school to harvest crops like some parents did. We attended school regularly with their approval.

I began my formal schooling at Five Forks Elementary School (Pamplin) and attended there for four years. My teachers there were Mrs. Pearl H. Baker and Mrs. Flossie Womack. I flourished under Mrs. Womack, an excellent teacher who awakened in me the thirst for learning and inspired me to do my best always. For my fifth year of schooling I moved to First Rock Elementary School (Prospect) where Mrs. Lydia Fisher was teacher. For the last two years of elementary schooling (sixth and seventh grades) I moved to Mary E. Branch II Elementary School (housed the old R. R. Moton High School Building). My sixth grade teacher was Mrs. Winston and my seventh grade teacher Mrs. West.

For the first two years of high school I was able to attend

the R. R. Moton High School which had been built a few years earlier to respond to the argument from the Black community that the county schools for Blacks were inferior to those for Whites. However, while the case of Prince Edward County vs. Board of Education was moving through the courts, the County Board of Supervisors, in sympathy with the politicians of Massive Resistance in Virginia, decided in the summer of 1959 to withdraw funding for the schools, which resulting in their being closed for five years rather than integrate.

When the schools did not open in September 1959, Samuel, Freddie and I found ourselves in disbelief that this was happening. We were devastated because going to school was an exciting experience for us, we were good students, and we were eager to learn. Samuel had just completed the tenth grade, Freddie the eighth, and I the ninth. In late September of that year, the former art teacher at Robert R. Moton High School, Mrs. Vivian Ross, informed Mrs. Minnie B. Miller, one of the former Home Economics teachers, that the principal of East End High School in Mecklenburg County, Virginia (also segregated), Mr. E. N. Taliaferro and his wife would be willing to take a child from Prince Edward County into their home for the academic year 1959-60. I remember distinctly that Mrs. Miller came to the field, where we were harvesting tobacco for our uncle, Mr. Thomas Allen, and informed my father of the offer from the Taliaferro family. Because I was the "loud mouth" among the three boys, I was the first one to speak up and said that I would go. There was no debate, our father did not insist that we "choose straws," and there was no discussion about which of us would be the more suitable individual to go to South Hill to attend school. Because schools also did not open in September 1960 and again in 1961, the Taliaferro family invited me back each year until I graduated in 1962. It was far from my thoughts at that time that the public schools of Prince Edward County, Virginia, would not open for another two years (they opened again in September 1964).

My brother Samuel stayed out of school for one year before being placed in the fall of 1960 in Moorestown Friends School, a Quaker high school in New Jersey. Thus he graduated in 1962 — the same year I did.

Freddie's fate was different, he stayed out of school for two years before being placed by a teachers' group from Northern Virginia, led by Mr. Robert Haygood, with a family in Arlington, Virginia. The group had come to Prince Edward County during the summer of 1961 to offer some type of enrichment program for the Black children. During that program he indicated that Mr. and Mrs. Ernest Johnson of Arlington, Virginia would be willing to take a child from Prince Edward County into their home so that the child might attend school. Freddie would spend two years in the Arlington, Virginia School System before returning home in the fall of 1963 to attend the Prince Edward Free School — a foundation supported by private funds. Freddie's graduation from high school had been delayed by two years, but he received his diploma in 1965, after having completed his senior year at the end of the first year that the public schools in the county were reopened.

This disruption in my education and that of my brothers Samuel and Freddie had a profound impact on us as individuals and on the family structure. The three of us certainly had mixed emotions about leaving home during the formative teenage years to live with families who were unfamiliar to us. And our parents, despite their anguish, were of different minds about us leaving home in those years to attend school away from home. Our father saw it as a threat to our livelihood since he would not have us to help him do the farm work. However, our mother, because of her regret that she never completed her formal education, was adamant that the last of her children should complete high school and receive their diplomas. And in her quiet and determined way she prevailed.

At East End High School four individuals had a particular influence on my life. The first was Mr. Taliaferro, the head of the family I stayed with and the principal of East End High School. He taught me the value of maintaining one's dignity in the face of racism, to have self-respect, and to be ambitious and focused on something worthy of one's talents and energies. It was Ms. Mary Tapp, my Latin teacher, from whom I learned to appreciate the nature of language and the influence of Latin on other languages, including English. Later when I would study German I came to appreciate how important my foundation in Latin was to my mastering the German language. Mrs. Anna Robinson, my homeroom teacher and my twelfth grade English teacher, taught me the mechanics of grammar, how to organize my thoughts, and how to express myself well. And her husband, Mr. Howard E. Robinson, the guidance counselor for whom I worked, was a role model for me because he taught me to work hard and to always give my best. He taught me that mediocrity was not an option.

After having graduated at the top of my class at East End High School in 1962, I enrolled in Berea College, Kentucky. I heard of Berea College from Helen Baker, a lawyer for the American Friends Service Committee, who had come to Prince Edward County to work on behalf of the education of Black children in the county. It was she who arranged for six students from the county to attend the Foundation School at Berea College, which was known for its success at "ungraded" education for youth from Appalachia who had gaps in their education and who needed remediation before they could complete their high school training and be accepted into the College division at Berea or any other place.

Berea College was founded in 1855 by Kentucky abolitionists and had a history of interracial education since its founding. However, this experiment was to cease in 1905 when the Day Law was enacted in Kentucky that made it illegal for Blacks and Whites to attend school together. It would be forty-five years later in 1950 when this law would be overturned and Berea College would resume its experiment in interracial education.

When I enrolled in Berea College, despite its reputation for interracial education, I was one of about a dozen Black students in my freshman class. The total Black student enrollment at Berea at the time was less than fifty (50) out of a student body of more than 1,200. There were no Black faculty members. While I was attracted by Berea's idealism, my main reason for applying to the College was because it had a Work Study Program and did not charge tuition (it still does not). This was important to me because my parents did not have the necessary financial means to send me to college and student financial aid was not readily available in the 1960s like it is today.

In reflecting back on those years at Berea, I realize how lonely the experience was for me, for I had never had contact with Whites in social settings and interpersonal relationships; I had never been treated as an equal by them. This being the case, this aspiring mathematician found an "existential" home in the study of German because the husband and wife instructors, Mr. Kris and Mrs. Amanda Kogerma—he Estonian and she Lithuanian—believed in me when I did not believe in myself. They saw my potential as a student of German. When they suggested that I had some ability in German and should think about teaching German, my retort was that Black people are not interested in learning German. They simply said to me "Then teach White folks German."

The statement by the Kogermas was extremely insightful for me and the turning point in the rebuilding of the self-image that racism in the South and the Prince Edward County situation had badly bruised if not shattered. I surprised myself by how I excelled in German and how liberating the immersion in a foreign language could be because it gave me an opportunity at role-playing. I could step outside my present situation, so to speak, and imagine myself in a very different one. As ironic as it may seem, in my enthusiasm for the German language and things German, it never occurred to me that I was excited about a language spoken by one of the most notorious racist dictators of the twentieth century — Adolf Hitler. This is perhaps because both Mr. and Mrs. Kogerma were enthused about German despite the fact that they had experiences both the Nazis and the Communists, both having grown up in Baltic countries.

This passion for German and things German first awakened at Berea College led me to pursue a Master of Arts degree in German at the University of Missouri-Columbia (1968) and a Doctor of Philosophy degree in German at the University of Cincinnati (1974). While at Cincinnati, I served as a Lecturer in German. Since that time I have held two professorships, one at the University of Virginia and the other at Wayne State University in Detroit.

During my six years at Virginia, I supervised the teaching assistants in German and launched my professional career. While the experience in the German Department and the encounter with excellent students academically was quite rewarding, the downside was the stigma of racism that permeated the atmosphere of the University and the pressure to publish above all else. In 1979 I moved to Detroit where I began my professional career at Wayne State University. For the past 30 plus years I have had a very successful and rewarding career as a professor of German Studies at this institution.

As far as professional achievement is concerned, I have had two Summer Fulbright Awards to the Federal Republic of Germany, have published two books and a number of articles, and have lectured at both national and international conferences. In 1984 I received the President's Award for Excellence in Teaching from Wayne State University. And finally, I have been a member of the College Board Advanced Placement Test Development Committee for German and served for a number of years as a Reader of Advanced Placement Examinations in German.

Tentatively, I plan to retire in a couple of years and spend my time doing volunteer work and traveling.

LINDA EDWARDS EDMUNDS

I started first grade at Five Forks School. In the fourth grade Mrs. Pearl Baker was my teacher. Mrs. Baker used to cook beans on the big potbelly stove. If students had beans at home, their parents would send beans for Mrs. Baker to cook. If a student had a piece of fatback meat, they brought it, so she could cook it in the beans and give the beans flavor. I didn't live far from the school and could walk there in ten minutes.

When I passed to the fifth grade, the schools were closed. I am not sure whether I went to classes in the basement of Ms. Flossie's house the first year the schools were closed; but I know I started going to her house the second year. A man named Mr. Anthony Jones had an old green truck and he put benches on the back. We would climb on the back like cattle. He would come around in the mornings and pick-up children and drive them to Ms. Flossie's. I don't remember all the children he picked-up, but I know Gladys Lawson rode on the back of the truck with us. Mr. Jones was her uncle.

Some of the students I remember being in the basement of Ms. Flossie's home were Lena Mitchell, Vivian Scott, and Ernest Williams.

Mr. Jones was married to Mrs. Della Althea Jones. Ms. Flossie used to call her Aunt Della.

My brother, Tony, had passed to the eleventh or twelfth grade when the schools were closed. I can't remember which grade, I was very young. Tony joined the United States Army and furthered his education.

My sister, Florence Edwards, was selected to participate in the Friends program and she went to Media, Pennsylvania, to school. Florence graduated high school in Media. Then she went on to Toccoa Falls Bible College in Toccoa Falls, Georgia.

I went to Ms. Flossie's the second and third years the schools were closed.

The fourth year of the school closing, Reverend Griffin arranged for me to be placed in a home in Hampton, Virginia. My mama just packed up my clothes one day and told me I was going away to school.

One Sunday evening Mrs. Lottie Jackson picked me up and drove me to Hampton, Virginia. Mrs. Jackson who taught at

First Rock School before the schools were closed now taught at a school in Hampton, Virginia.

I stayed with Mrs. Yvonne Boykin. She was a teacher at Y. H. Thomas High School. It was late in the school year and I remember school had already started when I arrived at Mrs. Boykin's. Mrs. Boykin had two little girls that were in elementary school. The first thing Mrs. Boykin's did was cut my hair. I don't know why she did that.

I went to Mary S. Peake Elementary School. I was placed in the fifth grade, with children much smaller than I. Remember I had passed to the fifth grade when the schools were closed and had been out of school for now my fourth year. I think Mrs. Boykin dropped us off each morning. The kids and everyone were nice to me at school, but it was hard being larger than the other children.

Mrs. Jackson would come home some weekends and would stop by Mrs. Boykin's house and pick me up and bring me to my parents.

When the school year ended, I was promoted to the sixth grade. When the Free School opened, I enrolled. I skipped the sixth grade and went to the seventh grade. When the Free School closed, I had completed the seventh grade and the next year I skipped the eighth grade and was placed in the ninth.

I graduated from high school in 1968.

In 1969 I married John Edmunds, Sr. He was from South Boston, Virginia. We have two children, John, Jr. and Tiffany. We have four grandchildren, as of today November 8, 2011.

———

CALVIN LESLIE LIGON

I was born in 1948 and started school when I was about six years old at Pamplin #10. Mrs. Hill was the teacher. She taught from the first to the sixth grades. In seventh grade you had to go to Mary E. Branch No. 2 in Farmville.

I was going to the fifth grade when the schools closed. Alma my little sister was around third grade.

When the schools first closed, me and my brother, Frank, crossed the Appomattox line. Frank was going to the sixth grade.

There was a man that lived in Prince Edward County, but he drove a school bus for Appomattox County. That was his job. We used to walk to his house or walk to the bus stop and meet him. We went to Carver-Price.

We only went a short time to Carver-Price. The principal called all of us in the office, about six of us from this area. He said, 'you have to live in Appomattox County to go to school here.'

Me and Frank went into the tobacco field and started working tobacco and stuff.

Miss. Alberta Sims opened a center in Pamplin for the children to go and learn. There was a lady named Miss. Bunch, I don't know what her real name was, we just called her Miss. Bunch. She had a house and a store hooked on to the side of the house. She ran a store. The store was on Highway 460, not quite a mile from where we lived. Miss. Bunch closed the store. The center Miss. Sims ran was inside the old store.

Willie Jenning, we called him Bill, he went to the center for a while. Bill passed. (deceased.) I never went to the center where Miss. Sims taught.

The center stayed open about two years and then Miss. Sims got a job teaching in Appomattox County.

Then after that school opened in 1963. Both of us went back. They put Frank in ninth grade and me in eighth grade. They said we were so old. I went to school for one year and then I quit. I didn't go the whole year of the Free School. I went back the next year when the regular school opened. I quit again; this time I think in May. I had a hard time getting back into studying. I went into the Job Corp. I stayed in the Job Corp for twenty-seven months and I came back home and started working.

After the regular school opened back up, Miss. Sims left Appomattox County and came back to Prince Edward County to teach.

————

CATHERINE DELORIS ADAMS

I was supposed to start school in September 1959. I was born February 9, 1953. My grandparents, Joseph and Mary, (Catherine chuckled. We were standing in the sanctuary of Zion Baptist Church, Prince Edward County, after Sunday worship service), raised me, Mary Cox Gray and Joseph Gray. We lived in Pamplin. My parents lived in New York. If I had started school, I would have gone to Pamplin #10.

For the next four years I just played. I stayed at home. We had our chores to do at home every day. Some people in my neighborhood went to other schools, some children went to school in Appomattox County. I think they had relatives there and went and stayed.

When the Free School opened, I went to Mary E. Branch, No. 2. I knew my ABCs when I started school and I could count. I could read a little. My grandma had worked with me a little. My brothers, Thomas and James, we called Jimmy, worked with me too. They had been to school. Tom was one year older than me and went to school one year. Jimmy was four years older than me. They worked with me at home.

In the Free School they went along with us to see how much we knew and how much we progressed. At the end of the year they promoted us to a grade. I was promoted to the fourth grade.

I think high school started at seventh grade. I started high school. I remember when we were in high school Tom was selected to be in a program and went to Massachusetts. I don't remember how it happened. The program was called ABC. That stood for A Better Chance. The family came to our house to visit and meet with my grandparents. The family invited me to go to Massachusetts too. When we got there, Tom stayed in a dormitory and I lived with the family. The boys in our family were very smart. I stayed the first semester. I didn't like the area. I thanked the family and came back home. I started high school again at home in the second semester. I don't remember what grade I was in when all of this happened, but I know I was in high school.

I skipped the eleventh grade. I had all of my credits to graduate and I was skipped.

I graduated in 1972.

———

LAURA JONES

I was born in Appomattox County, January 2, 1927, to William Anthony Jones and Della Althea Scott Jones. My mother was born in Prince Edward County, November 2, 1887. Dad was born October 17, 1889 in Appomattox County.

Mama went to school in Prince Edward County. I remember when I was a girl I often heard my grandmother, Alice Gillian Scott, talk about Mr. Watkins a teacher. Grandma was six years old she said when Lee surrendered to Grant. Grandma was born a slave girl.

Mama attended school at Sulphur Spring Baptist Church, there was a small school near the church. She went to the highest grade available in Prince Edward County during her youth. After eighth grade, she went off and attended Christianburg Institute in Blacksburg, Virginia, and graduated in 1910. Mama was the Valedictorian in the Class of 1910. She received the Gold Medal for Outstanding Performance and a scholarship to Cheyney State College in Pennsylvania (today Cheyney University of Pennsylvania) in Cheyney, Pennsylvania. Cheyney State was the first college founded to educate Black people in the United States.

On November 6, 1988 Mama was honored on Founders Day as the oldest living graduate of Cheyney State. Mama was one hundred years old at the time. We celebrated her 100th birthday on November 2, 1988.

Note of the Editor: "I have never been in a community where so many people lived to be one hundred years old or older," said the Editor.

My grandmother, Alice Gillian Scott lived to be 100, she died nine months after the one hundred year celebration. My mother lived to be 101 years old. Uncle Robert Scott (Father of Doris Scott Crawford) lived to be 102 years. Uncle Walter Scott lived to be 103 years old and he was the last of the children. The other brothers and sisters lived well into their nineties, as well as some cousins.

Mama came back to Virginia after graduating from Cheyney State. I believe she returned to Prospect. Mama was a school teacher in the Prospect area before she was married.

After Mama got married she moved to Appomattox County and taught in that area. She and Daddy were married August 7, 1921. Mama taught elementary school. I know she taught in Hixburg, between Prospect and Appomattox.

In later years Mama taught adult school in the afternoon and evening for grown people who wanted to learn to read and write. I remember I was a child when she was teaching adult education in Appomattox. That means she was teaching them in the 1930s.

We went to grade school in Appomattox County. We were still living in Appomattox County when we went to high school, but we stayed with my grandmother, Alice. School buses didn't come out to where we lived in Appomattox. My brother had to walk five miles to catch the school bus. We lived in Appomattox, but near the Buckingham County line. After I finished grammar school in Appomattox, to continue in high school I came to Prospect and lived with Grandma Alice. Otherwise I would have had to walk the five miles one way to the bus stop; or my parent could have paid a family in Appomattox rent so I could live with them. Since Granddaddy had died and Grandma wanted us to come and live with her, she was alone, it was convenient for everyone. My sisters and I graduated from Robert R. Moton in Farmville. I graduated in June 1944. The high school at that time was what is today the Museum.

Mama and Daddy had two boys and four girls, and they raised a foster child. They had seven grandchildren and eight great grandchildren.

After I finished high school and left home, Mama and Daddy moved to Prince Edward County. Daddy had never lived in Prince Edward, he always lived in Appomattox County, which was his home.

Mama worked as a Home Demonstration Agent or an Extension Agent. This person would go into homes and for example if a chair needed repairing Mama would show the mother of the house how to repair it. In that day people didn't throw things away, items were repaired and reused. Sometimes the women came together in groups and did quilting. Quilting lessons were given. The women gathered and did sewing, and this was basically a demonstration class in sewing. Mama taught women how to put a quality feminine touch in their home. I believe she showed women how to can fruits, vegetables, and meat.

I remember when the schools in Prince Edward County were closed and Mama mentioned helping to locate a place where she could work with the children. She and her sister, Aunt Pearl, ended up teaching at the Long Branch Sunday School Building in Five Forks.

Grandma Alice was married twice. Aunt Pearl was born during her first marriage. When Grandma Alice married a second time, my mother was an offspring from that union.

At one time, Aunt Pearl taught at Five Forks School. She taught there for many years. As far as I can remember, it was the only school where she taught. Aunt Pearl went to Hampton Institute.

Mama worked closely with Reverend Griffin. One summer college students from around the country, White and

Black, came to Prince Edward to assist with the children. Mama told us about it.

I was living in New Jersey and my sisters, Clara, Rosa, and Katherine and her family, always came home for revival beginning the second Sunday in August. One year when we came home some of the college students were still in the area. I remember they came over that Sunday for dinner and we met them. I remember one of them was from Florida; at least when my sister was in contact with her the lady was in Florida. This student and my sister Rosa stayed in touch for many years.

The students lived with families around the county, but several of them often came to Mama's house to relax.

There was a man who was a minister who contacted my family in later years. The gentleman came to Prince Edward again in the summer of 2011 and stopped by the house. The man was sharing that he was working with students in Prince Edward as late as 1967. It seems to me that college students were still coming at that time. It was in Prince Edward where he and his wife fell in love.

When we celebrated my mother's 100th birthday, some of the college students that had come to Prince Edward during the summers to work with the students came to the birthday party. The party was held at the community center in Prospect.

One of the college students invited Mama to her wedding in Montclair, New Jersey, and Mama came up and attended.

Mama and Daddy were married for sixty-one years.

ZION HILL

VINCENT EANES

I was born in the Zion Hill area on November 8, 1950, to Taylor and Gertrude Richard Eanes. I am the eleventh child out of twenty-one children. That's right, twenty-one children!

I started school at Branch No. 1 in Farmville. I went to school for two years and had been promoted to the third grade when the schools were closed.

During the years the schools were closed, I stayed around the house and I also worked in the tobacco fields. About twelve to fifteen of the twenty-one children in our house were caught up in the school closing. While the schools were closed, everybody worked on the farm. Daddy needed all the hands he could get to work tobacco, feed the hogs, milk cows, feed the chickens and do other chores.

Margaret, Lewis, Ralph, Jean, and Thelma were already out of school. The rest of us: Wilbur, James, Mack, Tom, Sonny, William, Yvonne, Nathaniel, Sylvia, Melvin, Roy, Larry, Carrie, Eunice, Quinton and me, most of us were impacted.

Finally, the Free School opened up. We all attended the Free School except Wilbur. He stayed with Daddy on the farm. He was the oldest at home and Wilbur chose to stay home. Daddy and Mama didn't make him stay at home. Wilbur had the option to go back to school.

When the Free School opened, there were no school

records. At first students were placed by age. You were taken to an area depending on your age and given a test. I was twelve and remember all the twelve and thirteen year olds went to the gym. Fourteen and fifteen year olds went to another place to be tested and so on.

According to my test scores, I was working below the first grade level, kindergarten. I was put in the first grade and was twelve years old. Even though I had completed two years before the schools were closed, I had forgotten everything.

The closing has to this day put a damper on the Prince Edward County community. I was affected very badly. I went from grade to grade up to twelfth grade. I was twenty-three years old when I graduated from high school in 1973. In fact, I was married while I was in twelfth grade. I met my wife, Shelia Wiley, and we were married. We have three boys: Vincent, Jr., Jawaski, and Rashad.

I am the only one in my family that attended college. I went to Lynchburg Seminary and College in Lynchburg, Virginia, (the institution has changed its name and is now Virginia University of Lynchburg). I graduated in 1993 with a Bachelor of Science in Religious Education. I worked for the Virginia Department of Transportation for twenty-five years as a heavy equipment operator. I'm retired now. I answered the call to the Christian ministry and I'm working in the Kingdom for the Great King.

In spite of what was done to me and so many others in Prince Edward County, I can still tell of the great power of Almighty God.

LUCY CELESTINE WOMACK EANES

I had five brothers and all of them were older. My youngest brother was seven years older than me. When I was growing up, my brothers were grown and working. Four were in the military and it was me and my parents at home. My parents were Benjamin Womack, Sr. and Amelia Scott Womack.

I started school when I was seven years old at Branch No. 1 in Farmville. My birthday came in December. When I went to school, there were children there from the community I knew, and I made many new friends. Mrs. Ethel Wilson was my teacher when I was in the third, fourth and fifth grades. Each year we thought we were leaving her and she met us at the next grade level. In the sixth grade, I had Mrs. Kelly. When I went to seventh grade, Mrs. West was my teacher.

We went to high school in the eighth grade at R. R. Moton High School. We were looking forward to going to the ninth grade and everyone was so happy. The news came that the schools were closed.

When we would go into town, Daddy would drive by the school because it was the closest and most direct route to downtown. You could see the big chain and lock on the doors. There was also a big chain across the driveway at the high school where the buses used to enter when the schools were opened.

I stayed out of school the first year, September 1959 to May 1960. I stayed to myself. I read a lot and went through the old school books I had at home.

The second year the schools were closed, Mrs. Ethel Wilson contacted my mother and father, and arrangements were made for me to go to school. Mrs. Wilson was teaching in Lynchburg, about fifty miles from Farmville. Mrs. Wilson rented a house in Lynchburg and took four school age children from Prince Edward County to Lynchburg with her to go to school during the 1960 to 1961 school year. I was the only one she took with her who was in high school. There was a girl in junior high school and two boys in elementary school. I attended Dunbar High School, which was where Mrs. Wilson taught. This would have been the 1960-1961 school year.

I returned to Dunbar for the 1961-1962 school year and lived with Mrs. Wilson. Mrs. Wilson came to Farmville each Friday and brought all of us home to see our parents and friends. Sunday evening was always a sad time because I knew I would be leaving my parents for another week. Being away from home was a crushing thing.

Mrs. Wilson asked me did I want to return to Dunbar High for the 1962-1963 school year. I said:

"I'll have to think about it. It looks like the schools may open back up and I want to be at home." To my dismay the schools didn't open.

There was a retired Black teacher in the Hampden Sydney community and she was interested in children who were not in school. She thought I would be a good candidate and contacted Mrs. Mozell Price in Appomattox County. Mrs. Price ran a summer camp for girls and was a supervisor at Carver–Price High School. The teacher from Hampden Sydney presented the idea to my parents. My parents discussed it with me and I said I would like to go and give it a try.

I went to Appomattox and lived with Mrs. Price. I did house work, cooked and had dinner prepared when she got home, and attended Carver–Price High School. I had to work for my room and board. I went to Carver–Price from September 1962 to May 1963.

When I came home for the summer in 1963, I heard that

the schools were going to open. I was delighted because I wanted to graduate from the high school in my home county.

Twenty-three seniors returned when the Free School opened. That year we had trips to Washington, D. C. and other places. When we went to Washington, D. C., the students were assigned to different homes in the Georgetown area. The students stayed in pairs at each home. We had a lot of teachers from many States and they exposed us to a lot.

Nothing could make up for the three teenage years I spent away from my parents.

Robert Kennedy came and visited the high school.

One of the greatest days of my life was the evening I lined up to get my high school diploma. I went to Saint Paul's College for one year, money got tight and I had to quit. Later I enrolled in a community college in Richmond.

All I can say to anyone who will listen is: 'Wake up, people. Don't let anything like what happened in Prince Edward County happen again.'

TUGGLE

CORNELL E. WALKER

The first school I attended was Mount Moriah across from Mount Moriah Baptist in the Tuggle community. The school was like an old house that had been turned into a school. It had grades first to six with one teacher. Mrs. Hazel C. Jackson was the teacher, probably the best teacher that Prince Edward County has ever had. Mount Moriah School was just one big room. There was a big pot belly stove in the middle of the room. In the winter if you sat in the back of the class you got cold, and if you moved to the front you burned up. The school had an outdoor toilet. There was a pump on the grounds. We filled the bucket and brought it back into the classroom for drinking water.

Daddy had an aunt and uncle named Frank and Ann Ross. When I was young, we were at Great-grand Aunt Ann and Uncle Frank's house. She told us that she could remember when a girl seeing smoke in Farmville and recalled seeing Lee's troops when they retreated.

My grandmother on my mother's side was a slave. I knew my grandmother very well. My grandfather, Hal West, was murdered. I am told he rode a white horse everywhere he went. He and grandmother lived in Israel Hill. He owned a lot of property and was preparing to buy some more. My mother said Granddaddy was told you can buy more land, but you will never do anything with it and he was killed by a White man.

Mrs. Jackson shaped the lives of a lot of people. She gave you more than an academic education. She had a way of bringing out the best in people. She made students assume responsibility early in life. Mrs. Jackson used the smarter students to work with the slower students. We had to make sure the slower ones came up to the same level as we. This set the tone for life early. The lesson learned was — always work to bring people up to your level. There was no financial pay for the work done in Mrs. Jackson's class, but another reward came to you for your work.

After sixth grade, I went to Branch No. 2 in Farmville. From there I went up to the high school, R. R. Moton High School.

In high school, there were four guys who always competed with each other. Joseph Hicks, James Lee, Samuel Cobbs and I competed endlessly. We thought we were pretty smart.

I had been promoted to the eleventh grade when the schools were closed. I stayed out of school for a year. There were no churches with learning programs in Tuggle.

Mrs. Beatrice Davenport was a teacher who lived in Tuggle. I used to cut her grass. When the American Friends Service Committee came around making inquiries about students going away to continue their education, Mrs. Davenport threw my name in the hat. I was selected to go to Media, Pennsylvania.

I stayed with a fine family, James and Gladys Austin. James worked for Scotts Paper and Mrs. Austin was a homemaker. This was a Black family. They were active in Second Street Baptist Church. There were four of us who went to the Media area: Florence Edwards from Prospect, John Shepperson from Hampden Sydney, and Hampton Scott. Media was a small town. John lived one block from me. Florence was two blocks away and Hampton lived on the other side of Media. The four of us didn't really know each other until we got to Media. Hampton attended Second Baptist also.

All of us, Florence, John, Hampton and I, attended Media High School. There were probably less than twenty-five Black students in the school. Two were in the same grade as I. I was in the eleventh. It wasn't an unpleasant experience but going from an all Black to a majority White school was different.

I returned to Media for my senior year of high school. When in twelfth grade, I was branded as being a Communist.

In a Social Studies class we were talking about capitalism and other governments and the freedoms we have here in the United States. I said:

"If we are so free, why did I have to leave home to go to school? If I was in Russia, I would *have* to go to school."

Many of the students couldn't believe that a county would close its schools rather than integrate.

I don't have a grand story, yet it is my story and that makes it grand. It's my story, a unique story. The experience of the closing of the schools prepared me for my next step in life.

I had three brothers: John, Franklin and Larry. My sisters were Estelle, Loretta, and Alease.

Larry stayed with a family in Charlotte County. He was not in a program such as the one sponsored by the American Friends Service Committee. Black families in neighboring counties took an interest in Prince Edward County students and that's how Larry ended up in Charlotte County.

Franklin was going to the twelfth grade. He didn't do anything the next year. In 1962 he joined the Army and later earned a GED while on active duty.

Estelle and Loretta had already graduated. Estelle was in Boston and Alease went to Boston to attend school. Alease was in seventh or eighth grade when the schools were closed. When Alease returned for the Free School, she was in eleventh grade. I know this to be the case because Alease was in the same grade as a young lady who became my wife in later years.

After I graduated from Media High School, I returned to Prince Edward County. I was a bus driver for the Free School and gassed up the other buses during the day.

The Free School was different. It was school without the academic structure to which students were accustomed.

Teachers had to scrounge to get supplies. There were times when I was in the building and teachers would ask me to go out and run errands.

One of the things that struck me was the risk a lot of parents took that we don't hear a lot about. Many parents were fired from jobs or were not hired for jobs because of their support or opposition to issues. Many Black people took a stand and the possibility for employment in the county or them being hired for a job was cancelled. They had to leave the county. Those people were the ones I admired.

Those boys with whom I competed in high school prior to the closure, Joseph Hicks, James Lee, and Samuel Cobbs, all ended up being fairly successful.

Unless this country learns to use and value all of its citizens it will go the way of Rome. No matter how great a nation, it is only as great as its people. I would say to the Prince Edward County government that over the past fifty years very little has changed and the good ole' boy politics still hinders the county's advancement.

NEW HOPE/ABELIENE

MAE WILLIE WATSON MORTON

Reverend L. Francis Griffin was the root of the school closing activity. I say activity because he picked it up and did everything for the people in Prince Edward County. He had a son we called Skip. Dr. Griffin was our keynote, our leader. Let me give you another name, Mr. Miller was very instrumental.

When Elliott was born, he was the first baby invited to participate in the baby contest to raise money for the NAACP in Prince Edward County.

I remember when Ralph Abernathy came to First Baptist Church. There was a huge crowd. I will never forget it. Anytime the outside speakers came there was a large crowd that attended. The police would stand outside with their billy-clubs. Reverend Abernathy's speech was directed to the local school situation. I remember that, but I can't remember anything exactly that was said.

Mrs. Mosley's husband was superintendent at New Hope Sunday School. Whenever there was a meeting at the church Mrs. Spencer would drill the boys and girls. Mrs. Spencer was the church clerk and a Sunday teacher.

Mrs. Betty Smith Marshall, Ben Marshall's wife, taught in Charlotte County.* Mrs. Marshall was from Charlotte County. Marriage brought her to Prince Edward County. When the schools were closed, she took her two daughters with her, and three other boys from the New Hope community to school in Charlotte County. The three boys were all out of same house. I will not give their names.

I was a little jealous, (Mrs. Morton started laughing), that she didn't take my boys.

There were three lawyers that came from Richmond to work with us.

Now as far as working with the women in this county I can name a few.

There was a lady named Mrs. Alice Earley and she was instrumental in doing everything she could and Mamie

Dell Brown Jackson, these two were hard workers; Mildred Womack Patterson, we were the women that did a lot of work with Dr. Griffin. There were no fellowship halls, so we met from house to house. We filled Reverend Griffin up with pound cakes. (Mrs. Morton laughed.) We made the cakes from scratch. There were only a few houses in our area. You didn't see houses all over. You saw a house here and there.

Now the Ku Klux Klan they had a meeting at the end of this place. (Mrs. Morton pointed down the road from her house to a wooded area.) They carved KKK on one of the oak trees. They had their meetings in the evenings and the White people around here then were snobbish. We couldn't get jobs. They would meet and declare that we couldn't go to school together.

Money was sent here to help the Black people and was put in the bank. That money was taken we were told and used for the White children. We never received the money.

In this community (New Hope) there were about fifteen children. I remember two White teachers that came.

The first summer they had classes for the children at New Hope (the Baptist church in the community) was the summer of 1962. There was a gathering at the lake and I remember carrying Steven in my arms as a baby.

I remember Mrs. Norma Becker teaching the children.

From September 1962 until May 1963 there was a Learning Center at New Hope Baptist Church. A lady named Ms. Lee taught. Ms. Lee was from South Africa. The building where they went to school was the same building where my husband went as a boy.

Reverend Griffin had us to do what we called selected buying. We didn't use the word boycott. I knew the areas of Kendrick, Chase City, Victoria, and other towns nearby and many people went to those towns to buy their groceries.

A lot of the children that were old enough went to Kittrell. Some went to Charlotte County. I sent Lyle to Charlotte County. He stayed in Keysville with my brother and my sister in-law. Mrs. Marie Mosley was his teacher. That was the way the children had to survive.

We would have a little outing down at the lake in the summer time.

In the meantime, there were two other ladies who lived around the curve, Mrs. Betty Mizer and Mary Barksdale. We would take the children in the morning, then let them play and then in the afternoon bring them back. One would teach alphabets in the morning and someone else taught in the evening before supper. That was how we organized our classes for the years the schools were closed.

There were no jobs. You had to live off of greens, turnip greens, and so forth.

You talk about canning, peeling apples, pears, and we raised some of the prettiest tomatoes. You talk about pretty gardens. Nobody went hungry and nobody got cold. I could make bed quilts, greeeaaatttt day. I learned to make bed quits and learned how to can. I could make succotash in half gallon cans.

Elliott (her son Lyle) was going to be six that November when we moved here. My husband left the area in the spring of 1960 to go away and work. I had to be like the western women who knew how to shoot a gun. There were snakes around and the KKK, who were the two-legged snakes. I could shoot too.

We would get obscene telephone calls. They would say they were coming to the house. I could shoot a gun so well until I would invite the caller to come. "Oh, please come by," (Mrs. Morton imitated her soft young innocent voice from the early 1960s), I would say. When I hung up, I would load my double barrel shot-gun.

White people would come around and ask do you want to sell your land. I guess they thought if they treated us bad enough and push us down enough we would sell and leave.

During the school closing we raised money to get funds to buy supplies for the Training Centers.

Note of the Editor: The Editor asked Mrs. Morton about families from her community that left Prince Edward County during the era of the school closure.

Wendell Brown and Ella Hurt got married and left. Both were high school age. The Neverson family left: Norma, David, and another sister went back to Washington. They were caught-up in the set-back. A lot of Black people just packed up and left.

We wrote letters to Robert Kennedy about what was going on in the county. Mr. Willie 'Buck' Carter told us not to write on professional paper; but while the schools were closed we wrote to Robert Kennedy and told him our children would be two and three years behind. Everyone who wrote received a reply from Robert Kenney's office.

While the schools were closed, sometimes I had to go away and work. I went to White Plains, New York, during the summer months and then returned home. I left the children with their grandparents. Sometimes I left in February and stayed until August or September. The children would stay with my husband's parents who lived not quite a mile from our house. I had in-laws and blood relative in White Plains.

I got married in 1951.

My husband went in the Army for two years and I purchased land in Prince Edward County.

The NAACP used to have fund raisers. The year Medgar

Evers was shot I raised the most money in the county and was crowned the queen. I remember I had to go to Washington, D.C. to a gala event.

I was in my thirties. It was tough times.

When Robert Kennedy came to Worsham School, I went over that day. I remember shaking his hand. I stayed at the school most of the day.

When the schools officially opened, we got a slate of teachers and many of them were not kind to the children. Prince Edward was one of the places where a person could seemingly slide in and get a job. We addressed the issue and started working on getting a good group of teachers to teach our little ones.

Once I worked at Worsham School after the schools opened. Mrs. Johnson was the principal. She said we need to teach these children how to eat greens. The children didn't eat them. I said:

"Mrs. Johnson, if you had eaten as many greens as these children, you wouldn't want to eat them either."

Mr. McIllwaine was not fair to the people. We had to sign petitions to have him relieved. It was hard times. I have been here fifty-three years.

Note of the Editor: The Editor asked Mrs. Morton did she know Vernon Johns and she offered the following remarks before our interview concluded.

Dr. Johns was the most dynamic and the greatest leader we had in this area. My nephew Lewis Watson used to work at the gas station own by Vernon, Jr. Mrs. Johns taught my husband when he was in school.

Mrs. Johns would sometimes put on whatever fitted and go. When Black people accepted everything White people did, the Johns left. The Johns were filled with wisdom and knowledge beyond education. The average person around here was glad to say, 'Cousin Vernon'. His leadership put him beyond the average person. Most times he was raggedy.

"Do you remember him using choice words?" the Editor asked.

"Any time he opened his mouth he used choice words."

The husband of Mrs. Morton added a few remarks.

When Vernon Johns was to speak, the people would be talking before the event and he would stand up and say – "Damn it," and the people would get quite and look around. Johns would say: "Now that I have your attention I can talk."

His farm was a few miles from here. He used to raise cattle and a few hogs. You go over there to work for him he would tell you off and then let you work. He would tell you what he wanted done in a hurry and he wanted it done that way.

Mrs. Johns would substitute for another class, but her course was music.

———

*Mrs. Betty Smith Marshall taught in Lunenburg County at Lunenburg Elementary School. See the story of Mrs. Avis Jenkins Gresby in this volume.

———

ELLIOTT LYLE MORTON

I can date my earliest memory related to Prince Edward

County. I clearly remember Eisenhower taking his second seat and my family moving to Prince Edward. Eisenhower's second term dates my relocation to Prince Edward County. I remember the Eisenhower event in particular because the first television I can recall watching was him taking the oath for his second term. Then I remember watching the parade and him standing up in the convertible. This would have been in January 1957. My middle brother, I recall, was born and his birthday was in June 1958. We moved about three quarters of a mile from New Hope Baptist Church. There were a few Black families scattered at a distance, but several other families built homes in the area and that gave me other children to play with. It was a wonderful thing to go to Sunday School at New Hope.

In the summer it was very hot, and we would have to come in and do something. Mom wouldn't let us stay outside in the heat, so we were already in a learning mode. But school didn't begin.

The first school I remember attending was at my mother's dining room table with some of the other children in the community. I remember Ivan and Raymond Miser, Garfield Barksdale, and I. There were four regular students at Mom's table, but she wasn't the only teacher. Mrs. Nora Baker, the Miser boys' grandmother, would come over and help teach sometimes. Mrs. Mary Barksdale, Garfield's mother, would also come and teach sometimes.

Having never heard of a community faculty from others that were schooled at home, the Editor asked: "How did they determine who taught and when?"

Reverend Morton smiled and explained.

It depended on who knew the most about a certain subject. Mom and Mrs. Baker knew music. Mrs. Barksdale and

Mrs. Baker knew agriculture. Mama and Mrs. Barksdale knew math. Mama was an excellent reader, even to this day. She would read and impress us with stories. Mrs. Miser and Mom together taught us life skills. These two taught us how to cook, measure, do fractions using the measuring cups in the kitchen. We had a practical type home economics class. They did whatever they could to get us to learn. This would have been the first year of the closing of the schools.

Mrs. Adie Patterson Spencer, the sister-in-law of Mrs. Mildred Patterson in Darlington Heights, came to New Hope on Saturday from Charlotte Court House to teach us. Mrs. Spencer was a school teacher. She taught at Central, but I don't know if she taught at Central High or Central Elementary. There was a one room building on the grounds of New Hope Baptist Church. I remember it had a stage and a large desk for the teacher. I don't know whether it was a small church in earlier days or a school.

When Mrs. Spencer came on Saturdays she had a good size group. There was the Evans family of about five; the Saunders family of two or three of school age, Herman was one and he had an older brother and a sister; then it was the Lee family, three people; there was Connie Hunter who was about five or six and I was there.

New Hope Baptist held worship service one Sunday a month. On the other three Sundays when there were no worship services Mrs. Spencer would teach school.

So, she taught classes on Saturdays and Sundays. Mrs. Spencer had a special interest in the children at New Hope Baptist Church because she was a member of that church, though she lived in Charlotte Court House. She was the church clerk. Mrs. Mildred Patterson's church membership was at New Hope and remains so until this day.

The boys and girls in the New Hope community had a dual learning track the first year the schools were closed. Mom and her associates taught us at home and Mrs. Spencer, a trained educator, taught us on Saturdays and Sundays.

In the late 1950s we didn't know what was going on when we saw the school buses pass going to the Academy. I was born in 1954 so I would have been around five years old.

I had a White friend in the community named Ronald Calhoun, we called him Ronnie. He was two or three years older than I. We would play and then Ronnie would go off to school. That was when I knew there were some differences. Ronnie had a tree house and we would sit in it and talk for hours. Then he would get upset because he had to go to school and I would get upset because I couldn't go to school. Ronnie went to the Academy. He went to the school in Farmville, they were bused in.

I can remember Mama and Daddy sitting in the dining room, that's where business was discussed, and talking with my paternal grandparents about whether we should stay in Prince Edward County. Mama and Daddy had just bought this house and ten acres of land. Dad didn't want his sons raised in the city. He had worked in New York and Fort Belvoir in Northern Virginia as a young man after leaving the military. He was a Korean War veteran. Mom wanted her children in a place where they could learn. Sometimes the discussions got a little heated and grandma and grandpa would have to referee.

In the summer of 1960 we had a full-blown school. I remember all the Patterson children from Darlington Heights were there.

I don't recall what college Ms. Lee attended. Clara

Patterson helped that year. Clara was very pretty and could make us learn. That summer we had all the Evans children, Saunders, Carry family, Connie Hunter, the Lee children, Mizer children, and my brother Jeffery. There were about thirty of us.

There were leaders in the community who met to ensure that each conclave had instructors. It was mix joy. I always enjoyed learning and being around other children, but I always wondered why was Ronnie always going to school and I was not. The most hateful thing was when the buses would be going to the Academy and we were walking along the road the White children would throw paper out of the buses at us.

There were some White students that attended Hampden Sydney College that treated us very nice.

I went to Charlotte Court House in first grade.

After the 1960 summer session ended, I remember sitting at the dining room table with Mom, Dad, my maternal grandmother, Aunt Ruth (Watson) and Uncle Ernest (my mother's brother). I was dismissed from the family meeting and shortly thereafter told to pack my bags because I was going to live with Aunt Ruth and Uncle Ernest in Charlotte Court House, so I could go to school.

Mom and Dad took me to the school early and had a meeting with Mr. Cooley, the principal of Central Elementary School. I don't know the story behind that meeting. I was drilled on: 'Where do you live?' 'How old are you?' I was told to give my aunt's address and not the Prince Edward County address. My parents and Mr. Colley coached me in my responses.

I went to first grade at Charlotte Court House. I vividly remember the first day of school at Central Elementary. We gathered in the cafeteria and were told to listen for our names and not to leave out of your seat. I was one of the last to be called and assigned a room and teacher because I was not from Charlotte Court House.

Mrs. Lillie Robinson was my first teacher. I found out in later life she was a distant relative.

I caught school bus Number 44 and attended Central Elementary School. I was both excited and afraid to get on that big bus. I had a cousin who was three years older and Wayne (Watson) took me under his wings. I remember him teasing me asking was I afraid. I would say 'No, just excited'. He would say: 'You look like you're about to cry.' Riding the bus caused me motion sickness. Mrs. Robinson would allow me to go into the classroom early each morning and put my head on the desk, so I could get myself together before class started.

I remember Mrs. Robinson would read stories to those of us who came in early and put our heads down on the desk. She read from Carter G. Woodson. I remember she would talk about preachers, preachers always fascinated me. I remember her talking about a preacher name Powell. (Adam Clayton Powell, Jr.)

The first play I was in I vividly remember.

Dad would pick me up on Friday evenings from Aunt Ruth and Uncle Ernest.

I remember Dad making up his mind to go back to New York to support the family and Mom staying in Prince Edward County.

We had a White teacher from South Africa and her name was Ms. Lee. She worked with the children in the New Hope area.

I distinctively remember the school closing forced the Black people in the county to come together. They may not have all agreed on everything, but the closure itself made everyone come together. All agreed that locking Black children out the schools was wrong and unacceptable.

We would go to NAACP rallies in Hampden Sydney with my grandfather. Mr. Buck Carter and others would teach the people how to pass the poll tax test, so they could register to vote.

Vernon Johns used to come to the community and I would be fascinated to hear him. The way he would pronounce his words and articulate was awesome. I remember hearing him preach at Triumph Baptist Church in Darlington Heights. Reverend Johns would politely curse across the pulpit but could get people to come together. I remember my grandmother saying: 'He shouldn't say things like that in front of children.' That made me want to listen to Reverend Johns all the more. (Reverend Morton started laughing.)

One of the phrases he would use was: 'The hell with how you feel about things, we need to get together.' My grandfather used to repeat the saying.

Looking back, I could tell Reverend Griffin knew how to maneuver. He had a lot of opposition in the community but could still rally the people. The preachers supported him in his effort to get the schools reopened.

Reverend Spraggs who was the pastor at Mercy Seat Baptist Church was very articulate. He was a soft-spoken man, but sometimes would have some hard words.

In the Prospect area there was Reverend Hendricks. Normally Reverend Hendricks was laid back, but when school issues came to the floor he got fired-up.

Reverend John Henry Allen at Saint James African Methodist Episcopal Church in Prospect was quiet but was with the community. He would never take the floor but would give advice.

King was at First Baptist Church and Vernon Johns was there that night also.

When the Free Schools opened, the bus stopped in front of our house. It was Bus #17. The news crew was outside. I remember Mama offered them coffee. The driver was Walter Jackson. Walter was about seventeen or eighteen.

I am an ordained minister in the United Methodist Church, and am a graduate of Radford University and Asbury Theological Seminary. My wife, the former Vera Dove, is from Rice, Virginia.

———

BURKEVILLE

———

FLOSSIE LEVELLA OLIVER-MOORE

I was born on May 7, 1942, to John Henry Oliver and Flossie Fears Oliver. My father was born in Nottoway County and my mother was born in Prince Edward County. I was born in Providence Hospital, Baltimore, Maryland. My father was employed by Bethlehem Steel in Baltimore and came home on weekends. My mother kept the house and farm going.

Daddy came home once and took Mama back with him to Baltimore. She went into labor and that's how I was born in that city. My grandmother, Mrs. Mary Elizabeth Jones Fears, (born in Nottoway County) was in Prince Edward and my brother was with her. After several months, my mother brought me back to Prince Edward County. Daddy remained in Baltimore. I have one brother and his name is Oakerlee Oliver, nine years older than I.

Daddy left Baltimore, returned to Prince Edward County and opened a store here in Burkeville. The store was on Highway 360. It was something like a grocery store. He sold beer, wine and all those things. The store had a piccolo inside.

The store was in the center of the two-lane highway. The highway department enlarged the roads making a dual highway, two lanes in one direction and two lanes with traffic going in the opposite direction. The store was torn down and a new store built.

After my mother and father were in the new store, they started serving cooked foods such as hotdogs, hamburgers, and barbeque. Mama had a hot plate under the cash register. This was where she made the hamburgers and barbeque sandwiches. Later my parents added a kitchen on to the store, as well as a barbershop and beautician shop. Mama did the store part and Mrs. Sally Holmes and Mrs. Lucile Wood were the beauticians. (Both Holmes and Wood are deceased.) Mr. George Hamlin and Mr. Earl Watson ran the barbershop.

My brother went to a church school at Morning Star Baptist Church. There was a little building on the side of the church which was the school.

I started first grade at a two room school named Levi Elementary School, located next to Levi Baptist Church in Green Bay. Mrs. Annie Mae Griggs was my first grade teacher. She lived in Farmville. She taught first and second grades. I think Mrs. Mammie Dell Brown taught third and fourth. Mrs. Brown came from Tennessee. Mr. James White, from

Farmville, taught fifth, sixth and seventh grades. To the best of my recollection, this was the order. There were two rooms and a divider that separated the teachers and their classes. Mr. White was there all the seven years I was at the school.

At Levi we had a small band of sorts. One student played the Xylophone and there were other small instruments.

In the early years at Levi we carried our lunch. When I was in the fourth or fifth grade, we had what was called a cafeteria. Mrs. Pinky Streat was the cook. There was another lady with her, it may have been Mrs. Mary Stokes, (not the Mary Stokes of Farmville). I am not sure who it was, but Mrs. Streat had a helper. They would serve us peanut butter, cabbage, and some sort of meat. I definitely remember the peanut butter and cabbage. (Mrs. Oliver-Moore started laughing.) I think we had a few crackers with the peanut butter. I believe the area where we used to hang our coats was converted to a make-shift area to prepare the food. Most of the food was cold food.

We had an outdoor toilet and a pump on the side of the school.

We played hopscotch, ring around the roses, and softball. I remember the children would get upset with me because I was a slow eater and they couldn't go out until I was finished. Back then they made you eat everything.

I remember the nurses would come around and check the students. Mrs. Nellie Coles was the county nurse. A dentist used to come around and check our teeth. My parents took me into town to the office of Dr. Miller.

When in sixth or seventh grade, we went to Farmville to R. R. Moton and wrapped the May Pole on May Day. That was a big thing and we thought Farmville was a big city. We also went to Farmville for the annual music festival. We sang 'Fariest Lord Jesus' and other songs. We had to recite the songs to the teacher, if you did not know the words you did not go on the trip to the music festival.

At Levi Elementary Mr. White served sought of as the principal or head teacher or whatever they were called in that day. I remember when we completed seventh grade we had a small ceremony and received a certificate. Mr. White gave us our certificate.

When I was promoted to the eighth grade, I went to R. R. Moton High School. I think the school was about two years old when I entered eighth grade. Mrs. Payne was my homeroom teacher. She was my homeroom teacher, but she taught music.

Mrs. Connie Rawlins taught social science. Mr. Stanton taught biology, Mr. L. White (brother of James White at Levi Elementary) taught science. Mrs. Glaze taught math, she was from Alabama. Mr. Whitley taught math or algebra. Mrs. Lee was the librarian and I used to assist her. I was thinking about being a librarian in high school.

I heard rumors about the schools being closed, but the rumors were discounted.

During the summer, shortly before the normal time for school to open, I remember some of us standing in front of the high school. In my mind now, I can see people standing at the high school in front of the gate with the pad-lock on it. I am not sure what we were doing. I know we were crying and just sad.

I had passed to the twelfth grade when the schools were closed. My family lived close to the Nottoway County line, but that county wouldn't accept me as a student in the high school. The first year the schools were closed, the surrounding counties would not allow Prince Edward County students to enroll in their schools.

Reverend Griffin talked to my father I know about me

going to Kittrell College. I am sure that at some point he spoke with my mother, as a decision of that magnitude both parents were involved. Then my parents talked to Reverend Dunlap. My parents told me about Reverend Dunlap and their encounters were primarily with him regarding Kittrell.

Reverend Dunlap was a pastor in the African Methodist Episcopal Church and Kittrell Junior College was sponsored by this denomination. Bishop Reid opened up the high school for us to come. Reverend Dunlap talked to Bishop Reid and the school administration and negotiated to allow Prince Edward County seniors to come and complete their last year of high school.

My parents packed up the car and drove me to Kittrell. We didn't go in the caravan that left Farmville.

After arriving at the school, I learned more about the high school department. The high school department was not fully operational at this time. The high school section at Kittrell reached its peak during an earlier period. In fact, the high school department was defunct and was revitalized to accommodate seniors from Prince Edward County. The Board of Trustees didn't hire teachers for the high school department. The teachers who taught us were on the college faculty. The president of the college, President Camper, had the faculty to arrange their teaching schedules to accommodate the Prince Edward County students. The college teachers did double duty regarding their teaching schedules. They taught in the junior college and in the high school department.

My parents made the sacrifice and paid my tuition. There may have been scholarships, but I did not get one. My parents paid. Parents that could pay did pay. I do remember working in the office of the school physician, Dr. James Green. I did some of the filing. I don't recall getting paid.

Robert Hamlin came to Kittrell after I was enrolled. Robert's father worked in pulpwood. He stopped by the store one day and Mama asked:

"What is your son doing?" Based on the reply, Mama explained: "Many of the children are at Kittrell. Why isn't Robert there?"

His father went home, made contact with the school, packed his son's belongings and drove Robert to Kittrell.

Robert can tell his story better than I and I hope he will get an opportunity to share his account.

At first, I was a little sad about being away from home, but once other students started showing up from home I became more and more at ease.

I graduated in May 1960 from the high school department and returned home. I felt comfortable at Kittrell and returned as a junior college freshman in August 1960. I participated in demonstrations in the town of Henderson near the school. We were picketing the eateries and restaurants.

The two years I was in the college program at Kittrell I served as the Year Book Editor and Chief, served on the Dormitory Council, was in the Drama Club, NAACP, and Library Club.

Back home, during the later years of the school closing Prince Edward County students stayed with grandparents, aunts, and uncles in surrounding counties to attend school.

After graduating from Kittrell Junior College, I took some summer classes at a college and the college didn't accept all of my credits. I enrolled at Claflin College, a Methodist institution in Orangeburg, South Carolina. The school accepted all of my credits from Kittrell.

When I was home in the summer of 1963, I remember demonstrating in town. I remember the dogs and them putting the water hose on us.

I graduated in 1965 from Claflin College.

I returned to Virginia and started teaching in Nottoway County. I met James Moore while he was teaching in Prince Edward County. June 14, 1969, we were married. We were blessed with three children: Janella who was an educator and vice principal at Friendly High School in Fort Washington, Maryland, passed on June 10, 2004; Trudy is an educator and researcher. James, Jr. graduated from Hampden Sydney in 2009.

I taught in the Nottoway County public schools for thirty-four years, teaching biology and retired.

As of the date of this interview, June 11, 2010, the original Levi School, where I started my education when a girl, is still on the same site. The pump is still on the side of the school. The church, Levi Baptist, has been remodeled.

VIRSO

LORRAINE JENNINGS HICKS

I was born in Tazewell, Virginia, April 11, 1936. I lived with Addison and Nannie Jennings in the Virso community. The Jennings owned their property. Virso was near Meherrin but was its own community. I started school at Virso School, which had two rooms and one teacher. Mrs. Lucille Franklin was the teacher. She was from Drake's Branch, which is in Charlotte County. She drove each day from Drake's Branch.

There was a heater in the middle of the floor that heated both rooms. There was no kitchen like other two and three room schools had. It had no electricity and the toilet was outside. We had to walk about a mile to the spring to get water. Sometimes she would name the two students who went to the spring to get the water. If a student had been bad in class that person wouldn't be chosen to go to the spring and get a pale of water. Getting the water was work, yet a treat because it got you out of the classroom. I lived about two or three miles from the school and had to walk. All of the children walked to Virso school, but the White children had school buses.

We went to school from September to May. We had plays at school and our parents would come. The performances were usually in the evenings. Virso went to the seventh grade and after that we came to Moton in town.

When we started at Moton, we had to walk to Highway 360 and that's where the bus picked us up. I had to walk about a half mile, but some students walked much further to catch the bus.

I started at R. R. Moton High School around 1949. This school today is the Museum.

I was in the Walkout (The Strike). That day we went to school as normal and went on to class. There were no loud speakers as I remember that an announcement was made over to come to the auditorium. I remember John Stokes coming to my classroom and making the announcement that an assembly was being held. I don't remember the whole class going out at that time, but there was a meeting in the auditorium and later that morning the entire class walked out. We went out of the front door and around to the side of the school. By that time the whole student body was outside. I don't remember much after that. We stayed out of school a week or two and then returned.

"Do you remember any of the students having signs or posters?" the Editor asked.*

I don't remember anyone having or holding signs.

The new school was built and then I went there and graduated in 1956.

————

*The Editor asked this question because it was printed in publications that students carried signs and posters the day of The Strike, but this is an embellishment. L. L. Hall and others noted that scenarios were added to The Strike as the years elapsed and many who had no direct involvement in April 1951 assigned themselves roles in succeeding years.

————

SYLVIA WALTON CHEATHAM

I was born September 22, 1946, to Rena Watson Walton and Samuel Walton. I started school at Virso around 1952 or 1953.

Mrs. Franklin was the teacher at Virso School the whole time I was there. The school had two rooms. Most of the children brought their lunch. You either brought your lunch or you had no lunch.

The school day started with prayer, then we would sing a church song. Then she would tell us to get ready to get down to work. There were about thirty students at Virso School.

I was there until I went to Mary E. Branch No. 2.

I remember going into town to Mary E. Branch No. 2 and then the schools closed. I was almost thirteen.

I did nothing when the schools were closed until it opened back up. I don't remember what grade they put me in. I stayed in school to the twelfth grade. I went three months in the twelfth grade. I went September, October and November 1968 and quit.

This is my story on Friday, May 18, 2012.

WILLIS JEAN COLEMAN BARNES

I was born July 13, 1947, at Farmville Hospital. My parents were Ben Coleman and Bessie Watson Coleman. I started school around 1953 at Virso School. Mrs. Lucille Franklin was the teacher. I lived about two and a half miles from the school.

Mrs. Franklin wore her hair parted down the middle in the top and would pull her hair back in a ball. She was medium complexion.

I remember us doing our morning devotion each morning. We said the Lord's Prayer, did our Bible verse, then said the Pledge of Allegiance to the flag.

I had passed to the seventh grade when the schools were closed. I don't remember going to Mary E. Branch No. 2.

There were seven children in my family: William Watson, Beulah Watson, Bennie Coleman, Jr. born in 1943, Alvin Thomas Coleman born in 1944, I was born in 1947, Diana was born in 1950 and Shirl in 1955. William and Beulah had graduated before the school shut down. Bennie, Jr., Alvin who we called Tommy, Diana, Shirl and I were locked out of the schools.

When the schools didn't open in September 1959, Mama

and Daddy sent Diana and Shirl to Aunt Geneva (Geneva Coleman Lambert) and Uncle Charlie (Charlie Lambert) in Charlotte County. Aunt Geneva and Daddy were sister and brother. Aunt Geneva and Uncle Charlie lived in Saxe. Diana had completed second grade at Virso School under Mrs. Franklin and Shirl was ready to start first grade. Diana and Shirl went to Bacon District School in Saxe.

Mama and Daddy would take Diana and Shirl to Saxe on Sunday evening and pick them up each Friday evening.

I stayed home and took care of the house for four years.

Tommy went to work and so did Bennie, Jr. They worked at Simmons Truck Stop on Highway 360 which was near our house.

When Tommy was old enough, he went to New York.

Diana and Shirl stayed with Aunt Geneva and Uncle Charlie for four years.

When the Free School opened, Diana and Shirl came back home. They went to the Free School and so did I.

I stayed in school until I reached the tenth grade and I dropped out. When the Free School opened, I had a child at home. I gave birth to my daughter Jacquline on October 7, 1962. It was very difficult trying to go to school and be a mother. I had no one to keep my baby. So, I quit school.

This is my story shared on Friday, May 18, 2012.

———

MABLE OTELIA WALTON

I started school at Virso School and Mrs. Franklin was the teacher. There was a man named Mr. Watkins and he was a substitute teacher. There were between twenty and thirty students at the school. Virso went to the fifth grade. I went to sixth and seventh grades at Branch No. 2.

I went to R. R. Moton High School in the eighth, ninth, and tenth grades. I had not heard anything about the school closing until the summer. The first I heard about it was in the summer.

The first year the schools were closed I stayed home. In the summer of 1960 I went to New York. When the schools reopened, I stayed in New York.

Bennie Coleman, Jr. got married when the schools were closed. His mother and father and my parents and family were very close. He was like a brother to me.

Going to school was the best years of my life. After I got to New York, I took a seamstress course.

_____

REDD SHOP

_____

EARL HUGHES

I first went to school in the Redd Shop area up to the second grade. The school I attended was Felden School. After I reached the second grade, my family moved to Green Bay and I started attending Mount Leigh School. Mrs. Sara White was the teacher.

When I passed to the fourth grade, that was when the

schools were closed. This was in June 1959. My family had the opportunity to send us to other relatives, my father's brothers and sisters or my mother's brothers and sisters when the schools were closed, but my father was not for it. He believed in the unity of the family.

I didn't do fourth, fifth or sixth grades.

When the schools reopened, and tests were given, I leveled out at the seventh grade. I tested at Branch No. 2 and with the test results I went to Moton High School at the seventh grade.

I guess I was a smart person. I did no studying the four years I was out of school. I believe we had a TV. I read no newspapers, books, magazines or anything during the four years. I don't know how I tested out at the seventh grade level.

I had to study hard in the beginning. Having completed the third grade and going to the seventh, I didn't know the information as I should.

From the seventh grade until I graduated from high school I had no real difficulties. I never was a troublesome person. I did my homework and I never got behind.

When school first opened, the Free School, I was one of thirty-two students that went to New York that school year. The thing we had in common was that all thirty-two of us had missed all four years of school before the Free School opened. I think there were thirty-five of us, but something happened, and three people did not make the trip. This was in December 1963 that we went to New York.

They placed one, two and three of us in private homes in New York. I can't remember the name of the people I lived with. They were older people and had a son. Their last name was something like Roseberg or Rosenberg. All the families brought the students to a church each morning where we gathered and prepared to move around the city for the day. The families we lived with provided everything while we were there. The family that took me in was extremely nice, some of the best people I ever met in my life.

We went to Madison Square Garden and went ice skating. We visited Time Square, the Empire State Building, and the United Nations. The United Nations was an eye opener.

After visiting these sites, we were taken to the home of Jackie Robinson. I still remember the barrel of nuts in his house. I couldn't imagine gathering that many nuts in a huge barrel. I remember all those trophies.

When I was in the tenth grade, two high school students were selected to go to Yale University and participate in a summer program. This was the summer of 1967. Paul Evans and I were selected. Yale University was selecting one or two students across the United States considered prominent students whose high school aptitude suggested they could become doctors, lawyers, etc. The administration at each school nominated the students. Mrs. LaVerne Pervall thought I was of this caliber and nominated me for the program. Students went to Yale to get the feel of what college life was like. The summer program was intended to motivate, direct, and stimulate you to go to college. I went to Yale by bus.

Math, Drama, and English were part of the summer curriculum at Yale. Drama was my focus. Once upon a time I thought I wanted to be an actor. Everything went well that summer. They were impressed with me and I was invited back. I returned the summer of 1968. I had just completed the eleventh grade.

When I went back, I was more familiar with the grounds and the people. I was in a production. Things went extremely well this particular summer. They wanted to recruit me to be a part of a drama group for a production. I would have had to report after graduating twelfth grade. I didn't think my parents would be for it.

Both summers at Yale were incredible. I was a little country boy, had never been anywhere or seen anything, it was great for me and not just only from the academic or book perspective. For me to have gone to Yale University those two summers it was like "*wow*' this was not possible.

I got in the program at Yale because of Mrs. LaVerne Pervall. She lived on Hill Street in Farmville and was the most influential educator in my life. Mrs. Pervall was responsible for me going to college. She became a Guidance Counselor my last year in high school and part of her job was to find out what kids wanted to do after graduating. She asked me what did I want to do and I said:

"I don't know what I'm going to do."

She said: "No, Earl, you have to consider college." I had never really thought about going to college and the first time college truly came into my mind was that day. As graduation drew near, one day she said: "We really need to get busy."

I applied and was accepted at Virginia Union University, Virginia State College and Cornell University. I graduated from high school in 1969 and entered Virginia Union University in the fall of that year. This was the only school that offered me money.

While at Virginia Union University, I was the first male on the cheerleading squad. I left college in 1973 and joined the United States Air Force. Four years later I was at Little Rock Air Force Base and the commander of the organization I was in said to me:

"You are going back to college. You are too close to finishing.

- 611 -

You need to get your degree." The Air Force had a program called Boot Strap. It was for enlisted members who were near completing a college degree. If selected for the program, you could go to college and complete your last year or semester. I went back to Virginia Union University and completed my degree in Mathematics.

While in the military, I traveled extensively. My overseas assignments were in Thailand, Turkey, Korea, Portugal, and the Philippines. I speak the language of Thailand and Turkey, and a little Portuguese. I had six State side assignments.

MICHAEL EVANS, SR.

I was born December 8, 1954. When I was supposed to start school, the schools were closed. I was living with my grandmother, Ethel Mae Evans. My mother was living in Richmond, Virginia, when I was born. When she decided to move to Newark with my stepfather, my grandfather Edward Thomas Evans told her to bring me here (Prince Edward County) to him and they would raise me. I called Grandma and Granddaddy Mama and Daddy. Mama and Daddy lived in the Redd Shop area.

My childhood in the Redd Shop area consisted of playing in the backyard at my grandmother's house. I was the only child in the house. Sometimes if I wanted to play with anybody I had to walk about a mile up the road. I went to my cousins, Keith Evans, Mitchell Evans, Cindy, Cherry Evans, and a lot more of my cousins. All of them were out of school. Everybody was out of school. None of them I named got to go away to school.

I didn't go to the church during the winter months for classes. I stayed with a lady named Miss Bolden during the week because my grandparents worked.

What turned me against the White folks in the neighborhood was one day one of my cousins named Gilbert Hines laid down in the road in front of the Academy bus and the judge of the county put Gilbert out of the state of Virginia for the rest of his life. He was about thirteen or fourteen when he laid in front of the bus. He was laying in the road when the bus came around the curve. It wasn't like he saw the bus and then laid in the road. He had to go to court. My great grandmother was raising him. Her name was Mary Evans. I remember hearing my grandparents talking about what had happen. After that event, I remember I didn't see Gilbert anymore. He didn't play with us anymore nor was he around us anymore. He went to Long Island, New York, to one of his uncles or aunts.

I went to the New Witt Learning Center in the summer. We used to walk up there. All the kids in the neighborhood would get together and walk. Mrs. Gladys Scott was our teacher. Classes were held inside the church. I remember going to Felden School a couple of times during the summer. I remember Ms. Liza Redd and Mrs. Mary Foster working with us. This was during the summer. Mrs. Scott worked with us during the summer months.

I only went to school for two summers before I started in the Free School. I had been taught to write my name and I could read a little bit when I started in the Free School. Mrs. Foster basically taught me to read and to write. I remember her hitting my knuckles with a ruler when we were with her during the summer.

When the Free School opened, I started at Worsham

Elementary School. I stayed at Worsham to the seventh grade. When I was in the sixth and seventh grade, they transported me each afternoon to the high school for band practice and junior varsity football practice. In the band I played the trumpet. In eighth grade I went to the high school, R. R. Moton High School. I was there when they changed the name to Prince Edward County High School. I graduated in 1974.

I went in the Marine Corps in 1974 and I got married in 1975 to Irene Patricia Coleman of Prince Edward County. I came out of the Marine Corps in January 1976. I was still in the service when my first son Michael, Jr. was born, I was over in Okinawa, Japan. Later my wife gave birth to another son, Marcus Evans. We later divorced, and I have another son named Jowan Ricardo. I raised six other children.

After getting out of the service, I came home and the first job I got was as an insurance salesman and that lasted about a year. Then I was hired as a mechanic at Avis Pontiac in Prince Edward County. I drove the wrecker primarily. I left there and went to Wide Load Mobile Home and pulled wide loads. Then in 1978 I went to the Department of Correction and started working at Deep Meadow Correction Center. I stayed there until 1984 and then I transferred to the Nottoway Correction Center. I stayed there until 1998 and then I retired.

I remarried in 2003 to Mildred Hicks from Nottoway County. She brought two children to the marriage.

Since I retired I have been working in my community. I am a Deacon in my church, New Witt Baptist Church, and I belong to the Prince Edward Elks Lodge #269.

When my cousin Gilbert was grown he would slip back into the county to visit his family. I got to see him whenever he slipped back in.

SHIRLEY ELIZABETH EVANS DOVE

I was born July 6, 1952. I was born and raised in the Redd Shop area. A mid-wife delivered me at home. I started first grade at Mary E. Branch No. 1 and I rode the bus into town to school. Mrs. Helen Bigger was my first grade teacher.

I finished the first grade and the schools were closed. I didn't start second grade as I should have. I didn't do anything much for the next several years. They had the Learning Centers in the churches. They had different things going on to help the children.

There was a man named Mr. Haskins who had an old truck and he used to pick up a lot of children. He would take a bunch of children from the community to a Learning Center and then come back for them when the session was over. His wife was named Sarah Haskins. I used to ride the truck. I don't remember the Center he took us to.

My two older sisters Sally and Eula and my older brother named Paul all three went to Washington, D. C. and lived in different homes.

One year a teacher in Richmond, Virginia, was going to take me in so I could go to school. She had already said she would take me. There was a committee picking out children to go and live with families. The committee contacted Mama, whoever the people were getting the homes for the children contacted her and told her they had a home for me in Richmond.

Mama said: "I'm not sending anymore of my children away from home to go to school."

I remained at home and learned as best I could. Mama tutored me somewhat at home.

I remember when Robert Kennedy came to Worsham Elementary School. I was in elementary school at Worsham.

I remember in elementary school Mrs. Herndon taught and she was the best teacher I ever had. She was crazy about her students.

That was a hard and hurtful thing for a lot of children when the schools closed. I did well in a lot of subjects, except Math. In all my other classes English and Science, I could do it. I didn't really care much for school.

I quit school in eleventh grade and I regret not graduating. I could have gone back and finished somehow, but when you get busy and raising a family some things don't get done.

I was very young when the schools were closed and can't remember a whole lot, but today, Saturday, September 22, 2012, I have told what I do remember.

I asked my older sister Sally to share her story. She will remember more because she was older.

———

SALLY MARIE EVANS LEE

I had passed to the fourth grade when the schools were closed. I was out of school the first two years. The third year the schools were closed I went to Washington, D. C. My sister Eulah and my brother Paul also went to Washington the third year the schools were closed.

I lived with a lady named Ms. Wood. She taught in the

Washington, D. C. public schools. She was a single parent and had a son and a daughter.

The next year, the fourth year the schools were closed, I went back to Washington, D. C. This year I stayed with the Taylor family. Mr. and Mrs. Taylor taught at Howard University. Both were professors.

Eulah and Paul also went back to Washington, D. C., but I can't remember anything about the families they lived with.

During my two years in Washington, D. C., I went to John Burroughs School on the Southeast side of D. C. and Georgetown Day School, a private school.

The families I lived with was like living at home. The families I stayed with were good people. They made sure I didn't get lonesome for home. I had chores to do. I would go out to games with friends, shopping, or enjoy the scenery of D. C. I would visit my sister and brother very often in D. C. I came home at Christmas and at the end of the school year.

When the Free School opened, I was put in the eighth grade. I graduated from R. R. Moton High School in June 1967.

———

GEORGE DOUGLAS BARKSDALE

I was born June 12, 1950, to Charlie and Rosa Brown Barksdale.

I started elementary at Felden School and Mrs. Foster was the teacher. I had passed to the fourth or fifth grade, I can't remember which, when the schools were closed.

Daddy drove truck for a saw mill. He hauled lumber to Roanoke, Farmville, and different sections of Virginia. Right after the closing of the schools Daddy had to drive a load of lumber to Farmville. The regular heavy forklift used to unload the lumber was broke and a lighter smaller forklift was used to unload the truck. The guy who operated the forklift put too much lumber on it and the forklift was raised up off the ground. The forklift spun around and struck Daddy on the knee. After Daddy got injured, we had to help around the house.

Me, Charlie, and Willie were at home during this time. I believe part of the main reason we missed the first two years out of school was because of Daddy's injury. Our older brothers and sisters had already gone off to school.

Charlie was coming up for the draft, so my parents wanted him to stay in school and get an education; but they wanted all of us to get an education.

My parents talked with Reverend Griffin and Mr. Clinton Lee and they told Mama and Daddy they had a program to send children to different counties or States. They located a family in Washington, D. C. for me and my brother Charlie T, his name is Charlie Thomas Barksdale. Charlie was a couple of years older than me.

In September 1961, the third year the schools were closed, me and Charlie stayed with the Richardson family. Ms. Richardson was a single parent and I believe she had one child, a boy whose name I can't remember. I think Ms. Richardson's first name was Lillian. Me and Charlie attended Holy Redeemer Catholic School. I graduated the end of the school year.

The fourth year the schools were closed, 1962-1963, I went back to Washington, D. C. Charlie and I were split up and I don't remember where he went that year. I stayed with Ms. Dorothy Brown. She was a single parent with two children.

Ms. Brown had a daughter named Audrey and a son named Billy. I attended Henry T. Blow School.

The Free School opened in Prince Edward County in September 1963, but I didn't attend. I was in Hampton, Virginia, that year with the Bassett family. I believe the man was named Andrew and his wife named Julia. They had a son named William, we called him Billy. I went to Robert R. Moton in Hampton.

My brother Charlie Thomas was with a Bassett family in Richmond this school year, and the two Bassett families were cousins if I am not mistaken. The Bassett family in Richmond the man of the house was a dentist. The Bassett family I lived with in Hampton the husband was a medical doctor and his wife stayed at home. She did volunteer or service work.

All three families I lived with were very loving.

When the Prince Edward County public schools opened in September 1964, I enrolled. I went to high school four years and graduated in 1968.

My brother Walter Junior stayed home the whole time and never went away to school. I'm not quite sure why he didn't go away. Walter knew how to drive the tractor and I didn't. That might have had something to do with it.

When I worked at the Buckingham County Correctional Facility in Buckingham County, Virginia, there was an inmate there and we thought we recognized each other. We started talking and figured it out. This was around 1988. He asked me one day:

"Do you remember Dot Brown." We called Dorothy—Dot. Dorothy's daughter was in college when I lived with the Brown family in Washington, D. C. and this fellow used to court Audrey. The inmate told me that Ms. Brown had become a preacher.

As of today, Monday, September 10, 2012, this is some of what I remember of my story from the years the schools were closed in Prince Edward County.

―――――

ONIE LOU BARKSDALE LAWRENCE

I was born May 5, 1946, in Prince Edward County at home to Rosa and Charlie Barksdale.

We had about twenty children going to school in our neighborhood. I was one of the smallest people for my age. We had to walk two and a half miles one way to Felden Elementary School. Mrs. Foster was the teacher. Trying to keep up with the big children was very hard. Each day I would go to sleep in school. Mrs. Foster told my parents to put a bed in the school, so I could take a nap each day and they did. Thank the Lord for our father he was our angel. When we had bad weather, he came and picked up our neighborhood children.

I went to Mary Branch No. 1 in Farmville in the fourth grade. I had passed to the fifth grade when the schools were closed.

Life was simple and plain when I was a girl. I had seven brothers and one sister, and we took care of each other. The children were Walter Junior, Annie Marie, me, Charlie Thomas, Willie Ernest, George Douglas, Earl, James Melvin and Leon. James and Leon were not school age. We were a very close-knit family. I wanted to be a filing clerk when I was a girl.

Me and Barbara Ann Botts were very close friends in school. She was the only child in her family, so we did many things together. Barbara's mother Ms. Geneva was a very loving and kind person. She would cook us Sunday meals, and took Barbara and me to different things and to places we wanted to go.

Mother and Father were hard working parents. Father worked at the saw mill, driving trucks. Every three years he would get a new truck. Daddy, my brothers and the neighborhood boys would help out other farmers. Sister would go and help others in tobacco. I would get sick each time I helped. So, babysitting the little children was my job. Mother worked at a nursing home.

Each year my parents would plant a big garden, large corn field, big wheat field, and a tobacco field. We raised many pigs, and cows, and chickens and my family shared with other families in the neighborhood. We raised most of our food.

I didn't go to school the first year the schools were closed. I helped Mama around the house. Sometimes we went to other peoples' house and had school. Most times we went to Aunt Rosa's house; Aunt Rosa and Uncle Willie Edward. Sometimes we went to Uncle Edgar and Aunt Mary Barksdale and their daughter Maggie Calhoun house. Uncle Edgar was my father's brother.

It was a long walk to Aunt Rosa's house. Aunt Rosa was a house wife, but she was smart. Me and my sister and some other children in our neighborhood walked with us to Aunt Rosa's house. Aunt Rosa didn't have children. It would be some children from her end that came to her house too and we all met up. Aunt Rosa had at least twelve children at her house that she taught. She gave us assignments. Aunt Rosa was my mother's cousin, but we called her Aunt Rosa.

Aunt Mary and Aunt Rosa felt they were smart enough to work with us.

In 1960 the brothers and sisters in my home that formed a close-knit family had to separate to go to school. The American Friends Service Committee sent some of us to different families where we would be able to go to school.

I went to Moorestown, New Jersey, in September 1960 to go to school. I lived with Mr. and Mrs. Charles Bound. Mrs. Bound was a teacher, but I can't remember what Mr. Bound did for a living. They had two daughters named Sharon and Charlotte and a boy named Charles, Jr. He was younger than the girls. Charlotte was my age. We stayed in church a lot. (Mrs. Lawrence chuckled.) I know Mr. Bound was a deacon in the church and Mrs. Bound was a deaconess. I think it was First Baptist Church. I worked in the church. Mr. and Mrs. Bound treated me like one of the family. I attended Moorestown Middle School.

The next year I didn't go back to Moorestown, I went to Portsmouth, Virginia. I attended Crestwood Middle School in Portsmouth. I lived with Mr. John and Mrs. Sally B. Smith. He was a cook at the ship yard in Norfolk and she was a school teacher. They had two daughters Brenda and Jackie. Jackie was around my age and Brenda was grown and married and was living in New York. Mr. Smith was a deacon and Mrs. Smith a deaconess in the church. Jackie and I sang in the choir at First Baptist Church in Norfolk.

One day I got a shock at school early in the school year. I was surprised to see my sister Annie Marie at school. I knew she was with a family in Portsmouth, but I didn't know we were at the same school. We were in the same class. I looked around and saw her in a class we were taking.

The next year I went back to Mr. and Mrs. Smith in Portsmouth. Jackie and I spent the summer with Brenda and her husband in New York. Mr. and Mrs. Smith treated me like one of the family. While in Portsmouth, I always came home at Christmas and at the end of the school year.

When I came back home they were marching and picketing downtown that summer. This was the summer of 1963. People were in training and I joined them. They trained on how to protect themselves when they shot water on us or hit us on the head. We met at First Baptist Church to get the training. Reverend Griffin was the pastor at this church in Farmville. This man named Robert Ellis and some people in the surrounding neighborhood would come and pick us up for training and sit-ins and picketing in front of stores.

I heard Martin Luther King, Jr. deliver his famous I Have A Dream speech. I went to the March on Washington with many other people from Prince Edward County.

I went to high school when I came back home in 1963. The Free School opened. I remember we went on a field trip to see the Washington Monument and the Lincoln Memorial. We spent the night with Black and White families in Washington. I graduated from high school in 1966.

I graduated from high school, got a job, and got married in 1966. I went to work at Keysville Mill. They later changed the name to Shaw Industrial Mill and E & B Carpet Mill. I was a textile machine operator. I worked as a twister operator. I ran the machine that twisted two ends of yarn together. Then it was sent to another factory to make the carpet. It was a good paying job and I loved it. I worked there for twenty-six and a half years before they closed down.

After the mill closed, I went to take a class at Southside Community College in Keysville, Virginia, for one summer and ended up in the wrong class. There were students that had just got out of high school. My counselor said that I did well, but I needed a couple more points to pass the class. Then I took three hundred hours of computer class to learn the basics and again ended up with students that had just gotten out of high school. This class taught me not to be afraid of taking on changes. I am teaching myself each day how to use the computer.

I have always wanted to be a filing clerk. I did volunteer work for the Farmville DMV as a filing clerk for a year. Then I became a file clerk for Home Health at Southside Hospital in Farmville for almost four years. I worked in an office with a group of ladies with no problems. I learned a lot and loved the job.

I was engaged for five years to Howard Lawrence. He was a hard-working young man. He could do almost any kind of job. We got married in 1966 and I moved to Keysville, Virginia, in Charlotte County. We have three daughters Sheri, Jonnie B. and Tonika. We have five grandchildren named Banetra, Krystale, Jazsmine, Thomas H. and Dajah. I thank my heavenly Father that they try to do the right thing and they love Grandma and Granddad. I have always helped out with my grandchildren because I know that they are our future. When they were younger I kept them in Sunday School and church, and they sang in the choir. I put them on the school bus each morning and went on school trips with them.

I always tell other grandparents to help with their grandbabies because they are the ones who will make this world a better place. Howard and I have been married for forty-six years. I have been an usher in church from the age of six years old and now I am sixty-six years old and love it.

Howard and I are now retired. We own a trailer court of twelve rented trailers. The trailer court is named Lawrence Lane Trailer Court. These trailers keep us busy and I am the filing clerk.

Having faith in our heavenly Father, you will always have

the best of everything. When I was in school, my mentor was a young person named Patricia. I liked the way she walked, talked, acted, and dressed. After I got to know her better, I knew that I wanted more out of life.

When I look back over my life now, I thank my heavenly Father for his Son Jesus Christ for being so good in leading and guiding. I know the Bible is our road map. I have had so much to happen in my life that I say I'm going to write a book one day.

I was just beginning to get my basic educational foundation when the schools were closed. Today I feel that if they had kept me back to get the basics that I missed I would be better off today. The closing of the schools impacted me, and I had to work harder to keep up with my classmates in school. I feel if I had stayed on a straight normal course with school I would have done much better educationally and in life in general. All of my grandchildren want to go to college. I had a teacher to tell me that I was going far in life because I had a lot of good common sense. Thank the good Lord for that.

For many years I sent a Christmas card to Mr. and Mrs. Smith in Portsmouth and I visited them periodically until they were deceased.

ANNIE MARIE BARKSDALE RICE

My parents were Charlie and Rosa Barksdale. I was born September 1, 1944.

I started to school at the age of six and I continued to get my education until the schools were closed when I was fourteen years old. I had passed to the sixth grade when the schools were closed, and I was at Mary E. Branch.

My father got hurt so I stayed home and cared for him.

I went to Aunt Rosa sometimes during the first year the schools were closed. Onie went to Aunt Rosa more than I did. I did a lot of cooking. When I was eight years old, I had already learned how to cook. I also had to milk cows and work in the tobacco field. When Onie went to the tobacco field she would always get sick, so she could go to Aunt Rosa. Her husband Willie Edward worked in Ashland, Virginia, near Richmond and came home on the weekends. Aunt Rosa was my great grand aunt; she was my mother's aunt.

The second year of the school closing I went to Dayton, Ohio. I went to Dayton on a train out of Farmville. I had never been on a train and I went by myself. I lived with Mr. and Mrs. Mumbeck at 805 Walton Avenue. I can't remember what they did for a living. They had a daughter my age and two boys. This was a White family and they were very nice. They treated me as I was one of their own. I can't remember the name of the school I attended in Dayton. I had chores to do after school and before. One of the fun parts of the school year was going to the fair with the 4-H.

Willie Bolden and his sister Bessie Bolden also went to Dayton. Willie and Bessie were from Redd Shop. I remember Tommy Hunter being in Dayton too.

The families in Dayton made it all nice for us and let us get together. They helped us not to be home sick. We had the company of each other.

I was more mature than many of the students at school. The girls were so into boys. I paid the boys no mind. I was gone away from my family the whole school year. When I came back home it was for the Christmas holiday, and at the end of the school year.

The next year, the third year the schools were closed, I went to Portsmouth, Virginia, and I happened to run up on my sister, Onie. I first saw her in class at Crestwood Middle School. I knew she was with a family in Portsmouth, but I didn't know we would be at the same school. I was so happy to see my Onie during the school year. I lived with a Pastor and his wife. I forgot his name and cannot remember his church, but I remember we were in church all the time. I think I came home at Christmas since Portsmouth was not that far away and I came home at the end of the school year. I had a wonderful school year at Crestwood.

I can't remember where I went the fourth year the schools were closed. When school ended, I came home for the summer.

My brother Willie Ernest went to Richmond at least one year and lived with a very religious family. When he came back home, Willie was more into the Bible, far more than he was before he left.

I participated in the demonstrations. Mr. Robert Ellis used to drive us around. He would drive us into town.

Then the next thing we knew the schools were opened. I started in the Free School but discontinued. It wasn't the same to me. All of the students were younger, and it didn't seem right to me being there with all of those kids.

After leaving school, I met my husband Charles Rice, Sr. I got married and raised three boys and two girls: Charles Rice, Jr., Joseph Timothy Rice, Garcia Nathaniel Rice, Mary Alvana Rice and Emma Marie Rice.

My first job was at Star Laundry in Farmville, Virginia. In 1964 to make a better life for us, we moved to Asbury Park, New Jersey. There I found work again working in laundry.

After the birth of our second child, we decided to move back to Virginia.

I did numerous jobs to make sure my family was cared for. After my last child was old enough to start school, I was hired at Hampden Sydney College working at the library and the President's house. I remained a faithful worker for twenty-five years until my health would not allow me to work.

———

EARL BARKSDALE

My earliest memories of the school closing in Prince Edward County was my mother and father, Rosa Barksdale and Charlie Barksdale, had to send my older brothers and sisters out of the county and State to go to school. I had some of my family to go to Ohio, Washington, D. C., and Portsmouth, Virginia, to live with other families and attend school. Some tried to get into school in neighboring counties, counties surrounding Prince Edward, but there was a lot of frustration involved. I stayed at home during the school closure. I was born December 12, 1953. When I was supposed to start first grade the schools were closed.

I had two younger brothers James and Leon. The three of us stayed home to help out on the family farm. We also helped other families and farmers with seasonal work.

My father's sister, Lizzie Scott, and his brother, Garfield Barksdale, was a big help in molding our lives. They both had children that were the same age or younger than me. They kept us when our parents worked, and this was an era when other people raised other peoples' children.

I recall that in Prince Edward County they had a program to work with boys and girls. The program was sent through the county, one was next to New Witt Baptist Church on Route 15. The little old Felden School with one large classroom was where teachers came to help teach us. The other one was an old school next to New Bethel Baptist Church on Route 15 next to Keysville.

Sometimes while we were walking to the old Felden School where I had to go, the White kids on the Academy buses would yell at us and we would yell back at them. One time we yelled at them first and the bus driver hit the brakes. (Mr. Barksdale started laughing.) We took off running down the road and into the bushes and they pulled off laughing at us.

Mrs. Foster and some other teachers came out to help tutor us. Mrs. Foster and the other teachers worked with us at the old Felden School mainly during the summer.

I also remember some people coming to our community and taking a census. They went to the different houses getting information about how many children were in the house and their ages.

The people gathering the information at the different homes didn't know the county. So, my father volunteered me to ride with them and show them around our neighborhood and other parts of the county. There was actually a large team of workers in the county, but the two that came to our house was a Black female and a White male.

My father assigned me to go with them and he told them:

"My son knows the majority of the people and the kids in the neighborhood."

"You ride and take them to all the people you know," my father said to me.

I rode with the man and the woman for a week or so. They came by and picked me up each day and I directed them to various sections. We pretty much scoured the county.

I remember some of the Black people were hurt and frustrated and didn't want to talk to the people I was guiding around the county.

We also went to some of the homes of White families whose children were not in school. We went to the Leigh Mountain and the Meherrin areas. We went to some houses and some of the people called us Niggers. Many of the poor White people were treated just as bad as the Black people were treated in the county. Many of the poor White people had to use the little money they had to pay for their children to go to the private schools. We stopped at the house of one White family and talked to them and they warned us of other White families to avoid. But the White gentleman who I was riding with said—'We'll cross that bridge when we get to it.' The KKK was very active at this time in Prince Edward County and some of the other counties.

The move was on to get the number of Black and White kids counted who had not been in school. I think this information was sent to the Government and the NAACP.

In the summer of 1963 we had a group of neighborhood people who came around trying to get children ready for school. They started having meetings at people's homes and met at some of the churches.

The Free School opened, and I went to Worsham Elementary School. I remember Lyle Morton, William Lambert, and Herman Saunders were there. They were all from the Hampden Sydney area and we were all in the same first grade class at Worsham Elementary. Mrs. Wilson, Mrs. Morton and Mrs. McClain were teachers that were very instrumental in getting us focused. We had to take a test to see what grade we was to start in that year.

There were a lot of old school bus break downs, some of the buses were very old. We got good working skills from Worsham and there were a lot of activities.

When the Free School opened, I had cousins that had been impacted by the closure. My uncle, Uncle Garfield Barksdale, had two children impacted, Garfield, Jr. and Patricia. Garfield, Jr. was around my age and Patricia was a little younger than me, she started school after the schools opened up. Aunt Lizzie's children were Leroy, Iniel and Barbara. Then Uncle Lee, Lee Barksdale, had two children impacted by the school closing. Their names were Larry and Nathaniel, both were older than me.

Rudolph Doswell was a big help in getting Black and White people children in school.

After the Free School year ended for the summer, they had programs in the summer to keep us involved.

After Worsham Elementary School, we went to Mary E. Branch in the town of Farmville.

To go to high school, I think you had to be in at least ninth grade. We had a lot of people to come to the classes to talk to us. Reverend Griffin came and talked to us about the closing of the schools and how it impacted our older brothers and sisters.

In high school I played on the Junior Varsity Football Team. Coach Perry, Coach Wilson and Coach Fuller were very motivating toward working as a team. Coach Wilson especially would ask us what we wanted to be when we grew up and what we wanted to do in life.

In my junior year of high school Coach Perry got me started driving school bus with my brother and father. I also drove in my senior year. I helped in the kitchen at school too, this was like a part-time job. I had met all my credits and had some free time as I was waiting for graduation.

After graduating, I came back and drove the school bus part-time, while I worked at W. A. Price and Sears and Roebuck in Farmville part-time.

Then I started working at the Department of Corrections in 1977. I have been working for the Department for thirty-five years.

I started out as a Correctional Officer; then was promoted to Correctional Corporal, Correctional Sergeant, Correctional Lieutenant, Correctional Captain, Correctional Major and then Correctional Assistant Warden. This progression was achieved when I worked at the Powhatan Correctional Facility in Powhatan County, Virginia. Later I was promoted to Warden Senior at the Dillwyn Correctional Facility in Buckingham County. That is where I am as of today, Saturday, October 13, 2012.

I am active in working on the re-entry of offenders into society. We are also trying to build a better healing environment for our workers and offenders.

I am pretty active in my church, New Witt Baptist Church in Prince Edward County. I am a Worship Leader and at present serve as Chairman of the Deacon Board. I'm also President of the New Witt Men and Company Choir. The New Witt Men and Company Choir will hold their Eleventh Anniversary tomorrow, October 14, 2012, at 3:00 p. m. Other groups will come and sing and share in the program.

Chapter Two

ACCOUNTS FROM SURROUNDING COUNTIES

AMELIA COUNTY

MACIO HILL

I was born in Winnabow, in Brunswick County, North Carolina. I started out at a six room school. Then we went to a consolidated school named Brunswick County Training School. Brunswick County Training School was the only Black high school in the county and was located in the town of Southport.

There was a time in Brunswick County when the Black children, depending on where they lived in the county couldn't attend high school because there were no buses to take them to high school. My wife's brother and sister went to high school in Wilmington, North Carolina. They caught a ride each day with workers going to that city. They attended Williston High School. Williston was closer than the actual county high school in which they should have been enrolled, but as I said no school buses were provided to transport teenage students from that end of the county to Brunswick County Training School. My wife's parents had to pay drivers to let their children ride to Wilmington to attend high school.

The sixth room school where my public education began was torn down and buses were made available. I entered Brunswick County Training School. After attending Brunswick County Training School for a year or two, I was enrolled at Williston High School in eighth grade. I rode with my father each morning, when he went to the ship yard in

Wilmington. I returned to Brunswick County Training School when I entered the ninth grade.

After graduating from Brunswick County Training School in 1951, I entered the United States Air Force. I was on active duty for three years and eight months. After being honorably discharged, I entered a community college sponsored by Fayetteville State College. The school was in Wilmington. I attended briefly and then entered North Carolina A&T. I transferred from North Carolina A&T and entered Elizabeth City Teachers College. I earned a degree in Elementary Education from Elizabeth City Teachers College.

After graduating, I was hired as a teacher in Amelia County, Virginia. Later I taught at Janesville Elementary School, a two room school. The other teacher was Mrs. Stone. The school went to the seventh grade. I had grades fifth, sixth and seventh. The school had a potbelly stove, and outdoor toilet, and every child brought their lunch. A person in the community would come and make the fire when it was cold.

I also taught at Russell Grove Elementary School in Amelia County. While at Russell Grove Elementary, I was elected president of the Amelia Teachers Association. This was the Negro teachers' association, as it was called in that era. The White teachers in the county had their own association.

Sometime in early 1961 a communication came from the Virginia Teachers Association (the Negro Association) of which Mr. J. Rupert Picott was president. The letter asked teachers to volunteer to spend several weeks during the upcoming summer teaching and tutoring Negro students in Prince Edward County. I don't remember whether the letter of request came directly to me as the president of the Amelia County Teachers Association or if all teachers received individual letters. I do recall that the letter was made available to all the teachers. The letter from Mr. Picott was sent to each Negro teachers association in every county in Virginia.

I was one of the Amelia County teachers that volunteered to go to Prince Edward County and work with the Negro children during the summer of 1961. The children in the county had already missed two formal years of education, from September 1959 to May 1961. Teachers from other counties in Virginia also volunteered to come to Prince Edward County that summer, as their county Teachers Association had received the same communication as we did in Amelia County.

I cannot discuss all of the particulars related to stipends and so forth for the teachers who traveled long distances and stayed with families in Prince Edward County during the week and returned home on the weekend to be with their own families. Volunteers such as me who lived only a short distance from Farmville were provided lunch each day and reimbursed for mileage. I was living in Amelia and drove approximately 35 miles one way to Farmville. We had wonderful discussions and staff development sessions as to how to go about teaching the children. Mrs. Vera Allen was the person most of us enjoyed in staff development. She was a wonderful person.

All the instructors who volunteered to work with the children and came to Prince Edward County in the summer of 1961 were certified trained school teachers that taught in the public schools. We all were assigned to different teaching sites scattered around the county. I had a class in an old two story white building, it was actually a house. It was in the heart of the Black section of Farmville.

I never will forget my first day teaching. I asked a little girl to go to the black board and write her name. She did not know her ABCs and she must have been around ten or eleven years old or older. She wrote some jagged upside-down markings. All the children that attended the site where I was assigned were willing to learn and we felt they made some progress during the summer. I had about ten children under my tutelage. As I remember, we taught about three or four hours each day with the school day ending around noon or shortly thereafter.

I don't recall how many teachers came to the county in the summer of 1961, but a good number came and offered their service.

My second encounter with youngsters from Prince Edward County came in the fall of 1962. I was the head teacher at Jetersville Elementary School in Jetersville, located in Amelia County. As the public schools in Prince Edward County were still closed, students started coming over to Amelia County in September 1962. A large number of students that lived in sections of Prince Edward County that bordered Amelia County began crossing the county line seeking an education. Students signed what was called Freedom of Choice forms, freely choosing the schools they wished to attend. Based on the information they gave me, they were admitted to Jetersville Elementary School. The children's parents drove them across the county line each morning and they caught the bus to Jetersville Elementary. Many of the students from Prince Edward County lived with relatives in Amelia County. Others were let off by parents each morning at the homes of friends in the county and the children caught the school bus or walked on to the school. Some Prince Edward County parents worked in Richmond or near Richmond and dropped their children off while passing through Amelia in the mornings and picked them up in the afternoons on the way home from work.

The student enrollment was increasing significantly in Amelia County, but the settled population in the community was not growing at the same rate. This disconnect aroused the curiosity of school board officials. The fall of 1962 student enrollment at Jetersville Elementary increased to the point where the Amelia County Superintendent, Mr. P. T. Atkinson, called me to his office. We had a long discussion concerning the placement of these kids, the Black students from Prince Edward County. We talked about reprisals that would happen as a result of integration in the schools. I remember telling him that many of the Black folks in the area were not afraid of the reprisals that would take place, and they would still eat fatback, corn-bread, and beans no matter what happened. The people were of the opinion that it was time for a change. At that point Mr. Atkinson told me he would talk with me at a later date. It is my feeling that he saw the need for children from Prince Edward County to receive some kind of education. I believe Mr. Atkinson was from Prince Edward County. I was an advocate for the boys and girls who were crossing the line from Prince Edward County to come to Jetersville Elementary. They needed to be in the classroom, even though county rules stated if a student was not a resident of Amelia County they could not attend school in the county. The Prince Edward County children attending Jetersville Elementary School weren't dismissed.

I think the summer programs in which teachers volunteered to go to Prince Edward County and work with the students lasted two summers, the summers of 1961 and 1962. I'm pretty sure 1963 was the last summer for the program, if they had anything that summer. The Free School opened in September 1963 and the county schools officially reopened in September 1964.

In my opinion Mrs. Allen was the master mind behind many of the wonderful programs that benefited the boys and girls in the county who didn't have the opportunity to leave, especially the summer programs. One of the most prominent names we hear repeatedly in the county is that of Mrs. Vera Allen.

Mr. Atkinson promised me a principalship, in spite of the position I had taken. Later I was placed in a principalship in Nottoway County where his friend was superintendent.

One of the most touching experiences I had during my educational tenure in Nottoway County involved a Black family, last name Nunnally. I think I have provided the correct spelling. The family moved to Nottoway County after the schools closed in Prince Edward County. The family had a son named Calvin. Calvin missed several years out of school before his family moved to Nottoway County. He graduated from Luther H. Foster High School, the Black high school in Nottoway County. Calvin was college material and it was evident to me. I told him I felt certain I could get him in the college I attended, Elizabeth City Teachers College. I made the proper contacts at my alma mater. We rode down one day and met with a friend of mine who was in charge of financial aid. Calvin's records were reviewed. In the fall of the year Calvin enrolled. Four years later he finished at the top of his class.

After I retired in 1991, I had another encounter with Prince Edward County students. The Prince Edward County Middle School needed a principal and I was invited to come out of retirement and lead the school. I accepted the offer and worked for three months. Since I was retired, I wanted to do something special for the children in that community. I requested that $100.00 a month be deducted from my pay and put into the student activity fund. I had a vision, but it was not welcomed. I worked three months and retired again.

In Prince Edward County families where children were nurtured, the children did well in spite of. In homes where children are nurtured and encouraged, they will rise up and excel though doors have been closed against them, even school doors.

Calvin has done extremely well. He has served as principal at Nottoway Middle School and later became head of the Educational Television Network in the State of Virginia. I am going to get his contact information, so he can be interviewed. His story needs to be published.

CUMBERLAND COUNTY

RUTH VIRGINIA FAWLEY JONES

I was born December 14, 1936, to Marshall and Lucile Randall Fawley. I was born in Cumberland County. I attended Sharon Baptist Church. There was a school next to the church call Sharon School. I think it was a two room school. Mrs. Helen Brown Randolph was the teacher. Mrs. Randolph taught my mother and all of her sisters and brothers.

Nina Randolph Newsome was my mother's sister and Aunt Nina graduated from Sharon. I imagine the school back then went to the sixth or seventh grade. My mama was born in 1901 or 1902.

My mother's parents were Frank and Mary Frances Lacy Randolph and they were from Cumberland County. Grandma used to tell us about slavery. She often told how the slave owner split her mother's head open with a boot. I also remember her telling how her mother told her about slave owners separating children from their parents and selling them. She also told how the slave owners would take the slaves for their own companions. My great-grandmother was named Nina Lacy. She was a slave and the mother of Mary Frances. Nina lived on a farm called the Allen Farm. I think Nina was a slave in Cumberland County, but there is no doubt that she was a slave.

Grandma used to make lie soap, what is called today Octagon soap. Granddaddy didn't talk much. Granddaddy raised race horses. He didn't train'em, but only raised'em and then sol'em. Maude was my favorite horse and she had a filly named Nellie.

When I was a girl, we had fun riding on the wagons and going on hay-rides. The hay-rides were wonderful. Some of the people in the neighborhood were relatives. They just put hay in the back of the wagon and made it nice and soft and you went for long rides. There was no special time for hay-ride.

We walked to Sunday School. It was about two miles from our house to Sharon Baptist Church. When I was girl, Reverend Shelton Anderson was the pastor. Reverend Joe Venerable also served as pastor for a while. Reverend Grant G. Cosby also severed Sharon when I was a girl. I remember him and his wife visiting Grandma and serving her communion more than once.

The spokesperson in the community was usually the principal or leading Black person. Mr. Robert L. Scales was the principal at Luther P. Jackson.

When I was a girl, I went to elementary school at Union Highway. It was one large open building. It was sectioned off first, second, and so on up to seventh grade. I think Sharon was closed. The school was about four miles away. We walked every day until one year my aunt came from New York.

Aunt Nina Randolph Newsome came home once a year. Aunt Nina talked to some people in the community to go to Farmville with her to speak to the superintendent. Only my mother in the end went with her. I think they caught a cab from Cumberland to Farmville. She and Mama met with Mr. McIlwaine. The White people tried to put her off, but she insisted. Aunt Nina said:

"The White children have a bus and the Negro children should also have a bus. If you don't give'em one I will go to higher authority."

He said: "They will have a bus."

Soon we had a bus. Mr. Andrew Booker was the driver. Later his wife Frances Booker drove. This was in the latter part of the 1940s.

I finished the seventh grade at Union Highway around 1947 or 1948. Then I entered Cumberland County Training School. There were separate buildings on the grounds. All of the buildings were brick, as I recall. The main building had elementary on the lower floor and the top floor was the high school. One of the buildings was a workshop.

When I went to high school, it was called Cumberland County Training School, but when I graduated in 1954 it was called Luther P. Jackson High School. He was the first Negro Surveyor in Virginia.

I recall there had already been some talk in the community about integration or desegregation before I left home in the summer of 1954.

ELSIE ALEXANDER

I went to school at Green Creek No. 5. I started school when I was four years old because I was able read. I started school in 1941. My older sisters and brothers and my mother were at home, which was how I learned to read. Mama was a housewife. Green Creek No. 5 was located on Cooks Road in Cumberland County. The teacher was Helen Randolph. The substitute teacher was Mrs. Juanita Wiley. Green Creek No. 5 was a one classroom school and had a cloakroom with a kitchen. There was a regular wood stove in the kitchen on which the cook prepared the food. Students got their lunch and returned to the classroom. The school went up to the seventh grade. After seventh grade, we went to Cumberland Training School. We rode the bus. The State provided transportation. The first year I had to walk about two miles from my house to catch the bus. The next year the bus came to the house.

I think the schools were numbered because there were so many small schools in the county.

They started building Luther P. Jackson High School when I was a junior. My class was the last to graduate from Cumberland Training School in 1952.

———

FLORENCE LAVERENE DEPTE

I started school in 1956 at Hawkes School. It had two rooms and a coat room out front. It was sort of cute how they made it. Hawkes was not near a church. We rode the bus to school. Mrs. Edna Smith taught me from first to third grades.

I had Mrs. Neely in fourth and fifth grades. Mr. L. L. Hall came to teach when I entered the sixth grade and he was my teacher in 1961.

I remember when I was in Mrs. Neely's class children came across the bridge to Hawkes. There was a girl name Aldreania or Aldrena Smith. She had a sister named Juanita Smith. They were in different grades. Aldrena was the oldest. I don't know if her family rented a house on the Cumberland side or came over each day from Prince Edward County.

I never asked any questions. I knew children from Prince Edward County started coming to Hawkes. I remember seeing these new faces that were not from the Sharon community. There were others that came to school at Hawkes, but I can't remember their names.

ELIZA MELROSE RANDOLPH REID

I was born in Cumberland County, September 10, 1923. My mother, Mrs. Helen Brown Randolph, was a teacher. She taught at Sharon School, Old Green Creek School, and Union School. She also taught in the lower end of Cumberland at Bonbrook School. There was only one school with the name Green Creek. When people say Green Creek No. 5, they are talking about the same Green Creek School.

The first school I attended was Sharon School. It was a two room school that went to the seventh grade. In elementary school Mrs. Florence Brown was the teacher, Mrs. Lottie M. Glades had the higher grades. School went from September to May.

Our day started at daybreak. We had to milk cows, feed the chickens, and feed the pigs. Then we got ready to go to school. We walked a short distance to school. It was near Sharon Baptist Church. Reverend Shelton Anderson was the pastor. I think he was the one who baptized me. We did the field work in the afternoon, when we came home.

When my sister, Alberta finished Sharon, there were no buses to take her to Cumberland Training School about twelve or fifteen miles away. She went to the town of Farmville, five miles away from our house and stayed with our grandfather, Mr. Jacob Randolph. He was a minister. He was the pastor of Race Street Baptist Church. He died in 1937. Alberta came home on the weekend.

When my sister, Juanita, and I finished seventh grade at Sharon there were still no buses. My father would drive us to the bridge each morning, let us out, and we walked all the way through the town of Farmville to the high school. The walk was probably a couple of miles.

After we had been going there about six weeks some local Negro families, as they were called in those days, purchased some buses. Some of the wealthy families in our area of Cumberland County got together and purchased buses. The Booker family had buses. Mr. Ardee Booker used to drive the bus most of the time. He had a brother named Norman Booker. Norman did the mechanical work on the buses. I don't know whether Mr. Ardee owned the buses or if all three Booker brothers owned the buses together. They had a brother named Sam who ran a store near the training school. The children used to go there a lot. They lived near the training school in an area called Booker Town. There were a large number of Booker families in the area.

We started going to Cumberland Training School. We

had to walk up to Highway 45, about two and a half miles to catch the bus.

The Washington family had a bus also. Mr. Albert Washington was the owner. His wife was named Hattie. I think his son drove the bus.

Mr. Washington and Mr. Booker made two trips each day in order to pick up all the children. They picked up children on the lower end of Cumberland first and took them to school. Then they came and picked us up.

A Mr. Brown had a station wagon of sorts that he picked up children in.

I think we had to pay a small fee to ride, the money was to help with upkeep. Some children had to stop riding the bus because their parents couldn't afford the fee.

After seventh grade, I went to the training school. I started at the training school around age thirteen and finished at age sixteen. I finished Cumberland Training School in 1940.

I think the county started providing buses before my last year of school, but the same men drove for the county.

I had niece in Farmville. She was the daughter of my husband's brother. She went to live in Buckingham County with her grandparents. (Mrs. Reid was speaking of when the Prince Edward County public schools were closed.)

My husband's brother owned a restaurant in Farmville. When Reverend Griffin would come by and sit, they would provide him a meal.

Mr. Lipscomb owned an old country grocery store here in Cumberland County. He sold almost anything. Mr. Lipscomb had a granddaughter in Prince Edward County and when the schools closed she started going Luther P. Jackson.

HELEN CAMPBELL

I started school during the 1949–1950 school year. I went to first grade at R. R. Moton, a two room school in Cumberland County. I can't remember any of the teachers' names. Back then the school was on a Route, but today it is Cooks Road. The school was next to Midway Baptist Church. We took our lunch. There was no electricity. The sunshine provided light for us. When it rained or was cloudy, you could hardly see, so we heard stories all day. There was an outdoor toilet.

In the second grade, I went to Hawkes. Mrs. Mary A. Neely was one of the teachers. I had Mrs. Leslie or Mrs. Lester, I can't remember the pronunciation. I did two years at Hawkes School.

My family moved to Amostown and I returned to R. R. Moton for one more year. I was in the fourth grade and Mrs. Butler was my teacher.

My family moved again back to the Sharon community. I went to Sharon School. There was one teacher, one classroom, and seven grades. There were twenty-five or thirty children in the one room. The seventh grade had the least number of students.

In the 1957–1958 school year, I went to Luther P. Jackson. By this time Sharon School had been lowered to the sixth grade and all seventh grade students went to Luther P.

When the schools were closed in Prince Edward County, I remember Dorothy Jo Hatcher and Darlene Walker walked across the bridge and caught the school bus to Luther P. Jackson High School. There were other students from the Farmville area that did the same, but I remember these two girls.

Mr. Howard Smith rented a house in Amostown, just

outside of Farmville, so his children could go to school in Cumberland County. There were about five children in that family.

———

WALTER RANDOLPH

I started school early because my grandmother was taking care of me. She was a teacher and took me to school with her. I was in class from around four years old and at five she pressed me forward. She taught at Green Creek and her name was Mrs. Helen Randolph. Green Creek was a one room school. When I was officially school age, Grandma transferred to Sharon School. I started legally at Sharon. Grandma retired in 1949 and Mrs. Florence W. Brown took over. This was Helen's sister-in-law. I stayed at Sharon School to the seventh grade. In the eighth grade I went to Luther P. Jackson. This was around 1954 or 1955.

I remember when the Prince Edward County Schools were closed. The talk in Virginia was Massive Resistance. Prince Edward County said—'We will not have it' and started an Academy.

"Do you remember any of the students that came from Prince Edward County to go to school in Cumberland County or any Prince Edward County families that moved to this county?" the Editor asked.

I can't remember any names other than the ones provided by Helen (Campbell).

We wondered — how could they have done it to those children? How could they have done such a thing?

- 648 -

———

ROBERTA GILLIAM FERGUSON

In 1944 I started school at Union Highway, a one room school. Mrs. Elizabeth Harris was the teacher. The school went to the seventh grade but was closed around 1949 or 1950.

I went to Sharon School for the fourth grade. We had to walk about two miles. There were a lot of children at Sharon, so we started going to Hawkes. At Hawkes School Mrs. Florence Brown was the teacher. The school board made the decision for us to go to Hawkes.

I went to Hawkes School in the fifth grade. This was around 1949. I was born in 1939. Hawkes School had two rooms and went to the seventh grade. There was an outdoor toilet and a pump on the yard for water. Mrs. Neely had fifth to seventh graders and Mrs. Leslie, she was from Alabama or Georgia, had first to fourth grades.

I went to Luther P. Jackson in 1953 in the eighth grade. The old Cumberland County Training School has two parts left. Most of the Cumberland County Training School has been demolished. I finished high school in 1957.

———

LILLY ANN ALLEN

The Editor left Farmville on the morning of November 8, 2004, in route to Cumberland County. The Editor was trying to find the home of the old teacher named Mrs. Brown who used to teach at the two room R. R. Moton School in Cumberland County. Carl Eggleston, Sr. first told me about her. She was his teacher when his parents enrolled their children at the school during the educational crisis in Prince Edward County. Eggleston said he had seen the senior educator recently but was unable to tell me where she lived. "Once you get in Cumberland County just ask anybody about Mrs. Brown and they can probably tell you where she lives," Eggleston said. The Editor was also in search of the daughter of one of the Booker brothers. Several people said that the woman lived in the town of Cumberland near the site of the old Luther P. Jackson High School. The Editor turned off the main road a short distance outside of Farmville, but had no idea where he was, other than in Cumberland County, and was unable to find his way back to the main road. He saw an elderly lady sitting outside in the cool morning air and stopped to chat with her. After she mentioned that she was from Cumberland County, the Editor asked her to share how life was in the county when she was a girl.

Mrs. Lilly Ann Allen began her story.

I was born June 5, 1929, in Powhatan, Virginia, and moved to Cumberland when I was a girl.

"How old were you when your family moved here?" the Editor asked.

I was under six. I hadn't started school when we moved. My mother was Mary Alice Allen and my daddy was Charles Ellis Allen. I married'a Allen.

We lived on Mount Olive Road. I went to a one room school called Sugar Fork School. Mrs. Mary Brown was the teacher. We walked to school, 'bout two miles one way. We went to school most'a the time, but sometimes we had to stay home and shuck corn, git wood, tote water from the spring and bring it up to the house.

Note of the Editor: Mrs. Allen appeared to be blind and the Editor felt he needed to guide the conversation a little more. The Editor slowly made a slight gentle motion with his right hand before her face. There was no reaction. The Editor determined she was blind or near blind.

"How did the school day begin?"

Each morning the firs' thing was you lined up outside and then go in and have singing. We always sung a church song. Each child said a Bible verse. Then the teacher would lead the Lord's Prayer for us. Mrs. Brown would work with the firs' grade a while then the secon' graders, and so on throughout the day. All the childr'n in one room.

The school went to the seventh grade. There was a branch that ran by the school. There was a spring by the branch and we would take the bucket to the spring, git water and bring it back to the school. There was a cooler in the room and we poured the water in the cooler. There was'a outdoor toilet. There wasn' no 'lectricity at Sugar Fork School. When we had a program at nigh', they use kerosene lamps to give ligh'. We had the Christmas program at school. Some of the bigger boys would go out to the woods and cut'a tree for the teacher to put in the class room. Mrs. Brown would put the tree in a corner and we would dress the tree. She didn' have no 'lectric cords and so forth 'cause wasn' no 'lectricity. So, she would let us put the red ribbons, and ferns out of the bushes on the tree. We got the green running cedar out of the woods and hung on the tree and all 'round the windows.

I had no 'lectricity' at home or school. My family attended Mount Olive Baptist Church. We walked to church each Sunday 'bout a mile or two. Mount Olive had no lights then. Mount Olive looked like a one room school at that time. Reverend John Booker, from Prospect, was the pastor. Reverend Booker baptized me in the spring. (A body of water.)

"What were some of the other one and two room schools in the area where you lived?" the Editor asked, trying to get a greater feel for the educational environment when she was a girl.

Some of the other one and two room schools I heard the people talkin' 'bout was Hawkes and Sharon School. There was a Cedar Fork School. I knew some child'rn who went there. I think Cedar Fork (s) School had one or two rooms. I never went there, but I know where it used to set.

When I passed to the eighth grade, I started goin' t' Cumberland County Training School. I rode the bus. Mr. Willie Brooks was the driver. I don't know whether he owned the bus, or it was a county bus. The training school had many rooms.

I went there t' 'leventh grade. That was the highest grade at the time. I was eighteen when I come out'a school.

———

EDWARD THOMAS BROOKS

Leaving Mrs. Allen, the Editor found his way back to the main highway and drove into the town of Cumberland, in Cumberland County. A man was seen exiting a store. The Editor stopped and said to the gentleman:

"Good morning, I am trying to find the daughter of one of the Booker brothers. She lives in town I was told."

"She lives right down the street," he said pointing. "She gott'a big mean dog. You betta' be careful."

Before leaving, the Editor asked the man to talk about the county and school when he was school age.

I was born 1937 and I started school around 1942.

I started at Berson Spring School. It had one room. I had to walk five miles one way to school. It went to the sixth or seventh grade. Mrs. Brim Hatcher and Mrs. Langer were teachers.

I started at the Cumberland Training School when I was in fourth grade nine years old. I would walk up to Highway 45 and the Booker bus would come along and pick me up and some other students. My sisters and brothers also rode the bus. Back in that time I don' remember my mama and daddy paying anything, but I know we rode the bus. Mr. Ardie Booker drove the bus.

Norman (Booker) owned the garage. Ulysses (Booker) owned the lunch room. Sam Booker owned the grocery store. There was a barbershop next to the grocery. Them Bookers' were tough people.

The areas where all the Bookers were was called Hicks Town. The Bookers owned that end of the town.

The Editor thanked Brother Brooks and then went to the house where the daughter of one of the Booker brothers lived. She was not at home. There was a big ferocious dog inside the house, meaner, the Editor thought, than Mr. Brooks described.

The Editor then visited the garage in town that the Booker brothers once owned. Mr. Brooks pointed it out to me earlier. Another gentleman now owned it. He shared some of the history of the garage with me.

———

LENA RUSSELL DOSWELL

I was born in Cumberland County, Virginia, October 25, 1928, to Frank and Maude Langhorne Russell. I started first grade at Cumberland County Training School, later named Luther P. Jackson High School.

In 1946 I left home and went to Saint Paul's College in Lawrenceville, Virginia. I was crowned the May Queen my junior year at Saint Paul's. I graduated in 1950. I was hired to teach at Halifax Training School. I taught there for one year. It was hard for me to get transportation home and the next year I got a job at Cumberland County Training School.

When the Prince Edward County public schools were closed, my husband, Rudolph Doswell, helped Roger Dove to go to Stanton and live with my sister Kathleen Russell Scott. I don't remember all the details, but Rudolph ended up talking to Kathleen and her husband Wesley Scott about Roger coming to live with them, so he could attend school. Kathleen and Wesley had four children: Deborah, Cheryl, Kathy, and Scott, Jr. Kathleen was a school teacher and Wesley her husband taught Industrial Education. Kathleen and Wesley were graduates of Saint Paul's College.

I taught in Cumberland County for approximately fifteen years and then I came to Prince Edward County.

When the Prince Edward County Free School opened, my husband Rudolph worked close with Dr. Sullivan to help get the Free School launched on time. Rudolph was a graduate of Moton High School and was deeply interested in the welfare of the students. Rudolph was the extension agent when the schools were open or before the closure. When Dr. Sullivan came to Prince Edward County, Rudolph drove the superintendent all around to help get him familiar with the county.

Rudolph rang the bell the first day to open the Free School and he said:

"We are ringing the bell to let the world know that the schools in Prince Edward County have reopened."

I came to Prince Edward in the summer of 1964 to teach in the Free School summer program. I taught summer school at Mary E. Branch No. 2. I taught first grade. The Cumberland County public schools where I taught had closed so I got a job in the Free School. It was a paid position.

People can read more about my husband's work with the Free School in *Bound For Freedom* written by Dr. Sullivan.

CHARLOTTE COUNTY

MARY FRANCES JACKSON GEE

I was born in Charlotte County, Virginia, in 1938. Out of a family of eleven I was the second child. I always loved Charlotte County for some reason. My father relocated to Prince Edward County when I was a junior at Central High School in Charlotte County. I was so upset when my father left that I cried, and a cousin offered to take me in until I finished school, but I wanted to be with my parents. Daddy was a sharecropper and thought he was bettering himself by moving to Prince Edward County. I came on to Prince Edward County and my education ended. I married Franklin Gee in 1959 and I went back to Charlotte County.

My sister Nancy Carol had been promoted to the eighth grade when the schools were closed. Franklin and I took her in the first year the schools were closed. She asked me could she come and live with us and go to school.

When Nancy Carol came, I went to Mr. Cooley's home, he was the principal and lived next door to the school. Mr. Cooley and I were in his living room. I explained that my sister was coming from Prince Edward County to live with us and I wanted to enroll her in school. He said:

"Fine, no problem."

Mr. Cooley was a different kind of person. If you asked him a question, he would answer it and move on. He answered my question about Nancy Carol being enrolled and left me sitting in the living room, thinking Mrs. Cooley would come and entertain me and she did. We sat and talked for a while. She was such a loving person. Mrs. Cooley, I believe, was a substitute teacher.

Mr. George Binford was the principal at the high school.

Franklin and I started our family. After our third child was born, that was when my siblings were brought into our home at the request of my mother. I believe Mama asked Franklin and me would it be alright if the others came—Shirley, Elizabeth, and Patricia.

When Shirley, Elizabeth and Patricia came to live with us, the Prince Edward County schools was in the third year of being closed. I didn't have to go and talk to Mr. Cooley about the three of them being enrolled. On the first day of school, Shirley, Patricia, and Elizabeth just got on the bus and went on to school. I made no arrangements for them.

The people, the teachers and administrators, knew my family because we had lived in Charlotte County earlier and I had attended Central Elementary and Central High School.

Lilly Mae Robinson who was a teacher at the elementary school knew my family. When she heard my sisters were in the school system, she was so delighted. She spoiled Patricia. The people knew everyone except Shirley and Patricia but got to know them.

Shirley, Elizabeth, and Patricia were all enrolled in the Charlotte County school system without a problem.

Home life was beautiful in our little four room house. There were nine of us in four rooms—Franklin, myself, our three children and Nancy, Shirley, Elizabeth, and Patricia.

There were families in Charlotte County or that lived near the Charlotte County line that took in students from Prince Edward County, so the students could attend school.

Annie Mae Hicks from Prospect stayed with Martha Carrington of Cullen, near Charlotte Court House, and attended Central High School.

Ms. Emma Johnson took in some girls from Prince Edward County.

There were other Prince Edward County children that went to school in Charlotte County but didn't move to Charlotte County. They remained at home with their parents.

The Jordan twins, Phyllis and Lillian, their father Mr. Charlie Jordan worked in pulpwood. Mr. Charlie Jordan had some of the guys that worked for him to drive the girls to Charlotte County each day and pick them up after school. I know this much because one of my husband's relatives, Gilbert Scott, worked with Mr. Jordan. One worker in particular, Luther Watson, drove the girls to and from school most times. Mr. Jordan owned the pulpwood company and had several trucks.

RUBY GREGORY GEE

I was a teacher at J. Murray Jeffress Elementary School in Charlotte County. When the Prince Edward County public schools were closed, I remember several teachers were hired to work in Charlotte County. The teachers were working in Prince Edward County when the public schools there were closed. Ms. Mary Redd, Mrs. Helen Bigger, Mrs. Mary Hendricks and Mrs. Flossie Womack taught at Central Elementary where Mr. Cooley was the principal. Mr. Cooley hired each teacher.

Mrs. Helen Dennis taught home economics at R. R. Moton High School before the schools were closed. She lived in Charlotte County and commuted. Mrs. Dennis never lived in Prince Edward County. In the fall of 1960 Mrs. Dennis brought two girls to Charlotte Court House to live with her so they could attend school.

Later I started teaching at Central High School and I taught many of the Prince Edward County students that came to Charlotte Court House to attend school. I taught Merel Hendricks and Angela Neverson. I also taught Mary Frances Hendricks and her sister, but I can't remember the sister's name. The two sisters stayed with Mrs. Helen Dennis. All the students I just named I taught them in high school. I taught John Evans in high school. Leroy Redd and his sister Jenette Redd I taught in high school. There were two Jordan sisters, as I recall. I probably taught many more Prince Edward County students, but I specifically remember these students. I was a home economics teacher and I only taught a few boys.

I was never questioned about any of the students in my classes. I never had to explain anything to the principal at the high school, who was Mr. George Binford, because he never asked. All I knew was that the students were on my roll and were from Prince Edward County.

There was the Topp family from Drakes Branch in Charlotte County. I knew the family. The father was named Johnny Topp. I can't remember his wife's name, but they moved to Prince Edward before the school closure. When the schools were closed, Mr. Topp sent the two boys to Washington, D. C. to live with relatives. He and his wife remained in Prince Edward County.

I went to Saint Paul's College in Lawrenceville, Virginia. Royce Bland was a student there at the same time. She was a teacher at R. R. Moton when the schools were closed. The Russell girls, Eunice Russell (McLendon-Whitehurst) and Lena Russell Doswell were at Saint Paul's at the same time. Lena was in my class.

ALETHEA DEPEE WELLS

I was born in Drakes Branch, Virginia, in 1925 to John and Naomi Lackland Depee.

I graduated from Saint Augustine College in North Carolina in 1945 and returned to Virginia. I started teaching at Nazareth School, a one room school, in the residential area of Phenix, close to Brookneal, in Campbell County. I taught in Phenix from 1950 to 1952. I was everything at the one room school, teacher, principal and janitor.

Then I went to Organ Hill School in Drakes Branch. This was a three room school. Then I taught at Duprees School from 1954–1959. Duprees was in Saxe. I took a break because

I had a child. I then went to Bacon District School in Saxe in Charlotte County from 1959 until 1983.

When I started teaching at Bacon District School in September 1959, the Prince Edward County public schools were closed. No Prince Edward students came to the Bacon District School area. All the students that came to Charlotte County went primarily to Central Elementary School and Central High School.

My sons, Eugene, Jr. and Peery, went to school in Charlotte Court House at Central High school with many of the Prince Edward students.

I knew many of the Prince Edward County students through my boys. I also knew many of the students through my husband who was a math teacher at Central High School. My husband Eugene graduated from Virginia Union University and was a member of Alpha Phi Alpha Fraternity, Inc.

As the both of us were educators, Eugene and I had conversations sometimes about the closing of the schools in Prince Edward County. We were for the students coming to school in our county. I believe many of the White people were for them attending school also because I never heard the White people in this county say anything negative about it.

My son, Peery, can tell you more about some of the Prince Edward County students that went to school with him. I will ask Peery to speak with you.

Note of the Editor: Mrs. Wells called her son and he came to the church and shared his story.

———

PEERY ALEXANDER WELLS

I started first grade in 1954 at Central Elementary and Mr. Douglas Cooley was the principal.

In September 1959 I was in the fifth grade. My fifth grade teacher was from Prince Edward County. She was one of teachers that lost her job when the schools were closed. Her name was Mrs. Mary Hendricks. She always had a smile but was very firm. Her husband was Reverend Haywood Hendricks. I went to school with some Hendricks' who were relatives of hers.

There were Prince Edward County students in the lower grades and the higher grades.

In September 1961 I entered the eighth grade, which was the beginning of my high school years. From my high school years, some of the students from Prince Edward County I remember were: Mary Frances Hendricks, Joyce Hendricks, Emanuel Smith, David Neverson, Angela Neverson, the sister of David. Alfred Redd was in the high school, he may have graduated before I entered high school. I know for a fact that he graduated, but I can't say what year. Phyllis Hendricks was the daughter of Mrs. Mary Hendricks, my teacher. There were a lot of students with the last name Hendricks out of Prince Edward.

———

LUNENBURG COUNTY

CHESTER STOKES

The Editor stopped at a gas station in Lunenburg County on Saturday, April 17, 2010, and saw two men sitting at a picnic table on the side of the building. One man was older and his age difficult to determine. The other gentleman was in his early twenties. The Editor parked and got out of his car, leaving the engine running and the door on the driver's side open because he only wanted directions to Saint Matthew Lutheran Church. Walking toward the two men, the Editor greeted them and introduced himself, and each man gave his name. All shook hands and the Editor said:

"I'm doing research. Can either of you tell me where Free State Road is? I'm trying to find Saint Matthew Lutheran Church."

"Just go t'da' sign down there," the older man said, pointing down the road, "turn righ, go a lil' ways and you'll see the church on the righ'." The man had a friendly air about him and the Editor could tell he was thoroughly familiar with local history.

"There used to be a school at the church many years ago, but it's closed now. I'm trying to find someone who remembers the school," the Editor said. "When the Prince Edward County schools were closed, some of the students attended Saint Matthew Lutheran School. I'm trying to find someone who was a student at Saint Matthew and remembers students from Prince Edward County coming to school there."

"I went to Saint Matthew, that was my school," the man said with great pride and added, "Mrs. Rahab Jackson was my teacher. The school is closed, but the part where the classroom was is still used. When they have a funeral or som'um, they slide the doors back to make mo' room." The Editor gathered that the old classroom now served as an overflow section for the church when there was a large attendance at a church event.

"Will you tell me about the school? Do you remember when the Prince Edward County schools were closed and some of the children from Meherrin in Prince Edward County used to cross the line and come to the school at Saint Matthew?" He quickly named several students. "Where can I plug up my laptop?" He pointed to an outlet near the picnic table on the side of the store/gas station. The Editor returned to his car, parked, got his laptop, plugged it up, sat at the picnic table, and typed as Mr. Chester Stokes talked.

When I was a boy, I went to Saint Matthew Christian School. I started there in September 1956. Reverend Frederick Ford was the pastor. He had a son named Frederick, Jr. Fredrick, Jr. was ahead of me in school. Reverend Ford had a daughter named Iris. Reverend and Mrs. Ford had seven or eight children. Most of the children dead now 'cept for Irish and the one we call Toby.

Mrs. Rahab Jackson was my teacher in elementary school. She taught all seven grades, first to seventh. Reverend Ford also taught. Mrs. Jackson and Reverend Ford did the teaching.

Everybody was in one big room with a coal stove in the middle of the flo'. I would say there was about twenty-five or thirty children in the school. There was the sanctuary and then a slidin' door that closed and separated the one big school room from the sanctuary. When they closed the slidin' doors, the chalk board was there for Mrs. Jackson to write on. In the summer we had Vacation Bible School in the big open room.

You had t' brin' your own lunch from home to school. We had about thirty or forty minutes for recess.

I took second grade work and third grade work in the same year and passed. I remember that because I had a brother one year older than me and I caught up wid' my brother. (Mr. Stokes smiled a little.)

I was doing fourth grade level work, when I was really in the third grade when the Prince Edward County Schools was closed.

My family lived on the east side of Free State Road where Saint Matthew School was located. Free State Road is Route 630. People who lived on the west side of Free State Road was in Prince Edward County. To get from the west side to the east side you just walked across the highway. That highway righ' there. (Mr. Stokes was pointing to the main road.) The west side of Free State Road is Meherrin.

The Prince Edward County students started crossing the highway to come over. I remember the Streat, the Reid, Bailey, and Stokes coming.

"Can you remember the children in the different families?" the Editor asked.

"Le'me see," he said, as though talking to himself and to the Editor at the same time. "Now in the Streat family there was William, Rachel, and Johnny." Mr. Stokes was counting individuals on his fingers while calling the names out loud. He paused and ended, "it migh'a been one mo' but I can't remember. In the Reid family," he commenced, calling names and holding up a finger for each person, "there was Wesley, Walter, Jimmy, Ida, Dora, Joseph, Mae, and they had a baby sister and I can't think'a her name. Then there was the Bailey family. There was William, Charles, Melvin, Bruce, Doris, Carrie, and Vivian. Most of the Stokes lived in Lunenburg County, but some Stokes children came from the Meherrin side in Prince Edward: Frank and William, but we called him Buck, (referring to William). Aunt Eva (Eva Crawley) ran The Chicken Shack on Second Street in Farmville. She used to brin' in her car James and Ralph, her two sons. She also brough' Clair and she brough' Marhall Thornton. Aunt Eva had'a 1958 Esel (Edsel). I think Ford made the car. Aunt Eva brought four or five every day."

Then Reverend Ford started teaching.

"You mean Reverend Ford started teaching because the number of students grew too large for Mrs. Jackson?" the Editor asked, seeking clarity.

Yea, dat's how Reverend Ford got involve in teaching. (This was emphasized. Mr. Stokes started talking excitedly.) You see, before it was just Mrs. Rahab Jackson when I started school. She was the only teacher. The school only had one teacher, Mrs. Jackson. But after the closing in Prince Edward and the children started crossing the road from Meherrin the class got too big for Mrs. Jackson. All the children were put together in the one big room, first to seventh grade. They had to break the class up. Mrs. Jackson had the lower grades and Reverend Ford had the higher grades. He lived next door to the church.

Meherrin is divided into two sections. One section of Meherrin is in Prince Edward County and the oth'a is the Meherrin section in Lunenburg County.

I started school at Saint Matthew because the nearest public school for me to start first grade was in Victoria fourteen and a half miles away. They sent a bus for eighth grade and up to go to high school in Victoria, Lunenburg High, but no bus was sent for elementary school students in my area.

Note of the Editor: After the interview, the Editor followed the directions given by Mr. Stokes, went to Saint Matthew Lutheran Church, parked, and walked around the grounds.

MILDRED H. JENKINS

Following the lead given me by Rebecca Lee Randolph on July 27, 2010, she told me that someone lived in the Jenkins house across from Lunenburg High School in Victoria, Virginia, and that it might be a member of the Jenkins family. "The name Jenkins is still on the mailbox," Mrs. Randolph said. The Editor set out to find the old school and the house, seeking someone who knew the giant school principal, Galvin Jenkins, in Lunenburg County that gave sanctuary to Prince Edward County students during the years of the academic crisis, but who has never been mentioned in a publication.

The Editor found the school and walked around the grounds, walked through some old facilities out back, then over to the ball fields. Upon leaving the school, he drove to a house positioned almost in front of the school. The name JENKINS was on the mailbox. The Editor parked, walked under a garage, and rang the bell at a side entrance. A lady opened the door. The Editor introduced himself, explained the project, that he had heard about Mr. Galvin Jenkins and wanted to speak with someone who knew him. She told me that the late Galvin Jenkins was her husband. I asked would she share some reflections about him for the project and she consented.

Mrs. Mildred H. Jenkins began her reflections.

Galvin was born and raised in the Rehoboth section of Lunenburg County, Virginia, and graduated from Lunenburg Training School in 1940. He entered Virginia State College and was drafted while a student and went off to war. After he was discharged, Galvin came back to school. I met him at Virginia State College. During the war, there were no more than one hundred male students on the campus. Galvin graduated in 1948.

After graduating, he applied to several schools and could not get in for what he wanted, which was Agriculture. He was accepted at Michigan State and went there and earned his master's degree.

He got a job teaching in South Hampton County, Virginia. I was from South Hampton County. He really wanted to return home to Lunenburg County and work in the school system. Finally, he got a job teaching at Lunenburg High School.

After teaching Agriculture at Lunenburg High School for several years, Galvin was appointed principal. William Craighead had been the principal, but he was appointed to a position with the State.

My husband didn't talk much about the children from Prince Edward County. If he was alive, he would sit with you all afternoon sharing information.

You should talk to my daughter Avis Gresby. She works in the Prince Edward County school district. She probably remembers some of the students from Prince Edward County that attended school with her.

MAJOR OWEN

After leaving the home of Mrs. Jenkins, the Editor was heading out of the town of Victoria and decided to stop at a café for lunch. As he got out of his vehicle, a gentleman was exiting the establishment. Greetings were exchanged. The Editor introduced himself and the gentleman introduced himself as Major Owen. Information about the project was quickly shared while standing in the parking lot.

"I am seeking information on Mr. Galvin Jenkins. I just left the home of Mrs. Jenkins," said the Editor to Mr. Owen. "Did you know Mr. Jenkins?"

"Yes, I knew him. Mr. Jenkins taught me Agriculture."

"Tell me a little about him as a teacher," the Editor encouraged. "Hold on, let me get some paper out of my car to write on."

"Well, I took Agriculture class. Mr. Jenkins wanted students to succeed. Whatever he could do to help he would do it. The farming knowledge I got from him in his class has remained with me."

The Editor asked: "Do you remember any students from Prince Edward County coming to your school when the schools were closed in Prince Edward?"

I remember Iris Fowlkes and Doris Cherry. I was in the sixth grade. Iris and Doris were around the fourth grade. They were from the Rehoboth area of Prince Edward. There were some other students, but I can't remember their names. We knew there were students in the school from Prince Edward County, but everyone kept quiet. That's how it was back then. That's how we had to survive.

The Editor thanked Mr. Owen for his time and for sharing, went in the café, and had lunch.

AVIS JENKINS GRESBY

I was born in Southampton County, Virginia, in the town of Franklin. We moved to Chase City soon after I was born. We lived in Chase City until 1966. Daddy starting teaching at Lunenburg High School and was named principal around 1961. I started school in 1959 and Daddy was not a principal at the time.

When I started first grade, the school was named Lunenburg High School. The elementary school, Lunenburg Elementary was next to the high school. These were the two schools in Victoria that Black children attended before integration. There were some outlying schools such as Kenbridge Elementary; it was a brick facility by 1959.

I remember several students from Prince Edward County that attended Lunenburg Elementary School. I remember a boy named Larry Winkler. I believe, I think he was in my class. I remember the name, even if he was not in my class. Polly Thornton was another student I recall. Theresa Alden (Clark). Mama taught Theresa in second grade and she was one year behind me. I was in the third grade, so this would have been the 1961-1962 school year. I have no idea how the Prince Edward County students came to school. I think one girl rode with a teacher.

Mrs. Marshall, the wife of Ben Marshall taught at Lunenburg Elementary School, she taught with Mama. Her daughters Ava and another whose name I can't remember was with me. Ava was not in my class, but a year, I think, behind me. The policy was a parent could enroll their children in school in the county where the mother or father taught.

I know for a fact that Mrs. Marshall taught at Lunenburg Elementary School. Mama and Daddy and Mr. Ben Marshall and Mrs. Marshall were good friends.

I finished seventh grade at the elementary school and then went across to the high school.

The White children went to Kenbridge High School in Kenbridge or Victoria High School in Victoria. Central High School was built and all students in the county had freedom of choice. You could attend Central or remain at Lunenburg High School.

In 1969 Lunenburg High School became Lunenburg Junior High and all the high school students went to Central High School. Lunenburg Elementary became Lunenburg Primary. The White elementary kept the name Victoria Elementary School.

I was a junior when I went to Central. I graduated from Central High School in 1971.

Daddy never talked about the children from Prince Edward County he accommodated. He may have talked to Mama about it. We just knew the children were from Prince Edward County. The children who came kept quiet about where they were from, but we knew where they were from because we knew the residents in our area. These were children we never saw in our church on Sundays or played with on the weekend or after school during the week. We only saw them at school.

———

BUCKINGHAM COUNTY

BETTY CARTER DAVIS

My family lived in a small community called New Canton in Buckingham County.

I graduated from Carter G. Woodson High School in Buckingham in June 1961. I was in the eleventh and twelfth grades the first two years the public schools in Prince Edward County were closed, the 1959-1960 school year and the 1960-1961 school year.

I remember two events from my senior year.

First, I recall a student came to live with my Aunt Mattie, Mattie Branch Mayo. Only one child came. The student was to stay with another family. She was to stay with an elementary school teacher. Something happened, and I cannot remember the details. Aunt Mattie took the little girl in until a family in the county could be found for her. The girl attended Steven J. Ellis Elementary School where Mr. Allen Gooden was the principal.

The second event I remember from the second year of the school closure was that arrangements were made for some high school students to enroll at Carter G. Woodson High School. Many names came by referral. The students were to live with friends or family or host families. The process was interrupted.

The students at first tried to enroll at Luther P. Jackson High School in Cumberland County, but there was an overflow at Luther P. Jackson. So, it was arranged for many of the high school students to come to our high school in Buckingham

County. People were anxious to help because these were students who were nearing graduation.

My Aunt Mary, Mary Royal, lived in Cumberland. She had sixteen children. I remember hearing Aunt Mary talk about the overflow at Luther P. Jackson High School.

The enrollment process for students to enter Carter G. Woodson High School was interrupted because of parental issues and host family issues that had legal implications.

When I graduated from Carter G. Woodson High School in the spring of 1961, there were no Prince Edward County students in my senior class.

After graduating from high school, I entered Virginia State College in Petersburg, Virginia. I attended Virginia State for a short period. Because of the declining health of my grandmother, I came home to take care of her. I later moved to Lynchburg, Virginia, and continued my education at Central Virginia Community College and Lynchburg College. Upon graduating from college, I started teaching in Amherst County, Virginia. I taught in the Amherst County public schools for twenty-five years and retired in 1999.

———

JOE CHAMBERS, JR.

When I was a boy, I attended S. J. Ellis Elementary which went to the seventh grade. When I passed to the eighth grade, I went to Carter G. Woodson High School. I remember new faces coming to our school because of the school closing in Prince Edward County. Ronald Branch and his brother John Branch came to school in Buckingham County. Their mother was Nurse Branch.

Ronald played on the high school basketball team. John was the oldest.

———

GWENDOLYN JONES

I know three students that came to Buckingham County to attend school when the public schools in Prince Edward County were closed. They were the sons of Odessa Moss Branch. The Branch family still lived in Farmville. The three sons were John, Ronald, and Barlow Branch — who are my cousins. The boys had an uncle here in Buckingham, Odessa's brother, who was James Archer Moss. They did not stay with him. Nurse Branch rented a house from Mr. Ulysses Washington, Sr. on Highway 15 South in Buckingham.

I started school at Slate River School, which was a one room school and had first to sixth grades. My mother, Ruth Hazel Jones, was the teacher. I remember the county school nurse, Nurse Odessa Branch, would come and check on the students.

In seventh grade I attended S. J. Ellis Elementary School for one year. I started at Carter G. Woodson High School in the eighth grade in the fall of 1962. The school had eighth through twelfth grades. The principal was George Frank (G. F.) Harris. I was in the graduating Class of 1967.

Barlow was in the Class of 69. He and my sister Velma went to Virginia State College.

———

OSCAR HOLMAN

I met a student from Prince Edward County that was impacted by the school closing.

When I was fourteen years old and in the ninth grade, I tried out for the football team at Carter G. Woodson High School. This was the 1964-1965 school year. There was a drill called the Bull Ring. One guy was in the middle of the ring and all the others were circled around him and the goal was to keep him in. The guy in the middle of the ring had a smile on his face. He knocked guys back one by one. He could have gotten out of the middle of the circle. He was naturally strong. I found out his name was Percy Tucker and he was a fullback. He lived with relatives in Buckingham. I did not make the team that year.

The next year I made the team. I remember we went to Prince Edward County to play R. R. Moton High School football team. Percy was playing for Moton High School. I did not understand at the time why he went to Moton. We were young and knew nothing about the politics of the day and what was going on. It was later that I learned that Percy went back to his home county to attend school.

The next time I met a student from Prince Edward County that had been locked out of the schools was when I went to Saint Paul's College. I started at Saint Paul's in August 1969. I ended up at Saint Paul's because when I was in high school teachers only talked to students about going to one of three schools—Saint Paul's, Virginia State College or Virginia Union.

There was a student at Saint Paul's named Mike Smith from Prince Edward County. The reason I remember him so well was because most of the freshmen were eighteen or nineteen years old, but Mike was in his early twenties. There were some other guys at school who were twenty-six or twenty-seven years old, but they were Vietnam veterans. Some had been to school, got drafted, and had come back. They were on the GI Bill, many of them were sophomores or juniors. Mike's situation was different.

Mike had a brother named Reginald, and he was known to most people as Reggie Smith. Reggie did not attend Saint Paul's College. I knew Reggie from my teaching days. After I graduated from college, I taught for thirty-three years. Reggie worked for the Virginia Department of Education. He used to come to Buckingham County shortly before the school year started and give an inspirational or motivational speech to the county teachers. I remember him coming to Buckingham several times to speak to us.

If my memory is correct, I believe Mike said he and Reggie went to New Kent County, Virginia, when the schools were closed.

After I graduated from college, I was on a pick-up baseball team. One time we went to Prospect in Prince Edward County to play a game. Some people said Percy was at the game. I did not get to see him and talk with him. They said he had lost one leg or both legs in Vietnam.

———

CHARLES WHITE

I attended Saint Paul's College. While a student, I pledged Alpha Phi Alpha Fraternity. I graduated in 1955. When I left Saint Paul's College, I returned home to live with my parents in Clifton Forge, Virginia, having a curfew at twenty-five years old. This was in 1955. I was waiting to be deferred.

I had turn down several teaching jobs. Everyone knew Saint Paul's turned out people who could teach a trade. I turned down about six offers. I got one from Fredericksburg, I believe. Dad said let the military take you off a job, if they draft you let them take you from a job. Some World War II veterans told me the same thing.

I got a letter from a man name George Frank Harris in Dillwyn, Virginia. I told my Black family doctor I was looking for a job. He had already encouraged me to come back and teach shop in Clifton Forge. He said you will be needed in Prince Edward County when I told him. When you meet with the superintendent he will ask you are you a member of the NAACP, you say yes, because if you say no he won't believe you.

I took a job in Buckingham County.

After the Supreme Court ruling, Prince Edward County said, 'we can't integrate because we are going to close our schools.'

Buckingham County's superintendent was Irving S. Driscoll. There were thirty something one and two room schools for Black students in Buckingham County. They had a list. There was Union Grove and other schools. He never visited the schools.

At the beginning of the 1959-1960 school year the superintendent held his meeting with the Black teachers. He told us he was not going to hire any of the teachers from Prince Edward County. He suggested that the Nigra teachers, as he called them, and the Negro Teachers Association should try and convince Negroes in Farmville to run Reverend Griffin out of town. He didn't hire any Black teachers from Prince Edward County.

There were three teachers in Prince Edward County that conducted workshops in teacher training programs in earlier years. They were Mrs. Connie Rawlins, Mrs. LaVerne Pervall and Mrs. Venessa Venable. Mrs. Rawlins went to Charlottesville to teach after the schools in Prince Edward County were closed.

Samuel Griffin was the principal at R. R. Moton High School in Prince Edward County. After the schools were closed, he was an assistant principal, he may have been a principal, but I think he was an assistant principal at one of the Black high schools in Charlottesville, Burly or Jefferson. I used to see him when we had games in the area.

Mrs. Josephine Bland taught at S. J. Ellis Elementary and she was from Prince Edward County. She was a senior at Saint Paul's when I was a freshman. She was permitted to bring her two children to school in Buckingham County.

If you worked in Buckingham County, you could bring your children to attend school. Nurse Branch served the community for the Negro schools, so she could bring her sons.

Buckingham County took the hardest position regarding teachers and Prince Edward County students coming to the county.

The superintendent said that he would personally approve student applications for admission to schools in the county.

They started a school closing committee in Buckingham County. There was a story in the Farmville Herald about Buckingham contemplating a school closing.

During the five years the Prince Edward County public schools were closed, Buckingham needed Math, English and History teachers at Carter G. Woodson High School but would not hire a teacher from Prince Edward County.

In 1964 Carter G. Woodson won the District Championship, won the regular basketball season championship, the basketball tournament, won the baseball championship and the track championship. I think it was the 4-40 State Championship.

Many guys played all the sports. Larry Jones won the FFA National Speaking Contest. Between 1964 and 1968 we had a thirty-five game winning streak in football. Alfred D. Wilson, Ferrell D. Johns, and I were the coaches. I also assisted with basketball. Wilson was the head coach of everything except football. Johns and I went to Saint Paul's together and we were roommates.

I brought the Explorer Scouting program to the county. The Explorer Scouts was for boys who were fourteen and over. We met during activity period at school. Ronald Branch was in the Explorer Scouts. In 1964 or 1965 I had more than 100 boys and it was unofficially the largest scout program in the country. The boys wore their uniforms once a week and the school looked like a military academy. We went on hikes and trips and they loved it.

I was a Boy Scout leader and the troops used to camp on my grounds.

Buckingham County had a freedom of choice program for schools. Parents could send their child to whatever school they desired. They knew parents would send Black children to Black schools and White parents would send their children to White schools. The scheme limited integration.

The principal at the White high school in 1969 was liberal minded and a high thinking person. White people always said with integration Black students would hold White students back.

Woodson had some smart students. Five of them, all Honor Roll, went to the White high school and did fine. One was the Valedictorian in the Class of 1969. The White principal instead of announcing it to the School Board first announced it to the student body. The School Board and Superintendent, when they learned about the announcement, encouraged him to change things in a way to prevent the girl from graduating Valedictorian. The principal would not change it. They fired him the next year.

It was announced around 1972 that Buckingham would integrate. Buckingham County was the last or among the very last to fully integrate its schools.

Some of the Black teachers had problems. Some White students would call Black teachers boy or girl as they were accustomed in their social setting. I had more White kids than Black in my class. I taught a building trade.

I taught fifteen years at Carter G. and two years in the integrated setting and left the school system. I opened Alpha Construction and ran it for five years. I employed some of my former students. One of my former students took my place as the building trade teacher after I left the school system.

Chapter Three

ACCOUNTS FROM COLLEGE STUDENTS

QUEENS COLLEGE &
HAMPDEN SYDNEY COLLEGE

JEAN LEANORE KONZAL

I grew up in Queens, New York, in the public housing projects. I was born into a working-class family. My parents were
committed to making the world better for working people.
My family could not afford to send me to college anywhere
except Queen's College. It was a free education.

I became interested and participated in a tutoring project
in south Jamaica, where a lot of African Americans and poor
families lived.

I cannot recall exactly how I got involved in the Prince
Edward County program. I think I answered an ad in the
college newspaper saying they were going to Farmville.
Fifteen to twenty students signed up and we were mentored
by Dr. Rachel Weddington and Dr. Sidney Simon. I believe
both were in the Department of Education. Weddington was
in Education and Psychology. Simon, I am not sure of his
specialty.

We spent about a year preparing to go to Prince Edward
County. We met in our group and learned about the history
of Farmville and what we could expect; and we learned educational strategies to work with the children. There was much
group work to be done, settling group conflict and such. We
dealt with the question of race and racism, which was a reality, as all of us were White except one student. Carolyn
Hubbard was a Black female. The professor who went with

us, Dr. Weddington, was also Black. She was the strength and support through it all. She kept a level head. We called her Doc. We called Dr. Simon — Sid.

A number of parents of our group members were not thrilled about having their children go South. My mother was especially frightened. My mother had a sister who acted as her mother in raising her, as my mother's mother died. My mother's sister was a Communist and went to Russia in the early 1930s. In the late 1930s they were part of Stalin's regime. My aunt, Jean Pincus, was killed in Russia. Mother never saw her sister again. There were many mass arrests and murders in that country at that time.

Mother was afraid I would go South and never return. I was nineteen at the time.

When we arrived in Prince Edward County, I lived with Mr. and Mrs. Fred Reid. They had two grandchildren, Tony and Butch. They lived on a farm. I remember it was located on a hill. It was hard walking up the hill. I was a city girl now with a cow outside my window and a rooster crowing and waking me up in the morning. (Dr. Knozal started laughing.) Myself and three other students lived with the Reid family: Phyllis Padow, Donna, whose last name I cannot remember, and Ina Gold and I stayed with Mr. and Mrs. Reid.

While I was in Prince Edward County working with the children, my mother received threatening telephone calls. The callers threatened me and called me all kinds of names.

I think most of the classes were held in the mornings. We focused a lot on reading and math. We had to do individual work because many of the children had various skill levels. Some children had not been to school for several years and others had been away and kept up their skill level.

The United Federation of Teachers were also in Prince

Edward County that summer. They were from New York also. We were all divided into small groups of children. There were centers in the outlying areas and in Farmville where the students gathered for classes.

The first group I taught was five and six year olds. Then I started teaching eleven and twelve year olds.

The real issue we encountered was more about the difference between city and country life and not race.

Initially the children were shy, but as the days went by they began to open up and trust us more. Their experience had not given them reasons to trust.

I had one of Reverend Griffin's daughters in my class. Mignon was her name. This was during my initial stage. I was teaching in the basement of First Baptist Church.

The Queen's College students worshipped at First Baptist Church each Sunday. This was an eye-opening experience for me, a Jew. I also remember Reverend Douglas who was the young Black pastor at Beulah African Methodist Episcopal Church, located across the street from First Baptist Church.

Some of the other students I remember from our group that went to Prince Edward County in the summer of 1963 were: Michael Wenger, Stan Shaw, and Deborah Yaffe.

————

CHARLES N. DAVIDSON, JR.

In the fall of 1962, I had arrived from Baltimore, Maryland, as a freshman student at Hampden-Sydney College in the midst of the massive resistance of white citizens to public school desegregation in Prince Edward County.

The public schools remained closed. Blacks were without

classroom and teacher. It was a dreadful and disdainful state of affairs that bore heavily upon the conscience of a handful of students and faculty alike at Hampden-Sydney College. Together we decided we would undertake something positive in response to the widespread injustice. We pledged to stand in solidarity with our black brothers and sisters.

To that end, a group of us participated in private meetings and conversations with members of the black community, including the Rev. L. Francis Griffin of First Baptist Church of Farmville. Each week during the academic year we made our way to the basement of that historic church to tutor disenfranchised black youth in the subjects they had been so heartlessly denied by the closing of the public schools in 1959.

Looking back these many years later, I think of it as by far the most important social undertaking of my career as a student at Hampden-Sydney. Since I had been afforded the privilege of an excellent high school and college education, there was no better way to share the fruits of my learning than with young African Americans who had fallen victim to the scourge of white racism.

I distinctly remember the warm, sunny day in May 1964, when Attorney General Robert F. Kennedy landed by helicopter on the lawn just a few feet beyond my dormitory room. He was one of only two visiting dignitaries in my time at Hampden-Sydney whom I remember having received a standing ovation from student body and visitors packed into the seats of Johns Auditorium.

Afterward, my classmate Louis Briel presented Robert Kennedy and Mrs. Kennedy with a portrait that Mr. Briel had painted of Robert's late brother, President John F. Kennedy. The Attorney General had come to visit the Free Schools of Prince Edward County, in support of public education for black citizens, and to champion the Civil Rights Bill of 1964, soon to be passed by the U. S. Congress despite all the voices of reactionary protest.

During the following year of 1965, a minority of us Hampden-Sydney and Longwood College students who belonged to the College Westminster Fellowship, meeting on Sunday evenings at Farmville Presbyterian Church, presented the officers and members of the fellowship's council, as well as the elders serving on the Session (the official board) of the church, with a proposal for initiating interracial dialogue within the larger community. The effort was to be facilitated by the publication of a journal named "Call to Commitment," an instrument of conciliation between the races and churches, black and white.

However, the fellowship's governing council defeated the proposal. Several members of the Presbyterian Church who did not want to see the journal come to light had influenced the decision from behind the scenes. Regrettably, both the Westminster Fellowship and the Farmville Presbyterian congregation remained racially segregated, fearful that a "troubling of the waters" would lead to a "mixing of the races."

We who represented the minority voice in the youth fellowship expressed our disappointment in the council's short-sighted decision. We were consciously aware of the fact that some of the most powerful citizens of Farmville, among the inner circle of persons who had led the public opposition to school desegregation, were members of the Presbyterian Church. The fellowship's council was so reluctant to "rock the boat" that it refused to bring the matter even before the entire fellowship for discussion, much less before the Session and the congregation.

Parenthetically, some of the professors and students at

Hampden-Sydney also prayerfully asked the college administration and its Board of Trustees to move toward facilitating the racial integration of the college's student body. While president of the Campus Christian Association my senior year, in collaboration with officers and members of the association who were likewise concerned and committed, we together continued to be advocates for justice for black citizens who for far too many generations had been deprived of the most basic human dignities and rights due them, including their most recent deprivation of the right to a quality public education. The days of white supremacy in the South and in Prince Edward County were surely numbered.

To whatever avail within the larger struggle for civil rights that our modest efforts at racial reconciliation may have contributed to bringing about needed social change in a deeply troubled time, we held fast to the belief, as did our black brothers and sisters, that the truth of the gospel — embodied in concrete acts of love and justice — would eventually prevail. The forces of resistance simply could not withstand the imperative of God's unconditional grace to transform a whole society.

That remains as true now as it was then.

Chapter Four

CONTRIBUTORS TRAIL

THE TRAIL OF CONTRIBUTORS

Mrs. Virginia Faggins Patterson, Mr. Russell Faggins, Mrs. Gwendolyn Wesley Crawley and her brother Mr. Howard Wesley, and the matriarch Mrs. Mildred Womack Patterson were interviewed by the Editor in that order on Saturday, August 11, 2001 at the Patterson family reunion in Darlington Heights, Prince Edward County, Virginia. This began the collection of stories for this publication.

For nearly two years the work moved slowly, and few interviews were secured.

Mrs. Adelaide Griffin was interviewed via telephone. Her niece Dr. Terri Griffin, who the Editor met during a teaching session in Lynchburg, Virginia, provided the contact information. Mrs. Ernestine Watkins Herndon, and Mrs. Bertha Earley Shepperson came to my designated office at Eggleston Funeral Home.

Dr. Ralph Reavis, Sr. invited me to be the guest lecturer at the M. C. Allen & Vernon Johns Preaching Lecture Series in Lynchburg, Virginia. In preparation for the lectures on Vernon Johns it seemed most appropriate to interview individuals who knew him and had engaged in professional and social contact with the man. Mr. Joe Berryman, who was born and reared in Prince Edward County, said he would take me there and introduce me to individuals that knew Johns. After scheduling his contacts, the Editor met Mr. Berryman in Lynchburg and he drove to Prince Edward County where we had lunch with Mrs. Vera Allen and Mrs. Elizabeth Johns Roebuck. The latter was a cousin of Vernon John.

Mrs. Allen urged me to telephone Mr. Macio Hill. She said he was one of the educators that came to Prince Edward County to work with children in the summer program. She provided the contact information for Mr. Hill.

No one was home at several houses where Mr. Berryman stopped. He stopped at the home of a clergyman not seen for several years. The man was intimately acquainted with Vernon Johns. Berryman shared with the wife why we stopped by. She sadly announced that her husband had Alzheimer's.

Mr. Berryman stopped at another house on a winding country road and knowing my interest in the school closure years he said to a woman standing on the porch: "Sister Dungee, this is Reverend Vaughn and he is interested in talking to people who were locked out of the schools. Weren't you caught up in that?" "Yeessss, I sure was." "Can you talk to him?" "Well," she started, "I ain't got time right now. I'm gittin' ready for Revival t'nigh; otherwise, I would talk t'im." "Can he call you?" Berryman asked. "Sure, he can." Mrs. Annie Marie Owens Dungee gave me her telephone number, gave me and Berryman some tomatoes out of her garden, and extended an invitation: "Try and come out to the Revival one night. We'll be goin' the rest'a the week." The Editor telephoned her about two weeks later.

The Editor called Mr. Macio Hill, explained the project, and mentioned that Mrs. Vera Allen strongly suggested that he be contacted. Mr. Hill invited me to his home to conduct his interview. After we had enjoyed an exceptionally exquisite home cooked meal prepared by Mrs. Hill, the task was tackled. Mr. Hill boasted of a Prince Edward County student that was locked out of the schools for four years, his family relocated to Nottoway County in the fifth year of the closure, the individual graduated at the top of his high school class several years later, at the top of his college class four years thereafter and was an outstanding teacher and principal in Virginia. "I will get the contact information for Calvin Nunnally. You have to get his story," Mr. Hill said emphatically.

The Editor sent Mr. Nunnally a letter and we later agreed on the evening he would be interviewed via telephone.

Mr. Carl Eggleston, Sr., the proprietor of Eggleston Funeral Home, Farmville, Virginia, who embraced the project, and gave me an office at his establishment to use and work out of when in the county asked one morning while the Editor was getting settled: "You just want to talk to some people who were locked out of the schools?" "Yes, I want to compile their stories and hopefully a book will be published," the Editor said. "I can get you some people," Mr. Eggleston replied. "There are plenty people around here. I was locked out of the schools too." Mr. Eggleston began to circulate the word that a gentleman was at his establishment compiling stories shared by individuals that were locked out of the Prince Edward County public schools. Chuckie Reid was interviewed on May 21, 2003.

Ms. Clara Medlyn Ligon, who at the time was a volunteer at the Moton Museum in Farmville, said to me upon learning of the project: "Has anyone told you about the lady that had a school in her house?" "No, I have not heard of her," was my response. "You have to talk to her. I will arrange for you meet Ms. Flossie." Ms. Ligon arranged for me to meet Mrs. Flossie Scott White Hudson at a center in Prospect where seniors gathered. Also, at the center on Wednesday, May 21, 2003, and shared accounts were Mrs. Gertrude Scott Stiff and Mrs. Alma Brown Robertson.

Mr. Travis Dawson Harris, Jr. was interviewed on May 22, 2003 at Eggleston Funeral Home. The proprietor arranged the interview. Harris said while preparing to leave: "There's a lady I'll contact when I get back to work and ask her to come by. "Thank you, I will be right here," the Editor assured. The next day Ms. Sara Deloris Earley came by and said Sheriff Harris encouraged her to come and share her story.

Ms. Clara Medlyn Ligon was interviewed during my May 2003 visit. She also directed me to Mr. James P. Young.

The Editor relocated from Washington, D. C. to Tampa, Florida, during the summer of 2003.

In Prince Edward County, on Monday, November 3, 2003, and Mr. Carl Eggleston, Sr. having announced my return to the community, Mr. Warren 'Ricky' Brown came by at the invitation of Eggleston. Reporting to my office one morning Mr. Eggleston was available and shared his story about being locked out of the schools. Later his mother Mrs. Ruth Eggleston, who was working in the front office of the establishment, allowed me to chronicle her story.

The Editor was back in Prince Edward County on May 17, 2004, and the town was busier than normal that morning. There was a huge canvass in front of the Moton Museum, rows of chairs neatly positioned, some seats occupied, news vans were parked nearby, and people were being interviewed by reporters. "What's going on in town today?" the Editor asked some older men seated on a bench at a small shopping center near the museum. "Some kind'a program, celebration," the men chimed unrehearsed. Still uninformed the Editor parked, walked across the street to the big tent, approached an individual under the huge canvass and asked: "What's going on?" With some surprise on her face, a lady said: "Today is the Fiftieth Anniversary of Brown verses the Board of Education." The date and event had escaped me. A local observance was being held because Prince Edward County, Virginia, (Davis vs School Board of Prince

Edward County) was one of the several law suits employed to strengthen the Brown vs the Board of Education litigation.

Many of the attendees looked to be in their fifties and sixties. They would have been among the students locked out of the Prince Edward County Public Schools between 1959 and 1964. After the program, the Editor approached a gentleman and asked was he in the county when the schools were closed. He said yes. An invitation was extended to him to walk across the street to the funeral home and share his reflections. "I don't have time. I have to be back in Richmond soon; otherwise, I would tell you my story." "Then tell it to me right here, right now," the Editor encouraged. My pen was in my hand. Either the lady with the gentleman gave me some paper or someone nearby gave me paper. Mr. Eddie Wiley started talking. He terminated the interview after about fifteen or twenty minutes, saying with regret: "I wish I could talk longer, but I got'a get back to Richmond."

After the Fiftieth Anniversary celebration concluded, Mr. Edward Thornton, Mrs. Shirley Jackson Brown, Mrs. Patricia Jackson Leverette and Ms. Jo Ann Randall came to my office at Eggleston Funeral Home and shared reflections.

When no more interviewees came, the Editor walked back across the street to the Moton Museum. He apologized to some ladies seated at a table for interrupting their lunch, explained the project hurriedly, and asked each to share her story from the years of the educational crisis. Mrs. Carrie Clark Bland and Mrs. Susie Manns Reid with great delight consented.

When Mr. Warren Ricky Brown learned that the Editor was back in the county, Brown stopped by my office at the funeral home on May 18, 2004, around 10:30 a. m., greeted me and said: "All you want to do is talk to people who didn't go to school, who got locked out?" "Yes, that's all." "Well, I can take you to some right now. There're some teachers at the school where I work." "Really," said the Editor, amazed and musing what a privilege it would be to compile stories from individuals that were locked out of the Prince Edward County public schools and as adults enjoyed their teaching career in that environment! The Editor got in his vehicle and followed Mr. Brown to the middle school.

Mr. Brown introduced me to the principal and briefly discussed the project. Mr. Brown escorted me to the library and he left. Shortly thereafter teachers and school workers that were locked out of the Prince Edward County public schools when they were girls came into the library one by one looking for the gentleman that was conducting the interviews. A man who was a school bus driver for the Prince Edward County Public School System also came by. He too was locked out of the schools when a boy. Mrs. Charlotte Herndon Womack, Mrs. Angeles Wood Christian, Mrs. Rosa Marie Bedford Johnson, and Mr. Cecil Watson told the Editor their stories. Cecil said he would ask his mother to tell what she recalled, as he remembered very little. After her interview, Mrs. Charlotte Herndon Womack contacted Ms. Sylvia F. Oliver, a substitute teacher, to inquire about granting an interview. Ms. Oliver told Mrs. Womack that she was unavailable but would be delighted to tell her story the next time the Editor came to Prince Edward County. Ms. Cynthia Lea Johnson, a teacher at the middle school, learned of the interviews and came by my office at the funeral home late that evening.

The Editor returned to the middle school on May 19, 2004 and had an audience with Mrs. Leola Miles Entzminger. She came to Prince Edward County, Virginia, as a young educator the second year the public schools were reopened and offered a rare account. Later in the day the Editor spoke via telephone with the mother of Mr. Cecil Watson, Mrs. Shirley Eloise Walton Watson Jennings.

In the afternoon around 2:00 p. m., the Editor was in the parking lot of a shopping center in Farmville and spoke to a gentleman standing outside his car. He greeted me and commented: "It's a hot one." "Yes, it is," was my reply. After talking for a few minutes, the man was asked about the period of the closing of the schools. He was told about the project and asked would he share his story. He agreed. The Editor retrieved some paper from his vehicle, went back to Mr. Alfred Frank Watson, and wrote as he talked while standing by his car.

On the evening of May 19, Mr. Warren Ricky Brown had arranged for the Editor to interview his mother, Mrs. Pearl Stokes Brown, and his brother, Mr. Walter McKinley Brown. Ricky, as he is called by his family and friends, also invited a friend to stop by named Mr. Hilton Lee, Sr. Mr. Lee was from the community of Rice. All three interviews were conducted at the home of Mrs. Brown.

One afternoon the Editor was walking around the apartment complex where Ms. Clara Medlyn Ligon lived and stopped to talk with a lady sitting on her front porch. She introduced herself as Ruth Virginia Fawley Jones who was from Cumberland County. Mrs. Jones was asked to expound on life when she grew up in Cumberland County.

Having heard about students from Queens College in New York that came to Prince Edward County in the summer of 1963 to work with pupils that had been locked out of the public schools for four consecutive years, the Editor sent a note to the Queens College message board in March 2004. He provided his email and telephone number and asked that any person who was a student at the college and went to Prince Edward County, Virginia, in the summer of 1963 contact him to assist with research. Dr. Jean Knozal responded in May 2004. She was interviewed by telephone on June 4, 2004.

Saturday, June 5, 2004, without any named prospects or recommendations for stories, the Editor drove to Meherrin to see the old New Bethel School on the grounds of New Bethel Baptist Church. A gentleman was leaving the church driving a truck as the Editor drove onto the grounds. Both drivers stopped. We introduced ourselves, had a brief conversation standing between the two vehicles, and then went inside the church, where Mr. Vincent Lowell Earley recounted events in his life during the years of the closure of the schools. Following our conversation, Mr. Earley guided me to the home of Mrs. Florence Wood Ayers. He said she was a person with whom the Editor should definitely speak.

Mr. Stanley Lorenso Wesley was interviewed on Monday, June 7, 2004, in my office at Eggleston Funeral Home.

The 'moving story,' as Mrs. Charlotte Herndon Womack described it, of Ms. Sylvia F. Oliver was drafted on Friday, June 11, 2004. Mrs. Dorothy Lee Allen, the sister of Mr. Hilton Howard Lee, Sr. granted an audience the same day. Hilton convinced his sister to share her story. Mrs. Allen contacted her younger sister Mrs. Cathlean Lee Kirby. Mrs. Kirby said she was unavailable this week but consented to see me on another visit.

Late Friday evening, June 11, 2004, the Editor stopped at the old Hendricks Store in Prospect. He explained the project to the young lady behind the counter. Her name was Ms. Marcella Ann Robinson. She said her memory was dim on the subject, but her older sisters could talk intelligently about the school closure years. She telephoned one of the sisters. Within fifteen minutes two women and a gentleman entered the store. Mrs. Doris Elizabeth Robinson Brown, Mrs. Elsie

Robinson Walker and her husband Mr. Cornell Walker were interviewed.

Cornell asked while we were sitting on a bench in front of the store: "Have you been to see Mr. L. L. Hall?" "No, but several people have mentioned his name as a person with whom I should speak." "His story needs to be included in the work or you don't have a history," Cornell said emphatically. "I'll speak with Mr. Hall and when you come to Prince Edward again I'll take you to see him. He doesn't give interviews anymore, but he'll do it if I ask him."

Saturday, June 12, 2004, the Editor rode back to Prospect and down a road near the Hendricks Store. After stopping at a home and discussing the project, Ms. Cynthia Vaughan shared her story.

The Editor was in Prince Edward County August 6-14, 2004, having returned for the Hampden Sydney Reunion on Saturday, August 7, 2004.

On Friday, August 6, 2004, the Editor was in Rice, saw a gentleman mowing his lawn, and stopped to get directions. While talking to him, the Editor gathered the man was among the students locked out of the schools. Being told about the project, the man said he had nothing much to tell. "Tell whatever you have, tell your story, no matter how little." Mr. Roy R. Miller disengaged his lawn mower, escorted me to his outdoor open garage where we sat, and he recounted his moving story.

The Hampden Sydney Reunion was held on the site where the building of the Beneficial Benevolent Society and Loving Sisters of Worship is located. Mrs. Rosa Marie Johnson Bedford and Mrs. Frances Goldman Scott invited me to this event when each was interviewed. Rosa Marie who was insistent about my coming to the reunion was in command on

Saturday, August 7. Many individuals came out from other sections of the county to see old friends who had return home for the event. Whether they were from the Hampden Sydney area or another section of the county, because they were present and were locked out of the public schools Rosa Marie encouraged individuals to share their story. In several cases people that were reluctant to rehearse their account for the record she in a regal yet stern convincing manner ordered them to repair to a spot on the grounds and give their account.

Stories were shared on Saturday, August 7, 2004, by: Mrs. Catherine Marie Johnson Jackson, Mr. Stanley J. Johnson, Mrs. Valarie Amelia Scott Brewer, Mrs. Josephine Baker Bourne, Mr. Tommy Hunter, Mr. James Edward Crawley, Mrs. Doris Dae Miller Johnson, Mrs. Eva Johnson Wilson, Mrs. Ernestine Hughes Smith, Mrs. Mary Virginia Peace, Ms. Sylvia Fowlkes, Ms. Sarah Dorothy Couch, Mr. Vincent Eanes, Mrs. Lucy Celestine Womack Eanes, Mr. Willie Sylvester Vaughan, Mr. Wyatt Vaughan, and Mrs. Leana Beatrice Evans Wormack. Thank you, Rosa Marie.

Rosa Marie said to me in the late evening: "Barbara Baker didn't come but she works in Farmville. I'll call Barbara and see if she will talk with you next week. Her sister Frances didn't come today either. I'll try and contact Frances next week too. I believe Frances was in the eleventh or twelfth grade when the schools were closed."

On Sunday morning, August 8, 2004, after the early worship service at Mercy Seat Baptist Church, the Editor met two men in the parking lot and wrote their accounts on paper as they talked. The two were Mr. Walter Wood, Sr. and Mr. Aaron Johnson.

Rosa Marie arranged for me to interview Mrs. Barbara Baker Simons the following week. While with Mrs. Simons, the Editor inquired about her sister Frances, who Rosa Marie mentioned. "When we are done, I'll call Frances and check if she can see you." At the end of our session Barbara called Frances. When she hung up, she gave me the directions to the home in the Meherrin section. The Editor left Farmville and found the home of Mrs. Frances Baker Streat, where a story as delicate as the lady that shared it was heard.

Mr. William Lee Streat, the husband of Frances, was born in the neighboring county of Lunenburg. He said he remembered youths from Prince Edward County attending school in his county during the closure years. "When I come to Prince Edward again, I would like to write your reflections," the Editor said, preparing to leave the home.

Ms. Clara Medlyn Ligon negotiated with Mrs. Flossie Scott White Hudson to have some of the individuals that attended sessions in the basement of her home during the school closure years to share their reflections. On August 11, 2004, the reflections of Mrs. Mary Frances Mitchell Jones, Mrs. Naomi Mitchell Carey, Mrs. Irene Mitchell Legin, and Mrs. Alberta Mitchell Ligon were gathered.

One evening during the week when at a restaurant in Farmville with Ms. Ligon a gentleman spoke to her. She introduced me and briefly shared about the project. "James has some information I am sure," she said convincingly. "Give me call. I can share a few things that might be of value." James Allen gave me his contact information.

Mr. Douglas Metteau Vaughan shared his stirring account during the week.

On Sunday, August 15, 2004, the Editor attended a service at Sharon Baptist Church in Cumberland County, Virginia. Inquiry was made with a gentleman about the old Sharon School once located next to the church. "You need to talk to my mother," he said. He invited me to come to the home of his mother Mrs. Eliza Melrose Randolph Reid. The editor shared in a delicious Sunday afternoon meal, after which he engaged in conversation in the front yard Ms. Elsie Alexander, Ms. Florence Laverene Depte, Ms. Helen Campbell, Mr. William Randolph, and Mrs. Roberta Gilliam Ferguson. The editor returned on a later occasion and interviewed Mrs. Eliza Melrose Randolph Reid.

Reverend John Otis Peterson, Sr., Pastor of Alfred Street Baptist Church, Alexandria, Virginia, invited me to preach the latter part of 2004. Learning the Editor would spend time in Prince Edward County on this visit, Reverend Ed Jackson, the Assistant to Reverend Peterson introduced me to Mr. Ralph Herndon who was born and reared in Prince Edward County. Mr. Herndon gave me the telephone number for his mother Mrs. Ernestine Watkins Herndon and his aunt Mrs. Ethel Watkins Wilson Fisher. The mother had already been interviewed.

When the Editor arrived in Farmville, he telephoned Mrs. Ethel Watkins Wilson Fisher. She was expecting my call.

"Have you talked with John Hurt?" Mr. Eggleston, Sr. asked. "No, I have not spoken to him." "You need to talk to John. He has been on the news and they had him up in Richmond to speak." Eggleston gave me the contact information. Mr. John Hurt was interviewed at the Prince Edward County Library on November 6, 2004.

Ms. Clara Medlyn Ligon arranged for me to interview Mr. Thomas R. Mayfield at the Moton Museum on Tuesday, November 9, 2004. While waiting for him to arrive, the volunteer welcoming guests that day, Mrs. Osa Sue Allen Dowdy, shared her story. Mr. Mayfield arrived at the scheduled time. When the Mayfield interview ended, Mrs. Dowdy informed me that she had called her sister and that Mrs. Ada Doreene Allen Whitehead would arrive soon. Mrs. Whitehead shared her wonderful story.

On Monday, June 6, 2005, the Editor was driving through Rice, headed in the direction of High Rock Baptist Church, and saw a gentleman sitting on a front porch absorbing the fresh early morning air. He had a coffee cup in his hand. With some reluctance the Editor intruded. The gentleman was told about the collection of stories and he informed me that his school days ended before the educational crisis struck. Still we talked, and Mr. Howard Hicks provided valuable information regarding the years leading up to the school closure. After his interview concluded, his wife Mrs. Lorraine Jennings Hicks rendered her account.

Mr. L. L. Hall agreed to grant an interview. Later in the day on June 6, 2005, Mr. Cornell Walker took me to the home of Mr. Hall.

Ms. Clara Medlyn Ligon took me to the worship service at Sulphur Spring Baptist Church, Prospect, on Sunday, May 18, 2003. After the worship service, Ms. Ligon stopped by the house of Mrs. Nannie Rebecca Harris Carr Hill to inquire about her condition. Ms. Fran Harris said that her aunt was still in a nursing facility. Driving in Prospect in June 2005, the Editor saw the same car in the yard that was parked the Sunday Ms. Ligon stopped by in 2003. The Editor stopped, reintroduced himself to Ms. Harris, and reminded her of the brief May 2003 visit. Mrs. Nannie Rebecca Harris Carr Hill was back at her residence. She and her niece Fran were interviewed on the same afternoon in June 2005.

Mr. William Junious Miser was interviewed on June 10, 2005, at the home of Mr. Cornell and Mrs. Elsie Walker. Cornell telephoned Miser and asked him to come to the house and talk with me. Later in the day Cornell and Miser rode me around Prince Edward County and pointed out sections that should be visited. Cornell was driving and the three of us were in his truck. After we had been riding a while, Cornell said: "We should take Wally to see Mr. Spencer." "Yea, he ought'a get some good information from Mr. Tracy Spencer," Miser added. Cornell drove to the Spencer land in Darlington Heights. The Editor and the project were introduced, and Mr. Tracy Spencer agreed to share reflections. Leaving the Spencer property, Cornell and Miser rode me through the Peaks community.

Saturday, June 11, 2005, the Editor engaged Mrs. Cathlean Lee Kirby, who was unavailable to tell her story in June of the previous year. Leaving the home of Cathlean in Farmville the Editor drove to Rice to the home of her cousin Mrs. Virginia Saunders Foster. Mrs. Kirby called and arranged for my appearance. Upon entering the home, Mrs. Foster introduced me to everyone in the house. One lady caught my attention, as she appeared to be within the age range of students locked out of the schools. Mrs. Gloria Ann Redd Lovelace said she was on her way to work. Mrs. Foster yielded and allowed the Lovelace interview to proceed, after which Mrs. Foster was interviewed.

Mr. William Lee Streat received a letter from the Editor informing him of my upcoming visit to Prince Edward County the latter part of 2005. An interview was conducted with him. During the same excursion to the county two individuals were seen under a canvass near a store. They were patiently waiting for travelers to stop and purchase some of their items. The Editor was on his way to Rice and stopped. Both parties looked to be in the age range of the group locked out of the schools. The gentleman said he was born and reared in another county. The woman said that she was caught up in the school lock down. Ms. Mary Barksdale shared her brief account.

During the summer of 2006, the Editor was driving through the countryside and decided to go to Peaks. He noticed a house where between eight and twelve children were playing in the front yard. The matriarch was sitting quietly and peacefully in a chair on the front porch. The Editor parked on the side of the country road and got out of his vehicle. While walking pass the children in the front yard, speaking to them, and having a briefing conversation with a girl about thirteen or fourteen, it was apparent that many lacked the reserved personality of rural youths. When on the porch with the matriarch, a New Jersey license tag on one of the vehicles parked in the yard caught my attention. The old lady on the porch introduced herself as Annie Mae Beasley Washington. She was aroused by the project, prepared to share her reflections without ado and noted: "I'm glad somebody is doin' dis kind'a work." After interviewing Mrs. Washington, Mrs. Beverly Beasley Hatcher, who now lived in New Jersey, was interviewed. Beverly was locked out of the schools when a girl.

Work brought me back to the Washington, D. C. area in the summer of 2007. My residence was in Alexandria, Virginia. From here the Editor journeyed to Prince Edward County when opportunity allowed.

Dr. Doris Scott Crawford, of Prince Edward County, was interested in the progress of the collection of stories. While the Editor was in Lynchburg, Virginia, for three lecture days, Dr. Scott arranged for me to meet with Mrs. Phyllistine Yvonne Ward-Mosley on March 25, 2010. Mrs. Ward-Mosley lived in Lynchburg.

Phyllistine matriculated out of State during her junior and senior years of high school. She said that there were events that occurred during the school closure years that her younger sister, Betty Jean, could talk about more intelligently. Phyllistine made the arrangements and the Editor drove to Prince Edward County on Saturday, April 17, 2010, for an 11:00 a. m. appointment with Mrs. Betty Jean Ward Berryman at her home.

There was a private Lutheran school in neighboring Lunenburg County that many students from Prince Edward County attended during the school closure years. When the session with Mrs. Berryman ended, the Editor drove to Lunenburg County in search of Saint Matthew Lutheran School. He stopped at a gas station in Lunenburg County to get directions to Saint Matthew Lutheran Church, where the private school had existed. The gentleman with whom the Editor inquired, Mr. Chester Stokes, gave directions. After sitting with Mr. Stokes for over one hour on a wooden picnic style table on the side of the gas station drafting his story, the Editor left to go and visit the site of the church, having a wealth of first-hand knowledge about Saint Matthew Lutheran School.

In a written communication to me on May 26, 2010, Dr. Doris Scott Crawford stated in part: "...the persons that I indicated that I would contact have graciously and enthusiastically agreed to speak with you. They are: ...Clara Patterson Taylor...Dr. Alfred Leon Cobbs..."Leon," as he was called by family and friends, thought you might be interested in talking to his brother Samuel...Catherine Alfreda Scott...."

Mrs. Phyllistine Yvonne Ward-Mosley put me in contact with Mr. Robert 'Bob' Hamlin and with Mrs. Flossie Levella Oliver-Moore. The three were students in the Kittrell Junior

College high school department the first year the Prince Edward County public schools were closed. The school was located in Kittrell, North Carolina.

The Editor drove to Burkeville to the home of Mrs. Flossie Levella Oliver-Moore on June 11, 2010. Before leaving her home, she inquired: "Have you spoken with Rebecca Randolph? She works at the School Board office." "No, I have not spoken with her." "When you come again, I want you to get her story," Mrs. Oliver-Moore said firmly. "If you arrange it, I will see her," was my response.

Several persons in Prince Edward County said: "You need to interview Barbara Botts." No one could tell me how to contact her. "I heard she lives in Richmond and holds a Ph. D," another person said on a later occasion. The Editor discovered a magazine article published in 2005 in which she was featured. On May 8, 2010, the Editor emailed Dr. Darlene Currie, a name randomly selected from a Richmond Public Schools Directory, explained the project, and that he was searching for an educator in Richmond named Dr. Barbara Botts. Days later Dr. Currie sent me the contact information for Dr. Barbara Botts Chapman, a retired educator. The Editor drove to Richmond on June 26, 2010 and interviewed Dr. Chapman.

Ms. Catherine Alfreda Scott, about whom Dr. Crawford informed me, was contacted. We agreed to meet at the Farmville Public Library on Tuesday, July 27, 2010, as she would be in Prince Edward County from New York during that time.

Before leaving the county that day Mr. Robert 'Bob' Hamlin was interviewed at the Moton Museum. Mrs. Rebecca Lee Randolph was interviewed the latter part of the afternoon, Mrs. Flossie Levella Oliver-Moore having arranged the meeting.

When opportunity permitted, the Editor journeyed to

Prince Edward County without anyone scheduled to interview. In late 2010 while on the way to Prince Edward County, in the town of Crewe, Virginia, a sign at a stop light caught my eyes. The town of Victoria was on the sign and the arrow pointing to turn. It came to my mind at the stop light that Mrs. Rebecca Lee Randolph shared that Lunenburg High School was in Victoria and that Mr. Galvin Jenkins, the principal gave sanctuary to Prince Edward County pupils during the school closure years, lived in Victoria. The Editor turned left when the light turned green and followed the road for about fifteen miles to Victoria. The old school was located and the house across the road from the school had the name Jenkins on the mailbox just as Mrs. Randolph said. The Editor was informed that Mr. Jenkins was deceased. His wife Mrs. Mildred H. Jenkins shared reflections. Leaving the home of Mrs. Jenkins, the Editor stopped for a noon snack at a café on the way out of town. He met Mr. Major Owen in the parking lot. Owen said he remembered the high school principal and some Prince Edward County students that came to the school during the educational crisis. Mr. Owen was interviewed in the parking lot of the café.

The Editor drove to Charlestown, West Virginia, to interview Mrs. Clara Patterson Clark Taylor on December 27, 2010. Dr. Crawford alerted Mrs. Taylor to expect me to contact her.

On February 1, 2011, my retirement became effective, allowing me to travel more freely.

In May 2003 Ms. Clara Medlyn Ligon called her nephew Arthur Lee Foster in Woodbridge, Virginia, and shared the news of the project. She told me that Arthur said he would be delighted to share his story, just call him and arrange a time. The Editor was unable to communicate with him because the contact information was misplaced. One day in early 2011 a slip of paper was exposed among a pile of papers on my desk in the den. The information on the paper was written in the hand of the late Clara Medlyn Ligon and had the contact information and the name Arthur Foster. A letter was sent to Mr. Foster on March 13, 2011. He called after receiving the letter and said he remembered the telephone call from Clara years before. Arthur arranged for me to come to his home on Monday, March 21, 2011.

Upon arrival, Arthur escorted me to the basement. In the basement sat a woman. "This is my wife, Ethel," he said, paused, and resumed giving her maiden name, "Ethel Poindexter." "Please to meet you, Sister Ethel," said the Editor, walking to the chair in which she was sitting to shake her hand. "Do you have a sister named Grace?" "Yes, Grace is the oldest," the wife answered. "I just downloaded a photograph of you and your sister last week from Ebony Magazine, 1963. Give me a minute to get my laptop operating and I will show it to you."

Arthur was interviewed first and then Mrs. Foster. Sister Ethel prepared a delightful snack for the Editor before he left their home. Arthur and Ethel said they would contact Grace and encourage her to share her story.

A letter was mailed to Mr. Samuel A. Cobbs on March 17, 2011, requesting an interview. He telephoned me immediately upon receiving my communication and we agreed the Editor would be at his home in Hampton, Virginia, on the morning of March 28, 2011. He shared his powerful story. We were done by early afternoon at which time his wife Sadie had lunch prepared for us. Before leaving the home, Sam said: "Wally, you need to talk with Aundré Carter. She's a Pearce now and lives in Pennsylvania." "Tell her what we are doing and see if she will agree to share her story." "You need to talk to my younger brother Freddie and my brother Leon."

On the morning April 6, 2011, Mrs. Avis Jenkins Gresby was interviewed in Farmville, Virginia. Leaving this appointment, the Editor drove to Appomattox to the home of Mrs. Grace Poindexter Forrest and interviewed her. "Mrs. Arnetta Coleman Winston West lives next door. She was a teacher in Prince Edward County when the schools were closed," Mrs. Forrest revealed. "Do you think she will see me?" the Editor asked, ready to walk next door. "She is not there right now. She spends the winter with her daughter in another State and comes back home when the weather warms up." "Please mention the project to her when she returns." Mrs. Forrest served an early afternoon meal and prepared me a sandwich to take and eat later on the road.

Mrs. Phyllistine Yvonne Ward-Mosley emailed me information regarding a reunion that was to take place April 22–24, 2011, in Prince Edward County. Hundreds of individuals that were locked out of the public schools were expected to be present. No interviews were secured on Friday. The Editor was introduced to Reverend Darrell Wade, pastor of Beulah African Methodist Episcopal Church, Farmville on Friday, April 22.

The next day the Editor was present for the second day of activities that lasted from mid-morning until early afternoon. Two persons that had been locked out of the public schools during the closure years approached me and shared their accounts. They were Mr. Freddie Cobbs and Mr. Anthony A. Farley. Mrs. Mary Jones Bannister graduated from Moton High School in 1957 but shared how the school closure impacted her younger brother and nieces and nephews.

Reverend Wade said: "When you came back to the county, there is a lady in the church that I want you to talk to; she knows a lot of history. Her name is Helen Walker." "I will let you know when I am coming again so you can set it up," was my reply. Wade, born and reared in South Carolina, was extremely interested in the project.

On Friday, May 20, 2011, the Editor returned to the county and at 10:45 interviewed Mrs. Helen Ruth Walker, arranged by Pastor Wade. When preparing to leave her home, Mrs. Walker said: "I wanted you to talk to my neighbor Grace Moton across the highway, but she went to visit some relatives; maybe you can see her the next time you come."

Leaving the home of Mrs. Walker, the Editor drove to Peaks, which was very near. Stopping at a home to make inquiry, a young lady said she knew nothing of the years of the school closure, but she would go inside and have her mother come out and speak with me. "How old is your mother?" the Editor asked. "Eighty-one." The family matriarch came outside and stood on the front porch where we exchanged introductions. The project was shared, and she was asked to recount what she remembered from the years of the closure of the schools. We sat on the front porch and Mrs. Sadie Scott Walker offered up her reflections. While interviewing her, the daughter of Mrs. Walker, who lived next door, came over to check on her mother. The Editor was introduced and upon learning that Mrs. Earnestine Walker Lee had been locked out of the schools she was asked to tell her story after the Editor finished with her mother.

The parsonage for Beulah African Methodist Episcopal Church had been vacant for over thirty years. When Reverend Darrell Wade came to the church in 2008, he began a revitalization effort. Though there was much work to be done at the parsonage, he said to me on an earlier occasion: "I know it costs you money to drive up and down the road. Two bedrooms are fixed up and you can use one whenever you are in the county. That will save you a little money." The Editor stayed at the parsonage on the night of May 20.

Mrs. Shirley Jackson Brown arranged for several individuals to assemble at Beulah African Methodist Episcopal Church on Saturday afternoon, May 21, 2011, in coordination with Pastor Darrell Wade, who allowed us to use the basement of the church to conduct interviews. The individuals summoned by Sister Brown were Mrs. Mary Frances Jackson Gee, Mrs. Lilly Jackson Scott, and Mr. Jerry 'Monster' Smith.

Samuel A. Cobbs forwarded to me the contact information for Mrs. Aundré Linell Carter Pearce in Harrisburg, Pennsylvania, and a letter was mailed to her on June 3, 2011. Mrs. Pearce was interviewed via telephone on July 1, 2011. In her account she shared about her uncle, Mr. Leeman Allen. "Where is your Uncle Leeman now?" the Editor inquired. "He still lives in Prospect." "Do you think you can get him to share his story the next time I am in the county?" "I'm sure he will," she affirmed.

A half dozen or so worshippers at Woodlawn United Methodist Church, Alexandria, Virginia, stood and introduced themselves to the congregation at the proper time on Sunday, August 7, 2011. Prince Edward County was mentioned by a few as their home. After the worship service, the Editor approached the group, explained the project, and asked who among them had been locked out of the schools. Mr. Rufus Dove said that he was caught in the school crisis. Mr. Dove was interviewed in the church fellowship hall after the worship service.

Several consecutive days were spent in Prince Edward County. Pastor Wade providing lodging at the parsonage.

Pastor Sylvia Shepard Meadows was interviewed in her office at the church in Farmville, on August 11, 2011, arranged by Pastor Darrell Wade. Then on to the home of Mrs. Grace Estelle Ferguson Moton, interview arranged by Mrs. Helen Walker. The day concluded with Mr. Leeman Allen, at his home in Prospect; his niece Mrs. Aundré Linell Carter Pearce arranged the audience.

Mrs. Eunice Russell McLendon-Whitehurst, an elementary school teacher in Prince Edward County when the schools were shut down, was interviewed at her home in Farmville on Friday morning, August 12, 2011. Her sister Mrs. Lena Russell Doswell was visiting. The story of Mrs. Doswell was also drafted at the dining room table.

On Saturday morning, August 13, 2011, Mrs. Grace Estelle Ferguson Moton escorted me into Farmville so we could have some material from her private files copied. She told me that we had to make haste because she was going to a Family Reunion at 1:00 p. m. "A family reunion would be a good setting to get some stories," the Editor said, having spoken out loud unintentionally standing in her kitchen. The words were uttered before realizing the implication. "You can be my guest," she replied. "Oh, no, I don't know any of the people and would not want to intrude." "Well, before we go into town we'll go right across the road and tell some of the people in charge that you are coming this afternoon." We drove across the road to a house where the Editor was introduced and strongly encouraged to be present later in the afternoon at the family reunion in the Peaks community. At the family reunion Saturday afternoon Mr. Leroy Carr, Mr. Phillip Walker, Mr. Leander Alfred Carr, Jr., Ms. Mable Booker and Mr. George Lee Jones, Jr. were interviewed.

Contact was made with Dr. Alfred Leon Cobbs on July 12, 2011. He said that he would draft his story himself. The Editor received it on August 23, 2011.

On Wednesday afternoon, August 31, 2011, the Editor was nearing Lynchburg, Virginia, where he had accepted a teaching position. Approaching Appomattox on Highway 460, he remembered Mrs. Grace Poindexter Forrest saying one of her favorite teachers lived in the house next door, but Mrs. West spent the winter months with her daughter in another State. Passing the home of Mrs. West on Highway 460 a light was on in the front room of the brick house. The Editor turned off the highway and into the yard, parked near the kitchen door and rang the bell. An older woman who possessed every conceivable feature of an educator opened the door. We exchanged greetings, briefly discussed the project, and with a smile Mrs. Arnetta Coleman Winston West invited me in to the kitchen where we sat, talked, and laughed and drafted her account.

On Wednesday, September 7, 2011, the Editor journeyed to New Hope Baptist Church, in the New Hope section of Prince Edward County, to attend the funeral of Mrs. Mildred Womack Patterson. It was at her home that the collection of stories started ten years earlier. At the fellowship dinner held in the annex after the funeral a gentleman said to me: "You're the book man." Unclear about what he meant, but believing he was referencing the compilation of stories, the Editor was slow to answer. Clarifying himself, the gentleman added: "You the man collecting the stories for the book? I was at the reunion in April when you spoke and asked people to tell their story." "Yes," the Editor replied, knowing Providence was at work, "I am the one collecting the stories. Where were you during the school closure years?" He quickly rehearsed some events, but my scribbling notes was a disservice to his story. "Your story is too rich, we need to get together and you take your time and tell it to me." Mr. Leon Hill gave me his address and telephone number. The Editor went into the fellowship hall, sat with Mrs. Gloria Perry Gibson and members of her family, dined, and returned to Lynchburg.

Mrs. Shirley Jackson Brown, on September 13, 2011, escorted me to meet with some senior citizens at their scheduled meeting held at Saint Michaels Church, Drakes Branch, Charlotte County, Virginia. The older sister of Shirley, Mrs. Mary Frances Jackson Gee, who lived in Charlotte County and a member of the group, arranged for me come. Mrs. Ruby Gregory Gee and Mrs. Alethea Depee Wells, both teachers in Charlotte County when the Prince Edward County public schools were closed, shared their memories of pupils coming to Charlotte County to attend school. After Mrs. Wells finished, she said: "You should talk to my son, Peery. He was a student and can tell you about some of the students from Prince Edward County that came to school in Charlotte County. He's at home. I'll call and ask him to come and speak with you." Mr. Peery Alexander Wells came to the church annex where we were gathered.

On the way from Drakes Branch, Sister Shirley stopped me by the home of Mrs. Dorothy Wiley Harris, the daughter of Mrs. James Wiley. The Editor had read about the Wiley family in a newspaper clipping. Sister Shirley explained the project to Mrs. Harris. The latter said she had graduated from R. R. Moton High School prior to the closure of the public schools, but there were younger children in her family that were impacted by the lock-out and she would communicate with them to see if any were willing to share their account.

Pastor Darrell Wade invited Reverend Alexander Isaiah Dunlap to come and preach at Beulah African Methodist Episcopal Church, Farmville, Virginia, on Sunday, September 25, 2011. Reverend Dunlap was the pastor at Beulah the first year of the educational crisis. He was the person responsible for getting Kittrell Junior College to receive Prince Edward County students, seniors especially, into the high school department the first year of the lock-out. This would be the first trip back to Farmville for Reverend Dunlap since leaving in the summer of 1960. When making hotel arrangements for the guest clergy, Wade had a conversation with the hotel desk clerk. He called me later and said: "There is a lady that works at the hotel in Farmville. She shared her story with me and I told her you would be in contact." While in Farmville on September 8, 2011, the Editor visited with Mrs. Pauline Elizabeth Holman Randolph. At the conclusion of our time together, she said: "You should talk to my brother George." "You arrange it and I will get with him."

Pastor Wade located as many former pastors of Beulah African Methodist Episcopal Church as possible and invited them to share in the worship service on September 25, 2011. One of the former pastors who returned that Sunday and was in the county during the school crisis was Reverend Franklin West. After the worship service, the stories of Reverend West and his wife Mrs. Marylene Council West were drafted during the fellowship dinner held in the basement after church.

Mr. Leon Hill recounted his story with me at the dining room table at his home in Prospect on Tuesday afternoon, September 27, 2011. Mr. Hill said as the Editor was preparing to leave: "I wan'a give you something." He left the dining room, went to another room, and returned with some papers. "I found this among the things of my late wife when I was cleaning up. I think she was writing her story; she was doing something sort'a like what you're doing." The Editor reviewed the pages and said: "Yes, she was writing her story." "You can have it," said Mr. Hill, "and do whatever you want with it." "I will retype it as it is written and include it in the book with the other stories. I cannot change anything because if I do it will no longer be authentic," stated the Editor. "I understand," said the giver. At the top of the typed account was the name Brenda Smith Potter.

On September 28, 2011, the Editor was at the home of Mr. George Notice Holman in Farmville.

Leaving his home, my journey took me to Prospect to try and locate Mrs. Mary Frances Hendricks Brown. Several people said to me: "You need to speak with Mary Frances Hendricks." She was not at home. The Editor was about to get in his vehicle and leave when a car rolled on the yard with two people inside. The car came to a stop, a gentleman got out on the front passenger side. The Editor walked to the driver side of the car, introduced himself, and said he was looking for Mrs. Mary Frances Hendricks. "I'm Mary Frances," the driver said in a soft tone, displaying no suspicion about the gentleman she was speaking with for the first time. The project was shared with her. The driver made no attempt to get out of her vehicle. She depended on the service of a motorized wheelchair. "Sure, I will tell my story," she said while laughing and displaying an anxiousness to report her account. Mrs. Brown remained in the automobile behind the steering wheel. The Editor stood at the driver side door and drafted the wonderful account as she talked and laughed from inside her vehicle and made me feel welcome on the grounds of her property.

Saturday, October 15, 2011, the Editor drove to the home of Mrs. Dorothy Wiley Harris in the New Hope area and rendezvoused with her sister Mrs. Oreatha Lois Wiley Banks at 5:00 p. m. Oreatha had driven from Richmond to visit her mother in a home for seniors in Keysville. We agreed that Oreatha, after spending the afternoon with Mrs. Minnie B.

Wiley, would stop by the home of her sister Dorothy for an interview before returning to Richmond.

The Editor felt compelled to go to High Rock Baptist Church, Rice, Virginia, on Sunday, October 16, 2011. During the period of announcements, Pastor Bernard S. Hill, Sr. allowed me to make remarks and the project was shared with the congregation. Brother Hilton Howard Lee, Sr., a long time standing member of the church and who gave his account years earlier, rendered additional remarks urging persons to tell about life during the school closure period. After the worship service, Mrs. Goldie Saunders Walker, agreed to share her story. She gave me her contact information. While on the church grounds after the worship service, rehashing my remarks made during the period of announcements, Mrs. Barbara Jones, an usher, said: "You need to talk to Clarence Nunnally. He was here during that time." Sister Jones called Brother Clarence, who was walking to his car, over to us. He told me what he remembered, and the Editor wrote the information on a piece of paper while standing in the church parking lot.

Dr. Kitty Smith arranged for Mr. James Hardy, Mrs. Dorothy Lockett Holcomb and Mrs. Gloria Allen Lockett to meet with me on Wednesday, October 19, 2011, in Farmville.

Mrs. Lockett said following her presentation: "You need to speak with Evangelist Lillie Jordan Johnson. She has a powerful story." Mrs. Lockett mentioned informally as we were talking after her session that she had a sister, Polly Allen Wise, that was a nurse. "You make the contact and I will get with Evangelist Johnson. I also want to speak to your sister, Polly," said the Editor.

Leaving Lynchburg, Virginia, on Thursday, October 20, 2011, to go home and see my mother in Sumter, South

Carolina, the evening found me in Concord, North Carolina, having made previous arrangements with Mrs. Shirley Ann Wiley Barnes for an interview. Shirley is the sister of Oreatha. Shirley shared her story while cooking dinner. By the time dinner was served her story was drafted.

Friday morning, October 28, 2011, the Walker family welcomed me to their home in Amelia County, Virginia. The story of Mrs. Goldie Saunders Walker was chronicled at the table, while her husband prepared a scrumptious breakfast— hash browns, bacon, eggs and coffee.

Mrs. Daisy Patterson Edwards was interviewed via telephone on Thursday, November 3, 2011. Days prior Mrs. Gloria Perry Gibson telephoned her cousin and requested permission for me to call.

Mrs. Gloria Allen Lockett contacted Mrs. Lillian Gloria Jordan Johnson as promised and an appointment was scheduled for early November. When the Editor arrived at the home in Prospect and entered the house, Mrs. Johnson introduced me to her mother. Upon hearing "This is my mother Libby Jordan," the thought entered my mind—'I know that name.' It came to me that Mr. L. L. Hall called Mrs. Libby Hill Jordan in June 2006 and asked her to speak with me. Mrs. Jordan, now almost one hundred years old, was shown her story on my laptop. She did not remember the telephone interview but acknowledged the accuracy of what was recorded. Then Mrs. Johnson was interviewed.

Having heard so much about the old Five Forks School an effort was made to find it. After driving a good distance on Five Forks Road and seeing nothing that resembled a school, the Editor pulled into a yard where a lady was engaged in yard work, parked, and got out of his vehicle. Greetings were exchanged, and the Editor said: "I am trying to find the old Five Forks School. A man told me a few weeks ago that it was still standing and was on this road." "The school is right there," she said, while pointing and added, "I went there when I was a girl." "The school is right where?" the puzzled Editor asked, seeing only houses. "Right there," she said again, pointing, and clarifying: "Somebody bought the school and turned it into a house. A family used to live there, but it's empty now; nobody lives there, it's been vacant for a while." "What did you do when the schools were closed?" the Editor inquired, determining she was within the age range for county residents that had been impacted by the school crisis. "I had passed to the fifth grade," she commenced. She was interrupted, the project explained, and she encouraged to give her full account. "I don't have much to share." "That is usually my sign that I am about to get some good information. Let me get some paper out of my car to write on," said the Editor. "Are you the man that spoke at the gathering in April and asked people to tell their story?" "Yes, I am." "I didn't speak with you because I didn't have much to tell." We stood in the front yard and Mrs. Linda Edmunds Edwards gave her account on Tuesday afternoon November 8, 2011. She told the world more than she will ever know.

Ms. Jacquelyn Nenee' Reid was interviewed on Tuesday, November 22, 2011, at the establishment in Farmville where she is co-manager, Bland-Reid Funeral Home.

Dr. Doris Scott Crawford arranged for me to preach at Sulphur Spring Baptist Church, Prospect, Virginia, on Sunday morning December 18, 2011. The church was without a pastor at the time. The collection of stories was briefly mentioned prior to the sermon. After the benediction, Mr. James Allen, Mr. Ernest 'Bill' Williams, Mr. Moses Ford, and Mrs. Laura Jones agreed to share reflections.

Mr. Moses Ford was interviewed on Saturday afternoon, January 7, 2012, in the house where he grew up in Prospect.

The Editor returned to Sulphur Spring Baptist Church on Sunday morning, January 8, 2012, to worship and met with Mr. Ernest 'Bill' Williams in the fellowship hall that afternoon. Mr. James Allen was scheduled for an interview afterward, but his cousin Bill had a lengthy session. Upon arriving at the home of Mr. Allen, his wife informed me that he was called out and had to go to Buckingham County.

Mrs. Laura Jones was interviewed on Thursday, January 19, 2012, at her home in Prospect.

On Sunday, January 22, 2012, Providence guided me to Calvary Baptist Church, Prospect, Virginia. A lady took me to the office of the pastor before the worship service started. The project of the collection of stories was shared with Reverend Darryl McCoy Brown. During the time of announcements, the Pastor said to the congregation: "I have told you many times that what happened in Prince Edward County should be written and you should tell your story. We have someone here today who will speak to that issue." Reverend Brown invited me forward and the vision was shared with the congregation. After the worship service, Mr. Raymond Ligon shared his story in the church annex. A lady found some paper for me to write on. Mrs. Aldrena Pryor Thirkill gave me her telephone number and address and invited me to come by her home that afternoon. During my time with Mrs. Thirkill, she suspended the interview at least twice saying: 'Let me call my brother Charles in New York, he remembers everything.' 'I wish I could talk to Charles Pryor', the Editor mused, but did not press the issue.

Reverend Carlton Jackson, Jr., Pastor of Pleasant Valley Baptist Church, Lynchburg, Virginia, and aware of the project, mentioned to me: "I have a clergy friend who is a pastor in Charlotte County, but he is from Prince Edward County. I believe he was affected by the school closure." "Would you check? If so, ask him would he share his story," the Editor said with delight. Reverend Jackson confirmed the status of his friend and Pastor Lewis Monroe Watson was interviewed via telephone on Tuesday evening, January 24, 2012.

Seeking clarification on an issue in the draft of Mrs. Aundré Linell Carter Pearce, she was called. During the conversation she said: "I was talking to a friend of mine a few days ago and told him about the project. He shared with me some of the things that happened with him during the years the schools were closed, and I was surprised. He lives in New York." "Tell him if he desires, I can do his story over the telephone as we did your story." Aundré emailed me on Wednesday, March 7, 2012: "I just had a long conversation with Charles Henry Pryor. He's the gentleman I'd tried to connect you with (Aldrena Thirkill is his sister). Hope you will have time to hear his story. This is his contact information..." Mr. Charles Pryor was interviewed on March 8, 2012, via telephone.

Providence moved me to drive to Prince Edward County on March 29, 2012. Driving along a side road a sign that read Pamplin caught my eyes. Shortly thereafter a man was seen moving on what seemed from a distance to be a riding lawn mower. The Editor turned off the main road and onto the dirt road hoping to catch the man, but the man disappeared before my maneuvers were completed and the dirt road accessed. Stopping at an abandoned house on the dirt road where another gentleman was standing in the yard, he was told about the project. "When I started first grade the schools had reopened," the man said and continued, "the fellow who was in front of you, he's the one you need to talk to." "He disappeared before I could get to him," was my reply. The Editor chatted with the front yard host about the community and how school was for him after the reopening. He abruptly ended his reminisces and said: "There he is now." The man the Editor first attempted to encounter pulled up in a truck, parked, and came into the yard. The front yard host explained my mission to his friend. The Editor asked the newest arrival where did he attend elementary school. "I went to Pamplin No. 10." "I have a photograph of that school. I will pull it up on my laptop," the Editor revealed. The laptop was retrieved from my vehicle, the three of us sat at a wooden picnic table of sorts on the side of the house, and the photograph presented. The older gentleman looked at the picture, choked momentarily, and sighed: "That's it." Mr. Calvin Leslie Ligon and the Editor sat at the old table on the side of the house and chronicling his account brought great delight to the both of us.

On March 4, 2012, a communication was sent to Dr. Charles Davidson asking him to draft his reflections and send the pages to me before the end of the month. He was a college student at Hampden Sydney College in Prince Edward County during the years of the closure of the public schools. His information was received before the end of the month.

Retired school teacher Mrs. Martha Carrington Morton was interviewed by telephone on March 29, 2012. Dr. Kitty Smith made the referral and gave me the telephone number.

Mrs. Oreatha Lois Wiley Banks and the Editor communicated extensively, as she had treasured artifacts from the school closure years in her private files. She agreed to submit some items to be included in the subsequent volume. In early 2012 she told me in a telephone conversation: "I have a friend from childhood who also lives in Richmond. I see her sometimes at church. I want you to talk to her. I told her about the project; her name is Jean Haskins." "Send me the telephone number and I will call." Mrs. Jean Haskins was interviewed via telephone on Thursday evening, April 19, 2012.

On March 28, 2012, the Editor met Mrs. Betty Carter Davis in Lynchburg, Virginia, through her daughter Ms. Kimely Davis. The daughter gave a presentation from her doctoral dissertation to a group of clergy. Her parents were in attendance. Learning the mother was from nearby Buckingham County, Virginia, she was asked about Prince Edward County students that came to her school during the closure years. Mrs. Betty Carter Davis shared her reflections. She contacted me days later and advised that others who might have meaningful reflections would be gathered on Saturday, April 21, 2012, for an Earth Day clean-up at Ellis Acres Memorial Park in Buckingham County. The Editor journeyed to Ellis Acres Memorial Park on the day of the clean-up campaign and was greeted by Mr. Wilbert Dean who Mrs. Davis identified as my point of contact. Mr. Joe Chambers, Jr., Ms. Gwendolyn Jones, and Mr. Oscar Holman were interviewed at Ellis Acres Memorial Park. Mr. Charles White was interviewed at his home.

The Editor was stirred inwardly on May 18, 2012, to drive to Prince Edward County to the Meherrin section, my goal was to locate New Witt Baptist Church and find someone in the vicinity that attended in the 1950s and 1960s. The church was located that afternoon. I saw a lady mowing her lawn and drove across the road, parked in her driveway, got out of my vehicle, introduced myself and asked could she tell me about Mrs. Gladys Scott who taught children in the church when the schools were closed. The woman, who introduced herself to me as Mable Lee Richardson Smith, said she did not know Mrs. Scott, but directed me to an older woman that lived miles down the road who perhaps knew Mrs. Scott. Mrs. Smith looked to be of the age of the generation locked out of the public schools. "What did you do when the schools were closed?" the Editor asked. "I wasn't here; my mother took me to Baltimore." "What happened before you went to Baltimore?" Mrs. Smith rehearsed her public school days in Prince Edward County prior to the lock-out. The project was explained hurriedly to her, and she was asked to share her account. She seemed reluctant but as we talked the idea became more appealing to her. As she was collecting her thoughts, Mrs. Smith said: "You need to talk to my brother, Willie Richardson." The Editor sensed she felt he had a more fascinating story. "Where is your brother?" she was asked, surmising my journey would take me to his house after leaving her home, at the same time saying to myself—'I have heard the name Willie Richardson.' "My brother lives in Baltimore," she replied while dialing a telephone number on her cell phone. Suddenly everything came back to me, where the name Willie Richardson was first heard. "Is your brother a dentist in Baltimore?" A big smile came on her face and Mrs. Smith blurted: "You know my brother?" "No, but a man named Arthur Foster told me about a Willie Richardson who is a dentist in Baltimore. I have been trying to find him since the early part of last year."

"Hey, Bro," Mable said turning from her conversation with me to the person on the telephone. "There's a man here collecting stories from people locked out of the schools. I told him he should talk to you. I'll put him on." She handed me the telephone. "Brother Richardson, how are you?" "Fine," he said. "I have been trying to find you. Arthur Foster told me when I interviewed him about a classmate that had become a dentist and that I should make every attempt to locate you."

Mr. Richardson started laughing and resounded: "Where is Arthur and how is he?" "He is fine and lives in Woodbridge, Virginia. I interviewed him last year." "Well, I'm on my way to a convention right now," the dentist said. "Let me give you my number and you call me tomorrow night at the hotel."

Some paper was found in my vehicle and the account given me by Mrs. Mable Lee Richardson Smith written thereon while standing in her front yard. When finished with her reflections, she said: "You should talk to Earl Hughes." "Where does he live?" "Right back there," she said, pointing to a thick wooded area. "Can I drive to where he lives and see him," the Editor was prepared to walk through the woods if necessary. "He's not there now." "When do you think he'll be back?" "He lives in Texas. He was here last week. He just left a few days ago. I have his telephone number, you can call him." "I need you to call first and prepare the way for me." Mrs. Smith called and spoke briefly with Mr. Earl Hughes. He gave permission for me to telephone him in a few weeks.

The Editor left the home of Mable Lee in search of the older woman she said might have known Mrs. Gladys Scott. After driving miles and seeing none of the landmarks Mable Lee mentioned, the Editor stopped, introduced himself to a gentleman sitting under a tree in his yard, and asked did he know the lady who was called by name. He said no. The gentleman was asked if he was familiar with the school closure years in Prince Edward County. Mr. Stokes said he was from a neighboring county, married a woman from Prince Edward and moved here. "My wife might be able to tell you something. She'll be home later this evening." The Editor said he would try and stop by later to talk with the wife.

The woman for whom the Editor was searching was located. She said she had no recollection of Gladys Scott. "Were any of your children locked out of the schools?" she was asked casually. "Yea," the mother said without emotion. "Le'me see," she said softly, and then called the names of her children she thought were impacted by the school closure. Some confusion was displayed. "Wai'a minute. Le'me call my daugh'a." The mother called the daughter. Upon hanging up, she turned to me and said: "The one I was on the phone wid, she said the schools had open up when she started." "The children you believe were locked out of the schools, what happened to them during those years? Did you send any of them away?" "No, wasn' nobody to sen'em t'. All our people was righ' here." She strained in thought, as the Editor had seen other mothers do. Then she conceded: "I don' know what happen wid' the child'rn when the schools was close."

Several hours of daylight were left and the Editor decided to drive this part of the county and soon saw a sign that read Virso. He turned on a road, saw a man mowing his lawn, pulled into the yard and parked. The man turned off his riding mower and came toward me. It was determined as he was walking in my direction that he was too young to have been impacted by the school crisis. We introduced ourselves and the project was explained. "When I started first grade, the schools had already open back up," he said. "Do you know anyone in the area in their late fifties or in their sixties?" the Editor inquired. "They could share information." The gentleman said he was unable to think of anyone. A lady came out onto the porch, whom the man said was his wife. Addressing me the lady said: "My mama wants to talk to you." The wife had heard the full conversation in the yard, called her mother and explained everything. 'Oh, good,' the Editor thought. 'I will drive to the home of the mother and interview her.' "Where does your mother live?" "She lives in New York," the daughter said. The husband gave me the telephone and a brief conversation was held with Ms. Mable Otelia Walton. She gave me permission to telephone her no matter how late my return to Lynchburg that night. The son-in-law retrieved the telephone. His mother-in-law named some people for him to take me to see. The son-in-law escorted me to see Mrs. Sylvia Walton Cheatham and Mrs. Willis Jean Coleman Barnes. No one was home at the third house approached.

It was dark when I returned to the home of Mr. Stokes. He introduced me to his wife, who he had already told about my earlier visit. Mrs. Stokes attempted to talk about the school closure years, but events were vague. "Let me call my sister, Leola. Leola is older, you can talk to her." Mrs. Stokes called, explained the conversation that had taken place at the house, then urged her sister to share with me anything recalled from the period of the school closure. Mrs. Stokes handed me the telephone and Mrs. Leola Watkins Bailey gave her account.

After returning to Lynchburg, the Editor telephoned Mrs. Mable Otelia Walton in New York late that night and drafted her reflections.

Mr. Earl Hughes was interviewed via telephone on Saturday, May 19, 2012.

A trip was made to Johnston Memorial Library, Virginia State University, Petersburg, Virginia, on May 24, 2012, to review photographs in the archives from the era of the closure of the public schools in Prince Edward County. The route from Lynchburg to Petersburg takes the traveler through Prince Edward County and on the return trip the High Bridge community was visited. Stories were still being sought from that section. Two men were seen working in the cemetery at High Bridge Baptist Church. The Editor drove onto the church grounds, parked, walked to the gentleman nearest my vehicle, and asked him was he from the High Bridge area. He said no, explaining he was from Rice but his mother's roots were in the church. "What is your name?" "Marvin Dove," the man answered. The Editor remembered having interviewed Mrs. Doretha Palmer Dove years earlier and she talked about High Bridge. The name and encounter were mentioned to him. "She was my mother," said Mr. Dove. He said that most of the people had moved from the area and securing stories from the High Bridge community would be difficult. "Were you locked out of the schools?" the Editor asked. Mr. Dove talked quickly of his boyhood. The Editor got a piece of paper out of his car and wrote as Mr. Dove shared his story.

Leaving High Bridge Baptist Church, the Editor drove to Prospect to see what fruits would fall from one of the rich trees in the area. He stopped by the home of the Ford family hoping to have a dialogue with Mrs. Alberta Stiff Ford. Clarification was needed on one issue that her son Moses was unable to provide when he shared his story earlier in the year. Mrs. Ford was at home and as Moses had informed her of his interview the mother was prepared to share.

The next stop was the home of Mr. James Allen. He was supposed to have been interviewed on Sunday, January 8, 2012. Slowing down near the house, Mr. Allen was seen sitting in a chair under a big tree in the front yard. The Editor drove into the drive way, parked, greeted Mr. Allen, and asked could we talk and have the conversation we had been trying to have for months. He was agreeable and under the big tree, which obviously served as a place of solace for him, shared his rich but painful story.

An interview was arranged with Mrs. Clara Louise Gibson Johnson by Dr. Kitty Smith for May 31, 2012, in Farmville. An interview was conducted on June 26, 2012, with Mrs. Polly Allen Wise via telephone, arranged by her sister, Mrs. Gloria Allen Lockett. Mr. Roger Dove was interviewed via telephone on June 30, 2012. His cousin, Mrs. Vera Dove Morton, prepared the way for the interview.

Dr. Doris Scott Crawford said to me in her office in the summer of 2012: "I thought about you the other day; I was talking to my cousin Lewis Fitch and he was talking about the time he was sent away to school." "Call him back and explain the project and that he should tell his story." Mr. Lewis Fitch, at home in New York, was interviewed by telephone August 13, 2012.

On Sunday, September 9, 2012, the Editor worshipped at New Witt Baptist Church, still trying to secure information on Mrs. Gladys Scott for the narrative book on the Prince Edward County school closure. A gentleman greeted me on the church grounds and introduced himself — Michael Evans. "I am here to worship, but I am engaged in research in Prince Edward County. I am trying to find someone who knew Mrs. Gladys Scott. She taught children in this church when the schools were closed." A smile came across the face of Brother Evans. "I knew Mrs. Scott from when I was a boy. She went to church here. I knew her husband too." Brother Evans escorted me inside and introduced me to the Pastor. Pastor Winston Bland permitted me to make remarks during the period of announcements in the worship service. Upon hearing about the collection of stories, the following individuals gave me their names and contact information after church: Mr. Michael Evans, Sr., Mrs. Mattie Irene Clark Bolden, Mrs. Shirley Elizabeth Evans Dove, Mr. George Douglas Barksdale, Mrs. Onie Lou Barksdale Lawrence, Mrs. Annie Marie Barksdale Rice and Mr. Earl Barksdale.

The majority of the interviews from the New Witt Baptist Church volunteers took place before the end of September and each by telephone—Mr. George Douglas Barksdale, September 10; Mrs. Onie Lou Barksdale Lawrence, September 11; Mr. Michael Evans, Jr., September 13; Mrs. Mattie Irene Clark Bolden, September 15; Mrs. Annie Marie Barksdale Rice, September 18; and Mrs. Shirley Elizabeth Evans Dove, September 22, 2012.

Mrs. Sally Marie Evans Lee was interviewed on September 26, 2012, via telephone. Her sister, Mrs. Shirley Elizabeth Evans Dove, prepared the way for the exchange.

On Sunday, September 30, 2012, the Editor journeyed to Triumph Baptist Church in Darlington Heights. Shortly after entering the sanctuary an usher asked: "Are you a preacher?" "Yes, I am. I came to worship today." "Let me take you to meet the Pastor," she said. In the study of the pastor the project was shared with him. Pastor James W. Morris allowed me to make a statement during the period of announcements. After the worship service, Mrs. Bernetta Stiff Watkins and Mrs. Joyce Stiff Hendricks gave me their respective telephone number. Mrs. Joy Cabarrus Speaks instructed me to come by her home that afternoon. Mrs. Speaks graduated before the educational crisis struck the county but provided valuable information on the years leading up to the tragedy.

Mrs. Joyce Stiff Hendricks was interviewed via telephone on October 4, 2012.

Mrs. Bernetta Stiff Watkins was interviewed at her home in Prospect, October 8, 2012. Upon arriving, Mrs. Watkins introduced me to her mother who was sitting watching the evening news. "This is my mother Mrs. Gertrude Stiff." The mother smiled and spoke. The Editor shook her hand and immediately recognized her facial features. "Mrs. Gertrude

Scott Stiff," said the Editor. "I interviewed you years ago. One morning you, Ms. Flossie and some others were at the center and we talked. I remember you telling me about riding the bus and your parents having to pay Mr. Hendricks a fee." She nodded and laughed. Mrs. Watkins escorted me to the dining room table where her account was drafted.

Mr. Earl Barksdale was interviewed via telephone on October 13, 2012. Mrs. Barbara Jamison Orr, of Charlottesville, Virginia, was interviewed via telephone on December 7, 2012. Mrs. Orr was an elementary school teacher in Prince Edward County when the school closure occurred. Her name and telephone number were given to me earlier in the year by her close friend Mrs. Ernestine Watkins Herndon.

The 2013 Christian Education Workshop for Lynchburg and Vicinity, was held on Saturday, March 16, 2013, and the Editor facilitated a group. Lunch was shared in the company of Dr. Carl B. Hutcherson, Jr. and Reverend Aloysious H. Nowlin. Nowlin said to Hutcherson: "I'm preaching in Prince Edward County tomorrow at Zion Baptist. They don't have a pastor." "I am conducting research in Prince Edward from the period of the school closure. May I follow you to the church?" "Sure, you can," Nowlin said. Following the morning worship service on Sunday, March 17, Ms. Catherine Deloris Adams was interviewed. With Ms. Adams the collection of stories and the Prince Edward County project concluded.

CPSIA information can be obtained
at www.ICGtesting.com
Printed in the USA
LVHW081729040319
609435LV00034B/1522/P